"Fr. Réginald Garrigou-Lagrange, O.P., was and is the greatest theologian of the twentieth century. Recognizing this fact is not to diminish other theologians of the postconciliar period who were lionized for lesser talents, but only to understand why his work is now experiencing an extraordinary and welcome revival among a new generation that is looking for a more stable footing. It's easy to understand his attraction when you begin to inhabit the comprehensive scope, coherence, and power of his thought, so well communicated here and throughout his corpus. We owe a great debt to Matthew Minerd for so masterfully translating Garrigou-Lagrange's monumental two-volume work on divine Revelation—a work of such exquisite depth and wisdom that one could confidently rebuild and refresh the entirety of Catholic theological education upon these forgotten and fecund foundations. We see here in these volumes, as if held high in a magnificent monstrance, the triumph of truth itself."

CHAD PECKNOLD
Associate Professor of Systematic Theology
The Catholic University of America, Washington, DC

"Whether one agrees or disagrees with him, Garrigou-Lagrange's treatise on divine Revelation is one of the most important and influential texts of twentieth century apologetics. It sets forth the common position of classical Thomism on issues such as the preambles and mysteries of faith, the nature of divine Revelation and faith, the motives of credibility, and related topics. A great deal of theology both before and after this text is a reaction to the principles and positions set forth here."

FR. JAMES BRENT, O.P.
Assistant Professor of Philosophy
Pontifical Faculty of the Immaculate Conception at the Dominican House of Studies, Washington, DC

"It is impossible to grasp what was going on in theology, whether Catholic or not, in the first half of the twentieth century without appreciating how central to it were the debates around divine Revelation, the act of faith, and apologetics. Even those Catholics who parted ways with neo-Scholasticism cannot be properly understood without a sense of the balanced and intricate account honed by such significant and influential figures as Fr. Réginald Garrigou-Lagrange, O.P. Combining linguistic skill with extensive knowledge of the Thomist tradition, Dr. Matthew Minerd has put a wider theological public in his debt by making available this fine and accurate translation of Garrigou-Lagrange's *De Revelatione*. A broader readership can now begin to rediscover not only the importance of this text as a point of reference for the history of theology but also its insights for the theological task today."

FR. SIMON FRANCIS GAINE, O.P.
Pinckaers Professor in Theological Anthropology and Ethics
Pontifical University of St. Thomas (Angelicum), Rome

"One does not have to be a Thomist to appreciate the brilliance and perspicacity of these tomes. They are among the timeless classics of a *faith seeking understanding* and will still shine brightly when many other works have been forgotten."

ULRICH LEHNER
William K. Warren Professor of Theology
University of Notre Dame, Notre Dame, IN

"We theologians today often fancy ourselves sophisticated, learned, and subtle. But how can we be so if we ignore the great theologians of the early twentieth century and eschew the scholastic tradition that they furthered? Garrigou-Lagrange's text *De Revelatione* is a treasure that, until the publication of this splendid translation, few could access. We have much to learn from this master, much to emulate, even if we take issue with him here or there. He defines his terms, establishes his starting claims, and clearly argues his case. If we today juggle two or three concepts about some topic, Garrigou-Lagrange works with not a few more, both distinguishing and uniting. Nor does he simply entrap us in a labyrinth. By his manifold consideration of each topic and his global vision of the whole, he presents to us a grand example of theological wisdom. This text, challenging and rewarding, promises abundant fruit for those who labor in its field. Dr. Minerd has done a great service in rendering this tome into clear and articulate English. Let us hope that young scholars and seminarians pick it up and read."

CHRISTOPHER J. MALLOY
Associate Professor of Theology
The University of Dallas, Dallas, TX

"Though published nearly a century ago, the relevance of Fr. Garrigou-Lagrange's *De Revelatione* perdures. In the work, Fr. Garrigou-Lagrange masterfully lays out the first principles of the defensive branch of fundamental theology called apologetics and proceeds to give an account of how one ought to consider the very possibility of revelation. Far from a topical handbook with *ad hoc* replies to various and sundry objections to the faith, the work attempts to provide a speculative account of apologetics, understood as a part of sacred theology. In this regard, it is not only important as an introduction to the understanding of the faith, that is, for beginners, but also for advanced students in theology. Aside from delineating the important role that prophecy and miracles play as extrinsic motives of credibility (often considered passé in our times), Fr. Garrigou-Lagrange emphasizes the properly supernatural character of faith, which requires an elevation through grace that perfects, without destroying, the deepest longings of the human heart. In providing us with a careful translation of Fr. Réginald Garrigou-Lagrange's *De Revelatione*, Matthew Minerd has performed an important service for the Church and for contemporary Catholic theology."

JOSHUA LIM
Tutor in Theology
Thomas Aquinas College, Santa Paula, CA

"This is a monumental effort of making Garrigou-Lagrange's fundamental theology more accessible to students and scholars alike. Garrigou-Lagrange upholds what so much of theology has abandoned over many decades: an understanding of revelation as divine speech, *locutio Dei*. These two volumes are valuable complements to other fundamental theologies, which, together and in dialogue with each other, can offer a more holistic understanding of divine Revelation, its possibility and credibility. In addition, the translation and re-publication of this masterpiece, along with other works by Garrigou-Lagrange, will undoubtedly affect the dynamics of twentieth-century Catholic historiography for the better: the Dominican master cannot be caricatured, ignored, or dismissed as a relic from a bygone era. He continues to teach today!"

ANDREW MESZAROS
Professor of Systematic Theology
Pontifical University, St. Patrick's College, Maynooth, Ireland

ON DIVINE
REVELATION

VOLUME TWO

ON DIVINE REVELATION

The Teaching *of the* Catholic Faith

Fr. Réginald Garrigou-Lagrange, O.P.

Translated by Matthew K. Minerd

EMMAUS
ACADEMIC

Steubenville, Ohio
www.emmausacademic.com

EMMAUS
ACADEMIC

Steubenville, Ohio
www.emmausacademic.com
A Division of The St. Paul Center for Biblical Theology
Editor-in-Chief: Scott Hahn
1468 Parkview Circle
Steubenville, Ohio 43952

The original French *De revelatione per ecclesiam Catholicam proposita*, 5th edition, was published in Rome in 1950 by Desclée et Socii.

Library of Congress Cataloging-in-Publication Data applied for
ISBN hardcover 978-1-64585-179-0 / paperback 978-1-64585-180-6 /
ebook 978-1-64585-181-3

Cover image: D. Nollet, *The Transfiguration of the Lord* (1694), St. Jacobs Church (Jakobskerk) Bruges, Belgium.
Cover design by Allison Merrick
Layout by Emily Demary

Table of Contents

Division of the Entire Work

On the Notion, Possibility, Necessity, and Discernibility of Revelation (Continued from Vol. 1)

SECTION V

On the Value of the Motives of Credibility Considered Each in Particular

Art. 4.   On the Probative Force of Miracles

Ch. 20. On the Value of Prophecy as a Motive of Credibility
Art. 1.   On the Notion of Prophecy
Art. 2.   On the Possibility of Prophecy
Art. 3.   On the Discernibility of Prophecy
Art. 4.   On the Probative Force of Prophecy

We have not yet come to the question concerning the existence of revelation but, rather, here remain concerned with the question of its credibility. Therefore, we must now consider the motives of credibility (or the signs of revelation) speculatively [*theoretice*], as regards their notion, possibility, knowability, and probative force. In book 2, in order to prove the existence of divine revelation, we will show historically that these signs of revelation did in fact once exist and, indeed, endure even now.

Inasmuch as it is concerned with the value of the criteria of revelation, this part of fundamental theology can be called apologetic *criteriology*.[1]

Although they are not more principal in nature, we must begin by discussing the value of the motives that are internal to us, for by these motives the man who does not yet believe is disposed to consider the other signs of credibility.

Then, after discussing these motives, we will take up the question of those that are external while, however, remaining intrinsic to religion. Likewise, we will consider how they are related to the other motives. In this way, we will take up the question of the unity of the whole of apologetics. Following these discussions, we will then discuss, at length, the value of miracles and of prophecy.

---

[1] [Trans. note: The terminology bears similarity to certain approaches to the scholastic curriculum of Fr. Garrigou-Lagrange's day. Criteriology developed as a kind of quasi-discipline especially in the nineteenth and early twentieth centuries, providing a mélange of epistemological discussions. For Fr. Garrigou-Lagrange, this office, though necessary, in fact falls to the sapiential discourse of metaphysics, which must reflect on its principles and on the possibility of its very constitution as a form of *sapientia*. This matter was taken up in the beginning of the first volume of this work. Moreover, for an overview of his position concerning the various disciplines in philosophy, it is necessary that one consult Réginald Garrigou-Lagrange, *The Order of Things: The Realism of the Principle of Finality*, trans. Matthew K. Minerd (Steubenville, OH: Emmaus Academic, 2020), 225–250.]

CHAPTER SEVENTEEN

On the Value of the Motives of Credibility That Are Internal to Us

{{2}}

SINGLE ARTICLE

§1. The internal motives of credibility are not utilized correctly by the partisans of the method of immanence.

§2. Individual internal motives *per se* can ordinarily convey probability, though not certitude, concerning the credibility of the mysteries of faith.

§3. Universal internal motives, when taken together, can supply a kind of moral certitude concerning the fact of revelation, and taken together, along with the correlative external motives that are intrinsic to religion, they constitute an irrefutable argument on behalf of the credibility of revelation.

§1. The Internal Motives of Credibility Are Not Utilized Correctly by the Partisans of the Method of Immanence

As is discussed in the encyclical *Pascendi dominici gregis*,[2] these new apologetes have too much affinity with the semi-supernaturalism of liberal Protestants and of modernists, both of whom ultimately tend toward naturalism itself.

A. CERTAIN RATIONALISTS also make use of internal motives in order to show that Christian ethics corresponds to our aspirations. However, they do not admit the supernatural origin of Christianity. Nay, like Kant and Hegel, they reject all supernatural dogmas or interpret them as being symbols of natural truths.

B. LIBERAL PROTESTANTS AND MODERNISTS, in almost the same way, make use

---

[2] See Pius X, *Pascendi dominici gregis*, no. 37 (Denzinger, no. 2103 [old]).

of internal motives drawn from our aspirations to religion. Thus, they show that the perfect fulfilment of these aspirations is found only in Christianity. However, this does not provide a foundation for proving that Christianity is revealed by God and, hence, is infallibly true and immutable in all of its dogmas and precepts. Nay, the modernists believe that Christianity is only a superior form of religious evolution and, hence, essentially changeable. And thus, they say that Catholicism, a religion founded upon authority, must give way to liberal Christianity (that is, religion of the spirit), wherein dogmas are only symbols that express the evolution of man's religious sentiment.[3]

Modernists do indeed make use of historical methodology, but they only thereby look to show that there is *"something unknown* hidden" in the history of the Church's miraculous life, akin to the natural mystery of evolution (for, already, this mystery is found in the appearance of plant life, sense life, and intellectual life, so *a fortiori*, it is found in the evolution of the religious sentiment). However, they do not thereby look to prove the supernatural origin of Catholicism.[4]

{{3}} C. THE PARTISANS OF THE METHOD OF IMMANENCE WHO ARE NUMBERED AMONG CATHOLICS (e.g., Blondel and Laberthonnière) do indeed hold, by faith, that Catholicism is a religion supernaturally revealed by God; however, in their apologetics, they make particular use of the method of immanence and assert that it holds primacy.[5]

Indeed, they argue, in particular, from the desire (or need) for religion, intending to show that this desire is fulfilled only in Christianity—nay, only in Catholicism. This gives rise to the practical necessity to embrace Catholicism in order to live uprightly.

Blondel argues as follows. Man wishes to be fully alive. Now, in the Catholic religion, and indeed in it alone, man finds the full development [*evolutionem*] of his life. Therefore, man *needs* the Catholic religion, which hence, is true, indeed, the only true religion. These new apologetes intend to lead men to the true religion through an analysis of what is naturally postulated by human action, and they strive to show that in the very nature of such action there is something that calls for the supernatural order.[6]

They do not completely reject *the value of miracles*. However, on account of their agnostic prejudices, they do not hold that miracles have an ontological value but,

---

3   See Louis Auguste Sabatier, *Les religions d'autorité et la religion de l'esprit* (Paris: Fischbacher, 1903). Here again, see the text of *Pascendi* cited in the previous footnote.

4   See Pius X, *Pascendi dominici gregis*, no. 35 (Denzinger, no. 3499).

5   See the end of the *Prolegomena* (Historical Overview of Apologetics, Considered in Relation to Methodology) in the first volume of this work. There, we set forth this new apologetic methodology inasmuch as it is opposed to that used in traditional apologetics.

6   These apologetes who, like Blondel, follow the paths paved by Kant and begin with the assumption of speculative agnosticism, must be distinguished from certain others, like Léon Ollé-Laprune, who also made use of internal methods while, however, holding that Kantianism is an "intellectual disease" and admitting the ontological value of the first principles of speculative reason, even independent from *praxis*.

rather, *solely have a symbolic value.* That is, they hold that miracles are not some kind of abrogation of the intrinsic laws of nature but, rather, are conceived by us as being such an abrogation (for[, according to them,] the laws of nature are not intrinsically fixed, as they are, however, in our static conception of them).

Therefore, miracles cannot be known as something brought about through God's special intervention as an utterly certain sign of the divine origin of our religion. Rather, they are only extraordinary sensible symbols compelling the attention of a nonbeliever so that he might consider the Catholic religion itself and, especially, its conformity with our nature's aspirations and exigencies.

In this way, they still do preserve the *primacy of the methodology of immanence*, for, according to them, this method enjoys not only temporal priority, inasmuch as it disposes the person who does not yet believe to an examination of religion, but even hold that this methodology has *a priority of value* inasmuch as, without it, other motives [of credibility] (e.g., miracles) do not have probative force.

CRITIQUE. In the first volume of this work (Prolegomena: On the Methodology of Apologetics), we set forth what contemporary theologians teach against this methodology. Now, however, three things need to be said in particular.

(1) *This new methodology of immanence gravely diminishes or destroys the probative force of miracles* on account of its *agnostic* prejudices.[7] This is so because it proceeds from (at least partial) agnosticism in relation to speculative reason, and it is not philosophically clear how it can arrive at true certitude concerning extramental reality.[8]

{{4}} (2) *It exaggerates our natural desire for supernatural life*, and this contains the danger of falling into Baianism and Immanentism. Hence, the

---

[7] *Indeed, this is so because it defines the truth* as being *the conformity of mind and life*, not the conformity of reality and the intellect. Thus, in order for a judgment to be true, it would need to be conformed to the exigencies of our life. However, this kind of conformity is known only through practical reason. Thus, according to them, extramental being is attained only in an indirect manner, in accord with the exigencies of human action. According to St. Thomas, only the truth belonging to the practically-practical intellect (i.e., the truth of prudence) is had through *conformity to right appetite* (see *ST* I-II, q. 57, a. 5, ad 3). However, rectitude of appetite depends on the first principles of reason, which themselves are true through *conformity to reality itself.* [Trans. note: That is, the first principles of practical reason, known through *synderesis* (in the case of the natural law) and through faith and *synderesis* (in the case of supernatural morality in the life of grace).]

[8] See Réginald Garrigou-Lagrange, "Chronique de métaphysique: Autour du Blondelisme et du Bergsonisme," *Revue Thomiste* (1913): 351–377; also see Garrigou-Lagrange, "Chronique: Les méthodes de l'apologétique," *Revue Thomiste* (1913): 478–489, a critical review of two works that are opposed to each other (*Immanence* by Fr. Joseph de Tonquédec, S.J., and the article "Méthode d'immanence" by Albert Valensin in the *Dictionnaire de l'apologétique*).

encyclical *Pascendi* says:

> And here We cannot but deplore once more, and grievously, that
> there are Catholics who, while rejecting immanence as a doctrine,
> employ it as a method of apologetics, and who do this so impru-
> dently that they seem to admit that there is in human nature a true
> and rigorous necessity with regard to the supernatural order—and
> not merely a capacity and a suitability for the supernatural order,
> such as has at all times been emphasized by Catholic apologists.[9]

(3) *This methodology does not prove the credibility or [seu] divine origin
of Christianity* and, hence, slides toward fideism. Indeed, in a way, it does
manifest the fact that Christianity is a beautiful and enticing religion, one
that is worthy of religious experience—nay, something morally necessary
today in order to live aright. However, this does not prove that the Catholic religion is to be irrevocably embraced with utter firm certitude through
divine faith as regards all of its dogmas and precepts, nor does it rule out the
possibility that perhaps someday in the future a religion that is more perfect
than Christianity might emerge. This proof remains inefficacious for two
reasons: on account of its agnostic prejudices and because it nearly exclusively makes use of internal motives.

Nor does it sufficiently preserve the Catholic notion of credibility
because, according to this form of apologetics, divine faith is more or less
the same as religious experience, which is found in all forms of religion.
Nonetheless, in various places, Blondel proposes various *good ad hominem
arguments*[10]—that is, those that can dispose an agnostic person to look into
the true religion and its notes.[11] Hence, when proposing the faith to agnostics, this methodology can be proposed as having *temporal priority*, though
this does not mean that it has, without any qualification, priority of value for
proving credibility.

---

[9] Pius X, *Pascendi dominici gregis*, no. 37 (Denzinger, no. 2103 [old]; Vatican trans.).

[10] [Trans. note: That is, taking the terms of argument accepted by a given person.]

[11] Moreover, even agnostics, notwithstanding their errors, are fortunately in a state of self-con-
tradiction, for they preserve *common sense* (or natural reason). Thus, they do not really doubt
the ontological value of the first principles of reason, which they only reject by forming an
imaginative fabrication along with sophistical reasoning. Thus, underneath these prejudices,
they retain the very nature of their intellect, along with *natural certitude regarding all common
[principles]*. Hence, some of them, when they sincerely examine the signs of the true religion,
really admit, in accord with common sense, the traditional arguments, even though they seem
to be more or less in doubt concerning them.

§2. Individual Internal Motives Per Se can Ordinarily Convey Probability, Though Not Certitude, concerning the Credibility of the Mysteries of Faith

Individual internal motives are drawn from the marvelous way that our loftiest aspirations are fulfilled, something that someone can experience in himself while reading the Gospel or while listening to the preaching {{5}} of the faith. Thus, the disciples on the road to Emmaus said: "Was not our heart burning within us, whilst he spoke in this way and opened to us the scriptures?" (Luke 24:32, DR).

These motives do provide probability, though *per se* and ordinarily they do not provide certitude. Indeed, the credibility of the mysteries of faith is made manifest inasmuch as these mysteries appear to our reason as having been revealed by God. Now, individual internal motives can manifest in a probable manner (though not certainly, at least ordinarily) that a given religion has been revealed by God. Therefore [, these motives cannot manifest the certain credibility of the mysteries of faith.]

The major premise holds on the basis of what we said in our preceding thesis concerning the notion and necessity of credibility. *The minor*, however, must be proven part by part.

(a) **These motives convey probability.** Indeed, while reading the Gospel or hearing preaching of the faith, the man who does not yet believe sometimes experiences within himself so great a feeling of peace that, to his eyes, this state of soul seems to arise from God himself, under the influence of actual grace: "Peace I leave with you: my peace I give unto you: not as the world giveth, do I give unto you" (John 14:27, DR). Thus, he enjoys within himself this interior peace that the world cannot give, a peace surpassing the powers of our nature. Hence, in some way, it is made manifest that the Gospel's teaching is something that has been revealed by God, not precisely because it is conformed to our natural aspirations (for then it would only be naturally excellent) but, rather, because it is *so profoundly* conformed to our loftier aspirations, and, likewise, so *freely given, that it seems to come from God alone*, inasmuch as only God can profoundly know and stir the human heart, inasmuch as he alone can intimately join together these extremes—namely, the loftiest conformity with our nature and the greatest gratuity.

Many have been able to experience this upon hearing what Jesus said in the Sermon on the Mount, before any miracles happen to be performed. Hence, it is said in Matthew 7:28 (DR): "And it came to pass when Jesus had fully ended these words, the people were in admiration at his doctrine." Hence, St. Thomas says in *Quodlibet* II, q. 4, a. 1: "If Christ had not performed visible miracles, there still would have been other methods for drawing men to faith, by which men would have been bound to submit thereto. Indeed, men were bound to believe upon the authority of the Law and the Prophets and, likewise, were required not to resist God's interior call within them."

In righteous believers, this experiential knowledge confirms faith and *proceeds from the gifts of the Holy Spirit*, which presuppose faith and charity. This is expressed in the words of Psalm 33:9 (DR), "O taste, and see that the Lord is sweet," and in those of St. Paul in Romans 8:16 (DR): "For the Spirit himself giveth testimony to our spirit that we are the sons of God."[12]

Something similar takes place (even if it is less certain) through "an interior instinct come from God drawing one"[13] *in those who approach faith*

---

[12] Thus, through the gift of understanding, the believer experientially "knows that given external appearances do not contradict the truth of faith . . . and hence that he must not draw back from those things which are held by faith" (*ST* II-II, q. 8, a. 2). However, this certitude of the gifts must not be separated from extrinsic criteria. See John of St. Thomas, *Cursus theologicus, In ST* I-II, q. 68, disp. 18, a. 5, no. 24.

[13] *ST* II-II, q. 2, a. 9, ad 3. For example, a certain rationalist, having now converted to the Catholic religion, frequently and sharply had fought against the faith and great piety of his bride, so much so that he was finally defeated by considering her extraordinary serenity and peace in the midst of grief-inducing affliction and sorrows. This peace, in which he already participated in some way, was the first motive of credibility that moved him, at least in a probable manner, leading him to consider the others and, ultimately, to believe. See Élisabeth Leseur, *Journal et pensées de chaque jour* (Paris: De Gigord, 1917), 36, where it was written in remembrance of her: "I have spoken of the miserable determination that I stubbornly persisted in contradicting all of her religious thoughts. My attitude began to change in 1908. When I saw her so sick with a liver disease which so regularly provokes so much hypochondria, impatience, and disgust, yet herself bearing it with such equanimity, I was quite struck with this sight, beholding a soul that exercised such mastery over itself and her body. Recognizing that she drew this superior power from her convictions, I ceased to attack them. In 1911, during her operation, my astonishment turned into respect and, in 1912, on the occasion of a trip to Lourdes, admiration. . . . At the Grotto . . . I hid so that I might not be seen by her and in order to avoid troubling her in her fervor. There I contemplated her. I had under my eyes the spectacle *of a fact that eluded me, one that I did not understand, but that nonetheless appeared quite clearly, "supernatural,"* and I could not turn my sight from this vision which enraptured me. I returned from Lourdes very troubled. . . . Oh! I was a rationalist, at least upon the surface, for Elizabeth acted upon me without me perceiving it. And this action became stronger throughout her final illness. I endlessly admired such moral strength in the midst of a true form of martyrdom. She was the one who comforted me between her seizures [*crises*]. . . . Drawing close to her bed, I experienced in her welcoming, smiling attitude, *an incomprehensible kind of peace and calm which existed within her.* Turning back to consider myself, I recognized what an insupportable patient I would have been for myself and for others, instead of such a source of serenity, such as appeared in her entire entourage, and from my depths, I inclined toward the sublime sentiment which sustained her and gave her such grandeur. . . . After her death, I found the 'Spiritual Testament' that she had drafted for me. . . . I understood the heavenly beauty of this soul, as well as the fact that she had accepted all of these sufferings . . . that her primary self-offering was for my conversion. . . . Her library was opened for my investigations, and the exegesis upon which I had so greedily fed myself once upon a time now appeared before my eyes in all of its indigence.

under the influence of actual grace.

{{6}} Thus, these internal motives in some way manifest the credibility of the mysteries of the faith. Indeed, they frequently provide great aid to the consideration of external motives when they are at work together.

(b) *However, per se and ordinarily, they do not suffice* for proving credibility, for *by them one only knows in a conjectural manner through internal experience that this internal effect of peace and joy is supernatural and not natural,* for a kind of interior peace and fulfillment of our natural aspirations could be found in Christianity if it happened to be only an excellent form of religious evolution (that is, a form of merely natural religion). Indeed, peace is found in non-divine forms of religion, as in Protestantism[14] and Buddhism.

Hence, in the annotations to the pre-conciliar schema for the [First] Vatican Council, we read, against liberal Protestants, who make use of internal motives in a nearly exclusive manner:

> That sentiment *according to ordinary providence is not subject to experience having a supernatural formal character,* and if it is separated from extrinsic criteria, it is open to the gravest of illusions. Whence, we even see that, on behalf of false religion and manifest errors, men call upon "an experience and internal sentiment," which they attribute to the Holy Spirit. Equally consistent with this confidence in "internal sentiment" and with a rejection of the motives of credibility is another error spread among many today, by which they dare to affirm that it is sometimes divinely ordained that one defect from the Catholic religion to another religion, if it is discovered that it does not satisfy internal experience and religious sentiment.[15]

Likewise, in *ST* I-II, q. 112, a. 5, St. Thomas shows that without special revelation man cannot determine with certitude whether he is in a state of grace, in accord with the word in 1 Corinthians 4:3–4 (DR): "Neither do I judge my own self . . . but he that judgeth me is the Lord." "But," adds St. Thomas, "in a conjectural manner, through signs, someone can judge that he is in the state of grace, namely, inasmuch as he perceives that he delights in God and scorns things of the world, and inasmuch as

---

Indeed, what weight could these barren denials have next to the *eminent power of the truth and life which overflows from the Catholic faith when it is accepted, understood, and practiced?*"

[14] [Trans. note: Obviously, Fr. Garrigou-Lagrange writes in a different era, in which ecumenical sensitivities were significantly less accentuated.]

[15] See *Acta Concilii Vat., Collectio lacensis,* vol. 7, 529. Jean-Michel-Alfred Vacant, *Études théologiques sur les constitutions du Concile du Vatican d'après les actes du concile,* vol. 1 (Paris: Delhomme et Briguet, 1895), 594.

a man is not aware of being guilty of any mortal sin."[16]

{{7}} Thus, *per se*, this individual fulfillment of our heart's aspirations is not a sufficient motive of credibility, for three things are required in order for a given fact to be a sufficient motive of credibility: (1) that it be intrinsically certain; (2) that it certainly be brought about through a special intervention by God; and (3) that its meaning be certain for confirming revelation.[17]

Individual internal motives, without others, per accidens and extraordinarily suffice. In such a case, an extraordinary grace supplies for external motives, as in the case of a prophet accepting revelation immediately from God under the light of prophecy and, likewise, in the case of private revelations or in certain *miraculous conversions*, like that of St. Paul.[18]

Hence, in *Quodlibet* II, q. 4, a. 1, ad 1, St. Thomas says: "Among those works which Christ performed while among men, we must also include His inner calling, by which He attracted certain men. Thus, Gregory says, in a given homily, that Christ interiorly drew Mary Magdalene through mercy, having also externally received her through His mercy."

Likewise, in Matthew 9:9 (DR), we read: "And when Jesus passed on from thence, he saw a man sitting in the custom house, named Matthew; and he saith to him: Follow me. And he arose up and followed him." And in Acts 16:14: "The Lord opened Lydia's heart to attend to those things which were said by Paul."

These individual internal motives have such a value only for particular men who have such experiences within themselves.

---

[16] Thomists generally admit that, without grace, man can love God *the Author of nature* with an imperfect love, one that merely notes his goodness [*merae complacentiae*] in an inefficacious manner. (See Billuart, *Summa sancti Thomae, De gratiae*, diss. 3, a. 4.) Hence, some (e.g., poets) who easily arrive at this inefficacious love can believe that this is an effect of grace and, nonetheless, can lack supernatural grace. Thus, without grace, it was possible for Plato to elevate himself to the contemplation of the beauty of the Highest Good in the *Symposium*.

[17] See Joachim-Joseph Berthier, *De locis theologicis* [1888 / 1900], 522 (on internal experience). Likewise, see Joseph de Tonquédec, *Immanence*, 288.

[18] And therefore, the apologete can argue from miraculous conversions. See Jacques-Marie-Louis Monsabré, *Introduction au dogme catholique*, vol. 3 [Paris: Bureaux de l'anné dominicane, 1888], conference 30, "Spiritual miracles," 333–365.

However, in other *non-miraculous* conversions, the supernatural intervention of God is not so clearly apparent, even though it frequently can be made manifest with great probability. See Thomas Mainage, *Introduction à la psychologie des convertis* (Paris: Gabalda, 1913), 123; *La psychologie de la conversion* (Paris: Beauchesne, 1915). In these works, the author intends to show, at least with great probability, that these conversions cannot be explained through natural causes—namely, through the natural activity of the subconscious, sensibility, intellect, or will. See in this second book the sections entitled "dualism in the souls of converts"; "conversion and the subconscious, the invisible teacher"; "God in the soul of converts." Likewise, see what we said in vol. 1, {{535}}–{{544}}.

§3. *Universal Internal Motives, When Taken Together, Can Supply a Kind of Moral Certitude concerning the Fact of Revelation*

Nay, taken together, along with the correlative external motives that are intrinsic to religion, they constitute an irrefutable argument on behalf of the credibility of revelation.

These universal internal motives are taken from the marvelous fulfillment of all of the moral and religious aspirations of humanity. They are called *universal* inasmuch as these aspirations are found in all men, at least in a vague manner and inasmuch as this miraculous [*mirabilis*] fulfillment agrees not only with one's individual experience but with the *general* experience of society renewed through Christianity. Moreover, the fulfillment in question is not any sort of fulfillment whatsoever but, rather, one that is extraordinary and miraculous [*mirabili*].

External motives drawn from the sublimity of the Church's teaching and from her marvelous religious life correspond to these internal, universal motives.

A. Taken together, these universal internal motives offer, *per se*, moral certitude concerning the fact of revelation.

{{8}} Indeed, *if all of our nature's legitimate aspirations, even its loftier ones, are marvelously satisfied—nay, surpassed—in some given religion*, this is a sign of this religion's divine origin, for solely by their natural powers, men would not be able to discover *so great a conformity and interior peace*, as is especially clear from what we said above concerning the moral necessity of the revelation of the sum of the natural truths of religion. Indeed, as we there said, men *morally cannot* readily arrive at firm, error-free knowledge concerning all the truths of natural religion. Therefore, if in some religion all the essential questions concerning God and the soul are harmoniously resolved, and all the aspirations of our nature marvelously satisfied and surpassed, *it is morally certain* that this religion is from God, especially if some legitimate aspiration is offended in other religions and philosophical systems, or at least if not all of them are satisfied in them.

In this way, one can have a kind of moral certitude concerning credibility, indeed, one that excludes, for the wise, every prudent doubt. Note, though, that I say, "for the wise," for not all can judge in a distinct manner concerning the value of this kind of motive. (Regarding the notion of moral certitude, see what we will say below in ch. 19, a. 3 concerning the discernibility of miracles).

Moreover, in order for this argument to offer this kind of moral certitude regarding the fact of revelation, three things are required:

(1) Against the agnostics, it is necessary that one presuppose *the ontological value of the first principles of reason*, especially the principles of causality and of finality. Nay, one must even presuppose natural certitude concerning the existence of God, a certitude that belongs to common sense and is defended by philosophical reasoning.

(2) One must argue not only from how the proposed religion is conformed to our aspirations and needs but also from how great and *marvelous a conformity it has, so that it would seem to come solely from God*—namely, inasmuch as this marvelous conformity and fulfilment *exceeds our natural powers and exigencies*, constituting a kind of moral quasi-miracle, as we said above. Hence, "marvelous" or "miraculous" [*mirabile*] is here not said merely oratorically but, rather, with a theological meaning, for it contains a probative middle term.

(3) Finally, one must argue *from all these aspirations taken together*, negatively and positively considered. In this way, it will be clear that only God can so profoundly know and satisfy men's hearts.

However, these *aspirations* are "the seeds of the natural virtues" in us concerning the ultimate end and the means [leading thereto]. That is, concerning the end, they are our aspirations to know God, to hope in him, to love him above all things, and to offer him internal and external worship. Likewise, concerning the means, they are inclinations to prudence, justice, courage, and temperance. However, we must insist in particular upon both *the desire for eternal beatitude* and *the conditional and inefficacious desire to see God through his essence*, which we spoke about in the previous volume, where we treated the topic of man's obediential potency (see vol. 1, ch. 12, §4).

Therefore, if all of these aspirations, without suffering any injury, are miraculously fulfilled—nay, *surpassed*—in some religion (as we will show below to be the case for Christianity when we consider the Christian virtues and the beatitudes set forth in the Gospel), this will be a sign of the divine origin of this religion.

{{9}} Preachers of the faith develop this argument in depth, inasmuch as in Christianity *knowledge of God* through faith arrives at the intimate secrets of the Heavenly Father and promises an eternal beatitude that consists in the immediate vision of God. *Hope* is given the greatest of reinforcements through the mysteries of the Incarnation and Redemption. *Charity for God* arrives at a holy and familiar friendship, especially in Eucharistic Communion. (What could be more conformed to our human aspirations than Holy Communion and, nonetheless, what is more freely given and not owed to us? Only God can thus join together this intimate conformity with the greatest of gratuity.) Likewise, in Christianity, *charity for one's neighbors* is extended even to the point that one sacrifices one's own life for the sake of others' souls, in the apostolate of missionaries and in other works of mercy. Internal and external *worship* are marvelously united in the sacrifice of the Mass. Christian prudence is neither carnal nor worldly but, rather, heavenly. *Justice* toward one's neighbors comes to be elevated through its connection to charity; *courage* pushes on to the heroism of martyrdom; *temperance* arrives at virginity; and *humility* is commended as a fundamental virtue, though it was overlooked by the pagans. Hence, Fr. Lacordaire argued from the three privileges of Christianity—namely, from charity, humility, and virginity. By contrast, allow faith and the Christian life to die away in a given region and nearly all at once vices, discord, and pride will appear once again.[19]

These supernatural effects are indeed not subject to common experience as having the formal character of being supernaturally produced by God. However, *their supernaturality indirectly shines forth* from man's inability (at least morally speaking) to arrive at such a teaching and form of life.

Likewise, solely by the powers of nature, men cannot arrive at *the peace*

---

[19] Concerning the value of the internal method in apologetics, see De Poulpiquet, *L'objet integral de l'apologétique*, pt. 2 (Internal apologetics, its necessity, method, and value.) On p. 342, he says: "See, at least to our eyes, the logical order to be followed in the subjective and objective study that constitutes internal apologetics.

"(1) One must obviously begin with the subject and show how, *de iure* and *de facto*, the response to a given interior aspiration or the solution to a given problem are necessarily of interest to the whole of man and to every man, likewise showing that it implicitly poses the religious question.

"(2) One must analyze, as exactly as possible, the specific characteristics of these subjective needs [and] the different postulates implied by a given desire so that it might be fully satisfied.

"(3) Having thus clearly delimited and specified the terms of the question to be resolved, one will then seek out the response to it. This new inquiry will aim to study: (a) the response that human reason, considered in itself, can give to it; (b) the response that it has in fact given in various philosophical systems; (c) the response offered by non-Christian religions; (d) the errors or insufficiencies contained in these different responses.

"(4) An exposition of the Christian solution will show that it addresses the aforementioned *lacunae* and, therefore, that it alone is fully satisfying the subject.

"(5) One will show how, *in fact*, the Christian solution has brought souls peace, light, and consolation, having transfigured their life."

And on p. 463: "*External* apologetics, which corresponds to our need for *truth* (and proves the *credibility* of dogma) must be supplemented by *internal* apologetics, which shows religion as something 'deserving of love,' and uncovers for us the point of intersection where all of our intimate aspirations for the *good* and the *beautiful* meet. . . . Apologetics is the demonstration of the *credibility* and the *desirability* of dogma."

Certainly, the "love-worthiness [*amabilitas*]" of the Christian religion is thus made manifest through the internal method. However, here too its *credibility* likewise already appears if one argues not only from its conformity with our aspirations but also from its *marvelous* conformity, which is at once so profound and gratuitous that it seems that it could only come from God.

experienced by the saints—namely, that which is found in their lives. Indeed, this peace differs essentially from the world's peace in at least two ways, as St. Thomas says: "First, as regards the end, for the world's peace is ordered to undisturbed enjoyment of temporal things, whereas the peace had by the saints is ordered to eternal goods (and is not diminished in an essential way through privation of temporal things). {{10}} However, secondly, they differ as imitation-likeness and truth, for the world's peace is a mere imitation of peace because it is only external in nature, whereas Christ's peace is true because it is both internal and external."[20] Now, this true internal peace proceeds from the fact that we efficaciously love God above all things with all our heart and love our neighbor as ourselves.[21] However, efficacious love cannot exist in us without God's aid, inasmuch as the order of agents must correspond to the order of ends.[22] As St. Thomas says, "Only God can remove all disturbance from our hearts." Whence, it is said, "May *the peace of God, which surpasseth all understanding*, keep your hearts and minds in Christ Jesus."[23] As St. Paul says in this same text, "Rejoice in the Lord always: again, I say, rejoice. . . . The Lord is nigh. Be nothing solicitous: but in everything, by prayer and supplication, with thanksgiving, let your petitions be made known to God." Likewise, one should consult biblical concordances at the entries for "desire," "blessed," "joy," "happiness," and "alleluia." Indeed,

---

[20] See St. Thomas, *In Ioann.*, ch. 14, lect. 7.

[21] See *ST* II-II, q. 29 (*On Peace*). Concord is a union of various hearts being in agreement on one thing. *Peace is the tranquility of order*, and this tranquility does indeed consist in the fact that all the movements of man's appetite are at rest.

Now, all desire peace, but some desire an apparent peace, which is only external, not internal. "Without sanctifying grace, no true peace can exist, but rather, only apparent peace" (ibid., a. 3, ad 1). Indeed, true internal peace proceeds from charity for God and neighbors and is defined by St. Augustine in his book *De verbis domini*: "Peace is serenity of mind, tranquility of soul, simplicity of heart, the bond of love, and the common possession of charity."

Therefore, peace is not a virtue but, rather, an effect of virtue, namely, of charity, and the end of all the gifts.

The peace of the carnal emotions is opposed to this peace. Concerning the former, Christ says in Matt 10:34 (DR): "I came not to send peace, but the sword." "This sword," writes St. Thomas in his commentary on this passage, "is the word of God, for some believe in it and others do not. Therefore, there consequently is war." "Peace between good and evil men cannot exist because peace involves an order of agreement, which cannot be had with the wicked." Cf. *In II Tim.*, ch. 2, lect. 4.

Also see *ST* II-II, q. 28 (*On Joy*): "Spiritual joy had concerning God is caused by Charity." And also see *ST* I-II, q. 70 (On the fruits of the Holy Spirit and their opposition to the works of the flesh).

[22] See *ST* I-II, q. 109, a. 6.

[23] St. Thomas, *In Phil.*, 4:7: "In the saints in via, peace surpasses everything experienced by men who do not have grace."

in these words within Sacred Scripture and in the writings of the classical doctors, we find what is expressed in modern apologetics by the words "aspiration" and "fulfillment." On all of this, see bk. 2, ch. 7 below.

B. Taken together, all of these internal motives offer moral certitude [of credibility], but they cannot be separated from the correlative external motives that are intrinsic to religion.[24] As we will show in the next chapter, together with them, they constitute an irrefutable argument.

---

[24] See Cardinal Dechamps (*Demonstrations de foi*, 1st conference, ed. Dessain), 1: "Hear and see. There are only two facts to be verified, one within us, the other without. They search after each other in order to embrace each other, and you yourself are the one who witnesses them both."

CHAPTER EIGHTEEN

On the Value of External Motives That Are Intrinsic to Religion

SINGLE ARTICLE

§1. The Church's teaching concerning the value of these motives

§2. A defense by reason that these motives, when taken all together, constitute an irresistible argument

§3. Concerning how these motives are related to the other motives, as well as concerning the unity of the whole of apologetics

§1. The Church's Teaching concerning the Value of These Motives

{{11}} As we said above, these motives are called "external" inasmuch as they exist outside of man's awareness, thus being opposed to our nature's internal aspirations to something divine. However, they are said to be "intrinsic" to religion inasmuch as they are drawn from the latter's excellence, purity, sanctity, and fruitfulness in everything that is good. For this reason, they are contrasted with extrinsic-external motives (e.g., miracles and prophecies), which are extrinsic signs in confirmation of the divine origin of religion.

And the [First] Vatican Council defines: "In fact, it is to the Catholic Church alone that belong all those signs that are so numerous and wonderfully arranged by God to make evident the credibility of the Christian faith." And immediately thereafter, it adds, with regard to external motives that are intrinsic to religion:

In fact, the Church by herself, with her marvelous propagation, eminent, holiness, and inexhaustible fruitfulness in everything that is good, with her catholic unity and invincible stability, is a great and perpetual motive of credibility and an irrefutable testimony of her divine mission.

Thus, like a standard lifted up among the nations (Isa 11:12), she invites to herself those who do not yet believe and at the same time gives greater assurance to her children that the faith that they profess rests on solid ground.[1]

In this declaration, the miraculous life of the Church is presented as being an irrefutable sign of her divine mission—that is, as a moral miracle, which clearly can be produced only by God. Nor is it proposed merely as being an extrinsic seal from God but, rather, as a manifestation of the divine life itself through certain visible notes.

Some say this represents a form of immoderate optimism in apologetics. {{12}}

Response: It is the optimism of the Holy Church founded on countless signs of the divine goodness and persevering in the midst of the miseries, failures, doubts, and errors of this life. However, the apologete is the minister of the *Ecclesia docens* of God, and she teaches not only the mysteries of faith but also the rational pathway to faith.

Now, in order for *the excellence of this marvelous life* to be made clear, the Council considered the issue *in relation to its four causes and its effects*: (1) in relation to its efficient cause ("with her marvelous propagation" —the note of apostolicity [*sic*]); (2) in relation to its final cause ("eminent holiness"), as well as in relation to the effects that manifest the end ("and inexhaustible fruitfulness in everything that is good"); (3) in relation to the material and formal cause together ("with her catholic unity"); (4) adding also "invincible stability" as a sign of the perfection of the whole work, which has such a miraculous and eminent appearance, exceeding natural powers, hence being "a great and perpetual motive of credibility and an irrefutable testimony of her divine mission."

The value of this motive is explained at greater length in the *Annotations to the Pre-Conciliar Schema*:

> Although less-educated believers do not know all of the motives of credibility distinctly nor are able to explain them to themselves, they nonetheless know, in a way that is accommodated to their own abilities, that the Church is one, holy, catholic, and apostolic, and in this they forever have before their eyes an unchanging, fully sufficient, and certain motive of credibility, or, rather, complex of motives, so that they would not now, as it were, "hastily believe with fickle hearts," but rather would rely upon the firmest of foundations for full certitude of credibility, always prepared, in a way appropriate to each of their conditions, to give an answer, truly through the Church and in the Church, whenever anyone asks about the reasons in support of what they hold in hope. For indeed, just as in the case of given natural truths, *prior to having a scientific demonstration*, all of mankind has *full certitude* concerning

---

[1] [First] Vatican Council, *Dei filius*, ch. 3 (Denzinger, nos. 3013–3014).

the providential dispositions of God in the natural order, even though this can indeed be more fully and distinctly explained in its foundations by philosophical inquiry, without this [certitude] being shaken by reasons that are brought forth [against it], so too *the divine goodness and wisdom in the order of supernatural providence disposes the Catholic Church to be eminent in those given characteristics, so that in them, prior to scientific inquiries*—which are quite inappropriate for the great host of men—*uneducated persons already have an easily knowable compendium of the motives of credibility needed for full certitude*, even though these motives can indeed be confirmed by apologetic disciplines by means of a more distinct and fuller explanation, though the prudent man cannot be led into doubt by reasons opposed to them, thereby being led to waver in his certitude concerning this matter.[2]

Also see what we will say below in ch. 19, a. 3 *concerning the moral certitude* involved in the discernibility of miracles.

§2. A Defense by Reason That These Motives, When Taken All Together, Constitute an Irresistible Argument

These motives can be considered in two ways: (A) negatively and (B) positively.

A. NEGATIVELY CONSIDERED, they are *immunity from manifest error, contradiction, deceit, and immorality.* Taken together in this way, they demonstrate that nothing could stand in the way of the proposed religion being revealed, though they do not thereby prove its divine origin but, rather, encourage the presumption that such an origin indeed exists.

Immunity from manifest error involves the lack of evident opposition to natural truths that are already known with certitude. Revealed truths can indeed be above reason, but they cannot be contrary to it, even though they frequently stand in opposition to philosophical systems that have not, in fact, demonstrated their conclusions, such as pantheistic evolutionism. Immunity from all contradiction is had from the coherence of the truths that are proposed as being revealed. {{13}} Immunity from deceit pertains above all to the mode of proposing religion, and immunity from immorality to the effects of this religion.

If all such negative notes are present, one will already be stirred to some presumption concerning the divine origin of the religion thus proposed, for as we proved earlier (in our thesis concerning the moral necessity of the rev-

---

[2]   *Acta Concilii Vaticani* in *Collectio lacensis*, vol. 7 (533).

elation of the natural truths of religion[3]), it hardly could be possible that man, without some special divine aid, would teach speculative and practical religious truths without any admixture with error.

This argument is confirmed through a consideration of other religions, wherein we can find obvious errors, deceit, and immorality. (In St. Thomas's works, see *SCG* I, ch. 6, where he compares Islam with the excellence and purity of Christianity.)

B. POSITIVELY CONSIDERED, the external motives intrinsic to religion are taken (1) from the sublimity of the doctrine proposed; (2) from the holiness of the religion's founder, its apostles, and its martyrs; (3) from its astonishing propagation; (4) from its fruitfulness in all that is good; (5) from its catholic unity; and (6) from its unconquered stability. Taken all together, these notes constitute an irresistible argument for the divine origin of this religion. Why? Because, as we must show, they cannot exist without *a special intervention by God.*[4]

Therefore, we need to argue from what is marvelous in God's principal work and from its harmony, in accord with what is said in Psalm 67:36: "Marvelous is God in his saints."

Let us begin by defining what harmony and sublimity are.

Harmony is the perfection of order. However, as Aristotle shows,[5] order is a disposition by way of priority and posteriority in relation to some principle. This is found analogically in magnitude, numbers, motions, knowledge, love, action, and in the hierarchy of beings. Hence, according to this definition, an order is more perfect to the degree that more things are disposed in a more united fashion in relation to some principle. Therefore, this perfection of order (or harmony) is all the greater to the degree that a more profound unity is found in a greater diversity, as in the universe, all of whose parts are ordered to each other and to God.[6]

Now, harmony is required for beauty, which, according to St. Thomas,[7] includes three things: integrity (as regards the multitude involved, at least, of power [*saltem virtutis*]), due proportion (as regards the unity of order), and clarity or splendor (as regards the manifestation of order in a number of parts or attributes). As regards human life, already in the natural life, beauty

---

[3] See vol. 1, ch. 13, a. 2.

[4] See Vacant, *Études sur le Concile du Vatican*, vol. 2, 150.

[5] See Aristotle, *Metaphysics*, bk. 5, ch. 11 (and lect. 13 in St. Thomas's commentary on this book). Likewise, see *ST* II-II, q. 26, a. 1, as well as "ordo" in the index to his works.

[6] See *ST* I, q. 21, a. 1, ad 3.

[7] See *ST* I, q. 39, a. 8. St. Augustine says, "Beauty is the splendor of order."

is an order of reason that *per se* and essentially is found in contemplation of the truth, though participatively in the moral virtues.[8]

On the nature of what is truly sublime. It seems that this term comes from the expression *sub limine caeli* [up unto the threshold of heaven], in order to designate that which is most loftily situated in the air. {{14}} And even if men abuse this word quite often, they say that, properly speaking, "sublime" signifies something that belongs to the loftiest and most extraordinary place in the order of beauty, especially that of intellectual and moral beauty. Now, from the aforementioned definitions of order, beauty, and harmony, we can say that *sublimity appears most especially in the loftiest and most intimate union of various things that are most distant from each other (e.g., of the loftiest and the lowliest).* On account of this distance, such a union, which at first glance seems to be impossible, is utterly marvelous and arouses tears of admiration. Such is the case for the way that the supreme mercy is inclined toward [lifting us out of] our misery, or the union of infinite justice with immense mercy. This is also true for the intimate reconciliation of the greatest strength and perfect sweetness found in martyrdom. By contrast, the discord found in the delusions of false mysticism rouse one to laughter.

Thus defined, the sublime, in the order of intellectual and moral beauty, is in a way akin to what a miracle is in the sensible order—namely, something extraordinary. Thus, as we will discuss below, just as a miracle is above (and not opposed to) nature, so too the sublime is above the customary order of things intellectual and moral and not opposed thereto.[9]

Modernists wish to see in this marvelous life of the Church only "something unknown"[10] that has not yet been historically and psychologically explained (namely, the natural mystery of religious evolution). By contrast, what we must show here is that something supernatural is indeed found in this marvelous life.

This sublimity at the basis of our argument is indicated by St. Paul in Ephesians 3:18–19 (DR) when he says: "You may be able to comprehend, with all the saints, what is the *breadth* and *length* and *height* and *depth*, to know also the charity of Christ, which surpasseth all knowledge: that you may be filled unto all the fulness of God." As is commonly held,[11] *breadth* is extension to all the parts of the universe, *length* to all times past and future, *height* to the loftiest mysteries of God, and *depth* to the worst evil or to obsti-

---

8   See *ST* II-II, q. 180, a. 2, ad 3.

9   See Charles Lèvêque, *La science du beau* [(Paris: A. Durand et Pedon-Lauriée, 1872)], pt. 1, ch. 8.

10   See Pius X, *Pascendi*, no. 35 (Denzinger, no. 3499).

11   See St. Thomas, *In Ep. Ad Ephesios*, ch. 3, lect. 5.

nacy to be punished, so that "all things cooperate in the good," to the salvation of souls and the glory of God.

The value of these various motives must be considered part by part, not merely in a rhetorical manner but indeed philosophically and theologically.

(1) **Purity and sublimity of doctrine.** The divine origin of a given teaching can be at least morally certain, on the basis of a threefold consideration of this doctrine: (a) considered in itself, (b) with regard to the way that it is proposed, and (c) with regard to the way it has been constituted.

(a) THE DOCTRINE CONSIDERED IN ITSELF. One sign of the divine origin of a religion is found in the doctrine that it proposes in the name of God, marvelously uniting *what is greatest and what is least,* supernatural things and natural things, the riches of the divine *mercy* and the misery of mankind, preserving the rights of *justice,* which are proposed to all men of all nations and times, gathering together *what is oldest* and *most new* so that even though the mysteries thus handed on may be obscure, they appear as being most excellently connected together with each other as well as with man's ultimate end. Thus, the Catholic liturgy [of the Roman rite] says, "God gives peace, reconciling in Himself *the lowliest with the loftiest.*"

{{15}} However, this is made manifest specifically [*in particulari*]:

(1) *As regards natural truths,* inasmuch as this doctrine exceeds, by far, all the systems of philosophers and other religions, proposing nothing that reason would show to be false, and *perfectly teaches all things* that pertain to natural religion concerning God's existence, nature, attributes, providence, and creation, as well as concerning man's origin, nature, and end, along with those truths concerning moral precepts and counsels, so that it fully suffices for rightly establishing a way of life for man and indeed perfectly responds to all of man's legitimate aspirations.[12]

---

[12] See *ST* I-II, q. 98, a. 1 (Whether the old law was good): "Just as a doctrine is shown to be true because it is in harmony with reason, so too a given law is shown to be good because it is in harmony with right reason. Now, the Old Law was in harmony with reason because it checked concupiscence . . . and also prohibited all things which are contrary to reason. Hence, it is manifestly clear that it was good . . . though it was imperfect." Also see *ST* I-II, q. 117, a. 1: "Now, the New Law is the law of perfection, for it is the law of charity . . . inclining one to works of virtue to be done for the very love of virtue, not on account of some extrinsic punishment or remuneration . . . and it is said to have spiritual and eternal promises which are the objects of virtue, especially of charity."

The divine doctrine is said to be living water for three reasons—namely, because it heals the weak, cleanses those who are soiled [with sin], and quenches those who thirst (cf. the end of St. Thomas's remarks on Isaiah 55).

It is also said to be wine for three reasons—namely, because it stings through argumen-

(2) *As regards mysteries as supernatural things proposed.* The divine origin of a religion is thus manifested inasmuch as these mysteries, as well as the duties correlative to them, *notwithstanding their obscurity and inaccessible loftiness*, seem to be *most greatly conformed to the naturally knowable attributes of God and to our nature's aspirations*, likewise calling for the mortification of the wicked inclinations of our sensuality and pride.[13]

This argument is reinforced if, as Pascal said, by these mysteries it should also explain both man's misery as well the nobility of his desires for supreme things, likewise offering a remedy for this misery.

By contrast, false mysticism proposes the absurd delusions of exultation, or falls into sub-rational sensualism.

The aforementioned doctrine is divine on account of these marvelous notes. For what human reason was not able to accomplish in so many philosophers, following upon the exertion of such great labors, manifestly surpasses, at least morally, the natural powers of man teaching this body of doctrine, or the powers of many men teaching this same doctrine firmly and without any division among themselves. At the very least, it is evident that, without supernatural assistance, it would be morally impossible to constitute this teaching as regards the sum of the natural truths of religion and to order so befittingly [such] mysteries, which are proposed as being supernatural.[14]

{{16}} As Cardinal Zigliara wrote:

Indeed, it is morally impossible that the man who says this on his own, that is, from the light of reason, would always and in all things pursue the truth, for sometimes he falls into error, often fluctuates between opposed opinions, and gets caught up in contradictions. However, where truth always exists, where no opposition exists in those things which are said by one person or (something even more marvelous, really) by many, who say that they speak through divine

---

tation, sets one ablaze through its enkindling power, and inebriates through its power of consolation (ibid.).

Likewise, it is called milk for three reasons—namely, on account of its beauty and sweetness, as well as on account of how easily it can be taken in (ibid.).

[13] See the prologue to *SCG* IV. Likewise, see *ST* II-II, q. 1, a. 7: "Thus, the articles of faith are involved in the doctrine of faith like how self-evident principles are involved in the teaching that can be had through natural reason. And there is indeed an order found in such principles, so that some are implicitly contained in others, just as all principles are reduced to this one: It is impossible to simultaneously affirm and deny [one and the same thing from the same perspective], as is clear from *Metaphysics*, bk. 4. And likewise, all the articles are implicitly contained in certain first things that are believed, namely, that God must be believed to exist and that He exercises providence concerning men's salvation."

[14] [Trans. note: Reading *ordinandi* for *ordinand* and *proposita* for *propositas*.]

inspiration, this is a sign that the doctrine in question does not come from man but, rather, from God, especially if the preaching of it is concerned with the loftiest mysteries of God.[15]

Also based on the goodness of this doctrine, it is manifest that it does not come from an evil spirit, something confirmed by comparing it with superstitions that suggest the basest of things concerning God.

Similarly, this argument is confirmed if the apostles enjoy such an abundance of wisdom that all of their adversaries are not able to resist them or contradict them. Hence, in 1 Corinthians 12:8–10 (DR), St. Paul places *words of wisdom* first among the various freely given graces when he says: "To one indeed, by the Spirit, is given the word of wisdom: and to another, the word of knowledge, according to the same Spirit; to another, faith in the same spirit; to another, the grace of healing in one Spirit; to another, the working of miracles; to another, prophecy; to another, the discerning of spirits; to another, diverse kinds of tongues; to another, interpretation of speeches."[16]

(b) DOCTRINE IN RELATION TO THE WAY IT IS PREACHED. This pertains to the "grace of words" [*sermonis*], which is given so that the divine truth may be readily accessible, delightful, and moving—in other words, so that it may illuminate the intellect, piously delight the affect, and efficaciously move the will to fulfill God's commands.[17]

(1) *In relation to its illumination,* a given harmony is marvelous if the loftiest myster-

---

[15] See Cardinal Zigliara, in *Propaedeutica ad sacram theologiam in usum scholarum, seu, Tractatus de ordine supernaturali,* 5th ed. (Rome: [Typographia Polyglotta Sacrae Congregationis de Propaganda Fide,] 1903), bk. 2, ch. 9, no. 4. Likewise, see Gonet, *Clypeus theologiae Thomisticae, De fide,* disp. 1, a. 8, 52 [*sic*]; Suarez, *De fide,* disp. 4, sect. 3; as well as what is said by Catholic apologetes and exegetes in general.

[16] The topic of freely given graces is explained by St. Thomas in *ST* I-II, q. 111, a. 4; II-II, q. 17[5]–8, and in *In I Cor.,* ch. 12, lect. 2. In the first text cited, in ad 4, he says: "*Wisdom and science* are not counted among the freely-given graces inasmuch as the former are numbered among the gifts of the Holy Spirit, that is, inasmuch as man's mind is moved by the Holy Spirit to those things which are of wisdom and science. Rather, *they are counted among the freely-given graces* inasmuch as they involve some *abundance of science* and of wisdom, so that man would be able not only to taste such things aright in himself but also would be able to teach others as well as to conquer those who contradict them. And therefore, what are clearly placed among the freely given graces *are words* of wisdom and *words* of science." And in ad 2: "Likewise, *faith* is not numbered among freely-given graces inasmuch as the former is a given virtue justifying man in himself but, rather, inasmuch as it involves a given super-eminent certitude of faith, by which man is rendered suitable to instruct others about those things that pertain to faith." Hence, Jesus says to his disciples, "*For I will give you a mouth and wisdom, which all your adversaries shall not be able to resist and gainsay*" (Luke 21:15, DR).

[17] See *ST* II-II, q. 177, a. 1 (Whether any freely given grace is connected to words).

ies are taught *with the greatest of authority*, together with *simplicity and humility*, in a way that is accommodated to the understanding of all men coming from various times and peoples. By contrast, philosophers often speak about the loftiest of things only in a probable manner, doing so with such abstractness that these truths can only be understood by the wise. Moreover, they often lack simplicity and humility. Similarly, neither could true illumination proceed from a false religion, which either tends toward the delusions of false mysticism or is inclined to naturalism, being unable to reconcile grace with nature.

(2) It is also miraculous that the preaching of the faith *brings holy delight by its own unction*, even though it *austerely proposes arduous precepts*. It duly offends the evil inclinations of the sinner and nonetheless profoundly draws his heart, bringing it peace. This intimate reconciliation of the greatest unction and austerity indicates that it involves God's special assistance. {{17}} By contrast, false religions are pleasing through a kind of false piety, do not impose difficult obligations, do not "raise the sword" against the spirit of error and evil, and do not bring true inner peace. They please men in order to achieve human acclaim and do not labor for the glory of God. If it sometimes is the case, as in that of Montanism or Jansenism, that they commend immoderate austerity, they lack unction and destroy harmony.

(3) Finally, the extraordinary *efficacy* of words is clear if countless hosts of people— not only men who are simple but also the wise—in contempt of visible things, are moved efficaciously to invisible and *utterly lofty* things, notwithstanding the countless hindrances involved therein, indeed sometimes in the midst of the tyranny of persecutors. This sign will be even greater if this doctrine *perpetually preserves its influence*, while other doctrines die off.

(c) Doctrine in relation to its origin. This argument can be perfected, and the impossibility (not only moral but also psychological) that this doctrine would be natural in origin can be made manifest, if it is historically clear that it appeared *without human preparation*—that is, neither being elaborated by the human genius of the person teaching it nor having been eclectically concocted from other sources. Therefore, St. Thomas says that it is loftier than a physical miracle, something "marvelous, [namely,] that simple men (like the Apostles), filled with the gift of the Holy Spirit, achieved the heights of wisdom and eloquence in a mere instant."[18] Above all, this *newness* must be reconciled with the utterly great *antiquity* of the religion in question, for there can only be one divine religion for all men.

However, this is historically verified in Christ, who said: "I have come

---

[18] *SCG* I, ch. 6. This is more miraculous in itself, and for the wise, though perhaps not for all men, for many men, inclined too greatly to sensible things, marvel more greatly at sensible miracles.

not to do away with the law and the prophets but, rather, to fulfill them." (See bk. 2, ch. 7 below, where we will historically set forth this motive, along with other similar ones.)

This excellent manner of teaching indicates the existence of a special intervention by God, "Who makes use of human language like a kind of instrument, although He Himself is the one who perfects the activity interiorly."[19]

A new sign is added if the preachers of the faith immediately "begin to speak in various tongues," which heretofore were wholly unknown to them, as is seen in Acts 2.[20]

Objection: The aforementioned argument is not scientific in character.

Response: It does not pertain to some particular science, like physics or psychology, but, rather, to wisdom (that is, the supreme science), which is concerned with the highest causes, as Aristotle says (*Metaphysics*, bk. 1, ch. 1). In other words, in accord with St. Augustine's terminology, it pertains to superior reason, not inferior reason.

It will be insisted, however: If a given doctrine proposes supernatural mysteries, this itself is obscure and requires miracles in confirmation of it. Therefore, it is not a motive of credibility by itself.

Response: A motive of credibility is present here (1) in the purity and excellence of this doctrine, inasmuch as it most perfectly hands on all the truths of natural religion, surpassing all philosophical systems and all other religions; also (2) in relation to obscure supernatural mysteries, inasmuch as *this obscurity essentially differs from the obscurity found in teachings that wander about incoherently*, illuminating in its own way all souls of good will and continually moving them to do good.[21]

{{18}} A miraculous sign is found in the intimate union of this obscurity with the mysteries' mutual harmony with each other, and in the reconciliation of the loftiest heights of reflection with the greatest simplicity, so that the deep things of God are thus handed on to little ones.[22]

And therefore, this doctrine appears obscure to us not on account of something it lacks as regards its truth and coherence but, rather, on account of its utterly great sublimity and brightness. Inasmuch as it is essentially supernatural, it is a loftier miracle than those things that are only supernatural from the perspective of the efficient causality involved in their production. Hence, it is too lofty to be intrinsically evident for us, something like

---

[19] *ST* II-II, q. 177, a. 1. Here he cites the words of St. Gregory the Great: "Unless the Holy Ghost fills the hearts of those who hear, in vain do the words of teachers sound forth in one's bodily ears."

[20] See *ST* II-II, q. 176 (On the gift of tongues).

[21] See 1 Cor 2:4.

[22] See Matt 7:29.

a light that is far too bright surpassing the powers of our intellect, just as the light of the sun surpasses the visual power of the night owl's eye.

Indeed, this sublimity of doctrine is above all apparent when one is subject to the Holy Spirit's internal illumination, though it can also be known in its effects by reason alone. By itself and without the internal light of faith, reason does not formally attain supernatural revealed truths. It knows the letter of the Gospel, not its spirit. And yet it nonetheless can know certain miraculous effects of supernatural truth, just as all people contemplating Christ's gentleness, humility, charity, and fortitude see there, as it were, rays of his supernatural life. Hence, many rationalists, like Renan, admit nobody has proposed (nor could anyone ever propose) a loftier doctrine than Christ's doctrine. And the scribes of the Pharisees said, concerning Christ: "Never did man speak like this man" (John 7:46, DR).

Hence, even if it is most highly fitting that a supernatural doctrine be confirmed through sensible miracles, already in its purity and sublimity we find a kind of sign of its divine origin. Nay, among the circumstances used in distinguishing a true miracle from a false one, it is quite common for one to include the goodness of the doctrine in question, in confirmation of which this given miracle was performed. Thus, without committing any vicious circle, *what remains obscure in a given doctrine is confirmed by the miracle, and the evident goodness of the doctrine confirms the truth of the miracle.* In this way, the spiritual and the sensible mutually aid each other, like intellection and sensation, in accord with the common axiom, "Causes are mutually related as causes to each other, though in different genera of causality."

(2) *The utterly great and obvious holiness of a religion's founder, apostles, and martyrs.* If this holiness is utterly great and obvious, it provides yet another sign, for such holiness cannot exist without *some special intervention by God.* Indeed, holiness is a virtue involving perfect purity from earthly things, as well as utterly firm union with God—indeed, ordering all of the acts of the virtues to God.[23] Now, the order of agents must correspond to the order of ends. Therefore, holiness cannot exist without God's aid,[24] and extraordinary holiness comes from God intervening in the world in an extraordinary manner.

However, this holiness appears most clearly in the heroic[25] exercise of all the virtues. "Common virtue perfects man in a human manner, *whereas heroic virtue* does so in a way that is super-human. Indeed, when the brave man fears something when it should be feared, this is a virtue; however, if he

---

[23] See *ST* II-II, q. 81, a. 8c and ad 1.

[24] See *ST* I-II, q. 109, a. 6.

[25] See Benedict XIV, *Doctrina de servorum Dei beatificatione et beatorum canonizatione,* bk. 3, ch. 21ff (*De virtute heroica*). Also see St. Thomas, *In VI Ethic.,* lect. 1.

does not fear it, it will be a vice. Now, if he fears nothing, trusting in God's aid, this virtue will be above the human mode of virtue, and such virtues are called divine."[26]

According to Benedict XIV (*De canonizatione sanctorum*, bk. 3, ch. 21), *four things are required so that heroic virtue can be said to have been proven*: (1) that the matter was *difficult*, above the common powers of men, (2) that the acts were performed *promptly* and readily, (3) indeed, being done *with delight*, (4) and not only once or rarely but, rather, *frequently*, on a given occasion. (Regarding Christ's holiness, see bk. 2, ch. 6 below.)

{{19}} St. Thomas says, "There are certain virtues had by those who have already achieved likeness to God. These are called 'perfect virtues.' Thus, prudence sees only the things of God; temperance knows no earthly desires; courage knows no passions; and, by imitating the Divine Mind, justice is united to it by an everlasting bond. We say that these virtues are had by the Blessed, or, in this life, by those who are utterly perfect."[27]

For example, St. Louis Bertrand remained at peace in the midst of the greatest dangers, and when he knew he had taken poison, which had secretly been given to him, he remained tranquil and trusted in God alone. In the midst of the most bitter of sufferings, he did not lament but, rather, said, "Lord, burn here and cut things off there, so that you may refrain from doing so eternally." Another holy priest, after being falsely accused of an atrocious crime, was suspended by his bishop, and immediately he gave thanks before the cross, as being unworthy of such grace. The holy deacon [*levita*] Vincent, having been taken from his horse and carried off to the gibbet, eagerly offered his executioners arguments so that they might hasten his demise, which they were delaying to bring about. And undaunted, he climbed up onto the grill of shining iron on his own, and unmoved there, standing erect in the light, looking to heaven, he prayed to God.[28] (Likewise see the other examples of heroic virtue given in the same text by Benedict XIV.)

As St. Thomas says in *ST* II-II, q. 124, a. 3:

> Now, of all virtuous acts, *martyrdom* most greatly demonstrates the perfection of charity, for a man's love for a thing is manifested all the greater to the degree that what he despises for its sake is dearer

---

[26] See St. Thomas, *In Matth.*, ch. 5 (beginning).

[27] *ST* I-II, q. 61, a. 5. (The virtues of those in purgatory can be heroic, though heroism is found most clearly in the virtues of souls that have been purified.) See Benedict XIV, *Doctrina de servorum Dei beatificatione et beatorum canonizatione*, bk. 3, ch. 21ff.

[28] See Thierry Ruinart, *Acta primorum martyrum sincera et selecta* (Verona, 1731), 325. In the same *Acta*, see SS. Perpetua, Felicity, Polycarp, Ignatius, et al. These will be set forth below in bk. 2, ch. 9, a. 2.

to him and that he chooses to suffer for its sake something more offensive to him. However, it is quite clear that of all the goods that man has in this present life, he loves life itself most of all and, on the other hand, hates death equally as much, especially when it is accompanied by the pains of bodily torment—and as Augustine observes (in his work, *Eighty-Three Different Questions*, q. 36), "even brute animals draw back from the greatest pleasures so as to avoid such pains." And for this reason, martyrdom clearly is the most perfect of human acts in respect to its genus, being the sign of the greatest charity, according to John 15:13 (DR): "Greater love than this no man hath, that a man lay down his life for his friends."

Hence, "*a martyr* is said to be a kind of *witness to the Christian faith*, displaying before our sight the idea that visible things should be scorned for the sake of invisible things, as is said in Hebrews 11:39."[29] "Indeed, nobody can scorn present things except out of hope for future goods. Indeed, such scorn is the principal means for overcoming the world. And therefore, because faith holds out invisible things to us, on account of which the world is to be held in scorn, therefore, our faith conquers the world."[30]

However, in order for true heroic virtue to be discerned as being something coming from God (in distinction from the false appearance of such virtue), beyond the four aforementioned conditions, {{20}} *we must consider the connection of the virtues* in prudence and in charity. Indeed, we see that some people are prompt to perform courageous deeds on account of their natural makeup or on account of some habits they have formed from custom, without however being ready to perform deeds of meekness, for nature is determined to one thing. However, if someone has all of the virtues at once and in a truly excellent manner, even those that are most distant from each other (like the greatest courage along with the heights of mercy, perfect love of the truth and justice simultaneously alongside the greatest mercy toward those who go astray), this is possible only through extraordinary assistance coming from God, who alone in his simplicity eminently contains utterly diverse perfections and can unite them together intimately within the human soul. This interconnection is the expression of a marvelous kind of harmony: "Charity is patient, is kind: charity envieth not, dealeth not perversely, is not puffed up; it is not ambitious, seeketh not her own, is not provoked to anger, thinketh no evil. It rejoiceth not in iniquity,

---

[29] *ST* II-II, q. 124, a. 4.
[30] St. Thomas, *In Ep. Ad Hebr.*, ch. 11.

but rejoiceth with the truth. It beareth all things, believeth all things, hopeth all things, endureth all things" (1 Cor 13:4–7, DR).

Hence, in bk. 3, ch. 21 of the aforementioned work, Benedict XIV says:

> If true moral virtues can be found among nonbelievers [*gentilibus*], this does not seem to cause any issue; moreover, they can attain to a heroic degree of virtue, considering the nature of the thing. However, in order to be established as being truly heroic, the full collection of all of the moral virtues is required. Now, no matter how many nonbelievers [*gentiles*] have been said to have heroic [virtue] on account of the excellence of a given moral virtue, they were lacking a number of other virtues and served the interests of [certain] vices, and therefore none of them was able to have been established as being *strictly heroic*, as is proven at length by Cardinals de Laurea and de Aguirre, and at great length by Théophile Raynaud.[31]

Therefore, a marvelous harmony is found in the preacher of the faith when he speaks in God's name with the greatest of authority, "as one having power,"[32] "not through persuasive words of human wisdom,"[33] with the greatest humility, without boasting, sincerely expressing oneself, out of zeal for God, with the greatest charity for one's neighbor, without fear but with unconquerable courage in the face of persecutions, yet combined with meekness so that *such a person would come to pray for those who persecute him.* This provides a sign of God's presence in him, for this marvelous harmony of heroic virtues, so very diverse among themselves, could not exist without some special aid given by God.[34]

Such a sign can only be denied if one is clearly filled with malice and perversity, as

---

[31] See *ST* I-II, q. 65, a. 1 and 3 (On the connection of the virtues in prudence and in charity). Also see the text of Benedict XIV cited above.

[32] Matt 7:29.

[33] 1 Cor 2:4.

[34] In his second sermon on the Visitation, discussing the *Magnificat*, St. Francis de Sales writes: "The union of the loftiest of charity with utterly profound humility is something quite admirable indeed, for these two virtues are so distant from each other that it seems that they could never come together in one and the same soul unless charity were to elevate it. And the more that it grows [*croist*], the more will it come to raise it above all that is not God. Humility does the complete opposite, lowering the soul below itself and all creatures, for what belongs to this virtue is that the greater that it is, the more does it lower the soul in which it is found.

"Therefore, I pray you to look upon the extreme character of these two virtues, and I assure you that you will ask, 'How can humility and charity be united and joined together?' Naturally speaking, this is impossible; thus, nobody other than Our Lord was able to unite these two virtues, and He showed the incomparable greatness of His power by uniting things that are distant from each other." They are connected like the tree's deepest root and its loftiest and most fruitful branch.

was the case for the Pharisees. {{21}} However, then, they who denied brought forth a new sign, for through their obvious malice, they prove the sufficiency of the aforementioned signs (see Acts 4:16).

By contrast, in the founders and preachers of false religions and sects, uncharitable fanaticism is substituted for the firmness of faith, or liberalism without true faith for charity. In false prophets, we find ostentation without humility, obsequiousness without dignity, being angry in difficult situations or rash without meekness and pusillanimous without courage.

Objection: Holiness needs to be confirmed through miracles. Therefore, by itself, it is not a motive of credibility.

Response: Eminent holiness, especially as we see in the constancy of the martyrs, already in itself is a sign, inasmuch as it quite clearly comes from God himself. Nonetheless, holiness is given certain attestation when it is confirmed by miracles. Nay, they confirm each other, though without involving any vicious circle, inasmuch as causes are causes of each other, though in different genera of causality. What remains obscure in holiness is confirmed by miracles, and what is already evident in holiness confirms the truth of miracles and excludes the possibility of [mere] marvels.

Second objection: However, it seems that without perfect charity—nay, even merely without charity—someone can offer his life as a martyr. Indeed, St. Paul says in 1 Corinthians 13:3 (DR): "If I should deliver my body to be burned, and have not charity, it profiteth me nothing." And many have died out of their fanaticism, undergoing torments for the sake of various religions and sects. Nay, without any special aid from God, soldiers undergo the brutalities of war.

Response: St. Thomas himself says:

> In the acts of the virtues, two things must be heeded, namely, *that which is done* and *the manner in which it is done*. Therefore, we must say that the act of offering oneself as a martyr or even the suffering of martyrdom can be performed not only by one having perfect charity but also by someone who lacks charity. However, he who has perfect charity does this promptly and with delight, as is clear in Laurence and Vincent, who even had humorous dispositions in the midst of their torments. However, this could not be done merely out of imperfect charity or, likewise, by him who lacks charity.[35]

Likewise, supernatural courage is something to be distinguished from natural courage, as well as from fanaticism, through the connection of virtues, inasmuch as it is joined with charity, humility, and prayer for one's persecutors.[36] For our discussion of arguments [on

---

[35] *Quodlibet* IV, q. 10, a. 1.

[36] See Benedict XIV, *Doctrina de servorum Dei beatificatione et beatorum canonizatione*, bk. 3, ch.

behalf of credibility] on the basis of the constancy of the martyrs, see bk. 2, ch. 9 below.

(3) *The wondrous propagation of religion.* The strength of this argument is set forth by St. Thomas in *SCG* I, ch. 6:

> Not the violence of arms, nor by the promise of pleasures, and—what is most miraculous of all—in the midst of the tyranny of persecutors, an innumerable host, not only of the simple but also of the wisest of men, flocked to the Christian faith. In this faith, things exceeding every human intellect are preached, the pleasures of the flesh are restrained, and it is taught that all things that are in the world are to be held in contempt. For the minds of mortals to assent to such things is *the greatest of miracles*, one that likewise is a manifest work of divine inspiration, so that men would come to seek only that which is invisible, doing so in contempt of that which is visible. . . . However, this marvelous conversion of the world to the Christian faith is the most certain evidence of the signs from the past (i.e., of miracles), such that it is no longer necessary that they be further repeated, since they are evidently apparent in their effect. Indeed, it would be *more marvelous than all signs* if the world were led by simple and humble men without miraculous signs to believe such difficult things, to perform such difficult actions, and to have so lofty a hope. . . .
>
> {{22}} But those who founded those erring sects followed the opposite path, as is clear in the case of Mohammed, who enticed people through promises of carnal pleasures, to which the concupiscence of the flesh rouses men. Likewise, he preached precepts that were conformed to these promises, giving free rein to carnal pleasures, and carnal men were quite ready to obey him in these matters. . . . He said that he was sent through strength of arms, signs which, however, are not lacking even in thieves and tyrants. Moreover, no wise men, trained in things divine and human, believed him from the start, but rather, he was believed by brutal men wandering in the desert, wholly ignorant of divine teaching, and through their number, Mohammed forced others to follow his law by violence of arms.

So that the value of this argument may be clear, we must manifest *the absolute disproportion* between this marvelous conversion of the world and natural causes, insisting *on the loftiness of the end to be obtained, the hindrances to its propagation, and the natural weakness of the apostles*, as St. Paul says in 1 Corinthians 1:25–29 (DR):

---

20 (On False Martyrs).

The weakness of God is stronger than men. . . . But the foolish things of the world hath God chosen, that he may confound the wise: and the weak things of the world hath God chosen, that he may confound the strong. And the base things of the world and the things that are contemptible, hath God chosen: and things that are not, that he might bring to naught things that are: that no flesh should glory in his sight.

Likewise, in 2 Corinthians 4:7 (DR): "*But we have this treasure in earthen vessels, that the excellency may be of the power of God and not of us.*" We must note this quite carefully: This weakness remains in God's instrument so that the supernaturality of the divine intervention may be made manifest more clearly.

Above all, one must argue from the fact that the *vitality of the Church is not diminished but, rather, is increased through persecutions*, as the Lord himself said: "Blessed are they that suffer persecution for justice' sake. . . . Blessed are ye when they shall revile you, and persecute you . . . for my sake. Be glad and rejoice for your reward is very great in heaven" (Matt 5:10–12, DR).

For a historical exposition of this argument, see bk. 2, ch. 9 below.

(4) *The fruitfulness of religion in everything that is good.* This fruitfulness must be considered in relation to the individual, family life, and society.

(a) *In relation to the individual*, inasmuch as his intellect is freed from errors concerning God, the world, and the soul, while the will is freed from the worst corruption of paganism.

(b) *In relation to family life*, inasmuch as the dignity of wives is here restored, the protection and education of children [fostered], and the harshness of slavery was tempered and, gradually, extinguished.

(c) *In relation to society*, inasmuch as legitimate authority, finding its foundation in God, is promoted, as well as due liberty, charity, and the [natural] laws common to all nations [*ius gentium*]. Thus, tyranny and license are shunned, as well as the interpersonal confusion arising from communism and the personal separation involved in individualism, with the harmony of individuals and society thus being established.

(d) *From all the works of mercy* and beneficence an argument is at hand too, here verifying the words of Christ: "Be ye therefore merciful, as your Father also is merciful" (Luke 6:36, DR), as well as those of Paul: "Who is weak, and I am not weak?" (2 Cor 11:29, DR); "put ye on therefore, as the elect of God, holy and beloved, the bowels of mercy" (Col 3:12, DR).

{{23}} In order to make this sign clearly manifest, we must distinguish the virtue of mercy from inefficacious, sense-derived commiseration. This sense passion is often found in fearful things [*in formidolosis*], whereas by contrast mercy presupposes goodness and courage and is a manifestation of the good through its own self-outpouring. Hence, St. Thomas says that it is the greatest of virtues inasmuch as "it falls to it to pour oneself forth for another and, what is more, to come to the needs of others. And this bespeaks the greatest of superiority. Whence, mercy is even *said to be proper to God*, and in it His omnipotence finds its greatest manifestation."[37] Indeed, in mercy *the inclination of the loftiest toward that which is least* is made manifest, as well as God's greatest goodness and omnipotence, inasmuch as "God is so omnipotent and good that He draws good even out of evil."[38] Hence, when a given religion manifests the greatest of mercy, this is a sign of its divine origin.

The strength of this argument will be even clearer if this fruitfulness in all that is good is found only in one religion, as is clear through an examination of history. See bk. 2, ch. 9 below.

Hence, in the annotations to the pre-conciliar schema to the [First] Vatican Council, we read: "Solely to the Catholic Church pertains the everlasting continuation of the motives of credibility found in the marvelous propagation and preservation of the Christian religion, *in the same effects which are both certain and worthy of admiration, indeed exceeding all natural causes*, found in the behavior and multitude of her martyrs, as well as (the moral continuation of) the perpetual manifestation of spiritual charisms."[39]

Christ himself indicated this sign, saying: "Even so every good tree bringeth forth good fruit, and the evil tree bringeth forth evil fruit" (Matt 7:17, DR). And St. Paul wrote to the Corinthians: "But as from God, before God, in Christ we speak. . . . Or do we need (as some do) epistles of commendation to you, or from you? *You are our epistle*, written in our hearts, which is known and read by all men: Being manifested, that *you are the epistle of Christ*, ministered by us, and written: *not with ink but with the Spirit of the living God*: not in tables of stone but in the fleshly tables of the heart" (2 Cor 2:17–3:3, DR). Indeed, the conversion of the Corinthians to Christ was known to all and served as an example for the conversion of others.

In these holy effects, the end of a religion is made manifest (inasmuch as the end, which is prior in the order of intention, is last in execution). Likewise, we here find a manifestation of the divine cause of religion, in accord with the axiom: The order of agents must correspond to the order of ends.

(5) *Catholic unity.* A new argument is furnished by the catholicity (or universality) of a religion (on the side of its material cause, or members), as

---

[37] *ST* II-II, q. 30, a. 4 (On mercy).

[38] *ST* I, q. 2, a. 3, ad 1 (as well as the text from St. Augustine cited in this response).

[39] *Acta Conc. Vatic., Collectio Lacensis*, vol. 7, 352. In the same place, there is a citation of Augustine, *De utilitate credenda*, ch. 17; and *Ad Volusian*, ep. 137, no. 15ff.

well as by its unity (on the side of its formal cause). It is suitable in apologetics to draw these two marks [of the Church] into one, inasmuch as unity is all the more miraculous to the degree that the Church is more universal.

Indeed, if men from all times and from among all peoples, be they uncivilized or civilized, *notwithstanding the profound diversity and opposition of their languages, inclinations, conceptions, political rules*, and so forth, come to be gathered together in the unity of faith, hope, and charity, as well as that of ecclesiastical rule and worship, so that dogmas never come to be defiled for the sake of the utility that a particular nation might draw therefrom, nor the essential principles of ecclesiastical rule revoked in order to meet the demands of secular power, this is a sign of God's intervention, {{24}} for he alone can produce and preserve such intimate unity in the midst of such diversity.[40]

This is made even clearer by considering the variation existing among the diverse sects that are not able to grow in extent without their dogmas coming to be defiled and also without allowing themselves to be unduly subordinated to secular powers. By contrast, the divine truth is made manifest in the fact that it is not unduly subordinated to any other power, not even the strongest (see bk. 2, ch. 9 below).

Hence, enumerating the signs of the true faith, Pius IX said:

This faith . . . revealing the salutary laws of Christ and acquiring greater strength every day from these most cruel persecutions, has pervaded the whole earth, land, and sea, from the rising to the setting of the sun, under the one standard of the Cross, and also, having overcome the deceits of idols and torn away the mist of errors and triumphed over enemies of every kin, it has illuminated with the light of divine knowledge all peoples, races, nations, however savagely barbarous and diverse in disposition, customs, laws, and institutions; and has subjected them to the most sweet yoke of Christ himself, "Announcing peace" to all, "announcing good."[41]

(6) *The unconquered stability of a religion.* Finally, the aforemen-

---

[40] See St. Thomas, *In De Trinitate Boetii*, q. 3, a. 3 (Whether the Christian faith is suitably called catholic / universal): "It is deservedly called catholic, inasmuch as it has been received by men belonging to all sorts of states of life." However, if someone were to object that the Christian faith has not been received by many and therefore is not universal, St. Thomas responds in ad 5: "The Christian faith is not called catholic (or universal) on account of its individualized extension but, rather, on account of how it has embraced all the various kinds of individuals who may receive it, for it has adherents drawn from among all of man's various conditions."

[41] Pius IX, *Qui pluribus*, no. 8 (Denzinger, no. 2779).

tioned arguments are confirmed by the unconquered stability of a religion that proposes itself as being revealed, for all things in the world are subject to change, with the generation of one thing involving the corruption of the other whence it comes, not only in the physical order but even in the social and political order. Nations rise and fall, as do political forms, and indeed so do religions, along with philosophical systems. *All things gradually spring forth, flower, and then come to their end,* "for the fashion of this world passeth away."[42] Hence, many today are concerned with writing about the history of religions, presenting the tale of their formation, development, and downfall.

By contrast, if only one religion remains the same, indefectible and unconquered in its stability, *notwithstanding the countless hindrances and causes of ruin it may have suffered,* if it is preserved without changing its dogmas, precepts, or authority structure [*in suo regimine*], above all if *it remains living in the midst of this immutability so that it forever renews itself*—if, for example, "there is growth and abundant progress in understanding, though in the same dogma, meaning, and judgment"[43]—then all of this stands as a sign of its divine origin, here bearing witness to an extraordinary participation in the divine immutability, which is not a deathlike immutability but, rather, a living one. In such a case, we have a verification of Christ's words: "Heaven and earth shall pass: but my words shall not pass,"[44] and "I say to thee: That thou art Peter; and upon this rock I will build my church, and the gates of hell shall not prevail against it."[45] And in the words of the Psalms: "(God is the one) who satisfieth thy desire with good things: thy youth shall be renewed like the eagle's."[46]

{{25}} By contrast, false religions and sects remain either lifelessly *in a deathlike immobility*, as is found in Islam, *or in a state of perpetual variation* through continuous accommodation to the undue demands of the age, tending likewise to naturalism or the denial of religion, as is clear in the case of Protestantism.[47] (Here too, see bk. 2, ch. 9 below.)

Conclusion. All of these motives intrinsic to religion, taken together, provide us with an irresistible argument. For if a religion in which all of these signs are found (the sublimity of doctrine, holiness, wondrous propagation, fruitfulness in all good things, catholic unity, and unconquered stability)

---

[42] 1 Cor 7:31 (DR).

[43] See [First] Vatican Council, *Dei filius*, ch. 4 (Denzinger, no. 3020).

[44] Matt 24:35 (DR).

[45] Matt 16:18 (DR).

[46] Ps 102:5 (DR).

[47] See Bossuet's *Histoire des variations des églises protestantes*.

were not from God, there would be an effect without a cause, without a *raison d'être*, for all of these goods can only arise from the fount of all goods.

Nor can it be said that this religion would be from God mediately through the natural evolution of religious sentiment, as the human sciences are mediately from God inasmuch as he is the author of our intelligence. Indeed, *the aforementioned notes are extraordinary* and *manifest an extraordinary intervention by God*. Moreover, this religion proposes itself as being supernaturally revealed and always affirms that this supernatural revelation is the fount of the whole of its truth, strength, and fruitfulness. Therefore, if this supernatural revelation were merely fabricated, all of the goods enumerated above would be founded on lies or delusions, and this is impossible, for real effects presuppose a real cause, not a fabricated one, good effects presuppose a good cause, and supernatural effects a supernatural one.

Finally, nor must one say that all of these goods come from natural religious sentiment, together with error or delusion, for by reason alone, it is clear that the omnipotent God, who is infinitely good, truthful, just, and provident, cannot permit all of these signs and goods to be found in some religion proposed as being revealed by God without, however, in fact having been revealed by him. God cannot permit mankind to be invincibly deceived in those things that are necessary for salvation, and he would permit this if all the aforementioned signs were joined together in conjunction with a fabricated revelation. Hence, even if no sensible miracles existed,[48] leaving only the moral miracle of the Church's miraculous life, the words of Richard of St. Victor would already hold true: "Surely, will we not be able to say to God with full confidence, 'Lord, if this is in error, we have been deceived by you, for these things were confirmed for us with such great signs and marvels, and by such things as can only be brought about by you'?"[49]

The objection of the modernists: The vitality of a religion that overcomes all hindrances, adversaries, hostilities, and battles, drawing to itself whatever teachings, cultural achievements, and ecclesiastical forms that are useful to itself, cannot indeed be *fully* explained through the laws of evolution, however much these laws appear unscathed throughout the history of this religion. Therefore, there is *something unknown* hidden in this history, something that is a worthy object of religious experience. However, this unknown element does not prove that God has supernaturally intervened, for perhaps what is here present is only a natural production of the loftiest form of religious evolution.[50]

{{26}} *Response*: Given their agnostic prejudices, modernists find themselves forced

---

[48] See St. Thomas, *ssold.* [*sic*] II, a. 6. [Trans. note: Perhaps this is referring to *Quodl.* II, q. 4, a. 1.]

[49] Richard of St. Victor, *De Trinitate*, bk. 1, ch. 2 (PL 196, 891).

[50] See Pius X, *Pascendi dominici gregis*, no. 35 (Denzinger, no. 3499).

to reach this conclusion. Indeed, they doubt the ontological and transcendent value of the first principles of reason and, hence, the value of the demonstrations of the existence of God as he who is essentially distinct from the world, as well as the demonstration of the possibility of supernatural revelation and of miracles. Nay, for them, miracles cannot involve the abrogation of laws of nature but, rather, are only the abrogation of the customary, subjective experiences that we fashion through our knowledge of natural phenomena. Therefore, even concerning the most openly miraculous of physical events, they say: This fact cannot be fully explained in accord with the laws that are now known; it contains something unknown. They must say the same thing concerning the Church's own marvelous life.

However, against their assertions, we defend the ontological and transcendent value of the first principles of reason, the value of the demonstrations of the existence of God as he who is essentially distinct from the world, the possibility of supernatural revelation, and in the next chapter we will metaphysically defend the possibility and discernibility of miracles. Now, presupposing all of these things, the argument drawn from the marvelous life of the Church is irresistible, as the Church herself says, provided that this marvelous life appears as being a moral miracle surpassing all created powers.

Therefore, against the immanentists, we must say: A given religion is made credible by divine faith, not inasmuch as it seems to be conformed to the exigencies of our nature but, rather, inasmuch as it *exceeds* these exigencies and can be constituted only by God, freely. Hence, if one is to argue from the conformity of this religion with the aspirations of our nature, one must make manifest *how this great conformity exists alongside such gratuity*, such that God alone could produce it.

§3. Concerning How These Motives Are Related to the Other Motives, as Well as concerning the Unity of [the Whole of] Apologetics

[Now, let us discuss the interrelation of these motives] (A) according to the partisans of the methodology of immanence and then (B) according to traditional apologetics.

A. *According to the partisans of the methodology of immanence*, internal motives have primacy—that is, not only priority of time (inasmuch as they dispose a subject to consider the other signs) but also a priority of value, for [according to them] without these motives, the others would remain too partial and, hence, inefficacious. [As they say,] the unity and power of the apologetic demonstration belongs to the practical order (that is, the order of life), in accord with the aspirations and exigencies of human action.[51]

---

[51] See Blondel, *L'action* (1893), 425–492. See the interpretation of this doctrine proposed by

This conception proceeds from a form of semi-agnosticism, which rejects the ontological value of miracles, in order to only admit their symbolic value, as well as from a form of semi-immanentism, which holds that our nature contains some kind of efficacious desire for supernatural religion—nay, specifically for the Catholic religion—in other words, a desire that also posits the requirement that it be fulfilled [*desiderium cum exigentia*].[52]

B. *According to traditional apologetics*, the subordination of the motives of credibility can be expressed as follows. (1) Internal motives are *per se* subordinated to external motives, though the former dispose one to consider the latter and, afterwards, also confirm them. (2) Among external motives, signs that are extrinsic to religion, like miracles and prophecies, are more knowable from our perspective, though motives intrinsic to religion are loftier in themselves. Finally, the strongest of these are those miracles that are most intrinsically concerned with religion, in which the prophecies are fulfilled and future beatitude announced.

{{27}} This calls for explanation.

(1) *Internal motives are per se subordinated to external motives.* This is so because our aspirations are subordinated to the religion in which they are fulfilled, as intelligence is subordinated to objective truth (or to being), just as love is subordinated to the good, for potency is designated in relation to act and acts in relation to their objects. Hence, in philosophy, *the supreme criterion of truth must be objective* and not subjective.[53] And the same holds true in apologetics: When judging concerning the rational credibility of religion proposing itself as supernatural, we must do so through a resolution to objective, external motives and not to the subjective exigencies of our nature. Moreover, if this religion is truly supernatural, it exceeds these exigencies and arouses loftier aspirations in us.

Hence, as we said earlier, when they are separated from external motives, internal motives are exposed to the gravest of illusions, and they cannot duly

---

Albert Valensin in the *Dictionnaire apologétique de la foi catholique*, 4th ed. (Paris: Beauchesne, 1931), 611 ("Immanence").

[52] See Joseph de Tonquédec, *Immanence: Essai critique sur la doctrine de M. Blondel* (Paris: Beauchesne, 1913), 163, 207.

[53] See Cardinal Zigliara, *Summa philosophica*, bk. 1, 228 (On objective evidence). Also see Édouard Hugon, *Cursus philosophiae Thomisticae*, vol. 1, *Logica* [Paris: Lethielleux, 1927], 375–379. The supreme criterion of truth cannot be external experience, nor consciousness, nor blind faith, nor some interior feeling felt by the soul, nor subjective evidence, nor some authority, but instead is evidence objectively considered [i.e., the evidential character of that which is known].

prove the divine origin of a given religion.

Against the tendency to subjectivism and humanism in matters of religion, we must recall the words heard by St. Augustine: "I am the food of those who are fully grown; *grow and you will eat me. But you will not change me into yourself*, as you change food into your own flesh, *but rather, you will change into me*." We must not judge divine things by resolving things to our level but instead must judge ourselves by resolving our notions to God. This is, properly speaking, wisdom—that is, science through the loftiest causes. Likewise, experiential wisdom, which is the gift of the Holy Spirit, judges all things in relation to God, supernaturally delighted in.

Nonetheless, internal motives drawn from our aspirations *dispose* the subject who does not yet believe so that he may consider the other motives. Thus, they have a priority of time, not of value, a priority standing on the side of the subject.

Indeed, as St. Thomas says:

> Just as the end is prior in intention and posterior in existence, so too, to the degree that something is closer to the end is it prior in proposition. . . . For this reason, *hope is said to open the way to faith*, not that it would already exist, but *that it is proposed as something future*. For example, when someone proposes eternal goods, he first wills those things, then willing to adhere to them through love, next willing to hope in them, and fourthly willing to believe in them, so that by believing thus he may hope in them, love them, and have them. . . . Thus, hope precedes faith by way of proposal but not in existence.[54]

Hence, on account of the fact that a religion draws to itself men who do not yet believe, they are roused by this to inquire into whether this religion is truly divine.

However, afterwards, internal motives drawn from the fulfillment of our aspirations *confirm* the other motives.

For, after the infusion of faith and charity, under the influence of the gifts of the Holy Spirit, the believer can experience more fully the profound peace that proceeds from the Gospel, which is known and loved[55] as is befitting to it, {{28}} in accord with the words of our Lord: "But the Paraclete, the Holy Ghost, whom the Father will send in my name, he will teach you all things and bring all things to your mind, whatsoever I shall have said to you. Peace I leave with you: my peace I give unto you: not as the world giveth, do I give unto you" (John 14:26–27, DR). And thus, the evident credibility of the mysteries of the

---

[54] *In* III *Sent.*, d. 23, q. 2, a. 5, ad 4. Also see *ST* II-II, q. 17, a. [8]. This analysis by St. Thomas contains what is true in the modern method of immanence while most excellently preserving the objectivity of our knowledge, as well as the supernaturality of the Christian religion.

[55] [Trans. note: Reading "cognitio et amato" as "cognito et amato."]

faith is confirmed by experiential knowledge, coming forth from the gifts of the Holy Spirit. These gifts perfect faith in a qualified manner (*secundum quid*), though, speaking without qualification (*simpliciter*), they are ruled by it, meaning that faith is therefore loftier than they are.[56]

No wonder, either, that internal motives first play the role of being a *disposition* and then, afterwards, that of being a *confirmation*, for generally, "just as on the way to generation a disposition precedes the perfection to which it disposes, in those things that are brought to their perfection in a successive manner, so too this same disposition naturally follows upon the perfection once it has been obtained. Thus, heat, which disposed to fire, is an effect flowing from the form of fire when the latter already exists."[57] Likewise, phantasms dispose to ideas, and afterwards they come to express them in a sensible way, for there is no knowledge without a conversion to the phantasms. Similarly, an antecedent emotion or passion precedes volition, and afterwards volition makes use of it as a consequent passion.

(2) *The marvelous life of the Church is loftier than a physical miracle, though it is not understood as easily.* Indeed, as Aristotle says in *Metaphysics* bk. 1, ch. 2: "The supreme causes of things are those that are the most intelligible . . . and they are known by men with the greatest of difficulty, for they are utterly remote from the senses." In other words, those things that are most intelligible in themselves are, from our perspective, more difficult to know, because our intellectual knowledge takes its origin in the senses.

St. Thomas applies this principle in order to show the fittingness of miracles as signs of invisible revelation, saying: "It is natural to man to discover intelligible truth through sensible effects. Hence, just as man, led along by natural reason, can arrive at some knowledge of God through natural effects, so too is man led through other supernatural effects to some supernatural knowledge of things to be believed in."[58] "Because those things that are of faith exceed human reason, they cannot be proven through human reasons but, rather, must be proven through arguments drawn from the divine power so that when someone performs works that only God can do, we may believe that the things that he says are themselves from God. This is akin to when someone brings letters, stamped by the king's ring, thus leading one to believe that what is contained in those letters does indeed proceed from the king's will."[59]

Hence, FROM OUR PERSPECTIVE, in apologetics, an extrinsic-external methodol-

---

[56] See *ST* I-II, q. 68, a. 8.
[57] *ST* III, q. 7, a. 13, ad 2.
[58] *ST* II-II, q. 178, a. 1.
[59] *ST* III, q. 43, a. 1. Also see *SCG* I, ch. 6.

ogy is easier, briefer, and safer. For *it is easier*, when speaking to the simple, to set forth obvious, splendid miracles (like Christ's Resurrection), supported by the testimony of many people, than it is to set forth the characteristics by which the excellence and sublimity of religion is recognized. This methodology is also *briefer*, for having already demonstrated that the truth of revealed religion is sufficiently evident on the basis of some miracle (e.g., Christ's Resurrection), the obligation to embrace it is thereby already clear enough, without needing to set forth the miraculous life of the Church through the whole of history, as well as the sublimity of her doctrine by diligently examining each of her dogmas and precepts. Finally, it is *safer*, for there is less danger of error involved in investigating into sensible facts like miracles than there is in carefully considering the exceeding excellence, purity, and immunity from error belonging to some doctrine, or in considering the moral effects of this doctrine. {{29}} This is especially the case because many dogmas remain very obscure, like that of the Holy Trinity, original sin, predestination, and eternal punishment. Hence, the [First] Vatican Council places among "external arguments for revelation, namely divine facts . . . miracles and prophecies in *particular*, which since they manifestly display the omnipotence and infinite knowledge of God are the most certain signs of the divine revelation, *adapted to the intelligence of all men*."[60] Indeed, they are the most befitting of signs, considering matters from our own perspective.

However, IN ITSELF, the miraculous life of the Church is a loftier motive, just as an intellectual and moral miracle is loftier than a physical one. Hence, St. Thomas, in *SCG* I, ch. 6, after enumerating sensible miracles—namely, "the miraculous curing of the weak, the raising of the dead, and alteration of heavenly bodies"—adds: "And what is *more miraculous*, there is the inspiration of human minds, leading simple and unlearned men, filled with the Holy Spirit, to possess at a single stroke the heights of wisdom and eloquence." And immediately afterwards he says concerning the miraculous conversion of the world to the Christian faith: "By which, the minds of mortals were led to assent to these things, and here we have *the greatest of miracles*, one that likewise is a manifest work of the divine inspiration, so that men would come to seek that which is invisible, doing so in contempt of that which is visible." Likewise, the [First] Vatican Council says that the Church's miraculous life is not only a motive of credibility but, indeed, "a *great* and *perpetual* motive of credibility and an irrefutable testimony of her divine mission." In this perpetuity, she surpasses all properly sensible miracles.

And therefore, souls going forward in the spiritual life increasingly come to see this miraculous life of the Church, no longer needing to take miracles into consideration. Similarly, the whole Church, now founded, no longer stands in need of miracles in the same way as she did at the time of her founding, for, as St. Thomas says in *SCG* I, ch. 6: "This great and marvelous conversion of the world to the Christian faith is the most certain witness from the signs from the past, so that it is no longer necessary that such

---

[60] [First] Vatican Council, *Dei filius*, ch. 3 (Denzinger, no. 3009).

signs be repeated, since they appear with the greatest of clarity in their effect, . . . although God does not cease, even in our own days, to work miracles through His saints in confirmation of the faith." St. Louis, the king, was invited to see a miracle, but he preferred to remain in adoration before the Most Blessed Sacrament in the obscurity of the faith that he already had. Therefore, the splendor of the Church, in itself, exceeds the splendor of miracles of the sensible order, even if the former is less obvious to our own eyes.

(3) *What are the stronger motives of credibility*? They are those miracles that are most intrinsically concerned with religion, in which the prophecies are fulfilled and future [things] announced.

Such is the case for *Christ's Resurrection*, which is at once a mystery of faith (the Resurrection of the Word) and a sensible miracle of the first rank (the glorious resurrection of a man), fulfilling a number of prophecies, providing a sign of Christ's victory over sin (which has death as one of its consequences), an exemplar of the Church in her ability to acquire power through persecutions, and a pledge of our future beatitude (which fulfills and indeed exceeds all of our aspirations). Hence, concerning this excellent motive, St. Paul says, "If Christ be not risen again, then is our preaching vain: and your faith is also vain" (1 Cor 15:14, DR). If Christ had not been victorious over death, he therefore would not have been victorious over sin, the wages of which are death. However, on account of *its perpetuity, and from our perspective as we now live on earth, the marvelous life of the Church* exceeds Christ's Resurrection [as a motive of credibility]; indeed, in her, an effect of the Resurrection is made manifest: "Christ conquers; Christ reigns; Christ commands."

Corollary concerning the unity of apologetics. Here we are not speaking of apologetics as though it were a science that would be distinct from sacred theology, for, as we already said in our prologue, apologetics is a {{30}} defensive office of sacred theology, which defends and explains revelation, likewise deducing conclusions from revealed truths.[61]

However, the unity of the defense of the faith (i.e., apologetics) is *a unity in the order of arguments*—that is, in the motives of credibility—for we must not merely mechanically juxtapose these proofs but instead must organically order them. Now, *per se*, this order must not be taken relative to our subjective aspirations or exigencies, as is wished by the partisans of the methodology of immanence but, rather, must be taken *relative to the end* toward which apologetics tends—namely, the evident credibility of the mysteries of faith, inasmuch as they are manifestly revealed by God. The various methodologies employed in apologetics are ways to the same end and, therefore, are ordered in relation to it.

Objection: However, the partisans of the methodology of immanence, following ways that are too subjective, say that the unity of apologetics must be taken through a

---

[61] See *ST* I, q. 1, a. 8.

resolution to the internal aspirations and exigencies that direct the inquiry undertaken by apologetics. Nay, were one not to consider these exigencies, other apologetic arguments would remain only inefficacious parts of the whole demonstration thus established.

Response: The order of agents corresponds to the order of ends,[62] and therefore, in order to arrive at the true end of apologetics (namely, evident credibility of the mysteries of faith),[63] the agent directing the apologetic demonstration must not be a natural aspiration or exigency of our will (or action) but instead is human reason, placed under the direction of faith. This is so because a natural exigency does not transcend the natural order, whereas reason, by contrast, can examine the value of the signs that are put forward by God himself in confirmation of revelation, just as it manifests the possibility and fittingness of this supernatural revelation, the true notion of which is given by God himself through revelation.

Hence, primacy, or *priority of value, belongs to the methodology that draws closest to this end, in short, the external method.*

Nonetheless, by way of temporal priority, we can first make use of an internal methodology so as to remove agnostic and naturalistic prejudices that would render any historical inquiry into miracles and prophecies useless. Indeed, they who believe that the dogmas of Christianity are absurd often do not wish to consider miracles, denying their power, lest they be compelled to admit something that is absurd to their eyes or something that would be too difficult to accept. By contrast, if they first understand, through a clear-eyed exposition, the conformity of the dogmas and precepts of Christianity (at least its principal ones) with our legitimate and supreme aspirations, then they may already begin to desire that they be able to acknowledge the truth of this religion.

Hence, (1) we must first set forth *internal motives*, drawn from the aspirations of our nature, just as Christ began his own preaching with the *beatitudes*, which fulfill and exceed our aspirations. (2) Then we must set forth the *excellence and sublimity of the Christian doctrine* with regard to the truths of the faith and precepts, just as Christ did in particular in the Sermon on the Mount; and we must simultaneously argue *from the holiness of Christ and the apostles, as well as from the marvelous life and fruitfulness of the Church.* (3) We must bring forward the *prophecies and miracles* that were performed in confirmation of revelation, {{31}} for a miracle is not performed prior to the proposal of the divine doctrine but, instead, afterward, as a sign in confirmation thereof, like the seal placed at the end of a letter. Thus, the evangelists, especially St. Matthew, first refer to Christ's words and

---

[62] See *ST* I-II, q. 109, a. 9.
[63] See, in the prolegomena to this work, vol. 1, {{3}} and {{43}}.

then, afterwards, to his miracles. Likewise, the apostles preached, "the Lord working withal, and confirming the word with signs that followed" (Mark 16:20, DR). Thus, the defense follows the proposal of faith, as it should. (4) Finally, *all the motives of credibility come to be confirmed through the experience of the gifts of the Holy Spirit.* Thus, the circle is perfected, and the unity of apologetics (that is, the defense of faith) preserved, just as the end is first in intention and last in execution.

CHAPTER NINETEEN

On Miracles as Motives of Credibility

Art. 1. On the notion of miracles
Art. 2. On the possibility of miracles
Art. 3. On the discernibility of miracles
Art. 4. On the probative force of miracles

ART. 1: ON THE NOTION OF MIRACLES

§1. Nominal definition
§2. The Catholic notion of miracles
§3. Heterodox notions of miracles
§4. Theological explanation of the Catholic notion of miracles
§5. Division of miracles

§1. Nominal Definition

{{32}} This nominal definition is clear from its etymology, as St. Thomas shows in *ST* I, q. 105, a. 7:

> The word "miracle" is derived from *admiratione*, astonishment or wonder. Now this arises when an effect is made manifest, while its cause remains hidden—as when a man sees an eclipse without knowing its cause, as the Philosopher says in *Metaphysics*, bk. 1, ch. 2. Now, the cause of an effect may be known by one person, while remaining unknown to others. Whence, something is wonderful to one man, but not to others (e.g., as an eclipse is to a country farmer but not to an astronomer). Now the term *miracle* is used because something is, *as it were, full of wonder, namely as having a cause completely hidden from all.* However, this cause is God. Therefore, we use the term "miracles" for whatever God does outside the order of causes which we know.

As Cajetan notes here, there is, therefore, "a difference between a *marvel* [*mirum*] and a *miracle* [*miraculum*], for the former is said of a part (that is, in relation to this [or that] thing), whereas the latter is only said of the whole (that is, in relation to all things). This conclusion finds its proof in the fact that God is a cause that is entirely [*simpliciter*] hidden. Whence, in using the words 'causes which we know,' St. Thomas means the same thing in the conclusion as what he says in the title of the article in speaking of *second* (or *natural*) causes."

This is explained at greater length in *De potentia*, q. 6, a. 2, and in *SCG* III, ch. 101, where St. Thomas draws a similar conclusion: "Therefore, properly speaking, the term 'miracle' is to be applied to those things which are done in a divine manner outside of the commonly observed order of things."

This notion can be had after the manner of a nominal definition, for it does stand in need of an explanation, added in *ST* I, q. 110, a. 4, so that one may philosophically determine {{33}} what is meant by saying that something is "outside" the commonly preserved order of things, and so that one may form a clearer idea about how miracles differ from extraordinary natural facts as well as from wonders and from divine, providential facts that are not, however, miraculous. All of these are already distinguished by common sense, but philosophical reason must set forth the root of this distinction.

§2. The Catholic Notion of Miracles

The [First] Vatican Council set forth the nature of miracles when it said:

> However, in order that the obedience of our faith be nevertheless in harmony with reason [cf. Rom 12:1], God willed that exterior proofs of His revelation, viz., divine facts, especially miracles and prophesies, should be joined to the interior helps of the Holy Spirit; as they manifestly display the omnipotence and infinite knowledge of God, they are the most certain signs of the divine revelation adapted to the intelligence of all men.[1]

Thus, according to the Council, *miracles are divine facts manifestly displaying God's omnipotence*. Therefore, according to the Church, miracles, properly so-called, must be above the powers of the whole of created and creatable nature, even above those of angels.[2] Thus, they essentially differ

---

[1]   [First] Vatican Council, *Dei filius*, ch. 3 (Denzinger, no. 3009).

[2]   See Jean-Michel-Alfred Vacant, *Études théologiques sur les constitutions du Concile du Vatican d'après les actes du concile*, vol. 2 (Paris: Delhomme et Briguet, 1895), 41. Here, Vacant rightly

from extraordinary natural facts, as well as from demonic wonders, which are mere simulacra of miracles. They also are distinct from ordinary divine facts, like God's daily creation of [spiritual] souls, which is done in accord with a given, regular order of things and cannot function as a sign of revelation.

In this declaration by the Council, miracles are distinguished from prophecies because what is being discussed here are miracles inasmuch as they pertain, properly speaking, to the physical order and not to the intellectual order. Nonetheless, externally manifested prophecy can be reduced to [the category of] miracles—that is, to God's miraculous intervention in the world, either in the physical order or in the intellectual / moral order.

§3. Heterodox Notions of Miracles

As we said earlier in this work,[3] there are two principal heterodox notions of miracles. (A) According to the first, which proceeds from *determinism*, a miracle is an extraordinary natural fact that has not yet been explained scientifically, something that religious sentiment attributes to God, like the hearing of a prayer. This is what many liberal Protestants think about these matters. (B) According to the other heterodox notion, which by contrast proceeds from agnosticism and *contingentism*, a miracle is not an abrogation of the laws of nature but, rather, of our manner of conceiving of the laws of nature. Such is the position held by a number of modernists.[4] {{34}} In both conceptions, miracles do not have an ontological value as divine seals but instead only have a symbolic value for provoking the soul to examine a religion as well as its conformity with our aspirations. These two notions, which seem opposed to each other, are ultimately reduced to naturalism, as we will explain in what follows.

---

says, "The Council presupposes that all miracles have God as their cause. Indeed, it places miracles among the order of divine facts, *facta divina*. It does not admit a broader notion of miracles, one introduced by modern apologists, extending the qualification of 'miracle' to facts that surpass man's powers, as well as those of sensible creatures—and, by consequence, to the interventions of angels and demons in our universe—along with God's interventions. This notion, thought up in order to deal with the difficulty experienced with regard to the problem of distinguishing angelic or diabolic deeds from those of God, does not in fact resolve this difficulty. Moreover, it has the disadvantage of giving the word 'miracle' a new acceptation, for it confuses the *miraculous* with angelic and demonic *marvels* [or *wonders*]." In the same text, Vacant cites, among the modern apologists who admitted this notion: Le Grand, *Dissertatio de miraculis* (see Migne, *Cursus completus sacrae scripturae*, vol. 23, col. 1117); Bruger, *De vera religione*, 2nd ed., 10; La Hogue, *Tractatus de vera religione*.

3   See vol. 1, ch. 6, a. 1, no. 3 (Heterodox notions of supernaturality).
4   For an exposition concerning these conceptions, see Joseph de Tonquédec, *Introduction à l'étude du merveilleux et du miracle* (Paris: Beauchesne, 1916), 86–122, 429ff.

A. *The heterodox notion of miracles founded on determinism*

Determinism holds that all things take place in a necessary manner, in accord with the determinate laws of nature, so that God himself could not act contrary to such physical laws, just as he cannot act in a way that would be contrary to mathematical or metaphysical laws. Hence, BARUCH SPINOZA, who after Descartes wished to reduce physical laws to mathematical laws,[5] absolutely denied the possibility of miracles: Just as God cannot make a square circle, so too it is impossible for him to raise someone from the dead.[6] Hence, Spinoza does not directly deny God's omnipotence but instead his freedom. According to Spinoza, God acts *ad extra* from a necessity of nature and therefore always acts in the same way, like the vital principle in plants. This error was already set forth and refuted by St. Thomas in *De potentia*, q. 6, a. 1.

THE DEISTS did indeed admit the essential distinction between God and the world, but they said God only has his general acts of will [*voluntates generales*], by which the laws of the world were constituted, but not particular acts of will concerning singular things, for this would be unworthy of divine providence. Hence, miracles are not possible. Such was also the position of the Averroists in the Middle Ages. Here too, see the same text from St. Thomas's *De potentia*.

NICOLAS MALEBRANCHE, however, in order to resolve the objections raised by determinism, said in certain works of his: "*A miracle is an effect depending upon general laws which are not known by us*, especially upon the general laws of the spiritual world, by which the angels act in the sensible world." And Malebranche seemed to hold that most miracles could be explained in this way.[7] However, according to him, there are other

---

5   See Léo Michel, "Le système de Spinoza au point de vue de la logique formelle," *Revue Thomiste* 5 (1898): 711–722.

6   Spinoza, *Ethica*, pt. 1, prop. 32: "The will cannot be called a free cause, but only a necessary one. . . . (For) it requires a cause, by which it would be determined."—Corollary 1. Hence it follows that God cannot act with a freedom of will.—Prop. 33: "Things could not have been produced in any other manner, nor in any other order, by God, than the one in which they were produced." And in the *Tractatus theologico-politicus*, ch. 6 (On Miracles): "The universal laws of nature are merely decrees of God, which follow from the necessity and perfection of the divine nature. Therefore, if something happens in nature which would contradict its universal laws, that would also necessarily stand in contradiction to the divine decree, intellect, and nature. . . . Finally, nature preserves a fixed and immutable order. From all that we have said, it follows with the greatest of clarity that the term *'miracle'* can only be understood in relation to the opinions of men, and that it *signifies nothing other than a work whose natural cause we cannot explain by analogy with some other happening that we are accustomed to experience*, or at least, cannot be explained by the person who writes or narrates the miracle." In the same text, Spinoza intends to prove that this definition for miracles is conformed to what is found in Sacred Scripture.

7   Nicolas Malebranche, *Entretiens sur la métaphysique*, ch. 12, no. 13, note: "*By the word 'miracles,' I mean effects which depend on general laws which we do not naturally know.*" According to Malebranche, just as, in accord with the laws governing the union of the soul and the body, we can hold back a stone that is falling, so too, in accord with the general laws of the superior

miracles, like the Incarnation, which exceed the powers of angels, and he seems to be speaking of these when he says, in another place, miracles do not depend on general laws but, rather, on God's particular will, and in this way they are distinguished from natural facts.[8]

{{35}} However, Malebranche's teaching diminishes the supernaturality even of these chief miracles, on account of his absolute optimism, according to which God was obliged to create the best world. Thus, all things that have been made, even the Incarnation and all supernatural deeds, would be morally necessary.

LEIBNIZ too, on account of [his] absolute optimism and the determinism of moral necessity, diminished the supernaturality of miracles. He says: "If the changing of water into wine at Cana was a miracle of the first rank (exceeding all of the powers of creatures), *God would have thereby changed the entire course of the universe*, on account of the interconnection of bodies, *or otherwise, he would have needed, even more miraculously, to prevent this interconnection*. Thus, this miracle required more than appears at first glance."[9] For according to Leibniz, all things are connected in virtue of the principle of

---

order (which he calls the order of grace), angels and Christ can immediately dispel an illness without God thereby intervening by a unique act of will [*voluntate singulari*], and these facts can be called miraculous.

[8]   He says in his work *De la nature et de la grâce*, sermon 1, a. 19 [Discourse 1, §57]: "Nothing that takes place in the world does not prove the feeling that God acts through general acts of will—if one makes exception only for miracles—which nonetheless would not be miracles differing from so-called natural effects, if it were true that God acts, ordinarily, through particular acts of will, since miracles are miracles only because they do not take place in accord with general laws. Thus, miracles presuppose these laws."

Against Malebranche, see Benedict XIV, *Doctrina de servorum Dei beatificatione et beatorum canonizatione*, bk. 4, ch. 2, no. 8. St. Thomas had already said in *ST* I, q. 22, aa. 2 and 3 that divine providence extends even *immediately* to singular things, although creatures do indeed execute his providence. Likewise had he already refuted absolute optimism in *ST* I, q. 19, a. 3; q. 25, aa. 5 and 6.

[9]   Gottfried Wilhelm Leibniz, *Essais de théodicée*, pt. 3, §249. Likewise, he says, in his work, *Discours de métaphysique*, ed. Henri Lestienne (Paris: Alcan, 1907), ch. 16 (p. 63): "Now, we need to explain how it is possible that God would sometimes have influence over men or over other substances by means of some extraordinary concurrence, since it seems that nothing ever happens in an extraordinary manner or supernaturally, given that all events take place only as consequences of what things naturally are. However, one must recall what we said earlier regarding miracles within the universe. They are always conformed to the universal law of the general order, even if they stand outside of the subordinate rules therein. And this is especially so because every person or substance is, as it were, a little world which expresses the great universe as a whole, thus enabling us to say, likewise, that *this extraordinary action of God upon this substance does not stop being miraculous, even if it is included* in the general order of the universe inasmuch as it is expressed by the *essence or individual notion of this substance*. This is why, if we were to understand everything expressed in our nature, nothing is supernatural there, for it extends to all things." Likewise, on p. 81, in the summary of chapter 31: "On the motives for election, foreseen faith, absolute decrees, and the fact that everything is ultimately reduced to

sufficient reason. Nonetheless, he says, in the same text, some great miracles exceed all created powers; such are the Incarnation and certain other actions of God that constitute miracles properly so-called—nay, mysteries. Nonetheless, these miracles, according to Leibniz, are morally necessary. Thus, in the end, he comes to diminish their supernaturality and gratuity.

At the same time, [ABBÉ CLAUDE FRANÇOIS ALEXANDRE] HOUTTEVILLE, in his French work on the truth of the Christian religion, proposed a new definition for miracles, which he thought to be necessary in order to resolve the objections raised by determinists. This definition caused no small tumult among philosophers and theologians. {{36}} He said that miracles are rare, stupendous, sensible effects exceeding human powers, *following in so hidden a manner from the laws of the communication of motions that we can in no way naturally know*, whether through experience or through reason, *that they are consequences of the same sorts of laws.* Thus, this author made a distinction, saying that miracles are rightly said to be natural inasmuch as they follow the order of nature (or the laws of motion), though they are called supernatural inasmuch as they cannot be foreseen by man solely through his natural powers. Houtteville strove to prove this opinion by appealing both to the fact that God acts through utterly simple and general laws and to the fact that nobody knows all of the possible effects of the general laws of the communication of motions.

The majority of theologians rose up against this opinion, believing that it destroyed the probative force of miracles.[10] However, some people, especially nonbelievers, embraced his position. This definition of miracles, as we said above (with Vacant[11]) cannot be reconciled with the definition that is found in the texts of the [First] Vatican Council. Indeed, if a miracle is produced in a hidden manner in accord with the laws of motion and by

---

God's reason for choosing to bring into existence a *given possible person, whose notion contains a given series of graces and free actions.* This removes the difficulties [involved here] in one single stroke." Indeed, according to Leibniz, *all miracles take place*, not according to mathematical necessity (as Spinoza wished), but *according to moral necessity (Discours de métaphyique,* ch. 13). According to him, all things are determined, *a priori,* by the principle of sufficient reason.

Leibniz retains nothing but the term "freedom" (whether human or divine). Something similar is found in the condemned propositions drawn from Rosmini. For example, in the 18th, we find: "The love by which God loves himself even in creatures, and which is the reason by which he determines himself to create, constitutes a moral necessity, which in the most perfect being always produces its effect; in fact, only this type of necessity leaves bilateral freedom intact in the many imperfect creatures" (Denzinger, no. 3218).

10 The words of Benedict XIV in *Doctrina de servorum Dei beatificatione et beatorum canonizatione* (bk. 4, ch. 2, no. 8) against Malebranche hold good against Houtteville: "Malebranche taught that in any given miracle of the Old Law divine angels did not execute their will. Rather, God was the one who executed the will of the angels, so that He was able to be said to have willed any of the aforementioned miracles, *not through a particular willing,* but rather, *through His general willing,* namely by doing whatever the angels willed. However, this utterly novel and dangerous doctrine was entirely overturned in a treatise [*dissertatione*] published in Cologne in 1685."

11 See Vacant, *Études théologiques sur les constitutions du Concile du Vatican,* vol. 2, 41.

the power properly belonging to the angels, they would not manifestly display the divine omnipotence [as the Council says that they do].

Finally, many LIBERAL PROTESTANTS reject the traditional notion of miracles on account of the determinism that they hold exists in the laws of nature.[12] For them, *a miracle is an extraordinary natural event that has not yet been explained by science, an event that can be attributed to God by religious sentiment, like the hearing of a prayer.* Hence, one and the same fact is natural for science (that is, in accord with the unknown laws of nature) and miraculous for religious sentiment (as an effect of the divine benevolence). Such was the position held by thinkers like Schleiermacher, Ritschl, and Sabatier.[13] {{37}}

---

[12] A[uguste] Sabatier, *Esquisse d'une philosophie de religion*, 1.1.3 (On miracles), 83: "The truth is that, today, the spectacular and sovereign regularity of the laws of nature and the harmony of the universe has penetrated all minds, and that our piety, when in the open daylight, does not rebel against these laws but, rather makes us consider them as being essentially religious, enabling us to contemplate, celebrate, and submit ourselves to them. . . . The scholastic theory (of miracles) is dead in the mind of those theologians who would like to still retain it today." Immediately before this, on page 81, Sabatier had said, "Spinoza also said, profoundly, that no historical testimony, gathered from the past, could ever have sufficient authority, if it were only human testimony, in order for a diligent and conscientious scholar not to be able to *doubt rather than speak of witnesses and historians instead of the constancy of the world's laws.* Bayle, Hume, Voltaire, Rousseau, Fontenelle, and a thousand others popularized an argumentation which, under their pens, became quite simple indeed. Thus, a new form of thought came into being, imposing itself with invincible strength upon apologists themselves. Themselves needing to take up the philosophical perspective, they so rationalized miracles that, in explaining their nature in order to admit them, they in truth only ended up denying them."

Likewise, see Jules Simon, *Religion naturelle*, 2nd ed., 284.

Nay, on page 90 of the aforementioned work, Sabatier admits ascending evolutionism, which holds that "*the more comes from the less*," contrary to the principle of causality and that of contradiction, likewise rejecting the possibility of miracles on account of the constancy of the laws of nature, as though the laws of nature were more necessary than the principle of contradiction. He admits absurdity while rejecting miracles, for there he says, "The scholastics say that the more cannot come from the less, and this is indeed correct in accord with abstract logic. However, reality scoffs at logic. All about us, it bears witness to the triumph of the opposite axiom."

[13] Schleiermacher defines the miracle as being any phenomenon that is ascribed to the Infinite by religious sentiment. Such a definition is merely subjective in nature—that is, relative to our religious knowledge. Nay, according to him, knowledge of miracles does not lead to faith but, rather, presupposes it.

According to Ritschl, miracles are extraordinary events to the degree that there can be witnesses to the divine benevolence so that one and the same thing would be natural according to science and miraculous according to religious faith.

Sabatier writes in *Esquisse d'une philosophie de la religion*, 87: "Reduced to its purely religious and moral meaning, for Jesus, a miracle was '*the answer to a prayer*,' abstraction being made from the phenomenal manner in which this answer was brought about. God manifests Himself in extraordinary events only so as to teach us how to recognize Him in the most ordinary of events. The child asks and the father bestows without the child being preoccupied with

Sabatier adds that Jesus and the apostles had such piety for and trust in God—indeed, to the highest degree—that they thereby looked upon both extraordinary and ordinary facts as being manifestations of providence. At the same time, they were able to have imperfect or erroneous scientific notions concerning the way that God acts in nature. However, Christ's religious outlook is not necessarily connected with these imperfect ideas and can be accommodated to contemporary science in our own day.

This definition of miracles represents an open denial of their supernaturality, retaining only the name, a vain exhalation of sound (*flatus vocis*), not the meaning, of what is meant by "miracles." So defined, miracles no longer have an ontological value as seals of God in order to confirm revelation with utter certitude but instead retain nothing more than *a symbolic value* in order to provoke the soul to an examination of religion and of its conformity with our nature's aspirations and exigencies. Nay, [according to these thinkers,] this symbolic value of miracles cannot be perceived unless one already has religious faith.[14]

B. *The heterodox notion of miracles founded upon agnosticism and contingentism*

At the end of the nineteenth century, many philosophers[15] and physicists,[16] follow-

---

the means used by the father in realizing his desire. The pious man adores the ways [of God], which he cannot understand. This trust in God's love and justice could be accompanied, in the minds of the apostles and of Jesus Himself, by imperfect or erroneous scientific ideas concerning the way that the divine action is exercised in nature. However, this confidence is not inextricably bound to these ideas and can easily enough be disentangled from them in order to then be placed into harmony with the outlooks held by contemporary science, as it was, in the minds of Jesus and of His apostles, in harmony with their own contemporary scientific view. The laws of nature, which we have come to be aware of in their sovereign constancy, immediately become, for piety, the expression of God's will."

[14] Already, Calvin, in *Institutio christianae religionis*, 1.8.5 and 12, said that miracles and prophecies are not sufficiently and efficaciously probative, except for those who already have internally accepted the Holy Spirit's private inspiration.

[15] See Émile Boutroux, *De la contingence de lois de la nature*, 74: "The most elementary and most general physical and chemical laws declare the relations which exist between things that are so heterogenous that it is impossible to say that the consequent would be proportioned to the antecedent and would result from it, for this reason, like the effect results from the cause. The only thing found here, for us, are the links given in experience, which are contingent like that same experience.... If this is so, the physical world is not immutable. The quantity of physical action can increase or diminish within the universe, either as a whole or in one of its parts."

And ibid., 156: "*In him (in God) power or freedom is infinite. It is the source of His existence*, which in this way is not subject to the constraint of inevitability. The divine essence, which is co-eternal with His power, is perfection in act [*perfection actuelle*]. It is necessary *with a practical necessity*; that is to say, it absolutely merits being realized and cannot be itself except by being freely realized.... Here, in this doctrine of the divine freedom, we have an explanation for the contingence which is presented by the hierarchy of forms and general laws of the world." This is a form of immoderate libertinism and contingentism that is radically opposed to the determinism of Spinoza.

[16] See Henri Poincaré's *La science et l'hypothèse*. On p. 113–119, he discusses his claim that first principles of mechanism, like the principle of inertia, are plausible hypotheses suggested by the

ing along the ways of Kantian agnosticism, exhibited the exaggerations of determinism and fell into the opposite excess, which is called "contingentism." {{38}} According to them, *the laws of nature* are not evidently necessary but instead are contingent. Nay, they held that we *indeed cannot prove that they are, in fact, fixed and stable. Rather, according to them, this stability only pertains to our subjective manner of conceiving things,* as Kant showed, and thus is something relative, for science can forever be perfected and these laws forever modified.

Therefore, a miracle is not evidently impossible (for physical science speaks about what is, not about what is possible or impossible). However, exceptions to the laws of nature frequently happen naturally without thereby constituting a miracle. Nay, as an intervention of the divine freedom over all the laws of nature, a miracle is something unknowable for us, for we do not know all the laws of nature, nor the extramental objectivity of laws that have already been determined. *A fortiori*, our knowledge cannot discern an immediate intervention in the world by some cause that would completely transcend the phenomenal order, for our reason is numbered among phenomena. *Hence, from our perspective, miracles cannot be the abrogation of the laws of nature as they are in things themselves but, rather, only an abrogation of apparent laws, inasmuch as they are subjectively conceived of by us*[17] (in the words of Blondel, abrogations "of anthropomorphic appearances," and in those of Fr. Laberthonnière, abrogations "of an order which is illusory").[18]

Hence, the ontological value of miracles cannot be scientifically and philosophically defended so that a special intervention by God would appear in order to confirm and prove the fact of revelation. [According to such thinkers] *miracles have only a symbolic value.* That is, they manifest to us God's presence in the world and in our life, and hence provoke the soul to an examination of religion and, especially, to consider the conformity

---

facts but are not experimentally demonstrated, nor proven *a priori*.

[17] See Maurice Blondel, *L'action* (1893), 396: "Now, can miracles—the impossibility of which cannot be asserted by any science, given that science makes its pronunciations concerning that which is real and not concerning the domain of what is possible—be anything other than a challenge to common reason, which is forever ready to confine itself within its *customary routines*? They are a provocation which likewise satisfies or irritates hearts, depending on how they are disposed to them. These sudden shocks are effective only to the degree that one grasps in them, *not the sensible marvel, what this is, but rather, its symbolic meaning*. And what is this meaning? No fact, however strange and disconcerting it may be, is impossible: *the idea of fixed laws within nature is nothing but an idol*. Each phenomenon is a particular case and a unique solution. *Ultimately, we can be sure that there is nothing more in a miracle than there is in the least of ordinary facts*. However, also, there is nothing less in the most ordinary of facts than there is in a miracle. And thus, we can see the meaning of these *exceptional shocks that provoke reflection, leading it to more general conclusions*. . . . Therefore, miracles are miraculous only for those who are ready to recognize the divine action in the most run of the mill events and acts."

[18] See his article in *Bulletin de la Société française de philosophie* (June 1911): 144ff; (Mar. 1912): 143. Also see Fr. de Tonquédec, [*Immanence*], 200–227.

of religion with the exigencies of our action. Nay, this symbolic value of miracles can only be perceived by minds that are already morally conscious of these exigencies, being disposed to acknowledge God's action in the midst of ordinary facts.

Some modernists went further still in diminishing the power of miracles. Indeed, they said, according to our manner of conceiving things, every phenomenon presupposes an antecedent phenomenon. Miracles, however, as conceived of by scholastic theologians, would be a phenomenon without a phenomenal antecedent. In other words, they would be contrary to the law / principle of causality and, hence, would be unthinkable. For at the very least, our subjective knowledge is ruled by the principle of determinism, and phenomena are conceived of as being successive moments in universal evolution. Therefore, a separated-off phenomenon, lacking any connection with preceding ones, is unintelligible. Therefore, *miracles cannot be admitted, unless there happens to be some law of miracles—* that is, unless there be an antecedent phenomenon from which a given miracle would as a rule follow. However, this phenomenon exists and is found in vigorous religious faith, which produces a miracle (e.g., extraordinary healing), just as our spiritual freedom ordinarily moves our bodily appendages. {{39}} *Therefore, miracles are extraordinary effects of vigorous faith* and a unique example of the superiority of spirit over matter. Nonetheless, at the same time, it is an effect of God inasmuch as faith comes from God.[19] Hence, it is said in the Gospel: "If you have faith as a grain of mustard seed, you shall say to this mountain: Remove from hence hither, and it shall remove: and nothing shall be impossible to you" (Matt 17:19, DR). And in Mark 6:5–6 (DR), it is said of Christ: "He could not do any miracles there (in his own homeland), only that he cured a few that were sick, laying his hands upon them. And he wondered because of their unbelief."

Modernists add that *physically speaking, a miracle is not something above nature but, rather, is only above our scientific knowledge concerning nature.* Science can neither affirm nor deny it. It is an extraordinary fact that has not yet been explained. False miracles in the physical order are not inferior to true miracles, but they do not have a religious value. True miracles can only be distinguished from false miracles through moral and religious criteria, which are known solely by faith (or religious experience). Hence, miracles proceed from faith, are known by faith, and confirm faith, inasmuch as they manifest its vitality,

---

[19] See Édouard Le Roy, "Essai sur la notion du miracle," *Annales de philosophie chrétienne* (Oct. 1907). [Trans. note: It appears that this sequence of articles actually was published in 1906.] If miracles are a purely physical work and a kind of absolute phenomenon arising in the midst of a phenomenal series without some relation to the phenomena that precede it, "it can be imagined, but not truly thought." "Miracles are conceivable only insofar as they are phenomena—only in function of the fragmenting up of reality, in other words, only in function of certain discursive forms elaborated by the human mind. . . . The miracle becomes intelligible if there is a law of miracles. . . . To affirm that it is possible is quite simply to affirm that faith is not only a source of illusory or [reading *an* as *ou*] true representations, but that it is an active force, capable of being balanced against physical forces."

in accord with what was said: "The tree shall be judged by its fruits."[20]

This conception of miracles is manifestly opposed to what is said in the Gospel[21] and does not differ in any significant way from the notion proposed by liberal Protestants like, for example, Sabatier. Hence, like determinism, this contingentism reduces miracles to extraordinary natural effects, which religious sentiment attributes to God inasmuch as they are a manifestation of the divine benevolence. Therefore, these two opposed conceptions are ultimately reduced to naturalism. However, already, in a way, they refute each other.

§4. Theological Explanation of the Catholic Notion of Miracles

As has been said already, according to the [First] Vatican Council, a miracle is a divine fact manifestly displaying the omnipotence of God. This traditional notion of the miraculous is explained as follows by St. Thomas in *ST* I, q. 110, a. 4:

> {{40}} Properly speaking, a miracle takes place when something is done outside the order of nature. However, it does not suffice for there to be a miracle if something is done outside the order of any given particular nature. Otherwise, anyone would perform a miracle by throwing a stone upwards, as such an action is outside the order of the stone's nature. *Therefore, in order for something to be called a miracle, it must be outside the order of the whole created nature. And this is something that God alone can do*, for whatever an angel or any other creature does by its own power is in accord with the order of created nature, thus meaning that such an action is not miraculous. Whence, God alone can work miracles.

---

[20] See the two articles by Le Roy under the same title from November and December 1907.

[21] See St. Thomas, *De potentia*, q. 6, a. 9 (*Whether the performing of miracles should be attributed to faith*). This text makes clear what are the relations between miracles and faith, according to the Gospel and to sound theology. "According to Gregory the Great in Dialogue 2.30, holy men perform miracles in two ways, namely by way of impetration *by prayer* that miracles may be divinely brought about and *by power*. Now, in both ways faith renders a man capable of performing miracles. Indeed, faith itself is what, properly speaking, merits that a prayer may be heard concerning miracles to be performed (which is proven in a number of ways)....Similarly, however, through faith man is most especially disposed to perform miracles by way of power. First of all, this is so because the saints are said to perform miracles from power not as kinds of chief authors of miracles but, rather, as divine instruments, declaring the divine command which natural things themselves obey when miracles are performed. Now, the divine word comes to dwell within us through faith, which is a kind of participation of the divine truth in us. Whence, through faith itself, man is disposed to perform miracles." St. Thomas adds two further reasons—namely, inasmuch as faith gives firmness of soul and elevation above sensible things. However, this only dispositively prepares for the performing of miracles.

(Ad 1) To the first objection, we must say that some angels are said to perform miracles either because God works miracles at their request, as when holy men are said to work miracles, or because such angels exercise some form of ministry in the miracles which take place, as in collecting the dust [of the deceased] in the general resurrection or by performing other such actions.

Therefore, going beyond the nominal definition to the real definition of miracles, strictly speaking, Catholic theologians say that a miracle is *a fact produced by God in the world, outside the order of action that belongs to the whole of created nature.*

(1) It is called *a fact* and not, however, a doctrine. Nay, in order that it be a sign, it must be a *sensible* fact.[22]

(2) It is said to be *produced by God*, at least as by its principal cause, for it does not exclude the activity of a wonderworker, who acts by God's power as an instrument.

(3) It is said to be *in the world*, not outside of the world.

(4) It is *outside the order of nature*, but not outside the order of divine providence, for miracles depend upon God's ordinate power, guided by his wisdom, even though it is here exercised in an extraordinary way.[23]

(5) Finally, it is said to be *outside the order of action that belongs to the whole of created nature* and not only outside the order of acting belonging to some particular created nature, for otherwise the throwing of a stone into the air would be a miracle. And it is said to be outside of the order of *action*, not of being, for the miraculous effect *effectively* exceeds all created powers

---

[22] Hence, merely spiritual miracles, like a vision had by a charismatic and other such extraordinary things, which are discussed in mystical theology, cannot be a direct testimony for others or a sign of mediate revelation. However, for the person who receives them, they can be immediate criteria of revelation, inasmuch as it is clear that such things certainly come to them from God.

[Trans. note: Although technically there are spiritual signs, such as the formal sign that is the *species expressa intellecta*, in which knowledge is attained.]

[23] *ST* I, q. 25, a. 5, ad 1: "Now, 'power' is understood as executing, 'will' as commanding, and 'intellect' and 'wisdom' as directing. Therefore, whatever is attributed to God's power considered in itself, He is said to *be able to do in accord with His absolute power.* Such things include everything in which the character of being is preserved [thus solely excluding that which implies contradiction]. However, whatever is attributed to the divine power inasmuch as it executes the command of His just will, God is said to be able to do by *His ordered power.*" However, this ordered power is called either *ordinary* (inasmuch as it is performed in accord with the ordinary course of things) or extraordinary (inasmuch as it is exercised outside of the established order of things). See *ST* I, q. 104, a. 3 and 4. "God can, through His absolute power, reduce creatures to nothing, but He does this *neither in accord with the ordinary course of things, nor miraculously,*" because a motive for such annihilation is lacking.

but does not entitatively exceed all created natures. Only intrinsically supernatural grace, which is a kind of formal participation in the divine nature, exceeds the order of being of the whole of created nature. However, by contrast, bodily resurrection supernaturally bestows natural life upon a corpse, not supernatural life.

Thus defined, miracles are *distinguished* (1) *from natural facts (even extraordinary ones)*, like fortuitous events, which are called fortuitous in relation to second causes and not in relation to providence, to which all things are subject; (2) *from diabolic marvels*, which are mere simulacra of miracles; {{41}} (3) from *divine* facts, or *effects that are ordinary*, as are the conservation of things in being, [God's] premotion [in created beings' activity], the daily creation of [spiritual] souls, and the justification of the wicked, which is not a miracle but instead the end aimed at by miracles.[24] Likewise, miracles are distinguished *from ordinary facts that are called providential* inasmuch as providence is more clearly made manifest in them (e.g., in accord with a favorable answer to a prayer).

Corollaries. First, "nothing can be called a miracle in comparison to the divine power, for all actions are of little account in comparison to the divine power. . . . However, something is said to be a miracle in comparison to the power of nature that it exceeds."[25]

Second, even if a miracle ought to be sensible as a sign, it need not be limited to being performed outside the laws of the *physical* order but can also be outside the laws of the *intellectual or moral* order (as in the cases of prophecy, the gift of tongues, and St. Paul's miraculous conversion). However, in order for it to be called a miracle and a sign, it must at least be manifested

---

[24] See *ST* I, q. 105, a. 7, ad 1: "Although creation and the justification of the ungodly are things performed only by God, they are not, properly speaking, miracles, for by their very nature, they do not proceed from any other cause. Thus, they do not occur outside the order of nature precisely because they do not belong to that order." Likewise, see *ST* I-II, q. 113, a. 10: "The justification of the ungodly sometimes is miraculous and sometimes not. The common and regular course of justification is to have God move the soul interiorly, with man being thereby converted to God, first through an imperfect conversion, so that afterwards his conversion may be perfect. . . . However, sometimes God moves the soul so vigorously that it arrives at perfect righteousness all at once, as happened in St. Paul's conversion, which was simultaneously accompanied by a miraculous external prostration of Paul upon the ground. Hence his conversion is commemorated in the Church as being something miraculous." And in ad 1: "Even though, as regards the good caused, certain miraculous works are of lower rank than the justification of the ungodly, they are beyond the accustomed order of such effects. Therefore, they have the character of being a miracle more greatly."

[25] *ST* I, q. 105, a. 8.

externally in some way, for otherwise it would not cause wonder.[26]

Third, although properly speaking a miracle exceeds all the powers of created nature, the term *miracle* is used *improperly* (or *in a broad sense*) for certain deeds that do not exceed the powers of angels and that, in consideration of the circumstances surrounding them, are attributed to good angels or to God. (For example, the fact that someone holy would walk upon the waters does not exceed all created powers. Hence, someone like Simon the Magician was able to be lifted into the air by some demonic power.)[27]

The properties of miracles[28]

(1) A miracle is said to be *arduous* inasmuch as it exceeds the powers of nature.

(2) It is said to be *outside of the hopes* or *exigencies of nature*, for nature is only obedientially, not naturally, ordered to it—namely, inasmuch as it obeys God in order to receive whatever he may will. However, it is not above the hope of grace, which comes from faith, through which we believe in the future resurrection.

(3) It is said to be *not customary*, "for it does not frequently take place, but rather, stands outside of the ordinary course of natural activity."[29]

(4) A miracle *is not contrary to nature* (i.e., it does not violate nature), whatever those who hold to naturalism might say. Rather, it accords with the obediential potency of nature—namely, with its primary aptitude by which any given creature naturally obeys God in order to accept whatever he may will, as our arm obeys our will.[30] {{42}} Thus, a miracle is not contrary to the laws of nature, *is not a violation of the laws of nature*, and indeed does not destroy them. Rather, it presupposes and confirms them, as an exception confirms the rule. For example, the dead do not *naturally* rise again. This law is so true that God alone can *supernaturally* raise the dead. Indeed, as we will discuss below, the laws of nature are hypothetically necessary—namely, on the supposition that all the various natural causes act in the appropriate conditions.

(5) Miracles are called *signs* because they manifest something supernatural—namely, either the divine origin of a given doctrine or the holiness of some servant of God.[31]

---

[26] See *ST* I, q. 105, a. 7, ad 3.

[27] See Benedict XIV, *Doctrina de servorum Dei beatificatione et beatorum canonizatione*, vol. 4, bk. 4, pt. 1, ch. 1, nos. 7 and 8; ch. 2, nos. 8 and 10.

[28] See *ST* I, q. 105, a. 7, ad 2; I-II, q. 113, a. 10; *De potentia*, q. 6, a. 2.

[29] *ST* I, q. 105, a. 7, ad 2.

[30] *ST* I, q. 105, a. 6, ad 1; *SCG* III, ch. 100.

[31] See *ST* II-II, q. 178, a. 2.

(6) They are called *portents* or *marvels* on account of their excellence.[32]

§5. Division of Miracles

A. This division is explained by St. Thomas in *ST* I, q. 105, a. 8, and is drawn in accord with the formal character of what a miracle is—namely, in comparison with the power of the whole of created nature, which is exceeded by miracles:

> Something is called a miracle in comparison with the power of nature, which it exceeds. Thus, the more the power of nature is exceeded, the greater is the miracle in question. Now, the power of nature is exceeded in three ways.
>
> First of all, it can be exceeded in the very substance of the deed in question (*quantum ad substantiam facti*)—as happens, for example, in the case of two bodies occupying the same place, that of the sun reversing its course, or that of the glorification of a human body. These kinds of things are absolutely beyond the power of nature and, thus, hold the highest rank among miracles.
>
> Second, something exceeds the power of nature, not in what is done but, rather, in the subject of its activity (*quantum ad subiectum in quo fit*)—as, for example, in the case of the raising of the dead and returning of sight to the blind, and other such things, for nature can give life, though not to the dead. Thus, such miracles are second in rank.
>
> Third, something exceeds nature's power *in the manner* (*quantum ad modum*) and order in which it is done—as when a man is immediately cured of a fever, without undergoing treatment or the usual course of nature's healing processes, or when the air is suddenly condensed into rain by divine power without some natural cause, as took place at the prayers of Samuel and Elijah (1 Kgs 12; 2 Chr 3:18). And these are the lowest kind of miracles.
>
> However, each of these kinds has various degrees, depending on the

---

[32] See *ST* II-II, q. 178, a. 1, ad 3.

different ways in which the power of nature is exceeded.[33]

{{43}} *Nevertheless, we must carefully note the difference between that which is substantially (quoad substantiam) miraculous and that which is essentially (quoad substantiam) supernatural.* A miracle *quoad substantiam* (e.g., the glorification of the human body) is only modally supernatural in relation to the way in which it is produced, not, however, essentially supernatural (that is, entitatively supernatural), as is sanctifying grace. The bodily brightness of glory is indeed supernaturally produced, but it is natural "as regards its formal character [*speciem*] and can be seen naturally by a non-glorified eye."[34] By contrast, sanctifying grace is supernatural *quoad substantiam* (that is, essentially supernatural) as a formal participation in the divine nature.

Hence, "quoad substantiam" is taken in the division of miracles as being a subdivision within modal supernaturality (that is, effective supernaturality [i.e., solely in relation to efficient causality, not formal causality]). By contrast, in the division of supernaturality, it is taken formally and intrinsically in opposition to that which is modally (that is, effectively) supernatural.

B. *The division of miracles is expressed in a different way* in De potentia, q. 6, a. 2, ad 3. There, St. Thomas says that miracles are commonly divided inasmuch as they are either *above, contrary to*, or *outside of* nature. However, this division generally [*quasi*] coincides with the preceding one. That which is *above* nature is, in particular, what exceeds nature as regards the substance of what is done. That which is *contrary to* nature is that which is contrary

---

[33] This division is explained by Sylvester of Ferrara as follows in his comments on *SCG* III, ch. 101, where he says: "As regards the greatness of miracles, we must consider the fact that it is not the same thing to say that *one of God's works is greater* than another one of His works and to say that it is *a greater miracle*, for one of God's works can be greater while, however, being less miraculous. This is so because something is said to be *a greater work of God* because it is nobler and more excellent, more fully manifesting the divine power. However, it is said to be *a greater miracle* because it more greatly participates in the formal character of what a miracle is, namely in the fact that something is done by God and that something else in reality would otherwise indicate that something else should have taken place. . . . Thus, we say that the creation of the universe and the justification of the ungodly is a greater divine work than is the sudden healing of someone from a fever, although this healing is a greater miracle, inasmuch as it more greatly participates in the formal character of what a miracle is, as is said in *ST* I-II, q. 113, a. 10, ad 1." Hence, it is not surprising that it is a greater miracle for two bodies to exist together in one and the same place than it is for the dead to be resurrected, for the first exceeds the powers of nature as regards the very substance of the action performed, whereas the second does so only in relation to the subject in which it is performed. However, according to St. Thomas, the glorious resurrection is a miracle belonging to the first order of miracles. Also, concerning this division, see Benedict XIV's celebrated work *Doctrina de servorum Dei beatificatione et beatorum canonizatione*, vol. 4, bk. 4, pt. 1, ch. 1, no. 7.

[34] *ST* III, sup., q. 85, a. 2c and ad 1.

to the natural disposition of the subject in which the miracle is performed. Finally, that which is *outside* of nature is that which is done outside of its customary mode of activity.

In this second division, "*contrary to nature*" is used *in an improper sense*, for, as St. Thomas proves in *SCG* III, ch. 100, no miracle is, properly speaking, contrary to nature but, rather, is done in accord with nature's obediential potency in relation to God. Nonetheless, improperly speaking, "it is said to be contrary to nature when nature retains a disposition contrary to the effect which God performs, as when He preserved the young men in the furnace uninjured, though the fire therein retained its burning power."[35]

The words "outside of nature" [*praeter naturam*] are *properly* said of miracles of the third order, though they are *commonly* used for any miracle when one says a miracle is that which is done outside the order commonly preserved in things. Thus, the common acceptation for the word "praeter" / "outside" contains the meanings of "supra / above," "contra / contrary to," and "praeter / outside" the order of nature, just as the modally supernatural contains the three orders of miracles.

ART. 2: ON THE POSSIBILITY OF MIRACLES

§1. The state of the question and its difficulty
§2. Demonstration of this possibility
§3. Resolution of objections

§1. The State of the Question and Its Difficulty

Having explained the orthodox notion of miracles, we now must discuss how it is that they are possible. As we have said, this possibility is something held *de fide*, but it can also be philosophically proven against those who deny such possibility.

(1) *Now, those who deny the possibility of miracles are above all drawn from the ranks of determinists*, who at least reject certain foundations of this thesis. These foundations are God's existence, his omnipotence, his providence, his freedom, and the non-absolute necessity of the laws of nature.

{{44}} Indeed, in arguing against determinists, it does not suffice that we solely bring forth the divine omnipotence, for as was said above, miracles do not merely depend on God's merely absolute power but, rather, depend on his power inasmuch as it is ordered, though extraordinarily, by his providence. Therefore, we must take up our argument precisely *upon the basis of God's omnipotence inasmuch as it lies under the divine freedom*, on

---

[35] *De potentia*, q. 6, a. 2, ad 3.

On Miracles as Motives of Credibility

which such a miraculous exception depends, for a miracle is the effect of an exceptional intervention by God in the world. Spinoza did not directly deny God's omnipotence but instead his freedom. Hence, the former rejected the possibility of miracles. The same holds for deists, who held that God does not have particular volitions but, rather, only general volitions. Leibniz, however, held that the divine choices are always morally necessary; in this way, he diminished the gratuity and supernaturality of miracles, as we discussed above.

If, as Spinoza wished, God were a non-free first cause, like the vital principle in plants, he could indeed produce effects exceeding the powers of finite nature, as the vital principle produces effects exceeding the order of physiochemical phenomena. However, these divine effects never would be miracles, for if God were not to act freely but, rather, from the necessity of his nature, he would always act in the same way, in accord with the customary order of things (e.g., he would conserve all things, move all things, and illuminate all intellects, but always in accord with the laws of nature, without any exception). These various errors were already set forth and refuted by St. Thomas himself, for example, in *De potentia*, q. 6, a. 1.[36]

---

[36] Against the ancient pantheists and the Averroists of his own time, St. Thomas said in *De potentia*, q. 6, a. 1: "Certain people held *that bodily things do not have some superior cause which would be the cause of their existence*. . . . And thus, they held that nothing could take place contrary to the course of nature because it is ordered necessarily by these bodily causes. However, this position is false because it is necessary that the first among beings itself be the cause of being in all the others, just as the hottest thing is the cause of hotness in all other things. . . .

"Others said that God is the cause of all beings through His intellect. However, they said that *God has a kind of universal knowledge of all things* inasmuch as He knows Himself and that He is Himself the first among beings, though *without having proper knowledge of each particular being*. . . . For this reason, they said that particular effects do not proceed from God except in a given order, through other causes, with the higher effects being more universal and the lower more particular. Thus, from this outlook, God cannot do anything contrary to the order of nature. However, this opinion is false, for since God knows Himself perfectly, He must know everything that is in Him in any way whatsoever. Now in Him there is the likeness of every one of His effects, inasmuch as nothing can exist without also imitating Him. Thus, it follows that He has proper knowledge of all things, as we have proven elsewhere (*ST* I, q. 12). . . .

"Others said that God produces things by natural necessity, meaning that His works are limited to the ordinary course of things in nature, thus meaning that He cannot act against it. However, this too is obviously false, for above all those things that act of natural necessity there must be something that determines nature to one mode of action, as we have proven elsewhere (*ST* I, q. 19, a. 4). Whence, it is impossible that God, who is the first agent, would act out of natural necessity.

"Therefore, having established these three points—namely, that God is the cause of existence in natural things, that he has proper knowledge and providence for each particular thing, and that he does not act out of a natural necessity—it follows that he can do something outside

(2) *However, other adversaries—namely, agnostics and contingentists—* deny our ability to discern miracles, rather than their intrinsic possibility. Nonetheless, many of them hold that *miracles are not intelligible if they are phenomena that lack some prior phenomenon* (that is, in opposition to the principle of causality). {{45}} Moreover, contingentists say the following: As they are defined by theologians, miracles presuppose the hypothetical necessity of the laws of nature so that they are marvelous and divine exceptions to them; now, the laws of nature are not fixed in this way but instead are contingent; hence, a divine exception is not distinguished in an absolute manner from natural exceptions to these laws.

Therefore, we must argue at once from the divine freedom and from the laws of nature. Many consider these two reasons separately. However, when this course is taken, the unity of this demonstration is not sufficiently clear. By contrast, St. Thomas considers, in one single argument, the customary course of nature inasmuch as it stands under the divine freedom.

§2. Demonstration of This Possibility

This question is treated at length by St. Thomas in opposition to medieval pantheists and Averroists[37] in *SCG* II: ch. 22 ("That God can do all things"); ch. 23 ("That God does not act out of natural necessity"); ch. 24 ("That God acts in accord with His wisdom"); ch. 25 ("How the omnipotent one is said to be unable to do certain things"); ch. 26–29 ("That neither divine intellect, nor the divine will, is confined to determinate effects"); and ch. 30 ("How there can be absolute necessity in created things") Also see, in bk. 3, ch. 98 and 99 ("That God can act outside the order of nature"). Likewise, see *De potentia*, q. 6.

In *ST* I, q. 105, a. 6, he proposes the fundamental argument, reducing to one single demonstration all the various proofs that are drawn either from the divine attributes or from the laws of nature that are not absolutely necessary. There he says:

> If we consider the order of things which depend on any given secondary cause, *God can indeed do something outside the order of things, for* He is not subject to the order of secondary causes. On the contrary, *this order is subject to Him, as*

---

the ordinary course of things in particular effects."

[37] The Averroists denied particular providence. According to them, God acts *ad extra* in accord with the necessity of his nature by producing from eternity (*ab aeterno*) the first intelligence that is immediately inferior to himself. However, this latter then would produce another, [with this sequence going on until] the last intelligence of heaven produces the sensible world, as well as knowledge in men, meaning that there would be only one intellect for all men. In this way did he deny personal immortality. See Maurice de Wulf, *Histoire de la philosophie médiévale*, 4th ed., [(Paris: F. Alcan, 1912)], 468.

proceeding from Him, not through natural necessity but, instead, by His own free choice. Indeed, He could have created another order of things. Whence, when He so chooses, God can do something outside this order created by Him—for instance by producing the effects of secondary causes without them, or by producing certain effects to which secondary causes do not extend.

This demonstration can be reduced to the following syllogism:

A superior, *free* cause, on which depends the application of *hypothetically necessary laws* without itself being confined to them, can act outside of the order of such laws.

Now, God is the omnipotent, free cause on whom depends the application of all hypothetically necessary laws that constitute the order of acting belonging to the whole of created nature, and the divine freedom is not confined to this order.

Therefore, God can do something outside of the order of action belonging to the whole of created nature (in other words, can perform miracles).

Now, there are three propositions to be proven in this demonstration—namely, the major premise and the two premises contained in the minor premise.

(1) *A superior, free cause, upon which depends the application of hypothetically necessary laws without itself being confined to them, can act outside of their order.* This proposition is made manifest (A) *a posteriori* by way of examples and (B) *a priori* through an analysis of the notions involved therein.

{{46}} A. *A posteriori.* By his own freedom, man can throw a stone in the air, thus acting against this hypothetically necessary law: A stone, left to itself, would naturally fall downward.[38] Likewise, a person who has a given artistic ability [*artifex*] acts outside of and above the particular laws of whatever he instrumentally utilizes. Thus, in plucking the strings of a harp, the musician produces an artificial effect through it, one that exceeds the natural power of the string left to itself, such that the non-musician does not know how to produce this effect through this string. Hence, St. Thomas says that the artisan draws out the artificial effect from the obediential potency of the thing that he uses and that obeys him. For example, "the fact that he would

---

[38] [Trans. note: Obviously, this example limps, though it could be charitably interpreted. In any case, the next two cases are clear examples of *obediential potency* as regards *a higher order*, namely, *human art and its products*, which, through its spiritual intelligibility, exceed the order of nature (*esse naturae*) in a string or wood. This is most obvious if one thinks of completely unformed string-like fiber and wood immediately taken from a tree.]

make a stool out of wood does not lay in the natural potency" of the wood but, rather, in its obediential potency.[39]

Nay, a person who has a given artistic ability [*artifex*] (for example, a musician of exceptional talent) can act outside and above the ordinary laws of his art, thus producing a work that is not only beautiful but, indeed, sublime (or extraordinary). Nonetheless, this happy exception neither destroys nor negates the ordinary law. Rather, it only suspends its application on account of the extraordinary motive involved therein. Thus, this exception confirms the law, for it is above, not contrary to, it.

B. *A priori*, through analysis of the notions involved therein, this major premise is evident. Indeed, if the application of hypothetically necessary laws depends on some free cause, this cause enjoys *freedom of exercise* as regards this application or non-application. Moreover, if[40] this free and superior cause is not confined to these laws, it also enjoys *freedom of specification* in relation to them, inasmuch as it can positively act outside or above them, as is clear in the examples cited above. For otherwise, this cause would be determined and necessitated to the application of these laws, thus being subject to them, meaning that it would be neither superior nor free in relation to them.

However, now we must prove our demonstration's minor premise, which contains two propositions.

(2) **The order of action belonging to the whole of created nature is constituted by laws that are hypothetically, not absolutely, necessary.** This is proven as follows. *Hypothetical necessity is that which is drawn* not from intrinsic causes but, rather, *from extrinsic causes* (namely, *the efficient and final causes*). *Now, the order of action belonging to the whole of created nature is constituted by laws drawn from the order of efficient causality.* Therefore, the order of action belonging to the whole of created nature is constituted by laws that are hypothetically, not absolutely, necessary.

{{47}} The definition of hypothetical necessity is found in Aristotle's writings[41] and

---

[39] St. Thomas, *Compendium theologiae*, ch. 104.

[40] [Trans. note: Reading *si* in place of *sic*.]

[41] See Aristotle, *Physica*, bk. 2, ch. 4: το ἐξ ὑποθέσεως ἀναγκαῖον. See St. Thomas's commentary, lect. 15 (On the kinds of necessity found in natural things). In lect. 6 on *Metaphysics*, bk. 5, ch. 5, St. Thomas states: "However, *absolute necessity* differs from other forms of necessity, for absolute necessity belongs to a thing in accord with what is intimate and proximate to it: whether it be its form, its matter, or the very essence of the thing—as when we say that an animal is necessarily corruptible because this follows from its matter, inasmuch as it is composed of contrary elements; and we also say that an animal is sensible because this follows from its form, and an animal necessarily is an animated, sensate substance because this is of its very essence.

"However, *necessity secundum quid* and not absolutely speaking is that kind of necessity which depends upon an extrinsic cause. Now, there are two kinds of extrinsic causes, namely,

is explained by St. Thomas in *ST* I, q. 82, a. 1:

> The term "necessity" is used in a number of ways, for something is necessary if *it cannot not be*. Now this may belong to something on account of an intrinsic principle: either *material*, as when we say that everything composed of contraries is of necessity corruptible, or on account of a *formal* principle, as when we say that it is necessary that the three angles of a triangle be equal to two right angles. In these cases, we have natural and *absolute* necessity. Necessity belongs to something in another way, on account of *something extrinsic*, namely either the end or the *agent*. Such necessity holds in relation to the end inasmuch as the end cannot be attained, or cannot be well attained. For example, food is said to be necessary for life, and a horse necessary for traveling. This is called "necessity of end," and sometimes also is called "usefulness / utility." On the part of the agent, something is necessary when someone is forced to do something by some [other] agent, so that he cannot act to the contrary. This kind of necessity is called "necessity of coercion."

Likewise, the possible or impossible is divided inasmuch as it is absolute or solely relative to a finite power.[42]

This division of necessity can be so written:

Necessity		impossibility	
absolute		*Absolute*, that which is intrinsically contradictory	
hypothetical	from the end / from the agent	*Relative*, to a finite power	

Hence, *absolute necessity* is that which, independent from whatsoever condition, cannot not be, nor be otherwise. It is founded immediately on the essence of the thing or on its intrinsic causes. For example, it is absolutely necessary that a triangle have three angles equaling two right angles, for this depends immediately on the essence (or formal cause) of the triangularity. Mathematical laws enunciating the properties of figures or of numbers are

---

final and efficient causes."

Absolute necessity is either *metaphysical* or *mathematical* in character.

Hypothetical necessity is twofold—namely, strict / physical (e.g., food is necessary for life) or *moral* (e.g., a horse is necessary for traveling a long distance).

[42] See *ST* I, q. 25, a. 3.

absolutely necessary, for mathematics abstracts from efficient and final causality, as Aristotle says on a number of occasions.[43] Likewise, metaphysical principles, which have the greatest of universality, are absolutely necessary (e.g., the principle of contradiction or the principle of causality holding that every contingent being has a cause).

Hypothetical necessity is that which cannot not be, presupposing some condition or extrinsic (efficient or final) cause. For example, presupposing that a given natural agent happens to act in natural conditions, a given effect is thus necessary. To take an example, if fire acts by its natural power, then it necessarily burns and does not freeze. However, this law does not rule out the possibility that the action of fire would be able to be impeded or modified by some preternatural cause. Similarly, on the part of the end, man must have two eyes in order to see well, but strictly speaking, one eye suffices in order that he be able to see, and man preserves his essence even if he happens to lack sight, just as a demented person, having lost the use of reason, nonetheless remains a man.

However, the order of action that belongs to the whole of created nature is constituted by the laws that express the mode of acting belonging to created agents. Therefore, the laws of nature are drawn *in accord with efficient causality* and hence are hypothetically, not absolutely, necessary. In other words, positing that all [the necessary] created causes (and only them) act in natural conditions, a given effect (e.g., the resurrection of a corpse) is impossible. {{48}} However, in the case of a miracle, a supernatural cause is added—namely, God.

These causal laws of nature are either positive or negative, but they are never absolutely necessary. *Positive laws* express *that which created nature can* do: presupposing that natural agents act in accord with natural conditions, then they necessarily produce this natural effect. However, these laws do not exclude the possibility that God would supernaturally intervene in order to impede or modify their natural effect. *Negative laws* express *that which created nature cannot do* (for example, nature cannot produce life in a corpse, presupposing that nature alone acts). However, these laws do not exclude the possibility that God would supernaturally intervene, if God exists above nature. Likewise, no created cause can make an accident remain in existence without a subject, nor make one substance transubstantiate into another. However, this does not mean that this would be impossible for God.[44]

---

[43] See *Metaphysics*, bk. 3, ch. 2, lect. 4; bk. 5, ch. 14 (lect. 16 of St. Thomas).

[44] Thus, to such hypothetically necessary laws are reduced the physical laws that are concerned with the very properties of things or with their essences, not metaphysically and in relation to what intrinsically constitutes them but instead inasmuch as they are considered in their

Finally, it is clear that these hypothetically necessary laws remain in force even in the case wherein their application is suspended by a superior cause (e.g., fire preserves its power to burn, even if it does not exercise this combustive power, just as a stone preserves its gravitational inclination, even if it is thrown upward). Hence, a miracle *is not a violation of the laws of nature*. In other words, miracles are not contrary to nature.

Therefore, the hypothetical necessity of the causal laws of nature is essentially distinguished from the absolute necessity of mathematical laws or of metaphysical principles. Only such absolute necessity excludes the possibility of miracles. Thus, it is not surprising that Spinoza denied that miracles are possible, for according to his Cartesian tendencies, he wished to reduce physical laws to mathematical laws, which abstract from final and efficient causality, thus rendering them absolutely necessary.

Nay, certain laws of nature are, properly speaking, contingent (e.g., that the earth is moved in one given direction rather than the opposite, for this is not determined by the nature of the earth, as is the case for the power of burning that proceeds from the nature of fire).

{{49}} (3) *God is the omnipotent, free cause upon whom depends the application of all hypothetically necessary laws, and he is not confined to them.* And there are two parts in this proposition.

A. *God is a free, omnipotent cause.* (a) Indeed, the First Cause must necessarily be immaterial and intelligent, for otherwise he could not produce

---

physical existence. Hence, an accident, which is a quasi-effect of substance, can miraculously remain in existence without a subject; and some created substance can be transubstantiated into another. (See Édouard Hugon, *Cosmologia*, 280.) See St. Thomas, *De potentia*, q. 6, a. 1, ad 11. Likewise, in *ST* III, q. 77, a. 1, ad 2, St. Thomas places the following objection before himself: "Not even a miracle can separate a thing from its definition. . . . However, it belongs to the very definition of what an accident is for it to exist in a subject. . . . Therefore, no miracle can make accidents exist without a subject in this sacrament (the Eucharist)." He responds to this objection by saying: "Since being is not a genus, *existence* (*esse*) cannot of itself be the *essence* of either substance or accident. Consequently, the definition of substance is not *a being through itself without a subject*, nor is the definition of accident *a being in a subject*. Rather, it belongs to the quiddity or essence of substance *to have existence not in a subject*, whereas it belongs to the quiddity or essence of accident *to have existence in a subject*. But in this sacrament, it is not in virtue of their essence that accidents do not exist in a subject, but rather, through the Divine power sustaining them. Consequently, they do not cease to be accidents, for the definition of accident (namely, the aptitude to [exist in] a subject, not actual inherence) is not withdrawn from them, nor does the definition of substance apply to them."

Likewise, substance—at least by [God's] purely absolute power—can exist without accidents, for substance is not an accident but, rather, has an aptitude to it, and this aptitude remains even if there is not, *de facto*, an act to which it is ordered, just as the reasoning faculty remains in the demented person, though not the exercise of reason. Similarly, one created substance can be transubstantiated into another, not through a created power but, rather, through an uncreated power. See *ST* III, q. 75, a. 4.

our intellects nor order the world, for the greater is not produced from the lesser. Now, the will follows the intellect (*ST* I, q. 19, a. 1), and *the divine will is free concerning particular things, which it does not need in order to have its infinite goodness in itself.* "Whence, since God's goodness is perfect and can exist without other goods, gaining no perfection from others," it follows that God is *free* to act *ad extra*—namely, to create or not create.[45]

Not only does God act freely *ad extra* but, moreover, *he acts there through will*, thus differing, for example, from man in human generation, in which case man freely generates, though not through will but instead because he is a given nature.

And St. Thomas proves this against pantheists and Averroists in *ST* I, q. 19, a. 4:[46]

First, indeed, this is seen in the very order of active causes. Since both intellect and nature act for an end, as is proven in *Physics*, bk. 2, ch. 5, *it is necessary that the natural agent have its end and the necessary means for attaining that end predetermined for it by some higher intellect*, as the arrow's end and definite movement is predetermined for it by the archer. *Whence, an intellectual and voluntary agent must precede agents that act by nature.* Therefore, since God is first in the order of agents, He must act by intellect and will.

Moreover, this is clear from the character of a natural agent, which has the property of producing one and the same effect, for nature acts in one and the same way unless it comes to be prevented from so acting. This is because the nature of an agent's activity accords with that agent's nature. Hence, for however long it has that nature, its acts will be in accordance with that nature, for every natural agent has a determinate being. Therefore, *since the Divine Being is not determined* and contains in Himself the fullness of the perfection of being, *He would act by a necessity of His nature only if He were to cause something undetermined and indefinite in being.* However, as we have already shown (*ST* I, q. 7, a. 2), this is clearly impossible. He does not, therefore, act by a necessity of nature. Rather, determined effects proceed from His own infinite perfection in accord with the determination of His will and intellect.

Finally, this is seen in how effects are related to their cause, for given that every agent produces its like, effects proceed from the agent that causes them in so far

---

[45] *ST* I, q. 19, a. 3.

[46] See also Cajetan's commentary. [Trans. note: The text of this quote comes from the *Summa theologiae*, not the commentary itself, though Fr. Garrigou-Lagrange does not make this clear in the citation, there merely writing "q. 19, a. 4 (Comm. Caiet.)".]

as those effects preexist in the agent causing them. Now, effects preexist in their cause according to the mode of the cause. Whence, *since the Divine Being is His own intellect, effects preexist in Him in an intellectual manner.* Therefore, they proceed from Him in an intelligible manner and, consequently, *in a volitional manner.* . . . Therefore, God's will is the cause of things.

(b) Moreover, God is omnipotent. In other words, *his power is infinite, for operative power follows upon existence,* and "the divine existence is infinite, inasmuch as it is not limited through receptive [potency]."[47] Indeed, if the divine existence were received into a finite essence, then it would be caused and not uncaused, self-subsistent existence.[48] Hence, God can do whatever is absolutely possible—namely, whatever is not contradictory in relation to existence.[49] "And whatever is attributed to God's power considered in itself, He is said to *be able to do in accord with His absolute power.* Such things include everything in which the character of being is preserved [thus solely excluding that which implies contradiction]. However, whatever is attributed to the divine power inasmuch as it executes the command of His just will, {{50}} God is said to be able to do by *His ordered power*,"[50] which is, as is immediately proven thereafter, either ordinary or extraordinary.

B. *The application of all hypothetically necessary laws depends upon the divine freedom, which is not confined to them.* (a) Indeed, the application of the hypothetically necessary laws of nature depends *upon the exercise of the action of the natural agent* [in question] and upon its end. Now, the action of any given created agent *depends upon the first agent*—namely, upon God, who acts *ad extra* in a free manner—for every created agent needs to be "premoved" by God in order that it may act.[51] And every natural end is subordinated to the ultimate, spiritual end intended by God, for the order of agents corresponds to the order of ends.

Hence, God can sometimes deny his natural concurrence, which is necessary for the activity of a created agent, just as he is not bound to create things or to conserve them in existence. Therefore, a contradiction is not involved in a natural action [*operatio*] falling short (e.g., as in the case of fire that does not burn), if God draws back his concurrence from it. In this, we can see God's freedom in relation to the exercise of acts (*quoad exercitium*).

---

47 See *ST* I, q. 25, a. 2.
48 See *ST* I, q. 7, a. 1.
49 See *ST* I, q. 25, a. 3.
50 *ST* I, q. 25, a. 5, ad 1; q. 104, a. 4.
51 See *ST* I, q. 2, a. 3; q. 105, a. 5.

(b) *Likewise, as regards specification, God is free in relation to the order of nature*, inasmuch as he is not confined to it. This is said against the medieval Averroists, as well as against the absolute optimism and determinism of moral necessity found in Leibniz and Malebranche.

As St. Thomas says in *SCG* II, ch. 26, "Lest someone should think that God's intellect or knowledge [*scientia*] can only reach certain effects, thus meaning that He acts by a kind of intellectual necessity, though not out of natural necessity, we still must show that His knowledge [*scientia*] or intellect is confined within no limits in its effects."

God can do other things than what he does, for

> the order placed in things by divine wisdom does not equal the divine wisdom. . . . Thus, it is clear that the whole idea of order which a wise man puts into the things which he makes is taken from their end. Thus, when the end is proportionate to the things made for that end, the wisdom of the maker is restricted to a given, definite order. However, *the divine goodness is an end which exceeds all proportion with created things*. Whence, the divine wisdom is not restricted to any particular order such that no other course of things could have come forth from it.[52]

Indeed, it is true to say that God could not have done *better*, "if the word 'better' is an adverb and implies the mode of activity of the one acting, for God cannot act with greater wisdom and goodness. However, if the word 'better' is a *noun* or implies something regarding the manner of existence of what has thus been created, in that case, then, He is able to do something better"[53] or, in other words, can create better things because "*God can do something better than any given thing that he has done*," given that there is forever an infinite abyss that separates the finite goodness of created things and his infinite. *And he even can make accidentally better the very things that he has made*, for example, by increasing their power (for example, human wisdom). Therefore, God is not confined to a given order of nature.

Conclusion. Therefore, God can act outside and above the order of acting belonging to the whole of created nature (or, in other words, can perform miracles). And *when he performs one, he does not act contrary to nature but, rather, acts in accord with its obediential potency*, by which all creatures are naturally suited to obey God, so as to accept whatever he may wish,

---

[52] *ST* I, q. 25, a. 5.
[53] *ST* I, q. 25, a. 6.

as the instrument obeys the artisan or as the arm obeys the human will.[54] {{51}} There is only one efficient cause and one end outside of which God cannot act—namely, himself, the very first cause and final end of all things.

Nor can it be said, with the deists, that only *general volitions* pertain to God's dignity but not *particular volitions*, governing through the mediacy of laws and not providing for particular things immediately. And St. Thomas responds in *ST* I, q. 22, a. 3, ad 1: "It belongs to a king's dignity to have ministers who execute his providence. However, the fact that he does not have a plan for those things which are done by them arises from a deficiency that exists in him, for every knowledge ordered to activity is perfect to the degree that it considers the particular things with which its action is concerned." "God, who has in His intellect the notion of all things, even the smallest, provides for all things, and He has given to whatever causes He has placed in charge of certain effects the power to produce those effects."[55]

Therefore, God can act outside of the order of nature, negatively or positively. He does so negatively by impeding the action of natural things (for example, the action of fire). He does so positively in three ways, as is set forth in the division of miracles, inasmuch as they exceed the power of nature: as regards the substance of what is done (e.g., bodily glorification), in relation to the subject in which it takes place (e.g., resurrection), or as regards the way it is done (e.g., a sudden conversion of water into wine).

These effects are possible for God's absolute power (inasmuch as they do not imply a contradiction) and for God's ordered, though extraordinary, power.

On the end of miracles. However, a proportionate end is required for this extraordinary intervention by God. *Now, the manifestation of the saving truth is a sufficient end for God to act outside the order of nature.* Indeed, St. Thomas says in *SCG* III, ch. 99 (*in fine*):

> Nor should we take this argument lightly, namely, that God does something in nature in order to manifest Himself to the minds of men, for as we showed earlier (ch. 17), all bodily creatures are, in a sense, ordered to intellectual nature as an end and, moreover, this intellectual nature's end is divine knowledge, as we also showed above. Therefore, it is not surprising that some change is made in bodily substance in order that provision might be made for the intellectual nature to be able to know God.

---

[54] See *ST* I, q. 105, a. 6, ad 1; *De potentia*, q. 6, a. 1, ad 18; *SCG* III, ch. 100.

[55] *ST* I, q. 22, a. 3; q. 14, a. 11.

Indeed, the whole of the bodily world is, as it were, nothing in comparison with the supernatural grace conferred upon this soul, "for the good of grace in one is greater than the good of nature in the whole of the universe."[56] Likewise, miracles can be performed "in order to demonstrate the holiness of someone, which God would like to propose to men as an example of virtue."[57] And sometimes, he miraculously "bestows upon man some particular benefit, namely, bodily health, beyond the common benefit set forth in miracles, namely so that they may lead men to knowledge of God."[58]

Corollary: *No creature can perform miracles through its own proper power; however, in order to perform a miracle, God can make use of men and good angels as instruments.*

{{52}} The first part of this follows from the definition of miracles, for they exceed all created powers (cf. *ST* I, q. 110, a. 4), and we will discuss below how we can discern effects that exceed all created powers and likewise can distinguish true miracles from false miracles (e.g., from wonders performed by demons).

The second part of the corollary is proven as follows. In order for rational creatures to be physical instruments of God, it is required and suffices that they receive from God some transient supernatural power, and by their own proper powers act dispositively in relation to the miraculous effect thus performed. Now, it is not difficult for God to confer this kind of power upon the rational nature, just as our soul instrumentally moves our members or external things. And thus holy men perform miracles not only by praying and asking for things but also by cooperating with God. "For God instrumentally uses either the internal powers of man, his speech, or also, some kind of external act."[59]

By contrast, no instrument is possible in the case of creation, for "the instrumental cause participates in the action of the superior cause only inasmuch as it acts dispositively through something that is proper to itself in bringing about the principal agent's effect. . . . And it cannot do something dispositively and instrumentally in relation to the effect of creation since creation is not brought about from anything presupposed which could be disposed through the action of an instrumental agent."[60]

Objection: A miracle can only be produced by a divine and infinite power. Now,

[56] *ST* I-II, q. 113, a. 9, ad 2.
[57] *ST* II-II, q. 178, a. 2.
[58] *ST* II-II, q. 178, a. 1, ad 4.
[59] *ST* II-II, q. 178, a. 1 and *De potentia*, q. 6, a. 4.
[60] *ST* I, q. 45, a. 5.

creatures cannot participate in infinite power. Therefore, creatures cannot instrumentally cause miracles.

Response: I concede the major premise but make a distinction regarding the minor premise. I concede that creatures cannot participate in infinite power as its own proper power. However, I deny that they cannot participate in an instrumental and transient motion coming from the omnipotent God. Indeed, this instrumental motion does not need to be proportioned to the subject in which it is received, except in a transient manner. Moreover, it is received in it on account of its passive obediential potency, which belongs to all things inasmuch as they are created beings. Therefore, a spiritual instrumental power can exist in a transient manner in a bodily instrument because it does not need to be proportioned to it, and it is received in it not inasmuch as it is bodily but, rather, inasmuch as it is a being.[61]

Thus, our intellective soul instrumentally makes use of its body in order to manifest its thoughts. Even if one's face is bodily, it is in some way intelligent—namely, instrumentally—inasmuch as it exists under the motion of the intellect and the will. Likewise does it express the virtues or the vices.

Whether an evil person can instrumentally perform miracles. As St. Thomas says, "Since the performing of miracles is a kind of divine testimony indicating the divine power and truth, if the power of performing miracles is given to demons, whose will is wholly turned to evil, God would stand in witness to their falsity, which is not suited to the divine goodness."[62] Hence, the demons can only simulate miracles through the alteration of bodies or through some sensual illusion brought about through the alteration of one's imagination.

"Miracles can be performed in order to confirm the truth of preaching by anyone who preaches the true faith and calls upon Christ's name, {{53}} which even the wicked do from time to time."[63] "However, miracles are always true witnesses to the purpose for which they are performed. Hence, wicked men who teach false doctrine never perform true miracles in confirmation of their teaching, although they may sometimes do so in praise of Christ's name which they invoke, and by the power of the sacraments which they administer."[64]

We have thus provided sufficient proof for the possibility of miracles, which God alone can perform as their principal cause.

---

[61] See Billuart, *Summa sancti Thomae, De sacramentis in genere*, diss. 3, a. 2, resolution of objections (*in fine*).

[62] *De potentia*, q. 6, a. 5.

[63] *ST* II-II, q. 178, a. 2.

[64] Ibid., ad 3.

§3. Resolution of Objections

There are two, mutually opposed series of objections concerning this matter. The first proceeds from determinism, whereas the second proceeds from contingentism.

I. Objections proceeding from determinism

These objections proceed from determinism inasmuch as it is applied to God or to the laws of nature. They can be proposed (A) in their ordinary form and (B) in their more recent form.

A. *Objections in their ordinary form*

First objection: A miracle is something outside of the orderly course of things [*est praeter ordinem*]. Now, the divine wisdom cannot act outside of the orderly course of things. Therefore[, miracles cannot be wrought by God.]

Response: A miracle is outside of the order of things inasmuch as things are subordinate to [a given] order, though not as regards the very notion of order, for it is ordered by God.

Second objection: A miracle would require alterations in divine will and providence themselves. Now the divine will and providence are immutable. Therefore, miracles are impossible.

Response: I make a distinction regarding the major premise. I concede the point if God had not decreed from eternity that there would be exceptions to these very laws. Otherwise, I deny the claim.

1. *It will be insisted, however*, that there can be no such exception. Indeed, to act in an exceptional manner outside the order of nature would be to act violently (i.e., contrary to nature). Now, it is not fitting to God that he act in a violent manner. Therefore[, there can be no such exception to the laws of the natural order].

Response: I make a distinction regarding the major premise. I concede the point if this action were not performed in accord with the obediential potency by which the creature is naturally suited to obey God. Otherwise, I deny it.

2. *Urging the point further*, one could say that this would be opposed to its obediential potency.

For, indeed, God cannot do something outside the order of metaphysical principles, especially outside the order of the principle of contradiction. Now, this fundamental principle is included in every necessary proposition, even in the laws of nature. Therefore, God cannot act outside the laws of nature.

Response: I concede the major premise, though I distinguish the minor. I concede that the principle of contradiction is included in every necessary proposition, in accord with the way that it is necessary. However, I deny that it is so included in such a way that every necessary proposition is absolutely necessary. Moreover, I distinguish the conclusion along the same lines: I concede that God could not act outside the laws of nature if they were absolutely necessary, but I deny that he could not do so if they are only hypothetically necessary.

For example, it is necessary that a dead person not rise so long as nature alone acts; however, this does not exclude the possibility that the dead could rise through God's supernatural intervention.

3. *Pushing back more, however*, the laws of nature are absolutely necessary.

The principle of causality, even though it holds from the perspective of the efficient cause, is nonetheless likewise absolutely necessary, and God cannot act outside of the order that it establishes. Now the laws of nature are laws of causality. Therefore, God cannot act outside of them.

{{54}} *Response*: No parity exists between the utterly universal principle of causality, on the one hand, and the laws of nature, on the other. Indeed, the former principle extends even to the divine causality, outside of which God obviously cannot act, for he cannot bring into existence an uncaused creature. By contrast, the laws of nature express a manner of acting belonging to created nature, and God can modify this manner of acting. The principle of efficient causality is hypothetical only in the sense that it is possible that a contingent beings not exist, though it is absolutely necessary that contingency depends upon the most universal first cause.

4. *Further insistence*: Even if the laws of nature are particular, nonetheless, they are absolutely necessary.

Indeed, even though mathematical laws are particular, they are absolutely necessary, and God cannot act outside of them. Now, the laws of nature are expressed mathematically and, hence, are likened unto mathematical laws. Therefore, the laws of nature are absolutely necessary, and God cannot act outside of them.

Response: I concede the major premise. God cannot, even extraordinarily, make a triangle whose three angles would not be equal to two right angles. However, I make a distinction regarding the minor premise. I concede that the laws of nature are likened unto mathematical laws as regards their quantitative (or numeric) expression. However, I deny that they are such as regards their very nature. For *mathematical laws are drawn from the formal principles* of figures or numbers and hence are absolutely necessary. By contrast, *the causal laws of nature are drawn from extrinsic causes*—namely, from efficient or final causality—and hence are hypothetically necessary. In other words, something that is mathematically impossible is absolutely impossible, whereas what is physically impossible is impossible for sensible nature, though not absolutely for every possible cause. Spinoza erred when he reduced physics to mathematics, for only mathematics abstracts from efficient and final causality.[65]

5. *Further insistence*: Even if they are distinguished from mathematical laws, the laws of nature are absolutely necessary.

Indeed, natural things have a determinate essence, whence flow determinate properties and a determinate manner of acting. Now, God cannot change what is essential to some given thing and simultaneously have that thing remain what it is. Therefore, God cannot change the natural manner of action in natural things.

Response: I make a distinction regarding the major premise. I concede that natural things have a determinate manner of acting as regards the *power of acting*. However, I deny that this is so *as regards the exercise of their activity*. I concede the minor premise. I distinguish the conclusion along the same lines as the major. As St. Thomas says in *De potentia*, q. 6, a. 1, ad 20: "In the furnace's fire, an order to burning remains, even though it did not burn the three young men therein."

6. *Further insistence*: Not even in relation to the exercise of a thing's activity can God act outside the laws of nature.

Indeed, God cannot do something outside the order of justice. Now, the order of justice is the rule of the very exercise of moral action, for the omission of due action is a sin. Therefore, similarly, God cannot act outside of the order of nature, by which the exercise of natural agents' action is ruled.

Response: As St. Thomas explains (in *De potentia*, q. 6, a. 1, ad 3), there is no parity here, for the order of justice directly designates an order to the ultimate end, outside of which God cannot act, whereas, by contrast, the laws of nature do not directly designate an order to the ultimate end but, rather, an order of one creature to another. Thus, God cannot, in an extraordinary manner, order us to despair or to hate God, for this would represent the denial of his infinite goodness.

7. *Further insistence*: Moreover, God cannot act outside of the particular moral precepts that rule the interrelationships between men. For example, God cannot, in an extraordinary manner, command murder. Therefore, similarly, God cannot act outside of natural laws.

Response: I deny the major premise. See what St. Thomas says in *ST* III, suppl., q. 67, a. 2: "There can be a divine dispensation even to the first principles of the natural law, for the sake of signifying or showing forth some divine mystery. {{55}} For example, we see the dispensation to the precept given to Abraham in relation to the slaying of his innocent son. However, such dispensations are not granted to all generally, but only to certain individual persons, as also is the case for miracles." Likewise, see *ST* I-II, q. 94, a. 5, ad 2 and q. 100, a. 8, ad 3: "When Abraham consented to kill his son, he did not consent to murder, for his son was due to be slain by the command of God, Who is Lord of life

---

[65] See St. Thomas, *De potentia*, q. 6, a. 1, ad 11.

and death, for He Himself inflicts the punishment of death on all men, both godly and ungodly, on account of the sin of our first parent. If a man executes that sentence upon the Divine authority, he will no more be a murderer than God would be." Likewise, see Cajetan's comments on this article:

> Just as this statement, "the dead cannot rise," is necessary (according to natural power) . . . and when God raises someone, He does not falsify that proposition or do away with it but, instead, acts above (not contrary to) nature, so too in the present case, this conclusion, "One must not murder," in the sense in which it is expressed, namely, by a private authority with certain other conditions, is a necessary conclusion; . . . however, since God orders the performance of an act which would be murder were he not to command it, he orders an action that is not outside or contrary to the precept but, rather, as it were, one that is above it, provided that he orders that the commanded act be performed by a superior authority.

B. *Objections raised by more recent forms of determinism*

Objection: Science presupposes the immutability of the laws of nature, for this provides the foundation for us to have infallible foresight concerning natural effects. Now, a miracle would disturb this immutable order and would impede our foresight. Therefore, miracles are impossible.

Response: I make a distinction regarding the major premise. I deny that science presupposes the metaphysical immutability that founds metaphysically infallible foresight [concerning natural effects]. I concede that it presupposes physical immutability as the foundation for physically certain foresight [concerning natural effects]. I contradistinguish the minor in the same manner.

Indeed, the natural law holding *that the dead cannot rise naturally* remains in force even if they do sometimes supernaturally rise. Nay, the law is thereby confirmed, for no natural agent but, rather, God alone can cause someone to rise from the dead. This does not disturb the law in question, for it takes place in few cases, just as natural exceptions also occur in a few cases. (For example, a man is sometimes born with six fingers on his hand.) Moreover, superior agents often alter the activity of inferior agents without the laws [of nature] being violated, as, for example, when the law of gravity is not destroyed by someone throwing a stone in the air, even though gravity is overcome by another through a superior force. Similarly, the vital powers of plants and animals make use of physical powers and surpass them.

1. *It will be insisted, however*, that at the very least there cannot be an exception to the fundamental principle of the conservation of energy. Now, a miracle would represent an exception to this principle, for through an extraordinary intervention, God would change the quantity of energy that exists in the world. Therefore[, miracles remain impossible].

Response: I make a distinction regarding the major premise. I concede it if that principle were utterly universal, like the principle of causality. However, I deny it if it is only particular and true for the physical agents with which the physicist is concerned. I distinguish the minor along the same lines. This principle is a hypothesis that is held commonly enough today for energy arising from physical actions, which are the object of external experience. (For example, an equal amount of energy exists between motion and heat when heat is generated by motion.) However, this law cannot be extended, without a vicious circle [*petitione principii*], to the energy that arises from God's invisible influence. In order to affirm this extension, one would need to prove that the world is a closed system, receiving nothing from God's invisible influence, and this cannot be proven by science. Rather, it is only a gratuitous postulate presented by materialism, which *a priori* denies the existence of God.

2. *Continued insistence*: At least we must say that there cannot be an exception to the principle of causality: "Every phenomenon presupposes an antecedent phenomenon." Now, a miracle would be a phenomenon without a phenomenal antecedent. Therefore, miracles are impossible.

Response: I make a distinction regarding the major premise. I concede that there cannot be an exception to the principle of contradiction, rightly understood: Everything that is done has a cause. However, there can be an exception to the principle of causality wrongly understood, along phenomenalist lines. {{56}} It suffices that there be a first, free cause existing above the phenomenal order.

3. *Continued insistence*: Nonetheless, a miracle can only be intelligible for us as being an effect of some phenomenal antecedent—namely, as an effect of living faith, which exceeds physical powers, just as our freedom moves our body.[66]

Response: I make a distinction regarding the minor premise. I concede the point along phenomenalist or evolutionist lines, and then a miracle would not be, properly speaking, a divine effect and would only have a symbolic value. However, according to the principles of sound philosophy, a miracle is intelligible as a fact that manifestly displays the divine omnipotence, as is said by the [First] Vatican Council.

4. *Continued insistence*: It is unfitting that a greater good would be forsaken for the sake of a lesser one. Now, in a miracle, a greater good is forsaken in this way for a lesser one—namely, the good of the universe for a given particular good. Therefore, it is unfitting that a miracle be performed.

Response: I deny the minor premise, for the order of the universe, in which its own good consists, is not destroyed through the performance of a miracle. Rather, the only thing that is removed is the order of a given particular cause to its effect (e.g., fire to burning). Hence, when a miracle is performed, a particular good is forsaken for the sake of a greater good and a loftier end.

---

[66] See the work of Édouard Le Roy cited above.

5. *Continued insistence*: However, as Leibniz says (in *Theodicy*, 3.249), the order of a given particular cause to its effect cannot be done away with without the entire course of the universe's activity thereby being altered, on account of the interconnection of all bodies with each other. Indeed, all things disposed by God are connected together in virtue of the principle of sufficient reason. Thus, this world is the best of all possible worlds.

Response: Leibniz's conception here, which is called psychological determinism or the determinism of moral necessity, is false. Yes, it retains the terms involved in discussing human and divine freedom, but it in fact does away with their very reality. Indeed, freedom does not require only deliberating intelligence, spontaneity, and the contingency that is found in the physical world. Beyond this, the dominating indifference of the practical judgment and the will are required, things that Leibniz denies (cf. *Theodicy*, 3.302).[67] Thus, not all things that are willed by God are necessarily connected in virtue of the principle of sufficient reason, and this world is not the best of all possible worlds. God can forever make better things. *Nor does man, by throwing a stone in the air, thereby change the entire course of the universe.* Moreover, the principle of *raison d'être*[68] must be understood analogically, not univocally. That is, it must be understood proportionally, or in various ways in things that are themselves necessary in various manners (namely, metaphysically or physically, and when physically either always or only in most cases, for matter is the principle of non-determination in physical things).[69] St. Thomas resolves this objection in *De potentia*, q. 6, a. 1, ad 21: "We must say that when God does something contrary to the course of nature, He does not destroy the whole order of the universe but, rather, only the course which is from the order of one particular thing to another."

---

[67] This indifference is founded on the absolute disproportion that exists between the universal good and the particular good. Hence, in order to proceed from the intention of the universal good (or of beatitude in general) to a given singular good, rather than some other, even if it is not equal, there only exists *a relatively sufficient reason*, not one that is absolutely sufficient and determining, for two finite goods, even if they are relatively unequal to each other, *are equally infinitely distant from the infinite good*, and only the infinite good, clearly seen, would draw our will in a necessary manner.

See *ST* I-II, q. 10, a. 2; I, q. 84, a. 1.

[68] [Trans. note: This is an excellent attestation to the fact that Fr. Garrigou-Lagrange clearly desired to distance the so-called "principle of *raison d'être*" from the Leibnizian principle of sufficient reason. Up to here, he referred to the *principium rationis sufficientis* but now slides into the *principium rationis essendi*.]

[69] We have refuted Leibniz's determinism at length in another work. See Réginald Garrigou-Lagrange, *God: His Existence and His Nature*, vol. 2, trans. Dom Bede Rose (St. Louis, MO: B. Herder, 1949), 268–350.

II. Objections proceeding from contingentism

Objection: Miracles presuppose the hypothetical necessity of the laws of nature. Now, the laws of nature certainly {{57}} are not hypothetically necessary but instead are contingent, for it is not rare that exceptions take place. Therefore, miracles are impossible or, at least, are not specifically distinct from natural exceptions.

Response: I concede the major, while distinguishing the minor premise. I will let the claim pass if one means that all natures are contradictorily identified with each other in universal becoming, as absolute evolutionism wishes things to be. However, I deny it if, in virtue of the principle of contradiction and identity, the natures of things are distinguished from each other. I distinguish the conclusion along the same lines.

Allow me to explain. According to absolute evolutionism, contradictory things are identified in becoming itself, as Heraclitus held among the ancients and Hegel in modern times. Hence, according to natural evolution, the more proceeds from what is less and the more perfect from the less perfect, and this is something more than a miracle—indeed, the production of the impossible itself. Nay, absolute evolutionism identifies necessity and contingency and hence denies the possibility of miracles, sometimes on account of the necessity of laws (as in idealistic evolutionism) and sometimes on account of their absolute contingency (as in certain forms of empirical evolutionism).

By contrast, in virtue of the principle of contradiction, being and nonbeing are radically opposed, and becoming is not self-explanatory, for it is not self-subsistent being. Consequently, there is a real and essential distinction between, on the one hand, God, who is immobile and completely simple, and, on the other, the changing and composite world. Hence, the law of created agents is not the same as the law of God's creative action. A creature cannot do whatever is possible for God, just as flesh cannot do what spirit can do. In the world, there are at least determinate laws that are hypothetically necessary: for created agents in general, for inanimate bodies, for living beings like plants, for animals, and for men. For example, there most certainly are laws like the following: Living things do not naturally return to life after their death; brute animals neither speak nor reason. The denial of these laws represents the contradictory confusion of all natures with each other. Nevertheless, natures are diverse, as well as whatever takes place on account of their activity (inasmuch as activity follows upon being and the mode of acting upon the mode of being).

1. *However, it is insisted that* in order to know hypothetically necessary laws, we must know the essences of things. Now, we do not know the essences of things. Therefore[, we do not know hypothetically necessary laws].

Response: I make a distinction regarding the major premise. I deny that we must know them intuitively and in a comprehensive manner. However, I concede that we must know them abstractively and imperfectly. I contradistinguish the minor premise along the same lines.

It suffices that we generically know what bodily living things are, even if we are not aware of what their specific differences are, in order that we might know, for example, the law stating that following upon death living things do not naturally return to life. Otherwise, induction of the laws [of nature] would be entirely impossible, bringing all physical science to ruin.

2. *Continued insistence*: Scientific classifications and laws are only representations that are useful for subjectively ordering phenomena. Hence, a miracle is only an abrogation of our subjective classifications, though not an abrogation of the laws of nature. Hence, it does not have an ontological value but instead only a symbolic one. Such was the position of Édouard Le Roy and Fr. Laberthonnière.

Response: I make a distinction regarding the major premise. I concede the point if it is considered in line with nominalism or conceptualism, denying it, however, if considered in terms of moderate realism. I distinguish the consequent in a similar manner. Contrary to what is held by the nominalism of empiricists and the conceptualism of subjectivists, moderate realism efficaciously defends the ontological value of the first notions and principles of reason, hence also defending the ontological value of miracles. On this, see what we said earlier, in vol. 1, ch. 9 (Examination of Agnosticism).

Indeed, positive science must not metaphysically determine what the nature of things is; however, it also must not admit the principles of a false philosophy (namely, nominalism or phenomenalism). *Otherwise, it would not be positive science but instead a form of positivistic science.* In reality, positive science must speak in accord with common sense—that is, in accord with natural reason concerning the substance of things, their powers, the soul's faculties, and so forth. {{58}} Our commonsense notions contain, vaguely, in the form of nominal definitions, the real definitions that are arrived at by philosophical reason. However, what common sense and sound philosophy understand by the term "humanity" is not an empirical collection of men but, rather, human nature, for otherwise, to say, "Peter is a man" or "Peter has humanity" would mean the same thing as saying, "Peter has a collection of men." Likewise, what common sense and sound philosophy mean by the term "human will" is not the collection of volitions but, rather, a given faculty. Thus, in virtue of the realism of our natural reason, classifications and laws, at least those fundamental laws that are established by science with certitude, designate extramental things and the real notions of things.

ART. 3: ON THE DISCERNIBILITY OF MIRACLES

§1. State of the question: The principal objection raised by adversaries
§2. The Church's teaching
§3. On certitude and its degrees in relation to the discernibility of miracles

§4. On the discernibility of miracles as regards the nature of the fact (or as regards their supernaturality)

§5. On the discernibility of miracles as regards the existence of the fact

§6. On false miracles and on magic, Spiritism, and hypnotism

§7. Resolution of objections

§1. State of the Question: The Principal Objection Raised by Adversaries

No few rationalists concede that miracles are possible. However, they hold either that they do not exist or that they cannot be distinguished from more or less extraordinary natural facts or from wonders. In the introduction to his work, *Vie de Jésus*, Ernst Renan wrote, "We do not say that miracles are impossible but, rather, that hitherto no miracle has been truly demonstrated." Kant held the same thing, as do agnostics in general. According to the modernists, like Édouard Le Roy, only religious faith can discern what is a miracle, for physically considered, a miracle does not differ from a natural fact, though, for religious faith, it is a symbolic sign of the value of faith itself.

The principal objection against the discernibility of miracles is: It is impossible to know with firm certitude that something that has been done exceeds all of nature's powers, for *we do not know all the powers and laws of nature*. Hence, that which is inexplicable through laws that are already known can come into existence through natural laws and powers that are unknown. Nay, agnostics add, as we said above: We do not know the laws of nature as they are outside of the soul in things themselves. Hence, that which seems to us to be an abrogation of these laws as they are in reality is, perhaps, only an abrogation of these laws as they are conceived by us. However, we already saw the resolution to this last difficulty at the end of the preceding article.

§2. The Church's Teaching

Against this error held by agnostics, the [First] Vatican Council defined: "If anyone says that no miracles are possible . . . or *that miracles can never be recognized with certainty* and that the divine origin of the Christian religion cannot be legitimately proved by them, let him be anathema."[70] And the corresponding chapter in *Dei filius* states: "which as they (miracles) manifestly display the omnipotence and infinite knowledge of God, they are {{59}} *the*

---

[70] [First] Vatican Council, *Dei filius*, can. 3.4 (Denzinger, no. 3034).

most certain signs of divine revelation adapted to the intelligence of all men."[71] And in Leo XIII's encyclical *Aeterni Patris*, miracles are called "established proofs, as it were, of unshaken truth."[72]

Indeed, miracles would not manifestly display the omnipotence of God if they were not discernible from natural facts. Likewise, in order that they might be utterly certain signs of divine revelation, they themselves must be known with certitude by reason alone, prior to the reception of faith, which is founded upon revelation. Indeed, as is defined in logic, a sign is that which, beyond the appearance it brings forward to the senses, makes something other than itself come into one's knowledge.[73] Thus, upon seeing smoke, we come to know the fire that exists under it. However, a sign is certain when it determinately signifies something and uncertain when it can signify many things (e.g., a red face).

Likewise, in the Anti-Modernist Oath we read: "I accept and acknowledge external arguments of revelation, that is, divine deeds, in particular miracles and prophecies as utterly certain signs of the divine origin of the Christian religion, and I hold that they are most excellently adapted to the understanding of all eras and men, even of our own days."

Above all, we must note that, as regards the discernibility of miracles, a natural certitude exists that is loftier than the *practical moral certitude* admitted by Georg Hermes. Indeed, along with Kant, Hermes held that speculative reason can only arrive at a merely subjective persuasion concerning objective reality, which itself can only be phenomenal and apparent in character. As regards practical reason, Hermes held, following Kant's thought on the matter, that it is autonomous. And whenever practical reason imposes some duty upon us, it obligates to all those things required for the fulfillment of that duty. Hence, according to Hermes, sometimes we find ourselves faced with the obligation to admit as being practically certain something that is theoretically uncertain (e.g., the obligation of admitting the testimony of the external senses, or the experience and honesty of men, or experience of

---

[71] Ibid., ch. 3 (Denzinger, no. 3009).

[72] Leo XIII, *Aeterni Patris*, no. 5.

[73] [Trans. note: Technically, according to the Thomist school, the *essence* of signification lies in the relational bringing of the other into cognition on the basis of something else ("that which represents something other than itself to a cognitive power"). The relation itself is the sign, no matter what the foundation may be. Thus, even the concepts (*species expressae*) formed by the internal senses and the intellect are *formal* signs. See John of St. Thomas, *The Material Logic of John of St. Thomas: Basic Treatises*, trans. Yves R. Simon, John J. Glanville, G. Donald Hollenhorst (Chicago: University of Chicago Press, 1955), q. 21, a. 1 (388–400). This point of doctrine was repeated many times, with good reason, in the work of John Deely.]

current or past things—and, hence, the truth of history and of miracles). Hermes said we cannot have physical certitude concerning the reality of a given man's death based upon the viewing of a corpse; however, we have the moral duty to bury the dead. Therefore, this duty requires us to admit, as something morally certain, the death of a man who must be buried. From this theory, it follows that our reason cannot prove the fact of revelation with utter certitude.

Already before the [First] Vatican Council, this Hermesian teaching was condemned by Pius IX in his encyclical *Qui pluribus*:

> Indeed, human reason, lest it be deceived and err in a matter of so great importance, ought to investigate diligently the fact of divine revelation so that it can know with certainty that God has spoken. . . . But how many, how wonderful, how splendid are the proofs at hand by which human reason ought to be entirely and most clearly convinced that the religion of Christ is divine . . . and that, therefore, nothing is more certain than our faith.[74]

Objection: The Church does not seem to admit that individual [human] reason can discern a miracle with certitude, for the Church reserves to herself judgment concerning the truth of miracles, for example, in the canonization of saints. (Such was the argument made by Maurice Blondel.[75])

Response: {{60}} The Church sometimes solemnly and officially judges concerning the truth of certain miracles and concerning the sufficiency of given signs for the manifestation of the holiness of the servants of God. Indeed, it is true that this official judgment does not fall to individual persons' reason. Likewise, the Church solemnly defined (e.g., at the [First] Vatican Council) as a dogma of faith: "The narrations concerning miracles contained in Sacred Scripture are not to be dismissed as being fables and myths."

However, this does not mean that individual reason is incapable of knowing miracles. Nay, the Church herself presents miracles as being "the most certain signs (of her divine mission), adapted to the intelligence of all men."[76] Therefore, miracles are naturally knowable with certitude before one comes to admit the divine mission and infallibility of the Church.

---

[74] Pius IX, *Qui pluribus*, nos. 7 and 8 (Denzinger, nos. 2778–2779).

[75] See Joseph de Tonquédec, *Immanence*, 223–229.

[76] See [First] Vatican Council, *Dei filius*, ch. 3 (Denzinger, 3009).

§3. On Certitude and Its Degrees in Relation to the Discernibility of Miracles

On certitude in general. Certitude is the firmness of the mind's adherence to some given knowable thing, without any fear of error. It does not suffice that the intellect be without fear; rather, the exclusion of fear must arise from a due motive (or foundation). On account of one's prejudices, ignorance, or passions, someone can be firmly persuaded that something is the case, even when it is in fact false. However, this accidental firmness does not suffice for the formal character of certitude. Moreover, we must not confuse *persuasion*, even when firm, which sometimes is concerned with false things, with certitude. The formal motive of certitude is always and essentially (*per se*) that which is true and causes a true judgment. Persuasion, even when firm, if it is considered later with diligence, can be set aside as being false. However, this is not so for certitude.

Certitude admits of degrees, not as regards the exclusion of the fear of erring but, rather, as regards the firmness of one's adherence, inasmuch as this firmness is founded essentially (per se) in metaphysical, physical, or moral necessity. (Similarly, spirituality admits of degrees, not as regards the exclusion of matter but, rather, as regards the perfection of spirit.)

These various degrees must be explained in relation to the present question:

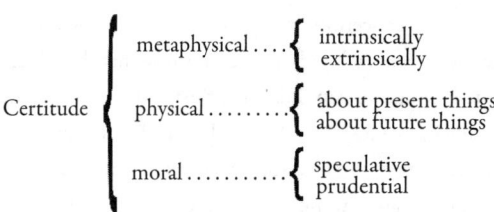

Metaphysical certitude, which is founded on metaphysical necessity, is had when the connection between the predicate and subject of a statement is absolutely necessary— that is, when it depends on the nature of its subject and predicate being made manifest through an analysis of those notions. Therefore, the denial of a metaphysically certain assertion implies a contradiction in an absolute manner. In this certitude, there is an absolutely necessary resolution to intelligible being, the formal object of the intellect, and to the first principles of reason. Hence, this certitude completely exceeds experience, even if the notions involved in the principles arise materially from experience through abstraction. Thus, it is metaphysically certain that every contingent being is caused and, hence, that there is a first, Uncaused Cause. Indeed, the denial of God's existence is radical absurdity, for were God no longer to exist, all things would become absurd, as we see, for example, in Hegel's absolute evolutionism. Likewise, as we will come to say, it is metaphysically certain that God alone can cause transubstantiation or raise the dead.

{{61}} Like those forms of certitude to be discussed below, metaphysical certitude can be *spontaneous* (as it is for common sense) or *critical / reflexive* (as it is in metaphysics).

Moreover, there is certitude that is *intrinsically metaphysical*, which is directly founded on metaphysical necessity, and certitude that is *extrinsically or metaphysical by* [*intellectual*] *resolution* inasmuch as something physically or morally certain cannot be denied without some metaphysical impossibility indirectly following from such a denial (e.g., that something comes into being without a cause).

Mathematical certitude is reduced to metaphysical certitude inasmuch as it is concerned with absolutely necessary propositions. Nay, from our perspective, mathematical evidence is clearer than is metaphysical inasmuch as it is less remote from the senses.

Physical certitude *is founded on the physical necessity* of the laws of nature, which are hypothetically necessary and do potentially undergo exceptions. This certitude is had, formally, by the mediation of experience (that is, formally by the mediation of the senses), and its resolution to being and to the first principles of being is only hypothetically necessary. This is particularly clear in foresight that is physically (not metaphysically) certain, for physical certitude concerning a future fact is less than physical certitude concerning a present fact in which it is empirically clear that there is no exception involved therein.

Even if physical certitude (whether *spontaneous* or *scientific*) is inferior to metaphysical certitude, it is a true form of certitude, fully excluding fear of error. Thus, I am physically certain concerning the existence of the table on which I am writing, and through reflection, we can firmly know that this is not a hallucination. For there are the laws and conditions for hallucination, and it is easy enough for me to verify whether these conditions in fact do exist.

Hence, *sometimes, intrinsically physical certitude can, through reflection, become extrinsically metaphysical* if its falsity were to lead to a kind of metaphysical impossibility. This is so if it were a question of all sensations taken together—that is, of the existence of the external world. Otherwise, a sensation would exist without that which is sensed, which is a contradictory claim; it would exist without an end, without an efficient cause, and [thus] without any *raison d'être*. However, nothing exists without a *raison d'être*.[77] This likewise holds true if we are speaking of general facts (e.g., heat generally expands iron; the falsity of countless experiences concerning this fact would lack a *raison d'être*). Likewise,

---

[77] [Trans. note: See Réginald Garrigou-Lagrange, "There Cannot Be Genuine Sensation Without a Real Sensed Thing," *Philosophizing in Faith: Essays on the Beginning and End of Wisdom*, ed. Matthew K. Minerd, trans. Thomas DePauw and E. M. Macierowski (Providence, RI: Cluny Media, 2019), 101–119.]

this holds for the case of some particular fact upon which the religious life of humanity depends. (e.g., Based on the experience of seeing Christ's scars, the Resurrection of Christ was quasi-physically certain for the apostles and for a number of disciples. If in these circumstances this knowledge concerning Christ's Resurrection were false, God would have permitted the whole of the Christian religion, which is fruitful in all good things, to be founded on an invincible error, which is contrary to the rational notion of providence.)

Moral certitude *is founded on moral necessity* and on the moral impossibility of the opposite being true.[78] For example, it is morally impossible that men would naturally arrive at perfect knowledge {{62}} of all the truths of natural religion. Hence, if this knowledge exists, it is morally certain that it comes from God who reveals. Likewise, it is morally impossible that a given intelligent and honest witness would lie in these particular circumstances. This certitude is had through the mediation of suitable human testimony. Yes, indeed, it is metaphysically and physically possible that a witness can be deceived and can deceive. Nonetheless, all things considered, his testimony seems evidently credible, and it produces true moral certitude and not merely great probability. For example, it is certain that my father, whose truthfulness I know well, is not lying when he tells me about

---

[78] As we said above (concerning the certitude required for the judgment of credibility), those who, joining Leon Ollé-Laprune (*La certitude morale*, 413–414), drawing back from the common terminology used by the scholastics, define moral certitude as "the firm adherence of the mind to historical or *metaphysical* truths influencing the moral life, an adherence that exists under the influence of moral dispositions with the concurrence of the will, even if an objective proof would *per se* suffice."

This definition of moral certitude is a cause of equivocation because it is not drawn from the *per se* motive for this certitude but, rather, from the dispositions that concur in this certitude *in a non-per-se* manner. It would follow that God's existence, proven by metaphysically valid arguments, would only be morally certain and that a philosopher, even one having great insight while, however, being wicked, could not arrive at certitude concerning God's existence without himself having the necessary moral dispositions. However, this is false. Sometimes great speculative understanding concerning God's existence is united to great wickedness, as we see in certain deists. Nonetheless, we must admit that the aforementioned definition can be admitted *ad hominem* against certain agnostics, especially in order to designate the commonsense certitude that remains in these philosophers even under their agnostic prejudices, indeed appearing to be firmer when they consider matters of religion with true simplicity of heart.

[Trans. note: Regarding this sense of *ad hominem* arguments, a sense wholly lost in contemporary parlance, see Tommaso Zigliara, *Summa philosophica*, vol. 1, 12th ed. (Paris: Briguet, 1900): "An 'absolute' demonstration is *one which proceeds from premises whose truth we admit and assume in order to then draw an inference, absolutely speaking*, as when we demonstrate the real existence of God on the basis of the contingent character of creatures, and other such demonstrations. However, a *relative* (that is, *ad hominem*) demonstration is *one which proceeds from principles which are admitted by the person we are arguing against and which we assume for the sake of refutation, setting aside the question of the truth of such principles*, as when someone assumes principles admitted by materialists or by rationalists, in order to convince them that their doctrine is false."]

the death of my brother. By contrast, testimony offered by some foreigner frequently furnishes only probability.

Moreover, against Georg Hermes, we must distinguish *speculative moral certitude* from *prudential certitude*. The first is concerned with a given fact, whether existing or past, and can be either spontaneous or critical (and then it is called historical certitude). The other—namely, prudential certitude—also called practico-practical moral certitude, is concerned with the moral fittingness of an action, especially concerning the golden mean to be observed in a given, utterly particularized act (e.g., in order to preserve, here and now, the virtue of humility). For, as St. Thomas says, following Aristotle: "The truth of the speculative intellect is taken *through the intellect's conformity to reality* [*ad rem*]. . . . Whereas the truth of the practical intellect (in prudence) is taken *through conformity to right appetite*"[79]—that is, to right intention—and this takes place when we must prudentially judge concerning contingent things to be done. Thus, someone who is invincibly unaware of the fact that a given wine contains poison can judge with practical certitude concerning the moral fittingness that this wine is to be drunk, while nonetheless erring speculatively. His judgment is conformed to right intention, not to reality.

Hence, sometimes intrinsically moral certitude can, through reflection, become *extrinsically metaphysical*, if its falsity would mean that a kind of metaphysical impossibility would follow. This is so in the case of the universal testimony of men, the falsity of which would be lacking in a *raison d'être*. The same holds true in the case of the testimony of many who, without any usefulness for themselves, would converge in order to tell a lie; nay, in such a case, they would speak falsely against what would be useful for them. So too is this true in the case of some morally certain miracle, paying heed to all the physical and moral circumstances, for God does not permit us to be deceived in a matter of such great importance, as will be made clearer in the next thesis concerning the probative force of miracles. This consideration, is, of course, extrinsic, but through it, intrinsically moral certitude does find itself to be reinforced.

§4. On the Discernibility of Miracles as Regards the Nature of the Fact (or as Regards Their Supernaturality)

Here we must respond to this objection: We cannot know with certainty whether some given extraordinary fact surpasses all the powers of nature, for we do not know all such powers; perhaps what seems to be a miracle can, in fact, be produced by unknown powers. Moreover, many things are held to be miracles when they can, in fact, be attributed to our imagination or to hypnotism.[80]

---

[79] See *ST* I-II, q. 57, a. 5, ad 3, as well as Cajetan's commentary on *ST* I-II, q. 57, a. 5, nos. 7 and 8.

[80] In this *theoretical* question concerning the discernibility of miracles, we must first consider the

Let us see (1) the response offered by certain recent thinkers and (2) the more profound solution.

I. *The response offered by a number of recent thinkers.* A number of authors who do not give sufficient metaphysical consideration to this question say the following: In order for us to be certain concerning the supernaturality of a given concrete fact, it is not necessary that we know all the powers of nature and be able to say how far their efficacy is able to extend; {{63}} rather, it suffices that we be able to practically decide what cannot be done in given, determinate circumstances. Now, *the laws of nature, in the same circumstances, are determined to the production of one effect, whereas, in the case of a miracle, the effect is produced by an agent that, in the same circumstances, brings about entirely different effects*, as though it were endowed *with freedom.*

If explained rightly, this response can indeed make manifest that such effects exceed the powers of sensible nature;[81] however, it does not follow from this that they exceed the power of imagination or of hypnotism (and, *a fortiori*, the powers of the demons).

Now, they respond to this difficulty concerning the power of imagination or hypnotism with the following: According to science, sicknesses that come from a given lesion of an organ cannot be healed in these ways. Moreover, not all miraculous facts are cases of healing of disease; indeed, many others are spoken of, such as the resurrection of the dead.

And they add that in order for the works of God to be distinguished from *diabolical wonders*, many signs must be considered:

(a) as regards *the nature of the work*, which sometimes manifestly exceeds created powers (e.g., the raising of the dead);

(b) as regards *the moral characteristics of the work*, namely: (1) as regards the person of the wonderworker; (2) as regards the manner in which the miracle is performed; (3) in particular, as regards its effects; and (4) as regards the teaching with which it is connected.

In this way, the majority of divine miracles are distinguished from diabolical marvels.

CRITIQUE: This response is true, but it *does not argue with sufficient profundity from the nature of a miraculous work*, which must be considered

---

nature of miracles, followed by the question of their existence. However, the reverse will be the case in the *historical* part of the work. See our discussion of Christ's miracles below, bk. 2, ch. 10, art. 1.

[81] See Étienne Hugueny, *Critique et catholique* [(Paris: Letouzey et Ané, 1910)], 287. Also see A. Bros, "Comment constater le miracle," in *Annales de philosophie chrétienne* (June 1906).

first and principally, for a miracle is the seal of God inasmuch as it is a work "which God alone can do," as St. Thomas says in *ST* III, q. 48, a. 1.

Indeed, moreover, some of the aforementioned authors, not giving sufficient consideration to the nature of a work of God, affirm too much when they wish to discern a miracle on the basis of the prior preaching by which it is obtained. They say that miracles are extraordinary facts that seem to exceed already-known sensible powers of nature—indeed, even those powers that are imaginable—for these extraordinary facts are not produced when these causes are posited, but, by contrast, the prayer of the wonderworker always precedes them, and without this prayer, the miracle is not produced. Thus, it inductively seems that the prayer is the moral cause of the miracle, while its physical cause is God, who, as he wishes, freely hears the prayer.

However, this explanation involves an exaggeration, and it does not even fully resolve the difficulty, for even a false wonderworker sometimes imitates a prayer prior to performing his wonder. Indeed, those who, with sincere heart, pray for a miracle without, however, always obtaining it sometimes obtain some providential assistance, though such assistance can fail to be, strictly speaking and certainly, miraculous. Hence, theologians generally hold that this prior prayer is one of the circumstances by which a miracle is discerned, though it does not constitute the first criterion for discerning a fact that exceeds natural powers, even those that are unknown.[82]

II. *The more profound solution.* {{64}} In response to the aforementioned objection, traditional theologians answer in a more profound manner, saying the following: Indeed, we do not *positively* know all natural powers; however, we *negatively* know what nature cannot do.[83] Indeed, we

---

[82] However, sometimes, not only does a prayer precede the miracle but also the wonderworker announces that the miracle is to be performed in the name of God the creator, in order to confirm his revelation, and in reality, performs this miracle in God's name. This is a sign of a true divine intervention. Hence, Billuart, as well as many other theologians, place, after the consideration of the nature of the miraculous work, as the second rule of the discernibility of miracles: "*A miracle performed in the name of God the creator, in defense of some given dogma,* never can be false nor lead one into error, for it would stand in contradiction to God's infinite goodness, wisdom, and truthfulness (1) that He would permit His name to be alleged in order to substitute a false miracle for a true one and (2) that He would suffer His name to be brought forward in witness of a falsehood by which men would necessarily and invincibly be led into error against what they owe to God and is necessary for one's salvation" (Billuart, *Summa sancti Thomae, De fide*, diss. 2, a. 2).

[83] Joseph de Tonquédec rightly says in *Introduction à l'étude du merveilleux et du miracle* (Paris: Beauchesne, 1916), 230: "There are cases wherein the bare possibility of the natural unknown will not even exist. One could rightly insist on the secret virtualities of nature, whether physical or psychological nature, along with our ignorance of them. On this side, there are boundaries that a sound intelligence will obstinately refuse to cross. We do not know the positive limits of

know certain *proper effects of God* that can only be produced by God and, hence, surpass all created powers, even powers that are unknown.

However, such knowledge is already had by common sense, or natural reason, and afterwards is perfected by philosophical reasoning.

(1) ACCORDING TO COMMON SENSE, in proposing the first rule for the discernibility of miracles, theologians generally say:

> There are certain effects which, by the common and constant sense of all men of whatsoever time and nature, are held to exceed all the powers of nature as something truly miraculous. Such things include, for example, the raising of the dead. In whatever place and at whatever time a truly dead man, as Lazarus was, rises, there is nobody who does not hold that such an occurrence is not truly and properly speaking a miracle. Whence, as is said of the man born blind in John 9:32 (DR): "From the beginning of the world it hath not been heard, that any man hath opened the eyes of one born blind." Whence, when there is such an effect, which the common and constant sense of all men, of whatever time and place, thinks to be miraculous, it must certainly be held to be a true miracle, for this sense, both constant and universal, possessed by all men of whatever time or nature, attentive to the infinite goodness, wisdom, and truthfulness of God, cannot be false. Otherwise, God who is the Author of common sense and of reason would either deceive us or permit us to be deceived, without any means of being able to discern error and to be freed from it, which stands in infinite contradiction to His goodness, wisdom, and truthfulness. And this would be quite especially the case if the error were concerned with something asserted as being a dogma.[84]

Therefore, *common sense* (or natural reason) *knows that certain effects are proper effects of God* and, hence, exceed all the powers of nature, *even those that are unknown.* For example, *only the Author of life can return a corpse to life*, illuminate someone born blind, and heal those who are sick with incurable diseases. {{65}} *Only the Author of matter can suddenly multiply a material*

---

natural forces, but we do know certain negative limitations of them. We do not indeed know how far they go; however, we believe that we can affirm that they do not go here or there. By combining oxygen and hydrogen, one will *never* obtain chlorine; by sowing wheat, one will *never* obtain roses; likewise, human speech will *never* suffice, by itself, to calm storms or to raise the dead. Against this, there is no possibility, even negative, which remains, not even a 'perhaps,' however remote one may suppose it to be [*si en l'air qu'on le suppose*], which can survive. If someone sows seed, believing that, perhaps, roses will come forth from grains of wheat, ... such a person is quite strange [*un anormal*]."

[84] Billuart, *Summa sancti Thomae, De fide*, diss. 2, a. 2.

substance or instantaneously convert it into another. Only the Author of the soul can slip into the soul and know the secrets of hearts, reveal with certainty future free actions, and suddenly convert the will to heroic acts. In all such cases, common sense declares: The finger of God is at work here.

This spontaneous knowledge of natural reason is, indeed, quite vague, though certain. In what objective medium does common sense perceive these truths? In the first principles of being, inasmuch as *being* is the formal and adequate object of our intellect. Indeed, natural intelligence perceives being in sensible things, just as sight perceives color; thus, common sense knows that contingent being depends upon the Necessary Being and vaguely discerns *the proper effects of the First Being*.[85] Therefore, in order to discern miracles, supernatural faith is not needed; rather, natural intelligence, which by its very nature exceeds the senses, suffices. However, this vague knowledge needs to be explained and defended by philosophical reason.

(2) According to philosophical reasoning, the aforementioned knowledge had through common sense is explained and defended through a resolution to *being* and to the first principles of being. In this way, the following two conclusions come to be established: (A) the supernaturality of many miracles of the first, second, and third order is metaphysically certain; (B) the supernaturality of others is generally morally certain on the basis of physical and moral circumstances.

A. *The supernaturality of many miracles of the first, second, and third order is metaphysically certain.* Indeed, it is metaphysically certain that God alone can produce (and, hence, immediately change) being inasmuch as it is being, prime matter, material substances without the mediation of accidents, the intellective soul, and the intellect and will. Now, many miracles of the first, second, and third order necessarily and evidently involve such immediate alterations. Therefore, it is metaphysically certain that these miracles can be produced by God alone.

The major premise. Here we must prove that such effects are proper effects of God. In this way, it will be made manifest that no cause inferior to God can produce them, for otherwise the power of this inferior cause would have the same specification as the divine power. Moreover, we must note that *only a universal cause that can immediately produce some universal effect* (whether in the depths of material things or in that which is separated from matter) *can immediately change that effect*, for this immediate change

---

[85] Concerning this, see what we said in our work *Thomistic Common Sense: The Philosophy of Being and the Development of Doctrine*, trans. Matthew K. Minerd (Steubenville, OH: Emmaus Academic, 2021), 126–128.

presupposes the same universality in the cause that immediately produces it. For example, the imagination, which cannot produce an intellectual judgment, cannot immediately change such a judgment but, rather, can only do so mediately—that is, through its own proper effect (namely, the phantasm). This principle will become clearer as we set forth the following examples.[86]

(a) *However, God alone can produce being inasmuch as it is being (or existence, absolutely speaking)* and not only inasmuch as it is this (e.g., Peter) or such (e.g., white). For to produce existence absolutely involves bringing about that effect from no presupposed subject (i.e., *ex nihilo*). {{66}} In other words, only God can create. Now, this is metaphysically demonstrated by St. Thomas (α) based on the universality of such an effect and (β) based on the manner of its production.[87]

(α) "It is necessary that we reduce more universal effects to more universal and prior causes. Now, among all effects, the most universal of all is existence [*esse*] itself. Whence, it is necessary that (existence inasmuch as it is existence) is the proper effect of the first and most universal Cause, which is God." Just as fire can ignite and light illuminate, Self-Subsistent Existence can produce existence absolutely.

(β) Similarly, this is made manifest from the way it is brought about: "Indeed, if a greater power is required in the agent to the degree that the (passive) potency is more remote from act, it is necessary that the power of the agent acting upon no presupposed potency, as is the case for the creative agent, be infinite, for there is no proportion between no potency and some potency, the latter of which the power of a natural agent presupposes, just as there is no proportion between nonbeing and being. And because no creature has, without qualification, infinite power, just as no creature has infinite existence, as we proved earlier in *ST* I, q. 7, a. 2, it follows that no creature can create" (*ST* I, q. 45, a. 5, ad 3).

Consequently, only God can *change being* [*ens*], *inasmuch as it is being, in its most profound depths*. By contrast, every created agent acts to bring about a determinate effect and does not extend itself to the whole nature of being.[88]

(b) *Only God can produce matter*[89] because matter can only be produced through creation—that is, from no presupposed subject—for it itself is the first subject of all natural changes. Consequently, only God can *immediately*

---

[86] Here, our concern is with the principal cause of miracles, for as we said above, a created agent can be the instrumental cause of a miracle.

[87] See *ST* I, q. 45, a. 5.

[88] This is proven as follows in *ST* III, q. 75, a. 4: Every agent acts inasmuch as it is in act (or the mode of activity follows upon the mode of being); now, every created agent is finite in its act (i.e., in a determinate genus and species); therefore, every created agent can bring about only a determinate effect and does not extend to the full nature of being.

[89] See *ST* I, q. 44, a. 2.

(or from within) change prime matter. On this, see what is said in *ST* I, q. 105, a. 1:

"God can immediately move matter to form (for example, suddenly bringing forth the form of wine from the matter of water) because being in passive potency can be reduced to act by an active potency which contains it within its power. Therefore, since matter is contained under the divine power, as something produced by God, it can be reduced to act through the divine power. And this is to move matter to form, for form is nothing other than the act of matter." And, as is said in *ST* I, q. 110, a. 2, this is proper to God, for he alone can produce matter and, hence, immediately change it. This immediate change is specified in the same manner as is immediate production. A cause that is inferior to God cannot change matter from within but only from without, by means of accidental alterations and local motions, as is clear in the case of substantial generation. This will become clearer from what we will say in what follows.

(c) *Only God can immediately change material substances*—that is, change them from within and not through the mediation of accidents. Indeed, as we have said, only God has immediate power over matter so as to be able to draw forth from it a new substantial form without the mediation of accidental dispositions. Therefore, God alone has immediate power to produce material substances without the mediation of accidents and, consequently, has the power to change them immediately (e.g., to immediately change the substance of water into the substance of wine).

{{67}} (d) *Only God has immediate power within the substance of the intellective soul, the intellect, and the will.*

(α) Only God can act immediately within the substance of the soul precisely as a substance. In other words, only he can act there without the mediation of accidents, as inferior substances must do. Moreover, the substance of the soul, precisely as spiritual and not able to be educed from matter, can only be produced by God through creation. Hence, it can be changed immediately by God alone (e.g., by being substantially joined anew to a body through resurrection, as we will discuss immediately below).

(β) Similarly, only God can subjectively move the intellect and the will in an immediate fashion, as is shown in *ST* I, q. 105, a. 3 and 4, because the order of agents must correspond to the order of ends. Now, the intellect and the will are essentially ordered to something absolutely universal—namely, to universal truth [*verum*] and to universal goodness [*bonum*]. Therefore, they can be subjectively moved only by a universal agent, which is at once the first intelligence and the first willing (that is, by God). And if such motions are extraordinary, as we will come to say, they pertain to prophecy or to graces of this kind or to miraculous conversions.

In this way, philosophical reasoning provides us with an explanation for the major premise of the demonstration. However, it is already *vaguely* known by common sense (or natural reason), whose formal object is *being*, and this is the source of the certitude had by common sense concerning the absolute supernaturality of the main kinds of miracles.

THE MINOR PREMISE is proven as follows. Now, many miracles of the first, second, and third order necessarily and obviously involve immediate changes of this kind, whether of being, of matter, of substances, of the soul, and so forth.

This is proven (1) among miracles of the first order for transubstantiation, even if this is an invisible miracle, as well as for the coexistence of two bodies in the same place; (2) among miracles of the second order for resurrection and the healing of one born blind; (3) among miracles of the third order for the sudden conversion of water into wine and for the multiplication of loaves.

(1) MIRACLES OF THE FIRST ORDER. (a) *Transubstantiation* is indeed an invisible miracle in the Eucharist and is held by faith alone. Hence, it does not have a value as a sign confirming revelation. However, it is metaphysically quite clear that transubstantiation can be produced only by God. Thus, it provides an illustration for our principle, enabling us then to understand how it is applied to other miracles.

Indeed, of its very essence, transubstantiation involves the changing of being inasmuch as it is being. Hence, it can only be produced by God. This is proven in *ST* III, q. 75, a. 4, for transubstantiation is not only a formal conversion with the same matter remaining, as happens in natural generation, but rather is the conversion of the whole substance of bread into the whole substance of Christ's body.

"The nature of being is common to both forms (i.e., of bread and of the body of Christ) and to both matters. And that which is of being in the one can be converted *by the Author of being* into that which is of being in the other, withdrawing that by which it was distinguished from the other."[90] No created agent can perform transubstantiation because

> every agent acts inasmuch it is in act. (Activity follows upon being, and the mode of activity upon the mode of being.) Now, any given created agent is determined in its act since it belongs to a determinate genus and species. Therefore, the action of any given created action bears upon some determinate act. Now the determination of any given thing in actual existence comes from its form. Therefore, no natural or created agent can act except by changing the form of that upon which it acts, {{68}} and for this reason, every change brought about in accord with nature's laws is a formal change. However, God is infinite act. Whence, His action extends to the whole nature of being. There-

---

[90] *ST* III, q. 75, a. 4, ad 3.

fore, He can bring about not only formal conversion, thus making diverse forms succeed each other in the same subject, but also the change of *the whole of being*, namely, so that the whole substance of one thing would thereby be changed into the whole substance of another.[91]

(b) According to St. Thomas, *the coexistence of two bodies in the same place* belongs to miracles of the first order—for example, as when following upon his Resurrection, Jesus entered the upper room "through closed doors" (John 20:26). The demonstration of the divine origin of this miracle is hinted at by the Angelic Doctor in *ST* I, q. 67, a. 1, and is more explicitly presented in *ST* III, suppl., q. 83, a. 3. It can be reduced to the following argument:

Two bodies cannot exist in the same place unless in this same place they remain distinct as regards their existence and as regards their matter. Now, two bodies in the same place cannot remain distinct as regards their existence and as regards their matter except by virtue of him who has immediate power over existence and matter, so as to *preserve in being and in matter the substantial distinction that naturally requires the distinction of positioning and place.* Just as an accident can remain without a substance only by the divine power, so too only by the divine power can one material substance remain distinct from another without having its own proper location.[92]

(c) Among miracles of the first order there is also placed the glorification of the body (or *glorious transfiguration*) inasmuch as it is derived from the glory of the soul, which can only be produced by God since it is supernatural *quoad substantiam*.[93] However, by reason alone, it is difficult to prove that this illumination of the body can only arise from the glory of the soul. Similarly, St. Thomas places among miracles of the first order "that the sun would reverse its course," at least in appearance,[94] or "*the alteration of the course of heavenly bodies*, which receive their unchangeable order from God

---

[91] *ST* III, q. 75, a. 4.

[92] This is how the argument runs in *ST* III, suppl., q. 83, a. 3. Likewise, in ad 4, it is said "that *one body cannot be locally present simultaneously in two places even through a miracle*—for the body of Christ is not locally present upon the altar—although it can miraculously take place that two bodies would be in the same place. This is because being in multiple places simultaneously is opposed to what it means to be an individual, on account of the fact that a being is *undivided in itself*. . . . Whence, a contradiction is involved in the claim that one and the same body would be locally present, at one and the same time, in various locations." Hence, according to St. Thomas, bilocation can only be apparent, inasmuch as a body is really present in one place, while in another place there is only an appearance of this body produced by God or by the angels.

[93] See *ST* III, q. 45, a. 2 on the Transfiguration.

[94] See *ST* I, q. 105, a. 8.

alone."[95]

(2) MIRACLES OF THE SECOND ORDER. Among these miracles, we find RESURRECTION. We must prove that here we find a change that God alone can produce. This is indeed admitted by common sense, inasmuch as it is commonly said that *only the Author of life can return the dead to life.* Nay, even nonbelievers do not say that resurrection can be brought about in accord with natural laws that are not yet known. Rather, they deny either the fact of such a person's death or the fact of resurrection in such cases.

We must here pass from the vague knowledge had by common sense (or natural reason) to more explicit knowledge through a reduction to principles that are *per se nota.* This demonstration can be proposed as follows.

{{69}} The soul is united to the body *through its substantial existence as a form.*

Now, resurrection is the substantial joining of a separated soul with the matter of a corpse, with no prior accidental dispositions mediating this rejoining.

Therefore, resurrection can only be produced by him who has immediate power over matter and the substantial existence of the soul—namely, by God.[96]

This is explained somewhat in *ST* III, suppl., q. 75, a. 3, though more profoundly in *De potentia,* q. 6, a. 7, ad 4, where it is said:

---

[95] Cf. *ST* III, q. 44, a. 2. [Trans. note: Needless to say, the final remark, however, bears witness to the defunct elements of St. Thomas's cosmology.]

[96] See *ST* III, suppl., q. 75, a. 3 (Whether the resurrection is natural or miraculous); *De potentia,* q. 6, a. 7, ad 4 (whether angels or demons can take on bodies). In the first text, we read: "Nature cannot be the principle of resurrection, even though resurrection finds the terminus of its activity in the life of nature. This is so because *nature is the principle of movement in the thing wherein that nature is,* either as the *active principle*—as in the movement of heavy and light bodies, as well as in the natural alterations of animals—or as the *passive principle*—as in the generation of simple bodies. Now, the passive principle of natural generation is the *natural passive potency* which *always has an active principle corresponding to it in nature,* as is said in *Metaphysics* 9, text 10. . . . Now, *there is no active principle of the resurrection in nature,* either with regard to the union of the soul with the body, or with regard to the disposition calling for that union, for *such a disposition cannot be produced by nature, except in a definite way by the process of generation* from a seed. Whence, even were the body to have a passive potency, or any kind of inclination, toward union with the soul, it would not be of such a nature as to sufficiently have the formal character of being a natural movement. Whence, strictly speaking, the resurrection is miraculous and not natural, except in a qualified sense, namely, on the side of the terminus which is natural life."

Thus, we indeed here have a proof that resurrection is not natural on the side of its cause, for nature is determined to one and only causes life in accord with determinate circumstances and dispositions that are the circumstances and dispositions of generation. Now, this does not explicitly prove that resurrection exceeds the powers of all possible created agents, even spiritual ones. However, this is made clear in *De potentia,* q. 6, a. 7, ad 4.

Nothing has power over its existence, for the power of any given thing flows from its essence or presupposes its essence. And because *the soul is united through its existence to its body as a form,* it does not lay in its power that it release itself from union with the body; and similarly, it does not lay within an angel's power that he unite himself to a body *in his existence* as a form. However, an angel can take on a body in the aforementioned manner, being united to it as a mover and as a figure to its shape.

And, in ad 14: "To exist in a given body can be understood in two ways. In one way, something can be there by being contained within quantitative boundaries, and this kind of presence is possible for demons. However, in another manner, something can be *within the essence of the thing as giving it existence* and activity, and this kind of presence is *proper to God alone,* even though God is not a part of any given thing's essence," though he is the cause of its existence.[97]

From these points, we have our demonstration.

The major premise is as follows: *The soul is united to the body through its substantial existence as a form.* This is proven in philosophical psychology. In the writings of Aristotle and St. Thomas there are three proofs for this: (A) inasmuch as the soul is the radical principle of man's vegetative, sensitive, and rational actions; (B) inasmuch as man's substantial difference is drawn from them; (C) because otherwise man's natural unity would be destroyed, for he would not be something that is essentially (*per se*) one but, rather, would be one in a nonessential (i.e., *per accidens*) manner, as for example, that which moves and that which is moved are accidentally united.[98]

---

[97] See *ST* I, q. 51, aa. 2 and 3.
[98] See *ST* I, q. 76, a. 1.

    A. *The radical principle of* man's vegetative, sensitive, and rational actions is his constitutive (or substantial) form. Now the soul is the radical principle of these actions. Therefore, the human soul is the substantial form of man's body. "For that by which something primarily (*primo*) acts is its form, . . . for nothing acts except inasmuch as it is in act (and is in act through its form, which is the determinative principle of its essence / nature). However, it is obvious that the first thing by which the body lives is the soul, . . . for the soul is the first thing by which we nourish ourselves, sense, and move locally, as well as likewise that by which we primarily (*primo*) understand. Therefore, this principle by which we primarily understand, whether it is called the intellect or the intellective soul, is the form of the body. And this is what Aristotle demonstrates in *De anima,* bk. 2, ch. 2."

    B. *The specifying principle of man* is his constitutive / substantial form. Now, the rational soul is man's specifying principle. Therefore, the rational soul is man's constitutive / substantial form. "Indeed, the nature of any given thing is revealed by its activity. However, man's proper action, inasmuch as he is man, is to understand (*intelligere*). . . . Therefore, it is necessary that man draw his nature from that which is the principle of this activity. However, any given thing's species is drawn from its form. Therefore, it follows that the intellective principle

{{70}} However, this doctrine is nothing other than an explanation for the vague apprehension had by common sense (or natural reason), and it has been defined by the Church.[99]

Now, the *minor premise* of our demonstration is the very definition of resurrection—namely, *the substantial joining of a separated soul with the matter of a corpse*, with no prior accidental mediating dispositions, so that a dead corpse immediately returns to life, manifesting within itself, in a permanent manner, the various activities of vegetative, sensitive, and intellective life. Indeed, this is the meaning of the term "resurrection," excluding all previous accidental dispositions that are necessary for the generation of a living being. Hence, resurrection *can only be produced by him who has immediate power within matter and the substantial existence of the soul.* Now, as we said above, this agent is God alone, who can change matter and the soul interiorly within their profoundest depths.

Also refer, at the end of this thesis's exposition, to the response to the objections raised against the value of this demonstration.

Also included among miracles of the second order is *the illumina-*

---

is the proper form of man."

C. *Man has natural substantial unity*, not accidental unity. In other words, he is something that is *per se*, not *per accidens*, one. Now, this union can only exist if the human soul is united to a body through its substantial existence as a form. Therefore[, the human soul is united to a body through its substantial existence as a form.] Indeed, otherwise, if the soul were united to the body accidentally through its action ("as mover") and not through its substantial existence, man "would not be something that is unqualifiedly one and, consequently, would not be unqualifiedly a being, for thus something is a being in the same way that it is one."

This demonstration presupposes the teaching concerning the substantial composition of bodies out of matter and form, which Aristotle proves by the substantial generation and corruption of bodies. It is obvious that not only do accidental corruptions exist in nature but also substantial corruptions—for example, the corruption of a lion. Such corruption leaves behind only remains, for *in these remains the properties of the vegetative and sensitive life* of the lion are no longer latently present. Therefore, it is no longer a substance. However, the existence of substantial corruption manifests the existence of substantial generation inasmuch as the same thing is the reason for opposites. Substantial transformation also is found manifestly in nutritive assimilation, inasmuch as food that is not yet living is made into our flesh or blood. And it cannot be said that our soul is only the principle of atomic organization, for that principle would not give first *substantial existence* and, hence, would only be accidental. Moreover, in any given atom, we can distinguish matter and the atom's constitutive form, for atoms are specifically (or, at the least, numerically) distinct and nonetheless agree materially [*conveniunt in materia*].

[99] See Council of Vienne, *Fidei catholicae* (Denzinger, no. 900); Lateran V, *Apostolici regiminis* (Denzinger, no. 1440); Pius IX, Letter *Eximiam tuam* to the Archbishop of Cologne, June 15, 1857 (Denzinger, no. 2828).

tion of those who are blind, especially those who are born blind.[100] And, as is recounted in the Gospel according to John 9:32 (DR), the man who was born blind said himself: "From the beginning of the world it hath not been heard, that any man hath opened the eyes of one born blind." Blindness, especially when congenital, is incurable, like a kind of partial death, the death of a given organ. {{71}} Hence, the argument brought forward for the case of resurrection proportionally holds good for the case of the illumination of a person born blind.

(3) MIRACLES OF THE THIRD ORDER. Among these miracles is included *the sudden conversion of water into wine.*

St. Thomas states in *In II Sent.*, d. 18, q. 1, a. 3, ad 4: "Although the conversion of water into wine was not something above the powers of nature as regards the substance of the thing done, nonetheless, it was above its powers as regards the mode of it being brought about, for nature cannot suddenly change water in a given vessel into wine. This is only possible through the digestion and maturation of grapes over time." Likewise, in *In IV Sent.*, d. 17, q. 1, a. 5, q. 1c, the conversion of water into wine is placed among miracles of the third order.

Now, because this alteration is brought about instantaneously, without the mediation of accidental alterations, it is the immediate educing of the form of wine from the potency of matter. Hence, it can only be produced by him who has immediate power within matter—namely God, who is not limited to moving matter externally but is he who alone can move it interiorly within its profoundest depths. In other words, in the matter of water, the form of wine is not in proximate potency but, rather, only in remote potency, so long as the preceding dispositions are lacking. Hence, the *sudden*, formal conversion of water into wine is not in the natural potency of the subject on account of the *manner* in which it is brought about but, rather, is only in the subject's obediential potency, which is subject to the divine power.

The same must be said concerning *the multiplication of loaves.*

St. Thomas says in *ST* III, q. 44, a. 4, ad 4: "The multiplication of the loaves was not brought about by way of creation but, rather, through an addition of extraneous matter which was transformed into loaves. Thus, Augustine says, in commenting upon John 6:1–14, 'Whence, He multiplies a few grains into harvests; thence in His hands He multiplied the five loaves.'" And St. Thomas adds, "It is manifest that grains are multiplied into harvests through a process of conversion." Likewise, in his comments on ch. 14 of the Gospel of Matthew, St. Thomas explains this multiplication as follows: "Some say that this can be brought about naturally, for just as matter is related to any possible form, so too is it related to any possible quantity. Now, it is foolish to say that matter would be

---

[100] See *ST* I, q. 105, a. 8.

related to any possible quantity, for the only way that this can be brought about is through the process of expansion [*rarefactionem*]. However, this process is determinate in natural things." Moreover, bread so condensed could not nourish five thousand men, as we read in Matthew, ch. 14.

Hence, St. Thomas concludes in *ST* I, q. 92, a. 3, ad 1: "Whence, given that no condensation is apparent in such multiplications, we must hold that there was an addition of matter involved, whether through creation or, more probably, through conversion," and he cites the same words from St. Augustine (*In Joan.*, tr. 24). He says that it is more probably through conversion, because there is no need here to have recourse to creation since this multiplication can be brought about through conversion.

If the multiplication of loaves was brought about through creation, it obviously could only have been brought about by God. It is more probably the case, however, that it was brought about through conversion, though certainly not transubstantiative conversion but, rather, through a sudden formal conversion, just as at the wedding feast of Cana water was turned into wine, with the same matter remaining. Hence, it can only be produced by him who has immediate power within matter—namely, by God.

Thus, the supernaturality of many miracles of the first, second, and third order is metaphysically certain and is confirmed through a consideration of the circumstances involved, as we will immediately discuss. {{72}} However, the existence of these miracles can be physically certain for those who witness them (e.g., for the witnesses of Lazarus's resurrection), as we will discuss below. The same must be said concerning many cases of healing, as will be discussed below in bk. 2, ch. 10, a. 3.

B. *The supernaturality of other miracles of the third order is in general known with moral certitude on the basis of physical and moral circumstances* (e.g., the sudden healing of a disease that would be difficult to cure).

Frequently, it is physically determinable that these facts exceed the powers of bodily agents, given the manifest disproportion involved and because the laws of nature are determined *to one* thing, whereas, in these extraordinary cases, the effect is produced by an agent that in the same circumstances would have brought about entirely *different* effects, as though that agent were endowed with freedom.

However, this does not mean that these effects exceed the powers of all created agents, even spiritual agents. Hence, we must consider, beyond the nature of the work done, its circumstances, not only those that are physical but also those that are moral and religious as well. Thus, we can discern whether a given fact arises from a good or evil spiritual agent, for if no evil is clear in these circumstances, then this extraordinary fact may legitimately be judged to come from God, at least mediately (namely, by the mediation of angels / good spirits). However, it is sometimes difficult to determine whether it exceeds the proper powers of the angels such that it could be produced by God alone as by its principal cause.

Concerning this matter, let us consider (1) what St. Thomas says; (2) what circumstances are, physically speaking; and (3) what moral circumstances are.

(1) *What does St. Thomas say?*

He responds:

> Signs performed by those who are good can be distinguished from those which are done by the wicked in at least three ways. First, they can be so distinguished *through the efficacy of the power* of the person performing them, because the good perform signs through the divine power, even to the point of bringing about things to which the active power of nature in no way extends, such as the raising of the dead and other things of this sort, which demons cannot truly do but, instead, can only bring about marvels that *do not last for a long period of time.* Second, such a distinction can be drawn *from the usefulness of signs,* because signs performed by those who are good are concerned with useful things, such as the curing of sicknesses, and other such things. However, signs that are performed by the wicked bring about harmful or vain effects, such as flying in the air, the stunning of the bodily members of persons, and other such things. . . . The third difference is found *in relation to the end* of the sign thus performed, for those signs which are performed by good men are ordered to the building up of faith and good morals, whereas the signs performed by the wicked are detrimental to faith and morals. Moreover, they differ *in relation to the way* in which they are performed, for the good bring about miracles by invoking the divine name in a pious and reverent manner, but the evil do so by certain absurd ravings, such as by cutting themselves with knives and other such disgraceful actions. Thus, signs that are performed by those who are good can manifestly be discerned from those which are brought about through the power of demons.[101]

Likewise, Benedict XIV said: "False miracles can be distinguished from true miracles through their efficacy, usefulness, manner of being performed, end, person, and occasion."[102]

---

[101] *In* II *Sent.,* d. 7, q. 3, a. 1, ad 2. Cf. *ST* I, q. 113, a. 4, ad 2.

[102] See Benedict XIV, *Doctrina de servorum Dei beatificatione et beatorum canonizatione,* bk. 4, ch. 7, nos. 14–22. This chapter cites as examples of false miracles the cases brought forth by certain Jansenists, who hoped to prove the holiness of a certain deacon named [François de]

However, in order for our knowledge to be more methodical and certain, {{73}} we must distinguish physical and moral circumstances from each other. Moreover, in the latter kind of circumstances, we must determine which are principle and which are secondary.

(2) *The physical circumstances* by which one can distinguish whether or not extraordinary healings and other such effects are natural are enumerated by Benedict XIV in *Doctrina de servorum Dei beatificatione et beatorum canonizatione*, bk. 4, pt. 1, ch. 8: "In order for a healing to be counted as being miraculous, the following conditions are needed: (1) the sickness must be grave and either impossible or difficult to cure; (2) [the sickness] should not be in its final stage so as shortly afterwards it should decline [in vigor]; (3) medicines must either not be employed or, if employed, they should be useless; (4) the healing must be sudden; (5) the healing must be perfect; (6) no purging or crisis must precede it, (7) and the sickness that was taken away must not return." These seven signs are explained one by one in this work by Benedict XIV, who makes use of a number of examples.

Likewise, the work treats separately the illumination of the blind brought miraculously, the marvelous healing of the deaf, dumb, paralyzed, and epileptic, as well as the miraculous healing of persons from leprosy, tumors, gangrene, and fever. Similarly, it treats of negative miracles such as sweating drops of blood, going for great lengths without food, certain spiritual miracles (such as miraculous conversions), the driving out of demons, the non-decaying of corpses, apparitions by the saints, as well as the imagination and its powers.

There are many scientific works recently edited by theologians and doctors concerned with the miraculous healings performed in the shrine of Lourdes.[103] Likewise, see shortly below concerning the effects of magnetism and hypnotism, as well as what is said in bk. 2, ch. 10, a. 3.

(3) *The moral circumstances* by means of which we can distinguish the aforementioned extraordinary facts from diabolical illusions are as follows.

In *ST* I-II, q. 7, a. 3, St. Thomas explains the seven circumstances of human actions, which are commonly enumerated in the following verse: *quis, quid, ubi, quibus auxiliis, cur, quomodo, quando*; who, what, where, by what aids, why, how, and when.

In this text, he states:

Pâris, who was buried in the cemetery of Saint-Médard in Paris.

[103] See the medical study by the medical doctor Antoine Vourch, with an introduction by Abbé Dubaquié, *Quelques cas de guérison de Lourdes et "la foi qui guérit,"* 2nd ed. (Paris, 1933). Likewise, see similar works written by Boissarie, Grandmaison, Dr. Van der Elst, Fr. Gemelli, Baustert, and especially Georges Bertin, *Histoire critique des événements de Lourdes: Apparitions et guérisons* (Paris: Lecoffre, 1908). Also, see what is said below in bk. 2, ch. 10, a. 3.

Whence, considering given acts, we must pay heed to "who" did it, "by what aids" or "instruments" he did it, "what" he did, "where" he did it, "why" he did it, and "how" and "when" he did it. . . .

The reason for this enumeration can be presented as follows. A circumstance is said to be something outside the substance of the act, yet in a way touching it. Now this takes place in three ways: first, inasmuch as it touches the act itself; second, inasmuch as it touches the act's cause; and third, inasmuch as it touches its effect.

Now, *it touches the act itself*, either by way of measure (as in *time* and *place*) or by qualifying the act as *how* (*quomodo*).

It touches the effect when we consider *what* is done.

It touches the cause of the act, depending upon the cause in question. In the case of the final cause, we have the circumstance *why*. In that of the material cause, or object, we have the circumstance *about what*. In the case of the principal efficient cause, we have the circumstance *who*. Finally, in the case of the instrumental efficient cause, we have the circumstance *by what aids*.

{{74}} NB: In ad 3, he says, *what, why,* and *who* are called circumstances not inasmuch as they are the object or specifying end or the agent himself but, rather, inasmuch as they are conditions on the side of the object, the end, or the agent.

However, what are the *principal circumstances* of human acts? St. Thomas responds in a. 4: "Properly speaking, acts are called human inasmuch as they are voluntary. Now, the motive and object of the will is the end. And therefore, the most principal circumstance of all is that which touches upon the act from the perspective of the *end*, namely, 'that for the sake of which' [something is done]. Now, accidents of the second rank are those which touch upon the substance of the act, namely *what* is done. But the other circumstances are more or less principal to the degree that they more or less draw close to the aforesaid accidents."

Hence, in order to know whether some extraordinary fact is a true miracle, after considering its nature and physical circumstances, we must consider why it is performed, what is performed, the person by whom it is performed, how it is performed, by what means it is performed, and where and when it is performed.

A. *Why (or propter quid).* The end of a miracle must always be the glory of God, for a miracle is a work of God, and the order of ends must correspond to the order of agents. A miracle coincides with the glory of God inasmuch as it confirms either a doctrine that is revealed by God or the holiness of some servant of his.

This end can be considered in two different ways: (a) inasmuch as it is first in intention, if[104] it is declared by the wonderworker prior to the production of the miracle; and (b) inasmuch as it is last in execution, for thus is it manifested in the moral effects of the miracle.

(a) From the first perspective, we have this rule: A miracle performed *in the name of God the Creator in confirmation of some revelation to be accepted by all* cannot be false, especially if the wonderworker *first announces it.* This is so because it stands in contradiction with the infinite goodness, wisdom, and truthfulness of God that he would permit his name to be alleged in order to substitute a false miracle for a true one and that he would suffer his name to be brought forth as a witness to a lie through which men would necessarily and invincibly be led into error against what they owe God and what is necessary to their salvation.[105]

(b) The end is also manifested in execution, and true miracles are discerned *by their effects* or fruits, for if they give rise, in a permanent manner, to worship of the Supreme Divinity [*cultus supremi Numinis*], the overturning of the worship of demons, reformation of morals in conformity with right reason, and concord of citizens and in social life, it is impossible that miracles of this kind would be performed by a demon to his own self-destruction. This rule is drawn from Origen (bk. 2, *Contra Celsum*).

By contrast, if certain wonderful things only serve to feed curiosity, if they provoke shameful or scurrilous actions, if they lend support to pride and disobedience and perturb the harmony and peace of society, they cannot come from God. In this way, many illusionary wonders from paganism, Islam, and Buddhism are excluded from being miracles.

B. *What is done.* If an extraordinary fact is in any way contrary either to the truth or to morals, or if it is ridiculous, it is the work of a demon, not of God. In this way, many illusory wonders attributed to the gods by paganism are ruled out [as not being true miracles]. So too, the illusory wonders spoken of in the books of Buddhism. For example, there is [the tale of] how the Buddha, about to do battle with the king of serpents, turned his whole body into fire; {{75}} and another time, he ran through the entire firmament of the heavens from east to west, simultaneously pouring water from one eye and fire from the other. Similarly, Mohammed's disciples relate the tale

---

[104] [Trans. note: Reading *si* for *sit*.]
[105] Such is Billuart's argument in *Summa sancti Thomae, De fide*, diss. 2, a. 2.

of him dividing the moon into two parts, gathering it with his sleeve, and then joining the two parts back into one. Likewise, the illusory wonders of the fakirs today are many, ridiculous, and useless (e.g., sitting on small pins).

C. *The person by whom it is performed.* True miracles are discerned on the basis of the morals and teaching of those who perform them. In other words, if they hand on a doctrine that honors God and is conformed to right reason, leading to good morals and favoring social life, and if the same people also bring together life and morals carefully in accordance with such a teaching, if they excel in zeal for God's glory, modesty, humility, and charity, then these sorts of miracles are true. Thus, without any vicious circle [*petitione principii*], the miracle confirms the teaching and is confirmed by it, for it confirms what is obscure in the given doctrine and in its origin, and is confirmed by the doctrine, inasmuch as the latter stands forth as an excellent means for manifesting and honoring God, as well as for bringing about the reformation of morals.

If, by contrast, the person acting is vicious, proud, wicked, fickle, inconstant, troublesome, impatient, and taking glory in his own defects of character, and if he proposes a teaching that is manifestly irrational, irreligious, and immoral, the illusory wonders that he performs are obviously not divine.

Indeed, as St. Thomas explains,[106] miracles can sometimes be performed by wicked men who preach the true faith and call upon the name of Christ. However, then, it is clear from the circumstances that a miracle can only be performed in confirmation of the divine truth and not in commendation of the life of the man used by God. "Whence," St. Thomas says, "wicked men who express some false teaching never perform true miracles in confirmation of their teaching, although they sometimes may do so in praise of Christ's name which they invoke and by the power of the sacraments which they administer."[107]

D. *How.* If something immoral, violent, cruel, or incongruous is discerned in the manner or acting, it is not a miracle. In this way, many of the illusory wonders of magicians are ruled out. Those who perform true miracles act in a pious, reverent, and utterly humble manner.

E. *By what aids.* True miracles are performed through invocation of the divine name—nay, in the name of God the Creator. If, by contrast, the means brought forth seem blasphemous, disgraceful, and absolutely ridiculous, it is not a miracle.

---

[106] See *ST* II-II, q. 178, a. 2.

[107] *ST* II-II, q. 178, a. 2, ad 3.

When considering this circumstance, one must take into account the persons, times, and places to which the divine action can accommodate itself.

F. *Where.* If it is among vain, unworthy men, so that in many ways it turns out as things do in cases of Spiritism or hypnotism, it is not a miracle.

G. *When.* When there is no necessity or fittingness in the miracle, it is not a true miracle, as takes place in the miracles of the fakirs or those of spiritualists. Thus, Christ did not wish to perform miracles before Herod merely in order to feed his curiosity.

{{76}} If all these circumstances taken together are in favor of the action being a miracle, it is morally certain that the extraordinary fact comes from God, at least mediately—namely, by the mediation of good angels.[108]

This intrinsically moral certitude is reinforced through a consideration of God's infinite goodness, wisdom, and truthfulness, for God cannot in such a case permit falsehood, which would give rise to invincible error in a matter of such great importance.

§5. On the Discernibility of Miracles as Regards the Existence of the Fact

Supposing that the aforementioned miracles are discernible as regards the nature of the fact (e.g., that resurrection, the multiplication of loaves, or the sudden conversion of water into wine exceed all created and creatable powers and can be produced by God alone), we still must discern whether a given case of resurrection is truly such or is instead only apparent (and the same holds for the case of the multiplication of loaves and so forth). Four things must be said concerning this matter.

(1) *In general.* To the extent that they are facts that are obvious to the senses, miracles are as easily observed as any other sensible facts. For example, the voice of the man who once was mute can be surely heard, as well as the command of the wonderworker healing him, just as much as one was able to hear the voice of someone who never was mute. And let it not be said that a miracle is a supernatural fact and therefore exceeds our knowledge. This is not true because such a miracle is only modally supernatural, in relation to how it is produced, not, however, entitatively, as is grace, for a miracle

---

[108] As Benedict XIV notes in *De canonizatione sanctorum*, bk. 4, ch. 2 (on the efficient cause of miracles), no. 8: "Indeed, philosophers, as well as theologians, both Christian and Jewish, hand on the traditions that the angels can act in sublunary bodies only if God so wills it. God makes use of the angels as His ministers." [Trans. note: Obviously, the language of the "sublunary" sphere reflects the defunct cosmology of the ancients.]

is intrinsically something natural, falling under the senses: When a resurrection is wrought, natural life is rendered unto someone in a supernatural manner.

Nay, because miracles are marvelous and disturb the ordinary course of events and excite more attention, *they must be tested more diligently*, and through such testing they are known with greater certitude. Some people are overly prone to recognize supernatural events, but in general we must face those who unbelievingly object, to whom a response must be given.

(2) *The existence of many miracles is physically certain for its witnesses* (e.g., resurrection, the illumination of someone born blind, the multiplication of the loaves, and the sudden conversion of water into wine).

The existence of any case of resurrection can be physically certain for those who witness it, for they can have (a) physical certitude in accord with the senses and with psychological laws concerning the reality of the death of some given man when his body already has a stench or when his heart stops. Granted, in certain cases, death is uncertain because of the lethargy involved, but this does not mean that all such cases are doubtful in nature, for the existence of death is physically certain when organs that are completely necessary for life (like the heart) not only do not exercise their essential functionality but, indeed, do not even have the possibility of exercising such functionality. (b) The witnesses of someone's resurrection can have physical certitude concerning the life restored to a corpse when the dead person rises, speaks about himself, senses, eats, and responds to questions, for then the functions of vegetative, sense, and intellective life appear in him, manifesting in him life inasmuch as it is something that is sensible *per accidens*.[109]

{{77}} *Objection*: According to theologians, a demon can simulate resurrection for some time by impeding the corruption of the body and by locally moving the members and tongue of the corpse so that it seems to speak.

Response: After examining the corpse, along with all the physical circumstances involved, it is manifest in such cases that this is not a true case of life, especially if one considers the eyes of the corpse, for a living gaze is not found therein but, rather, only a likeness of life and, gradually, signs of corruption. See *ST* I, q. 51, a. 2 (Whether angels can assume bodies and, in bodies that they assume, whether they can exercise vital actions). Likewise, see *ST* I, q. 114, a. 4, ad 5 and *De potentia*, q. 6, a. 7.

This false appearance of resurrection, which can indeed sometimes take place, does not destroy physical certitude concerning a true resurrection (e.g., that of Lazarus), for in this latter case, the signs of life and physical circumstances are not the same as in the

---

[109] See *ST* III, q. 55, a. 6; also see Benedict XIV, *De canonizatione sanctorum*, bk. 4, pt. 1, ch. 21 (On resurrection and on utterly certain signs of death).

former. Likewise, the possibility of hallucination does not destroy the physical certitude of sensation, for we can see that in such a case the causes and circumstances of hallucination are not present. See our discussion below in bk. 2, ch. 10, a. 2 (on the resurrection of Christ).

This physical certitude is indeed inferior to metaphysical certitude, but it does exclude all fear of error and can be either spontaneous or reflexive (that is, confirmed through reflection).

Similar certitude can be had concerning the healing of someone born blind, the multiplication of loaves, and the sudden conversion of water into wine, for these things and similar things are obvious to the senses.

Moreover, this certitude is reinforced by a consideration of the moral and religious circumstances of the miraculous deed. For example, see the Gospel account of the resurrection of Lazarus in John 11 and the illumination of the man born blind in John 9, in which we can see how the unbelieving Pharisees had physical certitude concerning the existence of these miracles, for they wished to have Lazarus killed "because many came to believe in Jesus on account of him" (John 12:11). Likewise, they cast out from the synagogue as a madman [*prae rabie*] the man who was blind from birth, who had been miraculously healed and was defending Christ (John 9:34).

(3) *Certain miracles of the third order seem to be only morally certain*, both as regards the existence of the fact, as well as with regard to its supernaturality (e.g., the sudden healing of fever). Indeed, as we have said, it is difficult to prove with either metaphysical or physical certitude that these facts, by their very nature, exceed all sensible powers and all created powers. Likewise, as regards the existence of the fact, a deceitful simulation is not always discerned with physical certitude, but moral certitude can be had through a consideration of moral circumstances.

This intrinsically moral certitude can be metaphysically strengthened through a consideration of God's attributes—namely, by being attentive to the infinite goodness, wisdom, truthfulness, and providence of God beneath all circumstances. Indeed, when all circumstances, whether physical or moral, are in favor of the miracle, if this in fact only was a merely apparent miracle brought about through a demonic deception, then this would imply that God would permit us to be invincibly led into error against something we owe to God himself and that is necessary to our salvation. [And this stands in opposition to his wisdom and providential care.]

{{78}} (4) *From historical human testimony, we can have moral certitude concerning the existence of miracles*. Once a miracle is recognized by witnesses as a sensible fact, it can be known with no less certitude by other men than are other historical facts. And in order to discern a miraculous fact that is narrated from a supposed or fabulous fact, it suffices (a) that it be a sensible fact that can be seen or heard (e.g., the resurrection of a dead person or the multiplication of loaves). Moreover, (b) it merely needs to be performed in the presence of many who can attentively see or hear it, who carefully assess it and are known for their honesty. Thus, in 1 Corinthians 15:5–6 (DR), St. Paul says, concerning Christ after his Resurrection: "He was seen by Cephas, and after that by the eleven. Then he was seen by more than five hundred brethren at once: of whom many remain until this present, and some are fallen asleep." And, finally, its certitude is guaranteed (c) if, in memory of this fact, public monuments are then erected, narratives written, or enduring burdens imposed. Such conditions, taken all together, establish the historical truth of the fact. Hence, if such a testimony is rejected, the whole of historical certitude will come into ruin, and no past or present facts will be able to be certain unless we see them ourselves, but nobody of sound mind holds such a position.

Now, just because a fact is extraordinary does not mean that its historical certitude is thereby diminished, for a historian precisely as a historian must not choose a particular philosophical system that is opposed to common sense (i.e., natural reason)—for example, determinism—for a historian must not explain a fact philosophically but, rather, must refer to it precisely as it was.[110] *Nonetheless, this historical certitude requires all the greater certitude to the degree that the fact in question is more extraordinary.*[111]

---

[110] See Charles-Victor Langlois and Charles Seignobos, *Introduction aux études historiques* [Paris: Hachette, 1899], 117–118: "Historically, the existence of the devil is much more solidly proven than is that of Peisistratos. We do not have a single word from a contemporary of Peisistratos speaking of seeing him. However, thousands of 'eye-witnesses' claim to have seen the devil. There are few historical facts established on the basis of so great a number of independent witnesses. Nonetheless, we no longer hesitate to dismiss the existence of the devil and to admit that of Peisistratos. This is because the existence of the devil would be irreconcilable with the laws of all the constituted sciences."

[111] See Charles De Smedt, *Principes de la critique historique* (Paris, 1883), ch. 2, 35ff. Also see Joseph de Tonquédec, *Introduction à l'étude du merveilleux et du miracle* (Paris: Beauchesne, 1916), bk. 2, chs. 2–4 (General rules and particular rules; cf. conditions relative to persons: §1 The ancients, 325; §2 the Middle Ages, 333; §3 The East, 352 [lit. 325]; §4 Believers, 359–392; §5 Non-professionals, 393; §6 The Masses—mental contagions and collective hallucination, 399.)

See ibid., 406: "Examples prove that a crowd which is dominated by the most intense religious enthusiasm, where expectations reach their paroxysm, utterly fail to see what it awaits. Only Renan would risk writing, with a ready pen, this broad-brush aphorism: 'Expectation *ordinarily* creates its object.' How many times have we not seen at Lourdes, at the procession of the Blessed Sacrament, the most imperious desire for a miracle, along with the most inflamed supplications, all come to nothing. One passionately desired to see and, yet, nothing took place. . . . The fact that attention can lead to hallucination is a particular and accidental case

Moreover, this historical certitude, which is, properly speaking, a form of moral certitude, can be strengthened through philosophical reflection: (1) when there are countless suitable witnesses whose false testimony would lack a *raison d'être*, for how would these many, various witnesses agree in one and the same deception or error without some use for themselves? {{79}} Moreover, (2) in a matter of great importance for salvation, God cannot permit invincible error, which would follow of necessity from this kind of false testimony. And finally, (3) a miracle can, as St. Thomas says in *SCG* I, ch. 6, "appear evidently in its effect"—namely, in the miraculous conversion of the world, which would have been "more miraculous than all other signs," [even] if it took place without [other] miracles.

Therefore, we must conclude that miracles can be known with certitude. Many, such as the resurrection, multiplication of loaves, and so forth, can be known by witnesses with physical certitude regarding the existence of the fact and with metaphysical certitude regarding the nature of the fact. However, other men can have moral certitude (which does exclude all fear of error) concerning them on account of historical testimony.

§6. On False Miracles and on Magic, Spiritism, and Hypnotism

As regards the question of miracles, we have sufficiently determined what *cannot* be brought about by the hidden powers of nature and of created spirits. Indeed, what they cannot produce are effects that are proper to God. Now, however, to the degree that it is possible, we must say what they can bring about. Regarding this matter, three things must be considered: (I) what is signified by the terms magic, Spiritism, and hypnotism, as well as what their correlative phenomena are; (II) an explanatory theory for these phenomena; and (III) the power of spirits to perform illusory wonders.

I. *The notions and phenomena of magic, Spiritism, and hypnotism*

(1) In general, *magic* is the power to bring about marvelous, unheard-of things. Two kinds of magic must be distinguished: *natural magic*, by which marvels are performed by making use of the hidden powers of nature or works of dexterity; *diabolical* (or *black*) magic, by which wonders are produced by the work of demons.

Although some wonders of this kind are mythical in character, nonetheless, a good number of them deserved to be believed in on account of

---

whose formula must not be universalized. More often than not, a crowd does not suffer from a hallucination." Moreover, a crowd can be divided, and thus, the affirmations of enthusiastic believers can run into strong oppositions.

the probity, piety, and teaching of their witnesses. This is also mentioned in Sacred Scripture. Thus, in Exodus 7:11 (DR): "And Pharaoh called the wise men and the magicians; and they also by Egyptian enchantments and certain secrets did in like manner." Likewise, in the New Testament there were the cases of the magical deeds performed by Simon the Magician, Elymas, and the Pythian girl (Acts 8:9–11; 13:8; 16:16). Likewise, Christ and Paul foretold that great signs and wonders would be performed at the time of the Antichrist: "insomuch as to deceive, if possible, even the elect" (Matt. 24:24, DR; cf. 2 Thess 2:9).

(2) *In our own era*, under the names of *magnetism*, *Spiritism*, and *hypnotism*, many phenomena are openly presented to the public. Indeed, many fraudulent cases crop up among these so that it is often difficult to distinguish true cases from false ones. Nonetheless, the phenomena that we will cite here are thought to be free from such fraudulence.

The term "magnetism" is used for signifying the art of obtaining marvelous phenomena, especially in man, by either physical or psychological means, and because Franz Mesmer ([1734][112]–1815) used magnetism in producing these phenomena, the term "magnetism" came to be attached to it.

Now, magnetism is divided, in accord with the variety of means used, into vulgar, hypnotic, and transcendental magnetism (which is called Spiritism nowadays, though it was called magic in earlier times). {{80}} *Vulgar magnetism* makes use of sensible means such as gestures, the fixing of the eyes, the touching of bodily members, and other such things. *Hypnotism* is vulgar magnetism itself, though with this distinction—namely, that in order to hypnotize (or to obtain magnetic sleep), it makes use of more or less scientific means, generally all those that tire out the senses and weaken the attention of the subject to be hypnotized (e.g., examination of the eyes, fixed gazing into a clear mirror, the influence of oxhydric light, and various excitations in the senses of sound and touch). However, certain parts in the body have a power by which hypnotism may be induced by means of pressure and, hence, are called hypnogenic zones. However, the principal means used here is verbal suggestion (which the other means supply for as needed). Hypnotists express in an imperative, verbal way the command to sleep, and immediately the subject falls asleep, thus coming to be extrinsically impelled and directed by the hypnotist. Finally, *Spiritism* calls forth interaction between mortals and spirits or the souls of the dead, which are evoked by means of given signs.

The phenomena of magnetism, hypnotism, and Spiritism can be reduced to three genera.

---

[112] [Trans. note: Original has "1783".]

(a) *First, there are the mechanical phenomena*, under which are contained the turning of tables and of other bodies, the motion of the human body or of some member thereof, and the attraction, elevation, movement, and suspension of certain bodies.

(b) *Second, there are physiological and sensitive phenomena*, such as convulsions, the trembling of bodily members, dilation and contraction of pupils and of nerves, magnetic sleep, major or minor insensibility, clearheaded sleepwalking, and the transposition (or translation) of senses as when one sees out of the back of one's head.

The school of Salpétrière admits three states in these hypnotic phenomena: lethargy, catalepsy or rigidity, and finally sleepwalking. In a hypnotic sleep, the hypnotized person communes exclusively with the hypnotist. In clearheaded sleepwalking, the hypnotized person seems to be equipped with wondrous abilities (e.g., the ability to see with one's eyes closed). They bring about hallucinations that are aural, visual, and even gustatory and olfactory in nature; the sweating of blood is produced. The hypnotist suggests a symphony, and immediately the patient hears music and is gladdened. Likewise, there can be suggestions that are to be completed after a lengthy passage of time. Thus, a hypnotist may suggest, "After a year, on a given day, you will do this, you will see this, you will hear this," and each of these are confirmed. Suggestion may also give rise to an apparent multiplication of personality, as when a woman believes that she is a soldier. These phenomena of suggestion seem to pertain, properly speaking, to the imagination; however, by means of it, they influence the intellect and the will.[113]

(c) *Finally, there are intellectual phenomena*, such as the knowledge of the internal affections of the soul, the predicting of future contingents (even free ones), as well as the ability to know the depths of the human body's organic composition, to scorn means for curing sicknesses, to discourse at length concerning scientific matters, to speak various unknown languages, and to work other such marvels.

These phenomena sometimes take place without the evocation of spirits, though {{81}} sometimes they are obtained after such evocations and thus, properly speaking, pertain to Spiritism. However, spirits of these kind do not immediately communicate with all people but, rather, do so through the mediation of some living person who, hence, is called a *medium*—that is, the passive medium utilized like a mere instrument by the

---

[113] If the hypnotist commanded someone to commit theft, the hypnotized person does indeed at first resist, but most are conquered by the more powerful will and commit theft. Concerning these things, see Coconnier, O.P., *L'hypnotisme française* (Paris: Lecoffre, 1897); Méric, *Le merveilleux et la science* (Paris: Letouzey et Ané, 1888). Concerning the power of suggestion in general, see Hippolyte Bernheim, *Hypnotisme, suggestion, psychothérapie*, 2nd ed. (Paris: Doin, 1903); Dr. Joseph Grasset, *L'hypnotisme et la suggestion* (Paris: Doin, 1904); Dr. Pierre Janet, *L'automatisme psychologique*, 10th ed. (Paris: Alcan, 1930); *De l'angoisse à l'extase* (Paris: Alcan, 1926); *La médecine psychologique* (Paris: Flammarion, 1928); Fr. Robert De Sinéty, S.J., *Psychopathologie et direction* (Paris: Beauchesne, 1934). Also see Fr. Angelo Zacchi, O.P., *Lo spiritismo* (Rome: Ferrari, 1922).

spirit. In Spiritism, there are apparitions, songs, writings, and scientific discussions that the spirits seem to send to us mortals from the other side. They give responses about things that have been suffered, about medical treatments to be performed, and so forth.[114]

Many facts of Spiritism are mere myths and frauds, though they cannot all be denied inasmuch as they are testified to by men of greatly proven character. Sometimes the presence of an evil spirit and of horror at sacred things is revealed in these matters, as can be seen in the violent shaking of a given table when a blessed rosary is placed upon it; likewise, these cases sometimes involve responses that are impious, heretical, and obscene for the mind, natural capacities, and dispositions of bystanders.

II. *Explanatory theories for the phenomena of hypnotism and Spiritism*

There are five explanatory theories for these phenomena.

(1) THE MATERIALISTIC THEORY strives to explain these phenomena by the aid of a given *fluid*, which they say is magnetic, and they maintain that it is so subject to the will—to say nothing about the fact that it is of service to the movement of one's limbs—that it can be sent forth outside of one and enter into other bodies. In this way, the magnetizing person would subject the magnetized person to himself. According to many, this magnetic fluid is the nervous fluid that would be a kind of animal heat; however, others hold that it is an ethereal and luminous fluid, while still others say that it is a universal substance, endowed with light, heat, and intelligence, and they call it God.

Critique. This last explanation is already rejected on the basis of our earlier refutation of pantheism. However, the preceding explanations are insufficient because a material fluid cannot produce all of the aforementioned phenomena, for spiritual phenomena, such as knowledge of things and of languages, exceed the power of matter.

(2) THE IMAGINATION THEORY has recourse to our imagination,

---

[114] Certain phenomena similar to those found in Spiritism are even claimed to exist, at least in principle, in *Modern Theosophy*. This society was founded by Helena Petrovna Blavatsky, a spiritualist, along with Henry S. Olcott in 1875. The doctrine, which Blavatsky would have borrowed from Mahātmā and the wise among the Tibetans, with whom she falsely claimed to have lived for a number of years, is above all copied from eastern religions, in particular Buddhism. This teaching was propagated energetically by Annie Besant and came to be altered, thus giving birth to a variety of schemata. With her support, the "Order of the Star in the East" was founded, which expected a new incarnation in Christ, and acknowledged Jiddu Krishnamurti as the New Messiah. In 1913, Rudolf Steiner separated himself from this form of Theosophy and founded the society of *Anthroposophy*. The teaching that he himself thought came forth from his own intuition agrees on many points with the teachings of Theosophy.

which is vigorously excited by the aid of the apparatus of magnetism. Hence, hysterical women in particular are more apt to undergo the action of hypnotism.[115]

Critique. This theory seems to provide a sufficient explanation for many hypnotic phenomena, though not for all spiritualistic phenomena. Indeed, St. Thomas already himself noted in *SCG* III, ch. 99: "Because the soul imagines something and is vehemently affected in relation to it, a change sometimes follows in the body, leading to healing or sickness, without the action of bodily principles, which by their own nature are ordered to causing sickness or health in the body." {{82}} Indeed, when the imagination acts with an intensity beyond measure, the strength of the other powers is thereby diminished. Hence, the power of the soul passes over through the imagination. Thus, hallucination becomes possible inasmuch as the images that once upon a time had come into the imagination [*ad phantasiam*] from the senses can again, in a reverse order, with the aid of the intermediary nerves, go back out to the senses. Thus, by making use of bodily dispositions, the hypnotist will be able to produce new images in the imagination [*in phantasia*] by means of which he will then be able to excite passions, actions, hallucinations, and locutions in the subject. The hypnotist even can stir up or bind the imagination [*phantasiam*] so that this faculty[116] would no longer be able to pay attention to its own *species*. In this way, the subject becomes incapable of perceiving those things that are present to him.[117] According to a number of authors, this perhaps does not imply that the influence of the hypnotist remains virtually in the imagination [*phantasia*] so that after a certain time it springs forth in act and overpowers [the subject's] memory.[118]

Nonetheless, the imagination theory cannot explain the ability to foretell future contingents, to know the depths of the human body's organic composition, to discuss at length concerning scientific things, and to speak various unknown languages.

---

[115] [Trans. note: Obviously, the present translator does not endorse the implications of the phrase "hysterical women."]

[116] [Trans. note: Technically, *phantasia* would involve the imagination properly so-called, the memory, and the cogitative power. However, the use of the singular here by Fr. Garrigou-Lagrange has necessitated the use of the term "imagination" in a loose sense.]

[117] However, the authority that the hypnotist exercises on the hypnotized person is explained as much through the consent given by the hypnotized person at the beginning of the process, by which he as it were hands over his own will, as through the influence that the hypnotist directly obtains within the subject's senses and nerves and indirectly obtains within his will. (See Coconnier, *L'hypnotisme française*, 374ff.)

[118] See Benedict XIV, *De canonizatione sanctorum*, bk. 4, final chapter (on the imagination and its powers).

(3) THE ANIMIST THEORY strives to explain these facts through powers innate within the human soul, which indeed are hidden from us and impervious to our powers of observation. This theory attributes to our soul certain vibrations, which it then can communicate to objects, by means of which similar vibrations are sent back into the soul itself. Thus, this is said to explain the occurrence of speaking tables [*locutiones tabularum*], words of gossip [*rumores*], songs, and[119] other such phenomena.

Critique. Like the theories already discussed, this one can explain certain facts of magnetism without falling into contradiction, though not all of them. Indeed, it is possible that there are vibrations that come forth from the human composite, by mediation of the air or the ether, thus influencing bodies at a distance. In this way, explanations have been provided for certain [mutual] attractions, the elevation of bodies, and a kind of telepathy,[120] but not for the ability to suddenly speak unknown languages or to hold lengthy discussions concerning the most difficult questions of philosophy or theology, as sometimes happens.

(4) THE SPIRITIST THEORY. Spiritists admit metempsychosis—that is, the passing of human souls from one body to another upon death. However, as they say, some souls remain in the air surrounding us, joined with a very delicate and fine form of body. Thus, spiritualists attribute the more noble phenomena of Spiritism to these souls.

Critique. The theory of metempsychosis is unfounded, being nether proven nor even persuasively argued on behalf of either *a posteriori* or *a priori*. Nay, it stands in opposition to the facts, for it seems impossible that our soul would have no memory at all[121] concerning its prior state, retaining absolutely no awareness thereof. {{83}} Moreover, as St. Thomas says in *SCG* II, ch. 73, no. 3: "The proportion between man's soul and man's body is the same as that between this man's soul and this man's body. Therefore, it is impossible that the soul of this man would be able to enter into any other body than his own." In other words, human souls are individuated through their ordering to this or that given body; however, the life that the soul is

---

119 [Trans. note: Reading *aliaque* for *aliaquae*.]

120 *Telepathy* properly so-called signifies: to sense at a distance, outside of the normal action of the senses or the intellect, what someone else is thinking or the things that are happening to such a person. It is either experiential or spontaneous and then is commonly emotional and thus is joined with friendship, consanguinity, etc. between persons. Ultimately *clairvoyance*, *psychometry* (knowledge by mediation of an object associated with them), and *crystalloscopy* (knowledge by means of a transparent body) are all reduced to *telepathy*.

121 [Trans. note: Reading *omnino* for *amnino*.]

naturally inclined to preserve is the life of the individual himself.[122]

Nor can one admit that the human soul has two bodies, one that has a material weight [*ponderabile*], from which it can be separated, and another that is delicate and fine, to which it is always united, by means of which it would be united to the aforementioned material body. This is not possible, for the soul is the immediate substantial form of the material body, which is truly animated; indeed, there is only one single radical principle of intellective life along with sensitive and vegetative life. As St. Thomas says in *ST* I, q. 76, a. 1 and 7: "One and the same man perceives that *he* senses and understands that *he* understands." Otherwise, man would not be something essentially (*per se*) united but, rather, would only be *per accidens* unified.

Moreover, this theory offered by spiritualists makes recourse to the souls of the dead only in an arbitrary manner—namely, as it were, only inasmuch as these souls are at hand to serve the desires of mortals. Hence, it is surprising that those souls would be used only by determinate persons who are called *mediums*. Moreover, these persons and spiritualists act in secret and, what is more, they refuse to acknowledge not only Catholic dogmas but also the natural truths of religion concerning God and the next life, as is clear in the books of the theosophists.

Finally, the separated soul cannot, by means of its natural cognition, know those things that are done here below, nor can it naturally move a given body since the only way that it can do this is by means of its own body.[123]

(5) The theory of Spiritualism explains the superior phenomena of spiritism through the intervention of spirits, which we call demons. The truth of this theory is established through the exclusion of the preceding [so-called] phenomena. Indeed, the superior phenomena of Spiritism must have a cause. Now, this cause can be neither a material fluid, nor the imagination, nor some power of the soul or something emitted from the soul, nor the souls of the dead. Therefore, we must have recourse to a superior cause, and this cause can be neither God nor a good spirit, for in the use of magnetism, hypnotism, or Spiritism, inasmuch as they are brought forth in order to detect *hidden things* [*occultorum*], there are so many things that are trifling, disgraceful, morally wrong, and irreligious that would be wholly unbefitting to God and his good angels. Therefore, it must be the case that the cause in question is an evil spirit, that which we call a demon. The response given in these kinds of wonders is that, even if it is most often

---

[122] Also, against the idea of metempsychosis, see Augustine, *De Genesi ad litteram*, bk. 7, ch. 10; *De civitate Dei*, bk. 10, ch. 30.

[123] See *ST* I, q. 89, a. 8; q. 117, a. 4.

the case that they vehemently kindle wicked passions,[124] likewise fostering vices and errors, sometimes they can be true and not counterfeit, because as St. John Chrysostom says, "The devil is sometimes permitted to speak true things so that his infrequent truthfulness may gain trust for his lie."[125] Thus, they can gain trust from the powers of reason, though they are contrary to faith, philanthropy, charity, and rational temperance so that Christian mortification would seem exaggerated, etc.

Hence, these wonders often enough clearly reveal the presence of an evil spirit, as well as dread at the presence of sacred things. {{84}} Nay, sometimes a demon enters the body of a man. Dwelling therein, it will act, making use of the senses and the person's bodily members, producing unusual actions. Often, the *Gospel* mentions people who undergo demonic obsession, referring to them as distinct people from those who are merely ill: "They presented to him all sick people that were taken with divers diseases and torments, and such as were possessed by devils."[126] And, according to the *Roman Ritual*, the signs of diabolic possession are "the speaking of unknown languages in many words or understanding the speaking thereof, the disclosure of things that are far away and hidden, the exhibition of powers above the natural capacities of one's age or condition, and other things of this kind which are significant signs when a great number of them occur." However, the *Ritual* adds, "(the exorcist) should not give easy credence to the claim that someone is undergoing demonic obsession; however, let him take note of the signs by which the obsessed person is distinguished from those who suffer from melancholy (literally, 'black bile') or some sickness."

Demons do not reveal themselves clearly to materialists. It suffices for them that creatures made in the image of God believe they draw their origin from ridiculous, weak, and lustful monkeys. If the demons were to manifest themselves to materialists, the latter would have a proof for the existence of spirits and a way toward faith in the existence of God. However, the demons do reveal themselves more clearly to the hidden depths of the Masonic sect.

III. *The power of spirits to perform illusory wonders*

(1) *The existence of spirits* (i.e., of angels) was denied in the past by the

---

[124] [Trans. note: Reading *passiones* for *passionis*.]

[125] [Trans. note: Fr. Garrigou-Lagrange cites work on Matthew's Gospel that, at St. Thomas's time, was attributed to St. John Chrysostom. Here he refers to the citation found in *ST* II-II, q. 172, a. 6. This text is, in fact, misattributed to St. John Chrysostom. It is instead an anonymous work known as *Opus imperfectum in Matthaeum*. For more information concerning this text, see *Incomplete Commentary on Matthew (Opus imperfectum)*, ed. Thomas C. Oden, trans. James A. Kellerman (Downers Grove, IL: InterVarsity Press, 2010).]

[126] Matt 4:24 (DR) and 8:16; Mark 1:34 and 9:24; Luke 8:30.

Epicureans and the Sadducees. Today, it is denied by atheists, rationalists, and indeed by liberal Protestants, who assert that the angels spoken of in Scripture are either good inspirations sent by God or men sent by God in order to instruct others.

By contrast, according to the Catholic Church, it is to be held on divine faith that the angels (that is, intellectual creatures that are distinct from God and more excellent than men) exist. Moreover, it is certain that the angels are purely spiritual.[127] The existence of the angels is frequently and openly asserted in Sacred Scripture.

Nay, reason itself persuasively argues on behalf of the existence of spirits, an existence that was admitted by many pagan philosophers such as Aristotle (who called them "separated substances"). Indeed, as St. Thomas says in *ST* I, q. 50, a. 1:

> What is principally intended by God in creatures is good, and this consists in assimilation to God Himself. Now, the perfect assimilation of an effect to a cause is brought about when the effect imitates the cause according to that by which the cause produces that effect, as heat produces heat. However, God produces creatures by His intellect and will. Hence, the perfection of the universe requires the existence of intellectual creatures. Now, intelligence cannot be the action of a body, nor of any bodily power, for every body is limited to the here-and-now. Whence, the perfection of the universe requires the existence of some incorporeal creature . . . which is knowable by the intellect alone.

Without the angels, the ascending series of creatures would seem to be cut off abruptly and, as it were, undeserving of the wisdom and omnipotence of the Creator, for human reason is a very weak participation in the intellectual light, given that it attains very few truths through simple intuition,[128] coming to know many only through the truly laborious work of reasoning. Therefore, in order for God's work to be fully wrought, it is suitable that there be purely spiritual creatures that would perceive the truth universally through simple contemplation, {{85}} creatures who

---

[127] See Lateran IV (Denzinger, no. 800) and [First] Vatican Council, *Dei filius*, ch. 1 (Denzinger, no. 3002).

[128] [Trans. note: On this language, see a text cited by Fr. Garrigou-Lagrange elsewhere, R. M. Jolivet, "L'intuition intellectuelle," *Revue Thomiste* 15 (Jan. 1932): 52–71.]

would be ministers of the Supreme Governor of things.[129]

(2) *The goodness and wickedness of spirits.* According to the Catholic Church, it is to be held on divine faith that certain angels, through their own fault, sinned and consigned themselves to eternal punishment. As was said at Lateran IV: "For the devil and the other demons were indeed created by God naturally good, but they became evil by their own doing."[130] However, others were confirmed in the good.

This knowledge had through faith perfects the apologetic thesis concerning the discernibility of miracles. Hence, it is useful for the apologete who, from on high, under the direction of faith, defends the probative force of miracles, inasmuch as miracles differ from deceptive diabolic wonders. Indeed, such was the way that they were defended by the prophets and apostles who were the first apologetes. Nonetheless, for those who hear apologetic preaching, it is not necessary to have foreknowledge concerning the obstinacy of the demons in evil. It suffices that by reason alone they see that extraordinary works that are not wholly good cannot be performed by God. Indeed, in reality, certain deceptive wonders of magic and Spiritism clearly manifest the intervention of a wicked spirit inciting one to vice and sacrilege.

(3) *What spirits can do in order to simulate miracles.* We do not know how far their power positively extends, but since they are creatures, they cannot do anything contrary to God's absolute will.

St. Thomas shows,[131] at least in general, how wicked spirits can simulate miracles in two ways: (A) by using powers of nature that are unknown to us; and (B) by altering man's imaginative powers [*phantasiam*], as well as his external senses, so that something would thus seem to be different from what it is.

A. *Indeed, spirits can move bodies through local motion,* just as man moves them,[132] "and, through local motion, they can cause other motions, namely by employing bodily agents in order to produce such effects, as a craftsman employs fire in order to soften iron."[133] And not only can they make use of powers of nature that are unknown to us, but they can even instrumentally move bodies to accidental effects that exceed the instrument's own proper form in order to, for example, imitate a human voice:

> In the production of effects of this kind, in comparison with man's own art, the angel's art is more efficacious and leads to better results . . . for they have great

---

[129] See *ST* I, q. 110 and 111.

[130] Lateran IV (Denzinger, no. 800). Also see 2 Pet 2:4.

[131] See *ST* I, q. 114, a. 4, ad 2; and q. 110, a. 4, ad 2.

[132] See *ST* I, q. 110, a. 3.

[133] Ibid., ad 2.

knowledge of the powers of natural things. . . . Hence, they can better choose the hour at which the power of a heavenly body is more likely to cooperate in producing the desired result. This seems to be the reason why necromancers observe the position of the stars when they invoke demons.[134]

Thus, spirits can simulate miracles, for example, by forming bodies from preexisting matter, assuming them, and visibly appearing in them.

B. *Likewise, they can alter man's imagination* [*imaginationem*], as St. Thomas explains in *ST* I, q. 111, a. 3:

> It is manifest that imaginative apparitions are sometimes caused in us by the local movement of our bodily spirits and humors, especially in sleep. . . . Indeed, the excitement of our spirits and humors may be so great that such appearances may even occur in those who are awake, as happens in those who are insane, and other such people. Thus, as this happens by a natural disturbance of the humors and sometimes also by man willing it by voluntarily imagining something that he experienced in the past, so too the same may be done by the power of a good or an evil angel, sometimes with stupor of one's bodily senses, and at other times without such stupor.

{{86}} And in ibid., ad 2:

> An angel alters the imagination, not indeed by impressing an imaginative form which was never previously received from the senses—for he cannot make a man born blind imagine color—but, rather, through the local motion of our bodily spirits and humors, as was said above.

Angels can also *alter the human senses* in two ways. They can do so externally, by externally setting something sensible before the sense power, whether it be something formed by nature or by forming something new, as he does when he assumes a body. Similarly, they can also move the spirits and humors internally, as was said earlier, whereby the senses would be altered in various ways, like how everything tastes bitter to a sick person because of the abundance of choleric humor in his system.[135]

By their own capacities and experience of the ages, the angels know physical secrets, as well as man's own innate characteristics, inclinations, and passions, and thus they can have better conjectural knowledge concerning future free actions than we do.[136] More-

---

[134] *De potentia*, q. 6, a. 3.
[135] See *ST* I, q. 111, a. 4.
[136] See *De malo*, q. 16, a. 7.

over, through certain bodily signs, angels can to some degree know man's thoughts.[137]

However, as was said earlier, *God alone can alter man's will from within*, for only God gives the intellectual nature its inclination to the universal good (for, indeed, the order of agents corresponds to the order of ends).

Likewise, God alone can physically influence our intellect. An angel does not illuminate man by giving him the light of nature or that of grace, but only by objectively strengthening its natural light and by manifesting the truth to it. As John of St. Thomas explains in his remarks on *ST* I, q. 106, a. 1, this strengthening is brought about not through a physical and subjective influence upon our intellect but, rather, through the objective medium by which the proposed truths are manifested in a loftier and more universal manner, as the teacher does for his students.

This provides a sufficient discussion concerning what spirits can do. With God's permission, wicked spirits can simulate miracles, but the good God does not permit men to be invincibly deceived in things that are necessary for salvation.[138] However, acting as God's instruments, good spirits can perform true miracles or, by their own powers, care for men, as the Church believes, namely, by preventing external damage from happening to us, aiding us in our difficulties, warding off demons, suggesting holy thoughts, and {{87}} sometimes inflicting punishments meant to heal us, as is explained in the treatise on the angels.[139]

§7. Resolution of Objections

There are two series of objections: (1) as regards the miraculous nature of the work, as well as regarding its supernaturality; and (2) as regards

---

[137] See *De malo*, q. 16, a. 8. Likewise, see the next chapter concerning prophecy.

[138] However, if it is asked why God permits demons to seduce, as well as cases of diabolic possession, St. Thomas responds in *ST* I, q. 114, a. 1: "This very assault by the demons comes from the demons' own wickedness. However, the ordering of such assaults is from God, who knows how to make orderly use of evil by ordering it . . . to the glory of His elect." Indeed, through assaults of this kind, the justice of God who punishes is manifested, as well as the need to have aid from God our help, along with a chance to exercise and strengthen our virtues. Indeed, already reason alone perceives the truth of this declaration by Sacred Scripture: "And God is faithful, who will not suffer you to be tempted above that which you are able: but will make also with temptation issue, that you may be able to bear it" (1 Cor 10:13, DR). Hence, in speaking of demonic possession in *In II Sent.*, d. 8, pt. 2, a. 1, q. 1, St. Bonaventure says: "However, the Lord permits this either to show His glory (for it is manifested in the casting out of demons), in punishment for sin (for avenging punishments are inflicted by evil angels), as a rebuke for a sinner, or for our education" (for the mystery of evil is thus revealed so that the mystery of grace might thereby appear with greater clarity).

[139] See *ST* I, q. 113.

the existence of the work.

A. *As regards the nature of the work.* It seems absolutely certain that, even if it happens to be extraordinary to the greatest degree, nothing that is done can exceed all created powers.

1. *Objection*: In order to affirm that some work by its very nature exceeds all of the powers of nature, we would need to know all of these powers. Now, we do not know all the powers of nature. Therefore[, we cannot affirm that some work by its very nature exceeds all the powers of nature].

Response: I make a distinction regarding the major premise. I deny it if it means that we would need to know all the powers of nature as regards *that which is positively possible*. However, I concede it if it means that we would need to know *that which they cannot do*. I contradistinguish the minor premise in the same way.

2. *Continued urging*: We do not absolutely know what the powers of nature cannot do.

In order to know absolutely (or metaphysically) what nature cannot do, we would need to determine that *a priori*. Now, we cannot determine *a priori* what pertains to nature. Therefore, this cannot be metaphysically certain.

Response: I concede the major premise but make a distinction regarding the minor premise. I concede that we cannot determine *a priori* what pertains in a particular manner to this or that given sensible nature. However, I deny that we cannot determine what pertains in general to *created nature inasmuch as it is distinct from God*. I distinguish the conclusion in the same way.

Allow me to explain. Indeed, it is clear *a priori* that a finite cause cannot produce the effects that properly can be performed only by the First Uncreated Cause, who alone can produce (and, hence, immediately alter) being inasmuch as it is being, matter, or spirit.

3. *Continued urging*: However, the proper effects of God cannot be determined. For example, it is not evident that the production of life from a nonliving being would be an effect proper to God.

Indeed, in Exodus 7, we read that the Pharaoh's magicians changed a staff into a snake through the power of demons. Now, this change presupposes the production of a living being from a nonliving being, just as happens in a case of resurrection. Therefore, the demons can also raise the dead.

Response: Many hold that these kinds of wonders were only hoaxes at the level of the senses. However, according to the literal meaning of the account, it seems more probable that his magicians produced true frogs and true serpents, carried in from elsewhere by the hidden power of demons. Moreover, these marvels performed by the magicians in Egypt must not be set in opposition to the true miracles performed by Moses, since the same biblical account makes clear that Moses conquered the magicians so that his serpent devoured theirs. Moreover, coming to the fourth wonder, the magicians' art stood inert, leading them to say to Pharaoh, "This is the finger of God" (Exod. 8:19). Hence, these wonders performed by the magicians could be distinguished from true miracles, at least on the basis of their physical and moral circumstances.[140]

4. *Continued insistence*: However, St. Thomas proposes[141] another interpretation for this fact, saying: "The demons did this through some collected seeds, which had the power to cause the sticks to rot and change into serpents." And St. Thomas said this because he held that inferior animals are generated from the rotting of plants, without any animal seed.[142] Therefore, the difficulty can be proposed, as follows: According to St. Thomas, it is not contradictory to say that a created cause can produce the sense life of inferior animals, using nonliving beings as the basis for this causation. Now, a greater power is not required *per se* in order to produce life from a corpse, for the effect specifying the action is always the sense life to be produced. Therefore, it is not contradictory to say that a created cause can produce the resurrection of a dead person.

{{88}} *First response*: St. Thomas admits this only for inferior animals because, in his day, physical scientists did not know about the unperceivable seeds from which inferior animals are generated. Now, however, it has been experimentally shown that every living being comes from a living being.

Second response: The hypothesis admitted by St. Thomas is not intrinsically contradictory. Indeed, it is not a question of spontaneous generation in the materialists' sense, for more would be produced from the less and the more perfect from the imperfect. Rather, when St. Thomas says that a created cause can produce inferior animals from nonliving animals, he presupposes the ordinary concurrence of the First Living Being.[143] And in this way, the rejection finds its resolution, for resurrection of a dead person likewise requires the concurrence of the First Living Being. However, in this case, such concurrence is

---

[140] See Billuart, *Summa sancti Thomae, De fide*, diss. 2, a. 2, §2.

[141] See *De potentia*, q. 6, a. 5, ad 8; *ST* I, q. 114, a. 4, ad 2.

[142] *ST* I, q. 91, a. 2, ad 2.

[143] See *ST* I, q. 70, a. 3, ad 3: "Since the heavenly bodies are moved movers, they have the character of being an instrument acting in virtue of a principal agent. Therefore, from their own power as movers, namely, as living substances, they can cause life." Likewise, see *De potentia*, q. 3, a. 11, ad 13: "Even if the heavenly bodies are not living, nonetheless, they act in virtue of the living substance by which they are moved, whether by angels or by God. Nonetheless, according to the philosopher, there are animated and living heavenly bodies." Likewise, see ad 14.

However, in the hypothesis admitted by St. Thomas, the fact that the ordinary concurrence of the first living being is required is clear from the fact that life is a simply-simple perfection and that God is the first living being. "However, that which is first and highest in any given genus is the cause of everything in that genus," as he says in *ST* I, q. 2, a. 3 (fourth way). Hence, just as being cannot be produced without the concurrence of the first being, nor action without the concurrence of the first agent, nor intellection without the motion of the first intelligence (*ST* I, q. 79, a. 4), nor free action without the concurrence of the first free action, so too neither can life be produced without the first living being. However, this concurrence is either ordinary (as in natural generation) or extraordinary (as in cases of resurrection). And in the second case, the life produced (i.e., returned) was not in the proximate potency of matter but, rather, only in its remote potency, over which God alone has immediate power.

extraordinary (i.e., miraculous). Only the Author of life can restore a corpse to life.

5. *Continued insistence*: Nonetheless, a superior power can do whatever an inferior power can do. Now, man can, even ordinarily, cause life—namely, through generation. Therefore, a created spirit can produce life, at least from a corpse in an extraordinary manner.

Response: I make a distinction regarding the major premise. I concede it if they are of the same order. I sub-distinguish it if they are of different orders. Here, I concede it if the superior cause were the cause of the whole being of the inferior cause. Otherwise, I deny it. I concede the minor premise, while distinguishing the conclusion along the same lines as the major premise.[144]

Allow me to explain. Even if our intellectual light is more perfect than physical light, it cannot physically illuminate but, rather, can only illuminate intellectually (in short, in a loftier manner). However, God, who is the creative cause of physical light can, without this light, produce its effect. Similarly, the angels cannot do what man does inasmuch as the latter is material, just as our intellect cannot sense, even though it is superior to the senses. By contrast, the divine power, which is the cause of the whole being of inferior causes, can produce, without them, their effects in a more perfect mode. See *ST* I, q. 110, a. 2, where St. Thomas proves that "every informing of matter is either immediately from God or from some bodily agent, though not immediately from an angel." Likewise, see the response to the first objection to that article.

6. *Continued insistence*: However, perhaps many things that are called miracles do not exceed the powers of the imagination when intensified beyond measure [*supra modum intensae*], for through the human soul's apprehension, the human body is altered, as is clear in those who become angry or fearful, and sometimes, also, this alteration goes so far as to cause sickness or health.

Response: In *ST* III, q. 13, a. 3, ad 3, St. Thomas says:

> If someone's imagination is strong, his body will naturally obey it in some things, for example, as when someone falls from a beam set high up, since the imagination of its nature is a principle of local motion. The same holds true as regards change regarding heat and cold, along with their consequences, for by their very nature, the passions of the soul, by which the heart is moved, follow the imagination. {{89}} Thus, by the excitement of the spirits (or humors), the whole body is altered. However, the other bodily dispositions, for example, the shape of the hand, or foot, and so forth, all of which have no natural relation to the imagination, are not altered by the imagination, no matter how strongly it acts.

---

[144] See *De potentia*, q. 6, a. 3; *De malo*, q. 16, a. 9 and 10.

Likewise, according to doctors, a death that is caused by some organic injury cannot be healed by the mediation of the imagination, even if excited beyond measure through hypnotism.[145]

7. *Continued insistence*: Nonetheless, facts that are called miraculous do not seem to exceed the powers of religious faith itself, for just as human freedom exceeds material powers and has sovereignty over them, so too, *a fortiori*, does a vehement religious sentiment that elevates freedom to the point of heroism. This is how modernists strive to explain many miracles.[146] Indeed, they cite Mark 6:5–6 (DR): "And he could not do any miracles there (in his homeland), only that he cured a few that were sick, laying his hands upon them. And he wondered because of their unbelief." Likewise, in Matthew 17:18, the disciples asked the Lord, "Why were we unable to cast out demons?" His response was: "On account of your lack of faith." Hence, as the modernists say, miracles are effects of faith. In this way, we have a phenomenon that is prior to the miracle, as is needed on account of the principle of causality: Every phenomenon presupposes a prior phenomenon. Nay, there is a law of miracles; namely, great faith extraordinarily exceeds the powers of matter.

Response: A response can be drawn from what St. Thomas says in *De potentia*, q. 6, a. 9 (Whether the working of miracles should be attributed to faith): "Holy men perform miracles in two ways, namely, by way of impetration by prayer that miracles may be divinely brought about and by power (as instruments of God). Now, in both ways faith renders a man capable of performing miracles." However, as is said in ad 19: "Faith is not the sufficient cause for the performing of miracles but, rather, only a kind of disposition thereunto." Hence, not all those who have faith perform miracles.

B. *Objections against the certitude concerning the existence of miracles* (for witnesses—for others)

1. *Objection*: There cannot be either physical or moral certitude concerning a fact that is contrary to the necessary laws of nature. Now, a miraculous fact is something of

---

[145] See Benedict XIV, *De canonizatione sanctorum*, bk. 4, final chapter (Concerning the power of imagination for producing extraordinary phenomena). This must be noted with respect to the society of "Christian Science," which was founded in ca. 1878 by Mary Baker Eddy. According to this Science [*sic*], man, who is truly a spirit, can have surge up within himself a capacity for healing all ills, whether physical or moral, just like the power Christ had so strongly once upon a time. Objectively speaking, neither Satan nor matter nor evil exist but, rather, only illusions of evil that must be healed through prayer and the spirit.

As regards the supernaturality of stigmata, see *Études Carmélitaines* (Oct. 1936); L. Sempé, S.J., "A propos d'un congrés sur la stigmatisation," *Messager du Sacré-Coeur* (May 1937): 286–296.

Likewise, see the section entitled "Stigmatization and Suggestion" in Réginald Garrigou-Lagrange, *The Three Ages of the Interior Life*, vol. 2, trans. Sr. M. Timothea Doyle (St. Louis, MO: B. Herder, 1948), 596–607.

[146] See Édouard Le Roy, "[Essai sur] la notion du miracle," *Annales de philosophie chrétienne* (Oct. 1907): [5–33, 166–191, 225–259].

this kind. Therefore, no witnesses can have such certitude concerning them.

Response: I make a distinction regarding the major premise. I concede that there can be neither physical nor moral certitude concerning a fact performed outside of the bounds of absolutely necessary laws. However, I deny that this holds for hypothetically necessary laws. Thus, there cannot be certitude concerning the existence of a square circle or concerning the existence of a living corpse. However, it is not contradictory to certitude that there be a resurrection of someone who was dead. Nay, witnesses can have physical certitude concerning it.

{{90}} 2. *Objection*: Some contend, with Renan, that miracles cannot be known with certitude unless they are performed before the scientific academy, indeed, many times.

Response: (1) If this were the case, God would need to await the establishment of academies. (2) Common sense (i.e., natural reason) suffices for knowing a sensible fact that is public and accommodated to being known by all. (3) At Lourdes, there now is a scientific commission of doctors tasked with examining miraculous healings, and likewise, doctors are gathered to render judgment concerning miracles involved in the beatification of saints.[147] (4) Finally, not infrequently, on account of their prejudices, arrogance, and passions, scientists are not equal to the task of judging concerning divine facts.[148]

3. *Objection*: Witnesses too can experience hallucination, whether it be natural or caused by a diabolical deception. Hence, they cannot have physical certitude concerning the existence of miracles.

Response: A hallucination or illusion can be diagnosed, first of all, on the basis of physical circumstances, for otherwise we could never have physical certitude on the basis of sensation. It is easy to verify whether a given case involves the conditions of hallucination or those of true perception. Moreover, the moral circumstances must be considered. In this way, a true fact is discerned from a demonic illusion. Likewise, Christ's miracles cannot be attributed to demons, for he himself cast out demons and said: "And if Satan

---

[147] See Benedict XIV, *De canonizatione sanctorum*, bk. 3, ch. 7.

[148] Hence, Jacques Marie Louis Monasabré in the second conference in his *Introduction au dogme catholique*, refutes the utterly vacuous Renan by showing "that he understands nothing concerning the dignity of God, nothing concerning the nature of miracles, nothing concerning his own end, nothing concerning the passions and mores of scientists, nothing concerning the weaknesses of our own poor minds, and finally, nothing concerning what He says." Likewise, Cardinal Louis Édouard Pie, *Troisième instruction*, *Oeuvres*, vol. 5 [Poitiers: Oudin, 1868], 105: "To set up as a principle the claim that a wonderworker does not deserve belief except inasmuch as he is set up before the tribunal of the principal representatives of nineteenth-century science and submits himself to the conditions of their program is to mock past centuries and the whole of mankind, refusing to allow that they would have had the modicum of good sense needed for observing facts which are utterly palpable. Moreover, this is to mock God, whom one supposes is able to flex to creaturely whims and to accept being ruled by His own creature at the very moment when He comes to manifest His greatest power. It is to condemn Him to not act as God precisely at the hour when He wishes to prove that He is God."

cast out Satan, he is divided against himself: how then shall his kingdom stand? . . . But if I by the Spirit of God cast out devils, then is the kingdom of God come upon you" (Matt 12:26–28, DR).

4. *Continued insistence*: This kind of demonic trickery cannot be discerned with firm certitude without supernatural aid, for as is said in Matthew 24:24 (DR): "For there shall arise false Christs . . . and shall shew great signs and wonders, insomuch as to deceive, if possible, even the elect." Therefore, human reason cannot, by itself, know miracles with certitude.

Response: In some cases, *per accidens*, supernatural aid is required in order to discern such trickery, on account of the multitude of wonders [performed]. However, *per se*, this aid is not required, for a miracle is, of its very nature [*ex se*], an obvious fact.

5. *Continued insistence*: Nonetheless, the Church reserves to herself judgment concerning miracles.

Response: As was said above, the Church reserves to herself solemn judgment, *ex officio*, concerning the truth of certain miracles in order to manifest the holiness of the servants of God. However, this does not mean that individual human reason cannot know miracles with certitude. By contrast, the Church herself holds that miracles are "irresistible signs of her divine mission, accommodated to the intelligence of all," as was said at the [First] Vatican Council.

6. *Objection*: However, frequently, in order to have certitude concerning miracles, it is necessary that we consider the doctrine that is to be confirmed by it. Now, this involves a vicious circle inasmuch as the miracle is confirmed by the doctrine that it ought to confirm.

Response: Without any vicious circle being involved, causes are causes of each other, though in different genera of causality.[149] In other words, if the doctrine is obviously immoral and impious, the miracle performed in confirmation of it is false; {{91}} if, in contrast, the doctrine obviously does honor to God and fosters peace, this is a new sign in favor of its miraculous character. Indeed, what remains obscure in the teaching is confirmed by the miracle. Thus, the clarity of the miracle and that of the doctrine mutually reinforce each other.

7. *Objection*: At least, as Hume says, there is not historical certitude concerning the existence of miracles, by means of testimony. Indeed, that which is morally impossible happens more readily than that which is physically impossible. Now, it is only morally impossible that a thousand witnesses would err, whereas it is physically impossible that a fact would exist outside the laws of nature. Therefore, it is easier for a thousand witnesses to err than for a fact to exist outside of the laws of nature.

---

149 [Trans. note: For a treatment of this principle at length, see the final chapter of Réginald Garrigou-Lagrange, *The Order of Things: The Realism of the Principle of Finality*, trans. Matthew K. Minerd (Steubenville, OH: Emmaus Academic, 2020).]

Response: Indeed, it is easier for a thousand witnesses to err than for metaphysical laws to be altered, for they are absolutely necessary and suffer no exception. It is even easier for a thousand witnesses to err than for something to be produced outside of physical laws *by a merely natural cause*, for this is physically impossible (that is, for nature itself). However, it is, as it were, infinitely easier for something to be produced *by the First Cause* outside of physical laws than it is for a thousand witnesses to err. Indeed, for God, to act outside the order of nature is neither physically nor morally impossible—nay, it is quite fitting in confirmation of the saving truth or the holiness of his servants. By contrast, it is both physically and morally impossible for a thousand witnesses to err—nay, even to a degree metaphysically impossible—for thence we would have a cause without an effect in such a case. If a thousand witnesses agree concerning something, it is metaphysically certain that the cause of this agreement exists, which cannot be assigned to anything other than the very evidence of the fact. Hence, Hume's objection is null and void.

8. *Continued urging*: Nonetheless, the testimony of a few cannot prevail against the universal testimony of mankind. Now, while two or ten witnesses profess that a dead person has resurrected, countless people from all regions of the world hold that the dead do not rise.

Response: The testimony spoken of here is not concerned with the same object. For universally, men hold that the dead do not *naturally* rise, nor *generally*. By contrast, two or ten witnesses profess that *someone* who was dead was *supernaturally* raised from the dead *in a particular case*. These two testimonies do not contradict one another. Nay, the second presupposes the first, just as the exception presupposes the law outside of which it takes place, for otherwise there would be no marvelous or extraordinary exception.

9. *Continued urging*: Nonetheless, this certitude concerning the existence of miracles cannot be historical. Indeed, on the basis of human testimony, we can accept natural facts as something historically certain; however, we cannot thus accept facts that are so extraordinary that they have no plausibility.[150]

Response: A miracle is a sensible fact that is obvious and, hence, naturally knowable by witnesses. Therefore, it is historical if it takes place before many attentive onlookers who carefully weigh out all of the circumstances of the fact, if public monuments are erected in memory of it, if stories are written about it, and so forth. Historical certitude is not diminished because a fact is extraordinary, for the historian precisely as a historian must not choose a particular philosophical system that is more or less opposed to natural reason and to deny facts that contradict this system. Rather, he must refer to facts as they were, in accord with the certain documentary evidence of them. Nonetheless, *historical certitude requires greater testimony to the degree that the fact in question is more extraordinary*.[151] This holds true, in particular, if the witnesses needed for asserting

---

[150] See Langlois and Seignobos, *Introduction aux études historiques*, 176.

[151] See Joseph de Tonquédec, *Introduction à l'étude du merveilleux et du miracle*, 264–293

the truth of the things spoken of have themselves suffered death.

Thus, without exercising sufficient criticism, the foes of Christianity enumerated certain miracles performed by nonbelievers [*gentibus*]. According to them, Vespasian supposedly healed the blind and lame and Apollonius of Tyana supposedly raised a dead girl, likewise performing many other miracles. {{92}} In reality, however, what is referred to concerning Vespasian has no witness but, rather, relies on his uncertain fame. Moreover, the lame and blind whom he is said to have healed were not, in the judgment of doctors, naturally unable to be healed, as is reported in Tacitus, [*Historiae*,] bk. 4, no. 81. As regards Apollonius, it was more than a hundred years after Apollonius's death that one Philostratus wrote his history, which was loaded with fables, and he refers to this raising up of a certain girl on the basis of uncertain rumors, without any testimony, and on the basis of his narrative it is not clear that the girl really was dead.[152] Finally, the fact that Apollonius was held to be an imposter thus ensured that he would have no sect.

By contrast, as we will show in the second book, Christ's miracles are historically certain. Nay, the evangelists themselves faced death for asserting the truth of the things that they narrated.

ART. 4: ON THE PROBATIVE FORCE OF MIRACLES

§1. The Church's teaching
§2. On the nature of this probative force, according to St. Thomas
§3. Demonstration of the value of miracles inasmuch as they are utterly
     certain motives of credibility
§4. Resolution of objections

§1. The Church's Teaching

The [First] Vatican Council defines, in *Dei filius*: "Miracles, . . . since they manifestly display the omnipotence and infinite knowledge of God, are *the most certain signs of the divine revelation, adapted to the intelligence of all men.*"[153] And likewise, in canon 3.4: "If anyone says that no miracles are possible and that, therefore, all accounts of them are to be dismissed as fable and myths; *or that miracles can never be recognized with certainty and that the*

(General rules). When critiquing the marvelous, what role must be played by the notions of possibility and impossibility, probability and improbability. These notions must be combined with the estimation of the value of witnesses. [Trans. note: This note is written in French, likely as a paraphrase of the sections in question. Also, reading *jouer* for *juer*.]

[152] See Louis-Claude Fillion, *Les miracles de Notre Seigneur Jésus-Christ*, vol. 1 [(Paris: Lethielleux, 1909)], 124.

[153] [First] Vatican Council, *Dei filius*, ch. 3 (Denzinger, no. 3009).

divine origin of the Christian religion cannot be legitimately proved by them, let him be anathema."[154]

Likewise, in the formula of the Anti-Modernist Oath prescribed by Pius X against modernism, we find it said: "Second, I accept and acknowledge external arguments of revelation, that is, divine deeds, in particular miracles and prophecies as *utterly certain signs of the divine origin of the Christian religion*, and I hold that they are most excellently adapted to the understanding of all eras and men, *even of our own days*."[155]

Hence, according to the Church, if certain men of our own era do not understand the probative force of miracles or hold that they only have a symbolic value, useful for drawing our attention, such assertions arise from their own agnostic prejudices.

Christ himself said: "The works that I do in the name of my Father, they give testimony of me. . . . But if I do, though you will not believe me, believe the works: that you may know and believe that the Father is in me and I in the Father" (John 10:25, 38, DR). Likewise, "If I had not done among them the works that no other man hath done, they would not have sin: but now they have both seen and hated both me and my Father" (John 15:24, DR). And "there is no man that doth a miracle in my name and can soon speak ill of me" (Mark 9:38, DR).

§2. On the Nature of This Probative Force, according to St. Thomas

According to the Holy Doctor, an argument based upon miracles, in order to prove the divine origins of some doctrine, is not a direct *a priori* demonstration (that is, from a proper cause, as is the demonstration of the soul's immortality on the basis of its spirituality), nor a direct *a posteriori* demonstration (namely, from a proper effect, as God's existence is proven by way of causality), {{93}} but rather, *is an indirect demonstration on the basis of an utterly certain sign*, which concludes that the thing in question is such, for otherwise absurdity or something impossible would follow. This indirect demonstration does not offer (as is the case in a direct / ostensive demonstration) vision of the truth of the reality in itself; however, it does exclude the fear of error, given the absurdity that would follow upon the denial of it.[156] What is directly manifested through a miracle is the intervention of the

---

[154] Ibid., can. 3.4 (Denzinger, no. 3034).

[155] Likewise, against fideism, see Theses Subscribed to by Louis-Eugène Bautain by Order of His Bishop, Nov. 18, 1835, and Sept. 8, 1840, no. 3 (Denzinger, no. 2753).

[156] See Cardinal Zigliara, *Summa philosophica*, vol. 1, 156 (Direct and indirect demonstration).

divine omnipotence, which "manifestly displays" this power, as the [First] Vatican Council says, and on this basis, the divine origin of the revealed doctrine is proven indirectly, though duly, presupposing the declaration of the prophet concerning the miracle's connection with the doctrine to be confirmed.

Now, the fact that this is St. Thomas's thought on this matter is clear in a number of his texts.

(1) In *ST* III, q. 55, a. 3, he expressly determines that an argument from miracles is a proof through a sign:

> There are two sorts of arguments. Sometimes, the term "argument" is used to indicate any kind of *account* [*ratio*] giving faith (i.e., certitude) concerning a matter that is in doubt, whereas at other times it refers to a *sensible sign* employed to manifest the truth, just as Aristotle himself also sometimes uses the term in his works (Cf. *Prior Analytics*, bk. 2; *Rhetoric*, bk. 1). Therefore, taking the term "argument" in the first sense, Christ did not demonstrate His Resurrection to the disciples by way of argument (because what exceeds human reason cannot be proven through human accounts). . . . However, if the term is taken in the second sense, Christ is thus said to have declared His Resurrection by means of arguments, inasmuch as He showed, through certain *evident signs*, that He resurrected (or that He was sent by God).

(2) Nonetheless, according to St. Thomas, this argument from miracles is *utterly certain*. Indeed, he says in *ST* III, q. 43, a. 1:

> Because those things that are of faith exceed human reason, they cannot be proven through human reasons but, rather, must be proven through arguments drawn from the divine power, so that when someone performs works that only God can do, we may believe that the things that he says are themselves from God. This is akin to when someone brings letters, signed by the king's ring, thus leading one to believe that what is contained in those letters does indeed proceed from the king's will.

Likewise see *ST* II-II, q. 178, a. 1. Also see *ST* II-II, q. 5, a. 2: "If, while announcing God's word, a prophet were to foretell something and give a sign, by raising a dead person to life, the intellect of the person who sees that sign would be convinced by such a deed that *he would clearly know that this is said by God*, who does not lie, although that future thing would not be evident in itself. Whence, the formal character of faith would not be destroyed by this certitude." Likewise, in *SCG* III, ch. 135: "Since those things that are known by faith surpass reason, the spoken words of the preachers needed to be confirmed by certain signs, *which would make it wholly clear that these words came from God*, provided that these preachers did things like healing the sick and the performance of other difficult deeds, which could be done only by God." And in *Quodlibet* II, q. 4, a. 1, ad 4: "It cannot happen that someone who announces a false teaching would perform true miracles, which can only be brought about by the divine power, *for were matters otherwise, God would be the witness to falsehood, which is impossible*." This final text makes clear why arguments from miracles provide a proof on the basis of an utterly certain sign, reducing the argument to impossibility or absurdity. Also see *In Ioan.*, ch. 9, lect. 3, no. 8; and see *In* III *Sent.*, d. 23, q. 3, a. 2, ad 2; d. 24, q. 1, a. 2, sol. 2, ad 4; d. 25, q. 2, a. 1, q. 4, ad 4.

§3. Demonstration of the Value of Miracles Inasmuch as They Are Utterly Certain Motives of Credibility

A. *Foundation for this probative force.*[157] {{94}} If a prophet proposing a doctrine as something revealed by God, while performing a miracle in confirmation of this revelation, did not truly receive this doctrine as something revealed by God, it would follow that God *would be the witness to falsehood*. Now, this inference is absurd. Therefore, the antecedent is also absurd. Hence, when miracles are performed in confirmation of some revealed doctrine, they are utterly certain signs of revelation.

Proof of the inference. Indeed, a miracle can be produced only by the divine omnipotence, under the direction of divine providence. Now, *providence extends* not only to the substance of the miracle to be performed but also *to all the circumstances* in which it is produced, the most important of which is the declaration made by the prophet concerning the connection of this miracle with this revelation to be confirmed. Thus, divine providence differs from our prudence, which cannot foresee all the external circumstances of our acts. Therefore, if a true miracle is indeed performed, along with all the circumstances that bear witness to the fact that it is done in confirmation of revelation, all the while without revelation actually being made, then God who alone can bring about a true miracle would be a witness to falsehood, either intentionally or at least permissively, inasmuch as he would thus have permitted a false prophet to misuse a true miracle.

Proof of the impossibility of drawing the inference. (1) *God cannot intentionally bear witness to falsity*, for through his very essence he is the First Truth. Were he to intentionally bear witness to falsity, the Unfailing First Truth would indeed fall short of what he is, something absurd.

---

[157] See Benedict XIV, *Doctrina de servorum Dei beatificatione et beatorum canonizatione*, bk. 4, pt. 1, ch. 4 (On the end of miracles); bk. 1, ch. 30, no. 10.

(2) *Nor can he do so permissively.* That is, God cannot permit a false prophet to misuse a true miracle in circumstances in which men would be invincibly led into deception. Indeed, were he to do so, God would simultaneously will and not will men to be able to arrive at their ultimate end, for he would perform a miracle by virtue of which error would in fact be accepted in place of truth in a matter that is necessary to salvation.[158]

Hence, miracles directly manifest a free intervention by the divine omnipotence and indirectly manifest the divine origin of doctrine in confirmation of which they are performed. As we read in the constitution *Dei filius* from the [First] Vatican Council: "miracles, . . . since they manifestly display the omnipotence . . . of God, are the most certain signs of the divine revelation." The transition from the divine attribute of omnipotence to that of the First Truth revealing is brought about on account of the impossibility of there being any contrariety among the divine attributes. Omnipotence and providence cannot act against the First Truth.

{{95}} This argument is confirmed by way of comparison to a king's seal placed as a stamp only upon truly authentic writings. Hence, the foundation for the value of miracles is the nature of this sign, which can be produced only by God, who is utterly truthful.[159]

B. *The condition for the probative force of miracles.* In order for a miracle to be an utterly certain sign of revelation, some necessary condition is required—namely, *the explicit or implicit declaration of the connection of this miracle with this revelation to be confirmed*—for otherwise, the miracle would indeed be an extraordinary intervention by God, but it would not be a fitting sign of God's doctrine.

This declaration can be *implicit*, though nonetheless manifest based

---

[158] Theologians generally agree with this, as can be seen in Salmanticenses, *De fide*, disp. 2, dub. 3, no. 64. However, along with certain other authors, they concede that it would not be contradictory for God to perform a miracle and a false prophet to strive to misuse it, provided that there simultaneously are other circumstances and signs by means of which one would be able to discern that the aforementioned miracle was not performed in confirmation of the doctrine proposed by this false prophet. For example, if God simultaneously declared in another way that the miracle was performed for the sake of other ends, or if the false prophet were to propose a doctrine opposed to prior, certain revelation, or if he were to teach something contrary to pure morality, and so forth. Then, of course, although we would see the performance of the miracle promised by him, we would be able (and indeed would need) to hold that this miracle is either false, apparent, or performed for the sake of other, very distant ends and hence in no way provides confirmation for what is proposed.

[159] Concerning the value of miracles, see A. de Poulpiquet, O.P., *L'objet intégral de l'apologetique* [(Paris: Bloud et Cie, 1912)], 61 and 69; *Le miracle et ses suppléances* [(Paris: Beauchesne: 1914)].

on its circumstances, by means of which it would be clear that the miracle is performed in confirmation of the doctrine previously proposed as being revealed by God. However, it can be an *explicit* declaration, either *directly* (if someone asserts that a given miracle is to follow in manifestation of the divine origin of a given doctrine) or *indirectly* (if someone announces himself to be sent by God and calls attention to a miracle that he performed earlier).

This declaration by the prophet, especially if it is explicit and direct, is confirmed by the miracle as a unified whole along with the revealed doctrine. In fact, the very connection of this miracle with this doctrine to be confirmed is revealed to the prophet by God, for otherwise the prophet himself could not announce the miracle to follow (for it is an extraordinary effect depending upon the wholly free will of God). Hence, we read in Exodus 4:1–19 that God manifested to Moses the miracles that he was to perform in confirmation of his divine mission so that the Israelites might believe. Likewise, Christ, sending forth his disciples to preach, said: "Heal the sick, raise the dead, cleanse the lepers, cast out devils" (Matt 10:8, DR). Thus, the prophets and apostles—that is, the first apologetes—knew from on high (namely, as revealed by God) the probative force of miracles before they performed them. Likewise, the teaching Church (*ecclesia docens*), in defining this probative force of miracles as a dogma,[160] infallibly judges it under the light of revelation, without a vicious circle, although the value of this motive of credibility can be known by the light of reason alone for those who come to faith. Hence, it is not surprising that, like the apostles, the apologete would speak from on high under the direction of faith to men who do not yet believe so that he may present them with rationally efficacious motives of credibility that are chosen and given by God himself. (See what we said earlier in the introduction to this work concerning the nature of apologetics.)

Moreover, miracles are motives of credibility accommodated to the intelligence of all, for they are sensible signs whose value is known on the basis of the principles of natural reason (i.e., common sense) concerning the truthfulness and omnipotence of God. However, in opposition to the objections against them drawn from the scientific order, they can be efficaciously defended both metaphysically and historically.

---

[160] See [First] Vatican Council, *Dei filius*, can. 3.4 (Denzinger, no. 3034).

§4. Resolution of Objections

{{96}} First, we will present the *a priori* objections, followed by those that are *a posteriori*.

1. *Objection*: Miracles only prove the fact of revelation through the mediacy of the declaration made by the prophet concerning its connection with this revelation to be confirmed. Now, this declaration is fallible and also perhaps feigned. Therefore, miracles cannot prove, at least apodictically (that is, with utter certainty) the fact of revelation.

Response: I make a distinction regarding the major premise. I concede it if this declaration is confirmed by the miracle in a unified manner together with the revealed doctrine; otherwise, I deny it. I distinguish the minor premise along the same lines.

2. *Continued insistence*: This declaration is not sufficiently confirmed, especially if it is indirect and made by calling attention to miracles that were performed in the past. Indeed, according to many theologians, it is not contradictory to say that a false prophet could misuse a true miracle performed for the sake of another end. Now, in such a case, the prophet's declaration would be false. Therefore, the prophet's declaration is insufficiently confirmed by the miracle.

Response: I make a distinction regarding the major premise. I concede it if it is clear, along with all the circumstances, that this miracle is performed for the sake of another end; otherwise, I deny it. We explained this earlier in the body of our thesis in the context of the Salmanticenses' argument concerning this point.

3. *Continued urging*: Nor in these circumstances does a miracle apodictically prove the fact of revelation.

According to Juan de Ripalda, God can perform a miracle in confirmation of some saving error. Now, a false form of revelation can be saving (e.g., false preaching concerning the end of the world can be saving as an exhortation to vigilance). Therefore, God can perform a miracle in confirmation of false revelation.

Response: With the Salmanticenses,[161] and nearly all theologians, I deny the major premise, for evil things must not be done so that good things may be brought about. Now, error, precisely as error, is not saving, and lies are, of themselves, evil. Therefore, God cannot *per se* influence one to err, nor to lie, even if, *per accidens*, salvation were to follow from it. Indeed, God would no longer be the First Truth through his very essence if this weren't so, and moreover, we would never be able to discern saving error from the truth[162] necessary for salvation. This would be to overturn the entire order of truth and morality.

4. *Continued urging*: Nonetheless, miracles cannot be the basis for scientific demonstration of the divine origin of some doctrine or of the fact of revelation.

Indeed, scientific demonstration is either *a priori* (i.e., from a proper cause) or *a*

---

[161] See Salmanticenses, *Cursus theologicus, De fide*, disp. 2, dub. 3, no. 71.

[162] [Trans. note: Reading *varitate* as *veritate*.]

posteriori (i.e., from a proper effect). Now, miracles are neither a proper cause nor a proper effect of revelation. Therefore, miracles cannot be the basis for scientific demonstration concerning the fact of revelation.

Response: I make a distinction regarding the major premise. I concede it as regards scientific demonstration, strictly speaking. However, I deny it for scientific demonstration in the broad sense. Indeed, the latter can be a demonstration through a sign. Now, if the sign is utterly certain, it provides the foundation for an apodictic demonstration through a *reductio ad absurdum* argument. As we said earlier, this holds for the case of miracles, through a reduction to this impossibility: God would be a witness to falsehood.[163]

{{97}} 5. *Continued urging*: The fact of revelation cannot be demonstrated from a sign either. Indeed, the fact of revelation, by means of which supernatural mysteries are manifested, is specified by these same mysteries and hence is supernatural *quoad substantiam*. Now, that which is supernatural *quoad substantiam* is also supernatural as regards how it is known, inasmuch as truth and being are convertible. Therefore, the fact of revelation cannot be naturally known with certainty on the basis of a sensible miracle but, rather, is only held by faith.

Response: I make a distinction concerning the major premise. I concede that *in itself* and *intimately considered*, the revealing action is supernatural *quoad substantiam*. However, as it is manifested *externally*, through the human testimony of the prophet and through miracles, it is known as something modally supernatural—namely, as a miraculous intervention by God in the intellectual order. Now, from this external perspective, the fact of revelation is known in the same manner as it would be known even if it were

---

[163] According to this distinction between scientific demonstration properly speaking and scientific demonstration broadly speaking (though apodictic), consider what is said by Cajetan in his comments on *ST* III, q. 55, a. 6: "Both the manifestation of Christ's resurrection through testimony and through arguments, that is through a sensible sign, was sufficient in its own category of argument, the former in the category of testimony, the other in that of sensible signs. And understand, also, that the sufficiency involved here is enough for causing the certitude of faith, not the certitude of science." Note that Cajetan is speaking of science properly so-called; he is not here excluding natural certitude as it is had through signs. Indeed, earlier, while commenting upon *ST* III, q. 43, a. 4, he had already said: "The miracles performed by Christ were sufficient for manifesting the deity itself, in three ways: substance, mode, and doctrine. Each of these are proven clearly (in St. Thomas's article). There, note what the author briefly comments [*pertransit*]: but if these three are fully considered, we can say that they contain the greatest of efficacy. Now, first indeed, as regards the resurrection of the dead and the illumination of the blind, it is clear that, so long as we set aside deceptive cases, such things can only be brought about by God. However, secondly, it is unthinkable that it would also be suitable for a demon to perform such things. And thirdly, it is completely convincing intellectually. Thus, if these three things are found together, *it is impossible* that we would not believe that Christ is God. For how would the false usurp for itself the divine name and claim, as though God would have been present as a lying witness in such a grand number of works properly belonging to the deity?"

solely modally supernatural—namely, as something ordered only to the manifestation of the natural truths of religion. However, in itself and intimately, it is supernatural *quoad substantiam* and from this loftier perspective is formally known only through faith, as we discussed earlier in the previous volume of this work.[164]

6. *Continued urging*: Finally, an objection is drawn from the facts: Miracles are found in all religions and, hence, they prove nothing.

Response: This is not the place to examine in detail the various wonders that are attributed to the various pagan partisans of Buddhism or Islam, as well as those belonging to the various sects of Christianity. For now, it suffices to say this does not prove that these wonders are true miracles and not the deceptive illusions performed by magicians. Nay, on the basis of both physical and moral circumstances, many things appear as being deceptive illusions.[165]

Finally, St. Thomas does not deny that miracles may be produced by God in false religions, but if they are true, which would need to be proven, they are never performed in confirmation of a false doctrine. In *ST* II-II, q. 178, a. 2, ad 3, the Holy Doctor says: "Miracles are always true testimonies concerning those things to which they lead men. Whence, wicked men who express some false teaching never perform true miracles in confirmation of their teaching, although they sometimes may do so in praise of Christ's name which they invoke and by the power of the sacraments which they administer." Likewise, in *De potentia*, q. 6, a. 5, ad 5, St. Thomas, following St. Augustine, refers to something read in historical texts concerning a certain vestal virgin who, as a sign of her preservation of chastity, carried water from the Tiber in a leaky vase without any water escaping from the vessel. Concerning this, the Holy Doctor says: "It is not unlikely, that as a commendation of chastity that the True God, through His good angels, would perform a miracle of this kind, retaining the water in the vessel, for if something good existed in the gentiles, it came from God. However, if this were done by demons, this does not stand against what we have said[, for . . . just as demons can move a body locally, so too can they hold back such movement]."

Hence, true miracles are always true testimonies concerning those things to which they lead men—namely, either in confirmation of revealed doctrine or as witnessing to someone's holiness. And these remarks suffice as regards miracles inasmuch as they provide an utterly certain motive of credibility.

---

[164] See sect. 4, ch. 14, a. 3 (How is the formal motive of infused faith known).

[165] See below, bk. 2, sect. 4.

CHAPTER TWENTY

On the Value of Prophecy
as a Motive of Credibility

Art. 1. On the notion of prophecy
Art. 2. On the possibility of prophecy
Art. 3. On the discernibility of prophecy
Art. 4. On the probative force of prophecy

ART. 1: ON THE NOTION OF PROPHECY

§1. The nominal and general definition of prophecy
§2. The Catholic notion of prophecy, inasmuch as it is a motive of credibility
§3. The heterodox notion of prophecy
§4. Theological explanation of the Catholic notion of prophecy
§5. The division of prophecy

§1. The Nominal and General Definition of Prophecy

{{98}} *Prophets*, in Greek προφήτης, in the Septuagint translation corresponds to the Hebrew word *nâbi'* and sometimes to the words *rôéh* and *hôzéh*. *Nâbi'* signifies "he who is inflamed in spirit and speaks to men on behalf of God" (see Exod 4:15; 7:1ff). *Rôéh* and *hôzéh* have the same general meaning as "he who sees" and designate those who enjoy the vision of God.

According to Eusebius of Caesarea (*Dem. Ev.*, bk. 5, prol.) and St. Thomas (in *ST* II-II, q. 171, a. 1), the word προφήτης comes from the words προ-φαίνω, "to make manifest before," or to foretell or appear. St. Thomas says, "They can be called prophets from the word φανός, namely, apparition, because things appear to them from afar."

Many others say that προφήτης comes from προφάναι, "to foretell." Many today hold this second etymology and say that προ- does not designate a

143

priority of time but instead means "on behalf of another." Hence, the word προφήτης would signify "he who speaks on behalf of another"—namely, "he who speaks to men on behalf of God." And, in reality, this is the signification of the Hebrew word *nâbi'*.

Hence, according to its general signification, the word *prophet* designates a servant of God who proposes divine revelation to us, and according to *this general acceptation*, the term *prophecy* means the same thing as *revelation*, as St. Thomas noted in a number of places.[1] In this sense, Hebrews 1:1–2 (DR) says: "God, who, at sundry times and in divers manners, spoke in times past to the fathers by the prophets, last of all, in these days, hath spoken to us by his Son."

{{99}} However, the term *prophecy* also has *a specific sense*, inasmuch as it is distinguished from discernment of spirits, from interpretation of words, and the other freely given graces enumerated in 1 Corinthians 12:10 and 14:6. *In that case, it signifies divinely given foreknowledge and the preaching of future events.*[2] In this way, it is distinguished from merely natural *conjecture* concerning the future, as well as from *divination*, which is attributed not to God but to demons. This particular sense is what we are going to talk about here, whereas by contrast, at the beginning of this treatise we explained the nature of revelation.

§2. The Catholic Notion of Prophecy, Inasmuch as It Is a Motive of Credibility

According to the [First] Vatican Council, *prophecies are "divine facts which, since they* manifestly display the omnipotence and infinite knowledge of God, are the most certain signs of the divine revelation, adapted to the intelligence of all men."[3] Similarly, see the Anti-Modernist Oath. And the Council cites 2 Peter 1:19 (DR): "And we have the more firm prophetical word: whereunto you do well to attend, as to a light that shineth in a dark

---

[1] See the prologue to *ST* II-II, q. 171: "Prophetic revelation extends not only to future human events but also to divine realities, both to those things proposed to all as matters of belief, thus pertaining to faith, and to higher mysteries which belong to the perfect and thus pertain to wisdom. . . . It also extends to the direction of human acts, which pertains to science, as will be clear below in q. 177." Likewise, see St. Thomas, *In I Cor.*, ch. 14:1. Likewise in the Old Testament, see Exod 4:16.

[2] See St. Thomas, *In I Cor.* 14:1: "The word 'prophecy' is not taken here *in its general sense*, namely, as we discussed earlier, but rather is taken *in a particular sense*, inasmuch as it is only a manifestation of future things."

[3] [First] Vatican Council, *Dei filius*, ch. 3 (Denzinger, no. 3009).

place." This notion is founded on the very words of the prophets.[4]

Hence, according to the Church, prophecy is a supernatural fact that can come only from God and displays his infinite knowledge [*scientiam*]. It proceeds from God's miraculous intervention in the world, though it differs from miracles properly so-called inasmuch as prophecy pertains not directly to the sensible order but, rather, to the intellectual order, even if it ought to be sensibly manifested so that it may become a sign of the divine origin of religion. The term *prophecy* is here taken by the Council as meaning the foretelling of future events, in accord with these words of Isaiah 41:23 (DR): "Shew the things that are to come hereafter, and we shall know that ye are gods."

§3. The Heterodox Notion of Prophecy

Today, liberal Protestants and rationalists reject the possibility of super-natural prophecy, just as they reject the possibility of revelation and of miracles.

And therefore, some reduce prophecy to *divinization*, which exists in all religions and is founded, according to them, on the overly great credulity of ancient peoples.

However, others identify prophecy with *living and firm religious faith*, which announces, with certitude, punishment to the ungodly, consolation to the oppressed righteous, salvation to the penitent, and the kingdom of God through the conversion of heart. However, these kinds of preaching proceed from firm moral and religious certitude, not from a miraculous intervention brought about by God. As they say, a prophet, often thinking upon the salvation of his brethren or homeland, cannot rest until he publicly announces his religious idea and fulfills the mission that he believes to be divine. {{100}} Later on, all kinds of fortuitous coincidences come to appear as being the fulfillment of particular things that he preached. Thus, Christ's disciples, imbued with messianic prejudices, strove to show that Christ's life fulfilled the prophecies that they called messianic. Such is the way that these things are explained by people like Spinoza, Renan, and liberal Protestants.[5]

---

[4] See Deut 18:21–22. [Trans. note: Fr. Garrigou-Lagrange also cites Sirach 68:24. The passage does not seem to be "XLVIII" instead of "LXVIII" either.]

[5] See Spinoza, *Tractatus theologico-politicus*, [trans. R. H. M. Elwes (London: George Bell and Sons, 1891),] ch. 1 (On prophecy), nos. 119ff (translation modified): "Returning, then, to the main object of our discussion, we find that the Scriptural phrases, 'The Spirit of the Lord was upon a prophet,' 'The Lord breathed His Spirit into men,' 'Men were filled with the Spirit of God, with the Holy Spirit,' and so forth are quite clear to us, and mean that prophets were

This heterodox conception of prophecy proceeds from the *a priori* denial of the supernatural order.[6]

§4. Theological Explanation of the Catholic Notion of Prophecy

Because[7] knowledge is specified by its object, we must consider the proper object of prophecy. Now, to this end, in *ST* II-II, q. 171, a. 3, St. Thomas distinguishes those things that are at a distance: (1) as regards their place, (2) on account of the shortcomings of human knowledge (thus, including super-natural mysteries hidden in God), and (3) on account of their indetermina-tion (thus, including future contingents). And the last are, of themselves, most greatly distant and therefore constitute the proper object of prophecy.

[Thus, as he says in that text:]

> We must consider the fact that, given that prophecy is concerned with those
> things *that are distant from our knowledge*, the more remote things are from our
> knowledge, the more do they pertain to prophecy. Now, there are three degrees
> of such things. The first such degree includes things that are distant from some
> particular man's knowledge, whether sensitive or intellective, but not from the

---

endowed with a peculiar and extraordinary power, and devoted themselves to piety with great constancy of soul. . . . Finally, the prophets were said to have God's spirit because men did not know the causes of prophetic knowledge. . . . As to the particular law of Nature by which the communications took place, I confess my ignorance." And in chapter 2, he writes: "It follows from what was said in the last chapter that, as I judged matters to be, the prophets were endowed with unusually vivid imaginations, not with unusually perfect minds."

Likewise, recently, Auguste Sabatier writes in *Esquisse d'une philosophie de la religion d'après la psychologie et l'histoire*, 91 and 94 (On prophecies): "No more than the Sibyls or the sooth-sayer Tiresias did the Hebrew seers have the miraculous gift of being able to read the future. The superiority of their inspiration came from elsewhere. It is found entirely in a purer idea of God, in more elevated idea of justice, in an essentially moral religion, in their indefectible faith, in the triumph of the law and the holy and merciful will of the Eternal One. Supported, on the one hand, by the sovereignty of their God and, on the other, by the inflexible law of moral conscience, they announced with assurance the punishment of the wicked, the conso-lation of the oppressed, the return of the captives, the healing of the sick, and salvation of all those who repent of their faults and change their lives. The Kingdom of God should be the effect of this kind of conversion of hearts and wills. Indeed, such was the character of the prophecies of John the Baptist, as well as those of Christ Himself. They in no way proceed from a special gift of a miraculous power of divination but, rather, from a firmer moral convic-tion, a life more profoundly rooted in God [*une vie en Dieu plus profonde*], and a more sincere and disinterested piety. . . . The moral notion of prophecy remains, but the notion of miracles has thus faded away."

6   See the article "Prophétisme" in the *Dictionnaire de la Bible*.

7   See *ST* II-II, q. 171–175 and q. 95 (On divination). Also see *SCG* III, ch. 155.

knowledge of all men. Thus, by his senses, a particular man knows things that are present to him *as regards their place*, though another man does not know of them by human sense, given the fact that they are removed from him. Thus, Elisha prophetically knew what his disciple Giezi had done in his absence (2 Kgs 5:26), and similarly, one man's *secret thoughts of the heart* are prophetically manifested to another, according to 1 Corinthians 14:25. Likewise, in this way, what one man knows by way of demonstration may be revealed to another prophetically.

{{101}} The second degree of such distance includes those things which surpass the knowledge which is possible for all men, not meaning that they themselves are unknowable but, rather, on *account of a shortcoming in human knowledge*. Such things include the mystery of the Trinity. . . .

The final degree includes things distant from the knowledge of all men by being *intrinsically unknowable*. Such are *future contingents*, whose truth is indeterminate.[8] Now, since that which holds universally and by something's very nature takes precedence of that which holds in a limited and relative sense, it follows that the revelation of future events is what is most proper to prophecy, thus seemingly giving "prophecy" its name. Hence, Gregory says (Homily I on Ezekiel): "And since a prophet is so called because he foretells the future, his name loses its meaning when he speaks of the past or present."

According to a better etymology, seeing the connection of *prophecy* with προφάναι (to speak on behalf of someone, to speak as representing another), the threefold gradation of prophecy can be expressed as follows. Prophecy in the broad sense is to speak in the name of God or by a divine instinct (see Exod 7:1; 1 Cor 14; passim.). However, because things said by a divine instinct are especially naturally hidden from human reason, prophecy therefore understood in a stricter sense is the communication of divine hidden things,

---

8   St. Thomas's words here stand in opposition to the theory of Molina or Suarez, holding that God knows conditioned, future free things *without any predetermining decree* of his will, as though these future things were *determinate* in themselves or on account of their circumstances and could be infallibly known through a divine super-comprehension of causes. Against this theory, see Billuart, *De Deo*, diss. 6, a. 4 (On the "middle science"), §1. This "middle science," invented in order to save human freedom, leads to determinism by circumstances, for without this determinism, God could [not] foresee *infallibly* what men would do or not do in given circumstances. In this text, Billuart writes: "The super-comprehension of a given cause cannot grasp in it something that it does not contain. Now, prior to the decree of the divine will, the effect of a second cause is not contained in as something determinately in the future but, rather, is indifferent in relation to being and non-being. Therefore[, super-comprehension of things cannot grasp such effects.]

be they in the past, present, or future (see Matt 24:8). Finally, because future contingents are most hidden, therefore, the strictest sense of the term *prophecy* is the announcing of these future things.

Hence, prophecy, understood in this particular sense, is rightly defined by Cassiodorus in accord with what it properly signifies: "A Divine inspiration or revelation, announcing the outcome of things with unchangeable truth."[9] Now, in order to make clearer what is objectively and subjectively required for it, *prophecy properly so-called* is defined: "*The infallible foretelling of a future contingent happening, which can be foreseen with certainty only by means of a supernatural light.*"

(a) It is called *infallible* so that it thus may be distinguished both from mere human conjecture (by means of which non-necessary future things can be foreseen with some probability) and from the divination of spirits (which is always fallible as regards future contingents).

(b) Likewise, it is said to be "the foretelling of a future contingent happening." This foretelling involves, primarily, foreknowledge, and secondarily, the speaking thereof. Now, there are two senses to the term *future contingent*. *Broadly speaking*, a future contingent sometimes seeks to exist of its very nature but is naturally able to be impeded through the concurrence of other causes, like when someone lives for a long time because of his robust physical makeup. However, *properly and strictly speaking*, a future contingent is that which, of its very nature, is indifferent to being and non-being, {{102}} as are things that depend upon free choice of the will. Now, the object of prophecy, strictly so-called, is that which is a future contingent, properly speaking.

It must be noted, though, that *a properly contingent future thing* is either *absolute* or *conditioned*. It is absolute when it does not depend upon any condition, except perhaps upon a condition that will take place, like Peter's conversion if Christ were to look upon him. It is conditioned when it depends upon a condition that will not take place, like the conversion of Tyre and Sidon if the Gospel were announced to them. And we will say, when we discuss the division of prophecy, that prophecy can be either concerned with an absolute future contingent (and then it is called prophecy of foreknowledge or of predestination) or with a conditioned future contingent (and then it is called prophecy of denunciation [*prophetia comminationis*]).

What we have said provides a sufficient determination concerning the proper object of prophecy, from which its definition is drawn.

(c) It is said that it is concerned with "what can be foreseen only by means of a supernatural light." Thus, it is clear what is subjectively required

---

[9] Cassiodorus, *In Psalt.*, prologue, ch. 1. See *Gloss. Lom.* at the heading "Psalterium." This definition is cited by St. Thomas in *ST* II-II, q. 171, a. 3, obj. 1.

for prophetic knowledge. Indeed, on account of its indetermination,[10] a future contingent, properly so-called, can only be known with certitude by God, as we will show below. As St. Thomas says in *ST* II-II, q. 171, a. 2: "Therefore, since prophecy extends to knowledge which is above natural knowledge, it follows that prophecy requires an intellectual light exceeding the light of reason." And, as the Holy Doctor says in the same place, "Indeed, it is necessary that manifestation be proportioned to the light through which it is brought about, just as an effect is proportioned to its cause. . . . Just as the bodily manifestation had through vision is brought about through bodily light, so too the manifestation of natural intellectual vision is brought about through the natural light of the intellect," and likewise is the manifestation of a supernatural intellectual vision brought about through a supernatural light.

First corollary. This prophetic light exists as something impressed upon the soul in a passing manner. As St. Thomas says in *ST* II, q. 171, a. 2:

Now, the prophetic light does not exist in the prophet's intellect as an abiding form, for *otherwise a prophet would always be able to prophesy at will,* which clearly is not the case. As Gregory the Great says (Homily I on Ezekiel): "Sometimes the prophet does not have the spirit of prophecy, nor is his mind always able to call it forth, thus, when he does not have it, he knows that its presence is due to a gift." Whence, Elisha said concerning the Shunammite woman: "Her soul is in anguish, and the Lord hath hid it from me, and hath not told me." And the reason for this is because the intellectual light existing in someone after the manner of an enduring and perfect form perfects the intellect principally in order to know the principle of those things that are made manifest through that light, as through the light of the agent intellect the intellect chiefly knows the first principles of all other things which are naturally known. However, the principle of those things which pertain to supernatural knowledge, which are manifested through prophecy, is God Himself, who is not seen through His essence by the prophets. However, He is seen in heaven by the blessed, who have a light of this sort, remaining as an enduring and perfect form, according to the words of Psalm 35:10: "In your light we will see light."

In *ST* II-II, q. 171, a. 3, ad 3, he adds: "*What is formal in prophetic*

___
[10] [Trans. note: Reading *indeterminationem* for *determinationem*.]

knowledge is the divine light, from whose unity the Prophecy draws its specific unity, although the things prophetically manifested by the divine light are various."

{{103}} **Second corollary.** *Prophetic knowledge involves two things— namely, reception or representation of a future contingent thing and infallible judgment concerning this thing.* As St. Thomas says in *ST* II-II, q. 173, a. 2:

> The gift of prophecy confers on the human mind something which surpasses its natural power in both of these respects, namely as regards its judgment, which depends on the infusion of an intellectual light, and as regards the acceptance or representation of things [so revealed], which is brought about by means of certain *species*. Now, human teaching is akin to prophetic revelation in the second respect, though not in the first, for a teacher represents certain things to his students through spoken signs, though he cannot enlighten them inwardly as God does.

Also see what we said concerning the notion of revelation in ch. 4, a. 1 of the first volume of this work.

Third corollary. *What is more principal in prophetic revelation is its supernatural light, not the representation of the future.* As St. Thomas says in the same text:

> However, what is principal in prophecy is the first of these two, since judgment brings knowledge to its completion. Thus, if certain things are divinely represented to someone by means of imaginary likenesses, as happened to Pharaoh (Gen 41:1–7) and to Nebuchadnezzar (Dan 4:1–2), or even through bodily likenesses, as happened to Belshazzar (Dan 5:5), such a man is not to be considered a prophet unless his mind be enlightened for the purpose of judgment. Rather, such an apparition is something imperfect in the genus of prophecy. Whence, some have called this "falling into prophecy," as also takes place in divination by dreams. *However, a man will be a prophet if his intellect is enlightened solely for the purpose of judging concerning things seen in imagination by others, as in the case of Joseph who interpreted Pharaoh's dream* (Gen. 41). However, as Augustine says (*Gen. ad lit.* 12.9), "Someone is especially a prophet when he excels in both respects, so that he may see in spirit likenesses signifying bodily things, and understand them by the liveliness of his intellect."

What we have said suffices as regards the notion of prophecy. Now we must pass on to its division.

§5. The Division of Prophecy

(See *ST* II-II, q. 174.) In order for a division to be *per se* and adequate, it must be drawn from the formal notion of the whole to be divided. Now, as was said, prophecy is the infallible preaching of future contingents. Hence, it can be considered in two ways: from the perspective of the object or that of the subject.

Thus, it is divided: (A) *by reason of the object known*, according to the extension of this object, or according to the nature of the future [contingent], be it absolute or conditioned; or (B) *by reason of the mode of knowledge* involved therein, prophecy is divided inasmuch as it is brought about through various kinds of visions, be they intellectual, imaginary, or sensible, or even inasmuch as it is brought while awake, in ecstasy, or in sleep. {{104}}

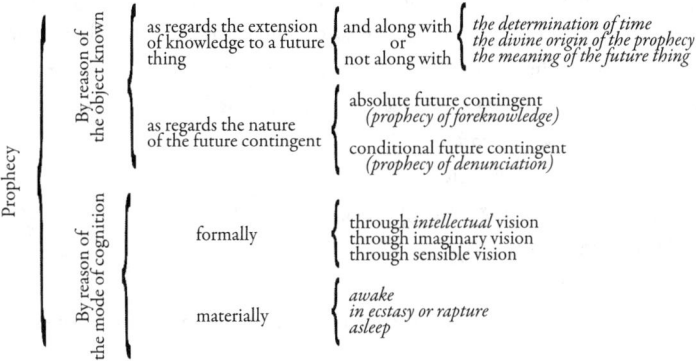

A. *By reason of the object known.* (a) AS REGARDS THE EXTENSION OF THE KNOWLEDGE INVOLVED, prophecy can be divided into four degrees, beginning with what is more perfect.

The first is the most perfect grade, wherein future things are known, along with the determinate future time, the meaning of the thing, and the divine origin of the prophecy itself.

Such is seen, for example, in Christ's announcement of his Passion and Resurrection: "From that time Jesus began to shew to his disciples, that he must go to Jerusalem, and suffer many things from the ancients and scribes and chief priests, and be put to death, and the third day rise again" (Matt 16:21, DR; see 17:22; 20:19). Likewise, Christ foretold to Peter: "This night, before the cock crows, you will deny me three times."

This exact foretelling of time is very rare.[11] God does not normally determine time mathematically in prophecies.[12]

The second degree: Here, the future is known along with its meaning, as well as the divine origin of the prophecy itself, though *the time of the future event is not determinately announced.*

Thus, Christ, in foretelling the destruction of Jerusalem, simultaneously foretold the signs of the end of the world and presented the first event as being the figure of the second. However, the time of the end of the world is not determinate, and its signs are not clearly and explicitly distinct from the signs of the destruction of Jerusalem (see Matt 24:1–36).

This temporal indetermination is not rare in cases of prophetic knowledge because of two seemingly opposed reasons—namely, on account of its loftiness and obscurity. Indeed, the prophet is in some manner elevated to divine knowledge of future things, and "for God a thousand years are like a day" (2 Pet 3:8). {{105}} Hence, *the prophet, contemplating things from on high, as it were, does not always consider the interval of time involved therein.*[13] However, on the other hand, St. Thomas says, "Just as the term 'faith' implies imperfection in knowledge, so too *'prophecy' implies a kind of obscurity* and distancing from intelligible truth."[14] This obscurity is frequent in prophecy, as is clear in the Book of Revelation and in the prophecies in the Old Testament. Moreover, temporal indetermination can be the occasion for exhortations to remain vigilant, as when Christ announced the end of the world (cf. Matt 24:36).

Third degree: Here the future thing is known, as well as its meaning, but *there is not certitude concerning the divine origin of the prophecy itself.*

St. Thomas says in *ST* II-II, q. 171, a. 5:

The prophet's mind is instructed by God in two ways. In one way, it is

---

[11] See Marie-Joseph Lagrange, "Les prophéties messianiques de Daniel," *Revue biblique* (1904): 495.

[12] See Marie-Joseph Lagrange, "Pascal et les prophéties messianiques," *Revue biblique* (1906): 540: "Indeed, the exact determination of time is extraordinarily rare. . . . The messianic hope should have been the spring of religious life for Israel, the awaited and implored event, and salvation inaugurated by desire, since prayer was able to advance the hour of its arrival. . . . The Messiah, the Liberator and Savior, was awaited with more impatience in times of anguish. The Jews knew of him very well, and one of the articles of their messianic faith is that the *sorrows of the Messiah*—the term is technical in nature—should precede His advent. Now, in the times of Herod and of Pilate, the nation could no longer conceive of any human hope of salvation."

[13] Thus, in the natural order, when we find ourselves upon a mountain, another loftier mountain to which we are traveling seems close to us because we do not consider the distance in its details.

[14] *ST* II-II, q. 147, a. 2, ad 3.

instructed through express revelation, while in another by a wholly mysterious instinct to "which the human mind is subjected without knowing the fact," as Augustine says (*Gen. ad lit.* 2.17). Therefore, the prophet has the greatest certitude about those things which he knows by an express revelation, and he knows for certain that they are revealed to him by God. Whence, it is written (Jer 26:15, DR): "In truth the Lord sent me to you, to speak all these words in your hearing." Otherwise, if he were not certain about this, the faith which relies on the prophet's utterances would not be certain. We can find a sign of the prophet's certitude in the fact that Abraham, having been admonished in a prophetic vision, prepared to sacrifice his only-begotten son, which he never would have done had he not been utterly certain concerning the Divine revelation.

However, sometimes, the prophet, considering the things that he knows by way of instinct, cannot fully discern whether his thoughts are conceived through a divine instinct or through his own spirit. And those things which we know through divine instinct are not all manifested with prophetic certitude, for this instinct is something imperfect in the genus of prophecy.

St. Gregory the Great says the same in his first homily on Ezekiel. And in Jeremiah 23:28 (DR) it is said: "The prophet that hath a dream, let him tell a dream: and he that hath my word, let him speak my word with truth." Likewise see *ST* II-II, q. 173, a. 4.

Fourth degree: Here the future thing is foretold, but the prophet is *unaware* not only of the divine origin of the prophecy but *also of the meaning of the thing that is foretold*.

Indeed, as St. Thomas says in *ST* II-II, q. 173, a. 4, he whose mind is moved to express certain words sometimes does not know what the Holy Spirit intends to express through these words, *as is clear in the case of Caiaphas*, as is read in John 11:49–51 (DR): "But one of them, named Caiaphas, being the high priest that year, said to them: You know nothing. Neither do you consider that it is expedient for you that one man should die for the people and that the whole nation perish not. And this he spoke not of himself: but being the high priest of that year, he prophesied that Jesus should die for the nation."

These are the principal degrees of prophecy, considered from the perspective of the extension of the object known.

Moreover, as regards the meaning of the foretold thing, and *on account of the supernaturality of this thing*, prophecy can be divided inasmuch as it is concerned with something that is essentially supernatural (e.g., the Incarnation of the Word, or the sending of the Holy Spirit) or with a future contingent of the natural order (e.g., the destruction of Jerusalem).

{{106}} In order to infallibly know a future contingent, it suffices that one have an intellectual light that is *modally supernatural*.[15] However, if the future contingent is supernatural *quoad substantiam*, it is not known formally as such, except under a light that is *supernatural quoad substantiam*, as we said above in our discussion of revelation. However, it is in fact the case that the great prophecies of the Old and New Testaments were ordered to the signification of essentially supernatural things, for not only were they some sign of revelation after the manner of a miracle, but moreover, they manifested the very revealed mysteries themselves progressively, announcing the future supernatural favors of God, especially the coming of the Redeemer. This religious signification was something essential and formal in them, and the foretelling of the events was subordinated to it so that the sign of revelation is subordinated to the revealed mysteries. Hence, it is not surprising if the prophecies were not to present a mathematical determination concerning a future contingent and forever contain a kind of obscurity, for they are concerned with the mysteries of God, not only illuminating the intellect but also drawing the heart.

(b) As REGARDS THE NATURE OF THE FUTURE THING ANNOUNCED, inasmuch as the future contingent in question is either *absolute* or *conditional*, prophecy is subdivided into absolute prophecy (prophecy *of foresight*) and conditional prophecy (prophecy *of denunciation* or promise).[16]

The prophecy of foresight designates foreknowledge of future events inasmuch as they are to be fulfilled in themselves and forever. However, prophecy of denunciation is not always fulfilled, but it foretells the order of cause to effect that sometimes is impeded by other supervening events.[17]

Thus, Jonah, sent by God, preached to the Ninevites: "Yet forty days and Nineveh shall be destroyed" (Jonah 3:4, DR). However, the Ninevites did penance, saying: "Who can tell if God will turn, and forgive: and will turn away from his fierce anger, and we shall not perish? And God saw their works, that they were turned from their evil way: and God had mercy with regard to the evil which he had said that he would do to them, and he did it not" (Jonah 3:9–10, DR) Likewise, Isaiah foretold to King Hezekiah in his illness:

---

[15] That is, it suffices that one have a light that is modally supernatural, as regards the manner of its production, i.e., something supernatural as regards *efficient causality*, like a miracle. However, reductively, it belongs to the order of miracles *quoad substantiam*, for that which is supernatural *quoad substantiam* (like sanctifying grace) is not the same as that which is a miracle *quoad substantiam* (like the glorification of the body).

[16] See *ST* II-II, q. 171, a. 6, ad 2; q. 174, a. 1. *De veritate*, q. 12, a. 10c and ad 7, 8, 9, 10 and 13; also, q. 12, a. 11, ad 2. *In Ieremiam*, ch. 18. *In Isaiam*, ch. 34 (middle) and *In Matth.*, ch. 1.

[17] See *ST* II-II, q. 174, a. 1.

Thus saith the Lord: Take order with thy house, for thou shalt die, and not live. And Hezekiah turned his face toward the wall, and prayed to the Lord, and said: I beseech thee, O Lord, remember how I have walked before thee in truth, and with a perfect heart, and have done that which is good in thy sight. And Hezekiah wept with great weeping. And the word of the Lord came to Isaias, saying: Go and say to Hezekiah: Thus saith the Lord the God of David thy father: I have heard thy prayer, and I have seen thy tears. Behold I will add to thy days fifteen years; and I will deliver thee and this city out of the hand of the king of the Assyrians, and I will protect it.[18]

This distinction between the prophecy of foresight and prophecy of denunciation was not invented in order to explain prophecies that are not fulfilled, but rather, God himself through the prophets explains the reason for this prophecy of denunciation. {{107}} Indeed, he said to Jeremiah (in Jer 18:7–8, DR): "I will suddenly speak against a nation, and against a kingdom, to root out, and to pull down, and to destroy it. If that nation against which I have spoken, shall repent of their evil, I also will repent of the evil that I have thought to do to them."

Likewise, the fittingness of the prophecy of denunciation is clear *a priori*, given how it manifests God's mercy. Indeed, God announces punishments so that he might turn a sinner from his sin and from damnation. Likewise, he can conditionally foretell a promise. However, conditional prophecy "is denominated more so from denunciation, because God is more inclined to relax punishment than to withdraw promised favors."[19] Hence, prophecy of promise is generally fulfilled and from this perspective pertains to prophecy of foresight.

Objection: Since the prophecy of denunciation is not fulfilled, it is false. Therefore, prophecy is not an infallible form of knowledge.

Response: St. Thomas writes on this point: "However, the prophecy does not cover over a falsehood, for the meaning of the prophecy is that inferior causes, whether they be natural causes or human acts, are such as to lead to such an outcome,"[20] though this disposition of things can be changed through penance.

When prophecy is made with an oath, then it is a prophecy of foresight,[21] as it is said in Psalm 109:4 (DR), "The Lord hath sworn, and he will not repent."[22]

---

[18] Isa 38:1–6 (DR).

[19] *ST* II-II, q. 174, a. 1, ad 2.

[20] *ST* II-II, q. 171, a. 6, ad 2. [Trans. note, the footnote also reads "et *De verit.*, q."]

[21] See St. Thomas, *In Ep. Ad Hebr.*, 7:21.

[22] "God is metaphorically said to repent inasmuch as He is akin to one who repents, that is, inas-

By contrast, as St. Thomas notes in *SCG* III, q. 155:

> When the revelation of prophecy is made according to the ordering of causes to effects (prophecy of denunciation), sometimes at the same time or afterwards a revelation is made to the same prophet concerning the outcome of the future effect, regarding how it may come to be altered (prophecy of foreknowledge), as when the healing of Hezekiah was revealed to Isaiah, and the freeing of Nineveh to Jonah.

Hence, prophecy of denunciation is changed only when it merits change, though it is fulfilled in some sense (ibid.).

B. *By reason of the mode of cognition*, prophecy is subdivided in two, inasmuch as the mode of cognition is understood either (a) formally in knowledge itself (b) or materially as regards the state of the prophet.

(a) FORMALLY, prophecy is made in three ways: (1) *through intellectual vision*, (2) *through imaginary vision*, and (3) *through sensible vision*.

We explained this earlier in ch. 4, a. 3, when we laid out the division of revelation. See *ST* II-II, q. 174, a. 2:

> That form of prophecy revealing a purely intelligible truth is more powerful than all others. . . . The prophet's mind is shown thereby to be loftier, just as in human teaching the hearer who is able to grasp the purely intelligible truth the master propounds is shown to have a better understanding than one who needs to be taken by the hand and helped by means of examples drawn from sense objects. Hence, it is said in commendation of David's prophecy (2 Sam 23:3, DR), "The strong one of Israel spoke," and soon thereafter (Sam 23:4, DR), "As the light of the morning, when the sun riseth, shineth in the morning without clouds."

Nonetheless, because the term *prophecy*, like the term *faith*, "implies a certain obscurity and distance from the intelligible truth, the term 'prophet' is more properly applied to those who see by way of imaginary vision. And nonetheless, the more excellent form of prophecy is that which is conveyed by way of intellectual vision, provided the same truth be revealed in either case" (ibid., ad 3).

{{108}} *However, imaginary vision* is more or less perfect, as is explained in *ST* II-II, q. 174, ad 1: (1) someone speaking under the appearance of being God is seen or heard; (2) or someone speaking under the appearance of an angel; (3) or someone speaking

---

much as He changes his sentence, though he does not change his counsel" (*ST* II-II, q. 171, a. 6, ad 2).

under the appearance of a human; (4) or only words are heard or seen; (5) or only symbolic signs are seen, like seven full ears of grain signifying seven years of plenty (Gen. 41). And the loftier the prophecy, the more express the nature of the sign.[23]

(b) Materially, as regards the state of the prophet, three kinds of prophecy can be made: (1) *while awake*; (2) *in ecstasy or rapture*; (3) *while asleep*.[24]

According to *ST* II-II, q. 174, a. 3: *"Visions received while awake pertain to a loftier degree of prophecy* (than those received while asleep), for the power of the prophetic light that draws one away, while awake, from sensible things to supernatural things seems to be greater than that which finds man's soul already withdrawn from them in sleep." Hence, perfect prophecy does not take place in sleep.

Ecstasy simply designates a mental excess, and *rapture* adds above this a kind of violence on the side of the mode of the activity, not on the side of the terminus.[25] The mind can be rapt away to divine things in three ways—namely, through imaginary likenesses, intelligible effects, and the divine essence. The first is attributed to Peter and John the Evangelist, the second to Adam and David, and the third to Paul and Moses.[26] However, in a way greater than the prophets, *Christ* was *above ecstasy and rapture*, and without ecstasy, while awake and conversing, he forever saw the divine essence, according to the common position held by theologians.[27]

Thus, the divisions of prophecy are sufficiently set forth, on the side of the object and that of the mode of cognition.

ART. 2: On the Possibility of Prophecy

§1. God can communicate prophetic cognition to man.

§2. God alone, through the power properly belonging to him, can give man prophetic knowledge of future contingents.

§3. God alone can communicate to man certain knowledge concerning thoughts of the heart. [Such knowledge] reductively pertains to prophecy.

§4. Resolution of objections.

---

[23] See *ST* II-II, q. 173, a. 2; q. 174, a. 1, ad 3.

[24] See *ST* II-II, q. 174, a. 1–3.

[25] See *ST* II-II, q. 173, a. 2, ad 1.

[26] See *ST* II-II, q. 175, a. 3, ad 1.

[27] See *ST* III, q. 10. [Trans. note: As relates to current debates concerning this topic, along with a defense of the Thomistic position, see Thomas Joseph White, "The Necessity of the Beatific Vision in the Earthly Christ," in *The Incarnate Lord: A Thomistic Study in Christology* (Washington, DC: Catholic University of America Press, 2017), 236–274.]

§1. God Can Communicate Prophetic Cognition to Man

Indeed, God can reveal to man those things that he knows. Now, he infallibly knows all future contingents and free actions. Therefore, he can communicate to man knowledge concerning future contingents.

The major premise was proven earlier in the discussion of the question of the possibility of revelation. By reason alone, we demonstrated the possibility of the revelation of truths that are not supernatural *quoad substantiam*, for by reason alone, it is clear that such natural truths can be expressed through our concepts. Now, future contingents exceed our intellect on account of their contingency / indetermination, not on account of intrinsic supernaturality, as is the case for mysteries like that of the Trinity, and after such events take place, they will be naturally and clearly knowable. {{109}} Hence, by reason alone, it is evident that God can announce to us such a future event by ordering our concepts in order to express such an event and by infusing the prophetic light into the mind of the prophet in order that he may infallibly judge concerning this matter. As was said above, it suffices that this be a light that is modally supernatural, corresponding to miracles of the first order.

The minor premise directly follows from the fact that God is the most universal cause of all things, acting through his intellect, and hence acting with foreknowledge of all things.

This minor premise can also be easily proven indirectly through an argument in the form of a *reductio ad absurdum*. Indeed, if God were not to know, infallibly and from eternity, all future contingents and free actions, his knowledge [*scientia*] would not be completely perfect and infinite, nor would it be measured by eternity but, rather, would be progressive, passing from imperfection to perfection, from potency to act. Nay, it would be passively determined by things as they gradually unfold. Thus, God would come to learn something, being thereby instructed by things.

However, all of this is impossible, for there can be no imperfection / potentiality in God, he who is Pure Act; nor can there be any progressive knowledge, nor any knowledge that depends upon creatures. God's knowledge [*scientia*] is not caused by things, like our own, but rather is their cause. Indeed, nothing can exist outside of the utterly universal First Cause, unless it is caused by him and first measured by God's practical knowledge [*scientia*], which, like the knowledge [*scientia*] that an artisan has, determines his works.[28] Hence, we must hold with utter certainty, even by reason alone, that

---

[28] See *ST* I, q. 14, a. 8.

God infallibly knows, from eternity, all future contingents and free actions, for eternity, existing all together in a single moment of duration, embraces all time, just as the top of a pyramid embraces all of its sides.[29] And revelation confirms this: "But all things are naked and open to his eyes, to whom our speech is" (Heb 4:13, DR); "you have understood all my thoughts from afar and have foreseen all of my paths" (Ps 138[9]:3)

In this treatise, we do not need to determine *how God knows future and free contingents*, nor how this foresight is reconciled with human freedom.[30] Concerning this point, it suffices that we note St. Thomas's words regarding this matter, for they contain the solution to this twofold problem. In *SCG* I, ch. 68, he begins by saying: "It is now necessary for us to show that God knows the thoughts of the mind and all the things that the heart wills in virtue of being their cause, since He is the universal principle of being." Having proven this through five arguments, he concludes the whole chapter as follows:

> The dominion that the will has over its acts, by which it has the power to will or not to will, excludes the determination of its power to one effect as well as any violence coming from a cause acting externally upon it. However, this does not exclude the influence of a higher cause from which it receives its being and activity. *Thus, the causality in the First Cause—that is, God—remains in relation to the motions of the will, so that, by knowing Himself, God can know such motions.*

Now, God is the cause of things through his will. Therefore, he knows future contingents and free actions in his will (that is, in his eternal decrees).

{{110}} St. Thomas develops [*evolvit*] this doctrine in *ST* I, q. 14, a. 5: "God knows things other than Himself in His divine power, which is the efficient [*effectiva*] cause of all things." Likewise, in *ST* I, q. 14 , a. 8: "*God's knowledge* [*scientia*] *is the cause of things, inasmuch as it has His will connected thereto*" (that is, the *divine decree*). This general principle is applied to [his] knowledge of future contingents in *ST* I, q. 14, a. 13:

---

29 See *De malo*, q. 16, a. 7.

30 [Trans. note: For further discussion on this topic by Fr. Garrigou-Lagrange, see Réginald Garrigou-Lagrange, *The One God: A Commentary on the First Part of St. Thomas's Theological Summa*, trans. Bede Rose (St. Louis, MO: B. Herder, 1943), 448–475; *Predestination*, trans. Bede Rose (St. Louis, MO: B. Herder, 1939), 59–229. For a recent treatment of this topic, see Taylor Patrick O'Neill, *Grace, Predestination, and the Permission of Sin: A Thomistic Analysis* (Washington, DC: Catholic University of America Press, 2019).]

And although contingent things become actual successively, none-theless God does not himself know such contingent things in a successive manner, as they are in their own being, as we do, but instead knows them simultaneously. This is so because His knowledge is measured by eternity, as is His being. *Now, eternity exists all together in a single moment of duration, thus embracing all time.* Whence, all things that exist in time are present to God from eternity, not only because He has the types [*rationes*] of things present within Him, as some say, but, indeed, because *from eternity, his Gaze looks on all things* as they are in their mode of being present [praesentialitate].

Thus, the center of the circle corresponds to all the points upon its circumference.

Nonetheless, our freedom is not injured by this, for "*since then the divine will is utterly efficacious,* it *follows* not only that things which God wills to be done are, in fact, done but also that *they are done in the way that He wills.* Now, God wills some things to be done in a necessary manner and others in a contingent manner."[31] "Necessity and contingency properly follow upon being inasmuch as it is being. Whence, the modes of contingency and necessity both fall under the foresight of God, who has universal care for all of being."[32]

On account of its transcendence, the divine motion "*brings forth all of being and all of its differences.*"[33] Thus, *even the free modality (which is a modality of being) of our actions is produced by the First Cause.* God prescinds only from evil, for evil is not being but, rather, a privation of a due good: "Just as the defect of limping is ultimately related to a curved shinbone, not to the motive power, which nonetheless causes whatever motion exists in this limping."[34]

"And just as by moving natural causes, God does not prevent their acts from being natural, so too *by moving voluntary causes, He does not deprive their actions of being voluntary. Rather, He is the cause of this very thing in them,* for He acts in each thing in accord with its own nature."[35] "And therefore, it would be more incompatible with the divine motion if the will were moved of necessity (i.e., without potency in relation to the opposite choice), for

---

[31] *ST* I, q. 19, a. 8.

[32] *ST* I, q. 22, a. 4, ad 3.

[33] See St. Thomas, *In* I *Perihermenias,* lect. 14: "The divine will must be understood as existing outside of the order of all beings, as a kind of cause *bringing forth the whole of being and all of its differences.* However, the possible and the necessary are differences of being. Therefore, the necessity and contingency found in things finds its origin in the divine will itself." Likewise, see *In* VI *Meta.,* lect. 3.

[34] *ST* I-II, q. 79, a. 2.

[35] *ST* I, q. 83, a. 1, ad 3.

this does not fall to its nature, than if it were moved *freely*, inasmuch as this befits its nature."[36]

Hence, *gently and strongly*, freely and infallibly, *God moves human freedom* to a given act rather than the opposed one,[37] *prescinding only from evil*. Not only does this motion not injure man's freedom but, moreover, it produces in the free act its very mode of freedom, which is a modality of being depending upon the cause of being inasmuch as it is being. The act remains free, for under the indifference of the practical judgment, it has a non-necessary relation to the particular good by which it is specified. {{111}} Nay, even if God were to will to do so, he could not move the will to a particular good in a necessary manner for as long as this good were judged to be freely deserving of choice and not satiating for the will, for under this judgment, potency in relation to the opposite choice remains.

Therefore, *all the Thomists* teach that God infallibly knows future contingents from eternity *in the eternal degree* by which he decreed to move all contingent and free causes to produce these contingent effects.[38]

Molina and *Suarez* teach, by contrast, that God knows conditioned future free actions, prior to [his] decree, either through a super-comprehension of second causes or in the truth (whether formal or objective) of future conditioned things. They call this divine knowledge his *middle knowledge* [*scientia media*], found between his knowledge [*scientiam*] of simple understanding and that of vision.

The Thomists respond: (1) A free determination, conditionally in the future and independent from the divine decree, *would be something that is not caused by God*. Thus, God would no longer be the most universal cause of all beings and of all the modalities of being. God's knowledge [*scientia*] would no longer be the cause of all things but, rather, would, in part, be caused by things.[39] (2) The *middle knowledge* [*scientia media*] thought up

---

[36] *ST* I-II, q. 10, a. 4, ad 1.

[37] Explaining the words of Phil 2:13 (DR), "For it is God who worketh in you, both to will and to accomplish, according to his good will," St. Thomas says in *SCG* III, ch. 89: "Some have said that God causes us to will and accomplish things inasmuch as He gives us the power to will, though not, however, that He makes us will this or that. . . . To such people, we can bring forth as obvious evidence words authoritatively drawn from Sacred Scripture. Indeed, it is said, in Isa 26:12 (DR): 'Lord, . . . thou hast wrought all our works for us.' Whence, not only do we have the power of willing from God but, also, its very activity.

"Hence, the very words of Solomon (Prov 21:1, DR), 'As the divisions of waters, so the heart of the king is in the hand of the Lord: whithersoever he will, he shall turn it,' show that the divine causality extends not only to the power to will but also to its very act."

[38] See Billuart, *Summa sancti Thomae, De Deo*, diss. 6, a. 4; Bossuet, *Traité du libre arbitre*, ch. 8.

[39] Hence, in their interpretation of St. Thomas, Molinists unjustly consider *ST* I, q. 14, a. 3 (Whether God has knowledge of future contingents) independent from a. 8 (Whether God's knowledge is the cause of things).

In a. 8, St. Thomas determines *in general* how God knows all things other than himself—

in order to save human freedom in fact destroys it, for *it leads to determinism by circumstances*. Indeed, the divine super-comprehension of our will cannot grasp in it something that is not contained therein. Now, prior to the decree of the divine will, an effect is not contained in a free second cause as something *determinately* in the future but, rather, is there as indifferent to being and non-being. Therefore, this effect cannot be infallibly foreknown by God unless one admits, with Leibniz, determinism on the part of circumstances. However, in that case, freedom comes to ruin. Likewise, prior to the divine decree, there is no *determinate* truth (whether objective or formal) concerning free future possibilities [*futuribilis liberi*], for otherwise, one would fall into determinism.[40] St. Thomas expressly says concerning future contingents, which are the proper object of prophecy: "Their truth *is not determinate*, and they are not knowable in themselves."[41]

Conclusion. Although the way that the divine foreknowledge and human freedom are reconciled remains mysterious, nonetheless, it is utterly certain, even through reason alone, that this foreknowledge exists. Hence, our conclusion stands firm: God can communicate to man knowledge of future contingents by impressing on the prophet's mind new *species* / images of things, or by ordering his already acquired *species* so that they may express future events, as well as by infusing the prophetic light needed for judging infallibly concerning what is thus received.

§2. God Alone, through the Power Properly Belonging to Him, Can Give Man Prophetic Knowledge of Future Contingents

(See *ST* I, q. 57, a. 3; II-II, q. 95 (On divination); q. 172, a. 1 and 5.)

Indeed, prophecy is foreknowledge and *infallible* preaching concerning future contingents, as something essentially distinct from conjecture regarding future things. Now, only God can, by his own proper power, infallibly know future contingents. Therefore, God alone can, by his own power, give man prophetic knowledge.

{{112}} *The major premise* is the definition of prophecy explained above.

The minor premise is proven from the fact that God alone is an utterly universal and eternal cause, himself alone in being perfectly immutable,

---

namely, in his causality. Afterwards, he determines, *in a specific manner*, how the divine science extends to evils, singular things, and future contingents. However, his solutions always presuppose the general principle: God's knowledge [*scientia*] is the cause of things.

[40] See Billuart, *Summa sancti Thomae, De Deo*, diss. 6, a. 4, §1 (Refutation of Molina and Suarez).

[41] *ST* II-II, q. 171, a. 3; likewise, see *In I Perihermenias*, lect. 14.

above the successive flow of thoughts. Hence, "He alone naturally sees all things in His eternity, which given its simplicity, is present to all time, embracing it. Now, all created intellects fall short of the divine eternity. . . . There is a form of duration [*est tempus*] in the angel's mind, in accord with the succession of his intelligible conceptions."[42]

However, if one pushes deeper into the matter and asks, "Why are future contingents present and determinate solely in God's eternity?" we may respond with St. Thomas: because God "in His providence establishes the mode of all things."[43] Indeed, future free contingents depend either solely on God's freedom (like miracles) or together on the divine freedom and human freedom. Now, God alone can infallibly know future things that depend solely upon his freedom, for he alone has natural knowledge concerning such things. Likewise, he alone can infallibly know future things that depend on human freedom, for he alone can move our freedom infallibly and freely with his gentle and strong power. Indeed, the order of agents corresponds to the order of ends, and God is the end of our will.[44]

Nay, theologians teach that the blessed, who immediately see the divine essence, do not know, in this, the free decrees of God as regards their termination in creatures but instead enjoy such knowledge inasmuch as God wills to manifest free future things to them.[45]

Nonetheless, *in a conjectural manner*, angels know many future contingents in their causes, as the doctor foreknows the health of the sick person and, likewise, as we foresee certain future free things conjecturally on the basis of the habits and physical dispositions of men by which they are inclined to one given thing. And the angels, whether good or evil, foresee such things much more keenly than we do, to the degree that they more perfectly know the inclinations of the causes of things and the inclinations of men. However, this conjecture is forever essentially different from the infallible knowledge had by the prophet, a knowledge that, therefore, can only be communicated to him by God.[46]

---

[42] *ST* I, q. 57, a. 3c and ad 2.

[43] *De veritate*, q. 8, a. 12 (Whether angels know future things).

[44] *ST* I, q. 105, a. 4. [Trans. note: Without grace, hope, and charity, God is the end of our will as *that in which the good in general is found*, not *in his inner mystery*. See Réginald Garrigou-Lagrange, "The Finality and Realism of the Will," in *The Order of Things: The Realism of the Principle of Finality*, trans. Matthew K. Minerd (Steubenville, OH: Emmaus Academic, 2020), 251–272; also see "Can the Possibility of the Beatific Vision be Demonstrated?," in *The Sense of Mystery: Clarity and Obscurity in the Intellectual Life*, trans. Matthew K. Minerd (Steubenville, OH: Emmaus Academic, 2017), 141–170.]

[45] See Billuart, *Summa sancti Thomae, De Deo*, diss. 4, a. 10.

[46] As regards the resolution to the objections raised against this conclusion, see what St. Thomas

However, God can give man this prophetic knowledge through the angels. In that case, the angel is an instrumental cause used by God, as also happens in the performing of miracles.[47]

§3. God Alone Can Communicate to Man Certain Knowledge concerning Thoughts of the Heart. [Such Knowledge] Reductively Pertains to Prophecy.

This knowledge, under the name "discernment of spirits,"[48] is numbered among freely given graces and is ultimately reduced to prophecy, broadly speaking.[49]

As St. Thomas says in *ST* I, q. 57, a. 4:

> *The thoughts of the heart can be known in two ways.* First, they can be known *in their effects.* In this way, they can be known not only by angels but also by men, indeed with all the greater subtlety to the degree that such effects are all the more hidden. {{113}} Indeed, thought is sometimes discovered not merely through an outward act, but also by the change in one's countenance, and doctors can discern some passions of the soul merely by taking one's pulse. Much more can angels, or even demons, make such discernments, to the degree that they more deeply penetrate those hidden bodily modifications. . . .

> In another way, thoughts can be known as they are *in the intellect*, and affections as they are *in the will*. Understood in this way, God alone can know the thoughts of hearts and affections of wills. This is so *because the rational creature is subject to God alone, and the only one who can act within it is He who is its principal object and last end*, something to be discussed in more detail later on (*ST* I, q. 105, a. 4). Therefore, all that exists in the will, and all things that depend only upon it, are known to God alone. Now, it is evident that the actual consideration of anything by someone depends entirely on that person's will, for a man who has a habit of knowledge, or any intelligible *species*, uses them at will. Whence, the Apostle says (1

---

says in *De malo*, q. 16, a. 7 (Whether demons know future things).

[47] See *ST* II-II, q. 172, a. 2, ad 3.

[48] See 1 Cor 12:10.

[49] *ST* I-II, q. 111, a. 4; II-II, q. 171, a. 3, ad 2.

Cor 2:11, DR): "For what man knoweth the things of a man, but the spirit of a man that is in him?" And we read in Jer 17:9, "Man's heart is unsearchable; who can know it? I, the Lord alone, am the one who searches it."

Objection: Angels naturally know, intuitively and through ideas infused into them, not only bodies but also souls—indeed, all the bodily and spiritual parts of the universe. Therefore, they naturally cannot foresee the secrets of our heart, though they can know them when they already exist. St. Thomas responds: "*The will's motion has no dependence on, or connection with, any natural cause.* Only the divine cause can influence the will. Consequently, the will's motion and the heart's thoughts cannot be known in any likenesses of natural things but, rather, only in the divine essence, which leaves its imprint on the will." That is, as John of St. Thomas explains in his comments on *ST* I, q. 57, purely internal acts, which depend solely on the free will and upon God, having no connection with natural causes, are known only by the person who is willing and by God, remaining hidden from created spirits. For they do not have a natural power to know any unrestricted kind of intelligible [thing] whatsoever but, rather, only that which pertains to the order of this universe, either as a part of it, or having a connection with it. Now, *purely internal free acts do not pertain to the order of the universe as a part thereof, nor as something having any connection with it.* For the order of the universe consists in the subordination and interconnection of natural causes by which inferior things are ruled by superior things.

In this, we see the excellence of our interior life, which is, properly speaking, under the dominion of God, above the order of the universe and the object of special providence, a kind of special universe unto itself (*unum versus alia omnia*, one thing set facing before all others, the soul facing toward the infinite God). One can fully [*perfecte*] write the history of a given city without mentioning the most holy interior life of a given soul living in this city, something known by God alone; what does history tell us of the interior life of St. Joseph or the Virgin Mary? This is the dominion of God alone, above history—nay, above the natural knowledge of the angels: "For he hath hidden me in his tabernacle; in the day of evils, he hath protected me in the secret place of his tabernacle" (Ps 26:5, DR).

§4. Resolution of Objections

As for the objections raised against the possibility of prophecy, see what was said earlier in response to objections raised against the possibility of revelation. However, one can also argue *against the supernaturality of prophecy*.

{{114}} 1. *Objection*: It seems that prophecy would be natural, for as the rationalists Ewald and Reuss say, he who already comes to attain some degree of perfection comes to have a lively conception of the object of his religious aspirations and of his brothers, thus foreseeing, at least in a vague manner, the development of the religious sentiment. This objection is not new but, rather, was proposed in nearly the same terms by St. Thomas in *ST* II-II, q. 172, a. 1: "It seems that prophecy could be natural. Indeed, as Gregory says (*Dialogue*, 4.26), 'sometimes the power strength of the soul by itself is sufficiently subtle for foreseeing certain things, and as Augustine says (*Gen. ad lit.* 12.13), the human soul, inasmuch as it is withdrawn from bodily senses, is able to foresee the future. Now, this pertains to prophecy. Therefore, the soul can acquire prophecy naturally."

Response: The Holy Doctor responds: "When the soul is withdrawn from bodily things, it becomes more adapted to perceive the influence of spiritual substances and, likewise, more inclined to perceive the subtle motions which take place in the human imagination through the impression of natural causes." Thus, such a person is better disposed to *make conjectures* concerning future contingent things, but he cannot know them *with certainty*, except through revelation, whenever he may wish to do so but, rather, inasmuch as God so wills.

2. *Objection*: Nonetheless, some people naturally foresee in sleep certain future things, as Aristotle notes in *On Divination in Sleep*, ch. 2.

Response: St. Thomas responds to this in *ST* II-II, q. 95, a. 6:

Dreams are sometimes the cause of future occurrences, for instance, when a person's mind becomes anxious on account of what it has seen in a dream, thus being led to do something or avoid something. . . . Sometimes, things which have occupied a man's thoughts and affections while he was awake recur to his imagination while he is asleep. This kind of cause of dreams is not causal in relation to future occurrences, so that dreams of this kind are related accidentally to future occurrences, and if they ever do concur in it, this will be by *chance*. However, sometimes the cause of dreams is an interior disposition of our body and humors . . . or an impression by external bodies, like the air. . . . Finally, the cause of dreams can be an external spiritual cause. *Sometimes*, it indeed *comes from God*, who through the ministry of angels reveals something to men in their dreams, as is related in a number of places in Sacred Scripture. *However, sometimes, through the activity of the demons*, certain images appear to people in their sleep, sometimes thereby revealing certain future things to those with whom they have made a forbidden pact.

3. *Objection*: At least from the prerequisites for prophecy, it seems that it is something natural, for that for which a natural disposition is required is itself natural. Now, prophecy requires a natural disposition, for prophecy can be impeded through a

vehement passion, and also through disordered concern with external things. Hence, too, we read, concerning the prophets in 2[/4] Kings 4:4 that "they lived together with Elisha," leading a kind of solitary life, lest worldly concerns would come to hinder the gift of prophecy.

Response: No natural quality sufficiently disposes one for prophecy. Nonetheless, some natural indispositions, such as vehement passions, can impede prophecy, "but the divine power, which is the cause of prophecy, removes such a natural indisposition."[50] Also, in *ST* II-II, q. 172, a. 4, St. Thomas adds, "Prophecy can exist without charity, for it is given for the good of the Church and not, directly, for uniting the Prophet's affections to God. . . . However, prophecy requires distancing from vehement passions or inordinate concern for external things."

4. *Objection*: If the gift of prophecy came from God alone, it would only be given to the best men. Now, there were also evil prophets, as we read quite clearly in Scripture concerning Balaam (Num 22:8), who is said to have been spoken to by God, although he was a prophet on behalf of demons. Likewise, we read in John 11:49–51 (DR): "But one of them, named Caiaphas, being the high priest that year, said to them: You know nothing. Neither do you consider that it is expedient for you that one man should die for the people and that the whole nation perish not. And this he spoke not of himself: but being the high priest of that year, he prophesied that Jesus should die for the nation."

{{115}} *Response*: St. Thomas says in *ST* II-II, q. 172, a. 4, ad 1 and ad 4:

> Sometimes, the gift of prophecy is given to a man both for the good of others and in order to enlighten his own mind. Such are those whom divine wisdom, giving itself through sanctifying grace to their minds, "maketh the friends of God, and prophets." However, others, receive the gift of prophecy solely for the good of others, thus being, as it were, instruments of the divine activity. . . . God's gifts are not always given to those who are the best, simply speaking, but sometimes are given to those who are best as regards the receiving of this or that gift. Thus, God gives the gift of prophecy to those whom He judges best to receive it from him.

Nay, God even uses the wicked for good ends on behalf of the good. Hence too, through the demons' prophets he announces certain truths so that the truth may be rendered more credible, given that even its enemies bear witness to it, and also so that men, by believing such prophets, may be more readily led onward to the truth. Hence, the Sibyls likewise foretold many true things concerning Christ.[51]

5. *Objection*: But, also according to Sacred Scripture, certain prophecies were made

---

[50] *ST* II-II, q. 172, a. 3, ad 3.
[51] *ST* II-II, q. 172, a. 6, ad 1.

by demons. Indeed, we read in 1[/3] Kings 18:19 (DR): "Gather unto me all Israel, unto Mount Carmel, and the prophets of Baal four hundred and fifty, and the prophets of the groves four hundred, who eat at Jezebel's table." However, these people worshiped the demons. Therefore, prophecy does not come solely from God.

Response: In response to this, St. Thomas says, in *ST* II-II, q. 172, a. 5:

> The demons, even by their natural knowledge, know certain things which are distant from men's knowledge, things which they can reveal to men: although those things which God alone knows are without qualification distant from men's knowledge, indeed most so. Therefore, prophecy, properly and simply speaking, is brought about solely through divine revelations. However, the revelation which is made by the demons may be called prophecy in a restricted sense. Whence, those men to whom something is revealed by the demons are called, in Scripture, prophets, though not simply speaking, but with an addition, for instance as in the expressions "false prophets," or "prophets of idols." Hence Augustine says (*Gen. ad lit.* 12.19): "When the evil spirit lays hold of a man for such purposes," namely for visions, "he makes him either devilish, or possessed, or a false prophet."

ART. 3: ON THE DISCERNIBILITY OF PROPHECY

§1. Prophecy, in itself, is naturally knowable with certitude.

§2. With utterly great certitude, many prophecies are able to be distinguished from human conjecture and from the divination of spirits.

§3. Certain prophecies, taken separately, can be distinguished from human conjecture or the divination of spirits only with moral certitude.

§4. Resolution of objections.

State of the Question—Catholics and rationalists completely disagree with each other on this point. According to the Catholic Church, as was stated at the [First] Vatican Council, "prophecies divine facts which, since they manifestly display the omnipotence and infinite knowledge of God, are the most certain signs of the divine revelation, adapted to the intelligence of all men."[52] Hence, they can be distinguished from human conjectures and the divination of spirits.

---

[52] [First] Vatican Council, *Dei filius*, ch. 3 (Denzinger, no. 3009).

By contrast, rationalists and liberal Protestants assert that even if supernatural prophecy were possible, it could not be distinguished from human conjecture, which sometimes is verified by the course of events.

§1. Prophecy, in Itself, Is Naturally Knowable with Certitude

{{116}} Indeed, prophecy is a sure prediction of a future event, with the truth of this prediction being made clear when the event comes to its fulfillment. Now, both the firm foretelling of a future event and its fulfillment can be known naturally with certitude. Therefore, prophecy, in itself, is naturally knowable with certitude.

Prophecy thus known naturally manifestly displays the infinite knowledge of God inasmuch as God alone can foresee future free choices with certitude, something admitted by natural reason. Thus, the order of the world manifests the existence of an ordering intelligence (that is, providence).

Objection: On the basis of the fulfillment of foretold events, prophecy is not distinguished with certitude from natural conjecture or from divination, for these latter predictions can also be verified by events, at least by way of fortuitous coincidences.

In order to resolve this difficulty, we must distinguish between prophecies that announce all the minute details of the circumstances and meaning of future free choices, and those that only vaguely point out something future. The former can be distinguished from each other with certitude, while the latter can be so distinguished with a kind of moral certitude.

§2. With Utterly Great Certitude, Many Prophecies Are Able to Be Distinguished from Human Conjecture and from the Divination of Spirits

This is clear according to (1) common sense (i.e., natural reason) and to (2) philosophical reason.

(1) ACCORDING TO COMMON SENSE. *To the degree that prophecy announces all the minute* circumstances and meanings of many future contingents long before the event, *so too is it all the less possible* that they be predictions that are confirmed by the fortuitous fulfillment of those details. Now, as we will come to show historically later on in this volume, many prophecies announce, (1) not in a doubtful and equivocal way but instead *certainly and determinately*, setting forth *the minute circumstances*, non-necessary *future things* that are, properly speaking, contingent and *free*. Indeed, they [often] announce (2) future things that are remote and *not close at*

hand, (3) indeed, things that are *many in number* and *complex*, (4) depending on *the freedom of many men* who do not intend to fulfill the prophecy (as in Christ's Crucifixion). (5) Nay, sometimes they announce miracles that depend *solely on the divine freedom* and hence cannot be foreseen without revelation, nor can be produced either naturally or fortuitously (as in Christ's Resurrection). Therefore, many prophecies can be distinguished, with the greatest of certitude, from the [mere] conjecture formed by men and spirits.

This argument is adapted to all intellects, as is the proof of God's existence on the basis of the world's order.[53]

{{117}} (2) ACCORDING TO PHILOSOPHICAL REASONING. Philosophical reasoning explains and defends the arguments of common sense, according to a resolution to the first principles of reason, and excludes explanations through the fortuitous coincidence of events or through natural necessity.

It is naturally or fortuitously *impossible* to foretell many future contingents firmly, long before their happening, with all of their minute circumstances. Many such future contingents depend on human freedom, and indeed, others are entirely extraordinary and can only be produced by the divine freedom, outside of mankind's natural expectations.

Now, in the messianic prophecies, which find their fulfillment in Christ, many things of this kind were predicted with firm certitude, at least four or five centuries before the event. For, as will be shown later on, these prophe-

---

[53] Some confirm this argument through a *computation of probabilities*. According to this computation, the probability in favor of the *fortuitous* fulfillment of the prophecies of the Old Testament is historically null. For example, as Pesch notes, if we were to suppose twenty events that were fortuitously predicted and that the probability against any given event were 10 to 1, already in two events together, you would have 100-to-1 odds that it would not happen. In three, this would increase to 1000 to 1. In twenty, it would be more than many thousands of thousands of a thousand to one. In other words, such probability would be morally null. In truth, when it comes to Christ, more than twenty clearly determined facts were predicted and fulfilled. Therefore, there is no probability that their fulfillment would have been merely fortuitous. Likewise, according to Hartmann, as regards natural finality, there was only a 15 in 10,000,000 chance that the various conditions for vision in the eye would have been coordinated without any ordering intelligence.

This computation of probabilities is founded on a given reasonable convention, though it is not necessary. (For example, it presupposes that the probability against a given foretold event is 10 to 1.) Moreover, this computation is something too quantitative / mechanical in character for resolving a problem of a higher order. Hence it does not sufficiently prove the point, for the fortuitous ordering of the world is not only morally improbable but absolutely so. Nay, it is evidently absurd, as we will say very soon, according to philosophical reasoning, which defends, through a reduction to the first principles, the absolute certitude of common sense.

cies predicted the universal propagation of monotheism (i.e., the kingdom of God),[54] the Davidic origin of the Messiah,[55] the qualities and supernatural gifts of the Messiah (Son of God,[56] Mighty God,[57] Prince of Peace,[58] judge of all,[59] and so forth), and finally, contrary to what the Jewish people were expecting, the suffering of the Messiah, his passion and disgraceful death,[60] and the conversion of the Gentiles.[61] (See our discussion below in bk. 2, sect. 3, ch. 12.)

Therefore, these predictions, so great in number, so certain, and so extraordinary, are not something fortuitous, nor something natural. No, they exceed human wisdom. And considering their object, end, circumstances, and fruits, they are not said to be diabolical but, rather, are divine, manifestly displaying the infinite foresight of God.

In order that this argument's strength may be even clearer, we must rule out two kinds of explanation—namely, (A) that they are chance in nature; (B) that they come about through natural necessity, as in the proof of the existence of God through the order of the world.

A. *How is prophecy distinguished from conjecture, which is verified fortuitously (that is, by chance happenings)? Chance is the per accidens cause of those things that rarely take place, either happily or unhappily, outside of the order of intention, as though it were intended.*[62] For example, someone digging a grave may accidentally find a treasure chest, or an arrow may accidentally kill a man as though it had been intentionally launched toward him.

Five things follow from this, by which the order of the world proves the existence of a Supreme Orderer of all things. (a) *Many things* cannot concur by chance *in order to bring about something that is essentially structured and unified (aliquid per se et unum)*, like the various conditions needed in the eye so that the act of vision may be possible. Otherwise, something unified, like vision, would be produced by a being that is *per accidens* and the perfect by the imperfect, thus meaning that the unity of an effect would lack a *raison d'être*. {{118}} (b) *From one per se principle*, there cannot arise by chance *many things that are connected in an essential and most excellent way,*

---

[54] See Isa 2:2–4; 18:7; 19:23–25; 23:15–18; 42:6–7.
[55] See Amos 9:11–12; Hos 3:3–5; Isa 11:1; Jer 23:5 and 33:14–18.
[56] See Ps 2:7.
[57] See Isa 9:5.
[58] See Isa 9:6–7.
[59] See Isa 11:3–5.
[60] See Isa 42:1–4 and 53.
[61] See Isa 54:10–11.
[62] See St. Thomas, *In* II *Phys.*, lect. 8.

as the various parts of the oak come forth from the acorn; chance (or the accidental conjunction of many things) is excluded by the simplicity of the *terminus a quo*. (c) *A fortiori, from one per se principle, something that is per se unified* cannot proceed by way of chance, like intellection from the intellective faculty or vision from the visual faculty. Chance (or the accidental conjunction of many things) is ruled out here on account of the simplicity of the *terminus a quo* and the *terminus ad quem* involved. And it is utterly manifest, in this last example, that the faculty *is ordered* to its correlative action, for potency is designated *in relation to act*, and every agent acts on account of its end. This is the principle of finality. (d) Similar things *that always or frequently take place* do not take place on account of chance, for otherwise their constancy would lack a *raison d'être*. (e) *Chance cannot be the first cause of the ordering of things*, for a *per accidens cause* presupposes the *per se* cause to which it befalls [*accidit*]. For otherwise, being *per accidens* (e.g., a musician-doctor) would be prior to the *per se*, and the order of things would come from the privation of order as well as the more would be produced from the less. (Nay, nothing is chance in relation to God but instead only in relation to other causes.[63])

These various principles, which make manifest the fact that the order of the world cannot come from chance, *proportionally* also manifest the distinction between the fulfillment of true prophecies and the fortuitous fulfillment of natural conjecture.

Indeed, (a) many things cannot concur, by chance, to bring about a unified, determinate thing, for otherwise the unity of the effect would lack a *raison d'être*. Now, in the fulfillment of many prophecies, *many things concur in order to bring about the determinately foretold thing, which is contingent and unified*. Therefore, this fulfillment is not fortuitous. For example, Christ announced his Passion and Resurrection, along with its principal circumstances. For example, in Mark 10:33–34 (DR): "Behold we go up to Jerusalem, and the Son of man shall be betrayed to the chief priests and to the scribes and ancients. And they shall condemn him to death and shall deliver him to the Gentiles. And they shall mock him and spit on him and scourge him and kill him: and the third day he shall rise again." Likewise, he foretold Peter's threefold denial, the indefectibility of the Church, and the circumstance of the destruction of Jerusalem. Similarly, the Old Testament prophets announced the various virtues of the Messiah, as well as the principal facts of his life.

(b) *From one per se principle*, there cannot arise by chance *many things*

---

[63] See *ST* I, q. 22, a. 2, ad 1.

that are connected in an essential and most excellent way. Now, from the primitive and simple promise of the Redeemer there have followed *many things that are connected in an essential and most excellent way*—namely, the series of messianic prophecies and the whole of Judeo-Christian religion, as we will show below. Therefore, this process cannot be chance in nature but, rather, is something ordered by God.

(c) *The unity of an ultimate consummation* [*unitas consummationis*], along with that of the perfection of countless souls, cannot proceed in a chance manner from one principle. Now, as we will discuss below, from the primitive promise of the Redeemer (which represents the commencement of all future prophecies), there proceeded the consummation of the whole of Judeo-Christian religion, which in Christ has come to restore to unity countless souls of good will. Therefore, this process is not chance in nature but, rather, is ordered by God.

(d) Similar things that *frequently* or always take place do not take place on account of chance. Now, the various Old Testament prophecies announce similar things, especially the Messiah / Christ and his works. Therefore, these prophecies are not fulfilled by chance.

{{119}} (e) *The whole of Judeo-Christian religion* cannot be from chance and unintended by God. Now, the whole of Jewish religion exists as a prophecy that is fulfilled in Christianity.[64] Therefore, the fulfillment of this general prophecy is not a chance occurrence. Nay, nothing is chance in relation to God but, rather, only in relation to other causes.

Hence, for the most part, true prophecies can be distinguished with the greatest certitude from conjectures that are fortuitously fulfilled.

B. *How prophecy is distinguished from conjecture, which is verified by a kind of natural necessity.* Many rationalists say the messianic hope naturally appeared in the writing of the Jews, and in a certain way, this hope created the Messiah, for the universal expectation of the Messiah so kindled their minds that when Christ appeared, his contemporaries bestowed him with the title and characteristics of the Messiah. However, he himself was at first unaware of this status but gradually persuaded himself that he was the Messiah, and his disciples, imbued with the same prejudices, strove with all of their skills to show that all of the so-called messianic prophecies were fulfilled in Jesus's life. (Such was the position held by Renan.)

---

[64] See Jules Touzard, *Comment utiliser l'argument prophétique* (Paris: Bloud, [1911]), 37–43. Also see Marie-Joseph Lagrange, "Pascal et les prophéties messianiques," *Revue biblique* (1906): 551–555.

Four things must be said against this so that our explanation may be fully filled out.

(a) Just as the order of the world cannot arise from blind necessity because, in such a case, the more perfect would be produced from what is less perfect, the greater from the lesser, and the intelligible from the unintelligible, so too the order of prophecies, as well as their fulfillment, cannot come from natural necessity, without a superior *ordering by divine providence.*

(b) Moreover, under the divine direction, the order of prophecies, as well as their fulfillment, is not natural, for what is announced is not a necessary or natural future thing, something determinately in natural causes, but, rather, *a future thing that is properly contingent and free in nature*—nay, something frequently *depending on the freedom of many* who do not intend to fulfill the prophecy, as is clear in the case of Christ's Crucifixion.

(c) Nay, the future contingent thus announced is sometimes a *miracle that depends solely on the divine freedom*, like the Incarnation of the Son of God, his Resurrection, the sending of the Holy Spirit, the marvelous propagation of the Church, and her indefectible duration. However, since miracles depend upon the divine freedom, they cannot arise from natural necessity nor from chance, and providence, which extends not only to the miracle's substance but also to its circumstances, cannot bring about a miracle that would *per accidens* verify a false prophecy, for then this latter prophecy would be admitted as being true and men would be deceived by God.

(d) Finally, as will be discussed below in bk. 2, sect. 3, ch. 12, *the messianic hope did not appear in a natural way* among the Jewish people. Nay, they were frequently unwilling to believe the prophecies and indeed killed the prophets.[65] Nor did the apostles and evangelists strive to reduce historical facts to their prejudices—namely, in order to show that in Christ's life the prophecies found their fulfillment, for this fulfillment is something completely historical, being testified to not only by the evangelists but also by other historians. {{120}} Nay, during Christ's Passion and Crucifixion, the apostles did not understand that all these things were done "so that Scripture might be fulfilled," and on the third day they were not willing to believe that Christ had risen from the dead.

Hence, many prophecies can be distinguished, with the greatest certitude, from human conjecture and from the divinations of spirits that are verified fortuitously or naturally. This certitude is strengthened through a consideration of divine providence, which cannot permit a false prophecy to be fulfilled in all the circumstances on whose basis it would be invinci-

---

[65] See Amos 7; Hos 4:5–14; Isa 28:7–13; Mic 3:5–7; Jer 9:14; 20:6, 26–29.

bly judged to be a true prophecy performed in confirmation of revelation. This cannot happen, especially if this revelation is proposed as something to be believed concerning something necessary to salvation, for God cannot permit men to be invincibly deceived in those things that are thus manifested as being entirely necessary for salvation.

§3. Certain Prophecies, Taken Separately, Can Be Distinguished from Human Conjecture or the Divination of Spirits Only with Moral Certitude

This moral certitude is had through the consideration of the various circumstances of the action (who, what, where, by what aids, why, how, and when), as was discussed above concerning the discernibility of certain third-order miracles.

In *ST* II-II, q. 172, a. 5, ad 3, St. Thomas says:

> The prophecy of demons can be distinguished from divine prophecy by certain, indeed, even external, signs. Hence John Chrysostom says (Hom. 19[66]) that "some prophesy by the spirit of the devil, such as diviners, but they may be discerned by the fact that the devil sometimes utters what is false, whereas the Holy Ghost never does." Whence, it is said in Deut 18:21–22 (DR): "If in silent thought thou answer: How shall I know the word that the Lord hath not spoken? Thou shalt have this sign: Whatsoever that same prophet foretelleth in the name of the Lord, and it cometh not to pass, that thing the Lord hath not spoken."

Therefore, one must examine whether circumstances of *weightiness, moral fittingness, and religion* are present or whether, by contrast, impiety, curiosity, and spiritual detriment to one's soul are present.[67] One must likewise consider the person who announces the future event. We know that although God can, absolutely speaking, make use of a wicked man for the good of others, in general he nonetheless only elevates good men in order to bring forth prophecies. Indeed, the wickedness of the agent does not directly

---

[66] [Trans. note: This text is, in fact, misattributed to St. John Chrysostom. It is instead an anonymous work known as *Opus imperfectum in Matthaeum*. For more information concerning this text, see *Incomplete Commentary on Matthew (Opus imperfectum)*, ed. Thomas C. Oden, trans. James A. Kellerman (Downers Grove, IL: InterVarsity Press, 2010).]

[67] As regards private revelations and prophecies, which are often uncertain, see St. John of the Cross, *The Ascent of Mount Carmel*, bk. 2, ch. 11, 14–30; bk. 3, chs. 9–12.

prove the falsity of the prophecy in question, though it arouses very strong suspicions. If, by contrast, *holiness of life* is found in the person announcing such a prophecy, deceit immediately seems to be missing from there, and it is safe and permitted that one opine that this fulfilled prophecy comes from God himself, for someone who is evil—namely, a demon—makes use of evil [men]. Hence, he who brings forward diabolic divinations is arrogant and makes an exhibition of himself in spectacles. See 2 Peter 2 concerning the punishment of pseudoprophets and wicked morals.

From all the circumstances taken together, one can have at least moral certitude concerning the divine origin of the prophecy that has been fulfilled.

§4. Resolution of Objections

{{121}} 1. *Objection*: Prophecy cannot, with certitude, be distinguished from divination, unless divination always announces false things. Now, demonic divination sometimes announces the truth, as theologians concede. Therefore, prophecy cannot be distinguished, with certainty, from divination.

Response: Prophecy can be distinguished, with certainty, from divination, even if divination sometimes announces something true, for at least on the basis of some circumstances, it is clear that this prediction does not come from God. Moreover, in general, divination is only true in a qualified sense. St. Thomas says in *ST* II-II, q. 172, a. 6:

> Just as the good is related to things, so is the true related to knowledge. Now, in things, it is impossible to find a thing which would be wholly devoid of goodness. Whence, it is also impossible for any knowledge to be wholly false, without some mixture of truth. Hence Bede says (in his commentary on Luke 17:12) that "no teaching is so false that it never mingles truth with falsehood." Hence, the teaching of the demons, by which they instruct their prophets, contains some truths that thus render it acceptable. For the intellect is led astray to falsehood by the semblance of truth, even as the will is seduced to evil by the semblance of goodness. Whence St. John Chrysostom says (Hom. 19[68]): "The devil is sometimes permitted to speak true things so that his infrequent truthfulness may gain trust for his lie."

Consequently, in his words, [the false prophet] extols philanthropy against Christian charity, the scientific spirit against the spirit of faith, liberalism against the obedience that is owed to God who reveals, merely rational moderation against Christian mortification, and so forth. The same is found in divinations.

---

[68] [Trans. note: See note 65 above.]

2. *Objection*: However, divine prophecy cannot be distinguished with certitude from conjecture or divination unless it is always fulfilled. Now, certain prophecies, even those that are divine, are not fulfilled, as Sacred Scripture itself admits. For example, Jonah, being sent by God, preached to the Ninevites: "Yet forty days and Nineveh shall be destroyed" (Jonah 3:4, DR), and nonetheless, this city was not destroyed. Likewise, Isaiah foretold the near-at-hand death of Hezekiah when he was ill, and nonetheless Hezekiah was healed (Isa 38).

Response: A prophecy that is fulfilled can be distinguished from conjecture or from divination, at least by means of the circumstances in which it is brought forward and fulfilled as was said. And then it is called a prophecy of foresight, which is the absolute prediction "of future events as they are in themselves."[69]

However, as we also said above, in the division of prophecy, there is another kind of divine prophecy—namely, prophecy of denunciation—by which "the order of the cause to the effect is announced (conditionally), an order which sometimes is imputed by other supervening things." Thus, punishment is foretold, in the form of a denunciation, in order to turn a sinner away from his sin.

In this way, as St. Thomas says (in *SCG* III, ch. 155):

> Isaiah foretold the future death of Hezekiah in accord with his order involved in his bodily condition and the lower causes related to outcome, and Jonah prophesied the destruction of Nineveh in accord with what its merits required. However, in both cases, things turned out differently, in accord with the work of God, who frees and heals. Therefore, the prophetic prediction of future events is a sufficient argument for faith, since, although men do know in advance some things concerning future occurrences, their foreknowledge concerning future contingents is not certain, as is the case for foreknowledge of prophecy. Indeed, even though prophetic revelation is sometimes fulfilled on the basis of the way that causes are ordered to a given effect, nonetheless, at the same time, or later, a revelation may be made to the same prophet concerning the outcome of the future event, as to how it is to be modified. For example, the healing of Hezekiah was revealed to Isaiah, as was the freeing of the Ninevites to Jonah.

However, God was the one who did this, as he himself says through the prophet: on account of Hezekiah's prayer and on account of the penance undertaken by the Ninevites.

Hence, at least on the basis of the circumstances involved, prophecy of denunciation can be distinguished from prophecy of foreknowledge, as well as from conjecture and divination. (See below, bk. 2, sect. 3, ch. 12, on the messianic prophecies and those of Christ himself.)

---

[69] *ST* II-II, q. 174, a. 1.

ART. 4: ON THE PROBATIVE FORCE OF PROPHECY

§1. The Church's doctrine {{122}}
§2. Rational demonstration of the probative force of prophecy
§3. Resolution of objections

§1. The Church's Doctrine

As was already said above, according to the [First] Vatican Council, prophecies are divine facts that, "[given that they] manifestly display the . . . infinite knowledge of God, are the most certain signs of the divine revelation adapted to the intelligence of all men."[70]

In this chapter of the Council's constitution, the probative force of prophecy is affirmed no less than the value of miracles, "which manifestly display the omnipotence of God." In reality, prophecy is a kind of miracle of the intellectual order, although it may be distinguished from a miracle strictly so-called, which pertains to the sensible order.

Moreover, it is declared that this probative force is adapted to the intelligence of all men. In fact, the apostles, especially St. Matthew, frequently argue from the prophecies of the Old Testament by showing that Christ's life and death were foretold in the Old Testament.

For example, see:

Matthew 1:22–23 (DR): "Now all this was done that it might be fulfilled which the Lord spoke by the prophet, saying: Behold a virgin shall be with child, and bring forth a son, and they shall call his name Emmanuel, which being interpreted is, God with us."

Matthew 8:17 (DR): "That it might be fulfilled, which was spoken by the prophet Isaias, saying: He took our infirmities, and bore our diseases."

Matthew 12:17–21 (DR): "That it might be fulfilled which was spoken by Isaias the prophet, saying: Behold my servant whom I have chosen, my beloved in whom my soul hath been well pleased. I will put my spirit upon him, and he shall shew judgment to the Gentiles. . . . The bruised reed he shall not break: and smoking flax he shall not extinguish. . . . And in his name the Gentiles shall hope."

---

[70] [First] Vatican Council, *Dei filius*, ch. 3 (Denzinger, no. 3009).

Matthew 13:13–14 (DR): "Therefore do I speak to them in parables. . . . And the prophecy of Isaias is fulfilled in them, who saith: By hearing you shall hear, and shall not understand: and seeing you shall see, and shall not perceive."

Matthew 21:4–5 (DR): "Now all this was done that it might be fulfilled which was spoken by the prophet, saying: Tell ye the daughter of Sion: Behold thy king cometh to thee, meek and sitting upon an ass and a colt, the foal of her that is used to the yoke."

Matthew 26:56 (DR): "Now all this was done that the scriptures of the prophets might be fulfilled. Then the disciples, all leaving him, fled."

John 15:25 (DR): "But that the word may be fulfilled which is written in their law: They hated me without cause."

Matthew 27:9–10 (DR): "Then was fulfilled that which was spoken by Jeremias the prophet, saying: And they took the thirty pieces of silver. . . . And they gave them unto the potter's field, as the Lord appointed to me."

Matthew 27:35 (DR): "That it might be fulfilled which was spoken by the prophet, saying: They divided my garments among them; and upon my vesture they cast lots."

§2. Rational Demonstration of the Probative Force of Prophecy

A properly divine sign (as it were, a seal properly belonging to God) confirms with the greatest certitude the divine revelation on account of which it was performed. Now, prophecy is a properly divine sign inasmuch as it can come solely from God. Therefore, prophecy performed in confirmation of revelation confirms this with utter certitude.

Indeed, prophecy *directly* and manifestly displays God's infinite knowledge, which alone extends to future contingents, just as miracles directly manifest God's divine omnipotence.

{{123}} However, like a sensible miracle, a fulfilled prophecy *indirectly* manifests the divine origin of revelation, in confirmation of which it is proposed, for otherwise God would be a false witness, placing his seal upon something confirming a counterfeit revelation. For example, the preaching and mission of Christ is divinely confirmed by the destruction of Jerusalem predicted by Christ.

However, *the connection* between a prophecy and the revelation to be confirmed is declared by the prophet either explicitly[71] or implicitly. Indeed, frequently, this connection is clear on the basis of the nature of the thing foretold when this thing intrinsically pertains to revealed religion, as when the Incarnation of the Son of God is foretold, as well as his Passion and Resurrection, the sending of the Holy Spirit, and the marvelous propagation and indefectibility of the Church.

However, sometimes prophecy, like miracles, takes place in order to confirm the holiness of some servant of God. Nevertheless, precisely speaking, the only thing that is certain in such a case is that to which the prophecy or miracle is ordered as a proof.

§3. Resolution of Objections

1. *Objection*: Prophecy proves nothing if even the wicked can prophecy. Now, in the Scriptures, we read that Balaam (Num 22) and Caiaphas (John 11:49) prophesied, even though both of them were wicked. Likewise, in Matthew 7:22–23 (DR), to those who say, "Lord, Lord, have not we prophesied in thy name," it is responded, "I never knew you." However, God knows those who are his, as is said in 2 Timothy 2. Therefore, prophecy does not have probative force.

Response: The wicked never prophesy or perform miracles in confirmation of their own wickedness or false doctrine, for otherwise God would be a witness to falsehood. However, sometimes they prophesy in commendation of the name of Christ, which they invoke, or in testimony to the holiness of some servant of God (*ST* II-II, q. 178, a. 2). Indeed, sometimes the gift of prophecy is given to men for the good of the Church alone, and in that case, it can exist without charity, for in that case, it is not ordered to the joining of the effect of the prophet himself to God but, rather, is only ordered to the use of others (*ST* II-II, q. 172, a. 4).

In general, however, God uses good persons, just as demons make use of the wicked. Nay, "prophecy requires the greatest elevation of one's mind to spiritual contemplation, which is indeed impeded through vehement passions and through inordinate occupation with external affairs" (*ST* II-II, q. 172, a. 4).

2. *Objection*: An obscure sign is not utterly certain. Now, prophecy, like faith, involves a kind of obscurity, as St. Thomas states in *ST* II-II, q. 174, a. 2, ad 3. Therefore [, it is not utterly certain.]

Response: *Prophecy involves a kind of obscurity* on account of one's distance from the

---

[71] For example, Matt 12:39–40 (DR): "An evil and adulterous generation seeketh a sign: and a sign shall not be given it, but the sign of Jonas the prophet. For as Jonas was in the whale's belly three days and three nights: so shall the Son of man be in the heart of the earth three days and three nights."

intelligible truth existing in the divine intellect and likewise because prophets are not accustomed to perceiving the future as clearly and distinctly as the present. Nay, sometimes, in prophecy, some given proximate fact is proposed as being the figure of another future and remote fact (e.g., the destruction of Jerusalem as a figure of the world's end), and one does not always clearly distinguish what pertains to the figure and what pertains to the reality. Finally, the earlier prophecies were more obscure because God only gradually revealed the messianic mystery.[72] {{124}} Moreover, another source of obscurity arises from the language used by the prophet, as well as from the circumstances in which he wrote, for these are only imperfectly known by us.

Nonetheless, prophecy remains an utterly certain sign of revelation inasmuch as it announces a complex future contingent, along with its circumstances. *A fortiori* is this the case if it foretells a future miracle that depends solely on the divine freedom (like the messianic prophecies that announce the miracles of the Messiah's life, and likewise Christ's prophecy concerning his Resurrection or concerning the propagation and indefectibility of the Church). Hence, a stronger argument is composed from all these prophecies taken together, just as in order to recognize the likeness between a man and his portrait, it is better to consider his entire picture rather than only a couple of traits, or just as in order to have a full sense of a book's meaning, one must thoroughly read and meditate on all of its parts.

This brings to a close our examination of the value of the motives of credibility that are extrinsic to religion. Take heed, however, that even if miracles and prophecies are something extrinsic to revealed religion, after the manner of a concomitant and confirmatory sign, nonetheless, many prophecies pertain intrinsically to the Christian religion, inasmuch as they announce Christ himself, his Incarnation, Passion, Resurrection, and the indefectibility of the Church. Likewise, certain miracles, such as Christ's Resurrection and Ascension, pertain intrinsically to religion and not only extrinsically, as does the healing of the man who was born blind.

Thus, we can more clearly see the harmony that exists among the various motives of credibility, whether they be internal to us (the marvelous satisfaction of all of the aspirations of the human heart), or external to us but intrinsic to religion (the marvelous life of Christ and of the Church), or extrinsic to religion (miracles and prophecies). The greater motives are those that, like the Resurrection of Christ, are at once a mystery of faith, a miracle, the fulfillment of prophecies, and the pledge of future glory.[73]

Now, however, turning to the second book of this treatise, we will take

---

[72] See *ST* II-II, q. 174, a. 6.
[73] See ch. 18 above (Concerning the subordination of the motives of credibility and the unity of apologetics).

up the question of the existence of divine revelation inasmuch as it is clear on the basis of Christ's testimony and historically confirmed by means of the various motives of credibility.

On the Existence
of Revelation

Introduction

CHAPTER ONE

On the Methodology and Division
of This Part of Apologetics

Single Article

§1. The two proposed methodologies: progressive and regressive
§2. On the value of the regressive methodology
§3. The union of the two methodologies

§1. The Two Proposed Methodologies: Progressive and Regressive

As all admit, Christianity is the most prominent religion among all the various religions found in the world today (namely, Christianity, Islam, and Buddhism). Hence, if revelation exists, it must first be sought out in Christianity. However, Christianity historically embraces within itself—as three stages—primitive religion, the Mosaic religion, and Christian religion properly so-called. Hence, in order to acknowledge the divine origin of Christianity, we can use two different kinds of methodology, either *a progressive one* or *a regressive one*—namely, beginning with a consideration of primitive religion or, by contrast, with an examination of Christianity as it is now proposed by the Catholic Church.

A. Up to the nineteenth century, many authors made use of *a progressive methodology*, proving successively and separately the divine origin (1) of primitive religion, (2) of Mosaic religion confirmed by the miracles of Moses and the prophets, and (3) of the religion of Christ and the Catholic Church. Even recently, this is the methodology used by Ottiger. {{126}} However, when this methodology is followed, this treatise comes to grow to an immense size or, otherwise, ends up leaving insufficiently unresolved countless difficulties proposed by adversaries against the Old Testament. It is better to leave the examination of these critical questions to those who are commentators on Sacred Scripture.

B. Hence, in the nineteenth century, many apologetes understandably made use of *a regressive methodology*. They began with an examination of Christ's religion, given that it is more known from our perspective. Considered in this order, the primitive testimony and *documents of the Old Testament are illuminated in light of the New Testament* through the fulfillment of the prophecies.

However, these more recent authors are divided among themselves:

(a) Many, like Brugère, intend to prove the divine origin of Christ's religion independent of any consideration of the life of the Catholic Church as it now exists. Hence, they first establish a *Christian demonstration* concerning the divinity of Christianity and then afterwards deal with the *Catholic demonstration* concerning the divine mission of the Roman Church.[1]

(b) Others, however, like Fr. Lacordaire,[2] Cardinal Deschamps,[3] and more recently Didiot,[4] *first consider the Catholic Church as it is alive today*, finding in her notes, as the [First] Vatican Council says, "a great and perpetual motive of credibility and an irrefutable testimony of her divine mission. Thus, like a 'standard lifted up among the nations' (cf. Isa 11:12), she invites to herself those who do not believe and at the same time gives greater assurance to her children that the faith that they profess rests on solid grounds."[5] Afterwards, on the basis of the Church's testimony, these apologetes then illuminate in a brighter light all the remaining historical parts of apologetics—namely, concerning Jesus Christ's life, doctrine, miracles, and the messianic prophecies. Finally, they receive from Christ's testimony the principal proof of the divine origin of the Mosaic religion and of primitive religion. This is, properly speaking, *a regressive methodology*, which can be called analytic and ascending, for it begins with the complex fact of the Church's life, then ascends to the principles of this life, whereas, by contrast, the opposite methodology is synthetic and descending.

§2. On the Value of the Regressive Methodology

This methodology is suitable (A) as regards a number of points and (B) so long as it is not proposed in an exclusive manner.

---

[1] [Trans. note: That is, the One Church, in union with the pope of Rome.]

[2] See Henri-Dominique Lacordaire, *Conférences*, vol. 1 (ed. in octavo), 201ff.

[3] Cardinal Deschamps, *La demonstration de la foi ou Entretiens sur la demonstration catholique de la revelation chrétienne* (*Oeuvres complètes*, vol. 1).

[4] Didiot, *Logique surnaturelle objective*, no. 317.

[5] [First] Vatican Council, *Dei filius*, ch. 3 (Denzinger, no. 3014).

A. *This methodology is suitable as regards a number of points.* (1) *This methodology is easier to follow inasmuch as it proceeds from currently existing realities, which are more known to us.* Thus, it is able to more greatly move souls to faith and is of the greatest use in apologetic preaching, as is clear in the conferences of Fr. Lacordaire.

(2) It is *briefer*, and, in a way, *firmer*, inasmuch as the resolution of historical and critical questions concerning the origins of Christianity are greatly corroborated through Catholic Tradition.[6]

{{127}} (3) In a way, this manner of proceeding *is conformed to the general methodology of fundamental theology*, as well as in relation to its apologetic part, which, as we said at the start of this text,[7] proceeds *under the direction of faith* and the Church's teaching.

(4) *It corrects the immoderate distinction between the Christian demonstration and the Catholic demonstration.* Indeed, this distinction really, in fact, is an argument *ad hominem*[8] to be used while arguing with Protestants. However, speaking *per se*, the Christian demonstration cannot be perfect unless it argues from the miraculous life of the Christian religion, which is nothing other than the very life of the Catholic Church manifested in her marks (*notis*). Indeed, the perfection of Christianity must not be manifested, as Protestants argue, independently from the perfection of the true Church of Christ. And by exaggerating the aforementioned distinction, many Catholic apologetes, while undertaking this Christian demonstration, nearly exclusively consider the motives of credibility that are extrinsic to religion (namely, miracles and prophecies). Hence, Protestants, especially liberal ones, have said that this [kind of] Catholic apologetics is overly extrinsic and is at fault for such "extrinsicism." Thus, proceeding in too *per accidens* a manner, these apologetes, while wishing to provide a better solu-

---

[6] See Ambroise Gardeil, "La réforme de la théologie catholique (Idée d'une methode régressive)," *Revue Thomiste* 11 (Mar. 1903): 18: "The light furnished by an isolated document drawn from the Tradition is far from adequate for illuminating everything that stirred the thoughts animating Christian consciousness in its origins. How many never-recorded things influenced its later development? And among the former, how many of them have come to us in a state which renders them acceptable for the critical historian? . . . Historical and critical documentation can indeed provide us with essays that sketch things out, hypotheses concerning the way in which things could have taken place, *true documentation*. It is impotent, however, for resurrecting *the full reality*. . . . It can say: that which is in the document exists; that which is not there is indeed perhaps true, but it does not exist for me. . . . As long as the critical question thus remains an open problem, the traditional teaching has the right to stand its ground: *melior est conditio possidentis* (the condition of the one who possesses is better)."

[7] See Prologue, ch. 2, a. 1, §3; a. 2; ch. 3.

[8] [Trans. note: That is, taking the terms of argument accepted by a given person.]

tion to certain demands raised by Protestants, nonetheless respond less well to other desires that they have.

(5) *Moreover, it is conformed to the [First] Vatican Council* inasmuch as the Council, in its treatment of revelation and faith in *Dei filius*, states, in the text cited above:

> However, to enable us to fulfil the obligation to embrace the true faith and persistently to persevere in it, God has instituted the Church through his only-begotten Son and has endowed her with manifest marks of His institution, so that she may be recognized by all men as the guardian and teacher of the revealed word.

> In fact, it is to the Catholic Church alone that belong all those signs that are so numerous and so wonderfully arranged by God to make evident the credibility of the Christian faith. In fact, the Church by herself, with her marvelous propagation, eminent holiness, and inexhaustible fruitfulness in everything that is good, with her catholic unity and invincible stability, is a great and perpetual motive of credibility and an irrefutable testimony of her divine mission. Thus, like a standard lifted up among the nations (cf. Isa 11:12), she invites to herself those who do not believe and at the same time gives greater assurance to her children that the faith that they profess rests on solid grounds.[9]

Afterwards, the Council, in its fourth session, produced another dogmatic constitution, *On the Church of Christ*, in which the intimate constitution of the Church was discussed, as well as the primacy of the Roman Pontiff. Hence, according to the order of the [First] Vatican Council, it seems better to compose a single Christian-Catholic demonstration, in which the whole of apologetics would come to its completion [*absolvitur*]. Afterwards, one must still produce the properly theological treatise on the intimate constitution of the Church, in which one must argue from faith, not solely from reason under the direction of faith, as one does in apologetics.

(6) Finally, this manner of proceeding in apologetics is *traditional, not new*, since the distinction between the Christian demonstration and the Catholic demonstration came into existence only after the appearance of Protestantism. {{128}} In defense of the divinity of Christianity, ancient apologetes always

---

[9] [First] Vatican Council, *Dei filius*, ch. 3 (Denzinger, nos. 3012–3014).

pointed out the motive[s] of credibility drawn from the Church's life.[10]

B. *This regressive method is not proposed as something exclusive.*
(1) *For, prior to speaking of the notes of the Church, the [First] Vatican Council affirms the value of the miracles and prophesies of Moses and Christ.* Indeed, it does not say that the miraculous life of the Church is the principal motive of credibility.[11] Moreover, Bautain had to subscribe to this proposition: "*Proof drawn from the miracles of Jesus Christ,* sensible and striking for the eye-witnesses, *has lost none of its force with its brilliance with regard to subsequent generations.* We find this proof with all certitude in the authenticity of the New Testament, in the oral and written tradition of all Christians."[12]

(2) In his encyclical *Providentissimus Deus*, no. 19, Leo XIII shows the *integral* authority of Sacred Scripture is not known in its full strength without the living magisterium of the Church, which, according to the word of the Council, "by its very self . . . is a kind of great and perpetual motive of credibility." However, he adds, "But since the divine and infallible magisterium of the Church rests also on the authority of Holy Scripture, the first thing to be done is to vindicate *the trustworthiness of the sacred records at least as human documents*" (no. 17). Hence, we must first argue apologetically *from the historical authority of the Gospels.*

(3) *Finally, it is more natural to set forth the historical testimony of Christ* concerning his divine mission, the mysteries to be believed, the precepts to be kept, and the institution of the Church *before considering the motives of credibility* that confirm this testimony, especially the life of the Church with her marks (*notis*). Indeed, a confirmation is more suitably proposed after the testimony to be confirmed.

§3. The Union of the Two Methodologies

It seems better to unite the regressive methodology with the progressive one, just as in many sciences the analytic (or ascending) methodology is united with the synthetic (or descending) one. This is also how we proceed in common knowledge, from the facts of experience and principles known

---

[10] Concerning this matter, see Johan Vincentius De Groot cites, in *Summa apologetica de ecclesia catholica* [(Ratisbon, 1906)], q. 1, a. 4, St. Irenaeus (*Adversus haereses*), Origen (*Contra Celsum*, praef, no. 3), St. Augustine (*De utilitate credenda*), St. Thomas (*SCG* I, ch. 6 and IV, ch. 35), Savonarola (*The Triumph of the Cross*), and among modern authors, Fr. Lacordaire and Cardinal Deschamps.

[11] See Vacant, *Études sur le Concile de Vatican*, vol. 2, 161 (Apologetics and the Vatican Council).

[12] Theses Subscribed to by Louis-Eugène Bautain by Order of His Bishop, Nov. 18, 1835, and Sept. 8, 1840, no. 3 (Denzinger, no. 2753).

by all to those things that are knowable only with greater difficulty. Hence, *we must first historically set forth Christ's own testimony* concerning his divine mission, which is more known than the testimony of Moses and the prophets and is more fundamental and lively than the declarations of the Councils. After this, *we then must hand on the motives of credibility that are more known to us*—namely, those things that remain in the miraculous life and doctrine of the Church *by which the as-yet-unbelieving man is disposed to consider miracles and prophecies from the past.*

Hence, this second part of apologetics is rightly divided as follows:

{{129}} Introduction: *On the historical authority of the Gospels.*

Section 1: *Christ's testimony* concerning his divine mission, concerning the mysteries to be believed and the precepts, as well as concerning the institution of the Church.

Section 2:
{
A. Confirmation of the testimony of Christ by motives internal to us, *based on the miraculous fulfillment of human aspirations.*

B. Confirmation of the testimony of Christ *by the sublimity of his doctrine, and the miraculous life of the Church.*
}

Section 3: Confirmation of the testimony of Christ *by his miracles and prophecies,* as well as *the prophecies in the Old Testament.*

Section 4:
{
A. Comparison of Christianity *with the Mosaic religion,* with a defense of the latter's divine origin.

B. Comparison of true Christianity *with other religions.*
}

Conclusion: *On the necessity of embracing the Catholic religion.*

CHAPTER TWO

On the Historical Authority
of the Four Gospels

Art. 1. The state of the question, the method, and opinions held
  by opponents {{130}}
Art. 2. On the authenticity and integrity of the Gospels
Art. 3. On the historicity of the Gospels

ART. 1: THE STATE OF THE QUESTION, THE METHOD, AND OPINIONS HELD BY OPPONENTS

The sources that discuss the existence, life, and teaching of Christ, indeed, having no small diffusion in the days of Christ's own life and at the dawn of Christianity, can be drawn from the pagans, the Jewish people, and Christians themselves.[1] The last are the most important, and thus we will only discuss a few of the former, indeed limiting that discussion to the first two centuries.

Pagan Testimonies
These testimonies are fewer in number. However, unjustly, adversaries have raised objections against the historical existence of Christ on the basis of the relative silence of these sources. Indeed, Palestine, on account of its limited chronicling, was very remote from the Romans and the Greeks, and in fact a complete history of the province of Syria did not exist even in Roman writings. Moreover, the life, sayings, and deeds of Christ were very foreign to the pagan mind, while, for the Romans, Christ was only one among the many people condemned as instigators. Finally, the Jewish people, with whom the Christians were more often confused at the beginning of the history of

---

[1] See Léonce de Grandmaison, *Jésus Christ* (Paris: [Beauchesne], 1931), vol. 1, 6ff; Giuseppe Ricciotti, *Vita di Gesù Cristo* (Milan: Rizzoli, 1941), 101ff.

Christianity, deserved only a little attention, according to them.

While the first century was quiet, in the second century Pliny the Younger (ca. 112) asked the emperor Trajan how he should act against the Christians in his province:

> They (the Christians) affirmed the whole of their guilt, or their error, was, that they met on a stated day before it was light, and addressed a form of prayer to Christ, as to a divinity, binding themselves by a solemn oath, not for the purposes of any wicked design, but never to commit any fraud, theft, or adultery, never to falsify their word, nor deny a trust when they should be called upon to deliver it up.[2]

At some point before AD 117, Tacitus wrote about Nero as the source of the rumor concerning the Christians' role in the burning of Rome:

> {{131}} Consequently, to get rid of the report, Nero fastened the guilt and inflicted the most exquisite tortures on a class hated for their abominations, called Christians by the populace. Christus, from whom the name had its origin, suffered the extreme penalty during the reign of Tiberius at the hands of one of our procurators, Pontius Pilatus, and a most mischievous superstition, thus checked for the moment, again broke out not only in Judaea, the first source of the evil, but even in Rome, where all things hideous and shameful from every part of the world find their center and become popular. Accordingly, an arrest was first made of all who pleaded guilty; then, upon their information, an immense multitude was convicted, not so much of the crime of firing the city, as of hatred against mankind. Mockery of every sort was added to their deaths. Covered with the skins of beasts, they were torn by dogs and perished, or were nailed to crosses, or were doomed to the flames and burnt, to serve as a nightly illumination, when daylight had expired. Nero offered his gardens for the spectacle, and was exhibiting a show in the circus, while he mingled with the people in the dress of a charioteer or stood aloft on a car. Hence, even for criminals who deserved extreme and exemplary punishment, there arose a feeling of compassion; for it was not, as it seemed, for the public good, but to glut one man's cruelty, that they were being destroyed.[3]

---

[2] Pliny the Younger, *Epist.* 10.96 (trans. William Melmoth and F. C. T. Bosanquet, Letters to Trajan, no. 97).

[3] Tacitus, *Annals*, 15.44 (trans. Alfred John Church and William Jackson Brodribb).

At around AD 120, Suetonius, referring to the same persecution as did Tacitus, says: "He likewise inflicted punishments on the Christians, a sort of people who held a new and impious superstition."[4] And in another place he states, "(Claudius) banished from Rome all the Jews, who were continually making disturbances at the instigation of one Chrestus."[5]

Eusebius (in *Ecclesiastical History*, 4.9) refers to a letter by Hadrian to Minucius Fundanus, the proconsul of Asia, in which the emperor established (in ca. AD 125) the rules concerning how one should proceed in rendering judgment against the Christians. Likewise, Christ and the Christians are named in passing in a certain letter by the same emperor (around AD 133) to the consul Servianus (Flavius Vopiscus, *Quaedrigae tyrannorum*, 8 in *Script. Hist. Aug.*).

Many sarcastic things were said about Christ and the Christians by a certain Hellenistic Semite, especially in *Peregrino* 11 and 13 (ca. AD 170), wherein the first lawgiver of the Christians is called a sophist and a magician who was crucified in Palestine. The *Letter of Mara bar Serapion* of Syria to his son Serapion (ed. Cureton, London, 1855) mentions the "Wise King" of the Jewish people, who, on account of his being murdered, were punished with the destruction of their capital, death, exile, and their dispersion, whereas he, through the laws that he established, lived on. However, we do not know the religion of the author of this letter, the source whence he drew this knowledge, and the precise time when it was written after AD 70 and before the last decade of the second century.

Jewish Testimonies

Flavius Josephus, the Jewish historian, toward AD 94, publicly wrote his *Jewish Antiquities*, in which there is found a famous testimony concerning Christ:

{{132}} Now there was about this time Jesus, a wise man, if it be lawful to call him a man; for he was a doer of wonderful works, a teacher of such men as receive the truth with pleasure. He drew over to him both many of the Jews and many of the Gentiles. He was [the] Christ. And when Pilate, at the suggestion

---

4   Suetonius, *The Lives of the Twelve Caesars* (Nero, 16; trans. Alexander Thomson and T. Forester).

5   Ibid. (Claudius, 25). Without any serious doubt, "Chrestus" here stands for "Christ" in the same way as, according to Tertullian (*Apol.*, 3) the pagans called Christians "Chrestiani," as also can be seen in the original text of the selection from Tacitus above too. The disturbance spoken of by Suetonius seems to have derived from controversies taking place between Jews and Christians, especially converts from Judaism, concerning the essential character of Christ [*qualitate Christi*], who the author erroneously thought lived in Rome at that time.

of the principal men amongst us, had condemned him to the cross, those that loved him at the first did not forsake him; for he appeared to them alive again the third day; as the divine prophets had foretold these and ten thousand other wonderful things concerning him. And the tribe of Christians, so named from him, are not extinct at this day.[6]

However, the authenticity of "the Flavian testimony" is disputed, and those who defend either its authenticity or interpolation are found equally between Catholics and non-Catholics.[7]

Talmudic Writings

The *Talmud* arose from the collections and the additions of "the traditions" (the Mishna and commentary upon it) and, following upon sure oral transmission, was finally fixed in writing in the fifth and seventh centuries. Much of what is contained in it goes back to the time of Christ, and that which pertains to him was later collected apart in the *Toledot Yeshu*. Since they are contradictory, calumnious, overly imaginative, and sarcastic—so much so that they are spurned by honest and learned Jews themselves—they do not have a historical value, though they at least bear witness to Christ's historical existence.[8]

Christian Testimonies

Beyond the canon of books contained in the New Testament, already in the second century many things were written in relation to Christ. Some of these writings, which are called "apocryphal," took on a form analogous to the New Testament, so that gospels, acts, letters, and apocalypses arose from both the impulse of devotion and frequently from heretical tendencies. However, there were other writings, called "pseudo-epigripha," taking the form of ecclesiastical documents, like constitutions, canons, [the] *Didascalia*. Finally, there were a number of so-called "sayings of Christ," which are

---

[6] Josephus, *Jewish Antiquities*, 18.3.3 (trans. William Whiston).

[7] See Ricciotti, *Flavio Giuseppi*, translation with commentary, vol. 1, app. 2 ("Testimonium Flavianum"), 173–185. The author admits the possibility of either judgment in this matter, whether on behalf of interpolation or authenticity. Indeed, he judges that the latter has greater probability of being true. No serious doubt exists concerning the authenticity of the passages concerning John the Baptist and his death (*Jewish Antiquities*, 18.5.2.) and concerning James, "the brother of Jesus who is called Christ."

[8] "Convincing as evidence against the extravagant hypothesis of a *myth of Christ* (for one does not hate, disfigure, or pursue partisanship concerning a legendary being) and, furthermore, indispensable for understanding Jesus's message, other documents drawn from Jewish origins have no right to figure in among the sources consulted concerning His life['s historical details]," Léonce de Grandmaison, *Jésus Christ*, 8.

found in the writings of the Fathers or in particular in certain codices[9] of the New Testament ("agrapha") or in papyrus scrolls ("logia"), which in general depend on the canonical books, apocryphal texts, and so forth. However, since in general these are devoid of historical value concerning Christ's life, or since there can at least be doubt concerning their independence from the books of the New Testament or from the tradition from which the written texts of the New Testament arose, this or that particular utterance having a merely probable value hardly can be brought forth as a separate argument for the historical details of Christ's life.

The principal sources from which we come to know of the teaching and the historical details of Christ's life are the books of the New Testament, among which the most important are the four Gospels. And in order to prove the existence of Christian revelation, it suffices that one vindicate the historical authority of the Gospels. {{133}} Moreover, today, adversaries no longer deny the historicity of the principal letters of St. Paul (1 Thess., Gal., [1 and 2] Cor., Rom., Phil.), and many rationalists like Harnack and Jülicher acknowledge that these letters were written from AD 49 to 59 or AD 53 to 64.

As regards the Gospels, here, we are not asking whether they are books that are inspired by God, whether they were received in the authentic canon of holy books, or whether they contain true doctrine. Rather, we are only asking whether they are historically truthful books, as regards the external facts recounted in them. However, in order to determine this, we must know (1) *whether they are genuine* / authentic (that is, written by the authors to whom they are attributed); (2) *whether they exist in their integral form* (that is, without being adulterated by later people); and (3) *whether they are historically truthful* in their recounting of the facts (in short, whether the Evangelists were neither deceived nor deceivers).

We do not wish to treat this question at length here, for it is better that it be set forth by commentators on Sacred Scripture, in the specific introduction to the New Testament.[10] Here, we will only gather together the principal arguments.

---

9   [Trans. note: Reading *codicibus* for *condicibus*.]

10   See Marius Lepin's article "Evangiles" in *Dictionnaire apologétique de la foi catholique*, vol. 1, col. 1598–1750. Also see [Rudolf] Cornley, *Introductio specialis in singulos Novi Testamenti libros* [(Paris: Lethielleux, 1886);] Alfred Durand's article "Critique biblique" in *Dictionnaire apologétique de la foi catholique*, vol. 1, 761–819; Eugène Jacquier, *Histoire des livres du Nouveau Testament* (Paris: Lecoffre, 1905). Among Protestant authors, see Frédéric Godet, *Introduction au Nouveau Testament*, vol. 2 (Neuchatel: Attinger, 1904); Hildebrand Höpfl and Benno Gut, *Introductio specialis in Novum Testamentum* (Rome: Anonima Libraria Cattolica Italiana, 1938).

§1. *Methodology*

The authenticity, integrity, and historicity of a given book can be proven either on the basis of extrinsic arguments (that is, testimonies drawn from writers at the same time or later times), or on the basis of intrinsic arguments (that is, ones drawn from the work itself, based on the way it was written or on the basis of the matters recounted therein).

(a) *Extrinsic arguments* present historical certitude concerning the authenticity of a given book, provided that the witnesses cited were substantial and that their testimony is not adulterated.

(b) *Intrinsic arguments* sometimes manifest that a given author could not have written a given book (e.g., because the way it was written pertains to a later era). However, internal notes do not suffice for positively determining the author and exact time of the composition of a given book. In general, they only provide probable certitude and, therefore, are only confirmations for external proofs.

(c) *Frequently, rationalists exaggerate the value of internal methodologies and hold external ones in scorn.* However, when internal methods are applied to a text, one's interpretation is often influenced by one's prejudices and passions, especially in determining the essential object of a given book. For example, according to Harnack, the essence of Christianity is the conception of God as the Father of all men. According to Loisy, the essence of the Gospel is the preaching of the heavenly kingdom of God that is one with the imminent end of the world. Following this arbitrary choice, the composition of the Gospels is explained on the basis of this general preconceived idea. Thus, Loisy excludes from the primitive Gospel whatever the Synoptic Gospels and the Gospel of John say concerning the institution of the Church, for according to him, Christ announced the imminent end of the world and did not intend to establish a Church. Moreover, by means of an internal method, we do not sufficiently know the "mentality" of the author so as to determine what does or does not pertain to the integrity of the books. Hence, it is not surprising that hypercritical people, who, as it were, exclusively make use of this method, arrive at contradictory conclusions. More often it is the case that they accept as being certain something that is only slightly probable. Nay, they wish to arrive at fully scientific knowledge through a way that leads only to probability. In this way of proceeding, *hypercriticism* appears as being *a lack of critical awareness*. The extremes touch each other.

{{134}} In his encyclical *Providentissimus Deus*, Leo XII states:

Professors of Sacred Scripture and theologians . . . with a similar
object in view, should make themselves well and thoroughly
acquainted with the art of true criticism. There has arisen, to the
great detriment of religion, an inept method, dignified by the name
of the "higher criticism," which pretends to judge of the origin,
integrity and authority of each Book from internal indications
alone. It is clear, on the other hand, that in historical questions,
such as the origin and the handing down of writings, the witness of
history is of primary importance, and that historical investigation
should be made with the utmost care; and that in this matter internal evidence is seldom of great value, except as confirmation . . . and
this vaunted "higher criticism" will resolve itself into the reflection
of the bias and the prejudice of the critics.[11]

§2. The Positions Held by Adversaries

Rationalists and many liberal Protestants judge historical facts on the basis of
their philosophical and subjective biases, holding *a priori* that the supernatural
does not exist or cannot be known, hence meaning that the supernatural facts
recounted in the Gospels cannot be true. However, according to them, all
facts must be explained in accord with natural laws and the natural progress
of human awareness. We refuted this principal of biblical rationalism earlier
when we discussed philosophical rationalism.

Following the exclusion of any possible supernatural element, in order
to determine the truth contained in the Gospel, these adversaries make
nearly exclusive recourse to the internal methodology, as seems fitting to a
subjectivist outlook.

Thus, by means of various systems of thought, they have striven to

---

[11] Leo XIII, *Providentissimus Deus*, no. 17 (Denzinger, no. 3286). Also see what is said about
modernist exegesis in Pius X, *Pascendi*, nos. 9, 18, and 34 (Denzinger, nos. 3479, 2086 [old],
2100 [old]). In the final text, we read: "The Modernists have no hesitation in affirming commonly that these books, and especially the Pentateuch and the first three Gospels, have been
gradually formed by additions to a primitive brief narration. . . . This means, briefly that we
must admit a *vital evolution*, springing from and corresponding with evolution of faith. The
traces of this evolution, they tell us, are so visible in the books that one might almost write a
history of them. Indeed, this history they do actually write, and with such an easy security that
one might believe them to have with their own eyes seen the writers at work through the ages
amplifying the Sacred Books. . . . They seem, in fact, to have constructed for themselves certain
types of narration and discourses, upon which they base their decision as to whether a thing is
out of place or not."

weaken the historicity of the Gospels:[12]

(a) THE FRAUD THEORY, which was stirred up by Hermann Samuel Reimarus (1694–1768): Christ was merely a man, a political agitator, who wished to free the Jewish people from the yoke of the Romans. With the rebellion having been rendered vain, with Christ dying as a rebel, his disciples changed his original intention and held forth Christ as someone beginning a spiritual renewal, freeing the whole of humanity through his death. {{135}} Hence, the historical facts were adulterated in accord with the new preconceived system, with many false things being invented (such as Christ's Resurrection) and other true ones being omitted, which they transformed into an adulterated history when they wrote the Gospels.

(b) NATURALISM: The fraud-hypothesis was rejected in general, for it cannot explain the effects of Christianity by appealing to so great an act of fraud. It was followed by naturalism, which was argued on behalf of by Heinrich Eberhard Gottlob Paulus (1761–1851), under the name of "rationalism": All supernatural things, which exceed the capacity of reason, are here eliminated by means of an explanation of the natural tendency in man, by which historical facts, especially extraordinary ones, and men of great abilities are exaggerated by tradition and transformed into legends, above all in Oriental writings. Therefore, Paulus himself admitted that there are natural facts in the Gospels, as a kind of historical nucleus, but all supernatural things, like Christ's miracles, are explained by the legendary tendency found in the Gospels. Thus, for example, Jesus did not multiply the loaves but, rather, had a few that he distributed, thus providing an example encouraging others to do likewise. Similarly, Christ did not walk on the water but, rather, only walked next to the water. Similarly, the dead people who, according to the Gospel, were supposedly dead and then raised to life were in fact only suffering from extreme drowsiness. And so forth.

(c) MYTHISM was proposed by David Friedrich Strauss (1808–1874), who, mocking the natural explanation proposed by Paulus, intended to prove that the Gospel accounts of miracles, the fulfillment of the prophecies and messianic expectations, and so forth, were all myths (personifications of a religious idea reduced to a historical form or conjoined with some historical person), gradually formed through a period of approximately 150 years after the death of Christ. These accounts were written under the falsified names

---

[12] Also see Marie-Joseph Lagrange, *Le sens du christianisme d'après l'exégèse allemande* (Paris: Gabalda, 1918); Léonce de Grandmaison, *Jésus Christ*, vol. 2, 130–218 (The Problem of Jesus); François-Marie Braun, *Où en est le problème de Jésus?* (Paris: Lecoffre, 1932); Giuseppe Ricciotti, *Vita di Gesù Cristo*, §§194–224 (The rationalistic interpretation of Jesus's life).

of the Apostles so that they might receive greater veneration. Very few of the particular details related in the Gospels pertain to the historical Christ; the remaining are ultimately reduced to an idealized Christ fashioned by the imagination of primitive Christianity.

Like the preceding systems, this form of mythism is commonly rejected by rationalists [today].

(d) The EVOLUTIONISM of the school of Tübingen, having as its author Ferdinand Christian Baur (1792–1860), in accord with the principles of Hegelian philosophy, proposed a system of tendencies: In a quasi-*a priori* manner, Baur believed that Christianity represents the necessary synthesis of two opposed tendencies, in accord with the Hegelian law of progress: Thesis and synthesis are reconciled in a higher synthesis. The sign of primitive contradiction supposedly would have been found in the debate between Peter and Paul spoken of in Galatians 2:14. Although this debate was concerned with a merely disciplinary matter, Baur concluded that the doctrine of St. Paul, who preached a universal form of Christianity, was utterly opposed to Peter's doctrine, which intended only the propagation and reformation of Judaism. Hence, the first Gospel written was that of Matthew, for it favors Petrinism (thesis). Then, the Gospel according to Luke was written, in which the Pauline tendency comes to light (antithesis). Finally, there were the Gospels according to Mark and John, which were attempts at a reconciliation (or a higher synthesis). In order to find the time needed for the aforementioned evolution (and this is the sole reason [for such speculations]), the New Testament writings were placed at a later time, and those that did not harmonize with this evolutionary schema were rejected as being non-authentic writings. Thus, according to him, the Gospel according to Matthew was not written before AD 130 and the Gospel according to Luke not before AD 150. The Gospel according to Mark and the Acts of the Apostles, which display a kind of neutral and reconciliatory spirit, thus were edited in an even later era. {{136}} Finally, the Gospel according to John was composed at around AD 170, while the only Pauline letters that were admitted as being authentic were those to the Romans and 1 and 2 Corinthians. Among those who belonged to this Tübingen School were Eduard Zeller, Albert Schwegler, [Karl Reinhold] Köstlin, and others.

Bruno Bauer (1809–1882) in a still more radical manner denied the historicity of all the books of the New Testament and, in the end, came to deny the historical existence of Christ.

(e) THE LIBERAL SCHOOL attempted a reconciliation between the traditional position and radicalism. Thus, Th[eodor] Zahn and B[ernhard] Weiss tended more so toward the first, whereas D[aniel] Schenkel, W[illibald]

Beyschlag, K[arl] H[einrick] Weizsächker, [Karl] Th[eodor] Keim, and Julius Wellhausen stirred up the latter position, while Heinrich Julius Holtzmann (d. 1910) represents the entire school, whose conclusions were repeated by Adolf von Harnack (1851–1930).

Having denied the historical value of the fourth Gospel, they held that the first Synoptic Gospel written was that of Mark (a position already put forward by Bauer), positing that it was written before AD 70, while some thought that there must have been some proto-Marcan text. Thus, the Gospels of Matthew and Luke would depend upon Mark. As regards the words of the Lord that are not found in Mark, according to von Harnack the sources for such dicta are found in various *Logia* that were composed by the Apostle Matthew around AD 50. They safeguarded the historical value of the Synoptic Gospels, with the exception of the first chapters of the Gospels of Matthew and Luke concerning Christ's infancy, as well as the miracle accounts, given that miracles are either natural, exaggerated facts, or words or psychological facts given a sensible representation, or things imagined in fulfillment of the Old Testament prophecies, brought about under Christ's spiritual influence, or, otherwise, things that we cannot explain. According to the liberal school, Christ, who was a mere man, preached a new moral doctrine, built upon the idea of a Father-God in heaven and fraternal charity. The kingdom of God that he announced was only purely spiritual and internal. Christ was the Son of God in a purely moral sense, just like other men; however, he understood God's paternity earlier and more fully than others. His messiahship is denied by some and admitted by others, who still do not agree about his nature [*qualitate*].

In France, we must also number among the members of this school people like A[lbert] Réville, É[douard Guillaume Eugène] Reus[s], [Louis] A[uguste] Sabatier, and others. Ernest Renan (1823–1892) declared himself to be an adversary of this school; however, he reached basically the same conclusions concerning the person of Christ and his miracles. According to Harnack, the Gospel of Mark was written in AD 65–70 by a disciple of Peter, the Gospel of Luke in 78–83 (nay, perhaps, in 60–70) and is genuine, the Gospel of Matthew in 70–75 by an unknown author, and the Gospel of John in 80–110, by some priest name John.

(f) ESCHATOLOGICAL MESSIANISM, which was argued on behalf of by J[ohann] Weiss (1892, 1900), A[lbert] Schweitzer (1906, 1913), and Alfred Loisy (1900, 1907): Christ, himself sharing in his era's apocalyptic ideas concerning the Messiah, announced a kingdom of God that was soon to come, which would be established in the world by God in his glory, following upon the tempestuous destruction of the wicked ruler of this age, setting up a kingdom of justice and happiness under the divine dominion. {{137}} And therefore, Christ's moral doctrine was only "for the time being." When his preaching was rejected by his contemporaries, Christ persuaded himself that his death would be able to accelerate the coming of the kingdom and that by means of it he himself would enter into messianic glory, and that he thence would return as Messiah on the clouds of heaven so as to judge the good and the evil and inaugurate the kingdom among those who are good (Weiss). According to Schweitzer, the eschatological idea took possession not only of Christ's doctrine but even of his whole life. At the beginning, he hid *the secret* of his messiahship (Wrede), preaching in parables because the common expectation was that the Messiah would be unknown in his preparation and must be rejected; however, in the end, before the Sanhedrin, he openly declared himself to be the Messiah and for this reason suffered death in order to save those whom he was to redeem. This teaching was accepted in summary form by Alfred Loisy and the modernists.

Here, the fourth Gospel is denied all historical value. Likewise, everything found in the Synoptic Gospels that is at variance with their eschatological idea, like the idea that the Church is a society instituted for future generations, is rejected as something being invented by the first Christians and falsely attributed to the historical Christ.

As is obvious, this historical school is rather arbitrary in its discernment of the historical elements of the Gospel and, above all, contradicts the rabbinical tradition, which held that the expected messianic era is not an eternal kingdom of felicity at the end of this world but, rather, was to be a historical era existing a rather long time [*satis diurnum*] prior to the future age, though still pertaining to this world. Nonetheless, this rather arbitrary school is still predominant in the writings of contemporary adversaries [to orthodox Catholicism].[13]

(g) THE METHOD OF HISTORICAL COMPARISON OF RELIGIONS: The books of the New Testament are documents coming from the primitive

---

[13] R[obert] Eisler (1929ff), giving new life to the teaching that was proposed once upon a time by Hermann Samuel Reimarus, argued on behalf of the idea of a *political messianism*, holding that Christ, as the leader of a seditious rebel band, first advocated only passive resistance against Roman domination, though ultimately endorsed strength of arms. When his followers were routed, he himself took refuge upon the Mount of Olives and afterwards was captured and punished with death for his seditious actions. Likewise, certain socialists hold that Christ was the prototype of rebels and as such was crushed with death by the public power. The religion founded by him was proletarian in nature, as a kind of communism (Karl Kautsky, 1908). According to others, however, Christ was neither a socialist nor a seditious rebel, but rather, a kind of early sprout in his teaching led to the development of Communism.

[Christian] tradition, which nonetheless not only underwent influence from the Old Testament (as David Friedrich Strauss already taught) but above all were influenced by prior and contemporary eastern religions, especially those in the Hellenistic world, as well as mystery cults. R[udolf] Seydel (1882ff), A[lbert] Edmunds (1902ff), and Gustaaf Adolf van den Bergh van Eysinga (1901) argued that *Buddhism* exercised such an influence. Other influences were argued on behalf of by others as well. Thus F[ranz-Valéry-Marie] Cumont (1896, 1900) invoked *Mithraism*, R[ichard August] Reitzenstein *Hermeticism* (1904) and *Hellenistic mystical religions* (1910), W[ilhelm] Brandt (1889ff) *Mandaeism*, and Wilhelm Bousset (1907) *Gnosticism*. Such explanations were also offered for St. Paul's teaching concerning the Spirit, grace, and the sacraments, especially those regarding Baptism and the Eucharist. Likewise, Alfred Loisy (1919) wrote of the great influence exercised by Hellenistic mystery religions upon St. Paul's Christianity.

The historical existence of Christ that had already been denied and reduced to a kind of solar myth (in Charles François Dupuis, 1742–1809) or an astral myth (in Constantin François de Volney, 1757–1820) {{138}} is now again reduced to the *myth of Jesus* (Joshua), continuously preserved in the ancient people of Israel (J[ohn] M[ackinnon] Robertson, 1900, 1902, 1910), or to the mystical cult of a certain pre-Christian *Jesus* existing both within and also outside of the Jewish people—which helps to explain the rapid propagation of the Christian religion (W. B. Smith, 1906, 1911)—or to the myth of the Babylonian god *Gilgamesh* (P[eter] Jensen, 1906, 1910), or to various myths all at the same time ([Andrew] Drews, 1909, 1928), or to the general idea of *"the divine being"* which gradually developed, having its reality only in the minds of those who believe (P[aul]-L[ouis] Couchoud, 1924).

This school of thought enjoys a number of followers in our own days.[14]

---

[14] Most recently, A[lfred] Rosenberg (1930ff), a defender of nationally rooted religion, rejecting the Old Testament as being a merely Jewish work (*Judenbible*), believes that the New Testament must be corrected of a great number of false elements coming from Palestine, Asia Minor, Syria, and Africa, elements that impede the recognition of the great personality of Christ. According to him, the great figure of Christ, which is presumed to be the type of the Nordic and Arian stock, nonetheless was neither the Son of God nor the Savior, and immediately after his death he came to be wrapped up in the Christian legends, superstitious stories, and sensual mysteries, like the story of the virginal birth, Christ's bodily Resurrection, his descent into hades, his ascent into heaven, the demonic obsessions recounted in the Gospels, his miracles, and the Christ-myth (a certain legend from Asia Minor concerning some Christ, someone who would free the slaves, a legend that came to be joined, in Palestine, with the messianic idea), which coalesced with which perverse Etruscan elements in Rome. Others of the same propensity have completely rejected Christ as being Jewish, like Mathilde Ludendorff

On the basis of the prejudiced opinion concerning the substantial dependence of the Gospels and the whole New Testament upon other religions, it flippantly discerns that supposed likenesses are to be found. However, the likenesses that do indeed exist can be easily explained by ideas that are, in fact, common to all men, being founded on the unity of human nature, on the basis of the natural fact that the same ideas and themes are expressed in the same words, on the basis of the analogy of the state of things, all of which remain unmoved in the midst of the substantial differences between Christianity and other religions. Nay, sometimes these adversaries make Christianity depend upon some religion that historically came after it, as is openly conceded in the case of Mandaeism today. The most ancient documents of Buddhism in a form that is accessible to us also come after Christianity, so that the influence of Christianity is possible within them, whereas the contrary cannot be proven.[15]

(h) THE MORPHOLOGICAL / FORM-HISTORY SCHOOL (*Formgeschichtliche Schule*): The Gospels do not immediately reach back to Christ and his life but, rather, were written by some redactor, who more or less perfectly gathered together, with some reason and in an artificial order, the oral tradition coming from a collective author—namely, primitive Christianity. This ecclesiastical catechesis of the Christian community developed as something that ultimately was fabricated, coming forth from the immanent life of the community and its own proper exigencies. Thus, for example, the accounts of Christ's baptism were invented as justifications for the Christians' baptismal ritual; the disciples' judgment concerning the Old Law was invented in order to drive home the new manner of living necessary for Christians in relation to the synagogue; and so too was the account of the apostles' calling written in order to attest to the authority of the apostles. {{139}} Therefore, those who are partisans of this methodology—such as K[arl] L[udwig] Schmidt (1919, 1923), M[artin] Dibelius (1919, 1926, 1933, and 1935), Rudolf Bultmann (1921, 1925, 1926, 1930), M[artin] Albertz (1921), and G[eorg] Bertram (1922 and 1928)—strive after this "paleontological Gospel" in order to determine the laws by which commonly, in oral tradition, the various *forms* of popular literature appear. Then, the parts of the Gospels are compared with these "infra-literary" forms, with which they are evaluated to possess even a common character and worth. Thus, they

---

(1933), who argues that Christianity has the effect of leading to idleness, hatred, wrathful cupidity, and other things. See "Amtliche Beilage: Studien zum Mythus des XX jahrhunderts," *Amtsblatt des [B]ischöflichen Ordinariats Berlin*, 1935, no. 2; also see the "Epiloge" for 1935.

[15] M. Ribaud, "Le bouddhisme et l'évangile" *Revue apologetique* 42 (1936): 68–87 and 150–157.

arrive at the classification of various forms such as apophthegmatic texts, paradigms, news-narratives, *paranesis* / exhortations, miracle-tales, legends, decrees [*sententia*], parables, and so forth. Finally, they show the various relations all these different parts of the Gospels have with the primitive life of the Church, such as the preaching, apologetic [*sic*] worship, and so forth, which will come to inspire the Gospel tradition.

The defenders of this outlook generally admit that Christ existed historically. However, they hold that very few truly historical elements [of his life] can be discerned, and then only with difficulty. Many followers of this methodology are found today in the eschatological school, as well as the historical-comparative school.

These are the principal schools of modern rationalists who have discussed the Gospels. As is clear from our survey, they all proceed along their various interpretive paths by using rather arbitrary methodologies. Hence, they perpetually change their positions. They only agree concerning a general principle, which we refuted earlier, though the whole of their criticism and exegesis depends on it: the denial of the supernatural order and of the possibility that God would intervene miraculously in the world.

However, presupposing the refutation of this false principle, we must now discuss the authenticity and integrity of the Gospels, gathering together the principal conclusions reached by Catholic critics.[16]

§3. The Church's Declarations

On July 3, 1907, in the decree *Lamentabili*, the Holy Office [of the Inquisition] condemned many of the modernists' propositions concerning this question. See nos. 12–18 (Denzinger, nos. 3415–3418), especially: "Until the time the canon was defined and constituted, the Gospels were increased by additions and corrections. Therefore, there remained in them only a faint and uncertain trace of the doctrine of Christ" (no. 15); "the narrations of John are not properly history but [rather] a mystical contemplation of the Gospel" (no. 16); "the fourth Gospel exaggerated miracles" (no. 17); "John claims for himself the quality of witness concerning Christ. In reality, however, he is only a distinguished witness of the Christian life, or of the lie

---

[16] See Pierre Batiffol, *Orpheus et l'évangile* (1910). This text contains an exposition and criticism of a number of these theories. For instance, see the chapter, "The Gospels: The Authenticity of Jesus's Discourses." Also see Marie-Joseph Lagrange, *Le sens du christianisme d'après l'exégèse allemande* (1918). In this book, Fr. Lagrange examines these various theories held by more recent rationalists and compares them with Catholic exegetical principles.

of Christ in the Church at the close of the first century" (no. 18).

The Pontifical Biblical Commission declared on June 19, 1911, and June 26, 1912, the authenticity, compositional time,[17] and *historicity of the Synoptic Gospels* (i.e., the Gospels according to Matthew, Mark, and Luke). {{140}} *As regards the synoptic question* (that is, the mutual relations among the first three Gospels), the same Commission affirms it is permitted that exegetes dispute these matters and appeal to hypothesis concerning traditions, whether written or oral, or even to speak about the dependence of one Gospel upon an earlier one or ones. However, it responded negatively to the following question: "Is what has been laid down above to be considered as observed by those who, unsupported by any testimony of tradition or by any historical evidence, readily endorse the so-called 'two-source' hypothesis, which strives to explain the composition of the Greek Gospel of Matthew and the Gospel of Luke mainly by their dependence upon the Gospel of Mark and the so-called collection of 'Sayings of the Lord'; and can they, therefore, freely advocate it?"[18]

Earlier, on May 29, 1907, the same Commission declared, with the approval of the Sacred Pontiff, that the *authenticity and historicity of the Fourth Gospel* is solidly proven by the historical arguments offered by tradition and is also confirmed by intrinsic arguments, notwithstanding the ways that this Gospel differs from the Synoptic Gospels.[19]

Art. 2: On the Authenticity and Integrity of the Gospels

By means of both extrinsic and intrinsic arguments, we can prove that the four Gospels were written by the authors whose names appear upon them—

---

[17] On June 26, 1912, the *Commission* responded negatively to both parts of the following questions (Denzinger, no. 3572): "*With regard to the chronological order* of the Gospels, is it permitted to depart from the opinion confirmed by the very ancient as well as the constant testimony of tradition that, after *Matthew*, who, as the first of all, wrote his Gospel *in his native language*, *Mark* wrote second in order, and *Luke* third; or on the other hand, is this opinion to be regarded as being opposed to that which asserts that the second and third Gospels were composed before the Greek translation of the first Gospel?"

Similarly, it responded *negatively* to both parts of the next question as well (Denzinger, no. 3573): "May the date of the composition of the Gospels of Mark and Luke be deferred up to the destruction of the city of Jerusalem; or can it at least be held, from the fact that in Luke the prophecy of the Lord concerning the destruction of this city seems to be more definite, that his Gospel was written after the siege had been begun?" See *Acta Apostolicae Sedis* (1912), 464.

[18] Ibid. (Denzinger, no. 3578).

[19] See Denzinger, no. 3398.

namely, by the two apostles Matthew and John and the two disciples of the apostles, St. Peter's disciple Mark and St. Paul's associate Luke.

§1. Extrinsic Arguments

Already in the third century, adversaries conceded that there was unanimous consensus concerning the authenticity of the Gospels. There also remains the testimony of the Apostolic Fathers, as well as that of other ecclesiastical authors—nay, even that of heretics and pagans as well.[20]

The testimonies of the first Fathers are fewer in number. Indeed, their writings were composed on given, particular occasions, which rarely provided an opportunity for citations from the Gospels. Nor were such references to the written Gospel greatly desired during these first days, when there still were people alive who knew the apostles and their disciples, and when oral tradition [concerning Christ] was still very strong. In particular, it is more difficult to discern in these first testimonies attestations to St. Mark's brief Gospel, since the allusions made to it are shared with the texts of the Gospels of Matthew and Luke, {{141}} and allusions that are proper only to it hardly ever appear. Hence, we will not cite it in these earlier testimonies.

The teaching of the twelve apostles (*The Didache*), ca. 80–100, was probably written in Syria and often more or less expressly alludes to Matthew and probably also to Luke.

In the Letter of Pope St. Clement to the Corinthians (ca. 95), Matthew is cited with sufficient clarity and has something very similar from St. Luke [as well].

The Letter of Pseudo-Barnabas (ca. 100), probably written in Alexandria, certainly cites St. Matthew, and a number of things in it (both ideas and words) perhaps presuppose knowledge of St. John.

Among Eastern Christians, in his letters, *the martyr St. Ignatius of Antioch* († 107) borrows equally from St. Matthew and St. John. He probably was also aware of St. Luke, and in response to certain Christians who perhaps were stirring up difficulties about certain doctrines, he expressly refers to a written Gospel in 8.2 of his *Letter to the Philadelphians*.

The letter of St. Polycarp to the Philippians (written a little bit after 107), composed by a man who still as a boy saw and heard St. John the Apostle, later becoming the bishop of Smyrna (Eusebius, *Historia ecclesiastica*, 5.24),

---

[20] Concerning all of these matters, see Franz Xaver von Funk, *Patres apostolici* (Tubingen: Laupp, 1901), vol. 1, 640–651; Lepin's article "Evangiles canoniques" in *Dictionnaire apologétique de la foi catholique*, col. 1605; Hildebrand Höpfl and Benno Gut, *Introductio specialis in Novum Testamentum* (Rome: Anonima Libraria Cattolica Italiana, 1938).

borrowed a number of things from SS. Matthew and Luke. Based on his use of the letters of St. John, one can also persuasively argue that he also had knowledge of his Gospel at the time when he wrote these letters.

The Shepherd of Hermas (ca. 150) seems to be familiar with all four Gospels, given his various allusions.[21]

The Second Letter to the Corinthians (written ca. 150), which was once upon a time falsely attributed to Clement of Rome, exhibits traces of SS. Matthew and Luke.

The Martyrdom of St. Polycarp, composed ca. 156 by a certain Marcion in the Church of Smyrna, makes allusion to SS. Matthew and John.

The Letter of the Churches of Lyon and Vienna, sent in 177 to the Churches of Asia and Phyrigia, argue that the Gospels of Luke and John were known in the Church in Gaul.

The Letter of St. Polycrates, the bishop of Ephesus, sent ca. 190 to Pope Victor, indicates knowledge of the Gospel of St. John.

The aforementioned testimonies allude to and cite the Gospels, without however naming them. However, the next testimonies mention the Gospels and their authors.

Papias, the bishop of the church in Hierapolis in Phrygia (Eusebius, *Hist. Eccl.*, 3.36), someone who heard John and was a companion of Polycarp, as a very old man (St. Irenaeus, *Adv. haer.* 5.33) wrote around 120 his *De explanatione sermonum Domini* in five books. His testimony is of the greatest importance, for it calls upon apostolic tradition, which he claims to have either immediately from the priests (according to many, this term refers to the apostles themselves and Christ's disciples) or by means of their disciples. In his surviving fragments of his works, he explicitly presents testimony to St. Matthew and St. Mark, not, as it were, by demonstrating that they are authors (something that seems to have been uncontroverted) but, rather, referring to their manner of writing and defending St. Mark, if one were to raise certain concerns regarding the ordering and integrity of his Gospel. In speaking of St. Mark, he says:

{{142}} And the presbyter (namely, John, according to many the Apostle himself) said this. Mark having become the interpreter of Peter, wrote down accurately whatsoever he remembered. It was not, however, in exact order that he related the sayings or deeds of Christ. For he neither heard the Lord nor accompanied Him. But afterwards, as I said, he accompanied Peter, who

[21] In this work, the following texts are cited: Matt 10:39; 13:38; 16:27; 19:17; 21:22; 28:18; Mark 9:47; 10:11, 23, 24; Luke 6:9; 9:24; 17:33; John 3:5; 10:13; 12:25, etc.

accommodated his instructions to the necessities [of his hearers], but with no intention of giving a regular narrative of the Lord's sayings. Wherefore Mark made no mistake in thus writing some things as he remembered them. For of one thing he took special care, not to omit anything he had heard, and not to put anything fictitious into the statements.[22]

However, concerning Matthew, he makes the following observations:

Matthew put together the oracles [of the Lord] (namely, the Gospels) in the Hebrew language, and each one interpreted them as best he could.[23]

St. Justin, a witness of both the East and the West, in *Apology* 1.66ff (ca. 155) testifies that in their gatherings on Sundays Christians read the writings of the prophets and the commentaries of the apostles, which are called *Gospels*. In his *Dialogue with Trypho*, in no. 103, he affirms that these Gospels were written by the Apostles and disciples. That this Gospel is the same as the four canonical books is manifestly clear based on countless allusions and citations that he makes, like more than twenty verses cited from the Sermon on the Mount. Moreover, he brings forth the messianic prophecies as they are in the First Gospel. He refers to the Annunciation and to a number of details of Christ's birth, which are only found in Luke. It seems that his writing even contains something drawn from Mark alone, as in the imposition of the surname "Boanerges" upon the sons of Zebedee. And his Christology, as well as a number of the formulas he deploys, presupposes the Gospel according to John. Hence, a number of rationalists hold that he had the three Synoptic Gospels before his eyes.

Tatian, a Syrian and disciple of St. Justin, though later a heretic, wove together in Syriac, around 170, a unified harmony of the four Gospels, called the *Diatessaron*.

St. Theophilus, the bishop of Antioch, in his *Apologia ad Autolycum*, ca. 180, in addition to citations of Matthew and an allusion to Luke, is the first to name John as the author of the fourth Gospel:

And hence the holy writings teach us, and all the spirit-bearing [inspired] men, one of whom, John, says, In the beginning was the Word, and the Word was with God, etc.[24]

---

[22] Papias, *Fragments*, 6 (trans. Alexander Roberts and James Donaldson).

[23] Ibid.

[24] Theophilus of Antioch, *Ad Autolycum*, 2.2 (trans. Marcus Dodds). See Marie Joseph Roüet de

St. Irenaeus, in his book *Against Heresies*, written in the final decades of the second century, brings forward very clear testimony concerning the four Gospels, whose authors he names, likewise assigning times to their composition:

> *Matthew* also issued a written Gospel among the Hebrews in their own dialect, while Peter and Paul were preaching at Rome, and laying the foundations of the Church. After their departure, *Mark*, the disciple and interpreter of Peter, did also hand down to us in writing what had been preached by Peter. *Luke* also, the companion of Paul, recorded in a book the Gospel preached by him. Afterwards, *John*, the disciple of the Lord, who also had leaned upon His breast, did himself publish a Gospel during his residence at Ephesus in Asia.[25]

{{143}} Now, the most distinguished witness is St. Irenaeus, on account of his erudition and intimate relationship with Polycarp, as well as with other immediate disciples of the apostles. Born in Asia, he stayed in Rome and was the bishop of Lyons. Hence, he is held to be an illustrious witness to the whole Church.

The *fragment* discovered by *Ludovico Muratori*, redacted [perhaps] in around AD 200, enumerates, among the inspired books recognized by the Roman Church in the second century:

> The third Gospel, the book according to *Luke*. Luke, himself a doctor, following upon Christ's ascension, having been taken up by Paul as someone zealous for the law, wrote in his own name, on the basis of (the general) opinion. . . . *The fourth* of the Gospels, is that of John, one of His disciples.[26]

However, nobody doubts that the Gospels of Matthew and Mark are discussed in the lines missing from this mutilated fragment.

Finally, at the beginning of the third century, *Tertullian*, an African, in his *Adversus Marcionem*, bk. 4, chs. 2 and 5 (written ca. 208) holds that it is beyond controversy to say that the Church had the four Gospels already at the time of the apostles.

Clement of Alexandria, in *Stromata* 3.13 and 1.21 (ca. 190) cites the names of the four Evangelists and distinguishes their books from apocryphal gospels.

Journel, *Enchiridion patristicum* (Freiburg: Herder, 1937), 11.182.

[25] Irenaeus, *Adv. haeres.*, 3.1.1 (PG 7, 844, trans. Alexander Roberts and William Rambaut).

[26] See PL 2, 173.

In his first *Homily on Luke, Origen* speaks like Irenaeus and affirms that these four Gospels are the only Gospels approved by the Church, naming their authors. Now, here we already see, whatever rationalists may say, the Church's critical sense, which rejected all of the apocryphal gospels. Indeed, from this time onward, there is a unanimous consensus concerning the authenticity of the four Gospels, as all profess.

AMONG THE HERETICS, especially *the Gnostics*, many admitted the authenticity of the four Gospels, from which they wished to erect their teaching concerning the *Aeons* (thus, *Basilides* and *Valentinus*). *Marcion* also chose St. Luke's Gospel as being the expression of the pristine doctrine rightly exposited by St. Paul.

Finally, among the pagans, as Origen indicates,[27] *Celsus* said that he knew many heretics who changed the Gospels in order to defend their errors.

The various *apocryphal gospels*, written in the second century, indirectly demonstrate the existence of the Gospels, whose narratives they imitate, filling out certain desiderata either out of piety or heretical intentions.

The authenticity of the Gospels is also confirmed on the basis of *textual history*. Indeed, *papyri* presenting certain Gospels go back to the second and third centuries. Likewise, there are the *Codex Sinaiticus* and *Codex Vaticanus B* going back to the fourth century.[28] Going back to the fifth century, there is *Alexandrinus A* and *Ephraem[i] C*. Versions of the *Old Latin* translation go back to the second half of the second century. *In Syriac*, there are the *Diatessaron* and *Evangeliorum separatorum* at the end of second and third centuries respectively. *Coptic* texts are found at the end of second century. *Gothic* texts are found at the middle of the fourth century. *The Vulgate* goes back to the end of the fourth century. These versions, which already call for a sufficiently long time, are found in copied codices, whose transcription again required some time. {{144}} Nay, study of textual families shows that the greater part of variant readings already existed in the second century. Thus, clearly, the text in question already had a longer history, so that we are ultimately led back to the first century for the autograph needed in order to account for all of this.[29]

---

[27] Origen, *Contra Celsum*, 2.13–16 and 5.52.

[28] [Trans. note: Dropping "ex 1500" at the start of this clause, as it is not clear what it is referring to. Also, reading *IV* for *VI*.]

[29] The authenticity of the fourth Gospel, forever fought against with such vigor, is expressly shown in the papyrus recently detected by Rylands, which accurately contains, according to our critique of the text, John 18:31b–33a, 37b–38. The most renowned paleographers ascribe the text to the first decades of the second century, and the fact that it comes from Egypt shows that St. John's Gospel had been in writing already for some time. See Ermenegildo Florit,

Conclusion. From all these documents, it is certain that *our Four Gospels were in use at around the end of the second century in a whole variety of churches and that their authenticity was recognized without doubt.* However, if these four Gospels were not written by the apostles and their disciples, *a whole host of morally impossible things would follow.* (1) How would the *Fathers, bishops, and believers* [of the early Church] have been able to have so flippantly accepted apocryphal books as the rule of faith? (2) Why wouldn't *heretics* and *pagans* deny their authenticity? (3) How were *various churches* able to be persuaded that the four Gospels, and them alone, are apostolic? It is morally impossible that believers dispersed throughout the world would have conspired in this kind of astonishing fraud without any protest being raised against it. (4) Hence, Catholic [biblical] critics insist: If the Gospels are not authentic, who were *their authors*? When did they write? Where? How is it that the names of such authors were able to remain unknown?

§2. Intrinsic Arguments

This authenticity is confirmed by means of internal arguments.

A. *As regards the Synoptic Gospels*, an examination of them clearly points out the fact that their authors were *unlearned and illiterate Jews* who did not know the Greek language and therefore used many Hebraisms. Moreover, these authors belong to the *first century*, for in their descriptions of places, mores, things, and persons, they refer without error to the smallest of circumstances, which would have been impossible for authors with even the least of intellectual culture writing in the second century after the devastation of Jerusalem and the destruction of the temple.[30] Finally, in the Synoptic Gospels, the prophecies concerning the military destruction of Jerusalem announce this event together with the ultimate end of the world, with very little distinction between the two. This makes clear that this prophecy was written before the event.

According to Catholic critics—and this is conceded as something probable by the rationalist Harnack—the first three Gospels were written between AD 50 and 70, more probably in 60 or a little bit before then, and the fourth Gospel between 80 and 100.[31]

Parlano anche I papiri (Rome: Scuola tipografica Pio X, 1943).

[30] See Guillaume Meignan, *Les evangiles et la critique au XIXe siècle* [(Paris: Palmé, 1864)], lect. 9–13.

[31] See Marius Lepin, *Jesus messie et fils de Dieu*, 3rd ed. [(Paris: Letouze et Ané, 1906)], introduction; also, his article "Evangiles canoniques" in *Dictionnaire apologétique de la foi catholique*,

{{145}} Rationalists and liberal Protestants acknowledge, with little difficulty, that St. Mark's Gospel was written around AD 70, though they hold that the others were written at the end of the first century.[32]

B. *As regards the fourth Gospel*,[33] whose authenticity is subject to attack in particular, internal criteria confirm that its author is *Jewish* (for there are many Hebraisms in it, and it is excellent in its accounts of Jewish customs and messianic concepts), that its author was *an eyewitness* [to the events recounted therein][34] (on account of his vivid description of personal characteristics, for example, of John the Baptist, Peter, Mary Magdalene, Martha, the Samaritan [woman], the man born blind, and so forth), that he was *an apostle* (for he is aware of the most minute of circumstances of Jesus's life, his intimate thoughts and prayers, his secret conversation with Nicodemus and with the Samaritan woman, etc.)—nay, that he is *John* (indeed the Apostle John is never named in this fourth Gospel but, rather, is only called "the disciple whom Jesus loved"). Now, this final point is easily explained by John's own modesty. However, this would be unintelligible if the fourth Gospel were a work written as a forgery. Moreover, in the final chapter, the authenticity of which is not rejected, in speaking of the "disciple whom Jesus loved," the text states: "This is that disciple

---

col. 1611: "In the opinion of all critics, the third Gospel is written by the same author as the book of Acts and was written prior to the latter. Now, the book of Acts comes to an end abruptly with the narrative of St. Paul's arrival in Rome in 62, simply mentioning that the Apostle was held in captivity for two years, without saying a word about his second captivity, nor about his death. The best explanation for this fact seems to be that the book of Acts was written soon after the events recounted therein, namely, in around 62 to 64. The third Gospel, being even older still, would therefore have been written toward the year 60, and the Gospels of St. Matthew and of St. Mark would have appeared in around the same era, perhaps some years earlier. Harnack himself recently declared that criticism must be disposed to regard the plausibility of this sort of hypothesis. See Harnack, *Die Apostelgeschicte* (Leipzig: Hinrichs, 1908), 221." See also Batiffol, *Orpheus et l'évangile* (Paris: Gabalda, 1910), 132.

[32] We can summarize the conclusions held by the principal rationalists and [liberal] Protestants concerning the time when the Gospels were composed:

	RENAN	H. HOLTZMANN	B. WEISS	HARNACK	ZAHN
Mark......	76	68	69	65–70	64
Matthew ...	84	67	70	70–75	Aram. 62/ Gk. 85
Luke.......	94	70–100	80	60–83	75
John.......	125	100–133	95	80–110	80–90

[33] See Lepin, *L'origine du quatrième évangile* (Paris: Letouze et Ané, 1907).

[34] See Piux X, *Lamentabili*, no. 18 (Condemnation of the opposition proposition, held by modernists) (Denzinger, no. 3418).

who giveth testimony of these things and hath written these things" (John 21:24, DR).

However, the differences between the fourth Gospel and the Synoptic Gospels does not prove anything against its authenticity but, rather, manifests (1) that John wished to *provide* those matters that were missing in the Synoptic Gospels, in particular describing what happened in Judea and not only in Galilee. And likewise, intending to assert Christ's divinity more explicitly, to this end, he gathered together, in an ordered fashion, the Lord's miracles and words. He does not contradict the Synoptic Gospels but, rather, hands on a supplement to them. Moreover, (2) the diversity *comes from the individual differences of the writers, and from the variety of charisms*, something spoken of by St. Paul in 1 Corinthians 12:4–10 (DR, slightly modified): "Now there are diversities of graces, but the same Spirit.... To one indeed, by the Spirit, is given the word of wisdom: and to another, the word of knowledge, according to the same Spirit.... To another, faith in the same spirit;... to another, prophecy;...to another the interpretation of words." Now, John was given the interpretation of Christ's words and *words of wisdom*, which are spoken of by St. Paul in 1 Corinthians 2:6–10 (DR):

{{146}} Howbeit we speak wisdom among the perfect: yet not the wisdom of this world. . . . But we speak the wisdom of God in a mystery, a wisdom which is hidden, which God ordained before the world, unto our glory. . . . But, as it is written: That eye hath not seen, nor ear heard: neither hath it entered into the heart of man, what things God hath prepared for them that love him. But to us God hath revealed them by his Spirit. For the Spirit searcheth all things, yea, the deep things of God.

According to Harnack, St. Paul wrote these sublime words in AD 53. Why, therefore, could not the disciple who reclined on the breast of the Lord not write the fourth Gospel in the first century? The Spirit breathes where he wills, and how could the Lord's most beloved disciple write about his beloved Master in any other way? However, the other Evangelists received, instead, words of science and of faith, "for they principally hand on those things which pertain to Christ's humanity."[35] Nay, *the apparent disagreement*, which is itself found among the Gospels, in a certain manner *manifests their authenticity*, for as Brugère said: "If the books that circulated under the names of the Apostles were written by later authors, they were written

---

[35] St. Thomas, *In* III *Ioann.*, lect. 1.

either frankly and without any intent to deceive or cunningly and with such an intent. Furthermore, if the first, why do they contain so many various, minute *points of agreement* in them? If the latter, why so many various *points of disagreement*?"

§3. On the Integrity of the Gospels

This integrity (i.e., non-corruption) involves the authenticity of all of its parts. Indeed, in order to duly prove the divine origin of Christianity, it suffices that we historically defend the substantial integrity of the Gospels—that is, as regards its teaching and its most important facts. Now, today, following upon the diligent examination of manuscripts, versions, and the citations of the Fathers, non-Catholic critics themselves nearly all admit that no fact represents a substantial adulteration in the text of the Evangelists from the time of its final redaction—namely, for the Synoptics, from AD 70 to 90 and for John, from AD 110 to 120. Indeed, there are many variant readings, but the majority of them are only verbal transpositions, synonyms, or orthographic modifications. About ten of them pertain to matters of doctrine, but these texts do not contain anything essential regarding Christ's preaching or the most important facts of his life, nor do our own apologetic arguments rely on these texts.[36]

Moreover, as is historically clear,[37] the variants introduced by heretics were immediately discerned. It would have been difficult, without the knowledge of the bishops and the faithful, to corrupt the Gospels, which were preserved with the greatest of veneration and were constantly read. The Gospels were dispersed and utterly well-known throughout the world, with many copies in any given diocese. Now, it would have been morally impossible for all of these to be corrupted.

ART. 3: ON THE HISTORICITY OF THE GOSPELS

{{147}} Among[38] rationalist thinkers, Bruno Bauer was not ashamed to assert

---

[36] See Lepin, "Evangiles canonique," *Dictionnaire apologétique de la foi catholique*, col. 1613 (The principal passages of disputed authenticity: the final passage in Mark 16:9–20; the sweating of blood in Luke 22:43–44; the episode involving the adulterous woman in John 7:53–8:11; the Trinitarian formula of baptism in Matt 28:19; the attribution of the Magnificat to Mary in Luke 1:46; the angel of the pool in Bethesda in John 5:3–4). Also see the same author's work, *Jesus messie et fils de Dieu*, 3rd ed., 55–57 (on the historical value of the Gospel's infancy narratives).

[37] See Henri Wallon, *De la croyance due à l'évangile*, 2nd ed. [(Paris: Adrien Le Clere, 1866)], 45ff.

[38] See Lepin, "Evangiles canoniques," *Dictionnaire apologétique de la foi catholique*, cols. 1684–

that the Evangelists were deceivers, and Renan and others likewise did not balk at saying that they were suffering from hallucinations.[39] Today, many critics acknowledge the *sincerity* of the Evangelists,[40] but in order to exclude everything supernatural from the Gospels, liberal Protestants and modernists choose to believe that the historical person of Christ was transfigured by the disciples' faith, through a kind of *process of idealization*. Therefore, everything that goes beyond historical conditions must be set aside regarding him.[41]

§1. The Historicity of the Synoptic Gospels

Contemporary adversaries, compelled by historical evidence, admit that the three Synoptic Gospels were written not at the end of the second century (as Strauss wished) but, rather, between AD 60 and 90, by perfectly sincere authors who made use of written documents and agreed with each other in substance. However, once one has posited these points, it is no longer possible for one to claim that a process of idealization / transfiguration took place.

(a) *This kind of idealization is something improbable*, for as the rationalists themselves profess, the Synoptic Gospels refer to matters pertaining to the political, moral, and religious state of the Jewish people. Therefore, how could they have conveyed in a less accurate way the facts and sayings

---

1702. Also see the discussion of the historicity of the Gospel narratives in Pierre Batiffol, *The Credibility of the Gospel ("Orpheus" et l'évangile)*, trans. G. C. H. Pollen (New York: Longmans and Green, 1912).

[39] Nay, Renan wrote in *Vie de Jésus*, 6: "My reason for rejecting the miracles recounted by the Evangelists is not based on my prior demonstration that the latter do not deserve absolute belief on my part; rather, the reason why I say the Gospels are legends is because they recount miracles. They can contain history, but certainly, not everything therein is historical."

[40] The Evangelists certainly were not *hallucinating*. How would all of them suffer from hallucination concerning the same facts, through the whole of their life, and in the same manner? To the contrary, they were "slow to believe," as Christ says, not having exceeding credulity. And one would even need to say that Christ's greatest foes suffered from hallucination as well, for they were not able to deny his utterly evident miracles. Finally, this kind of hallucination would have been something more extraordinary than all of the miracles found in the Gospel.

Nor can we say that the Evangelists were *deceivers*. Their probity and simplicity are clear from how they lived. They could not hope to receive any temporal or eternal advantages from such deception but, rather, could expect only persecutions. They followed a way of life that is utterly opposed to one that would have led to being favored by others. Nay, they sealed their witness with their own blood and, without fanaticism, died in the midst of torments with great humility and patience. Finally, how would this deceit have borne such fruit in all good things and holiness through the course of nineteen centuries?

[41] See Pius X, *Pascendi*, no. 9 (Denzinger, no. 3479).

of Christ that they intended *especially* and *faithfully* to narrate?[42] The transformation and deformation of the historical details of Christ's life do appear
in the apocryphal gospels, in which we read of Christ performing countless
astounding wonders, even in his childhood. However, nothing similar is
found in the simple and serious narratives presented by the Evangelists.

{{148}} (b) *Moreover, it was morally impossible,* between AD 60 and
90, to adulterate or transform facts that would still have had *many living
witnesses.* Hence, Strauss said, in order to admit the formation of myths, it
is unavoidably necessary that the Gospel narratives were written at the end
of the second century (a position today rejected by all). *A fortiori,* as Jean-
Jacques Rousseau[43] and, later on, John Stuart Mill[44] admitted, *neither such
Galilean fishermen* nor the first Christian writers *could ever have thought up
or perfected the words of Christ* or made up his marvelous life and the morals
set forth in the Synoptic Gospels. How could they have united such loftiness
with such simplicity? As is clear in the apocryphal texts, the human transformation of Christ's teaching and life destroys its harmony, sublimity, and
simplicity.

(c) *Finally, this idealization is contrary to the facts,* as Lepin shows.[45]
Indeed, *the Synoptic Gospels affirm Christ's divinity* (as well as the satisfactory character of his death) *much less clearly and expressly than does St. Paul,
who, nonetheless, had written some of his letters by AD 50 or 53.* Instead, these
Evangelists narrate things that pertain to the Savior's humanity, his infirmities, sufferings, and sorrows. Likewise, they frequently note the apostles'
imperfections and erroneous prejudices. However, they would not have done
this if they wished to transfigure Christ's deeds and words so as to manifest
his divinity, which had been openly and distinctly preached by St. Paul in
his letters from the years 50 to 53.[46] {{149}} Nay, when St. Paul thus affirms

---

[42] See Luke 1:1–4 (DR): "Forasmuch as *many have taken in hand to set forth in order a narration*
of the things that have been accomplished among us, *according as they have delivered them unto
us, who from the beginning were eyewitnesses* and ministers of the word. It seemed good to me
also, having diligently attained to all things from the beginning, *to write to thee in order,* most
excellent Theophilus, *that thou mayest know the verity of those words in which thou hast been
instructed."*

[43] See Jean-Jacques Rousseau, *Émile,* ch. 3.

[44] See John Stuart Mill, *Three Essays on Religion* (1884), 252ff.

[45] See Lepin, "Evangiles canoniques," *Dictionnaire apologétique de la foi catholique,* col. 1703ff.

[46] See below in the following chapter concerning Christ's own testimony regarding his divinity,
as well as the principal texts for St. Paul: Rom 1:3–4, 8:3, 32; 9:5; Gal 4:4–6; 1 Cor 1:24,
30; 2 Cor 4:4; 5:19; Col 1:15; 1:19; 2:9 (*"For in Him* [Jesus] *dwelleth all the fulness of the
Godhead corporeally"*); Phil 2:5–7 (DR) ("For let this mind be in you, which was also in Christ
Jesus: Who *being in the form of God,* thought it not robbery *to be equal with God* but emptied

Christ's divinity, he did not announce to the Churches something new and unheard of but, rather, speaks about it as of a dogma that had already been received and believed in by the whole Christian community. Moreover, it is certain that already on the day of Pentecost, the apostles taught that Christ is the true Messiah,[47] the Son of God, and the Author of life.[48]

Hence, in the primitive Church, there was no progressive idealization of Christ's deeds and words. Rather, once one acknowledges the sincerity of the Evangelists, it is necessary to admit the historicity of their narratives. As Wallon has noted, if critics were to raise as many difficulties for themselves regarding documents like Caesar's *Commentaries*, whose authenticity is proven by so few testimonies, as they do for the Gospels, very few documents indeed could be historically demonstrated. Thus, a new confirmation of our thesis is had from the impossibility of disproving the historicity of the Synoptic Gospels after such great exertion in critical labors.

---

himself, taking the form of a servant, being made in the likeness of men, and in habit found as a man").

Now, the time of the composition of the Epistles of St. Paul is assigned as follows by the Catholic critics Cornely and Jacquier and by the rationalists Harnack and Jülicher.

	CORNELY	JACQUIER	HARNACK	JÜLICHER
1 Thess.	53	50–52	48–49	53–54
2 Thess.	53–54	50–53	Id.	Id.
Gal.	51–54	53–58	53	55–57
1 Cor.	58	55–58	53	56–57
2 Cor.	58	Id.	Id.	57–59
Rom.	59	55–59	53–54	58–59
Eph.	63	62–64	57–59	62–63
Col.	63	Id.	Id.	Id.
Phlm.	63	Id.	Id.	Id.
Phil.	63	Id.	Id.	62–64
1 Tim.	65	63–67	90–110	110–125
Titus.	65	Id.	Id.	Id.
2 Tim.	66–67	66–67	Id.	Id.

However, as we said above, according to Catholic critics, the three Synoptic Gospels were written between the years 50 and 70. It is more probably the case that they were written around the year 60 or a little thereafter, and Adolf von Harnack concedes that this is probable for the Gospel of Luke.

Nay, rationalists generally acknowledge, without difficulty, that the Gospel according to St. Mark was written around AD 70.

[47] See Acts 2:36.
[48] See Acts 3:13–15.

§2. The Historicity of the Fourth Gospel

As is seen in the propositions condemning liberal Protestants and modernists, they assert:

> The narrations of John are not properly history but, rather, a mystical contemplation of the Gospel. The discourses contained in his Gospel are theological meditations on the mystery of salvation, lacking historical truth.

> The fourth Gospel exaggerated miracles, not only to have them appear more extraordinary, but also in order that it might become more suitable for showing forth the work and glory of the Word Incarnate.

> John claims for himself the quality of witness concerning Christ. In reality, however, he is only a distinguished witness of the Christian life, or of the life of Christ in the Church at the close of the first century.[49]

In recent days, Catholic critics, especially Lepin, have written against modernists concerning such claims.[50] It seems best merely to summarize the arguments set forth by this celebrated author.

The principal end of the fourth Gospel *is indeed dogmatic,* for it is written in particular to clearly manifest that Jesus is the Son of God, as is seen in the final lines in John 20:31 (DR): "But these are written, that you may believe that Jesus is the Christ, the Son of God: and that believing, you may have life in his name." However, this does not mean that the deeds and words of Christ recounted in this Gospel are not historical. Nay, in order to prove something of such great importance, a truthful [*sincerus*] author must bring forth only utterly certain facts and words, which are even selected in relation to their truth and importance. Now, the author of the fourth Gospel did not fail in applying this rule, for nowhere does he say that he is proposing allegories or parables but, on the contrary, describes facts and refers to words by setting forth all the various relevant circumstances of persons, time, and place.

---

[49] See Pius X (Holy Office), *Lamentabili*, nos. 16–18 (Denzinger, nos. 3416–3418).

[50] See Lepin, *La valeur historique du quatrième évangile* (1909); "Évangiles canoniques," *Dictionnaire apologétique de la foi catholique*, vol. 1, col. 1694–1750; M.-J. Lagrange, *L'évangile de S. Jean*, 3rd ed. (1927) and also the 5th edition of this text.

{{150}} We can consider the historicity of facts and words separately.

A. *The historicity of facts.* Some adversaries object that many of the facts recounted in this Gospel are not found in the Synoptic Gospels. Hence, they do not seem to be historical.

The following three arguments can be made in response to this.

(a) *These facts are never proposed by the author as being allegories or parables* but, rather, are presented as being real events.

(b) *The few facts that it holds in common with the Synoptic Gospels are referred to by the author of the Fourth Gospel in nearly the same manner* as they are by SS. Matthew, Mark, and Luke. Allegory is not found more frequently in such matters in the fourth Gospel than in the others. See the testimony of John the Baptist (John 1:19–34 and the Synoptics), the casting out of the sellers and money changers from the temple (John 2:13–16), the multiplication of loaves (John 6:1–13), the walking upon water (John 6:16), the anointing of Jesus in Bethany (John 12:1–8), Christ's triumphal entry into Jerusalem (John 12:12), and the whole narration of the Passion (John 18–19).

(c) *Nor is it surprising that this Gospel would recount many facts omitted by the Synoptic Gospels,* for in general it does not exposit in its own turn the things that were already said by the other Evangelists and thus were known to all the faithful, but rather *completed the account offered by the texts that preceded it.*[51] Indeed, the text writes nearly nothing concerning Jesus's ministry in Galilee but instead recalls the deeds that were done in Judea. Nor does it refer again to the institution of the Eucharist but, rather, to the promise of this sacrament through the multiplication of loaves (ch. 6). It says nothing about the raising of Jairus's daughter from the dead, the widow of Naim, or the confession of St. Peter in Caesarea. However, this Gospel alone recounts the miracle performed at the wedding feast of Cana, the story of how Nicodemus approached Jesus, the conversion of the Samaritan woman, the healing of the man born blind and of the paralytic at the Pool of Bethesda, and the resurrection of Lazarus. Moreover, it minutely describes these facts, giving their circumstances of place and time, considering also the various customs and traditions of the Jewish people, not seeming more allegorical than the narration that it shares with the Synoptic Gospels. See, for example, the narratives concerning the conversion of the Samaritan woman, the

---

[51] See Rudolf Cornely, *Historica et critica introductio in U. T. libros sacros,* vol. 3, [Paris: Lethielleux, 1886,] 252. "Just as the Synoptic Gospels give particular attention to setting forth those things that took place in Galilee, St. John is almost solely concerned with those that took place in Judea."

curing of the man born blind, and the description of the Pool of Bethesda.

B. *The historicity of the words [of the fourth Gospel].* Rationalists object that a great distance separates the words of the fourth Gospel from those referred to in the Synoptic Gospels, as regards both the doctrine set forth as well as the form of the preaching: The Synoptic Gospels, above all, narrate moral precepts in a simple style, whereas John teaches the loftiest dogmas concerning the Word Incarnate in a more sublime style. Now, it is said: Christ could not have preached in such diverse ways in the same circumstances.

Catholic critics respond by saying that this difference must not be exaggerated, and in reality, it proves nothing against the historicity of the Fourth Gospel.

(a) *Indeed, in the Synoptic Gospels, we often have only the substance of Christ's words,* as is clear, for example, in Luke's recounting of the Sermon on the Mount, which St. Matthew refers to at much greater length. [Likewise,] there are four beatitudes in Luke, whereas eight are recounted in Matthew. {{151}} Hence, it is not surprising that John recounts the Lord's words more extensively and abundantly, especially as regards the loftier mysteries, for it is beyond a doubt that he would have wished to supply a number of points omitted from them. For example, this Gospel presents Christ disputing with the Pharisees, whereas in the other Gospels, Christ often speaks to the people. Thus, we have a ready explanation for why the Fourth Gospel and the Synoptic Gospels employ manners of speaking that are often quite different.

(b) *Moreover, the dogmatic aim of the fourth Gospel must be taken into consideration.* John properly intended to shed greater light on Christ's divinity, which by this point in time was being denied by the Gnostic Cerinthus and by the Ebionites. Hence, he collected, in particular, all the deeds and words of the Savior by which his glory and divinity were manifested. However, in so doing, he does not contradict the Synoptic Gospels, for they do indicate Christ's divinity, though less explicitly. Moreover, whereas the Synoptic Gospels proposed a kind of catechism for the simple, John, like St. Paul, "speaks wisdom among the perfect," and he hands on lofty mysteries rather than moral precepts. However, he does not omit the latter either, though he reduces all things to charity toward God and neighbor.

(c) *Finally, John's manner of writing corresponded to the sublimity of the doctrine set forth therein.* His style is often majestic, magnificent, and livelier, and this bears witness to his particular character and special vocation. Indeed, he was the disciple whom Jesus loved, the one who laid his head upon the Lord's breast, and the person to whom Jesus gave his mother as he was dying. Hence, more profoundly understanding Christ's words, he more easily preserved them in his memory. Nor, in the words imputed to Christ, did he set forth his own ideas rather than those of the Lord, for in many places it is clear that John distinguishes his own comments from the very words of Christ. See, for example, John 2:21 ("But he said this concerning the temple of his body"), 12:33 ("However, he said this regarding the death that he was about to die"), and also 7:39.

(d) *As regards the apparent contradictions* between the fourth Gospel and the first three, see Cornely.[52] By the consent of all [Catholic critics], these apparent contradictions are *entirely accidental in character*, and they do not touch upon either the substance of the historical details of Christ's life or his doctrine, but rather, are concerned with questions of chronology, as well as the number or order of his miracles. This actually provides a new sign of the Evangelists' honesty, for if they had deceitfully written under the name of the apostles, they would not have left behind these apparent differences. Moreover, as Catholic commentators show, profound knowledge [*scientia*] is often present where there appears to be contradiction. Thus, for example, the Synoptic Gospels speak about the Pharisees and Sadducees where John recalls the Priests and the Pharisees. However, at this time, the Priests were the Sadducees, meaning that there is no contradiction here but, rather, an accurate relating of things.

CONCLUSION: Thus, we have a sufficient proof for the historical authority of the Gospels. And *very few, if any, non-sacred books have such evident historicity*. The first mention of Herodotus is made by Aristotle, a hundred years after his death, and the second by Cicero (that is, four hundred years later). [The existence of] Thucydides is first alleged by Cicero—namely, after three centuries. {{152}} The same holds true for many other profane writings whose authenticity and historicity are admitted in general. Hence, among rationalists, Strauss confessed that he did not fight against the authenticity of the Gospels for historical reasons but, rather, on account of their moral consequences.[53] The same holds for Renan, as was said above. Zeller likewise declared that the historical account of Christ's Resurrection must not be believed in, although it is established on the basis of utterly certain testimonies.[54] Therefore, when they hold that the evangelical witnesses concerning supernatural facts must be rejected, rationalists are not moved by historical reasons but, rather, by other motives.

---

[52] See ibid., 268, no. 73ff.

[53] See David Strauss, *Das Leben Jesu für das deutsche Volk* (Bonn: E. Strauss, 1895), xxii.

[54] Eduard Zeller, *Vorträge und Abhandlungen: Erste Sammlung* (Leipzig: Fues, 1875), 543.

SECTION I

Jesus Christ's Testimony

Ch. 3. Jesus Christ's Testimony concerning His Divine Mission {{153}}
Single Article

Ch. 4. Christ's Testimony concerning the Mysteries to Be Believed and
the Precepts to Be Kept
Art. 1. His Teaching concerning God
Art. 2. His Testimony concerning His Divine Filiation and the
Redemption
Art. 3. His Testimony concerning the Christian Life
Art. 4. His Testimony concerning the End of the World, the Final
Judgment, and Eternal Life

Ch. 5. Christ's Testimony concerning the Establishment of the Church
in Order for Revelation to Be Guarded and Infallibly Proposed
until the End of the World
Single Article

Ch. 6. In View of His Wisdom and Holiness, Christ's Testimony
concerning Himself Is Deserving of Faith
Single Article

Having proven the historical authority of the four Gospels, on their basis, especially that of the Synoptic Gospels (whose historicity is more readily admitted by adversaries), we must now determine the nature of Jesus Christ's testimony (1) *concerning his divine mission*, (2) *concerning the mysteries to be believed and the precepts to be kept*, and (3) *concerning the establishing of the Church* so that revelation may be infallibly preserved up to the end of the world.

This threefold testimony pertains to the treatise on revelation, for the

· 223

first assigns the origin of this revelation, the second its object, and the third the necessary condition for its uninterrupted preservation and proposition. Finally, we must consider whether this testimony is deserving of faith on account of Christ's character, wisdom, and holiness.

Therefore, we must distinguish four chapters in this section.

We must set forth this testimony at great length, using Christ's very own words, so that in our later discussions we may present in full force the apologetic arguments drawn from the sublimity of Christ's doctrine, from its moral effects, and from the marvelous fulfillment of all our legitimate aspirations in Christianity. Moreover, as many today note, *already, a plain exposition of Christian doctrine provides its apologetic defense,* for many non-believers reject the faith not so much on account of their ignorance of its signs (e.g., miracles) but, rather, on account of prejudices that they have against the mysteries and precepts of Christianity.

CHAPTER THREE

Jesus Christ's Testimony concerning His Divine Mission

Single Article

§1. State of the Question

{{154}} Not[1] all rationalists agree concerning the existence of this testimony.

(a) A few, like Wellhausen, Schmidt, Wrede, and others, say that Christ did not affirm that he was the Messiah but, rather, declarations of this sort were ascribed to him by his disciples, who believed in his messiahship especially after his death, for they believed that he had been raised from the dead.

(b) However, most rationalists, like Harnack and O[skar] Holtzmann, hold that Christ affirmed his messiahship. Nevertheless, some, such as Weiss and Loisy, say that Christ was not aware of his messianic dignity from the start, and when he exercised his ministry, he did not then speak of [his] end such that he would have taught that he was the Messiah, nor were his miracles concerned with that either. Nonetheless, near the end of his life, he came to teach that he was the Messiah or, rather, that he would be the ruler of the heavenly kingdom, which was soon to come, along with the end of the world.[2] Our thesis is set up against these thinkers.

---

[1] See Marius Lepin, *Jésus messie et fils de Dieu*, 3rd ed. (1906), 78–218; Pierre Batiffol, *L'enseignement de Jésus* (Paris: Bloud, 1905).

[2] All of these propositions were condemned in the decree *Lamentabili*, nos. 28, 33, and 35 (Denzinger, nos. 3428, 3433, and 3435).

§2. Jesus Openly Affirmed That He Was the Messiah Announced by the Prophets

From the beginning of his ministry, Jesus bore witness to the fact that he was sent by God, and with the passage of time, he asserted with increasing explicitness that he was the Messiah and Savior.

The term *Messiah* (Hebrew, *Masiah*; Greek [*Sept.*], Χριστός, Μεσσίας, in John 1:42 and 4:25; Vulgate, *Christus*) means the same thing as "anointed one" (from the Hebrew word *masah*, "to anoint")—namely, the one anointed by God in order to have the office of the High Priest. According to the Old Testament, the Messiah will be *the high priest* (Lev 4:3, 16), *a prophet* (1 Chr 19:16), *the king and founder of the kingdom of God* (Ps 18[7]:51; 20 [19]:7; 72[1]; 89[8]:39 and 52; Isa 61–62), and *the Savior* (Ps 2:2; 45[4]:8; Dan 9:24).

However, the Jewish people came to misinterpret [adulteraverant] the notion of the Messiah and in Jesus's time expected a political Messiah, who would reestablish the kingdom of Israel and bestow upon them temporal domination over all nations.[3] {{155}} Therefore, *Jesus had to gradually correct this erroneous prejudice* and show his disciples that the Messiah announced by the prophets was not to be a temporal ruler but, rather, the humble and patient savior, *who comes to give his life as a ransom for many* (Matt 20:28). Hence, Jesus did not begin his preaching by explicitly declaring to the people that he was the awaited Messiah, for he did not wish to present himself as being a temporal ruler. (Nay, when the people tried to make him a king, he fled to the mountains, as we see in John 6:15). Nor did he wish to suddenly, and without any preparation, remove these prejudices, for the Jewish people would not understand his true spiritual mission unless they were gradually disposed to accept it. Hence, on many occasions, Jesus said to the various people whom he miraculously healed, "Tell no one" (Matt 8:4; Mark 1:44; Luke 5:14—Mark 5:43; Luke 8:56—Matt 9:30; Mark 7:36; 8:26[4]), because these miracles would have quickly revealed his messianic dignity.

Therefore, Jesus *progressively* manifested himself as being the Messiah, indeed doing so in various ways, inasmuch as he spoke either privately and intimately or publicly before the people. We can distinguish two stages in

---

[3] Hence, the wicked Herod intended to kill this Messiah (cf. Matt 2:13). Nay, Christ's own disciples and the apostles themselves somewhat preserved this prejudice all the way up to the Ascension (cf. Luke 24:21 and Acts 1:6).

[4] Also see the article "Messie" in the *Dictionnaire de la Bible*.

this progressive manifestation: (A) the beginning of his ministry; (B) the final year of his life.

A. *At the beginning of his ministry*

(a) Publicly before the people. (1) Jesus declared his doctrinal and messianic mission inasmuch as he *"came into Galilee, preaching the gospel of the kingdom of God* and saying: The time is accomplished and the kingdom of God is at hand. Repent and believe the Gospel" (Mark 1:14–15, DR; cf. Matt 4:17). He chose his disciples "and said to them, 'Come, follow me, and I will make you fishers of men'" (Matt 4:19). "And Jesus went about all Galilee, teaching in their synagogues, and preaching the gospel of the kingdom, and healing all manner of sickness and every infirmity, among the people" (Matt 4:23, DR). In the Sermon on the Mount, he perfected the Mosaic Law in his own name, asserting many times: *It was said of old ... But, I say to you ...* (Matt 5:21–24). He taught like one *having power* (Matt 7:29; Mark 1:22; Luke 4:32).

(2) He responded to the Pharisees, telling them that he is *the Lord of the Sabbath* (Matt 12:8), *is greater than Jonah and Solomon* (Matt 12:41–42), *and more than David* (Mark 12:35–37).

(3) Likewise, in the synagogue in Nazareth, after having read the words of Isaiah concerning the future Messiah: "The spirit of the Lord is upon me. Wherefore he hath anointed me to preach the gospel to the poor, he hath sent me to heal the contrite of heart. . . . And he began to say to them: This day is fulfilled this scripture in your ears." And when the unbelieving people heard him, they said, "Is not this the son of Joseph?" And Jesus said, "Amen I say to you, that no prophet is accepted in his own country" (Luke 4:21–25 DR; Matt 13:54ff; Mark 6:1–4).

(4) He even expressly declared his messiahship *after the curing of the paralytic* in the Pool of Bethesda in Jerusalem on the Sabbath. The Jews accused him, as though he were breaking the Sabbath. *He responded that he was sent by God and claimed for himself all the rights that pertained to the Messiah—* namely, the power to bring about what the Father does, raising the dead, exposing the hearts of men, and leading his believers to eternal life. {{156}} Nay, many of the words in this response make manifest not only Christ's messiahship but also his divinity.

Indeed, John 5 (DR) deserves to be read in whole:

"My Father worketh until now; and I work. . . . For as the Father raiseth up the dead and giveth life, so the *Son also giveth life to whom he will.* For neither does the Father judge any man: but hath given all judgment to the Son. . . . He who honoreth not the Son honoreth not the Father who hath sent him. Amen,

amen, I say unto you that *he who heareth my word and believeth him that sent me hath life everlasting.* . . . For as the Father hath life in himself, so he hath given the Son also to have life in himself. . . . But I have a greater testimony than that of John, for the works which the Father hath given me to perfect, *the works themselves, which I do, give testimony of me, that the Father hath sent me.* And the Father himself who hath sent me hath given testimony of me. . . . *Search the Scriptures.* . . . And the same are they that give testimony of me. . . . I am come in the name of my Father, and you receive me not. . . . For if you did believe Moses, you would perhaps believe me also: for he wrote of me."

(b) PRIVATELY, however, speaking in a more intimate manner, Jesus more quickly manifested his messiahship. (1) From the beginning, following upon the testimony of John the Baptist and his first discussion with Jesus, Andrew went to find "first his brother Simon and saith to him: We have found the Messiah, which is, being interpreted, the Christ" (John 1:41, DR). Likewise, Philip and Nathanael confessed, "Rabbi, thou art the Son of God. Thou art the King of Israel" (John 1:49, DR).

(2) Jesus "having called *his twelve disciples* together, he gave them power over unclean spirits, to cast them out, and to heal all manner of diseases, and all manner of infirmities, . . . commanding them, saying: . . . And going, preach, saying: The kingdom of heaven is at hand. Heal the sick, raise the dead. . . . For it is not you that speak, but the spirit of your Father that speaketh in you. . . . He that receiveth you, receiveth me: and he that receiveth me, receiveth him *that sent me*" (Matt 10:1, 7, 20, 40, DR). "And he that despiseth you despiseth me; and he that despiseth me despiseth him that sent me" (Luke 10:16, DR).

(3) "Now when John the Baptist had heard in prison the works of Christ: sending two of his disciples he said to him: Art thou he that art to come, or look we for another? And Jesus making answer said to them: Go and relate to John what you have heard and seen. *The blind see, the lame walk, the lepers are cleansed, the deaf hear, the dead rise again, the poor have the gospel preached to them*" (Matt 11:2–5, DR). However, these words manifest the fulfillment of the prophecy of Isaiah (Isa 35:5), which the Jews understood as applying to the Messiah.

(4) Coming to the first village in Jerusalem, Jesus spoke *with Nicodemus,* one of the leaders of the Jews, who came to Jesus at night and believed in him because of his miracles. Then, Jesus declared to him that he descended from heaven and is the only-begotten Son of God.

"No man hath ascended into heaven, but *he that descended from heaven, the Son of man who is in heaven.* . . . For God so loved the world, as to give *his only begotten Son*, that whosoever believeth in him may not perish, but may have life everlasting. . . . He that believeth in him is not judged. But he that doth not believe is already judged: because he believeth not in the name of the only begotten Son of God" (John 3:13–18, DR). In this response, Jesus quite obviously teaches his messiahship, nay, even his divine filiation.

{{157}} (5) He said the same thing to the Samaritan woman. "The woman saith to him: I know that the Messiah cometh (who is called Christ): therefore, when he is come, he will tell us all things. Jesus saith to her: I am he, who am speaking with thee." And the Samaritans, after hearing him, said: "We ourselves have heard him and *know that this is indeed the Savior of the world*" (John 4:25–42, DR).

All these testimonies belong to the beginning of Jesus's ministry; however, at the end of his life, he came to speak even more explicitly than before, not only to his disciples but to the people in general.

B. *In the last year of his life*

(1) During the final year of his life, Christ manifested to his disciples the full perfection of his messianic dignity. Nay, by means of the words that he used, he hinted at his divinity.

"And Jesus came into the quarters of Caesarea Philippi, and he asked his disciples, saying: Whom do men say that the Son of man is? . . . (And then, later on, insisting more strongly,) But whom do you say that I am? Simon Peter answered and said: 'Thou art Christ, the Son of the living God, ὁ Χριστὸς ὁ υἱὸς τοῦ Θεοῦ τοῦ ζῶντος.'" (Matt 16:13–15, DR; see Matt 16:13–19; Mark 8:29 reads "You are Christ"; Luke 9:20 states, "The Christ of God"). Now, these words at least mean that Christ is truly the Messiah, and they were approved by Christ as being inspired by the Heavenly Father.

(2) On the feast day of the Jews, Jesus went up to the temple and taught. "And the Jews wondered, saying: How doth this man know letters, having never learned? Jesus answered them and said: *My doctrine is not mine, but his that sent me.* . . . Jesus therefore cried out in the temple, teaching and saying: You both know me, and you know whence I am. And I am not come of myself: but *he that sent me is true*, whom you know not. I know him, because *I am from him*: and he hath sent me" (John 7:15–29, DR). Then, the leaders and Pharisees sent ministers to seize him, but nobody was able to place a hand upon him, and the ministers returned, saying: "Never did man speak like this man" (John 7:46, DR).

On the following day, Jesus returned to the Temple, and he taught, saying, "I am the light of the world. He that followeth me walketh not in darkness but shall have the light of life. The Pharisees therefore said to him: Thou givest testimony of thyself. Thy testimony is not true. Jesus answered and said to them: . . . I am one that give testimony of myself, and *the Father that sent me giveth testimony of me*" (John 8:12–18, DR). And continuing:

> And he that sent me is with me: and he hath not left me alone. For I do always the things that please him. . . . If you continue in my word . . . the truth shall make you free. . . . *I speak that which I have seen with my Father.* . . . If God were your Father, you would indeed love me. For *from God I proceeded and came.* For I came not of myself: but he sent me. . . . Which of you shall convict me of sin? If I say the truth to you, why do you not believe me? He that is of God heareth *the words of God.* . . . Amen, amen, I say to you: If any man keep my word, he shall not see death for ever. The Jews therefore said: Now we know that thou hast a devil. . . . Art thou greater than our father Abraham who is dead? Jesus answered: . . . Amen, amen, I say to you, *before Abraham was made, I AM.* (John 8:29–59, DR)

These last words declare something more than Christ's messiahship, but the Pharisees, unable to hold the eternal character of this claim [*aeternitatis verba*], nor able to understand them, considered them to be blasphemous and "took up stones therefore to cast at him" (John 8:59, DR).

{{158}} A bit later on, the Jews surrounded him and said, "How long dost thou hold our souls in suspense? If thou be the Christ, tell us plainly. Jesus answered them: I speak to you, and you believe not: the works that I do in the name of my Father, they give testimony of me. But you do not believe, because you are not of my sheep" (John 10:24–26, DR). Nay, Jesus then affirmed his dignity, which went beyond his dignity as Messiah, adding, "I and the Father are one. The Jews then took up stones to stone him. Jesus answered them: . . . Do you say of him whom the Father hath sanctified and sent into the world: Thou blasphemest, because I said, I am the Son of God?" (John 10:30–36, DR).

(3) WHEN JESUS TRIUMPHALLY ENTERED JERUSALEM, "the multitudes that went before and that followed, cried, saying: Hosanna to the son of David; *Blessed is he that cometh in the name of the Lord: Hosanna in the highest*" (Matt 21:9, DR; Mark 11:10). "And some of the Pharisees, from amongst the multitude, said to him: Master, rebuke thy disciples. To whom he said: *I say to you that if these shall hold their peace, the stones will cry out*" (Luke 19:39–40, DR). On the same day, entering the temple and casting out the money changers, he said, "It is written, *My house shall be called the house of prayer*; but you have made it a den of thieves" (Matt 21:13, DR; Mark 11:7; Luke 19:46). In doing this, Christ acted as a teacher.[5]

---

[5] Many rationalists, like Harnack and Holtzmann, hold that Christ's entry into Jerusalem

(4) DURING HIS PASSION. Before the Sanhedrin, the chief priest said to him, "I adjure thee by the living God, that thou tell us if thou be the Christ the Son of God. Jesus saith to him, *Thou hast said it*. Nevertheless I say to you, *hereafter you shall see the Son of man sitting on the right hand of the power of God and coming in the clouds of heaven*" (Matt 26:63–64, DR; cf. Mark 14:60–64). Then the chief priest tore his garments, saying, "He has blasphemed." In this response, Jesus declared, at the very least, that he is the Messiah and that the right to sit at the Father's right hand and to judge men belongs to him.

(5) AFTER HIS RESURRECTION, he confirmed his disciples in faith, and going with certain disciples to the town of Emmaus, he said, "O foolish and slow of heart to believe in all things, which the prophets have spoken. *Ought not Christ to have suffered these things, and so to enter into his glory?* And beginning at Moses and all the prophets, he expounded to them *in all the scriptures the things that were concerning him*" (Luke 24:25–27, 44–45, DR). By means of such words, he clearly affirmed that he is the Messiah announced by the prophets. So too when he said his eleven disciples, "As the Father hath sent me, I also send you" (John 20:21, DR; cf. Matt 28:18–20; Mark 16:18).

CONCLUSION. All of *these testimonies*, as Harnack himself admits[6] against Wellhausen, *are so connected with the whole of the Gospel narrative* that were they done away with, nearly nothing would remain concerning Jesus's historical existence, and in particular, his death would remain inexplicable. *Nor was there sufficient time for the progressive idealization of Jesus's life to take place*, for already on the day of Pentecost, the apostles taught that Jesus is the Messiah and the Author of life.[7]

{{159}} Moreover, one cannot say, with Loisy, that Jesus only affirmed that he was perhaps the Messiah of a future kingdom soon to be established with the coming end of the world, for in many texts Jesus asserts that he already is the Messiah. However, "the kingdom of heaven is like to a grain of mustard seed, . . . which is the least indeed of all seeds; but when it is grown up . . . it becometh a tree" (Matt 13:31–32, DR). Thus, the kingdom of God began with Christ's preaching, was manifested in glory through his Resur-

---

obviously shows that Christ wished to claim the title of Messiah for himself.

6 See Harnack, *L'essence du christianisme* [Paris: Fischbacher, 1902], 140.

7 See Acts 2:36 and 3:13–15. According to Catholics and conservative Protestants, the *Acts of the Apostles* were written by St. Luke before AD 70. Harnack says that it was written between AD 78 and 83 or, perhaps, between 60 and 70. On the authenticity and historicity of Acts, see the second article (on the divinity of Christ) in the next chapter.

rection and Ascension, and finally will come to its consummation after the last coming of the Messiah.

CHAPTER FOUR

Christ's Testimony concerning the Mysteries to Be Believed and the Precepts to Be Kept

{{160}} Christ's[1] teaching can be reduced to four fundamental headings: (1) concerning the one God and the Trinity, (2) concerning the divine filiation of Jesus himself, as well as the satisfactory power of his death, (3) concerning the Christian life, and (4) concerning the end of the world, the final judgment, and eternal life.

These are the mysteries of the Trinity, the Incarnation, the Redemption (and the sacraments), the life of grace, and the future life, along with their correlative precepts and counsels.

We will devote four articles to discussing these teachings, putting off to the next chapter the discussion of Christ's testimony concerning the Church, given the particular difficulties involved in that discussion, though also so that we may devote special treatment to the intimate connection of the instituting of the Church with the whole of Christ's doctrine.

According to liberal Protestants and modernists, Christ did not teach a determinate body of doctrine but, rather, began a kind of religious movement.[2] Let us here consider what can be gathered from the Synoptic Gospels,

---

[1] See Bossuet, *Discours sur l'histoire universelle*, pt. 2, ch. 19 (Jesus Christ and his teaching); Batiffol, *L'enseignement de Jésus* (Paris, 1906); Rose, *Études évangeliques* (1905), 12–156; Vigouroux and Lesetre, "Jésus-Christ," in *Dictionnaire de la Bible*, col. 1480–1497; Léonce de Grandmaison, "Jésus-Christ," in *Dictionnaire apologétique de la foi catholique*.

[2] In its decree *Lamentabile*, the Holy Office condemned these two propositions: "Christ did not teach a determined body of doctrine applicable to all times and all men but, rather, inaugurated a religious movement adapted or to be adapted to different times and places"; "Christian doctrine was originally Judaic [*sic*]. Through successive evolutions, it became first Pauline, then Joannine, and then finally Hellenic and universal" (*Lamentabile*, nos. 59 and 60; Denzinger, nos. 3459 and 3460).

the Gospel according to John, and St. Paul's letters.

ART. 1: HIS TEACHING CONCERNING GOD

§1. According to the Synoptic Gospels

Jesus always presupposed, as an utterly certain and received dogma, the Old Testament teaching concerning *the One Creator God, and he himself confirmed it.*

{{161}} "Hear, O Israel, the Lord is your God, and He is the One God" (see Mark 12:29, 32). He created creatures (Mark 13:19). He is the *Lord of heaven and earth* (Matt 11:25, 26), is in heaven (Matt 5:34–35, 45–48) as though upon a throne, whereas the earth is his footstool (Mark 5:35). *He is perfect* (Matt 5:48). *God is the [only] one who is good* (Matt 19:17). He is *omnipotent*: "Those things that are impossible for men are possible for God" (Luke 18:27). *He knows all things and sees the hidden depths of our hearts* (Matt 6:4, 6, 18). He knows what we need before we ask for them (Matt 6:8). He can do what he wills (Matt 20:15).

In relation to men, God is above all their FATHER, he who is most provident, merciful, and just.

Be perfect, as your Heavenly Father is perfect (Matt 5:48; 16–45). "Therefore, you will pray: Our Father, who are in heaven, hallowed be thy name" (Matt 5:9, 15–18). The divine *providence* is universal and extends *to the least of individual things*: "Behold the birds of the air . . . and your heavenly Father feedeth them. Are not you of much more value than they?" (Matt 6:26, DR; also 30 and 32). "Seek and it will be given to you" (Matt 7:7). "Our Father is *merciful*" (Luke 6:36), "making the sun rise upon the good and the wicked" (Matt 5:45). He is patient (Mark 12:2–5) but vindicates his servants concerning their adversaries (Luke 17:1–8). He calls all men to labor in his vineyard (Matt 20:1–15). He demands work proportioned to the gifts given to each person (Matt 25:14), giving a higher or lower place in heaven to those for whom it is prepared (Matt 20:23). As the *Supreme Judge*, he renders unto each person in accord with that person's work (Matt 16:27, as well as in the parable of the talents in Matt 25:35–36). His son "shall say to them that shall be on his right hand: Come, ye blessed of my Father, possess you the kingdom prepared for you from the foundation of the world. . . . Then he shall say to them also that shall be on his left hand: Depart from me, you cursed, into everlasting fire, which was prepared for the devil and his angels" (Matt 25:34–46, DR; 18:34–35; 22:11–13). Nonetheless, before the final judgment, God can remit one's debt (Matt 18:25). He assiduously seeks after the sinner, like the shepherd seeking out a lost sheep (Luke

15:1–7), and mercifully receives the repentant prodigal (Luke 15:24).

God the Father has a SON *equal to himself:* "And no one knoweth the Son but the Father: neither doth any one know the Father, but the Son, and he to whom it shall please the Son to reveal him" (Matt 11:27, DR). Also see the next article concerning Jesus Christ's divine filiation.

Finally, concerning the HOLY SPIRIT, Jesus says: "And I send the *promise of my Father* upon you" (Luke 24:49, DR); "when (the enemies of the kingdom of God) shall deliver you up, take no thought how or what to speak, . . . for it is not you that speak, but the spirit of your Father that speaketh in you" (Matt 10:19–20, DR); "the Holy Ghost shall teach you in the same hour what you must say" (Luke 12:12, DR); "he that shall speak against the Holy Ghost, it shall not be forgiven him, neither in this world, nor in the world to come" (Matt 12:32, DR; Mark 3:29).

As is clear from the context, he says this against those wicked persons who, compelled by the evidence of the signs of the Holy Spirit, nonetheless do not wish to believe, or even attribute such miracles to a demon.

{{162}} The distinction and equality of the three divine persons is affirmed by Christ when he says to his disciples: "Going therefore, teach ye all nations: *baptizing them in the name of the Father and of the Son and of the Holy Ghost*" (Matt 28:19, DR; see the next article for a discussion of the authenticity of this formula).

§2. According to John

"*God is a spirit*: and they that adore him must adore him in spirit and in truth" (John 4:24, DR). Jesus calls him Father, saying, "My FATHER worketh until now. . . . For as the Father raiseth up the dead and giveth life, so the Son also giveth life to whom he will. . . . For as the Father hath life in himself, so he hath given the Son also to have life in himself" (John 5:17–21, 26, DR). "*Holy Father*, keep them in thy name whom thou hast given me. . . . Sanctify them in truth. . . . *Just* Father, the world hath not known thee" (John 17:11, 17, 25). "For God so loved the world, as to give his only begotten Son" (John 3:16, DR). "I and the Father are one" (John 10:30; also, 17:11, 21; likewise, see the next article concerning Christ's divine filiation).

The HOLY SPIRIT is called the Paraclete: "But when the Paraclete cometh, whom I will send you from the Father, the Spirit of truth, who proceedeth from the Father, he shall give testimony of me" (John 15:26, DR). "He shall abide with you and shall be in you. . . . He will teach you all things and bring all things to your mind, whatsoever I shall have said to you" (John 14:17, 26, DR). "For he shall not speak of himself, but what things soever he shall hear, he shall speak. And the things that are to come, he shall shew you. He shall glorify me: because he shall *receive of mine* and shall shew it to you. All things whatsoever the Father hath are mine. Therefore I said that he shall receive of me and shew it to you" (John 16:13–15, DR). These texts make clear the fact that the Holy Spirit is God, indeed a distinct person from the Father and from the Son, by whom he is sent. The mystery of the Trinity was explicitly revealed by Jesus himself.

The same doctrine concerning God is found in St. Paul's letters.

ART. 2: His Testimony concerning His Divine Filiation and the Redemption

§1. State of the Question

The opinions of the modernists, as well as many liberal Protestants, concerning this matter can be found in the propositions condemned by the decree *Lamentabili*:

> No. 27: "The divinity of Jesus Christ is not proved from the Gospels. It is a dogma that Christian conscience has derived from the notion of the Messiah."

> No. 30: "In all the evangelical texts, the name 'Son of God' is equivalent only to that of 'Messiah.' It does not in the least way signify that Christ is the true and natural son of God." (Likewise, see no. 31.)

> No. 38: "The doctrine concerning the expiatory death of Christ is not evangelical but, rather, is only Pauline."[3]

A number of rationalists, like Renan, B[ernhard] Weiss, H[ans Hinrich] Wendt, and Adolf von Harnack, acknowledge that Christ has some kind of divine filiation, superior to his messiahship.[4] However, they deny that Jesus is true God in virtue of this filiation.

---

[3] See all of *Lamentabile*, nos. 27–38 (Denzinger, nos. 3427–3438).

[4] See Renan, *Vie de Jésus*, 440: "Rest now in your glory, noble founder and initiator [*noble initiateur*]. Your work is complete. Your divinity has its foundation. . . . Henceforth beyond the reach of fragility, you will assist, from the lofty heights of divine peace, in the infinite consequences of your acts. You will no longer be distinguished from God." And ibid., 464–474: "In order to make Himself be adored to this degree, he must have been worthy of adoration. . . . The faith, enthusiasm, and constancy of the first Christian generation can only be explained if we presuppose, at the origin of the entire movement, a man having colossal proportions. . . . This sublime person, who each day still presides over the world's destiny, we may indeed call Him divine, not in the sense that Jesus would have absorbed everything that is divine or that

{{163}} *Among conservative Protestants*, many, like Godet and, in England, Stevens, Gore, Ottley, and Sanday, all defend Christ's divinity, not only on the basis of the fourth Gospel and the letters of St. Paul but also on the basis of the Synoptic Gospels themselves.[5]

Therefore, let us see what we can find in the Synoptic Gospels, the Gospel according to John, and in the letters of St. Paul concerning these two mysteries of the Incarnation and the Redemption.

In order to understand the state of the question, we must note the fact that Jesus is called the *Son of God* more than fifty times in the Gospel. The question we face is: *In what sense must this expression be understood?*

In Scripture, the term *son* is said *in relation to man* in two ways. Strictly and properly, it signifies a living being coming forth from another living being in conformity with its nature. In its broad and metaphorical sense, it designates a disciple or adopted heir. *In relation to God*, it is also used in two manners. In a broad sense, it is applied to men who participate in God's spirit and life. Thus, Christians are called "sons of God," τέκνα Θεοῦ. However, in its proper and strict sense, it is said of the second person of the Trinity: ὁ υἱὸς τοῦ Θεοῦ, *the only-begotten One, who is in the Father's bosom* (John 1:18). This name, "Son of God," sometimes is perhaps equivalent, in the Gospel, only to the name *Messiah*—namely, when it is attributed to Jesus by those who do not yet seem to know of his divinity.[6] However, merely by the Synoptic Gospels themselves, it is certain that Jesus said that he is the Son of God in the proper, strict, and loftiest sense—namely, inasmuch as he declared that he had a divine nature, not only a participation in this nature (that is, a sharing in it through grace).[7]

§2. Christ's Testimony, in the Synoptic Gospels, concerning His Divinity

In[8] the Synoptic Gospels, Jesus declares his divinity in two ways: (1) by claiming for himself rights / privileges that alone belong to God; and (2) by affirming that he is the Son of God.

A. ***Christ attributes divine rights to himself.*** There are seven particular themes that we can consider.

He would be identical with it but, rather, in the sense that Jesus is the individual who enabled His fellows to make the greatest step toward the divine."

On the opinion held by these contemporary rationalists, see Lepin, *Jésus messie et fils de Dieu*, 228ff.

5   On the opinion held by these Protestants, see ibid., 237.

6   Mark 3:11: "The unclean spirit . . . shouted saying: 'You are the Son of God.'"

7   Christians are themselves said to be "sharers in the divine nature" (2 Pet 1:4).

8   See Lepin, *Jésus messie et fils de Dieu*, 267–371.

(1) *Jesus is greater than every creature*, in accord with his own testimony. He is greater than Jonah, Solomon, and David (Matt 12:41–52), who called him Lord (Mark 12:36; Matt 22:45). He is greater than Moses and Elijah, who appeared next to him on the day of the transfiguration (Matt 17:3). He is greater than John the Baptist (Matt 11:3, 11) and greater than the angels, for they "ministered to him" (Mark 1:13; Matt 4:11) after the temptation in the desert. {{164}} Indeed, the angels are *his*: "The Son of man shall send his angels, and they shall gather out of his kingdom all scandals" (Matt 13:41, DR; also 16:27, 24:31).

(2) *He demands faith, obedience, and love in relation to himself, to the point of denying all contrary affections and even to the point of sacrificing one's life.*

"He that loveth father or mother more than me, is not worthy of me; and he that loveth son or daughter more than me, is not worthy of me" (Matt 10:37, DR; Luke 14:26). These words would be the sign of odious and intolerable pride if Jesus were not God. Likewise, he says: "Amen I say to you, there is no man who hath left house or brethren or sisters or father or mother . . . *for my sake* and for the gospel, who shall not receive a hundred times as much, now in this time . . . with persecutions: and in the world to come life everlasting" (Mark 10:29–30, DR). And again, "he that is not with me, is against me: and he that gathereth not with me, scattereth" (Matt 12:30, DR). Likewise: "Blessed are those who suffer persecution for the sake of justice . . . for my sake."

(3) *He speaks as the Supreme Lawgiver*, completely equal to the divine authority in giving the old law. Completing and perfecting this divine law, and freeing it from the false interpretations of it by the teachers of his days [*rabbinorum*], he says many times over, "It was said of old . . . However, I say to you . . ." (Matt 5:21–48). Likewise, he prohibited divorce, which Moses had permitted on account of the hardness of men's hearts (Matt 5:32; 19:9). He says that he is the lord of the Sabbath (Mark 2:27, 28).

(4) *He performed miracles in his own name*, telling the paralytic and a number of dead people to "rise" (Matt 9:6; Mark 2:5; 5:41; Luke 7:14). In the midst of the storm, he said to the sea: "'Peace, be still.' And the wind ceased." (Mark 4:39). The apostles performed miracles in Jesus's name (Matt 7:22; Acts 3:6; 4:10).

(5) *He claimed for himself the right to be able to forgive sins*, which according to the Jews was a privilege belonging to God alone:

And Jesus, seeing their faith, said to the man sick of the palsy: Be of good heart, son, thy sins are forgiven thee. And behold some of the scribes said within themselves: He blasphemeth. And Jesus seeing their thoughts, said: Why do you think evil in your hearts? Whether is easier, to say, Thy sins are forgiven thee: or to say, Arise, and walk? But that you may know that the Son of man hath power on earth to forgive sins, then saying to the man sick of the palsy: Arise, take up thy bed, and go into thy house. And he arose, and went into his house. (Matt 9:2–7, DR, slightly modified)

Likewise, he attributed to himself the power of being able to refresh souls: "Come to me all you that labor and are burdened, and I will refresh you" (Matt 11:28, DR). Nay, he claimed for himself the right to give others the power to remit sins (Matt 18:18).

(6) *He attributed to himself the power to judge the living and the dead*: "You shall see the Son of man sitting on the right hand of the power of God and coming with the clouds of heaven" (Mark 14:62, DR; also 8:38; 13:26). "And he shall send his angels with a trumpet and a great voice: and they shall gather together his elect from the four winds, from the farthest parts of the heavens to the utmost bounds of them" (Matt 24:31, DR).

(7) *He promised to send the Holy Spirit*: "And I send the promise of my Father upon you" (Luke 24:49, DR). Therefore, the Holy Spirit is not inferior [to him].

{{165}} Finally, *he receives adoration* (Matt 8:2; 28:9, 17; Mark 5:6), whereas by contrast, Peter, Paul, Barnabas, and the angels all reject such adoration, stating that they do not deserve it (Acts 10:25–26; 14:14; Rev 19:10; 22:8).

B. *In the Synoptic Gospels, Jesus affirms many times that he is the Son of God in a proper and strict sense.* (1) "*All things are delivered to me by my Father. And no one knoweth the Son but the Father: neither doth any one know the Father, but the Son,* and he to whom it shall please the Son to reveal him" (Matt 11:27, DR; Luke 10:21).

Jesus said these words after uttering reproaches against the cities of Chorazin and Bethsaida, then giving thanks for his disciples' faith: "I confess to thee, O Father, . . . because thou hast hid these things from the wise and prudent, and hast revealed them to little ones" (Matt 11:25, DR). The authenticity of this text is admitted by the majority of Protestant critics. Now, in this text, the equality of the Father and the Son are declared in relation to knowledge and knowability. However, this kind of *equality* rests upon consubstantiality, as St. Thomas notes: "For the substance of the Father surpasses every intellect, since the essence of the Father is said to be unknowable, like the substance of the Son."[9] The Son is only known by the Father and therefore, like the Father, exceeds all created knowledge. Hence, he is God. Among the modernists, Loisy admitted this traditional

---

[9] See St. Thomas, *In XI Matth.*

explanation of this text. Nay, he added that its sense is substantially the same as that of John 1:18 (DR): "No man hath seen God at any time: the only begotten Son who is in the bosom of the Father, he hath declared him."[10] These two texts sit at the same lofty heights. No distance separates them, he says. However, against nearly all critics—not only those who are Catholic but also Protestants, even liberal ones[11]—Loisy unfoundedly holds that this declaration, even as contained in Matthew and Luke, was not a genuine expression stated by Christ himself but, rather, was ascribed to him by the later Christian tradition.[12]

(2) *Christ's response to Peter's confession.* "Simon Peter answered and said: *Thou art Christ, the Son of the living God.* And Jesus answering said to him: *Blessed art thou, Simon Bar-Jona: because flesh and blood hath not revealed it to thee, but my Father who is in heaven*" (Matt 16:16–17, DR; Mark 6:29; Luke 9:20).

Some say that it is impossible to prove historically that Peter affirmed anything more in this confession than Jesus's messiahship, for in Mark 8:29 he only says, "Thou art Christ," and in Luke 9:20, "Thou art the Christ of God." Only in Matthew do we read "Thou art Christ, the Son of the living God." Nonetheless, Jesus's response makes it clear enough that, even historically speaking, Peter affirmed more than his messiahship, for the signs of messiahship were already manifest for the apostles from the start of Jesus's ministry, and many of them acknowledged it (e.g., Andrew, Philip, and Nathanial in John 1:41 and 49). Jesus also set forth these signs for John the Baptist's disciples (Matt 11:4). Hence, mere messiahship did not require such revelation. Nay, on the basis of the text from St. Matthew cited above, "no one knoweth the Son but the Father" (Matt 11:27, DR), we can argue as follows: If Peter was only able to know what he affirmed concerning Jesus as something coming from the Father, this is a sign that he affirmed his divine filiation. {{166}} However, it does not follow that Peter at this time knew through faith the nature of this divine filiation as explicitly as it would come to be defined later on by the Church.[13]

(3) *The formula of Baptism.* In Matthew 28:18–20 (DR), following the account of Christ's Resurrection, we read:

And Jesus coming, spoke to them, saying: *All power is given to me in heaven and in earth.* Going therefore, teach ye all nations, *baptizing them in the name of the Father and of the Son and of the Holy Ghost.* Teaching them to observe all things whatsoever I have commanded

---

[10] See Loisy, *L'évangile et l'église*, 47.
[11] The authenticity of this text is admitted by rationalists and liberal protestants like Weiss, Keim, Wendt, Oskar and Heinrich Holtzmann, Stapfer, et al.
[12] Against Loisy's opinion here, see Marie-Joseph Lagrange, "L'évangile et l'église, par Alfred Loisy," *Revue biblique* (Apr. 1903): 304; also see Lepin, *Jésus messie et fils de Dieu*, 323.
[13] See Lepin, *Jésus messie et fils de Dieu*, 332.

you. And behold *I am with you all days, even to the consummation of the world.*

The person who has power over all things in heaven and earth has power over every creature, which belongs to God alone. Likewise, in the baptismal formula, the Son appears as being equal to the Father and the Holy Spirit. However, if he were not God, he would be infinitely lower than the Father and the Holy Spirit.[14] In the final words, he promises divine assistance up to the consummation of the world. Nay, he says, "I am with you," thus confirming what had been written concerning him: "They shall call his name Emmanuel, which being interpreted is, God with us" (Matt 1:23, DR; Isa 7:14).

(4) *Jesus's response to Caiaphas.* In Matthew 26:63–65 (DR), when Christ appeared before the Sanhedrin, the chief priest, rising up, stated to him:

I adjure thee by the living God, that thou tell us if thou be the Christ the Son of God.[15] Jesus saith to him: Thou hast said it. Nevertheless, I say to you, hereafter you shall see the Son of man sitting on the right hand of the power of God and coming in the clouds of heaven. Then the high priest rent his garments, saying: He hath blasphemed. What further need have we of witnesses? Behold, now you have heard the blasphemy.

In this response, Jesus appears as being something more than a messiah, for the mere dignity of being a messiah does not involve divine filiation, sitting at the right hand of God, and the exercise of the loftiest power. Hence, as we read in all three Synoptic Gospels, Caiaphas rent his garments, saying, "He has blasphemed."[16] And as regards this point, the Synoptic account is illuminated by the fourth Gospel, wherein we read in 5:18 (DR), after the curing of the paralytic in the Pool of Bethesda: "Therefore the Jews sought the more to kill him, because he did not only break the Sabbath but also said God was his Father, *making himself equal to God.*" Likewise, in John 10:31, after Christ said, "I and the Father are one," the Jews took up stones in order to cast them at him.

---

[14] As regards the authenticity of this baptismal formula, see Lepin's article "Evangiles canoniques" in *Dictionnaire apologétique de la foi catholique*, col. 1621. Without any legitimate motive, Loisy denies this authenticity, but he is forced to admit: "The use of this formula is attested to in *Didache* 7.1, and one is justified in believing that it was universally received in the Churches by the beginning of the second century" (*Les evangiles synoptiques*, vol. 2, 751).

[15] In Mark 14:61 (DR): "Art thou the Christ, the Son of the Blessed God?" In Luke 22:66 (DR): "If thou be the Christ, tell us"; and 22:70 (DR): "Art thou then the Son of God?"

[16] Concerning this set of texts in the Synoptic Gospels, see Lepin, *Jésus messie et fils de Dieu*, 289 (note).

This explains why Caiaphas, not unaware of Christ's earlier declarations, asked him the question in order to give a fatal response to it. Hence, we read in John 19:7 (DR), in the Passion narrative: "The Jews answered him: We have a law; and according to the law he ought to die, because *he made himself the Son of God.*"

(5) *There is the question raised by Jesus to the Jews concerning Christ the Son of David* in Matthew 22:41–46 (DR):

> {{167}} And the Pharisees being gathered together, Jesus asked them, saying: What think you of Christ? Whose son is he? They said to him: David's. He saith to them: How then doth David in spirit call him Lord, saying: The Lord said *to my Lord, Sit on my right hand,* until I make thy enemies thy footstool? *If David then call him Lord, how is he his son*? And no man was able to answer him a word.

Likewise, see Luke 20:44 and Mark 12:37.

The authenticity of this text is admitted by particularly liberal critics.[17] However, the Lord spoken of in the Psalm is superior to David and equal to the first Lord—namely, to God the Father.

(6) *The parable of the murdering workers in the vineyard.* The authenticity of this parable is admitted by the majority of critics.[18] In Mark 12:2–12 (DR) (see Matt 21:31–46 and Luke 20:1–19) we read:

> And at the season (the lord of the vineyard) sent to the husbandmen a servant to receive of the husbandmen of the fruit of the vineyard. Who, having laid hands on him, beat him and sent him away empty. And again, he sent to them *another servant*: and him they wounded in the head and used him reproachfully. And again, he sent another, and him they killed: and *many others,* of whom

---

[17] See H[ans Hinrich] Wendt, G[ustave] Dalman, B[ernhard] Weiss, E[dmond] Stapfer, P[aul] Wernle, and O[skar] Holtzmann. (Cf. Lepin, *Jésus messie et fils de Dieu*, 306). Loisy seems to deny the authenticity of this text, though for only one reason, for according to him, the divinity of Christ affirmed in this text was only gradually deduced from the notion of Messiah by Christian consciousness.

[18] Loisy doubts the authority of this parable because it includes a very detailed prophecy concerning Christ's death. According to him, it is more natural to say that this parable was conceived through a kind of process of idealization following upon Christ's death. However, this is nothing more than an *a priori* denial of the supernatural order. On this, see Lepin, *Jésus messie et fils de Dieu*, 309ff: all of Christ's preaching would need to be rejected, with nearly nothing remaining historically concerning Christ.

some they beat, and others they killed. *Therefore, having yet one son, most dear to him, he also sent him unto them last of all,* saying: They will reverence my son. But the husbandmen said one to another: This is *the heir.* Come let us kill him and the inheritance shall be ours. And laying hold on him, they killed him and cast him out of the vineyard. What therefore will the lord of the vineyard do? He will come and destroy those husbandmen and will give the vineyard to others. And have you not read this scripture, The stone which the builders rejected, the same is made the head of the corner. By the Lord has this been done, and it is wonderful in our eyes.

And they sought to lay hands on him: but they feared the people. For they knew that he spoke this parable to them. And leaving him, they went their way.

The application of this parable was obvious: The servants sent by the lord of the vineyard were the prophets, and Jesus himself will say more clearly, a little later on, to the Pharisees in Matthew 23:31–37 (DR):

Wherefore you are witnesses against yourselves, that you are the sons of them that killed the prophets. Fill ye up then the measure of your fathers. You serpents, generation of vipers, how will you flee from the judgment of hell? Therefore behold I send to you prophets and wise men and scribes: and some of them you will put to death and crucify. . . . That upon you may come all the just blood that hath been shed upon the earth. . . . Jerusalem, Jerusalem, thou that killest the prophets and stonest them that are sent unto thee, how often would I have gathered together thy children . . . and thou wouldst not?

Therefore, if the servants of the Lord are the prophets, his most dear son is something more than a prophet or the Messiah but, rather, truly is his son. The same point as that expressed in this parable is expressed in full also in the beginning of the Letter to the Hebrews:

God, who, at sundry times and in divers manners, spoke in times past to the fathers by the prophets, last of all, in these days, hath spoken to us by his Son, whom he hath appointed heir of all things, by whom also he made the world. Who being the brightness of his glory and the figure of his substance and upholding all things by the word of his power, making purgation of sins, sitteth on the right hand of the majesty on high. (Heb 1:1–3, DR)

{{168}} CONCLUSION. Therefore, against the modernists, we must say: *In the Synoptic Gospels, Jesus's declarations concerning his eminent dignity transcend mere messiahship and express the divine filiation that belongs to Christ in an altogether proper manner.* Moreover, *this divine filiation* is not only superior to messiahship (which, as was said earlier, is conceded by many contemporary rationalists, like, for example, Harnack) but, moreover, *establishes Christ as being above all creatures, equal to God, and himself God,* the Second Person of the Trinity.

§3. Confirmation from the Acts of the Apostles

Nor can it be said that the aforementioned declarations were gradually formed through a kind of process of idealization, following upon Christ's death and then ascribed to him, *for the time that would have been necessary for such idealization was lacking,* given that *we can certainly say that, from the day of Pentecost, the apostles taught that Jesus is not only the Messiah but, indeed, is God.*

This certitude is had on the basis of the Acts of the Apostles, whose authenticity is historically certain.[19] This book refers to *St. Peter's publicly spoken words,* in which we read:

> The God of Abraham and the God of Isaac and the God of Jacob, the God of our fathers, hath glorified *his Son Jesus,* whom you indeed delivered up.... But you denied the Holy One and the Just: and desired a murderer to be granted unto you. *But the author of life* you killed, whom God hath raised from the dead: of which we are witnesses. . . . And the faith which is by him hath given this perfect soundness (to the crippled man who was sitting at the door of the temple) in the sight of you all. (Acts 3:13–16, DR)

---

[19] See Eugène Jacquier, *Histoire des livres du Nouveau Testament,* vol. 3 (Paris: Lecoffre, 1908). See also J.-B. Semeria, "Les Actes des Apôtres," *Revue biblique* (1895): 328; Vincent Rose, "La critique nouvelle et les Actes des Apôtres," *Revue biblique* (1898): 325–342. Not only all Catholics and conservative Protestants (like Barde, Blass, Plummer, Headlam, and Zahn), but even many rationalists (like Renan, Reuss, Harnack, et al.) attribute the full text of the Acts of the Apostles to St. Luke, the companion of St. Paul. According to Catholics and conservative Protestants, it is more probable that the Book of Acts was written around 63–64, or at least before AD 70. Among the rationalists, the school of Tübingen said that it was written around AD 150. However, by force of the historical evidence, the rationalist Harnack says that it was written between AD 78 and 83 or perhaps even between 60 and 70. See Adolf von Harnack, *Die Apostelgeschichte* (Leipzig: Hinrichs, 1908), 211.

Now, the author of life spoken of here is none other than God himself. Then the chief priest and elders asked Peter in whose name he had performed this miracle, and he responded:

> By the name of our Lord Jesus Christ of Nazareth, whom you crucified, whom God hath raised from the dead, even by him, this man standeth here before you, whole. *This is the stone which was rejected by you the builders, which is become the head of the corner. Neither is there salvation in any other.* For there is no other name under heaven given to men, whereby we must be saved. . . . (However, the Priests and temple functionaries) could say nothing against it . . . and charged (Peter and John) not to speak at all, nor teach in the name of Jesus. (Acts 4:10–18, DR)

Shortly thereafter, when the apostles were freed from prison by an angel, they were interrogated once more by the chief priest: "But Peter and the apostles answering, said: We ought to obey God rather than men. The God of our fathers hath raised up Jesus, whom you put to death, hanging him upon a tree. Him hath God exalted with his right hand, to be *Prince and Saviour*, to give repentance to Israel and remission of sins" (Acts 5:29–31, DR). Now, God alone is the savior of souls, forgiving their sins. At the council of Jerusalem, in order to establish that the Gentiles are not bound to observe the Mosaic Law, Peter said: "Now therefore, why tempt you God to put a yoke upon the necks of the disciples which neither our fathers nor we have been able to bear? *But by the grace of the Lord Jesus Christ, we believe to be saved*, in like manner as they also" (Acts 15:10–11, DR). {{169}} Similarly, in many places, Jesus is called "Lord" by Peter (cf. Acts 2:36; 11:20). *He was made the Lord of all* (Acts 10:36) *by God, the judge of the living and the dead* (Acts 10:42). Finally, in Jesus's name, the apostles performed miracles, conferred baptism, and the deacon St. Stephen said, while dying, "Lord Jesus, receive my spirit" (Acts 7:58, DR).

   In these public words proclaimed by St. Peter immediately after Pentecost, we have testimony to the primitive Church's faith, already believing that Jesus is the Son of God, the Author of Life, the Lord of all, the Savior of all, the Judge of the living and the dead. Therefore, against the rationalists Weiss, Oskar Holtzmann, and Loisy, we must say: *There cannot have been a process of idealization between the primitive documents of Christianity and the composition of the Gospels*; indeed, these primitive documents do not describe Jesus as being merely human and only the son of David.

   Moreover, adversaries would need to explain *how so substantial an alteration would have taken place without any complaint*; how, at a time when the memory of the apostolic preaching was so vivid, could this dogma of Christ's divinity have been introduced, against the will of Jewish converts, who adhered so firmly to monotheism, and against the will of all the first Christians, and then spread throughout the whole world? To the contrary, history makes it clear that there were heretics, such as the Ebionites, who denied Christ's divinity, being immediately and unanimously condemned by the Church, as is clear from the writings of the Apostolic Fathers.

§4. A Second Confirmation Drawn from St. Paul's Letters

In his letters, St. Paul, expressly *affirming Christ's divinity*, does not, however, announce it to the churches like something new and unheard of but rather *speaks about it as though it were an already-received dogma*. Now, the chief letters of St. Paul (1 and 2 *Thessalonians, Galatians,* 1 and 2 *Corinthians, Romans, Ephesians, Colossians,* and *Philippians*) were written by St. Paul from AD 48 to 59 or 50 to 64, as is admitted by many rationalists, including Harnack and Jülicher.[20]

Here, it suffices to refer to the principal testimonies from St. Paul concerning Christ's divinity.[21]

- Romans 1:3–4 (DR): "Concerning his Son, who was made to him *of the seed of David, according to the flesh,* who was predestinated the *Son of God in power, according to the spirit of sanctification,* by the resurrection of our *Lord* Jesus Christ from the dead."
- Romans 8:3 (DR): "God, sending *his own Son* in the likeness of sinful flesh and of sin, hath condemned sin in the flesh."
- Romans 8:32 (DR): "He that spared not even *his own Son,* but delivered him up for us all, how hath he not also, with him, given us all things?"
- Galatians 4:4–6 (DR): "But when the fulness of the time was come, God sent *his Son, made of a woman, made under the law*: That he might redeem them who were under the law: that we might receive the adoption of sons. And because you are sons, God hath sent the *Spirit of his Son* into your hearts, crying: Abba, Father."

Therefore, according to St. Paul, Jesus is the Son of God according to the Spirit of sanctification and from the seed of David according to the flesh.

Moreover, St. Paul affirms the eternal preexistence of the Son of God, prior to the Incarnation, in 2 *Corinthians* 4:4 (DR): "The god of this world . . . hath blinded the

---

[20] See the discussion above concerning the historicity of the Gospels.
[21] See Vincent Rose, "Études sur la théologie de St. Paul," *Revue biblique* (1903): 349. Also see Ferdinand Prat, *La théologie de St. Paul* [(Paris: Beauchesne, 1912)].

minds of unbelievers, that the light of the gospel of the glory *of Christ, who is the image of God*, should not shine unto them." Colossians 1:15–19 (DR):

> *Who is the image of the invisible God, the firstborn of every creature. For in him were all things created in heaven and on earth, visible and invisible, whether thrones, or dominations, or principalities, or powers. All things were created by him and in him. And he is before all; and by him all things consist.* And he is the head of the body, the church: who is the beginning, the firstborn from the dead, that *in all things he may hold the primacy: because in him, it hath well pleased the Father that all fulness should dwell.*

{{170}} In this text, the Son of God is openly said to be the Creator, just as in Romans 11:36 (DR), it is said of God, "For of him, and by him, and in him, are all things."[22]

Likewise, in 1 Corinthians 23–30 (DR): "But we preach Christ crucified: unto the Jews indeed a stumbling block, and unto the Gentiles foolishness. But unto them that are called, both Jews and Greeks, Christ, *the power of God and the wisdom of God*. . . . But of him are you in Christ Jesus, who of God is made unto us wisdom and justice and sanctification and redemption." Colossians 2:9–10 (DR): "*For in him (Christ) dwelleth all the fulness of the Godhead corporeally. And you are filled in him, who is the head of all principality and power.*" 2 Corinthians 5:19 (DR): "For *God indeed was in Christ*, reconciling the world to himself." Philippians 2:5–7 (DR): "For let this mind be in you, which was also in Christ Jesus: *Who being in the form of God*, thought it not robbery *to be equal with God*, but emptied himself, taking the form of a servant, being made in the likeness of men, and in habit found as a man." The expression, "being in the form of God," ὅς ἐν μορφῇ Θεοῦ, the word μορφή (i.e., "form") signifies the divine essence / nature, as is clear from the words following upon it: "to be equal with God."[23] There can be no clearer affirmation of the glorious preexistence of the Son of God prior to the Incarnation.

Likewise, see Romans 9:3–5 (DR): "I wished myself to be an anathema from Christ, for my brethren . . . *of whom is Christ, according to the flesh, who is over all things, God blessed forever. Amen.*"[24]

---

[22] See St. Thomas, *In I Col.*, lect. 4.

[23] See Prat, *La théologie de St. Paul*, vol. 1, 445; also see J. Labourt, "Notes d'exégèse sur Philipp, II 5–11," *Revue biblique* (1898): 402[–415].

[24] *A particular* difficulty does exist in this text with regard to a matter of punctuation. Tischendorf Gebhardt in his edition reads, "from whom is Christ, according to the flesh. Who is over all things, God blessed forever. Amen." If the period is placed after "according to the flesh," the last line is only an invocation to God. However, according to the editions of Nestle,

Finally, in *Hebrews*[25] 1:2–3 (DR): "In these days, (God) hath spoken to us by his Son, whom he hath appointed heir of all things, *by whom also he made the world. Who being the brightness of his glory and the figure of his substance and upholding all things by the word of his power*, making purgation of sins, *sitteth on the right hand of the majesty on high*." And likewise, in 1:10 (DR), the words of the Psalm are applied to him: "Thou in the beginning, O Lord, didst found the earth: and the works of thy hands are the heavens." He is declared to be superior to the prophets, to Moses, and to the angels, as the eternal mediator and priest: "Whereby he is able also to save for ever them that come to God by him; always living to make intercession for us" (Heb 7:25, DR).

And by speaking thus, St. Paul intended to affirm something that was already believed in the Church, not something new.

§5. Christ's Testimony, in St. John, concerning His Divinity

Just as in the Synoptics, in the fourth Gospel, Jesus on many occasions calls himself *the Son of Man*. The use of this term is a sign of his humility and of the subjection of his humanity to his Father.[26] However, he especially affirms, again and again, the fact that he is *the Son of God* and *Lord*.

{{171}} "You call me Master and Lord. And you say well, for so I am" (John 13:13, DR). "The hour is come. Glorify *thy Son*, that thy Son may glorify thee. As thou hast given him power over all flesh, that *he may give eternal life* to all whom thou hast given him. . . . And all my things are thine, and thine are mine" (John 17:1–10, DR).

> The Jews sought the more to kill him, because he did not only break the sabbath but also said God was his Father, *making himself equal to God*. Then Jesus answered and said to them: Amen, amen, I say unto you, the Son cannot do anything of himself, but what he seeth the Father doing: for what things soever he doth, these the Son also doth in like manner. . . . For as the Father raiseth up the dead and giveth life: *so the Son also giveth life to whom he will*. For neither does the Father judge any man: *but hath given all judgment to the Son*. That all men may honor the Son, as they honor the Father. . . . For as

---

Westcott-Hort, Weymouth, Weis, and many other liberal critics, there is only a comma there, after "according to the flesh." All the Fathers of the Church read this text as affirming Christ's divinity, as do all Catholic exegetes. See Alfred Durand, "La divinité de Jésus Christ dans St. Paul," *Revue biblique* (1903): 550.

[25] According to Jacquier, *Histoire des livres du Nouveau Testament*, this letter was written by St. Paul himself before AD 70. According to the rationalist Harnack, it was probably composed by Barnabas between AD 65 and 96, perhaps before 70.

[26] See Batiffol, *L'enseignement de Jésus*, 196–197.

the Father hath life in himself, so he hath given to the Son also to have life in himself. (John 5:18–26, DR)

"You are from beneath: I am from above. You are of this world: I am not of this world" (John 8:23, DR; 3:13; 7:28).

"For from God I proceeded and came" (John 8:42, DR). *"I came forth from the Father* and am come into the world: again I leave the world and I go to the Father. . . . And yet I am not alone, because the Father is with me" (John 16:28–32, DR). And it is a question of filiation, properly so-called, for Jesus says: "Amen, amen, I say to you, *before Abraham was made, I AM"* (John 8:58, DR). *"And now glorify thou me, O Father, with thyself, with the glory which I had, before the world was, with thee . . .* because thou hast loved me before the creation of the world" (John 17:5, 24, DR).

Moreover, Jesus sees God: "Not that any man hath seen the Father: but he who is of God, he hath seen the Father" (John 6:46, DR). "As the Father knoweth me, and I know the Father" (John 10:15, DR). *"All things whatsoever the Father hath are mine.* Therefore, I said that he shall receive of mine (the Spirit of Truth) and shew it to you" (John 16:15, DR). "Philip, he that seeth me seeth the Father also. How sayest thou: Shew us the Father? Do you not believe that *I am in the Father and the Father in me?"* (John 14:9–10, DR; 17:21). Nay, *"I and the Father are one"* (John 10:3; see 17:11). The Jews understood this as meaning "the Father's dignity is the same as mine," for they immediately "took up stones therefore to cast them at him." Similarly, he said, *"I am the way, and the truth, and the life.* No man cometh to the Father, but by me" (John 14:6, DR).

These declarations by Christ express the same thing as do the words recounted in Matthew (Matt 11:27, DR) and Luke (10:22): "All things are delivered to me by my Father. And no one knoweth the Son but the Father: neither doth anyone know the Father, but the Son, and he to whom it shall please the Son to reveal him." And this latter declaration is not inferior to the words of John in the prologue to his Gospel: "In the beginning was the Word: and the Word was with God: and the Word was God. . . . And the Word was made flesh and dwelt among us (and we saw his glory, the glory as it were of the only begotten of the Father), full of grace and truth. . . . No man hath seen God at any time: the only begotten Son who is in the bosom of the Father, he hath declared him" (John 1:1, 14, 18, DR).[27]

---

[27] Likewise, see 1 John 1:1 (DR): "That which was from the beginning, which we have heard, which we have seen with our eyes, which we have looked upon and our hands have handled, of the word of life."

§6. Jesus Christ's Testimony, in the Gospels, concerning the Mystery of Redemption

Modernists hold that the doctrine concerning Christ's atoning death is not something found in the Gospels but, rather, is only Pauline.[28] Let us now consider Christ's declarations in the Gospels.

A. *In the Synoptic Gospels.* {{172}} "The Spirit of the Lord is upon me. Wherefore he hath anointed me to preach the gospel to the poor, he hath sent me to heal the contrite of heart" (Luke 4:18ff, DR; Mark 1:38). "For I am not come to call the just, but sinners" (Matt 9:13, DR). "*For the Son of man is come to save that which was lost.* . . . Even so it is not the will of your Father, who is in heaven, that one of these little ones should perish" (Matt 18:11–14, DR; Luke 9:56). "Even as the Son of man is not come to be ministered unto, but to minister and *to give his life as a redemption for many*" (Matt 20:28; Mark 10:4–5). On many occasions, he announces his Passion to his disciples, saying: "The Son of man shall be *betrayed* to the chief priests and the scribes: and *they shall condemn him to death. And shall deliver him to the Gentiles to be mocked and scourged and crucified: and the third day he shall rise again.* . . . Can you drink the chalice that I shall drink?" (Matt 20:18–22, DR; Mark 10:34; Luke 18:32). However, the disciples did not yet understand this lofty mystery. Before the Passion, instituting the Eucharist, Jesus said: "*This is my body, which is given for you. Do this for a commemoration of me.* . . . *This is the chalice, the new testament in my blood, which shall be shed for you*" (Luke 22:19–20, DR; Matt 26:28; Mark 16:24).[29]

B. *In the Gospel according to John.* "As the Father hath loved me, I also have loved you" (John 15:9, DR). "I will not now call you servants. . . . But I have called you friends" (John 15:15, DR). "*I am the good shepherd. The good shepherd giveth his life for his sheep*" (John 10:11, DR). "My sheep hear my voice. And I know them: and they follow me. *And I give them life everlasting* . . . . And no man shall pluck them out of my hand" (John 10:27–28, DR). "I am the light of the world. He that followeth me walketh not in darkness, but shall have the light of life" (John 8:12, DR). " I am the resurrection and the life: he that believeth in me, although he be dead, shall live. And everyone that liveth and believeth in me shall not die forever" (John 11:25–26, DR; 17:2). "Amen, amen, I say unto you: *He that believeth in me hath everlasting life.* I am the bread of life" (John 6:47–48, DR). "He that believeth in me, as the scripture saith: Out of his belly shall flow rivers of living water"

---

[28] See Pius X (Holy Office), *Lamentabili*, no. 38 (Denzinger, no. 3438).

[29] See Rose, *Études sur les Evangiles*, ch. 7.

(John 7:38, DR). "Abide in me: and I in you. . . . *I am the vine: you the branches.* He that abideth in me, and I in him, the same beareth much fruit: for without me you can do nothing" (John 15:4–5, DR). " No man cometh to the Father, but by me" (John 14:6, DR; 6:44–45).

"For this came I into the world; that I should give testimony to the truth" (John 18:37, DR). *"For God so loved the world, as to give his only begotten Son*: that whosoever believeth in him may not perish, but may have life everlasting" (John 3:16, DR; cf. 3:17–18). "I am come that they may have life and may have it more abundantly. . . . As the Father knoweth me, and I know the Father: *and I lay down my life for my sheep.* . . . Therefore doth the Father love me: because I lay down my life, that I may take it again. *No man taketh it away from me: but I lay it down of myself.* And I have power to lay it down: and I have power to take it up again. *This commandment have I received of my Father"* (John 10:10–18, DR). "Greater love than this no man hath, that a man lay down his life for his friends" (John 15:13, DR).

"Unless the grain of wheat falling into the ground die, itself remaineth alone. But if it die, it bringeth forth much fruit. . . . Now is my soul troubled. And what shall I say? Father, save me from this hour. {{173}} *But for this cause I came unto this hour.* Father, glorify thy name. . . . Now is the judgment of the world: *now shall the prince of this world be cast out. And I, if I be lifted up from the earth, will draw all things to myself.* Now this he said, signifying what death he should die" (John 12:24–33, DR). Therefore, these words, thus distinguished from this observation made by John, are the very words of the Lord.

Therefore, Christ clearly and openly taught the dogma of the Redemption,[30] and it is utterly false to say, with the modernists: "The doctrine of the expiatory death of Christ is not evangelical but, rather, is only Pauline."[31]

C. *St. Paul.* St. Paul explains this evangelical doctrine, saying: *"For all have sinned* and do need the glory of God. Being justified freely by his grace, through the redemption that is in Christ Jesus, whom God hath proposed to be a *propitiation*, through faith *in his blood"* (Rom 3:23–25, DR). "For as by the disobedience of one man (namely, Adam), many were made sinners: so also by the obedience of one, many shall be made just" (Rom 5:19, DR). God "spared not even his own Son but delivered him up for us all" (Rom 8:32, DR). "Christ also hath loved us and hath *delivered himself for us, an oblation and a sacrifice to God for an odor of sweetness"* (Eph 5:2, DR).

D. *Christ instituted the sacraments in order to apply his Redemption*

---

[30] Rivière, *Le dogme de la rédemption* ([Paris: Lecoffre,] 1905), 68–99.
[31] Pius X (Holy Office), *Lamentabili*, no. 38 (Denzinger, no. 3438).

[*through the ages*]. "Going therefore, teach ye all nations: *baptizing* them in the name of the Father and of the Son and of the Holy Ghost" (Matt 28:19, DR). "And taking bread, he gave thanks, and brake; and gave to them, saying: *This is my body*, which is given for you. *Do this for a commemoration of me*. In like manner, the chalice also" (Luke 22:19–20, DR). However, the Eucharist presupposes the Sacrament of Holy Orders. The nature and effect of Baptism and the Eucharist are explained in John 3:3–5 (DR): "Amen, amen, I say to thee (Nicodemus), unless a man be born again, he cannot see the kingdom of God." (Water is the material instrument and the Holy Spirit the efficient cause of grace, by means of which we are reborn to the divine life.) However, concerning the Eucharist, it is said in John 6:50–55 (DR): "This is the bread which cometh down from heaven: that if any man eat of it, he may not die. . . . The bread that I will give is my flesh, for the life of the world. . . . Except you eat the flesh of the Son of man and drink his blood, you shall not have life in you."

Moreover, Jesus said to the apostles after the Resurrection: "Receive ye the Holy Ghost. *Whose sins you shall forgive, they are forgiven them: and whose sins you shall retain, they are retained*" (John 20:22–23, DR). This is the institution of the Sacrament of Penance, which presupposes the Sacrament of Holy Orders.

E. *Concerning good and evil angels.* According to Christ's own teaching, there are *many* good angels and many demons.

"Thinkest thou that I cannot ask my Father, and he will give me presently more than twelve legions of angels?" (Matt 26:53, DR). *The holy angels* are in heaven (Mark 12:25). They "*always see the face of my Father* who is in heaven" (Matt 18:10). {{174}} "There shall be joy before the angels of God upon one sinner doing penance" (Luke 15:10, DR). They care for little ones (Matt 18:10). "So shall it be at the end of the world. The angels *shall go out and shall separate the wicked from among the just* and shall cast them into the furnace of fire" (Matt 13:49–50, DR). "The Son of man shall send his angels, and they shall gather out of his kingdom all scandals, and them that work iniquity. And shall cast them into the furnace of fire: there shall be weeping and gnashing of teeth" (Matt 13:41–42, DR). "Whosoever shall confess me before men, him shall the Son of man also confess before the angels of God" (Luke 12:8, DR).

Demons (i.e., wicked angels) also are said to exist. On many occasions, Christ casts them out (Matt 13:39; 25:41; Mark 5:8; 1:25; Luke 4:35; 9:1; 11:18). They are *spirits*: "He cast out the spirits with his word" (Matt 8:16, DR). "And when *an unclean spirit* is gone out of a man he walketh through dry places seeking rest, and findeth none. Then he saith: I will return into my house from whence I came out. And coming he findeth it empty, swept, and garnished. Then he goeth, and taketh with him seven other spirits more wicked than himself, and they enter in and dwell there; and the last state of that man is made worse than the first. So shall it be also to this wicked generation" (Matt 12:43–45, DR; Mark 5:9; Luke 8:30; 11:24–26).

Jesus gave his apostles the "power to cast out demons" (Mark 3:15). However, he said concerning certain demons: "But this kind is not cast out but by prayer and fasting" (Matt 17:20, DR; Mark 9:28). Satan is said to be the prince of demons: "And if Satan cast out Satan, he is divided against himself: how then shall his kingdom stand? And if I by Beelzebub cast out devils, by whom do your children cast them out? Therefore, they shall be your judges. *But if I by the Spirit of God cast out devils, then is the kingdom of God come upon you*" (Matt 12:26–28, DR; Mark 4:15). Jesus says to the apostles: "Simon, Simon, behold Satan hath desired to have you, that he may sift you as wheat. But I have prayed for thee, that thy faith fail not" (Luke 22:31–32, DR).

In the fourth Gospel, Satan is called "*the prince of this world*" (John 16:11). Jesus says to the Pharisees: "You are of your father the devil: and the desires of your father you will do. He was a *murderer* from the beginning: and he stood not in the truth, because truth is not in him. When he speaketh a lie, he speaketh of his own: for he is a liar, and the father thereof" (John 8:44, DR). However, before his Passion, Jesus says to his apostles: "The prince of this world cometh, and in me he hath not anything" (John 14:30, DR). And "the prince of this world is already judged" (John 16:11, DR).

Art. 3: His Testimony concerning the Christian Life

Let us now briefly consider the relation of the Law of the Gospel with the Mosaic Law, in particular considering the most important Christian precepts, councils, and virtues.

§1. The New Law of Christ Perfects the Old Mosaic Law

"Do not think that I am come to destroy the law, or the prophets. I am not come to destroy, but to fulfil" (Matt 5:17, DR).

From the beginning of his preaching, Jesus, in the Sermon on the Mount (Matt 5 and 6), *purified the Old Law of the interpretations of the scribes and Pharisees, bringing it to completion and perfection as regards the moral precepts.* (a) Regarding *murder*, "it was said to them of old: Thou shalt not kill. . . . But I say to you, that whosoever is angry with his brother, shall be in danger of the judgment." {{175}} (b) Regarding *adultery*, "whosoever shall look on a woman to lust after her, hath already committed adultery with her in his heart." (c) He declares *marriage* to be indissoluble. (d) He prohibits oaths in general, lest they be made without a just cause. (e) *Regarding love for one's enemies*: "You have heard that it hath been said: An eye for an eye, and a tooth for a tooth. But I say to you not to resist evil: but if one strike thee on thy right cheek, turn to him also the other. . . .

Love your enemies: do good to them that hate you: and pray for them that persecute and calumniate you." [(f)] *As regards the purity of one's intention*: "Take heed that you do not your justice before men, to be seen by them: otherwise you shall not have a reward of your Father who is in heaven. . . . That thy alms may be in secret. . . . And when ye pray, you shall not be as the hypocrites, that love to pray. . . . that they may be seen by men."

However, from the beginning of his ministry, Jesus *implicitly announces the abrogation of the ceremonial precepts*: "Nobody putteth a piece of raw cloth unto an old garment. . . . Neither do they put new wine into old bottles. Otherwise the bottles break, and the wine runneth out" (Matt 9:16–17, DR; 2:21–22; Luke 5:36–39). Nay, Jesus announces the destruction of the temple in Jerusalem: "They shall not leave in thee a stone upon a stone: because thou hast not known the time of thy visitation" (Luke 19:44 [DR]; 21:6; Matt 24:2). And he says to the Samaritan woman: "Woman, believe me that the hour cometh, when you shall neither on this mountain, nor in Jerusalem, adore the Father. You adore that which you know not: we adore that which we know. For salvation is of the Jews. But the hour cometh, and now is, when the true adorers shall adore the Father in spirit and in truth. For the Father also seeketh such to adore him" (John 4:21–23, DR).

Thus, as St. Thomas says, "The old law is said to be eternal simply and absolutely as regards the moral precepts; however, even in the ceremonial precepts it lasts as that which figured the realities that they foreshadowed."[32]

§2. *The Christian Virtues*

However, in order to give particular consideration to the precepts of the evangelical law and the Christian virtues, let us see what Christ taught regarding true holiness / justice (in a general sense) concerning: faith, hope, and charity; prayer; humility, mortification, self-denial, and patience; prudent diligence, fidelity, vigilance, and zeal. For indeed, there are particular Christian virtues that lay beyond the natural virtues defined by the Greek philosophers—namely, prudence, justice toward others, fortitude / courage, and temperance. However, these latter virtues are elevated in the Christian life[33] and are connected with charity, according to the words of St. Paul: "Charity is patient, is kind: charity envieth not, dealeth not perversely, is not puffed up; is not ambitious, seeketh not her own, is not provoked to anger, thinketh no evil . . . beareth all things . . . endureth all things" (1 Cor 13:4–8, DR).

When rightly ordered, this simple exposition already provides an apologetic argument drawn from the sublimity of Christ's doctrine.

---

[32] *ST* I-II, q. 103, a. 3, ad 1.

[33] See *ST* I-II, q. 61, a. 5; q. 63, a. 3 and 4.

(1) *True holiness*[34]

"*Seek ye therefore first the kingdom of God*, and his justice" (Matt 6:33, DR). "*Be you therefore perfect, as also your heavenly Father is perfect*" (Matt 5:48, DR). "Not everyone that saith to me, Lord, Lord, shall enter into the kingdom of heaven: but he *that doth the will of my Father who is in heaven*, he shall enter into the kingdom of heaven" (Matt 7:21, DR).

{{176}} "Take up my yoke upon you, and learn of me, because I am meek, and humble of heart: And you shall find rest to your souls. For my yoke is sweet and my burden light" (Matt 11:29–30, DR). "For whosoever shall do the will of God, he is my brother, and my sister, and mother" (Mark 3:35, DR; Luke 8:19, 21). "Blessed are they who hear the word of God and keep it" (Luke 11:28, DR).

"Not that which goeth into the mouth defileth a man: but what cometh out of the mouth, this defileth a man. . . . But the things which proceed out of the mouth, come forth from the heart, and those things defile a man . . . evil thoughts, . . . adulteries, . . . false testimonies, and blasphemies" (Matt 15:11–19, DR; Mark 7:15–23; Luke 11:39). "*If thy eye be single, thy whole body shall be lightsome*" (Matt 6:22, DR). "Take heed therefore that the light which is in thee be not darkness" (Luke 11:35, DR). He who gives alms, prays, or fasts so that he may be seen by men "has already received his reward" (Matt 6:2–16). This represents a commendation of *purity of intention*, which is the source of that *peace* that the world cannot give (John 14:27).

Thus, we see the Christian life has as its exemplary end, rule, manner of tending to the end, and its fruits.

(2) *Faith*

In the Synoptic Gospels, Jesus declares on many occasions that faith is absolutely *necessary for salvation*: "Go ye into the whole world and preach the gospel to every creature. He that believeth and is baptized shall be saved: *but he that believeth not shall be condemned*" (Mark 16:15–16, DR).

External confession of faith is also required: "Everyone therefore that shall confess me before men, I will also confess him before my Father who is in heaven. But he that shall deny me before men, I will also deny him before my Father who is in heaven" (Matt 10:32–33, DR). Jesus says to the sick who come to him in order to ask to be healed: "Do you believe that I can do this unto you?" (Matt 9:28, DR). And after the healing, he adds: "Thy faith hath made thee whole" (Luke 17:19, DR; Matt 9:22; Mark 5:34). He reproaches the Jews for their disbelief: "O unbelieving and perverse generation, how

---

[34] As St. Thomas says in *ST* II-II, q. 81, a. 8, holiness is a specific virtue—namely, the virtue of religion. However, it is also a general command, referring all of the acts of the virtues to God or, through this, disposing one to worship of God. It implies two things that are necessary for the application of the mind to God—namely, purity and firmness.

long shall I be with you? How long shall I suffer you?" (Matt 17:16, DR; Mark 9:18; Luke 9:41). He says to Peter when the latter was walking fearfully on the water: "O thou of little faith, why didst thou doubt?" (Matt 14:31, DR). And upon the calming of the storm, he said to his disciples: "Where is your faith?" (Luke 8:25). "What do you fear? Do you not yet have faith?" (Mark 4:40). He praised the *power of faith*: "For, amen I say to you, if you have faith as a grain of mustard seed, you shall say to this mountain: Remove from hence hither, and it shall remove: and nothing shall be impossible to you" (Matt 17:19, DR; 21:21; Luke 17:6; Mark 11:23). Nay, *the soul is justified through living faith*, for Jesus says to Mary Magdalene, who was a sinful woman in the city: "Many sins are forgiven her, because she hath loved much.... Thy sins are forgiven thee" (Luke 7:47–48, DR). And St. Paul says in Romans 4: Justification is not from works of the law but, rather, from faith in God, which was reputed to him unto justice.

A. *In the Gospel according to John,* Jesus not only preaches the absolute necessity of faith but also more profoundly manifests its object, its supernatural cause, and its effects.

(a) *The necessity of faith*: "He that believeth in him (namely, the Son of God) is not judged. But he that doth not believe is already judged: because he believeth not in the name of the only begotten Son of God" (John 3:18, DR). "Therefore, I said to you (namely, the Pharisees) that you shall die in your sins. *For if you believe not that I am he, you shall die in your sin*" (John 8:24, DR).

{{177}} (b) *The object of faith*: "We speak what we know and we testify what we have seen: and you receive not our testimony. If I have spoken to you earthly things, and you believe not: how will you believe, if I shall speak to you heavenly things?" (John 3:11–12, DR). And he says to his disciples: "But I have called you friends *because all things, whatsoever I have heard of my Father, I have made known to you*" (John 15:15, DR).

(c) *The cause of faith*: "This is the work of God, that you believe in him whom he hath sent" (John 6:29, DR). "No man can come to me, *except the Father, who hath sent me, draw him*. . . . But there are some of you that believe not. . . . Therefore did I say to you that no man can come to me, unless it be given him by my Father" (John 6:44, 65, 66, DR; likewise, see St. Thomas's commentary on this). "But you do not believe, because you are not of my sheep. *My sheep hear my voice. And I know them, and they follow me*" (John 10:26–27, DR). And St. Paul writes: "For by grace you are saved through faith: and that not of yourselves, for it is the gift of God" (Eph 2:8, DR).

Nonetheless, the motives of credibility, more than being merely sufficient, are indeed even manifest for nonbelievers: "But if I do (the works, that is, the miracles of my Father), though you will not believe me, believe the works: that you may know and believe that the Father is in me and I in the Father" (John 10:38, DR; 14:12). "The works themselves, which I do, give testimony of me" (John 5:36, DR).

(d) *The effects of faith*: "If you continue in my word, you shall be my disciples indeed. And you shall know the truth, and *the truth shall make you free*" (John 8:31–32, DR).

"Amen, amen, I say to you, he who believes in me has eternal life, and I will raise him up on the last day" (John 6:40, 47). "He that believeth in me, the works that I do, he also shall do; and greater than these shall he do, because I go to the Father" (John 14:12–13, DR).

(3) *Hope*

Hope is commended in the Gospel when prayer is discussed, as well as God's mercy and providence.

For example, "Ask, and it shall be given you. . . . Or what man is there among you, of whom if his son shall ask bread, will he reach him a stone? How much more will your Father who is in heaven, give good things to them that ask him?" (Matt 7:7–11, DR; the same is found in the other Gospels too). "Be not solicitous for your life, what you shall eat, nor for your body, what you shall put on. . . . Behold the birds of the air. . . . Your heavenly Father feedeth them. Are not you of much more value than they? . . . Seek ye therefore first the kingdom of God, and his justice, and all these things shall be added unto you" (Matt 6:25–33, DR). Likewise, see the parables that illustrate God's mercy. For example, in the *parable of the prodigal son*: "And when he was yet a great way off, his father saw him and was moved with compassion and running to him fell upon his neck and kissed him" (Luke 15:20, DR).

(4) **Charity**

A. *Toward God.* "Thou shalt love the Lord thy God with thy whole heart and with thy whole soul and with thy whole mind. This is the greatest and the first commandment" (Matt 22:37–38, DR; Mark 12:35; Luke 10:25–28). "Many sins are forgiven her, because she hath loved much" (Luke 7:47, DR).

"If you keep my commandments, you shall abide in my love" (John 15:10, DR). "He that loveth me shall be loved of my Father: and I will love him and will manifest myself to him. . . . If any one love me, he will keep my word. And my Father will love him and we will come to him and will make our abode with him" (John 14:21–23, DR). "And I will ask the Father: and he shall give you another Paraclete, that he may abide with you forever" (John 14:16, DR).

{{178}} B. *Charity for our neighbors.* "And the second (commandment) is like to this: Thou shalt love thy neighbor as thyself. On these two commandments dependeth the whole law and the prophets" (Matt 22:39–40, DR; Luke 10:25–28; these two fundamental commandments were already found in Deut 6:5 and Lev 19:18).

"All things therefore whatsoever you would that men should do to you, do you also to them" (Matt 7:12, DR; Luke 6:31). And in the *parable of the Good Samaritan* (Luke 10:25–27) Jesus responded to the question, "Who is my neighbor?" stating that even foreigners and enemies in need of aid are one's neighbor.

Jesus said to his disciples: "A new commandment I give unto you: That you love one another, *as I have loved you.* . . . By this shall all men know that you are my disciples" (John 13:34–35; 15:12–17). "If then I being your Lord and Master, have *washed your feet*; you also ought to wash one another's feet" (John 13:14, DR). "Holy Father, keep them in thy name whom thou hast given me: that they may be one, *as we also are*" (John 17:11, 21–23, DR).

In practice, you not only are not to kill but even not to get angry at your brother, indeed, not even saying to him shameful words (Matt 5:21–22). "Woe to that man through whom scandal comes about," especially if he scandalizes one of these little ones (Matt 18:6–7). "*Judge not*, that you may not be judged. For with what judgment you judge, you shall be judged. . . . How sayest thou to thy brother: Let me cast the mote out of thy eye, and behold a beam is in thy own eye?" (Matt 7:1–5, DR; Luke 6:37–42). Nonetheless, sometimes we must judge, though without pride, for it is said, "Give not that which is holy to dogs; neither cast ye your pearls before swine" (Matt 7:6, DR).

"Give to him that asketh of thee" (Matt 5:42, DR). "Leave there thy offering before the altar and go first to be reconciled to thy brother. . . . Be at agreement with thy adversary betimes, whilst thou art in the way with him" (Matt 5:24–25, DR). "But if thy brother shall offend against thee, go, and rebuke him between thee and him alone. If he shall hear thee, thou shalt gain thy brother" (Matt 18:15, DR). And we must not forgive injuries only "seven times; but till seventy times seven times" (Matt 18:22, DR). "*Love your enemies: do good to them that hate you*: and pray for them that persecute and calumniate you. . . . If you love them that love you, what reward shall you have? do not even the publicans this? (Matt 5:44–46, DR).

"But yet that which remaineth, *give alms*: and behold, all things are clean unto you" (Luke 11:41, DR). "Make unto you friends of the mammon of iniquity (namely, by giving alms): that when you shall fail, they may receive you into everlasting dwellings" (Luke 16:9, DR).[35] And it is said to the wicked rich man: "Son, remember that thou didst receive good things in thy lifetime, and likewise Lazarus evil things: but now he is comforted and thou art tormented" (Luke 16:25, DR). Riches are considered as being a minister of divine providence, for the benefit of others. Nay, Jesus gives a young man the following *counsel*: "*If thou wilt be perfect, go sell what thou hast, and give to the poor*, and thou shalt have treasure in heaven: *and come, follow me*" (Matt 19:21, DR). (The closing words contains the counsel of obedience beyond the counsel of poverty.)[36] And since the young man

---

[35] In *ST* II-II, q. 32, a. 7, ad 1, St. Thomas notes, with St. Augustine: "Riches are only wicked for those who are themselves wicked, placing their hope in them."

[36] See *ST* I-II, q. 108, a. 4 (Whether the new law fittingly adds the counsels to the commandments / precepts): "The difference between a counsel and a commandment / precept is that a precept involves necessity, whereas a counsel is left to the choice of the person to whom it is presented." The commandments / precepts of the New Law are concerned with things that are necessary to salvation, whereas counsels are concerned with those means by which a man more readily and expeditiously can achieve the end of eternal beatitude. Christ's counsels are reduced

went away sad, Jesus said to his disciples: "Amen, I say to you, that a rich man shall hardly enter into the kingdom of heaven" (Matt 19:23, DR). {{179}} "Lay not up to yourselves treasures on earth. . . . But lay up to yourselves treasures in heaven where neither the rust nor moth doth consume" (Matt 6:19–20, DR).

Jesus confirms the precept related to honoring one's parents: "*Honor thy father and mother*; And: He that shall curse father or mother, let him die the death" (Matt 15:4, DR). And he condemns the false traditions of the Pharisees concerning this matter. As regards civil society and authority, he says: "*Render therefore to Caesar the things that are Caesar's*; and to God, the things that are God's" (Matt 22:21, DR).

Thus, charity does not destroy but, rather, perfects religion [and] justice between men. It requires us to take into account not only the rights of others but also to consider other men as being like ourselves, children of our heavenly Father. Thus, they must be loved for God and in God.

(5) *Prayer*

A. *Its necessity and conditions.* Jesus preached: "Ask, and it shall be given you: seek, and you shall find: knock, and it shall be opened to you" (Matt 7:7, DR; Luke 11:9; Mark 11:24).

"We ought always to pray and not to faint" (Luke 18:1, DR). The apostles asked, "Lord, teach us to pray, as John also taught his disciples" (Luke 11:1, DR). On the Mount of Olives, he told them, "*Pray, lest ye enter into temptation*" (Luke 22:40, 46, DR). After predicting the destruction of the temple and the city of Jerusalem, he says: "Watch ye, therefore, praying at all times, that you may be accounted worthy to escape all these things that are to come" (Luke 21:36, DR). "Whatsoever you shall ask the Father in my name, that will I do: that the Father may be glorified in the Son. If you shall ask me anything in my name, that I will do" (John 14:13–14, DR; also John 15:7, 16; 16:23–24).

Regarding the conditions of prayer: "And when you are praying, speak not much, as the heathens. For they think that in their much speaking they may be heard" (Matt 6:7, DR). "*And when ye pray, you shall not be as the hypocrites, that love to . . . pray in the synagogues, . . . that they may be seen by men.* . . . But thou when thou shalt pray, enter into thy chamber, and having shut the door, pray to thy Father in secret" (Matt 6:5–6, DR). In the parable of the Pharisee and the Publican, Jesus teaches that we must *pray with humility*, for "every one that exalteth himself shall be humbled: and he that humbleth himself

---

to three, namely, to poverty, continence, and obedience, all which are opposed to "concupiscence of the eyes, concupiscence of the flesh, and the pride of life" (John 2:16). See *ibid.*, ad 1: "Considered in themselves, the aforementioned counsels are expedient to all; however, on account of some indisposition in certain people, they are inexpedient for them." And in *ibid.*, ad 4: Many of Christ's counsels are concerned with precepts, though only as holding that we must have our souls prepared to do them. For example, man must be prepared to bless his enemies (or do other such things). This represents something that is required and, therefore, is a precept. The precepts are the ends of the counsels (see *ST* II-II, q. 189, a. 1, ad 5).

shall be exalted" (Luke 14:11, DR). Moreover, we must pray *with faith and trust*: "And all things whatsoever you shall ask in prayer believing, you shall receive" (Matt 21:22, DR); likewise, with *perseverance* (Luke 11:8) and forgiving if we hold something against someone (Mark 11:25). The prayer of two or three gathered together is of the greatest efficacy (Matt 18:19–20).

B. *The Lord's Prayer* (Matt 6:9–13; Luke 11:2–4). Jesus taught us a brief, perfect, efficacious prayer that infinitely surpasses all the prayers of the pagans and is understandable by all, whether learned or not. In the Lord's Prayer, we seek not only all the things that we can desire uprightly but also in the order in which they ought to be sought.

As St. Thomas explains,[37] our end is God. Hence, we must first seek the glory of God: "Our Father, who are in Heaven, hallowed be thy name." Second, there are the words "thy kingdom come," through which we seek the arrival of the glory of God's kingdom. However, merits order us to the aforementioned end; Hence, we say: "Thy will be done, on earth as in heaven." {{180}} Likewise, various aids assist us in reaching this end, whether they be temporal or spiritual. This is touched on in the words "Give us this day our daily bread" (Lucan version), whether this is understood as indicating temporal bread or sacramental bread (that is, the Eucharist), for in Matthew, this petition is expressed as "give us this day our supersubstantial bread."

However, three kinds of things can turn us away from our ultimate end: first, the sins that we commit ("forgive us our trespasses, as we forgive those who trespass against us"); second, temptation ("and lead us not into temptation"—namely, do not allow us to be overcome by temptation); third, evil whether present or future, as a punishment or a fault ("deliver us from evil").

(6) *Humility, mortification, self-denial, and patience*

Jesus highly commends these virtues, which are most efficacious in removing impediments to salvation.[38] Indeed, without them, we cannot have the other more active Christian virtues, such as diligence, fidelity, and zeal.

A. *Humility*: "Learn from me, because I am meek, and *humble of heart*" (Matt 11:29, DR). "Woe to you, Pharisees, because you love the uppermost seats in the synagogues and salutations in the marketplace" (Luke 11:43, DR; Matt 23:5). Jesus says to his disciples: "Amen I say to you, *unless you* be converted, and *become as little children*, you shall not enter into the kingdom of heaven. Whosoever therefore shall humble himself as this little child, he is the greater in the kingdom of heaven" (Matt 18:3–4, DR; Mark 9:34–36; Luke 9:48; 22:24–27). "Because everyone that exalteth himself shall be humbled: and he that humbleth himself shall be exalted" (Luke 14:11, DR; 18:14). Likewise, "Suffer the

---

[37] See *In* VI *Matt* and *ST* II-II, q. 83, a. 9.
[38] See *ST* II-II, q. 161, a. 5, ad 2 and 4.

little children, and forbid them not to come to me: for the kingdom of heaven is for such" (Matt 19:14, DR). Nothing like this was said by the philosophers.

B. *Mortification*: St. Paul often recommends mortification: "If by the Spirit you mortify the deeds of the flesh, you shall live" (Rom 8:13, DR); "always bearing about in our body the mortification of Jesus" (2 Cor 4:10, DR); also see Colossians 3:5. This kind of mortification separates Christian temperance from the natural temperance defined by the Greek philosophers.[39] "But I say to you, that whosoever shall look on a woman to lust after her, hath already committed adultery with her in his heart. *And if thy right eye scandalize thee, pluck it out and cast it from thee.* For it is expedient for thee that one of thy members should perish, rather than thy whole body be cast into hell" (Matt 5:28–29, DR; also 18:9). Likewise, Jesus commends *the mortification of anger, of rash judgments,* and so forth. (Matt 5:22; 7:1). However for past sins, Jesus preaches, like John the Baptist: "*But except you do penance, you shall all likewise perish,*" like those upon whom the tower fell in Siloam (Luke 13:5, DR). And to the precept a counsel is added: "For there are eunuchs, who were born so; . . . and *there are eunuchs, who have made themselves eunuchs for the kingdom of heaven. He that can take, let him take it*" (Matt 19:12, DR).

C: *Self-denial*: Self-denial is absolutely necessary for every Christian: "*If any man will come after me, let him deny himself.* . . . For he that will save his life, shall lose it: and he that shall lose his life for my sake, shall find it" (Matt 16:24–25, DR). "He that loveth father or mother more than me, is not worthy of me; and he that loveth son or daughter more than me, is not worthy of me" (Matt 10:37, DR). "For what doth it profit a man, if he gain the whole world and suffer the loss of his own soul?" (Matt 16:26, DR). "*Enter ye through the narrow gate*: for wide is the gate, and broad is the way that leadeth to destruction, and many there are who go in thereat" (Matt 7:13, DR). And Jesus also adds the counsel: "*And everyone that hath left house, or brethren, or sisters,* or father, or mother, or wife, or children, or lands *for my name's sake, shall receive a hundredfold, and shall possess life everlasting*" (Matt 19:29, DR).

{{181}} D: *Patience*: Patience is required in affliction. "If any man wishes to come after me, let him . . . *take up his cross,* and follow me" (Matt 16:24, DR; Luke 9:23; 14:27). "And he that taketh not up his cross, and followeth me, is not worthy of me" (Matt 10:38, DR). "In your patience you shall possess your souls" (Luke 21:19, DR). This virtue of patience is connected to fortitude / courage.[40] In particular, the person who gives up all things for Christ's sake is promised "a hundredfold in this life" "with persecutions" and "eternal life" (Mark 10:30).

(7) *Prudent diligence, fidelity to God's grace, vigilance, and zeal*

A. *Prudent diligence* in the good use of God's gifts is commended *in the parable of the talents*. Recompense and the very joy of the Lord is given to the servant who had received

---

[39] See *ST* I-II, q. 63, a. 4: "Infused temperance and acquired temperance differ in *species*."
[40] See *ST* II-II, q. 136, a. 4.

five talents and profited by making another five, so too for the one who had received two and profited by making another two. However, to the one who had received one and hid it in the soil, the Lord said: "Wicked and slothful servant. . . . Take ye away therefore the talent from him and give it him that hath ten talents. For to everyone that hath shall be given, and he shall abound: but from him that hath not, that also which he seemeth to have shall be taken away" (Matt 20:15–28, DR; Luke 19:25). "Unto whomsoever much is given, of him much shall be required: and to whom they have committed much, of him they will demand the more" (Luke 12:48, DR).

B. *The fidelity of God's grace* is often praised: "*Well done, good and faithful servant, because thou hast been faithful over a few things, I will place thee over many things*" (Matt 25:21, DR). "He that is faithful in that which is least is faithful also in that which is greater" (Luke 16:10, DR). Nay resistance to God's grace and *contempt for the divine inspiration merits terrible castigation*, as is taught in *the parable concerning those who are invited to the great banquet*. All of the people invited responded to the Lord, saying, "Hold me excused." Then, the Lord gathered together into his house the poor, lame, and blind and said of those who were first invited, "none of those men that were invited shall taste of my supper" (Luke 14:24, DR; Matt 22:2–3). Likewise, in another parable, *concerning the fruit tree that does not bear fruit*: "Cut it down therefore. Why cumbereth it the ground?" (Luke 13:7, DR). Likewise, St. Stephen said of the Jews: "You always resist the Holy Ghost. As your fathers did, so do you also" (Acts 7:51, DR). *The parable of the sower* illustrates the same moral doctrine: Just as seed is received in different ways in rocky soil, thorns, and good earth, so too men more or less faithfully accept the word of God and bear fruit (Matt 13:3–23), and to those who despise the word of God it is announced: "By hearing you shall hear, and shall not understand: and seeing you shall see, and shall not perceive" (Matt 13:14, DR). And it is said of Jerusalem: "*And they shall not leave in thee a stone upon a stone: because thou hast not known the time of thy visitation*" (Luke 19:44, DR).

C. *Vigilance.* "*Watch ye therefore, because you know not what hour your Lord will come*" (Matt 24:42, DR; Mark 13:33; Luke 12:4). This is illustrated in the *parable of the ten virgins* who go forth to meet the bridegroom and the bride, five being foolish and five being prudent (Matt 25:1–13). Likewise, in the parable of the servants who expected their lord: "Blessed are those servants whom the Lord, when he cometh, shall find watching" (Luke 12:37, DR). This vigilance pertains to prudence: "*Beware of false prophets*, who come to you in the clothing of sheep, but inwardly they are ravening wolves. By their fruits you shall know them" (Matt 7:15–16, DR). "For there shall arise false Christs and false prophets" (Matt 24:24, DR). However, to the apostles, it is said: "Behold I send you as sheep in the midst of wolves. Be ye therefore wise as serpents and simple as doves" (Matt 10:16, DR).

D. *Zeal.* The words of Psalm 68[9]:10 (DR) are applied to Christ: "The zeal of thy house hath eaten me up." {{182}} Jesus himself says: "I am come to cast fire on the earth. And what will I, but that it be kindled? And I have a baptism wherewith I am to be baptized. And how am I straitened until it be accomplished?" (Luke 12:49–50, DR). Jesus promises repayment for works of zeal: "Then shall the king say: . . . Come, ye blessed of my Father. . . . *For I was hungry, and you gave me to eat.* I was thirsty, and you gave me to drink. I was a stranger, and you took me in. Naked, and you covered me. Sick, and you visited me. I was in prison, and you came to me. . . . *As long as you did it to one of these my least brethren, you did it to me*" (Matt 25:34–40, DR). However, zeal is especially expressed in the loftier beatitudes, which Jesus speaks about at the beginning of the Sermon on the Mount.

(8) *The Beatitudes*

As is seen in the Sermon on the Mount in Matthew 5, the Beatitudes contain merits and rewards. As St. Augustine explains,[41] merits are the acts of perfect virtues and of the gifts of the Holy Spirit.[42] However, the rewards are already had inchoately in this life and will be experienced in full perfection in heaven. Hence, these beatitudes contain the full perfection of the Christian life and are set forth by Christ from the beginning of his preaching, for beatitude is what man desires above all else, that which draws him to the performance of virtuous deeds.

This preaching bears witness, in a striking and preeminent manner, to the sublimity of Christ's moral doctrine.

The first three beatitudes involve drawing back from evil (i.e., from sin), whereas the later ones involve drawing onward toward that which is good and best—namely, toward God—in accord with the acts of the active life and the contemplative life.[43] The beatitudes ascend to God, whereas by contrast the "Our Father" descends from God's glory to our needs.

While the world says that felicity is found in affluence by possession of external goods, in pleasures, and in honor, Jesus says, "Blessed are the poor in spirit for theirs is the kingdom of heaven." This beatitude proceeds from humility and the gift of the fear of the Lord, against carnal desire [*cupiditas*] and the spirit of pride. Similarly, he says, "Blessed are the meek, for they shall inherit the land." That is, blessed are those who do not grow angry, who do not desire vengeance against their enemies and domination over others. This merit proceeds from gentleness and piety. "Blessed are those who mourn, for they

---

[41] St. Augustine, *De sermone Domini in monte.*

[42] Announcing the Messiah, Isaiah 11:2–3 (DR) had enumerated these gifts of the Holy Spirit, saying: "And the spirit of the Lord shall rest upon him: the spirit of wisdom, and of understanding, the spirit of counsel, and of fortitude, the spirit of knowledge, and of godliness. And he shall be filled with the spirit of the fear of the Lord." Among these gifts, those enumerated first are those that are superior; however, the beatitudes are enumerated in an inverted order— that is, in an ascending order.

[43] See St. Thomas, *In V Matth.* and *ST* I-II, q. 69, a. 3.

will find consolation." That is, blessed are those who are afflicted, who do not seek consolations in carnal desires or in vain things but, rather, know through experience that what is truly and profoundly evil is sin, thus leading them to mourn for their own sins. Such people receive a consolation that is infinitely superior to worldly delights.

The fourth and fifth beatitudes pertain to the active life. The prideful person says: Blessed is the man who lives and acts as he wishes, is under nobody else, stands at the head of others, and exercises his sovereignty. Jesus says: "Blessed are those who hunger and thirst for justice, for they will be filled." Such blessed hunger and thirst for justice will be fulfilled. "Blessed are the merciful, for they shall obtain mercy." That is, blessed is he who does not oppress those placed under him, who gives good counsel for the afflicted; God will be merciful to him.

The sixth and seventh beatitudes pertain to the contemplative life. Certain philosophers hold that beatitude is already found in speculation concerning the truth and care little for purity of heart. {{183}} However, Jesus says: "Blessed are the pure of heart, for they will see God." Indeed, already in this life, they receive understanding of divine things. Nor is beatitude to be sought after solely in human virtue or dignity without ordering that to God. Hence, it is said: "Blessed are the peacemakers, for they will be called sons of God." Such people are those who are truly wise and blessed, not because they are peaceful in a human way but, rather, because they consider all things in relation to God, thus finding and communicating true peace. This peace, which the world cannot give (John 14:27), is the fruit of divine contemplation (Gal 5:22).

Finally, the eighth beatitude is the most perfect of all, expressing the perseverance that is had through union with God, notwithstanding the unjust disturbances that may befall one: "Blessed are those who suffer persecution for the sake of justice, for theirs is the kingdom of heaven." This merit proceeds from heroic patience in persecutions, by which the soul is at last purified, so that superhuman beatitude is found in the midst of torments themselves. These sublime words were entirely novel, above mankind's common sense and natural reason. They manifest supernatural wisdom and self-abnegation to such a degree that good Christians themselves do not understand this beatitude sufficiently well when persecution comes. However, John Chrysostom said: "He who seeks such glory before God does not fear being brought to ruin before men." Nay, Jesus insists: "Blessed are you when men come to speak ill of you and persecute you, uttering every kind of evil against you untruthfully, for my sake. Rejoice and be glad, for great is your reward in heaven, for so too did they persecute the prophets before you."

No comparison can be made between this Christian ethic with even the noblest of the ethics proposed by the noblest of pagan philosophers. The absolute superiority of Christ's doctrine is manifestly clear. He himself said, concerning good works that proceed solely from a natural inclination: *"Do not also the heathens this? Be you therefore perfect, as also your heavenly Father is perfect"* (Matt 5:47–48, DR).

Art. 4: His Testimony concerning the End of the World, the Final Judgment, and Eternal Life

§1. Concerning the End of the World

We must set forth the principal declarations that Christ made concerning this matter, for many liberal Protestants and modernists hold that Christ announced the end of the world was something soon to come. If he said this, his testimony would have obviously been false and, hence, not divine.

A. *The signs of the end of the world and the second coming of the Messiah.* These matters were announced by Jesus, for instance, in Matthew 24:24–31 (DR) (see also 26:64; Mark 13:21–27; Luke 17:20, 36; 21:25–27):

> For there shall arise false Christs and false prophets and shall shew great signs and wonders, insomuch as to deceive (if possible) even the elect. Behold I have told it to you, beforehand. If therefore they shall say to you: Behold he is in the desert: go ye not out. Behold he is in the closets, believe it not. For *as lightning cometh out of the east and appeareth even into the west: so shall also the coming of the Son of man be.* Wheresoever the body shall be, there shall the eagles also be gathered together. And immediately after the tribulation of those days, *the sun shall be darkened* and the moon shall not give her light and the stars shall fall from heaven and the powers of heaven shall be moved. And then shall appear the sign of the Son of man in heaven. And then shall all tribes of the earth mourn: {{184}} and they *shall see the Son of man coming in the clouds of heaven with much power and majesty.* And he shall send his angels with a trumpet and a great voice: and they shall gather together his elect from the four winds, from the farthest parts of the heavens to the utmost bounds of them.

B. *The time of the final coming of the Son of God remains uncertain.* According to Matthew 24:36 (DR), Jesus said: "*But of that day and hour no one knoweth*: no, not the angels of heaven, but the Father alone." However, in the Gospel according to Mark: "But of that day or hour no man knoweth, neither the angels in heaven, nor the Son,[44] but the Father. Take ye heed,

---

[44] According to the traditional interpretation of this passage, these words do not mean that the Son of God does not know the day of his second coming but, rather, that he did not receive the command to reveal this day, for as he says in John 12:49 (DR): "For I have not spoken of

watch and pray. For *ye know not when the time is*" (Mark 13:32–33, DR, and also vv. 34–47).

However, many rationalists,[45] liberal Protestants, and, in particular, Loisy[46] hold that Jesus held that the end of the world was something soon to come, or at least this is how the apostles materially understood the Lord's preaching.[47] Rationalists draw their argument particularly from two texts. In Matthew 24:34 (DR), after foretelling the destruction of Jerusalem and the Judgment Day, Jesus says, "This generation shall not pass till all these things be done," and in Matthew 16:28 (DR), before his transfiguration, Jesus said, "Amen I say to you, there are some of them that stand here, that shall not taste death, till they see the Son of man coming in his kingdom" (see also Mark 8:39 and Luke 9:27).

These two texts from Sacred Scripture are indeed difficult, for in the same discourse, Christ speaks both about the end of Jerusalem and the end of the world; and since the first event is the figure of the second, it is not easy to discern what pertains to the first and what to the second. However, the words of a given author, especially one who is wise, must be understood in such a way, if possible, *that contradictions are not seen to be there*. Now, as Catholic exegetes show,[48] as well as a number of conservative Protestants,[49] the rationalists' interpretation is not founded on the text of the Gospel but instead is opposed to it on a number of points.

(1) Jesus says, "The kingdom of heaven is like to a grain of mustard seed (which grows gradually), which a man took and sowed in his field . . . and becometh a tree, so that the birds of the air come, and dwell in the branches thereof" (Matt 13:31–32, DR). Likewise, in the parable of the sower, he shows how the divine seed gradually grows up to the time of the harvest. He sends the apostles not only to the people of Israel but says to them: "Go ye into the whole world and preach the gospel to every creature" (Mark 16:15, DR). "Going therefore, teach ye all nations" (Matt 28:19, DR; Luke 24:47).

---

myself: but the Father who sent me, he gave me commandment what I should say and what I should speak." Hence, before his Ascension, he said to his apostles: "It is not for you to know the time or moments, which the Father hath put in his own power" (Acts 1:7, DR), and thus, as St. Jerome states, commenting on Matthew 24:36, "He shows that He Himself knew, but that it was not expedient that it be known by the apostles."

45 Like Renan and Stapfer.

46 See Loisy, *L'évangile et l'église*, 5–7, 24, III.

47 Such was the position held by Psessensé, Reuss, A. Réville, and Bovon.

48 See Marie-Joseph Lagrange, "L'avènement du fils de l'homme," *Revue biblique* (1906): 382–411; Lepin, *Jésus messie et fils de Dieu*, 2nd ed., 385–399.

49 Such as Godet and Sanday.

He expressly says, "And unto all nations the gospel must first be preached," before his second coming (Mark 13:10, DR). "And I say to you that *many shall come from the east and the west*, and shall sit down with Abraham, and Isaac and Jacob in the kingdom of heaven" (Matt 8:11, DR; Luke 13:29). {{185}} Likewise, to Peter: "Thou art Peter; and upon this rock I will build my church, and the gates of hell shall not prevail against it" (Matt 16:18, DR).

(2) Moreover, it does not follow from the words of the Lord that the end of the world must immediately follow upon the destruction of Jerusalem. Nay, he announces in Luke 21:24 (DR): "Jerusalem shall be trodden down by the Gentiles till the times of the nations be fulfilled."[50]

(3) Up to the Ascension itself, Jesus says to the apostles, "It is not for you to know the time or moments, which the Father hath put in his own power" (Acts 1:7, DR), just as he had said before his Passion, "But of that day or hour no man knoweth, neither the angels in heaven, nor the Son, but the Father. Take ye heed, *watch* and pray. For ye know not when the time is" (Mark 13:32). Thus, the day is uncertain, and nobody can be sure of his state, for in any given state, one is taken and another left (Matt 24:38–45). And as St. Jerome says, therefore the Lord wished to make the day uncertain so that man may forever be in a state of expectation regarding it. Thus, the first generation remained forever vigilant in expectation of it.

(4) The words recounted in Matthew 24:34, following upon the twofold preaching of the destruction of Jerusalem and the end of the world, "this generation shall not pass till all these things take place," are understood in different ways by various commentators—namely, either as pertaining to the generation of all the faithful and the end of the world, or as pertaining to the present generation and the ruin of Jerusalem. We can also say this present generation will not pass away until all of these things really *take place*, or at least in figure, for the destruction of Jerusalem will be the figure of the end of the world (and Christ did not always distinguish the time of the prior event from the time of the latter). Finally, others understand this as saying that the Jewish people will not pass away until the end of the world comes, for in many places in Sacred Scripture, "generation" refers to the

---

[50] In Matt 24:29 (DR), we do indeed read: "*Immediately after the tribulation of those days*, the sun shall be darkened." However, the words "immediately after" refer to the first signs of the end of the world and not to the destruction of Jerusalem, for immediately before this, we read: "For there shall arise false Christs . . . and shall shew great signs and wonders, insomuch as to deceive (if possible) even the elect. . . . As lightning cometh out of the east and appeareth even into the west: so shall also the coming of the Son of man be. Wheresoever the body shall be, there shall the eagles also be gathered together."

[Jewish] people [*pro gente*].[51] Moreover, as St. Peter says, in speaking of the second coming of the Lord, "*One day with the Lord is as a thousand years, and a thousand years as one day,*" (2 Pet 3:8, DR), for God sees all things in eternity. However, a prophet is elevated in some way to have knowledge of future things as they are in the divine name (see our discussion below in ch. 11 concerning the prophecies of Christ.)

(5) However, when Jesus said, prior to his transfiguration, "There are some of them that stand here, that shall *not taste death*, till they see the Son of man coming in his kingdom" (Matt 16:28, DR), some refer these words to the transfiguration and others refer them (as seems better) to the destruction of the Jerusalem temple or the synagogue, along with the expansion of the Church.[52] Here it is not a question of the end of the world, for Jesus said: "Of that day or hour no man knoweth . . . but the Father. Take ye heed, watch and pray. For ye know not when the time is."[53]

{{186}} (6) Nay, St. Paul says in 2 Thessalonians 2:2–4 (DR): "*Be not easily moved . . . as if the day of the Lord were at hand.* Let no man deceive you by any means: for *unless there come a revolt first*, and the man of sin be revealed, the son of perdition . . . so that he sitteth in the temple of God, shewing himself as if he were God." Therefore, the time of Christ's final coming remains uncertain.

§2. On the Last Judgment

Jesus said: "They that have done good things shall come forth unto the resurrection of life: but they that have done evil, unto the resurrection of judgment" (John 5:29, DR; see 6:39–40, 44). (Against the Sadducees, he affirms the resurrection again.)[54] "The Son of man shall send his angels, and they shall gather out of his kingdom all scandals, and them that work iniquity. And shall cast them into the furnace of fire: there shall be weeping and gnashing of teeth. Then shall the just shine as the sun, in the kingdom of their Father. He that hath ears to hear, let him hear" (Matt 13:41–43, DR; also see 13:40, 49–50).

"Woe to thee, Chorazin, woe to thee, Bethsaida: . . . it shall be more

---

[51] See Num 10:30; 13:28; Lev 20:18; Ps 44[5]:19, etc. Also, concerning this text in Matthew, see Louis Billot, *La Parousie* [(Paris: Beauchesne, 1920).]

[52] As is said concerning the death of John the Apostle in John 21:20ff.

[53] See Maldonatus's commentary on Matthew. [Trans. note: This is likely referring to the Spanish Jesuit theologian and author on scripture, Juan Maldonado (ca. 1533–1583).]

[54] In Matt 22:30 (DR): "For in the resurrection they shall neither marry nor be married but shall be as the angels of God in heaven." Also see Mark 12:27 and Luke 20:38.

tolerable for Tyre and Sidon in the day of judgment, than for you" (Matt 11:21–22, DR). "But I say unto you, that every idle word that men shall speak, they shall render an account for it in the day of judgment. For by thy words thou shalt be justified, and by thy words thou shalt be condemned" (Matt 12:36–37, DR). "The Son of Man . . . [will] render to every man according to his works" (Matt 16:27, DR). However, the Lord will be able to give equal grace to the last workers as to the first (Matt 20:14).

Already in this life, judgment has begun: "He that believeth in him is not judged. . . . And this is the judgment: because the light is come into the world and men loved darkness rather than the light: for their works were evil" (John 3:18–19, DR; also see 12:47–48). "He that believeth in the Son hath life everlasting: but he that believeth not the Son shall not see life: but the wrath of God abideth on him" (John 3:36, DR).

However, Jesus says *concerning the damned*: "These shall go into everlasting punishment" (Matt 25:46, DR) and shall be cast "into the furnace of fire: there shall be weeping and gnashing of teeth" (Matt 13:42, DR; also see 13:50; 18:8; 25:41; Mark 9:44–45; Luke 13:28). The wicked rich man in hell said, "I am tormented in this flame," and Abraham responds to him that "between us and you, there is fixed a great chaos" (Luke 16:24–26, DR). However, this suffering is said to be eternal properly speaking and not only hyperbolically, for Christ consistently affirms this eight times, when he speaks of "the unquenchable fire of hell, where the worm does not die and the fire is not extinguished" (Mark 9:42–47). Moreover, as regards its duration, this punishment is likened to the reward given to the righteous: "And these shall go into everlasting punishment: but the just, into life everlasting" (Matt 25:46, DR).

§3. On Eternal Life

Jesus says: "But they that shall be accounted worthy of that world and of the resurrection from the dead shall neither be married nor take wives. Neither can they die any more for they are equal to the angels and are the children of God, being the children of the resurrection" (Luke 20:35–36, DR); "they shall go into life everlasting" (Matt 25:46; Mark 10:30); "then shall the just shine as the sun, in the kingdom of their Father" (Matt 13:43, DR). {{187}} The Son of Man will say to them: "Come, ye blessed of my Father, possess you the kingdom prepared for you from the foundation of the world" (Matt 25:34, DR). "Your reward is very great in heaven" (Matt 5:12, DR). "*They shall see God*" (Matt 5:8, DR). "Now this is eternal life: That they may know thee, the only true God, and Jesus Christ, whom thou hast sent" (John 17:3,

DR). "Father, I will that where I am, they also whom thou hast given me may be with me: that they may see my glory which thou hast given me, because thou hast loved me before the creation of the world" (John 17:24, DR).

"In my Father's house there are many mansions" (John 14:2, DR). The number of the elect is not revealed, but Christ says: "Enter ye in at the narrow gate: for wide is the gate, and broad is the way that leadeth to destruction, and many there are who go in thereat. How narrow is the gate, and strait is the way that leadeth to life: and few there are that find it!" (Matt 7:13–14, DR; Luke 13:24).[55]

However, all must hope, for God calls all men to labor in his vineyard up to the last hour (Matt 20:1–16), and for the least act of charity, which is not destroyed through sin, he gives eternal reward: "For I was hungry, and you gave me to eat . . . as long as you did it to one of these my least brethren, you did it to me" (Matt 25:35–40). Indeed, the life nourished in us by the Eucharist is the beginning and seed of eternal glory: "He that eateth my flesh and drinketh my blood hath everlasting life: and I will raise him up in the last day" (John 6:55, DR; also 6:56–59).

---

[55] As St. Thomas says in his commentary on Matthew's Gospel: "The way of the flesh is delight, and this is prompt in coming, but the way of the spirit is hidden."

CHAPTER FIVE

Christ's Testimony concerning the Establishment of the Church in Order for Revelation to Be Guarded and Infallibly Proposed until the End of the World

SINGLE ARTICLE

{{188}} Here,[1] we will take up the question concerning the instituting of the Church, especially whether Christ instituted *a living and infallible magisterium* in order to uphold and propagate his teaching. Moreover, we are here concerned with what he said concerning the constitution of the Church, its properties, and *us*. Finally, it is a question of whether Christ's testimony concerning the Church is intimately connected with all of his doctrine.

Here, however, we must not begin to constitute a properly theological treatise on the Church. Rather, it suffices here that we devote our attention *to the historical*[2] question

---

[1] See Pierre Batiffol, *L'église naissante et le catholicisme* [4th ed.] (Paris: Lecoffre, 1909), chs. 1 and 2; Yves de la Briére, "Église," in the *Dictionnaire apologétique de la foi catholique*.

[2] In the properly theological treatise concerning the Church, the various theses discussed there are proven not only historically but also positively from revelation already held through supernatural faith. Indeed, many authors, not without cause, divide the treatise on the Church into its apologetic part and into its properly theological part, although it seems better to place this apologetic part into the treatise on revelation for the reasons stated above, for thus the unity of the apologetic demonstration is better preserved, as well as the unity of the theological treatise on the Church. [Trans. note: As Fr. Garrigou-Lagrange notes very early in the first volume of this work, technically, the most appropriate place for the treatise on the Church is after the treatise on the Incarnate Word.]

concerning this specific case of Christ's testimony, so that we may see the "irrefutable" value *of the great and perpetual motive of credibility* drawn, as the [First] Vatican Council states,[3] from the miraculous life of the Church manifested through her marks [*notis*]. Indeed, this miraculous life is at once a moral miracle and the fulfillment of this *prophetic testimony*. Thus, the full apologetic demonstration (namely, as Christian and Catholic) would find its perfection as a unified whole, and rightly so indeed, since true Christianity is nothing other than Catholicism.

Certainly, many authors put off this exposition of this special testimony, placing it after the treatise on revelation, in the beginning of the theological treatise on the Church. However, when this is done, the unity of the apologetic demonstration is not preserved sufficiently well, and the value of the motives of credibility intrinsic to religion become less apparent. Hence, today, in the treatise on revelation, we must refute the theories held by rationalists, liberal Protestants, and modernists, who hold that Christ did not announce the Church but, rather, only *the kingdom of God that was soon to come in the future. If this were true, Christ's testimony would have been false* and, hence, not divine.

§1. State of the Question

All concede that Jesus established the Church implicitly and mediately, insofar as he preached a doctrine that many men embraced. {{189}} However, it is asked whether he himself immediately and explicitly established a *hierarchical* religious society in order to preserve and propose revelation in an infallible manner up to the end of the world.

(1) *Many rationalists and liberal Protestants*, like Harnack, Hoeffding, Sabatier, Stapfer, and Ménégoz, hold that it was foreign to Christ's own mind that he was establishing a Church as a society, since he was persuaded that the kingdom of heaven is one with the end of the world, which was soon to come. Hence, according to them, Jesus only taught men how to honor, love, and perfectly subject themselves to God as their Father. Thus, Harnack and Sabatier hold *that the kingdom of God is merely internal*, as though Christ only enunciated the dispositions of soul needed for entering this kingdom: penance, faith, and filial love for the Heavenly Father. Indeed, according to Harnack,[4] this represents the entire essence of Christianity.

Afterwards, by a solely natural process, the hierarchy of the Church would have come into existence, given the need to institute some rule of faith in opposition to heresies. However, these liberal Protestants reject the infallibility of this rule, just as they also reject the infallibility of Scripture, accepting only conscience as the rule of faith. Thus,

---

[3]   [First] Vatican Council, *Dei filius*, ch. 3 (Denzinger, no. 3013).
[4]   See Harnack, *Essence du christianisme* (French translation, 1907), 75–81.

they admit a "religion of the Spirit," which they oppose to the "religion of authority."[5]

(2) *Modernists* like Alfred Loisy[6] and George Tyrrell[7] not only teach that Christ believed that the end of the world was soon to come but, moreover, thus proclaimed that *the kingdom of God is merely eschatological*—that is, in the future following upon the consummation of this age, with the coming of the Messiah on the clouds of heaven (παρουσία). However, they held that Jesus instituted the beginnings of the society from which the Church arose. According to the modernists, this Church is not infallible but only needs to be obeyed like a social authority, whereas the first and foremost rule of faith would be each person's conscience illuminated by the Holy Spirit. See, to this end, propositions 6 and 52–56 condemned in *Lamentabile*:[8]

No. 6: "The 'learning Church' (*ecclesia discens*) and the 'teaching Church' (*ecclesia docens*) collaborate in such a way in defining truths that it only remains for the 'teaching Church' to sanction the opinions of the 'learning Church.'" (This is democratism, which is opposed to the existence of hierarchies.)[9]

No. 52: "It was far from the mind of Christ to found a Church as a society that would continue on earth for a long course of centuries. On the contrary, in the mind of Christ the kingdom of heaven together with the end of the world was about to come immediately."

No. 53: "The organic constitution of the Church is not immutable. Like human society, Christian society is subject to a perpetual evolution."

No. 54: "Dogmas, sacraments, and hierarchy, both their notion and reality, are only interpretations and evolutions of the Christian intelligence that have increased and perfected by an external series of additions the little germ latent in the Gospel."

No. 55: "Simon Peter never even suspected that Christ entrusted the primacy in the Church to him."

No. 56: "The Roman Church became the head of all the churches not through

---

5   Auguste Sabatier, *Les religions d'autorité et la religion de l'esprit* (Paris: [Librairie Fischbacher,] 1904), 47–83.

6   Alfred Loisy, *L'évangile et l'église*, ch. 3 (Regarding a small book), 157–186; also, on p. 90, "Simple reflections."

7   See George Tyrrell, *Lex orandi* [(Longmans, Green & Co., 1903)].

8   See Denzinger, nos. 3406 and 3452–3456.

9   See Pius X, *Pascendi*, nos. 23 and 28 (Denzinger, nos. 3492 and 2104 [old]).

the ordinance of divine providence but merely through political conditions."

(3) *Conservative Protestants* hold that Christ instituted a supreme and infallible authority that would safely preserve and propagate revelation. However, they hold that Scripture is the sole rule of faith, and they intend to determine certain fundamental articles of Christian doctrine in order to be able to avoid anarchy. (*Lutherans* say that the true Church is invisible and ruled by presbyters delegated by the people who are equal, by divine right, to the bishops. *Episcopalian-Anglicans* admit that a visible society was instituted by Christ and is ruled by the bishops.)

{{190}} (4) *Greek schismatics* acknowledge an infallible authority, which they place in the body of bishops acting collegially. However, they hold that the jurisdictional primacy of the Roman Pontiff is not of divine right. They admit the authority of the first seven ecumenical councils. According to them, the Church is an aristocratic regime.

(5) *Catholics* hold that Christ established the Church as a hierarchical and monarchical society, having a supreme and infallible authority in matters of faith and morals not only in the college of apostles and bishops but also in the head of this college—namely, the Roman Pontiff, the successor of Peter, who represents Christ on earth.[10] In particular, the [First] Vatican Council states in *Dei filius*, regarding the institution of the Church for the sake of infallibly proposing revelation: "However, to enable us to fulfill the obligation to embrace the true faith and persistently persevere in it, God has established the Church through His only-begotten Son and has endowed her with manifest *marks* (*notis*) of his institution so that she may be recognized by all men as the guard and teacher of the revealed word."[11]

Therefore, we see in the Gospels, whose historical authority we already have proven, the following points to be taken up in what follows: (a) what the kingdom of God preached by Christ is; (b) whether Christ instituted a hierarchical and lasting Church; (c) whether he intended to confer, in perpetuity, infallibility upon this Church in order for her to propose revelation; and (d) finally, whether he fitted this Church with visible marks (*notis*). By way of confirmation, we will then see together in the Acts of the Apostles and the Letters how the Apostles understood this testimony offered by Christ. Indeed, we must not look to the Gospel to find a complete and scientific delineation of the Church, for the Church grew, just like a mustard seed. However, we do need to look into her essential foundations as they were explicitly determined by Christ.

---

[10] See Council of Trent, *Decree on the Sacrament of Orders* (Denzinger, no. 1767); Pius VI, Constitution *Auctorem fidei*, no. 50 (Denzinger, no. 2650); [First] Vatican Council, *Pastor aeternus* (Denzinger, nos. 1821ff).

[11] [First] Vatican Council, *Dei filius*, ch. 3 (Denzinger, no. 3012).

§2. What Is the Kingdom of God Preached by Christ?

It is a spiritual kingdom, though not a merely internal one nor one that is solely eschatological or future.

(1) *It is a spiritual, non-temporal kingdom.* In the time of Christ, the Jews understood the messianic prophecies solely in their material sense, expecting above all a temporal and national kingdom. Hence, the wicked Herod feared the coming of the Messiah (Matt 2:3). Likewise, after the multiplication of the loaves, the people wanted to make Jesus a king, but he headed for the hills (John 6:15). When the Pharisees asked when the kingdom of God would come, Jesus responded: "*The kingdom of God cometh not with observation.* Neither shall they say: Behold here, or behold there. *For lo, the kingdom of God is within you*" (Luke 17:20–21, DR). Likewise, Jesus said to Pilate: "*My kingdom is not of this world*" (John 18:36, DR).

Therefore, it is a spiritual kingdom, not a temporal one. In order to enter it, what is required are penance and faith: "*The kingdom of God is at hand. Repent and believe the Gospel*" (Mark 1:15, DR). Likewise, one must have filial love for the Heavenly Father. This is the greatest commandment (Matt 22:3; 5:3–12). And he adds: "Love your neighbor as yourself" (Matt 22:39). Nay, "Love your enemies: . . . That you may be the children of your Father who is in heaven" (Matt 5:44–48, DR). "*For I tell you, that unless your justice abound more than that of the scribes and Pharisees, you shall not enter into the kingdom of heaven*" (Matt 5:20, DR). "You will pray thus: Our Father . . ." (Matt 6:6).

{{191}} (2) *However, the kingdom of God is also and at the same time external, visible, and social.* The whole essence of Christianity is not found merely in filial love for God the Father, for the kingdom of God takes the form of a flock: "Fear not, little flock, for it hath pleased your Father to give you a kingdom" (Luke 12:32, DR; Mark 14:27). The apostles are in this flock, and it is said concerning them: "Come after me; and I will make you to become fishers of men" (Mark 1:17, DR; Luke 5:10). This society is called the *Church,* ἐκκλησία, when Christ, speaking about fraternal correction, says: "*And if he will not hear them: tell the church. And if he will not hear the church, let him be to thee as the heathen and publican*" (Matt 18:17, DR).

If the kingdom of God were merely internal, it would correspond solely to the good, but on the contrary, *it contains both the good and the wicked,* as is clear from the parable of the good seed and the weeds. Likewise, it is said: "*Again the kingdom of heaven is like to a net cast into the sea, and gathering together of all kinds of fishes. Which, when it was filled, they drew out, and sitting by the shore, they chose out the good into vessels, but the bad they* cast forth" (Matt 13:47–48, DR; also see 13:36–48).

(3) *The kingdom of God is not only future / eschatological.*

(a) *It already is present.* The Pharisees asked, "When will the kingdom of God come?" To which Jesus responded, as just cited: "The kingdom of God cometh not with observation. Neither shall they say: Behold here, or behold there. For lo, *the kingdom of God is within you*" (Luke 17:20–21, DR). By contrast, Christ's coming on the clouds of heaven will be observable. However, even now, the kingdom of God is not merely present as an internal kingdom within the Pharisees' hearts, for they themselves do not believe, but rather is ἐντὸς ὑμῶν, "in your midst," just as Jesus had said earlier to the Pharisees: "But if I by the finger of God cast out devils, doubtless the kingdom of God is come upon you" (Luke 11:20, DR).

(b) Nor is the end of the world something to come immediately in the future (see previous chapter), for the kingdom of God is *progressive, like the mustard seed,* which slowly grows and "becometh a tree, so that the birds of the air come, and dwell in the branches thereof" (Matt 13:32, DR). Nay, "*this gospel of the kingdom shall be preached in the whole world,* for a testimony to all nations: and then shall the consummation come" (Matt 24:14, DR). "Many shall come from the east and the west" (Matt 8:11, DR). Likewise, in the parable of the murdering vineyard workers, Jesus says to the Pharisees: "Therefore I say to you that the kingdom of God shall be taken from you and shall be given to a nation yielding the fruits thereof" (Matt 21:43, DR). As we explained above, Christ said, concerning the end of the world: "But of that day and hour no one knoweth: no, not the angels of heaven, but the Father alone" (Matt 24:36, DR).

(c) Moreover, as was said above, the kingdom in this world [*regnum mundi*] *is made up of good and wicked,* of the wealthy and the poor. Now, these differences will no longer exist in heaven after the end of the world. Therefore, the kingdom of God is not merely eschatological / future.

Thus, the kingdom of God that Jesus preached was already present, in a hidden manner, in righteous souls, and in a visible manner in the newborn ecclesiastical society, and he likewise announced its future consummation in heaven after the end of the world. This makes clear the falsity of the thesis held by liberal Protestants and modernists.

§3. Christ established the Church as a Society That Is Hierarchal and Existing into Perpetuity

This point stands against Protestants, even those who are conservative.

{{192}} A society is a union of men formed in order to accomplish some one thing. Now, a *hierarchy* (ἱερὰ ἀρχή) means *a sacred ruler instituted by divine right*. The Church would not be hierarchical but instead a form of democracy if the people in the Church were to exercise power either through themselves or through their delegates, as Calvinist Presbyterians wish, holding that the authority of the presbyters is delegated by the people. Similarly, according to modernists, the Church's rule must be reformed and, as they say, constructed along the lines laid out by modern consciousness, which wholly leans in the direction of democracy.[12] By contrast, the Catholic Church declares that she was instituted by Christ as a *hierarchical and monarchial society*—that is, constituted under one head having supreme power.[13]

As regards the historicity of the texts by which this instituting is proven, conservative Protestants admit, as something historically certain, that Jesus himself gave to Peter and the apostles the power to teach, rule, and sanctify the faithful. However, they hold that Christ did not intend to confer this power to the successors of Peter and the apostles in perpetuity. By contrast, liberal Protestants hold that the Gospel texts lean in the direction of a perpetual hierarchy but ultimately only express the faith of Christian consciousness as it was at the end of the first century, not being genuine declarations of Christ. The reason adduced by such liberal thinkers is that the kingdom of God preached by Christ was merely internal or merely eschatological, which was already refuted above. Moreover, these critics reject, in particular, the historicity of Christ's own declarations after his Resurrection because they hold that the miracle of the Resurrection is impossible or, at least, uncertain, a claim that we will refute below.

By contrast, Catholic exegetes note that the historicity of all these texts, whether before or after the Resurrection, are confirmed by the very fact that they are few in number and brief, found here and there throughout the Gospel, in a context where something else is being discussed. They certainly are not artificially put together in order to prove some thesis based on declarations that are unjustly ascribed to Christ.[14] Moreover, before his

---

[12] See Pius X, *Pascendi*, no. 28 (Denzinger, no. 2104 [old]).

[13] See Denzinger, old systematic heading "II. The Essence of the Church." Also see *Statuta ecclesiae antiqua*, can. 90 (Denzinger, no. 326); Trent, *Decree on the Sacrament of Orders* (Denzinger, no. 1769); Pius VI, Brief *Super soliditate petrae* (Denzinger, no. 2592); [First] Vatican Council, *Pastor aeternus*, intr. (Denzinger, no. 3051).

[14] See Yves de la Brière, "Église," in the *Dictionnaire apologétique de la foi catholique*, col. 1238; E. Dublanchy, "Église," in *Dictionnaire de théologie catholique*, col. 2115: "The authenticity of these texts is sufficiently assured for us by the constant and universal Christian tradition, solemnly affirmed by the [First] Vatican Council (sess. 4, ch. 1) and proven by numerous testi-

Resurrection, Jesus had promised the power that he then gave to them after his Resurrection.

(1) *Christ instituted a hierarchical and monarchical society* by conferring on the apostles the threefold power of teaching, ruling, and sanctifying the faithful, as well as by conferring immediately upon Peter primacy in teaching and jurisdiction.

We must note the progress of Christ's declarations from the beginning of his ministry up to the Ascension.

A. *He chooses twelve Apostles* whom he calls by name, teaching them and *sending them to preach the kingdom of God* first to the children of Israel: "These twelve Jesus sent . . . saying: . . . go ye rather to the lost sheep of the house of Israel. And going, preach, saying: The kingdom of heaven is at hand. Heal the sick, raise the dead, cleanse the lepers, cast out devils: freely have you received, freely give" (Matt 10:5–8, DR; Mark 6:7–13; Luke 9:1–6).

{{193}} B. Then, after Peter's confession in Caesarea, Jesus said to him, in the form of a promise: "And I say to thee: *That thou art Peter* (Kepha) *and upon this rock* (Kepha) *I will build my Church*, and the gates of hell shall not prevail against it. *And I will give to thee the keys of the kingdom of heaven. And whatsoever thou shalt bind upon earth, it shall be bound also in heaven: and whatsoever thou shalt loose on earth, it shall be loosed also in heaven*" (Matt 16:18–19, DR).[15] In this declaration, Christ promises to Peter a primacy that is not only one of honor but, indeed, one of jurisdiction,[16] for Christ is here speaking to Peter alone, to the exclusion of the others, and promises to him the supreme power of ruling the Church, for he will be *the foundation* of the Church that will be built upon him. He will receive the "keys of the kingdom of heaven," and "whatsoever he binds upon earth will also be bound in heaven." These words not only express the power to interpret a law that is already established but, rather, the right to impose and lift various obligations in the spiritual order, indeed in so efficacious a way that whatsoever Peter binds on earth will also be bound in heaven. Therefore, it is a question of primacy of jurisdiction.

However, the primacy of teaching is expressed more explicitly in Luke 22:31–32 (DR), when prior to his Passion, Christ says to Peter: "Simon, Simon, behold Satan hath desired to have you, that he may sift you as wheat.

---

monies found in Leo XIII's Encyclical *Satis cognitum* (June 29, 1896)."

[15] See Batiffol, *L'église naissante et le catholicisme*, ch. 2 (94–113, The Church in the Gospel, the status of Matt 16:18–19).

[16] See the explanation of this text in [First] Vatican Council, *Pator aeternus*, intro. (Denzinger, no. 1822) and in Dublanchy, "Église," in *Dictionnaire de théologie catholique*, col. 2116.

But I have prayed for thee, that thy faith fail not: and thou, being once converted, confirm thy brethren."

C. *To the twelve apostles,* Jesus said, around the middle of his public life: "Amen I say to you, *whatsoever you shall bind upon earth, shall be bound also in heaven*; and whatsoever you shall loose upon earth, shall be loosed also in heaven" (Matt 18:18, DR). By these words, Jesus promises to them the power to bind and loose—that is, the power of ruling the Church—though not in the same way as what he said earlier to Peter, for to Peter alone is promised the same authority as that which is promised to the other apostles forming a single body with Peter, as will be clearer upon considering the testimonies to be discussed below.

Moreover, they were promised the special assistance of the Holy Spirit in preaching the Gospel: "But the Paraclete, the *Holy Ghost,* whom the Father will send in my name, *he will teach you all things* and bring all things to your mind, whatsoever I shall have said to you" (John 14:26, DR; 15:26–27); "he will teach you all truth" (John 16:13, DR).

D. Finally, *after his Resurrection,* Jesus *gave* the power that he had promised, both to the apostles and to Peter.

To the apostles, he gave the power of teaching, ruling, and sanctifying the faithful in the whole world: "And Jesus coming, spoke to them, saying: All power is given to me in heaven and in earth. *Going therefore, teach ye all nations: baptizing them in the name of the Father and of the Son and of the Holy Ghost. Teaching them to observe all things whatsoever I have commanded you*" (Matt 28:18–20, DR; Mark 16:15, DR: "Go ye into the whole world and preach the gospel to every creature"; Luke 24:44–49). "Peace be to you. As the Father hath sent me, I also send you. When he had said this, he breathed on them; and he said to them: Receive ye the Holy Ghost. *Whose sins you shall forgive, they are forgiven them: and whose sins you shall retain, they are retained*" (John 20:21–22, DR).

{{194}} *To Peter,* however, he conferred the supreme power that had been promised to him earlier. Jesus says to Simon Peter: "Simon, son of John, lovest *(diligis)* thou me more than these? . . . *Feed my lambs.*" And he says again: "Simon, son of John, lovest *(diligis)* thou me? . . . *Feed my lambs.*" And he says to him a third time: "Simon, son of John, lovest *(amas)* thou me? . . . *Feed my sheep*" (John 21:15–17, DR). These words are said only to Peter, conferring upon him *primacy, for* the word *feed* (βόσκε ποίμαινε) designates, in both profane and sacred authors, power in society. However, this power *is given solely to Peter.* Therefore, it establishes his primacy. And it is given to him *over the whole Church,* for the words "feed my lambs . . . feed my sheep" designate all of the Christian disciples, whatever their dignity may be. Thus, Christ corroborates the words that he said earlier to Peter: "But I have prayed for thee, that thy faith fail not: and thou, being once converted, confirm thy brethren" (Luke 22:32, DR).

Thus, it is clear that Christ established the Church as a hierarchical society, conferring upon the apostles the power to teach, rule, and sanctify the faithful, likewise conferring upon Peter primacy of teaching and jurisdiction. This was how Peter understood this as well, for after Christ's Ascension, he exercised the supreme authority in the Church, as is clear in the Acts of the Apostles.[17] It is also how matters were understood by St. Paul,[18] who teaches that the Church is built "upon the foundation of the apostles"[19] and is the mystical body in which the perfect hierarchy is found.[20]

---

[17] See Acts 1:15ff regarding the election of Matthias to the number of the apostles; Acts 2:14 and 3:6 in the preaching of the Gospel; Acts 9:32 in his visiting of all the Churches throughout Judea, Galilea, and Samaria; Acts 10:20, in the conversion of the Gentiles when he is sent by the Holy Spirit to Cornelius; in Acts 15:7 and 12 (DR) at the Council of Jerusalem: "And when there had been much disputing, Peter, rising up, said to them: Men, brethren, you know that in former days God made choice among us, that by my mouth the Gentiles should hear the word of the gospel and believe.... And all the multitude held their peace," and the apostles established by common decree that the Gentiles were not to be bound by the Mosaic Law.

[18] Paul acknowledged Peter's primacy when he said in Gal 1:18 (DR): "Then, after three years (after my conversion), I went to Jerusalem to see Peter: and I tarried with him fifteen days." In Gal 2:11 (DR), he does indeed write, "But when Cephas was come to Antioch, I withstood him to the face, because he was to be blamed." However, in doing this, Paul did not deny Peter's authority but instead only feared that his overindulgence of Jewish converts and their legal observances would turn Gentiles away from the Christian faith.

[19] See Eph 2:19–22 (DR): "Now therefore you are no more strangers and foreigners: but you are fellow citizens with the saints and the domestics of God, *built upon the foundation of the apostles* and prophets, Jesus Christ himself being the chief corner stone, in whom all the building, *being framed together*, groweth up into a holy temple in the Lord. In whom *you also are built together into a habitation* of God in the Spirit."

[20] St. Paul often describes the Church as being the *mystical body of Christ*. See the following texts. Eph 1:22–23 (DR): "And (God) hath subjected all things under his feet (that is, Christ's feet) and hath made him *head over all the Church*, which is his body and the fulness of him who is filled all in all." Eph 4:16–26: "*We are members of each other.*" Eph 5:23 and 30 (DR): "The husband is the head of the wife, as Christ is the head of the church. He is the saviour of his body.... Because we are members of his body, of his flesh and of his bones." Col 1:16, 18, 24 and 2:10 and 19. In 1 Cor 12, St. Paul shows how Christ provides for the Church in all the various states of her members, enumerating there the various charismatic graces of the Holy Spirit. See 1 Cor 12:12 (DR): "All the members of the body, whereas they are many, yet are one body: So also is Christ." Likewise, in 1 Cor 12:26–27 (DR): "And if one member suffer any thing, all the members suffer with it: or if one member glory, all the members rejoice with it. Now *you are the body of Christ* and members of member [*sic*]." See Rom 12:4–8 (DR): "For as in one body we have many members:... So *we, being many, are one body in Christ*; and every one *members one of another*. And having different gifts, according to the grace that is given us."

{{195}} (2) *Christ instituted this hierarchical society as something to exist in perpetuity.* Indeed, after saying to his apostles, "Going therefore, teach ye all nations: baptizing them . . . teaching them to observe all things whatsoever I have commanded you," Jesus adds, *"and behold I am with you all days, even to the consummation of the world"* (Matt 28:20, DR). "You shall be witnesses unto me . . . even to the uttermost part of the earth" (Acts 1:8, DR). However, this office of teaching, ruling, and sanctifying the faithful is not maintained solely and properly by the persons of the apostles. Therefore, it will belong also to their successors, who will maintain this same office. In this way, the unity and integrity of the faith will be preserved up to the end of the world so that the faithful may be able to safely come to supernatural faith. Thus, St. Paul often declares that this power had been given to Timothy and Titus through the imposition of hands,[21] and he says, concerning the bishops instituted in the various churches: "The Holy Ghost hath placed you bishops, to rule the church of God which he hath purchased with his own blood" (Acts 20:28, DR; 14:22).

Likewise, Christ intended that *the primacy* be *perpetual*, passing on to Peter's successors. Indeed, he said: "Thou art Peter; and upon this rock I will build my church, and *the gates of hell shall not prevail against it"* (Matt 16:18, DR). That is, the Church is indefectible, though it cannot subsist without a foundation and supreme power. And, in fact, the bishops admitted the primacy of the Roman Pontiff in Peter's successors. The preeminence of the Roman Church is acknowledged in the writings and facts of the first three centuries, and afterwards it comes to be so clearly [*diserte*] expressed that its existence could not be placed into doubt.[22]

§4. Christ's Testimony concerning the Infallibility of the Church

Christ affirmed that he conferred perpetual infallibility upon the Church in order to preserve and propose revelation.

Doctrinal infallibility is not mere *de facto* inerrancy but, rather, *de iure* inerrancy, in virtue of divine assistance. This assistance and special aid, by means of which error in matters of faith and morals is always safely defended against, differs both from inspiration, which involves a positive [divine] motion in order for one to write infallibly, as well as from revelation, which involves the manifestation of a truth that heretofore had been unknown.

---

[21] 1 Tim 4:15; 2 Tim 1:6; 5:17–22; Titus 2:5.

[22] See De Groot, *De ecclesia*, q. 14 and 15; E. Dublanchy, "Église," *Dictionnaire theologie catholique*, cols. 2119–2136.

Protestants, even conservative ones, by the very fact that they deny that Christ instituted a perpetual hierarchy with the power of teaching, reject the infallibility of such a hierarchy, which according to them is not founded on the Gospel.

Modernists hold that the teaching Church (*ecclesia docens*) is infallible only insofar as it sanctions / confirms the commonly held opinions of Christian conscience, opinions that can change in accord with the development [*evolutionem*] of religious sentiment, philosophy, and the sciences.[23]

(1) ***Christ conferred this infallibility on the college of the apostles and their successors.***

A. When he sent them to preach the Gospel, he added: "*And behold I am with you all days*, even to the consummation of the world" (Matt 28:20, DR). {{196}} Jesus did not say this to all the faithful but, rather, to the college of apostles, and he promised that he would remain with them for all days, up to the end of the world, teaching them his doctrine so that they might faithfully propose it.[24] Now, this special assistance from Christ in order to teach the truth of faith obviously implies infallibility, as when he himself said, in the same text: "All power is given to me in heaven and in earth." Hence, in Mark 16:16 (DR), after the words, "Go ye into the whole world and preach the gospel," he adds, "he that believeth not shall be condemned." According to these texts, the Church's magisterium is infallible of itself, not from the consent of the faithful, inasmuch as it would confirm their common opinions, as the modernists wish. On the contrary, the faithful are bound to believe what the Church teaches as being *De fide*.

B. Likewise, Christ promised this infallibility to the college of apostles when he said: "And I will ask the Father, and he shall give you another Paraclete, that he may abide with you forever, *the Spirit of truth*. . . . *He will teach you all things* and bring all things to your mind, whatsoever I shall have said to you" (John 14:16–17, 26; 15:26–27). "But when he, the Spirit of truth, is come, he will teach you all truth" (John 16:13). This promise implies the special assistance of the Holy Spirit, inasmuch as the latter is the one who teaches the truth, indeed doing so in order to propose Christ's doctrine.

C. *Such was how the apostles understood Christ's promises*. Indeed, when they established their decrees [at the Council of Jerusalem]: "For it hath

---

[23] See *Lamentabile*, no. 6 (Denzinger, no. 3406) and Pius X, *Pascendi*, nos. 23–28 (Denzinger, nos. 3492ff [Old. nos. 2091–2095]).

[24] Indeed, this is the biblical sense of these words: "I am with you." See Gen 31:3; Deut 32:8; Jer 30:10; Luke 1:28; Acts 18:9–10.

seemed good to the Holy Ghost and to us" (Acts 15:28, DR). Likewise, in their preaching: "And we are witnesses of these things and the Holy Ghost" (Acts 5:32, DR). And in anathematizing errors: "Bringing into captivity every understanding unto the obedience of Christ" (2 Cor 10:5, DR), "though we, or an angel from heaven, preach a gospel to you besides that which we have preached to you, let him be anathema" (Gal 1:8, DR). They write, saying, "The church of the living God, the pillar and ground of the truth" (1 Tim 3:15, DR). "That henceforth we be no more children tossed to and fro and carried about with every wind of doctrine" (Eph 4:14, DR). "O Timothy, keep that which is committed to thy trust, avoiding the profane novelties of words and oppositions of knowledge falsely so called" (1 Tim 6:20, DR). "We are of God. He that knoweth God heareth us. He that is not of God heareth us not. By this we know the spirit of truth and the spirit of error" (1 John 4:5–6, DR). "Therefore, brethren, stand fast: and hold the traditions, which you have learned, whether by word or by our epistle" (2 Thess 2:14, DR). Likewise, later on, in order to refute heresies that arose, the Fathers argued on the basis of the infallible magisterium of the Teaching Church (*ecclesia docens*)—that is, of the apostles and the bishops, whose general councils they held as being the authentic instrument of the truth.

(2) *Christ conferred this infallibility directly and immediately on Peter and his successors.* This is had in accord with the college of the bishops of the Church, to whom infallibility was promised[25] in the very declarations of Christ, by means of which the perpetual primacy of teaching and jurisdiction were conferred to Peter.

A. "That thou art Peter; and upon this rock I will build my church, and the gates of hell shall not prevail against it" (Matt 16:18, DR). {{197}} However, if Peter, when he speaks *ex cathedra* in order to define that something is *De fide*, were not infallible, he would not be a solid foundation for the Church.

B. "I have prayed for thee, that thy faith fail not: and thou, being once converted, confirm thy brethren" (Luke 22:31–32, DR). However, Peter would not be able to truly and efficaciously confirm his brethren's faith if he could err when he defines those things that are *De fide* or if his definitions were not irreformable of themselves but, rather, only from the Church's consent.

C. "Feed my lambs. . . . Feed my sheep" (John 21:15–17, DR). However, if Peter were not infallible in Christ's doctrine to be defined, he could not

---

[25] See [First] Vatican Council, *Pastor aeternus*, intro. and ch. 4 (Denzinger, nos. 3054 and 3065–3075).

truly feed Christ's flock with the word of truth.

Now, this privilege of infallibility, by the very fact that it pertains to the primacy of teaching, is transmitted along with it to Peter's successors so that they may be able to confirm their brethren in the faith.

In fact, during the first four centuries of the Church's life, the Roman Church was held as being the center of the unity of the faith and the safe norm of orthodoxy against heresies.[26] However, from the fifth century, the infallibility of the Roman Pontiff comes to be affirmed with increasing clarity by the popes themselves, by the Fathers, and by the councils.[27] Finally, we must note that, in order to establish the apologetic proof of the divine origin of Catholicism, it is not necessary to know with critical and historical certitude whether Christ intended to directly and immediately confer upon the Roman Pontiff [*Summo Pontifici*] the privilege of infallibility. It suffices to know with moral, historical certitude *that Christ declared that he himself was instituting a hierarchical Church, giving it infallibility* to propose revelation, *conferring it perpetuity*. However, we have proven this presupposing the historicity of the Gospels. Moreover, it is infallibly and supernaturally certain for the faithful on the basis of the definitions of the Church herself.

§5. Christ Constructed His Church as Having Visible Marks (Notis)

This is also morally and historically certain, presupposing the historicity of the Gospels, from the very declarations of Christ.

A. *The state of the question.* The marks (*notae*) are the *visible signs* by means of which, among all religious groups, the Church is discerned as being true. However, in order for this to be so, it is necessary that these signs

---

[26] At the end of the second century, there is the very clear testimony of St. Irenaeus in *Adversus haereses*, bk. 3, ch. 3, cited by the [First] Vatican Council in *Pastor aeternus*, ch. 2: "For this reason, 'because of her more powerful principality,' it was always 'necessary for every Church, that is, the faithful who are everywhere, to be in agreement' with the Roman Church" (PG 7, 849). In this same text (Denzinger, no. 3057), the Council cites also the testimony of St. Leo the Great and St. Ambrose, as well as that of the preceding councils.

[27] See St. Innocent I, Letter *In requirendis* to the Bishops of the Synod of Carthage (Denzinger, no. 217); St. Zosimus, *Epistula tractoria* (Denzinger, no. 231); Council of Arles, *De gratia et praedestinatione* (Denzinger, nos. 330–342); St. Hormisdas, *Libellus fidei* (nos. 363ff); Leo IX, *In terra pax hominibus,* (Denzinger, old no. 351; [no longer included in Denzinger]); Sixtus IV, *Licet ea quae de nostro mandato* [Denzinger, no. 730 cited; cf. nos. 1411–1419]; Leo X, *Exsurge Domine*, no. 28 (Denzinger, no. 1478); Pius IV, *Iniunctum nobis* (Denzinger, nos. 1869–1870); Decree of the Holy Office (Dec. 7, 1690), no. 29 (Denzinger, no. 2329); Alexander VIII, "Articles to the French Clergy," no. 4 (Denzinger, no. 2284); [First] Vatican Council, *Pastor aeternus*, ch. 4 (Denzinger, nos. 1832 and 3073).

belong to the true Church of Christ, and to it alone, as *essential properties*.

Among Protestants, liberal Protestants, who hold that Christ in no way intended that the Church be a visible society, teach for this very reason that she does not have visible marks. Such is the position of Harnack.[28] However, many conservative Protestants admit two marks of the Church: preaching of the pure word of God and right administration of the sacraments. Nevertheless, these two marks are not obvious. Nay, they are the very things that must be manifested by means of visible signs.[29]

{{198}} However, the Roman Church [*sic*], in the Niceno-Constantinopolitan Creed (AD 381), proposes four notes of her divine institution: "*And in one, holy, catholic, and apostolic* Church."[30] And she ever teaches this against heretics.[31] Likewise, the Greek schismatics and High Church Anglicans hold that Christ's Church *de iure* has four marks, though they differ from us as regards the *de facto* application of these marks. Therefore, we must consider what is had concerning this matter on the basis of Christ's own declarations.

B. *On the basis of Christ's testimony, it is clear that the four aforementioned marks are set out by him.* Indeed, Christ established the Church as a visible society, namely, one in which authority would be exercised in a visible manner (by teaching, ruling, and sanctifying through the administration of the sacraments), with its members united by visible social bonds—that is, through the external profession of the same faith, external obedience to the same pastors, and participation in the same sacraments.

As regards these visible marks, we can say the following.

(1) *Christ intended his Church to be visibly united.* Here it is a question of the property of visibility by which the Church, in her profession of faith, ruling activity, and worship is undivided in herself and divided from any other.

Indeed, the subordination of all the faithful to the same supreme jurisdiction and magisterium is something *visible*.

However, already, the fact that Christ established the Church as a hierarchical and monarchical society (that is, constituted *under one supreme head*) means that he willed that the Church be *per se* visibly united. This

---

[28] See Harnack, *L'essence du christianisme* (French translation, 1907), 327–329.

[29] See De Groot, *De ecclesia*, q. 5, a. 1. Also see Yves de la Briére, "Église," in the *Dictionnaire apologétique de la foi catholique*, col. 1271.

[30] Denzinger, no. 150.

[31] See Innocent III, Letter *Eius exemplo* to the Archbishop of Tarragona (Denzinger, no. 792); Boniface VIII, *Unam sanctam* (Denzinger, no. 468); Holy Office, Letter to the Bishops of England on Sept. 16, 1864 (Denzinger, nos. 2886–2888).

property belongs to the Church on account of her constitutive form.

Nay, Jesus said this expressly. He compares the Church to a kingdom, a city, a house, and a sheepfold. However, these figures bear witness to visible unity. In particular, Jesus says about the kingdom: "Every kingdom divided against itself shall be made desolate" (Matt 12:25, DR). Moreover, he openly said: "And other sheep I have that are not of this fold: them also I must bring. And they shall hear my voice: *And there shall be one fold and one shepherd*" (John 10:16, DR). Immediately before his Passion, he gives this solemn testimony: "Holy Father, keep them in thy name whom thou hast given me: *that they may be one, as we also are....* And not for them only do I pray, but for them also who through their word shall believe in me. *That they all may be one, as thou, Father, in me, and I in thee; that they also may be one in us.*" And he wills this unity as a visible sign, for he immediately adds: "*that the world may believe that thou hast sent me. And the glory which thou hast given me, I have given to them: that they may be one, as we also are one. I in them, and thou in me: that they may be made perfect in one: and the world may know that thou hast sent me and hast loved them, as thou hast also loved me* (John 17:11, 20–23). This unity should shine far and wide *so that the world may know* Christ's divine mission.

Christ willed *unity*: (a) *in the profession of faith*, "teach ye all nations... to observe *all things whatsoever* I have commanded you" (Matt 28:19–20, DR); (b) *in ruling*, "Thou art Peter.... I will give to thee the keys" (Matt 16:18–19, DR) and "Feed my sheep" (John 21:17, DR); {{199}} (c) *in worship*, through unity of baptism, "baptizing them in the name of the Father and of the Son and of the Holy Ghost" (Matt 28:19, DR), and in unity in the Eucharist, "Do *this* for a commemoration of me" (Luke 22:19, DR).

In fact, as we read in Acts 4:32 (DR), in the newborn Church, "And the multitude of believers had but one heart and one soul."

St. Paul marvelously sets forth the same doctrine, especially in Ephesians 4:3–16 (DR):

> Careful to keep the unity of the Spirit in the bond of peace. One body and one Spirit: as you are called in one hope of your calling. One Lord, *one faith, one baptism....* And (Christ) gave some apostles, and some prophets, and other some evangelists, and other some pastors and doctors for the perfecting of the saints, for the word of the ministry, for the edifying of the body of Christ, until we all meet into the *unity of faith* and of the knowledge of the Son of God....
> We may in all things grow up in him who is the head, even Christ: *from whom the whole body, being compacted and fitly joined together, by what every joint supplieth*, according to the operation in the measure of every part, maketh increase of the body, unto the edifying of itself in charity.

Hence, Paul wrote to the Corinthians: "Now this I say, that every one of you saith: I indeed am of Paul; and I am of Apollo; and I of Cephas; and I of Christ. Is Christ divided?" (1 Cor 1:12–13, DR). And "the bread which we break, is it not the partaking of the body of the Lord? *For we, being many, are one bread, one body: all that partake of one bread*" (1 Cor 10:16–17, DR).

However, as regards heretics, St. Paul says, in order to preserve the unity of the Church: "A man that is a heretic, after the first and second admonition, avoid" (Titus 3:10; cf. 2 Pet 2). And he openly and vehemently fought against pseudo-apostles who corrupted the word of God (2 Cor 11:13ff; Gal 2:4; 1 Tim 6:3), for there can be no unity except in truth. Likewise, St. John never separates charity from truth: "Whosoever revolteth and continueth not in the doctrine of Christ hath not God. . . . If any man come to you and bring not this doctrine, receive him not into the house nor say to him: God speed you" (2 John 9–10, DR). Such are the requirements of unity, even according to him who ever said: "Dearly beloved, let us love one another: for charity is of God" (1 John 4:7, DR).

(2) *Christ intended his Church to clearly and supremely manifest the aforementioned sort of holiness.* Holiness implies cleanness (ἅγιος, without earth) and firm union with God. A society is said to be *visibly* and *eminently* holy inasmuch as it has in itself the principles and means that are efficacious for producing conspicuous holiness, and *in fact* bears witness, without pause, to the effects of such splendid holiness—namely, superior virtues in a great number of its members and, in certain ones, heroic virtues that quite clearly exceed the natural moral powers of humanity. These virtues are visible in their effects—namely, in their exceptional piety toward God, absolute self-denial, and the greatest of charity for one's neighbors.

Now, this lofty holiness should belong as *an essential property* of the Church instituted by Christ, on account of the end to which this society is ordered, just as unity belongs to it above all on account of its constitutive form, for indeed, Christ gave the Church her order in order to foster eminent and supernatural holiness.

{{200}} While praying before his Passion, he expressly said: "Holy Father, keep them in thy name whom thou hast given me. . . . *Sanctify them in truth.* . . . And for them do I sanctify myself, *that they also may be sanctified in truth*" (John 17:11–19, DR). Already, from the start of his ministry, he had said in the Sermon on the Mount: "*Unless your justice abound* more than that of the scribes and Pharisees, you shall not enter into the kingdom of heaven" (Matt 5:20, DR). And setting forth the new law in its perfection, he had commended *in the Beatitudes* and *counsels* the loftiest degree of the virtues of humility, chastity, self-denial, charity, and love for our neighbors. In order to produce this holiness, *he instituted the Eucharist*: "The bread that

I will give is my flesh, for the life of the world. . . . He that eateth my flesh and drinketh my blood hath everlasting life . . . [and] abideth in me and I in him" (John 6:52, 55, 57, DR). Likewise, *he promised the Holy Spirit*: "I will ask the Father: and he shall give you another Paraclete, that he may abide with you forever" (John 14:16, DR).

Moreover, Jesus intended that this eminent sanctity be *visible*: "*You are the light of the world*. A city seated on a mountain cannot be hid. Neither do men light a candle and put it under a bushel, but upon a candlestick, that it may shine to all that are in the house. So let your light shine before men, that they may see your good works, and glorify your Father who is in heaven" (Matt 5:14–16, DR). "*Even so every good tree bringeth forth good fruit*" (Matt 7:17, DR). "I have chosen you; and have appointed you, that you should go and should bring forth fruit; and your fruit should remain" (John 15:16, DR). "*I am come to cast fire on the earth*. And what will I, but that it be kindled?" (Luke 12:49, DR).

Nay, Jesus promises preachers of the faith *extraordinary signs of holiness* and of the divine origin of the Gospel: "And these signs shall follow them that believe. In my name they shall cast out devils. They shall speak with new tongues. They shall take up serpents: and if they shall drink any deadly thing, it shall not hurt them. They shall lay their hands upon the sick: and they shall recover" (Mark 16:17–18, DR). And this is seen throughout the whole history of the Church in the apostolate of the holy preachers of the faith.

St. Paul sets forth this mark of Christ's Church as follows: "Husbands, love your wives, as Christ also *loved* the church and delivered himself up for it, *that he might sanctify it*, cleansing it by the laver of water in the word of life, that he might present it to himself, *a glorious church, not having spot or wrinkle* or any such thing, but *that it should be holy and without blemish*" (Eph 5:25–27, DR). This holiness will be consummated in heaven. However, on earth, even if the Church must be visibly holy in her doctrine, her means [of sanctification], and her fruits, nonetheless sinners still exist in her, as is set forth in the parable of the wheat and the weeds, for both weeds and good seed will exist in the field of the Church: "Suffer both to grow until the harvest" (Matt 13:30, DR)—that is, up to the end of the age. Even this presence of sinners in the Church is an occasion for eminent virtues, patience, mercy, and zeal for reparation: "Do good to them that hate you: and pray for them that persecute and calumniate you" (Matt 5:44, DR).

(3) *Christ intended that his Church be universal / catholic—that is, spread out through all peoples.* In its general meaning, *catholicity* (καθ᾽ ὅλον) signifies universality or totality. {{201}} Inasmuch as it is applied to the

Church,[32] catholicity *of right* (or *virtual* catholicity) is the Church's right and aptitude to spread throughout all people. *De facto* catholicity (or *actual* catholicity) is her progressive visible diffusion so that, in particularly well-known nations, a noteworthy number of men gradually become members of the Church. This progressive catholicity is called *formal* insofar as it is joined with unity.

However, in many of his declarations, Christ made manifest that he intended that the Church be universal not only *de iure* but also *de facto*. This mark (*nota*) belongs to the Church in particular as considered from the perspective of her members, just as the earlier ones belong to her from the perspective of her form and end.

Indeed, *de iure*, Christ intended to bestow a teaching and means of salvation that are apt and sufficient for all men, for he compared the Church to a "mustard seed, which . . . when it is grown up, it is greater than all herbs, and becometh a (great) tree" (Matt 13:31–32, DR). Likewise, he said, "For God so loved the world, as to give his only begotten Son: that whosoever believeth in him may not perish, but may have life everlasting" (John 3:16, DR). Likewise, in speaking of our Savior, St. Paul says, "Who will have all men to be saved and to come to the knowledge of the truth. For there is one God and one mediator of God and men, the man Christ Jesus, who gave himself a redemption for all" (1 Tim 2:4–6, DR; Rom 1:16), or, as St. John says, "For the sins of the whole world" (1 John 2:2).

However, Christ also intended that his Church have a progressive, *de facto* universality, saying to the apostles, in a way that was at once a command and a prophecy: "*You shall be witnesses . . . even to the uttermost part of the earth*" (Acts 1:8, DR). "*Go ye into the whole world and preach the gospel to every creature*" (Mark 16:15, DR). "*Going therefore, teach ye all nations; . . . and behold I am with you all days, even to the consummation of the world*" (Matt 28:19–20, DR). Earlier, he had said, "Many shall come from the east and the west, and shall sit down with Abraham, and Isaac and Jacob in the kingdom of heaven" (Matt 8:11, DR; Luke 13:29). And in the parable of the sower: "He that soweth the good seed is the Son of man. And the field is the world" (Matt 13:37–38, DR).

Indeed, Jesus said to the apostles from the start, "But go ye rather to the lost sheep of the house of Israel" (Matt 10:6). However, this only pertained to the beginning of the preaching of the Gospel. He himself healed

---

[32] The very term is applied to the Church in the writings of the most ancient of Fathers (e.g., in St. Ignatius of Antioch, *Letter to the Church at Smyrna*, no. 8: "Wherever Jesus Christ is, there is the Catholic Church."

the pagan centurion's boy (Matt 8:5–10) and the daughter of the Canaanite woman (Matt 15:23–28). And he said to the Pharisees, "The publicans and the harlots shall go into the kingdom of God before you" (Matt 21:31, DR). Likewise, after the day of Pentecost, his disciples, "began to speak *in various languages*" (Acts 2:4, 8), and a great number of nations heard their own tongues being spoken. Then, Peter, as he himself says, was sent by the Holy Spirit to the Gentiles (Acts 10:20). Finally, Paul became the teacher of the Gentiles and said: "For as many of you as have been baptized in Christ have put on Christ. There is neither Jew nor Greek. . . . For you are all one in Christ Jesus" (Gal 3:27–28, DR; Rom 1:13–15; 3:22–23; Eph 2:13–16; etc.).

Nay, St. Paul bore witness that the promises were at least partially fulfilled even in his own days when he said, concerning the apostles: "Their sound hath gone forth into all the earth (Rom 10:18, DR). "(The Church) is in the whole world and bringeth forth fruit and groweth" (Col 1:6, DR).

{{202}} However, Christ proclaimed a *moral* and *relative universality* for his Church, not one that is physical and absolute: "Because the light is come into the world and men loved darkness rather than the light: for their works were evil" (John 3:19, DR). And he predicted persecutions, for *many will not wish to believe*: "If the world hate you, know ye that it hath hated me before you" (John 15:18, DR). In the end, "many false prophets shall rise and shall seduce many. And . . . and the charity of many shall grow cold" (Matt 24:11–12, DR). Nonetheless, "*this Gospel of the kingdom shall be preached in the whole world, for a testimony to all nations: and then shall the consummation come*" (Matt 24:14, DR; Mark 13:26).

(4) *Christ willed that his Church be apostolic—that is, that it forever be the same society as that which the apostles founded.* Here we are speaking of the *legitimate, public,* and *uninterrupted succession of the Church's pastors from the apostles, identical in their profession of faith, sacraments, and rule.*[33] Hence, as apostolicity is not only mere material succession of pastors but, rather, *formal succession,* it must be united with the marks (*notis*) of unity and catholicity, for otherwise there would not be identity of one and the same society.

---

[33] It does not suffice, as Protestants wish, that there be apostolicity *of doctrine,* through preaching that is conformed to the teaching of the apostles, for this conformity is not always sufficiently visible, since false prophets and heretics propose their preaching as being something conformed to the Gospel. Nor would succession through power of *orders* suffice, as the Anglicans wish, for this succession is not of itself and always visible, without rightful declaration by legitimate authority. Moreover, continuous succession in *legitimate rule* is required so that one and the same society might be preserved.

This continuous and legitimate succession is *visible*, especially as regards its *rule*, just as it is visible in the continuous and legitimate succession involved in a civil society that has this or that political rule. A succession of this kind in the Church excludes interruption, which can be brought about through heresy or schism (namely, through separation from the supreme authority of the Church). Therefore, this mark of the Church pertains in particular to its efficient instrumental cause (the apostles), just as the aforementioned marks pertain to the other three causes (formal, final, and material).

So conceived, apostolicity is *an essential property* of Christ's Church, for as was said above, Christ established the Church as a *hierarchical* and *perpetual* society, in which authority / jurisdiction must be transmitted in an uninterrupted fashion.

He expressly said to the apostles, "As the Father hath sent me, I also send you" (John 20:21, DR), and "Going therefore, *teach ye all nations*. . . . I am with you all days, *even to the consummation of the world*" (Matt 28:19–20, DR). He says to Peter, "*That thou art Peter; and upon this rock I will build my Church*, and the gates of hell *shall not prevail* against it" (Matt 16:18, DR). Hence, a church not built upon this foundation, but, rather, in separation from the supreme authority of Peter and his successors, is not the true church of Christ.[34]

{{203}} Likewise, St. Paul wrote to the Ephesians: "You are no more strangers and foreigners: but you are fellow citizens with the saints and the domestics of God, *built upon the foundation of the apostles* and prophets, Jesus Christ himself being the chief corner stone" (Eph 2:19–20, DR). And concerning the preachers of the faith, he says, "And how shall they preach unless they be sent"—namely, by legitimate authority (Rom 10:15, DR). Hence, in Acts 14:22, Paul and Barnabas were selected to establish "presbyters throughout the particular churches." And Paul writes to Titus: "For this cause I left thee in Crete: that thou . . . shouldest ordain priests in every city, as I also appointed thee" (Titus 1:5, DR). Finally, speaking similarly about the glorious Church in heaven, St. John says in Revelations 21:14 (DR): "And the wall of the city had *twelve foundations*, and in them, *the*

---

[34] [Trans. note: The comment does not, however, apply in the broader sense of church, truly attributed to Orthodox Churches, but instead is here concerned with the One Church as such. Even before the Second Vatican Council, this language was recognized on a number of occasions. To this end, one can consult the pre-conciliar schema *De ecclesia*, ch. 11, note 6. For an appropriate understanding of the language of Church and sister churches, see the 2000 CDF document, "Note on the Expression 'Sister Churches.'" However, this qualifying comment is not meant to minimize what is lacking in those Churches that do not recognize the pope as the visible head of the One Church of Christ.]

twelve names of the twelve apostles of the Lamb."

(5) **Conclusion concerning the marks of the Church.** These four visible marks manifest the four causes of the Church. Unity in the profession of faith, rule, and worship especially bears witness to her formal constitutive. Her eminent holiness reveals the inchoate attainment of her loftiest end. Her catholicity denotes her extension to all peoples, to all men who wish to be saved. And finally, her apostolicity reveals her instrumental efficient cause—namely, the apostles sent by Christ.

However, if all these visible marks, especially eminent holiness, are found ceaselessly in a given Church and in that Church alone, this Church and it alone is Christ's Church. Moreover, if all of these visible marks in fact do perpetually exist in some Church, by that very fact, *they constitute a great moral miracle*, as was shown earlier,[35] and likewise *a miraculous fulfilment of the most illustrious of the prophecies of Christ.*[36] Hence, we will see below,[37] in arguing from the marvelous life of the Church throughout the course of history, how these four notes are, as the [First] Vatican Council said, "a great and perpetual motive of credibility and an irrefutable testimony of her divine mission"[38]

§6. The Aforementioned Testimony of Christ concerning the Church Is Most Excellently Consistent with the Whole of His Preaching

This connection is especially clear in relation to Christ's teaching concerning the kingdom of God, the salvation promised to all men, the Eucharist, the remission of sins, and so forth. All of these not only are consistent most excellently with the things that are announced concerning the Church but, indeed, cannot be understood without them: How could Christ's teaching be preserved and propagated if there were not instituted an *authority in whom we could place our faith safely*? A religious society, like every society, cannot stand firm without a living and supreme authority. Moreover, the dogmas handed on by Christ are understood with difficulty, full of mysteries, and therefore can be easily corrupted. Likewise, his austere commands, opposed to all vices, could easily fall into oblivion, and as experience shows, ritual worship easily can slide into superstition.

---

[35] See bk. 1, ch. 18 (On the value of external motives that are, however, intrinsic to religion).

[36] In order to know the fulfillment of his *prophecy*, one must first have historical knowledge about the aforementioned testimony by Christ concerning his perpetual and indefectible Church. However, this historical knowledge is not prerequired in order to discern the marvelous moral *miracle* of the Church's life. This miracle of itself manifests the divine origin of Catholicism.

[37] See sect. 2, ch. 9.

[38] [First] Vatican Council, *Dei filius*, ch. 3 (Denzinger, no. 3013).

{{204}} Nor would it suffice, whatever Protestants may say, that we have inspired Sacred Scripture without the Church's *living and infallible magisterium*. Indeed, difficulties arise concerning the inspiration and meaning of Sacred Scripture, and in order to resolve them, a proximate, safe, and complete rule of faith is required, one whose existence is clearly obvious to all and aptly suited to resolve controversies. Otherwise, many would find it impossible to know those things that must be believed and done in order to arrive at salvation.

Hence, Jesus's testimony on this matter is perfectly consistent with the whole of his preaching. And this suffices as regards the exposition of Christ's teaching for our purposes here.

CHAPTER SIX

In View of His Wisdom and Holiness, Christ's Testimony concerning Himself Is Deserving of Faith

Single Article

{{205}} *State of the Question*—Here, our concern is particularly aimed at the testimony that Christ gave concerning his divine messianic and doctrinal mission. In order that it be deserving of faith, two things are required and will suffice if present: that it be clear that Christ was neither a deceiver nor someone who was deceived.

Today, however, all adversaries confess that Christ was *not a deceiver* but, on the contrary, was the most perfect exemplar of every virtue. Hence, he himself was persuaded that he was divinely sent. Nonetheless, certain rationalists hold, with Ernest Renan and Adolf Harnack, that Jesus was *deceived up to a point*, and that this persuasion that he had concerning his divine mission was nothing more than a lively awareness of his union with God.

However, this cannot be admitted if we consider, simultaneously, (1) the object and mode of the testimony offered by Christ, (2) his wisdom, and (3) his holiness.

§1. Christ's Testimony concerning His Divine Mission Was Something He Expressly Proposed, Indeed as Something to Be Believed by All

As we have already noted, from the beginning of his public life up to its end, Christ clearly and expressly affirmed that he was sent by God in order to reveal to men that teaching that is necessary for salvation. Many liberals, like G[ustaf] Dalman and P[aul] Wernle, assert that nowhere in the Gospels does Jesus appear uncertain concerning his divine mission. Moreover, he proclaimed this divine mission as something to be believed by all, on pain of eternal damnation: "Amen, amen, I say unto you that he who heareth my word and believeth him that *sent me* hath life everlasting: and cometh not into judgment, but is passed from death to life" (John 5:24, DR). "He that believeth in me hath everlasting life" (John 6:47, DR). "He that believeth in him (namely, the son of God) is not judged. *But he that doth not believe is already judged*: because he believeth not in the name of the only begotten Son of God" (John 3:18, DR). "He that believeth and is baptized shall be saved: *but he that believeth not shall be condemned*" (Mark 16:16, DR). This last text is also expressly concerned with the necessity of believing in the divine mission of Christ, in whose name men are to be baptized.

{{206}} Nay, the disciples understood Jesus that "to undergo martyrdom for Christ's sake is something falling under a [necessary moral] precept, namely, because man must have a soul that is prepared to allow himself to be killed rather than to deny Christ or mortally sin."[1] Indeed, Jesus himself had said: "And fear ye not them that kill the body, and are not able to kill the soul. . . . Everyone therefore that shall confess me before men, I will also confess him before my Father who is in heaven. *But he that shall deny me before men, I will also deny him before my Father who is in heaven*" (Matt 10:28, 32–33, DR).

However, if Christ had been deceived in this expression and continuous affirmation, *this deception* (or hallucination) would not have been merely transitory but instead *perpetual*, indeed about a matter of the greatest importance—namely, *about the very foundation of the doctrine to be believed in.* Now, nobody of sound mind can persuade himself that he has been divinely sent by God, is greater than all the prophets, in whom all must believe under pain of damnation, unless such a person were to receive from God utterly certain internal or external signs of his divine mission.

Nay, we would look upon a carpenter from Nazareth as though he were, *quite properly speaking, out of his mind*, if he were to make up such a tale and say that he was going to come on the clouds of heaven in order to judge the living and the dead, not blushing when he spoke thus: "He who loves father or mother more than me is not worthy of me," "before Abraham was I am," and "have confidence in me, for I have conquered the world."

However, this kind of pathological state is manifestly excluded if we consider Christ's wisdom and holiness, even before considering his miracles.

---

[1] See St. Thomas, *Quodlibet* IV, q. 10, a. 2 (Whether the suffering of martyrdom for Christ's sake is something that falls under a precept). Also see *ST* II-II, q. 124, a. 1, ad 3; a. 3, ad 1.

§2. Christ's Wisdom Excludes This Kind of Insane Deception

(a) As is even confessed by adversaries, Christ *ought to be numbered among the wisest of men, as is clear from his teaching and work.* Indeed, far surpassing all philosophers, he gives to us a marvelous solution for all of the essential problems concerning God, man, and the next life (see below what we will come to say about the sublimity of his teaching). With the greatest of simplicity, he teaches the loftiest mysteries, precepts, and counsels as things proposed to little ones. Finally, by his own work, he restores mankind in an unparalleled fashion, renewing man in all the virtues. In this, we have a witness to his utterly eminent wisdom and rectitude of judgment, which rule out the possibility of insanity and perpetual deception concerning the very foundation of the doctrine he proposes.

(b) *In fact, all admired Jesus's wisdom, as is recounted in the Gospels.* In the temple, in the midst of the teachers of the law, when he not even yet an adolescent, "all that heard him were astonished at his wisdom and his answers" (Luke 2:47, DR). After the Sermon on the Mount, "the people were in admiration at his doctrine" (Matt 7:28, DR). Nay, the scribes [*ministri*] of the Pharisees sent to trap him respond: "Never did man speak like this man" (John 7:46, DR).

(c) Christ's *prudence and perspicacity* are clear, in particular, *in his responses to the Pharisees.* They tempted him with questions, like that concerning the woman caught in adultery (John 8:7) and the census owed to Caesar (Matt 22:15–21). Likewise, the Sadducees captiously asked him about the resurrection (Matt 22:23–32). And Jesus always refuted them with his utterly lofty authority and sharp genius so that St. Matthew notes: {{207}} "And no man was able to answer him a word: neither durst any man from that day forth ask him any more questions" (Matt 22:46, DR).

(d) *With the greatest* tranquility of soul, *he judges concerning all things,* even when he is afflicted with the gravest of injuries. For example, when the Pharisees said to him, "This man casteth not out devils but by Beelzebub the prince of the devils," Jesus responds to them, "Every kingdom divided against itself shall be made desolate: and every city or house divided against itself shall not stand" (Matt 12:24–25, DR). When the Jews said to him, "You have a devil," Jesus responded, "I have not a devil, but I honor my Father. And you have dishonored me. But I seek not my own glory; there is one that seeketh and judgeth. . . . It is my Father that glorifieth me. . . . And you have not known him: but I know him. *And if I shall say that I know him not, I shall be like to you, a liar.* But I do know him and do keep his word" (John 8:49–55, DR).

(e) *Nay, Jesus humbly and fittingly asserts the reason for his rectitude of judgment* when he says: "I cannot of myself do anything. *As I hear, so I judge. And my judgment is just, because I seek not my own will* but the will of him that sent me" (John 5:30, DR). Likewise, when the Jews said to him, "How doth this man know letters, having never learned?" Jesus responded, "My doctrine is not mine, but his that sent me" (John 7:15–16, DR). John the Baptist had said concerning him: "He that cometh from heaven is above all. *And what he hath seen and heard, that he testifieth*: and no man receiveth his testimony. . . . For he whom God hath sent speaketh the words of God: for God doth not give the Spirit by measure. The Father loveth the Son: and he hath given all things into his hand. He that believeth in the Son hath life everlasting: but he that believeth not the Son shall not see life: but the wrath of God abideth on him" (John 3:31–36, DR).

(f) Finally, *Jesus speaks with authority like the supreme teacher* when he says something that nobody had said: "Amen, amen, I say to you: If any man keep my word, he shall not see death forever" (John 8:51, DR). "I speak that which I have seen with my Father" (John 8:38, DR). "You believe in God: believe also in me" (John 14:1, DR). "I am the light of the world. He that followeth me walketh not in darkness" (John 8:12, DR). "I am the way, and the truth, and the life. No man cometh to the Father, but by me" (John 14:6, DR). And the words of St. Paul find their greatest confirmation in Jesus: "The spiritual man judges all things and is himself judged by no man." "For he was teaching them as one having power, and not as the scribes and Pharisees" (Matt 7:29).

All of these facts indicate an utterly eminent wisdom and are not the words of a man who is insanely deceived concerning the very foundation of his teaching. Moreover, this is all corroborated through the authority of Jesus's life, which we will now turn to discuss.

§3. Christ's Holiness Perfectly Confirms His Testimony

Great philosophers often do not do what they teach in their ethics. However, whatever Jesus said, he kept and did. Pseudo-mystics, even if they sometimes are gifted with great speculative intelligence, err in particular due to the vain enthusiasm and ardor coming from their spiritual pride, deceiving others in their wake. Nothing like this is found in the case of Christ.

By contrast, as adversaries themselves admit, Jesus appears to us without having any defect, as the perfect exemplar of holiness, epitomizing all the virtues. {{208}} And his humility is not less than his magnanimity, his meekness than his courage / fortitude, his mercy than his justice. No, in him, the most varied of virtues, possessed to a heroic and supreme degree, are united in a sublime harmony, and as we will soon show, this is a moral miracle in confirmation of his testimony.

Holiness involves two things: (A) purity from sin and imperfections; (B) all the virtues and, in particular, firm and continuous union with God. All of these things will here be considered in an apologetic manner, not by arguing from faith but, rather, from historical testimony, distinguishing loftier virtues from false holiness or [*seu*] pseudo-mysticism.[2]

A. *Jesus was without any sin and defect.* Thus, in response to the Jews seeking to find a reason to kill him, he was able to say, without any contradiction: "Which of you shall convince me of sin?" (John 8:46, DR). And, in fact, as is recounted in the Gospels, "And the chief priests and the whole council sought false witness against Jesus, that they might put him to death, and they found none" (Matt 26:59–60, DR). But one time, because Jesus confessed that he was the Christ, the Son of God, "Then the high priest rent his garments, saying, 'He hath blasphemed'" (Matt 26:65, DR). Judas himself confessed, "I have sinned in betraying innocent blood" (Matt 27:4, DR). And Pilate said, "I am innocent of the blood of this just man. Look you to it" (Matt 27:24, DR).

The holiest of men feel sorrow on account of their own sins and imperfections. Christ alone, though utterly humble, was aware of no sin. His disciples, who perfectly knew his intimate life, as well as all of its external circumstances, had been able to write of him, in his hour of sorrow and ultimate anguish or in the moment of his glorification: "Who did no sin, neither was guile found in his mouth" (1 Pet 2:22, DR); "and in him there

---

[2] See Bossuet, *Discours sur l'histoire universelle*, pt. 2, ch. 19: "The wisest of the philosophers found . . . that the most virtuous of men must be a person who, on account of the perfection of his virtue, drew the jealousy of all, so that he would only have his conscience at his disposal, seeing himself be exposed to every kind of injury, to the point of being placed on the cross, without his virtue being able to give him even the small relief of being able to exempt himself from such suffering (cf. Socrates in *Republic*, bk. 2). Does it not seem that God would have placed this marvelous idea of virtue in the mind of a philosopher only to be able to render it effective in the person of His Son and to enable us to see that the righteous man has another kind of glory, another kind of peace, and finally another kind of happiness than that which can be had on earth?"

See Pascal, *Pensées* (ed. Havet), 268: "Without any riches, without any outward display of knowledge, Jesus Christ *exists in his own order of holiness*. He did not invent anything, nor did he exercise his reign, but rather was *humble, patient, holy before God, terrible to the demons, and sinless.* Oh! With what great pomp and what incredible magnificence has he come to the eyes of the heart which there see Wisdom!" "Never was a man so radiant, never had a man such infamy."

Also see the 36th conference of Henri-Dominique Lacourdaire (The intimate life of Jesus).

is no sin" (1 John 3:5, DR); "him, who knew no sin" (2 Cor 5:21, DR); "but one tempted in all things like as we are, without sin" (Heb 4:15, DR).

B. *Christ had all virtues, even of the greatest diversity, in a heroic state.*[3] {{209}} In particular, we will specify his charity and piety toward God, his charity and mercy toward men, and his perfect self-denial, humility, and meekness, alongside the greatest of courage / fortitude and patience while undergoing martyrdom.

(a) *Christ's charity and piety toward God* is utterly perfect. His ultimate desire is that the glory of the Father in heaven might increase: "I must be about my father's business" (Luke 2:49, DR). "My meat is to do the will of him that sent me, that I may perfect his work" (John 4:34, DR). "For I do always the things that please him. . . . I honor my Father. . . . I seek not my own glory" (John 8:29, 49, 50, DR). Before his Passion, he prays thus: "Father, the hour is come. Glorify thy Son, that thy Son may glorify thee. . . . I have glorified thee on the earth; I have finished the work which thou gavest me to do" (John 17:1–4, DR). Before this, he had said: "Therefore doth the Father love me: because I lay down my life, that I may take it again. . . . This commandment have I received of my Father" (John 10:17–18, DR). At the moment of his greatest sacrifice, he says: "My Father, if this chalice may not pass away, but I must drink it, thy will be done" (Matt 26:42, DR). Indeed, obedient to the point of death, even death upon the Cross, glorifying God, he cried out in a loud voice, "Father, into thy hands I commend my spirit" (Luke 23:46, DR) and "It is done" (John 19:30).

In pseudo-mysticism, false love of God often destroys love of neighbor and leads to spiritual pride. By contrast, in Christ, the greatest of charity toward God confirms his love for his parents, his ungrateful homeland, and his fellow men. Nay, in him there is the fount of love for all men, inasmuch as they are sons of God.

(b) *Christ's charity and mercy for men* was of the greatest perfection because it was at once of the greatest profundity, universality, and efficacy. In general, our love is profound only for a few number of relatives [*parentes*] and friends, and when it comes to be extended outward to more distant circles, it becomes less intense and less efficacious.

---

[3] See Marie-Joseph Lagrange, *L'évangile de Jésus-Christ* (1928), 612–616 (a comparison of Jesus and Socrates): "Socrates is indeed the hero of . . . civic justice. He wished to die for the sake of this virtue, fulfilling this duty to the end, for the sake of its own, proper dignity. And he offered a magnificent example, . . . though it was powerless to draw men toward morality, indeed not even indicating the way that leads to God. Thus, the ideal that was conceived of by the most idealistic of the Greeks proves to be quite inferior to that which was traced out by the Evangelists concerning Jesus, who came to preach the truth and died for it."

Christ's charity is concerned directly with that which is most profound and noble in all men—namely, their soul, inasmuch as it is made in the image of God and is ordered to eternal life. As he himself said, Jesus is the *shepherd of souls*; he knows them, calls them by name, and leads them (John 10:3–14). Hence, he loves all, whatever their conditions, not only Jews but also Gentiles, not only the just but sinners, especially the poor, the sick, and the afflicted, whom he heals and strengthens. He went about doing good, healing bodies and souls, and mercifully receiving the prodigal son and the penitent Mary Magdalene. He rejected nobody and called the traitorous Judas himself his friend.

This charity likewise had *the greatest of efficacy*. He said, "Greater love than this no man hath, that a man lay down his life for his friends" (John 15:13, DR). And "I am the good shepherd. *The good shepherd giveth his life for his sheep*" (John 10:11, DR). "For God so loved the world, as to give his only begotten Son: that whosoever believeth in him may not perish, but may have life everlasting" (John 3:16, DR). "The Son of man is not come to be ministered unto, but to minister and to give his life a redemption for many" (Matt 20:28, DR). "This is my body, which is given for you. . . . This is the chalice, the new testament in my blood, which shall be shed for you" (Luke 22:19–20). {{210}} Up to the end, he showed mercy toward sinners and those in error. On the cross, he said to the penitent thief, "This day thou shalt be with me in paradise" (Luke 23:43, DR), and for those who tortured him, he prayed, "Father, forgive them, for they know not what they do" (Luke 23:34, DR).

However, this utterly great mercy never slid into overindulgence or foolish leniency. For Christ, fraternal correction is an act of charity.

"But if thy brother shall offend against thee, go, and rebuke him between thee and him alone. If he shall hear thee, thou shalt gain thy brother" (Matt 18:15, DR).[4] Never did Christ's mercy lead him to forget God's eternal rights. *It did not exclude a just and inflexible severity* toward the obstinate Pharisees. Nay, his holy indignation motivated him against these adversaries of the kingdom of God and of the salvation of souls:

> But woe to you, scribes and Pharisees, hypocrites, because you shut the kingdom of heaven against men: for you yourselves do not enter in and those that are going in, you suffer not to enter. . . . Woe to you, blind guides, . . . you

---

[4] See *ST* II-II, q. 33, a. 1 (Whether fraternal correction is an act of charity): "Fraternal correction is not opposed to forbearance to the weak. . . . It is concerned with bringing about the correction of sins." And in a. 6: "If a sinner is incorrigible, the common good is observed in this way when the order of justice is preserved."

are like to whited sepulchers, which outwardly appear to men beautiful but within are full of dead men's bones and of all filthiness. . . . You are the sons of them that killed the prophets. . . . You serpents, generation of vipers, how will you flee from the judgment of hell? (Matt 23:13–36, DR)

This indignation in no way is opposed to charity but, rather, proceeds from it—namely, from zeal for the glory of God and the salvation of souls. Likewise, he cast out the money changers from the temple because they made the house of God into a business place (John 2:15). Thus, he perfectly preserved the order of charity, which false charity destroys or overthrows.[5]

Thus, in Christ we have a marvelous reconciliation of the holy rigor of justice and immense mercy. As in God himself, the intimate character of this reconciliation remains hidden, but its existence indicates a supernatural perfection, for he who is naturally inclined to justice often falls short in mercy, and vice versa. {{211}} However, in Christ, "Mercy and truth have met each other: justice and peace have kissed" (Ps 84[5]:11, DR); nevertheless, the rigor of justice is always subordinated to charity, from which it proceeds.[6]

(c) *Self-denial, humility, and meekness.* Jesus said: "He who wishes to come after me must deny himself, take up his cross, and follow me." He himself always scorned pleasures, riches, and honors to such a degree that he

---

[5] See *ST* II-II, q. 26, where St. Thomas discusses the order of charity, stating that man must love God more than his neighbor, more than himself, and a better neighbor more than another.

An objection, however, is raised by some liberal Protestants, who confuse true charity with false charity (or liberalism): These movements of anger and vengeance in Christ indicate a lack of meekness.

Response: With St. Thomas, we can say, as he does in *ST* III, q. 15, a. 9: "Sometimes, the desire for vengeance is sinless—nay, is laudable—namely, when someone desires vengeance in accord with the order of justice, and this is called *anger through zeal.*" Also, in ad 2: "Anger which goes beyond the order of reason is opposed to meekness; however, this is not the case for anger which is measured and reduced to its due mean by reason, for meekness is the mean in matters of anger." And in ad 3: "*In us* . . . if the activity of one power is intense, that of another is weakened. This is why any kind of movement of anger, even if it be tempered by reason, dims the mind's eye in him who contemplates. However, *in Christ*, through the regulation of the divine power, every power was allowed to do what was proper to it, and one power was not impeded by another. Therefore, just as the joy of his mind in contemplation did not impede the sorrow or pain of the inferior part, so too, conversely, the passions of the inferior part in no way impeded the act of reason."

Likewise, in *ST* II-II, q. 157, a. 2, ad 1: "*Clemency and meekness are not opposed to severity* (but, rather, to cruelty, rage, and ferocity)." "For inflexible severity is concerned with the infliction of punishments when right reason requires this, whereas clemency reduces punishments also in accord with right reason, namely, when and where this is necessary. And therefore, they are not opposed, for they are not concerned with the same things."

[6] See *ST* I, q. 21, a. 4.

did not have "a place to lay his head." He did not come "to be served but to serve." No more did he seek after the favor of princes than did he look for the applause of the masses, and when they looked to make him a king, he fled to the mountains (John 6:15).

Quite justly was he able to say to his disciples: "Learn of me, because I am meek, and humble of heart" (Matt 11:29, DR). Indeed, he remained in obscurity for thirty years, prohibited his miracles and transfiguration from being spread abroad (Matt 9:30; 18:9), and did not seek his own glory but, rather, his Father's (John 8:49–50). He did not desire a reputation from great teachers but, rather, spent his time evangelizing the poor in particular, choosing ignorant men as his apostles, and on many occasions commended humility. Nay, at his Last Supper, he washed their feet (John 13:13). In his Passion, he suffered all kinds of humiliations for our salvation, doing so with the greatest of meekness, "like a lamb led to the slaughter."

However, this humility and meekness never passed over into timidity or pusillanimity. In a most excellent manner, Christ reconciled it with *dignity, magnanimity*, and *perfect honesty*. "But let your speech be yea, yea: no, no" (Matt 5:37, DR). Due to his perfect honesty, many departed from him (John 6:67). And he laid blame to the disciples' vices and the crowd's disbelief. During his Passion, after being struck by the servant of the High Priest, he responded appropriately: "If I have spoken evil, give testimony of the evil, but if well, why strikest thou me?" (John 18:23, DR). And when Pilate asked him if he was a king, Jesus responded with majesty: "Thou sayest that I am a king. For this was I born, and for this came I into the world; that I should give testimony to the truth. Every one that is of the truth heareth my voice" (John 18:37, DR). Likewise, he said to Caiaphas: "Hereafter you shall see the Son of man sitting on the right hand of the power of God and coming in the clouds of heaven" (Matt 26:64, DR). Thus, a man of the greatest humility and, at the same time, magnanimity, was condemned on the accusation of intolerable pride[7] and blasphemy.

(d) *The greatest fortitude, perseverance, and patience in martyrdom.* His firmness remained forever unshaken, being diminished neither by the disbelief of the Jews, nor by the slowness and fearfulness of his disciples, nor through the utterly bitter cup of his Passion. In the midst of the most awful of torments, he showed incredible patience and strength of soul, not by putting on the affected freedom from pain expressed by Stoics, or through bitter disdain for his torturers, but rather by praying for them and crying out trustingly: "Father, into your hands, I commend my spirit." And saying this,

---

7 [Trans. note: Reading *superbiae* for *superbia*.]

he breathed his last breath. However, those nearby, seeing all that was done, glorified God, saying, "Indeed this was a just man" (Luke 23:47).

{{212}} *This meekness for his torturers* shows the supernaturality of this heroic fortitude united to it, inasmuch as both come not from self-love but, rather, from the greatest of love for God and for souls.[8]

(e) *This harmony and perseverance in heroic virtues is a moral miracle.* Christ would not have had all of the virtues, indeed in such utterly great diversity and at such a heroic and supreme degree, without a special intervention by God. For, as was said above,[9] holiness (that is, virtue involving perfect purity from earthly things as well as utterly firm union with God) cannot exist unless it comes from God, inasmuch as the order of agents must correspond to the order of ends, and extraordinary holiness comes from God, intervening in the world in an extraordinary manner. However, Christ's holiness is clearly supra-human, for given that nature has a single determination [*determinatur ad unum*], we see some people, either from their natural makeup or from some habit, are prompt in doing acts of fortitude while they are nonetheless not prompt in performing acts of meekness. However, if someone were to have, simultaneously and with great excellence, all virtues, even those that are utterly distant from each other—like the greatest fortitude and the greatest meekness, perfect love for truth and justice and, at the same time, the greatest of mercy toward those who err and toward sinners—this could be only through an extraordinary aid coming from God, who alone in his simplicity eminently contains perfections that have such utterly great diversity and who alone can unite them together in an intimate manner in the human soul.

Mere mental quickness cannot simulate this harmony of the virtues, for such versatility does not pass from one virtue to another dissimilar one but, rather, passes from a sin by way of excess to one by way of defect—for

---

[8]   Rousseau himself said in *Émile*, bk. 4 (The Profession of Faith of the Savoyard Vicar): "Is it possible that the sacred personage, whose history it contains, should be himself a mere man? Do we find that he assumed the tone of an enthusiast or ambitious sectary? What purity, what sweetness in his manners! What an affecting gracefulness in his delivery! What sublimity in his maxims! What profound wisdom in his discourses! . . . How great the command over his passions! Where is the man, where the philosopher who could so live and so die, without weakness and without ostentation? . . . Yes, if the life and death of Socrates are those of a sage, the life and death of Jesus are those of a God." [Trans. note: Since this was written in Latin in the original, this text was drawn from the translation found at https://sourcebooks.fordham.edu/mod/1782rousseau-savoyard.asp; originally found in *French and English Philosophers: Descartes, Rousseau, Voltaire, Hobbes* (New York: P. F. Collier, 1910).

[9]   See earlier in this same volume, bk. 1, ch. 18 (On the value of motives external to us, though intrinsic to religion), §2, 2 (Holiness and heroic virtue).

example, from immoderate fear to rashness, from irrational love to utter lack of affection, from thoughtlessness to craftiness, from indifferentism (or liberalism) to fanaticism (or sectarianism). Thus, to take a concrete example, consider Jean-Jacques Rousseau in his own life and in his works.

This argument is rounded off and brought to perfection by consideration of Christ's *perseverance* in all the virtues. However, due to human nature, with its weaknesses, and free choice's readiness to turn this way or that, it is impossible for someone to persist fixedly for a considerable length of time in the full host of heroic virtues, without a special intervention by God.[10] Thus, Christ's holiness is truly supra-human and miraculous.[11]

Conclusion. Therefore, Christ's testimony finds a perfect confirmation in his wisdom and holiness, {{213}} for God cannot perform a miracle to the benefit of error. Thus, it is impossible that we admit that Christ was deceived or was a deceiver when he declared over and over that he was sent by God.[12] Hence, this testimony, confirmed by divine authority, is certainly deserving of faith. Already here, we have a motive of credibility that is adequate, of itself, in relation to a supernatural end.

---

[10] See *ST* II-II, q. 137 (On perseverance), a. 1 and 3.

[11] See Pascal, *Pensées* (ed. Havet), 271: "Who taught the evangelists the qualities belonging to a perfectly heroic soul so that they could depict it so perfectly in Jesus Christ? Why do they present him as being weak in his agony? Do they not know how to depict a resolute death? Yes, certainly, for the same St. Luke depicts the death of St. Stephen more strongly than that of Jesus Christ. Therefore, they make him capable of feeling fear before the necessity of dying arrives and then make him altogether brave. However, they make him so troubled when he afflicts himself, whereas when men afflict him, he is altogether strong."

[12] In his *Theologia fundamentalis*, thesis no. 31, Ignaz Ottiger, S.J., holds that this conclusion is morally certain, and this is generally held by Catholic apologetes. See, for example, Hugo Hurter, *Theologia dogmatica*, vol. 1, thesis 15; Christian Pesch, *Praelectiones dogmaticae*, vol. 1, nos. 146–149; Adolphe Tanquerey, *Theologia fundamentalis*, 14th ed., 205.

Confirmation of Christ's Testimony through Motives That Are Internal to Us, as Well as by Motives That Are Intrinsic to Religion

{{214}} Motives that are internal to us are drawn from the way that Christianity miraculously fulfills human aspirations. By contrast, those external motives that are intrinsic to religion are drawn from the sublimity of its teaching, as well as from the miraculous life of the Church. Hence, this section will be divided into three chapters.

Inexhaustible Spiritual Fecundity and Especially in the
Perseverance of the Martyrs

Art. 3. The Church's Catholic Unity and Unconquered Stability

Confirmation of Christ's Testimony through the Way That Christianity Miraculously Fulfills Human Aspirations

SINGLE ARTICLE

§1. State of the Question

Already in bk. 1, ch. 18, we speculatively discussed the value of motives that are internal to us, and we established this hypothetical proposition: If all the legitimate aspirations of our nature, even the loftier ones, *are satisfied in a marvelous manner—nay, surpassed* in some religion and in it alone—it is *morally certain* that this religion was instituted by God himself, for it is at least morally impossible that man would arrive at such a marvelous fulfillment merely by his natural powers. However, in contrast to the claims of liberal Protestants and modernists, it does not suffice to argue solely from the conformity of Christian teaching with our natural aspirations. This would only prove that Christ taught the most perfect form of natural religion.

   Now, however, we must set forth a verification of this sign in Christianity. Therefore, we must enumerate the principal aspirations of our nature and ask how they are satisfied in Christianity and not outside of it.

A. *The religious and moral aspirations* of our nature, as we said above, are nothing other than the seeds, within us, for the natural virtues concerned with our ultimate end and the means necessary to reaching it. In relation to the end itself, there are the aspirations *to know God* with firm certitude as the principle and end of all beings, *to hope in God* as the one who provides the necessary assistance for reaching our end as well as *future beatitude* following upon the sufferings of this life, and *to love God above all things*, not only affectively but effectively, so that the whole of our moral life would in fact be ordered to our ultimate end.[1] As St. Thomas says:

{{216}} It is *impossible* that *man's beatitude would be found in some created good*, for beatitude is a perfect good which wholly brings the appetite to a rest. Otherwise, the end in question would not be an ultimate end if something more still remained to be desired. Now, the object of the will, which is the human appetite, is the universal good, just as the object of the intellect is the universal true. From this, it is clear that the only thing that can still man's will is the universal good, which is not found in some created good but, rather, only in God, for every creature has a participated good.[2]

Likewise, we have within ourselves an inclination to offer God *the internal and external worship* owed to him. These various aspirations follow from the first, which is nothing other than the desire to firmly know the first and highest truth.

Concerning the means, there are inclinations *to the moral virtues*—namely, to prudence, justice, fortitude, temperance, and the conjoined

---

[1] See *ST* II-II, q. 26, a. 3: "*Natural love* has its foundation on the natural goods bestowed on us by God. In virtue of this love, *so long as man's nature remains unimpaired, he loves God above all things and more than himself.* However, beyond man, every single creature loves God through such natural love as well, each in its own way, namely, either by an intellectual, rational, animal, or at least a natural love (as, for example, stones do, as well as other things lacking of knowledge) *because each part naturally loves the common good of the whole more than its own particular good.*" Likewise, see *ST* I, q. 60, a. 5: "Indeed, we see that the part naturally exposes itself for the sake of preserving the whole body. Otherwise, if man were to love himself more than God, it would follow that natural love would be *perverse* and not perfected through charity but, rather, destroyed."

[2] *ST* I-II, q. 2, a. 8; q. 3, a. 1. Also see Ambroise Gardeil, "Les exigences objectives de l'action'" (On the necessity that there be an ultimate end, which can only be God; how this exigency is expressed by St. Augustine, St. Thomas, and Pascal), *Revue Thomiste* 6 (1898): 125–138, 269–294; "L'action: Ses ressources subjectives" (Can we possess God?), *Revue Thomiste* 7 (1899): 23–39; "Les ressources de vouloir," *Revue Thomiste* 7 (1899): 447–461.

virtues, which are admitted by all moralists.

B. *The natural desire for the future life* must be made manifest in particular. The existence of this desire is (a) clearly attested to by our own awareness, (b) proven by reason, and (c) confirmed by the consent of mankind.

(a) Our soul experiences a kind of desire to live forever, even though our body is mortal. There are those who do indeed inflict death upon themselves, but such persons detest not life itself but, rather, the miseries of life, nor would they do away with their life if they could have one that is more blessed.

(b) However, it is clear to reason that this desire is not like the sense inclination that animals have for preserving their bodily life, which of itself is subject to corruption. Indeed, as St. Thomas says in *ST* I, q. 75, a. 6, "In knowers, desire follows knowledge. However, the senses only know being inasmuch as it is subject to the here and now, whereas the intellect grasps being [*esse*] *absolutely* and in a way that is not subject to any particular time. Whence, *all beings that have an intellect naturally desire to exist forever*. However, a natural desire cannot be in vain." Moreover, as nearly all spiritualist philosophers say, *in this life, virtue does not always meet with success, nor are vices atoned for with due punishments*. Therefore, because just retribution is not fully had in this life, we naturally and reasonably hope in a future life, in which there would be a full manifestation of justice (or of the moral order).[3]

(c) Hence, the future life is desired by mankind in general. This desire is found in all religions,[4] and it manages to persevere, notwithstanding the existence of wicked passions and the sophistries of materialists.

C. *Moreover, we have within us a natural desire to see God as he is in himself.* {{217}} We showed this fact more fully earlier (in bk. 1, ch. 12), and we explained it in line with what St. Thomas says in *ST* I, q. 12, a. 1. Indeed, many obscurities remain in the most perfect natural knowledge concerning God that is had on the basis of our knowledge of created things, especially as regards the intimate reconciliation of certain divine attributes (e.g., justice and mercy) and as regards the divine permission of evil. Hence, we naturally desire to know God not only in an abstractive manner in the mirror of creatures but, rather, intuitively and immediately. As we said above, this desire is indeed natural, though it is conditional and inefficacious (i.e., it is a velleity).

---

3 This is conceded by Kant.
4 See Alexander Le Roy, *The Religion of the Primitives*, trans. Newton Thompson (New York: Macmillan, 1922), 282ff.

This condition is always present in it: if God would will to elevate us to supernatural vision of his essence.

These are our nature's principal intellectual, moral, and religious aspirations. Now we must consider whether they are satisfied outside of Christianity or, rather, only in Christianity.

§2. Imperfect Solutions Offered by Natural Reason, Philosophical Systems, and Other Religions

The aforementioned aspirations are insufficiently responded to by: (a) *natural reason*, (b) *philosophical systems*, and (c) *other religions*.

(a) *Natural reason.* As we showed above, natural reason cannot morally arrive at firm, unencumbered, error-free knowledge concerning the full array of naturally knowable truths pertaining to religion. Indeed, it arrives at certitude concerning God's existence, but doubts remain for natural reason as regards God's essential attributes, the conditions of our future life, and many other matters of great importance.

(b) *Philosophical systems.* Certain absolutely erroneous systems of philosophy, such as materialism, pantheism, and agnosticism sate our natural aspirations much less than does natural reason, and they do incredibly grave harm to those that are chief and the loftiest. However, other systems (e.g., those of Plato and of Aristotle) that approach more closely to the truth do not go without manifest error concerning certain attributes of God (e.g., the divine freedom), nor do they speak about the future life with firm certitude—or when they do, they confuse it with the transmigration of souls (or metempsychosis), which does not suitably respond to our aspirations. Likewise, the ethics set forth by these systems is highly inferior to Christian ethics and contains a number of manifest errors. However, modern philosophers who have separated themselves from the Church do no better job than the ancients at resolving the chief problems of philosophy but instead fall into agnosticism or pantheism / determinism.

(c) *Other religions.* We will here consider only the principal religions that remain in the world.

Buddhism teaches nothing concerning God and holds that man is subject to metempsychosis until the point when he acquires perfection in "nirvana." However, this loftiest perfection does not appear as being something positive, as the greatest beatitude, but, rather, is the extinction of all desires in the soul, a kind of annihilation. Moreover, among the people a kind of polytheism / idolatry is practiced.

Islam contains many true things that were borrowed from Judaism and

Christianity (namely, monotheism, immortality of the soul, and bodily resurrection). However, the paradise that it promises is a place where believers are occupied with sensible and carnal pleasures more than with the vision of God. Moreover, it also teaches fatalism.

Finally, *Protestants*, given that they are separated from the Catholic Church, do not have a firm rule of religious certitude and hence are divided among themselves and, forever fluctuating about, are carried away with every passing wind of doctrine. {{218}} Indeed, conservative Protestants hold that there is one authority, not one that is living but, rather, a written authority—namely, Sacred Scripture. However, since this rule is not always evident in its inspired character, nor complete, nor obvious to all, nor readily able to settle controversies, many sects have arisen. Hence, liberal Protestants reject any given authority, even that of Scripture, thus coming to corrupt and deny the chief truths of Christianity (e.g., Christ's divinity). Nay, they frequently arrive at agnosticism, no longer retaining firm certitude concerning the divine transcendence or the personal immortality of souls.

In no way do we find in these religions and sects the marvelous fulfilling of the human aspirations to certain knowledge of God, for his aids and retribution, and to religious unity of souls in God, loved above all things.

§3. The Christian-Catholic Solution

By contrast, the Christian-Catholic solution to these matters not only *satisfies* our soul's natural desires but, moreover, *surpasses* them. That is, it arouses loftier and livelier desires.[5]

---

[5] The strength of this argument is not clear unless its parts are considered together, as in the following synoptic chart:

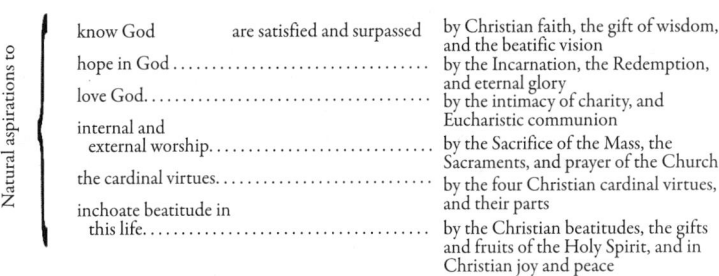

This is the synopsis of the whole of moral theology. Thus, it is clear that this argument is entirely traditional, though the Doctors of the Church did not develop it in apologetics

(1) *In response to our aspirations to firmly know God* there corresponds the *doctrine of faith* proposed as something divinely revealed, confirmed by divine signs, and explained by the living, *infallible* magisterium.[6] {{219}} However, this revelation promises us, in the present life, knowledge of the intimate secrets of the Heavenly Father, *wisdom* inspired by the Holy Spirit, and in the future life, *beatific and immediate vision of the divine essence*, which exceeds every natural desire, in accord with the words of St. Paul in 1 Corinthians 2:9 (DR): "Neither hath it entered into the heart of man, what things God hath prepared for them that love him."

(2) *Man's natural hope for future beatitude* is not only fulfilled but is elevated, for indeed, by reason's own natural judgment, we can confidently expect aid from God for doing the moral good, as well as natural beatitude in the next life, but not the *Incarnation* of the very Word of God, nor his death on the Cross for our *redemption*, nor *the eternal glory* promised to the faithful. However, on the basis of all these things, it is clear that God wills that all men be saved, thus rousing our hope more loftily: "For God so loved the world, as to give his only begotten Son: that whosoever believeth in him may not perish, but may have life everlasting" (John 3:16, DR).

(3) *The natural inclination to love God above all things* could never have been extended to the point of being a desire for holy and familiar *friendship with God*, or *charity*, which is proposed to all of us, especially in

---

but instead in theology properly so-called, or in ascetical and mystical books. See St. Augustine, *Confessions*; *On the Sermon on the Mount*; *Treatise on John's Gospel*; St. Bernard, *Opera omnia*; St. Thomas, *ST* I-II (the treatises on beatitude and on the virtues and the gifts of the Holy Spirit); Bl. [St.] Albert the Great, *On Adhering to God*; St. Catherine of Siena, *Dialogue*; Thomas à Kempis, *Imitation of Christ*; St. Teresa, *Opera omnia*; St. Francis de Sales, *Treatise on the Love of God*; Bossuet, *Élévations*.

[6] See Fr. Lacordaire, *Conférences de Notre Dame*, conf. 1 (On the necessity that there be a teaching church and on what is characteristically distinct about it): "Man is a being that is taught . . . . What do you want from me? The truth? Therefore, you do not have it in yourselves. Therefore, you are seeking it. You wish to receive it. And you have come here in order to be taught. . . . Our first indigence is that which we feel for the truth, just as our first wealth is that of the soul for the truth. . . . And it is not only each individual man who finds himself to be taught. There are also the nations and the centuries. . . . They experience the yoke of authority. . . . For us Christians who are delivered by the Church, we live neither in the present century, nor in the last century, nor in the next. No, we live in eternity. We do not wish to submit ourselves to the teaching of a given century, nor that of a given nature, nor that of a given man, for these teaching are false because they are variable and contradictory."—conf. 3: "Why do you not laugh when I say that I am infallible, not me, but the Church, of whom I am a member and who has given me a mission? Once again: why do you not laugh? It is because the history of the Church gives her some right, even in your eyes, to present herself as being infallible." Also see Cardinal Deschamps, *Oeuvres*, vol. 1.

Eucharistic Communion, and this is a pledge *of eternal communion*. What could be *more conformed* to our aspirations and yet something more *freely given* [*gratuitum*]? In this, we see the greatest of harmony, something only God could bring about.[7] Indeed, harmony is unity in diversity. Now, the greatest diversity seems to exist between absolute free giving and profound conformity. Nonetheless, these find themselves to be most closely united in the Eucharist. Thus, in general, the supernatural gifts of God differ from his natural gifts on account of their free and gratuitous character, as well as from the deluded ravings of false mysticism on account of these supernatural gifts' conformity with our rational nature. In this, we have a fulfillment of our aspirations exceeding the common order of things, indeed a miraculous fulfillment.

On this point, see the words of Christ to the Samaritan woman: "If thou didst know the gift of God and who he is that saith to thee: Give me to drink; thou perhaps wouldst have asked of him, and he would have given thee living water. . . . He that shall drink of the water that I will give him shall not thirst for ever. *But the water that I will give him shall become in him a fountain of water, springing up into life everlasting*" (John 4:10–14, DR).

{{220}} Hence, St. Augustine wrote in *Confessions*, bk. 1, ch. 1: "O Lord, you made us for you, and our hearts are restless until they rest in you."

Likewise, *our natural love for our neighbors* is surpassed in Christianity, for it proclaims to us that our neighbors must be loved for God's own sake, for God's glory, since they are our brothers in this life as members of the mystical body of Christ and hereafter sharers in eternal glory.

(4) *Worship.* In Christ's religion, internal worship is proposed as being "adoration in spirit and in truth." External worship is subordinated to it, with the most marvelous expression of such external worship being the sacrifice of the *Mass*, the commemoration of the sacrifice of the Cross, and the offering of the most pure victim by the most holy priest. The sweetness of

---

[7] See *ST* II-II, q. 23, a. 1 (Whether charity is a form of friendship), and in his Office of the Most Holy Sacrament, he wrote, concerning Eucharistic communion: "*Oh, how pleasant* [*suavis*], *Lord, is your Spirit,* who in order to show your sweetness [*dulcedinem*] to your sons, having given the most pleasant bread, coming down from heaven, *fill the hungry with good things, and send the rich and disdainful away empty.*"

St. Augustine similarly said: "*To diseased eyes the light is offensive, though it is loveable to the pure.*" (See the Church's office for the conversion of St. Augustine.)

Thus, the apologetic argument drawn from the marvelous fulfillment of our aspirations fills the hungry with good things but sends others away empty. For a living expression of this argument, see the post-communion prayers in the [Roman] Missal for nearly all masses.

the mysteries of Christ is splendidly expressed in the Church's prayers.[8]

(5) *The inclinations of our nature to the moral virtues*, similarly, are not only fulfilled but, moreover, are roused more loftily in Christianity. Indeed, *Christian prudence*, ordering all things to the kingdom of God, shunning care for temporal goods, infinitely exceeds not only worldly prudence founded on a kind of utilitarian calculus but also right, natural prudence, which is ordered solely to moral goods. *Christian justice* is forever connected to charity and, hence, is elevated and tempered by mercy. *Christian fortitude* not only relies on our own natural powers but, beyond this, upon God's grace, and every Christian must be ready to suffer martyrdom rather than to place his faith in doubt. Similarly, *Christian temperance* exceeds naturally acquired temperance by far: "For according to the rule of reason in matters of desire and the eating of food, the mean stands in not doing harm to the body's health and not impeding the act of reason. However, according to the rule of the divine law, man must chastise his body and reduce it to servitude."[9] As St. Paul says, this is necessary so that we may live according to

---

[8] For example, in the following hymns:

Jesu, the very thought of Thee,	O hope of every contrite heart	But what to those who
with sweetness fills my breast,	O joy of all the meek, to those who fall,	find? Ah, this nor tongue
but sweeter far Thy face to see,	how good to those who seek,	nor pen can show: the love
and in Thy presence rest.	but how great to those who find!	of Jesus, what it is none but
		His loved ones know.
		(trans. Caswall, alt.)

This represents the most perfect expression of our apologetic argument, in which we truly and properly show *how good Christ is to those who seek*, but *how great to those who find him*!

Likewise, expressing supernatural joy:

When once Thou visitest the heart,	O Jesu! Light of all below!	May every heart confess Thy name,
then truth begins to shine;	Thou font of life and fire!	and ever Thee adore;
then earthly vanities depart;	surpassing all the joys we	and seeking Thee, itself inflame
then kindles love divine.	know, and all we can desire.	to seek Thee more and more.
		(trans. Caswall)

[9] *ST* I-II, q. 63, a. 4 (On *the specific* distinction between the Christian moral virtues and naturally acquired moral virtues). Also see *ST* I-II, q. 61, a. 5 (whether the cardinal virtues are fittingly divided into *political, perfective, perfect, and exemplar* virtues). See [Antonin] Massoulié, O.P., *Méditations de S. Thomas*, pt. 2 (On the illuminative life), ch. 11: "We must begin at the first degree and be led there in accord with these principles: never do anything which you cannot account for; . . . be persuaded that the opinion of the vulgar, the so-called spirit of the world, is the most inconstant of rules; do nothing solely in accord with pleasure, for pleasure is not permitted for its own sake, being the most changing of things and opposed to virtue. However, this is not the degree where one must come to an ultimate rest. There, you only meet with

the spirit, not the flesh. {{221}} Along with mortification, Christ commends humility as the fundamental virtue, for without God's grace, no man can perform saving works.

(6) *Moreover, we desire inchoate beatitude in the present life.* Now, according to Christian doctrine, the Christian virtues are perfected by the *gifts of the Holy Spirit* as regards both contemplation and action, and the *beatitudes* proceed from these gifts. Blessed are the poor in spirit, the meek, the merciful; blessed are those who mourn, who hunger and thirst for righteousness; blessed are the pure of heart, the peacemakers; blessed are those who suffer persecution for the sake of righteousness. This beatitude, which the martyrs sometimes found in persecution itself, surpasses every natural power. Thus, we have the *fruits of the Holy Spirit* enumerated by St. Paul: "charity, joy, peace, patience, benignity, goodness, longanimity, mildness, faith, modesty, continency, chastity" (Gal 5:22–23, DR).[10] The marvelous fulfillment of our aspirations is already had in this life so that St. Paul's words are confirmed: "Rejoice in the Lord always: again, I say, rejoice. . . . Be nothing solicitous: but in everything, by prayer and supplication, with thanksgiving, let your petitions be made known to God. And *the peace of God, which surpasseth all understanding*, keep your hearts and minds in Christ Jesus" (Phil 4:4–7, DR). As Christ said, "This is a peace which the world cannot give." And likewise he had said, "If any man thirst, let him come to me and drink. He that believeth in me, as the scripture saith: Out of his belly shall flow rivers of living water" (John 7:37–38, DR).

Above all, holy souls enjoy this profound peace, though men who do not yet believe, who read the Gospel or the lives of the saints with sincerity and good will, find in Christ's doctrine, under the influence of the solicita-

---

philosophers; in this domain, only reason rules. . . . As St. Augustine says (*City of God*, 19.20), true wisdom is not found in the choices of prudence, in the acts of temperance, and in respect for rights through justice if all of this is not ordered to the eternal beatitude which has been promised to us. . . . Therefore, we must pass on to the second degree (*the purifying virtues*), where reason obeys and grace commands, *where the virtues begin to be Christian.*"

Also see Marie-Albert Janvier, O.P., *Exposition de la morale catholique.* See the *Morale spéciale*, vol. 7, dedicated to Christian prudence, in its distinction from human prudence through its end, its light, and its means. Likewise, see Mgr. Charles Gay, *De la vie et des vertus chrétienne considérées dans l'état religieux.* In particular, see what is said in this work concerning humility, poverty, mortification, chastity, obedience, and temptation, and you will see the *specific* difference (nay, the difference of orders) that exists between the infused Christian virtues and the naturally acquired moral virtues spoken of by Aristotle in his *Ethics.*

[10] [Trans. note: In the original, no actual footnote accompanies this citation. It is possible that the first line of the next note was meant to be associated with this mark in the body.]

tions of grace, the principle of peace, and thus they are invited to believe.[11] This is clear *on the basis of experience*, not only individual experience but that of the *common* experience had by Christians and those who *sincerely seek God*: "If any man will do the will of him (namely, of my Father), *he shall know of the doctrine, whether it be from God*, or whether I speak of myself" (John 7:17, DR).[12]

CONCLUSION. From this miraculous fulfillment of all the aspirations of humanity, taken all together, we have moral certitude concerning the divine origin of Christianity and Catholicism.[13] {{222}} This argument is strengthened if we consider what happens upon the death of faith and the Christian life in a soul or in a region, for nearly all of a sudden, there appears once more vices, discord, pride, presumption, corruption, and in the end, the worst of things, barren sorrow and desperation.[14]

---

[11] See *ST* I-II, q. 70 (On the fruits of the Holy Spirit). Also see *ST* II-II, q. 2, a. 9, ad 3: "He who believes has sufficient inductive basis upon which to believe, for he is moved by the authority of the divine teaching confirmed by miracles, and what is more, *by an interior instinct from God inviting him to conversion.*"

[12] In the midst of the Areopagus, St. Paul said in Acts 17:26–27 (DR): "God hath made of one, all mankind, to dwell upon the whole face of the earth.... *That they should seek God, if happily they may feel after him or find him*, although he be not far from every one of us."

[13] See what we said earlier, speculatively, concerning the value of the motives of credibility that are internal to us, those that are not solely individual but, indeed, universal (bk. 1, sect. 5, ch. 17).

See Albert Janvier, O.P., *Exposition de la morale catholique*, Morale spéciale, vol. 4 (Charity and its effects): 1st conference, *Joy* (How the joy of charity bears it aloft over all earthly joys, through its essentially spiritual character and through its solidity); 2nd conference, *Interior peace* (it includes a permanent tranquility, which demands that the soul's central desire be fixed, and this tranquility progresses when all desires tend toward one and the same object; it finds its crowning when our desires are filled through the possession of the good to which they aspire); 3rd conference, *Social peace*. In vol. 4 (Feelings and acts contrary to charity): 4th conference, *disgust for divine things, acedia*. (This voluntary disgust for divine things is contrary to charity and leads to despair; the source of this disgust is sensuality, disordered attachment to temporal goods; on the man of pleasures, the man dedicated to money, and the ambitious who find heavenly pursuits insipid.)

Also see Ernst Hello, *L'homme*, pt. 1, 28 (Indifference): "Of all the follies that the devil inspires, behold that which is most suited to him: *the truth is tiresome*. The truth! But it is, in fact, beatitude. The truth! But it is, in fact, the principle of ecstasies! It is what all known splendors strive to symbolize. Satan is the prince of boredom and the ennui of despair.... God is the master of joy. Let indifference look upon itself and therefore, let it judge itself!" And on 213: "A man who knows nothing about Christianity and is not embarrassed because of this ignorance, would be embarrassed if he were equally ignorant concerning the historical details of Scipio's life. The vain man loves to know about the first bit of indifferent news, but when it comes to sublime things, he takes pride in his ignorance."

[14] See [Hippolyte] Taine, *Les origines de la France contemporaine. Le régime moderne*, vol. 2, 118–119: "In Italy during the Renaissance, in England under the Restoration, in France under the

This conclusion is admitted by many Catholic apologetes, without any affinity with Protestantism or modernism, for they propose it as a way toward consideration of external motives. To this end, see the works of Hettinger, Albert Maria Weiss, and Léon Ollé-Laprune.[15]

§4. Objections

{{223}} Naturalism denies the aforementioned satisfaction of human aspirations: (1) in relation to the dogmas of Catholicism; (2) in relation to its ethics; and (3) in relation to the imperative manner that this teaching is to be proposed.

First objection: *Certain dogmas*, like that of the Trinity, do not seem to correspond to our inclinations and remain far too obscure. Nay, some of them seem to be contrary to our inclinations and to reason, such as the idea of eternal punishment.

Response: The aforementioned argument is not the main argument for credibility,

---

Convention and the Directory, man was seen to become pagan, as in the first century. By the same stroke, he found himself like man at the time of Augustus and Tiberius, namely, overrun by pleasures and hardships: he abused others and himself. Brutal and calculative egoism once again had the upper hand. Cruelty and sensuality spread abroad. And society became a cut-throat and wicked place." Likewise see [Félix] Le Dantec, *L'athéisme*.

[15] See [Franz] Hettinger, *Apologie du cristianisme* (French translation), III, 22–69. Albert Maria Weiss, *Apologie des Christentums vom Standpunkt der Sitte und Cultur* (Freiburg im Breisgau, 1889), in French, passim. Juan Arintero, *Desenvolvimiento y Vitalidad de la Iglesia* (Salamanca, 1908), vol. 2, 64–112; vol. 4, 344–365; vol. 3, 13–114. [Louis-Victor-Emile] Bougaud, *Les christianisme et les temps présents*, 8th ed. (Paris, 1901), all throughout. [Léon] Ollé-Laprune, *Le prix de la vie*, 4th ed. (Paris, 1897); *La vitalité chrétienne* (1901).

Cf. Christian Pesch, S.J., *Praelectiones dogmaticae*, 4th ed., vol. 1, no. 258: "We can also include among internal criteria that *internal experience* by means of which, through those things that follow theoretically and practically upon Christ's doctrine, one senses in oneself its excellent and marvelous effects, stillness of soul, zeal for the virtues, weariness with worldly things, desire for heavenly things, the diminution of wicked passions, the growth of humility, chastity, patience, charity, and peace which surpass every sentiment. If, on the contrary, with this religion everything grows dark and is born of to the depths, with the passions growing and the virtues falling into despair, then, we can be certain that this is not a minor indication that this doctrine does not have God as its author. However, by means of this internal experience, many men have come into contact with Christ's teaching, which still must be examined, and each such person can take up the same risk of following this teaching provided that he strive to set up his life in line with this teaching" (cf. Suarez, *De fide*, disp. 4, sect. 6, no. 4). Likewise, see [Joseph] Kleutgen, *Theologie der Vorzeit*, vol. 4, no. 190ff; A. Schmid, *Apologetik als Spekulative Grundlegung der Theologie*, 226ff: ["]But (against what is held by Protestants) men who are not yet Christians lack this experience, and nonetheless must embrace Christ's teaching as being divinely revealed. Hence, Christians themselves do not all, nor always, have the same internal experiences. Therefore, another criterion is needed." Hence, we must not argue solely from individual experience but, rather, *from the common experience* of Christians and those who sincerely seek God.

but it does dispose one to consideration of the others that are taken from the sublimity of Christ's teaching, from the life of the Church, and from prophecies and miracles. Therefore, in treating of the sublimity of this teaching, we will briefly discuss the way that the Trinity and eternal punishment are suitable in relation to naturally knowable divine attributes (and, hence, with reason). However, already we can see that eternal punishment, even if utterly contrary to the sinner's inclination, is not contrary to the rational desire for future sanction so that the wicked may not prevail but instead may be punished, indeed, in perpetuity, if their fault is irreparable and would remain forever impenitent.

Second objection: Christian ethics does not seem to be accommodated to the ordinary circumstances of our life, but rather, it contains an immoderate and mystical elevation that is suited only to certain men who are separated from the world.

Response: This objection does not distinguish well enough between what Christian ethics teaches about the *precepts / commands* that must be kept by all and *counsels* proposed to those who sincerely desire true spiritual perfection. Now, the common precepts do indeed seem exaggerated to the tepid, who do not care about their eternal salvation and think only of temporal things. However, in such spiritual *mediocrity*, the natural aspirations of the human heart already are greatly diminished, and in such a case one definitely is not thinking about their marvelous or extraordinary satisfaction.[16]

---

[16] See Ernest Hello, *L'homme*, bk. 1, ch. 1 (The mediocre man): "The mediocre man thinks that Christianity is a kind of useful precaution and that one would be imprudent to dispense with it. Nonetheless, in his depths he detests it. Sometimes, also, he has a kind of conventional respect for it, the same kind of respect that he has for books currently in the vogue. However, he has a horror for Catholicism. He looks upon it and sees something exaggerated. He loves Protestantism much more, believing that it is more moderate. He is the friend of all principles, as well as all of their contraries.

"The mediocre man can have esteem for virtuous men and for men of talent. He feels fear and horror at saints and men of genius. He looks upon them and sees something exaggerated. He admits the sisters of St. Vincent de Paul, given that their action is performed, at least partially, in the visible world. But of the Carmelites, he says: what good are they?

"Indeed, he wishes that Christianity be denied, though let this be done politely, with a kind of moderation in one's words. He has a kind of love for rationalism, and in a bizarre turn of affairs, a love for Jansenism as well. He adores the profession of faith of the Savoyard Vicar. He rues the fact that the Christian religion has dogmas. He would like it to teach *only a morality*, and if you tell him that its morality flows from its dogmas as a consequence flows from a principle, he will be sure to tell you that you are speaking exaggerations.

"In order to avoid being critiqued by him for being intolerant for everything that is thought with strong adherence, one would need to take refuge in absolute doubt . . . though one would need to hold such doubt in the form of a modest opinion, which reserves the rights of the contrary opinion. He is modest and proud: submissive before Voltaire and in revolt against the Church. The mediocre man feels neither greatness nor misery. He is neither delighted nor precipitous. He remains at the penultimate rung of the ladder, unable to climb upward and too lazy to descend. Everything above him seems ridiculous, and the infinite seems to him to be nothingness."

{{224}} *Third objection*: The Catholic Church's manner of proposing doctrine is too imperative in character.

Response: If we were here concerned with philosophical opinions to be imposed, this would indeed represent an abuse of authority. However, this is not the case if it is a question of the infallible proposition of the doctrine of salvation to be believed in on account of the authority of God who reveals. There are not motives of credibility lacking in order to believe in the Church's infallibility. Nay, this infallibility most excellently corresponds to our natural desire for the truth, freeing us from doubts, as well as from the errors of false philosophy and sects. And once it is rejected, as is seen in Protestantism, there can be no settling of the controversies that arise, and the unity of faith dies off among believers who gradually withdraw from religion and decline toward naturalism.

Fourth objection: There is not such great conformity of Christianity with our natural aspirations, for many are driven away by the Christian mysteries and precepts.

Response: In Christianity, the satisfaction of our nature's legitimate aspirations is all the more marvelous to the degree that the wicked inclinations of concupiscence and pride are themselves offended and corrected, for thus we have a reconciliation between meekness and fortitude, as well as between mercy and justice, and this is a splendid sign of the truth. However, it is therefore not surprising that *Christ and the Church* are *simultaneously a center of the most profound attraction and of vehement repulsion*, for as St. Augustine says, "To diseased eyes the light is offensive, though it is loveable to the pure." Nay, as will appear more clearly in the next two chapters, many of the Church's adversaries, like the Pharisees and those following them, so vehemently and perpetually fought against her that in this extraordinary contention we find a new sign—namely, the fact that their open malice manifests the holiness of the religion that they wish to destroy. Thus too is Simeon's prophecy concerning Jesus verified: "Behold this child is set for the fall and for the resurrection of many in Israel and for a sign which shall be contradicted" (Luke 2:34, DR).[17] Christ brings peace, though not as the world gives it. No, his peace exceeds everything we can imagine.

---

[17] See, on this, Bossuet, *Elévations sur les mystères*, 18th week, 12th–20th elevation.

CHAPTER EIGHT

Confirmation of Christ's Testimony through the Sublimity of His Doctrine

{{225}} Already, in bk. 1, ch. 17, in our speculative discussion of the value of motives that are external to us, though intrinsic to religion, we determined whence the sublimity of a doctrine must be drawn. Thus, in three articles, we must consider this sublimity (1) *in the doctrine itself*, (2) *in the way that it is proposed* and perpetually preserved, and (3) *in the way that it was established* (namely, without any human preparation). This gives us the division of this chapter.

ART. 1: THE SUBLIME HARMONY OF CHRISTIAN DOCTRINE CONSIDERED IN ITSELF

As we said in bk. 1, ch. 18, sublimity is something utterly lofty and extraordinary in the order of beauty, especially intellectual and moral beauty, and it appears especially in the utterly lofty and intimate union of things that are most distant from each other (e.g., the highest and the lowliest of things). On account of this utterly great distance, this union, which at first glance seems impossible, is utterly marvelous, giving rise to tears of admiration and seeming like an intervention by God, like the inclination of the supreme mercy toward our misery. Thus, in it we find a sign of the divine origin of the doctrine proposed in God's name, a doctrine that marvelously unites in itself *the highest* and *the lowliest of things*, *supernatural* and *natural things*, the riches of the divine *mercy* and the *misery* of mankind, preserving the rights of *justice* and simultaneously joining together *the oldest of things* with *the newest*, reconciling *the obscurity* of the mysteries with *a wisdom* that is accommodated to all men's understanding.

Thus, we will consider how Christian doctrine appears as regards:

§1. natural truths concerning God and man,

§2. supernatural mysteries,

§3. precepts and counsels,

§4. the harmony of the whole of Christian doctrine.

Many rationalists do indeed hold that Christ was a profound teacher of virtue, who, in a figurative manner that was accommodated to all, admirably renewed and vigorously preached the ancient positions held by Jewish wisdom. However, they add that Christ never proposed a properly dogmatic doctrine to be believed on pain of eternal damnation. In our exposition of Jesus's own testimony, we already saw the falsity of this judgment rendered by rationalist thinkers. {{226}} Now we must show against them the sublimity of Christ's dogmatic and moral doctrine.[1]

§1. Natural Truths concerning God and Man

Christian doctrine greatly surpasses all systems proposed by philosophers as well as other religions, proposing nothing that reason shows to be false and *perfectly teaching* everything pertaining to natural religion.

A. *Regarding God.* According to right natural reason, there is one God, the principal and end of all beings, existing from himself, pure spirit, eternal, infinitely perfect, really and essentially distinct from the world, utterly wise and exercising the loftiest providence, good, merciful, and a just lawgiver and remunerator.

Now, Christianity teaches all of these truths explicitly and indeed much more perfectly than other religions or various philosophical systems.

Therefore, Christianity most perfectly teaches all those things concerning God that pertain to natural religion.

The major premise is admitted by spiritualists, and these truths are at least implicitly (or vaguely) contained in the object of common sense (i.e., natural reason had by all men), though they are more or less corrupted in

---

[1] See Jean-Baptiste Gonet, *Clypeus theologiae Thomisticae, De fide*, disp. 1 (A useful and pleasant digression), §2 (The truth, holiness, and efficacy of our faith, argued on in light of its credibility). Likewise, see Bossuet, *Discours sur l'histoire universelle*, pt. 2, ch. 19 (a most renowned chapter: Jesus Christ and his doctrine); Antonino Valsecchi, *Dei fondamenti della religione e dei fonti dell'empietá* (1765), bk. 3, chs. 8–12; Lacordaire, *Conférences* 14–37; Monsabré's preaching from Lent 1880 in *Exposition du dogme catholique*, vol. 8 (Paris: Édouard Baltenweck, 1879), 109–160 ("Vie de Jésus, le docteur") and Lent 1890; Abbé de Broglie, *L'histoire des religions*, ch. 10 (326ff); André Bovet, *De la science de Jésus-Christ comme argument apologétique* (Thesis at Fribourg, Switzerland, 1895).

various religions outside of Christianity. (See the preceding chapters and also, at the end of this treatise, see the comparison of Christianity with other religions.)

The minor premise. Now, according to the Christian faith, we can say the following.

(1) THERE IS ONE GOD WHO IS INFINITELY PERFECT (without any vestige of polytheism), *who is an utterly pure spirit* ("God is a spirit," as is said in John 4:24, thus rejecting all forms of anthropomorphism), *existing from himself* ("I am who am," Exod 3:14), *immutable* (in whom there is no change, nor any shadow of alteration, Jas 1:17), *eternal* (who is, who was, and who will be, Rom 16:26 and Rev 1:8), *omnipresent* and *immense* (whose throne is heaven and earth his footstool, Matt 5:34 and Acts 7:49; in whom we live, and move, and have our being, Acts 17:28), *intellectually knowing all things* ("who sees in secret," Matt 6:4; "and is greater than our heart, knowing all things," John 3:20) and *utterly wise* (who alone is wise, Rom 17:27, and whose judgments are incomprehensible, his ways unsearchable, Rom 11:33), *volitionally omnipotent* (all things are possible for him, Eph 3:20; who made heaven and earth, Acts 4:24 and 14:14), *utterly free* (who does all things in accord with the counsel of his own will, Eph 1:1 and Rom 9:6), and *utterly holy* (who alone is good, Matt 19:17 and John 17:11; who is light and in whom there is no shade at all, John 1:5), and *he is utterly blessed* and sufficient unto himself (who does not lack anything while, at the same time, himself giving all things life and inspiration and indeed all things, Acts 17:14; 1 Tim 1:11; 6:15).

{{227}} (2) AD EXTRA, GOD IS A MOST PROVIDENT, MERCIFUL, AND JUST CREATOR.

He is the Creator of all beings (who made heaven and earth, the sea, and all that is in them, Acts 4:24 and 14:14; who created all things, Eph 3:9; and is the α and the ω, the alpha and the omega, Rev 1:8), *he who conserves all things* (bearing all things through the word of his power, Heb 1:3). However, this doctrine concerning creation and concerning *utterly free creation* lacks every vestige of *pantheism* (whereas, by contrast, Eastern religions like Buddhism, and many philosophies, held and still hold a form of emanationism), likewise lacking any *dualism* (which was admitted by Plato and the Platonists in his theory of uncreated matter, as well as in the Persian religion—namely, the doctrine of Zoroaster concerning the dual principles of good and evil). Likewise, the dogma of creation is in no way vitiated *by determinism* (whereas, by contrast, many philosophers, like Leibniz, wrongly thought that God created from necessity, not indeed absolute necessity but, rather, out of moral necessity, as though God would not have been infinitely good and wise had he not created, as though he stood in need of something to be added to his perfection by means of creating).

Moreover, according to the Christian faith, God is *the provident governor of things* ("He feeds the birds of the air, and yet surely are you not greater than them," Matt 6:26; "place all of your cares upon him, for he cares for you," 1 Pet 5:7). Divine providence is not only general (as many ancient thinkers said and, afterwards, the Averroists and deists), but also extends *to utterly singular things*. Nonetheless, this teaching is essentially distinct from the *fatalism* held by Muslims or the *pessimism* of Calvin and many Protestants who hold that God positively and from eternity wills all of men's sins. By contrast, it is said in Psalm 5:5 (DR): "Thou art not a God that willest iniquity."

Finally, inasmuch as he is infinitely good and utterly holy, God is *utterly truthful* and *faithful*, *utterly just* ("he renders unto each person in accord with his works," Rom 2:6), *utterly bountiful* ("he who fees the birds of the air and clothes the lilies of the field," Matt 6:26–30), and *merciful* (who always is ready to forgive those who turn back, Luke 15:20; rich in mercy on account of his utterly great charity, by means of which he loves us, Eph 2:4).

Thus, the Christian teaching concerning God perfectly sets forth all the divine attributes *and does not diminish any of them in order to affirm another*. In this it differs from other religions, heretical sects, and more or less erroneous philosophical systems.

B. ***Regarding men.*** According to right natural reason, man, even if he is mortal, has a spiritual, immortal soul, endowed with freedom and placed under the moral law, founded upon God who is the supreme lawgiver and remunerator.

Now, Christianity teaches these truths much more perfectly than do other religions and philosophical systems.

Therefore, it teaches most perfectly concerning man, just as it does concerning God, all the truths pertaining to natural religion.

The major premise is admitted by all spiritualists, and at least implicitly, these truths are known by common sense (i.e., natural reason).

{{228}} *The minor premise.* According to Christian faith, man is created by God, in his image (Eph 4:24; cf. Gen 1:26; Wis 2:23), is not made up of his body alone (which men can kill, Matt 10:28) but also has a spiritual soul (which only God can cast into Hell, Matt 10:28; and which is called to future glory, Rom 8:18; 2 Tim 4:7, 8). It was created in order to know the true God, to love him above all things, and to fulfill his will so as to thus arrive at eternal life (John 18:3; 1 Tim 2:4; Matt 6:33; 6:21; 25:46).

All these truths are proposed in Christianity not only with great probability but as things to be believed with the greatest certitude. Now, on the basis of this, we can have moral certitude concerning the divine origin of Christianity, for, as was proven earlier, without God's special assistance, it is morally impossible for man to know—firmly, readily, and in an error-free manner—all the natural truths pertaining to religion (see vol. 1, ch. 13, a. 3).

§2. Regarding Supernatural Mysteries

The sublimity of Christian teaching is made manifest inasmuch as these mysteries, notwithstanding their *obscurity*, appear to us as being "*the light of life*" on account of their conformity with the naturally known attributes of God and with our aspirations. This sublimity is especially seen in the intimate union *of the utterly lofty life of the Deity* with the mind and heart *of poor men of good will*, mediated through the redemption brought about by *Christ*. This must be set forth for the principal mysteries of the Christian Faith.

(1) *The mystery of the Most Holy Trinity* is the most supreme mystery of all, as well as the most obscure, but its obscurity does not arise from absurdity or incoherence. Rather, in it we see harmony, which indicates a brightness that is far too radiant for our intellect. Indeed, this is not a form of absurdity, for we do not say that God is one and three from the same perspective but, rather, say that he is one and utterly simple as regards his nature and that he is three as regards the divine Persons.

The fittingness and harmony of this mystery is made manifest most commonly by theologians on the basis of two principles:[2] *The good is essentially self-diffusive*; and *the loftier a given form of life is, all the more is that which emanates from it all the more intimate.*[3] Hence, it is fitting that the

---

[2] See *ST* I, q. 27ff and *SCG* IV, ch. 11. The latter article seems to contain the Holy Doctor's loftiest words concerning this mystery. Likewise, see throughout St. Bonaventure's *Itinerarium mentis in Deum*.

[3] This principle is enunciated by [Ps.-]Dionysius in *De Divinis nominibus*, ch. 4. (See lect. 1. of Aquinas's commentary.) Also, it is cited by the Angelic Doctor in *ST* III, q. 1, a. 1; *ST* I, q. 5, a. 4, ad 2 (as regards finality), q. 6, a. 1 and 2 (as regards finality and efficient causality). Likewise, it is found throughout the writings of St. Augustine. St. Thomas elsewhere says something equivalent: Only perfect beings generate, or every agent acts inasmuch as it is in act. See Bossuet, *Elévations sur les mystères*, week 2, 1st elevation: "Why wouldn't God have a Son? Why would the blessed nature be lacking in this perfect fecundity which It gives to Its creatures? . . . I know quite well that an immortal nature has no need, as does our mortal and weak nature, to renew itself, to perpetuate itself, by substituting in its place children which will be left in the world when one comes to leave it. However, in itself, independent of this necessary compensation, is it not beautiful to produce another self through abundance, through

Greatest Good be maximally self-diffusive—namely, fruitful *ad intra*—*in the intimate depths of* his nature. {{229}} The application of the aforementioned twofold principle appears with increasing clarity as we ascend up the scale of beings. Fire generates fire *ad extra*, and a plant likewise generates a plant, though the plant's vital action is already immanent. In animals, sense knowledge is something loftier and more intimate than vegetative actions. Man's intellective life is even more intimate, for our intellect conceives the internal word (or the expressed idea). However, this internal word remains highly imperfect, for it is a changing accident and does not fully express the intellect itself from which it proceeds. Here, we do have a kind of spiritual generation, though one that is most imperfect. In the Highest Good, there must be a life that is maximally perfect and immanent. Therefore, it is fitting that he have the greatest fecundity inasmuch as he fully diffuses himself forth, in the most profound manner, communicating not only an imperfect and accidental expression of his nature but, rather, the whole of his utterly simple nature, without any division or multiplication—namely, so that the Word proceeding from him remains intimately united, according to a numerical identity of nature. This is the greatest form of self-diffusion and, simultaneously, the greatest intimacy of union—in short, the most perfect form of spiritual generation: "Thou art my son, this day have I begotten thee" (Ps 2:7, DR). Thus, as is said in the Nicene Creed: "We believe in one God, the Father almighty. . . . We believe in one Lord, . . . the Only Begotten Son of God, born of the Father before all ages. God from God, Light from Light, True God from True God, begotten, not made, consubstantial with the Father."

However, since this procession takes place by way of intellection, another also is suitable for it, here by way of love—namely, by means of which the Father and the Son communicate not only an imperfect expression of their love but, rather, the whole of their being to the Holy Spirit. As is said in the Athanasian Creed: "And in this Trinity, nothing is before and nothing after, nothing is greater or less, but all three persons are co-eternal and co-equal."

Thus, notwithstanding its obscurity, this mystery appears to us in a way as being *the harmony of the fecundity of the divine life and the unity of God*. Why would one deny this infinite fecundity? Is it a form of imperfection? Through this dogma, we also have a manifestation of the *most perfect intellectual life and love*: three persons living on the same truth, through the same intellection, on the same infinite good, through the same friendship, without any trace of egoism.

---

plenitude, by way of an inexhaustible communication, in a word, through fecundity and the richness of a blessed and perfect nature?"

Moreover, by this mystery, we have a confirmation for the refutation of pantheism. Creation appears as being freer and in no way necessary, for even if God were not to create, we would still find in him the greatest fecundity, and thus would already have a full verification of the principle: *The good is essentially self-diffusive, indeed all the more intimately so to the degree that it is more perfect.* Therefore, this principle does not imply pantheistic emanationism, as Plotinus wished. Hence, this supernatural mystery is not opposed to natural truths concerning God but, rather, is conformed to them and corroborates them.

(2) **The mystery of the elevation of our nature to the supernatural order** is suitable, as we showed above.[4] (1) *On our side*, inasmuch as our nature contains an obediential / elevable potency for the supernatural order, something that appears in our natural, conditional, and inefficacious desire to see God through his essence, for knowledge of God in the mirror of creatures is highly imperfect and remains obscure, especially as regards the intimate reconciliation of certain divine attributes.[5]

{{230}} (2) *On God's side*, it is befitting to the Highest Good that he would communicate himself to us in accord with what is most intimate in him—namely, according to his divine life, precisely as divine—for the good is self-diffusive, indeed all the more intimately so to the degree that it is more perfect.

(3) *It is befitting to man, from the beginning of creation*, that he be elevated to the supernatural order, for in the natural order, the perfect precedes the imperfect, as act precedes potency, and things were established by God at the start so that they may be the principles of others. Therefore, the first man was established in a perfect state as regards nature and grace, inasmuch as reason was placed under God, while the inferior powers were placed under reason and the body under the soul. Thus, he was able to instruct others, to govern,[6] and to communicate to them supernatural life together with human nature itself by way of generation, for *original justice* was a gift that was divinely given to the whole of human nature.[7]

Moreover, once we have admitted this mystery concerning the original justice and perfection of man, we can more readily explain *the loftiness of our aspirations*, which remain vigorous, notwithstanding our inordinate passions, errors, doubts, and defects. According to St. Thomas, this sorrow-

---

[4] See vol. 1, ch. 12, §4 (Theses concerning the possibility and suitability of revelation).
[5] See *ST* I, q. 12, a. 1.
[6] See *ST* I, q. 94, a. 3; q. 95, a. 1.
[7] See *ST* I, q. 100, a. 1.

ful state of opposition is a *probable* sign of the original elevation of the first man.[8]

(3) *The mystery of original sin*, according to which, "by the disobedience of one man, many were made sinners," is indeed obscure to us, for at first glance, a defect derived from the beginning of our existence seems to exclude the notion of fault, which conceptually involves the idea of being voluntary. However, original sin must not be conceived of as being something voluntary through our own will but, rather, through the will of our first parents, for it is not a personal sin committed by us but, rather, *a sin of nature*, contracted inasmuch as we have received from our first parents human nature stripped of original justice, according to the words of Ephesians 2:3 (DR), "by nature children of wrath." Hence, according to St. Thomas, original sin consists essentially in the deprivation of original justice, as something that was voluntary through the will of our first parents.[9] The Catholic doctrine in this matter is the golden mean and peak between and above *Pelagianism*, which denied original sin, and *Protestantism*, which exaggerated this sin as though man's free will were now extinguished.[10]

{{231}} However, as understood according to the mind of the Church, *this mystery is not opposed to reason* for the following reasons.

A. *It is not opposed to reason in relation to the divine justice*, since original sin is only a privation of grace and of the preternatural gifts—that is, of *something that is not owed* [to human nature as such]. God was indeed able to have given grace to mankind on the condition that Adam, the head of humanity, not sin, and thus extend even to gratuitous and supernatural gifts the inheritance and solidarity that is naturally found between father

---

[8] See *SCG* IV, ch. 52. Pascal eloquently sets forth this argument in *Pensées* (ed. Havet, 141–143): "Thus, what kind of chimera is this man? What a novelty! What a chaos! What a subject of contradiction! What a prodigy! Judge of all things and imbecilic worm upon the earth! The custodian of truth and a cesspool of uncertainty and error! At once the pride of the universe and its refuse! . . . We have an idea of happiness, and we cannot reach it. We perceive an image of the truth, but we possess only mendacity. We are incapable of being absolutely ignorant but also of knowing with certitude. In this way, it is clear that we once existed in a degree of perfection from which we unhappily have fallen!" Though, on account of his Jansenist tendencies, Pascal does not distinguish clearly enough, in man's first state, between nature and grace, likewise failing to acknowledge the free character of our first elevation. Therefore, he exaggerates the consequences of original sin, diminishes the powers of reason far too much, and hence, according to him, the sorrowful opposition existing between our aspirations and our misery is a sign that is not only probable but, indeed, *manifest*, that the first man was originally elevated in this manner.

[9] See *ST* I-II, q. 81, a. 1; *De malo*, q. 4, a. 1.

[10] See Trent, *Decree on Justification*, can. 5 (Denzinger, no. 1555).

and children in relation to natural gifts. Indeed, already often in human judgment, when someone commits the crime of high treason, the parent's sin falls upon the head of his children, whereas by contrast, the child of a distinguished man is honored.[11]

B. *Nor does it contradict the divine wisdom and goodness* to permit (or tolerate) the fall of Adam and his children. As St. Thomas says:[12] "*God permits evils to take place in order to draw a greater good from them.* Whence it is written in Romans 5:20 (DR): 'Where sin abounded, grace did more abound.' Therefore, too, in the blessing of the Paschal candle, we say: 'O happy fault, that merited such and so great a Redeemer!'" In fact, according to revelation: "By one man's offence death reigned through one; much more they who receive abundance of grace and of the gift and of justice shall reign in life through one, Jesus Christ" (Rom 5:17, DR). (On this, see the Salmanticenses' thesis concerning the motive of the Incarnation.)[13]

---

[11] According to St. Thomas in *ST* I-II, q. 81, a. 3: "Children are never inflicted with *spiritual punishment* on account of their parents, unless they share in their guilt, either in their origin or by imitation, for every soul immediately belongs to God. However, sometimes by Divine or human judgment, children receive *bodily punishment* on their parents' account, inasmuch as the child, as to its body, is something of its father."

[12] *ST* III, q. 1, a. 3, ad 3.

[13] In *Cursus theologicus, De Incarnatione*, tr. 21, disp. 2, no. 29, the Salmanticenses, along with Capreolus, [Pedro de] Godoy, and Jean-Baptiste Gonet, provide a more profound explanation for this Thomist thesis than do many other Thomists, teaching: "In His first intention, God decreed Christ not only according to substance but even as regards the circumstances of passible flesh and precisely as He who would redeem from Adam's sin. And, at the same time, by the same act, he willed the permission of the aforementioned sin.... Thus, between the aforementioned objects, which are not connected of themselves, *he decreed* and established *this mutual dependence in different genera of causality, namely, on the one hand, that Christ would be the end for whose sake (finis cuius gratia) that passive permission of the aforementioned sin would be allowed,* as well as the end of the redemption of mankind and of all the divine deeds pertaining both to the order of nature and of grace, *and on the other hand, that the permitted sin would be the matter with which the redemption was concerned (materia circa quam),* and mankind would be the end to which *(finis cui)* this was given. Whence, in the line of final causality *for whose sake,* God first willed and saw Christ, then other things; however, in the line of material causality, as well as the line of final causality *to which,* He first willed and saw the permission of sin, the remedy of this, and those other things that pertained to this, before Christ."

This interpretation is more profound and simpler than what is proposed by Billuart (in his thesis concerning the motive of the Incarnation). Not only does it provide a better resolution for Scotus's objections but, moreover, it most excellently corresponds to the general axiom, "Causes are causes of each other, though in different genera [or lines] of causality," and also is conformed to St. Thomas's teaching concerning the order of predestination. For the Holy Doctor teaches in *ST* I, q. 23, a. 4 and 5 that predestination to glory is intrinsically prior to grace (or merits) according to the line of final causality, though vice versa in the line of meritorious causality, which is reduced to line of causality exercised by the disposition of the

{{232}} C. *Nay the present condition of humanity is thus better explained* once the existence of original sin is admitted. St. Thomas also says:

> There are *probable* signs of the existence of original sin in mankind. Indeed, since God exercises care for human acts, rewarding good works and allotting penalties for bad ones, . . . on the basis of the penalty itself we can be sure concerning the fault. Now, mankind commonly suffers various penalties, both bodily and spiritual. The greatest bodily penalty is death, and all the others are ordered to it, namely, hunger, thirst, and other such things. However, the greatest spiritual penalty is the frailty of reason, making it difficult for man to arrive at knowledge of the truth, likewise meaning that he readily falls into error and that he cannot entirely overcome his animal appetites but, instead, is constantly overshadowed by them.

> However, it could be said that defects of this kind, both bodily and spiritual, are not penalties, but instead natural defects necessarily following upon matter. . . . Nonetheless, if we consider matters aright, we will be able to judge *with probability*—presupposing divine providence, which has connected a suitable perfection to each perfectible thing—that God united a superior nature (i.e., the soul) to an inferior one (i.e., the body) in order that the *former might rule the latter*, and that, if some obstacle to this dominion should occur because of some failure on the part of nature, it would be removed by His special and supernatural favor.[14]

D. Finally, the mystery of original sin is confirmed *by the various traditions of the peoples of the world*, written down in the works of pagan poets and philosophers, in which we find a more or less explicit acknowledgment of the existence of a fall. Thus, Hesiod speaks of the fate of Prometheus, who, after stealing fire from heaven, not only underwent cruel punishments but

---

matter in question. Moreover, God does not permit evils to be done except so that he might draw something better from that. Thus, God predestined St. Augustine to a given degree of glory and permitted Augustine to fall into sin so that acknowledging his sin, he was humbled, converted, and thus arrived at glory. Likewise, God predestined St. Stephen to a given degree of glory with the golden crown of martyrdom and permitted the sin of his persecutors so that St. Stephen might arrive at the glory of martyrdom. Thus, God predestined Christ to the glory of the Redeemer and permitted Adam's sin so that Christ would become the Redeemer of humanity. See *ST* I-II, q. 79, a. 4; I, q. 20, a. 4, ad 1; III, q. 24, a. 3 and 4.

[14] *SCG* IV, ch. 52.

also was the cause of evils for mankind.

Hence, as Pascal has said, without this mystery, man is more incomprehensible than is this very mystery for man himself, for this doctrine resolves the enigmatic problem of the coexistence, in man, of such weakness and misery alongside such great aspirations to sublime things.[15]

{{233}} (4) *The mysteries of the Incarnation and the Redemption* bring to us a remedy for original and personal sin, and also appear as being most excellently connected with all the aforementioned mysteries.

A. THE INCARNATION OF THE WORD does not involve a contradiction, as though it were a mixture / confusion of the divine nature and the human nature. It is defined as being the intimate union of both natures in an unconfused and non-mixed manner in one and the same person so that Christ, existing as one person, would be true God and true man. Already in the natural order, the body and the soul are united without confusion in one and the same person, which is simultaneously, though according to different [principles] spirit and matter.

Nay, the possibility and suitability of the Incarnation are persuasively argued on behalf of both (a) from God's side and (b) from the side of human nature, especially for our redemption.

(a) *From God's side.* Indeed, as St. Thomas says, "It pertains to the notion of the good that it communicate itself to others. (The good is self-diffusive).

---

[15] See Pascal, *Pensées* (ed. Havet, 142–143): "Heed well then, O proud man, what a paradox you are to yourself. O weak reason, humble yourself, and be silent, O foolish nature. *Learn well that man infinitely exceeds himself,* and learn from your Master your true condition, which you know not. Listen to God.

"For, in the end, if man had never been corrupted, he would have enjoyed in his innocence both truth and felicity with assurance. And if man had only ever have been corrupted, he would have no idea either of the truth or of beatitude. . . .

"Certainly, nothing offends us more brusquely than this doctrine (concerning original sin), and nonetheless, without this mystery, the most incomprehensible of all, we find that ourselves are incomprehensible for ourselves. The twists and turns of the knot that is our condition take place in this abyss so that *without this mystery man is more inconceivable than is this very mystery for man himself.*"

Likewise, Bossuet (in his sermon for the profession of Mme. De la Vallière, at the end of the first point): "O God! What therefore is man? Is he a prodigy? Or, rather, is he an inexplicable enigma? No, good sirs, we already explained the enigma. *What is so very great in man is something which remains from his first condition, and what is so very base in him, something seeming to be so ill-matched to his very first principles, is the wicked effect of his fall.* He resembles a building that has fallen into ruin. . . . In his origins, he was founded upon the knowledge of God and love for Him; through his depraved will, he fell into ruin. . . . Still, God's impression remains upon man, *impressed strongly enough so that he cannot lose it, yet so weakly there that he cannot follow it.*"

Whence, *it pertains to the notion of the Highest Good, namely God, that He would communicate Himself to the creature in the loftiest manner*. Now, this is indeed what takes place through the joining of a created nature to Himself so that in one person there would be all three of these: the Word, a soul, and a body."[16] Thus, we have an indication, from God's side, concerning the possibility of this mystery.

The suitability [or fittingness] of this mystery is persuasively argued for on the basis of the fact that it falls to the divine *mercy* to raise man up from sins, provide him with the most perfect assistance, and not only grant him pardon: "For God so loved the world, as to give his only begotten Son: that whosoever believeth in him may not perish, but may have life everlasting" (John 3:16, DR). Finally, it falls to the divine *justice* to obtain a worthy satisfaction for sins. "Now, a sin committed against God has a kind of infinity, on account of the infinity of the divine majesty, for an offense is all the graver to the degree that the one who is offended is greater. Whence, in order for an appropriate satisfaction to be made, it is necessary that the act of the person making satisfaction have an infinite efficacy, as something being of God and man."[17] Indeed, on account of the divine person eliciting such an act, one of Christ's acts of charity has an infinite value for meriting and making satisfaction.

(b) *On the side of man, it is not contradictory* to speak of a union with God taking place in a person [i.e., through hypostatic unity]. Indeed, *personality* (by which man has power over himself, existing and acting through himself) *is all the greater to the degree that it intimately depends on God and dominates inferior things*. Thus, moral personality is loftier in the righteous man than in the man who has given himself over to the passions. Likewise, in the intellectual order, the personality of a man of great genius has an eminent place, as someone who is, so to speak, inspired by God. *A fortiori*, the personality of the saints is marvelous, for they do not act in accord with their own judgment, nor according to their own will, but, rather, according to the judgment and will of God. Through self-denial, the saints arrive at intimate union with God and, hence, come to perfectly dominate their passions as well as all inferior things. Thus, St. Paul was able to say: "With Christ I am nailed to the cross. And I live, now not I: but Christ liveth in me" (Gal 2:19–20, DR). In a way, *the saints share one and the same judgment and willing with God*, according to a full conformity. {{234}} *The most perfect union* would exist if human nature and the divine nature were united

---

[16] *ST* III, q. 1, a. 1.

[17] *ST* III, q. 1, a. 2, ad 2.

without confusion *in one and the same divine person* and *one and the same divine existence*. However, this marvelous union is found in the Incarnation of the Word, wherein the supreme personality is manifested, along with the greatest of intimacy with God and domination over inferior things.[18]

Hence, just as all men attribute to themselves the acts of their body and soul, so too Christ was able to attribute to himself divine perfections and human perfections: "*I* speak that which I have seen with my Father" (John 8:38, DR); "*I* am the way, and the truth, and the life" (John 14:6, DR); "*I* and the Father are one" (John 10:30, DR); "*I* am the resurrection and the life" (John 11:25, DR); and so forth. The word *I* designates the uncreated personality of the Word, to which Christ's human nature is united.

"And the Word was made flesh and dwelt among us, and we saw his glory, the glory as it were of the only begotten, . . . full of grace and truth" (John 1:14, DR).

Therefore, the possibility of the Incarnation is hinted at inasmuch as it belongs to God to communicate himself in the loftiest manner, and it is fitting to man to be united to God with the greatest of intimacy. This twofold truth is corrupted in pantheism, but in the Incarnation of the Word, it shines forth in its full radiance. Pantheism absurdly mixes together created nature and uncreated nature, whereas the dogma of the Incarnation distinguishes both natures, though it unites them together in the closest of manners in the Person of the Word.[19]

Moreover, on the side of humanity, not only does the Incarnation of the Word seem possible but, indeed, it is maximally befitting *in order to redeem mankind*, for nothing can move us more efficaciously to the good and lead us away from evil, as St. Thomas explains in *ST* III, q. 1, a. 2. Indeed, our faith is more certain when based on the conviction that God himself is the one speaking (without any mediation through prophets). Hope finds a stronger foundation too, and charity is roused all the more strongly: "By this hath the charity of God appeared towards us, because God hath sent his only begotten Son into the world, that we may live by him" (1 John 4:9, DR). "Greater love than this no man hath, that a man lay down his life for his friends" (John 15:13, DR). And the most perfect exemplar of all the virtues is pro-

---

[18] See *ST* III, q. 4, a. 2, ad 2: "The assumed nature is not lacking its own, proper personality on account of some *defect* befalling the perfection of human nature but, rather, on account of an *addition*, which is above human nature, namely its union with a divine person." Also see ibid., ad 3.

[19] See the Athanasian Creed: "Just as the rational soul and body make up one man, so too, God and man are one in Christ; they are entirely one, not through a confusion of substance but, rather, through a unity of person."

posed to us, as well as a remedy for presumption and pride. Hence, the words of Augustine [*sic*]: "God became man so that man may be made God"[20]— that is, one who participates in the divine nature and eternal felicity.

B. THE MYSTERY OF THE REDEMPTION already appears as something befitting on the basis of what we have said. According to the Christian faith, it finds its consummation in the *sacrifice of the Cross*, whose commemoration, continuation, and application is had in the celebration of the Mass. The ways this sacrifice is befitting are set forth in an express manner in the particular treatise devoted to this sacrament in theology proper. Here, within the bounds of apologetics, it suffices for us to propose them in general, as did the apostles themselves, especially St. Paul. *Concerning the sacrifice of the Cross*, they said: "*But God commendeth his charity towards us*, because when as yet we were sinners according to the time, Christ died for us" (Rom 5:8–9, DR). "Christ also suffered for us, leaving you an example that you should follow his steps" (1 Pet 2:21, DR). {{235}} "For you are bought with a great price. Glorify and bear God in your body" (1 Cor 6:20, DR). "Christ . . . hath delivered himself for us, an oblation and a sacrifice to God for an odour of sweetness" (Eph 5:2, DR). "We were reconciled to God by the death of his Son" (Rom 5:10, DR).[21]

Moreover, upon the Cross, infinite justice and infinite mercy are reconciled with each other, in accord with the words of Psalm 84[5]:11 (DR): "Mercy and truth have met each other: justice and peace have kissed." This is, properly speaking, the sublimity and splendor of the Cross.[22]

Finally, as regards the application of Christ's merits, THE SACRAMENTS are maximally befitting, inasmuch as they perfect man in relation to the principal acts of the spiritual life, both individually and socially, as St. Thomas explains most excellently.[23] Through Baptism, man is spiritually regenerated and is strengthened through Confirmation. Through the Eucharist spiritual

---

[20] [Trans. note: This dictum is usually cited from St. Athanasius.]

[21] See *ST* III, q. 46, a. 3.

[22] Whence, the Church sings [in the Roman Rite on Good Friday]:

Abroad the regal banners fly,	O lovely and refulgent Tree,
now shines the Cross's mystery:	adorned with purpled majesty. . . .
upon it Life did death endure,	Hail Cross, of hopes the most sublime; . . .
and yet by death did life procure.	grant to the just increase of grace,
	and every sinner's crimes efface.
	(trans. Blount, alt.)

[23] See *ST* III, q. 65, a. 1.

life is nourished or preserved. Through Penance, health is restored. Through Extreme Unction, the remainders of sin are removed and man is prepared for his final glory. Moreover, in relation to society, Matrimony is for the natural propagation of the species and a remedy for concupiscence.[24] Finally, the Sacrament of Holy Orders is for the spiritual ruling and sanctifying of the multitude.

As St. Thomas says in *ST* III, q. 73, a. 3 and a. 5: "THE EUCHARIST is, as it were, the consummation of the spiritual life and *the end of all the sacraments*, for by the sanctifications brought about by all the sacraments, we are prepared to receive or to consecrate the Eucharist."[25] In this, we see the marvelous harmony that exists in Catholic worship, wherein Christ's *sacrifice* is preserved in perpetuity: "*For the victim is one and the same*: through the ministry of priests, *the same now offers himself, who then offered himself on the Cross*; only the manner of offering is different."[26] The Mass is the sacrifice of Christ, "always living to make intercession for us" (Heb 7:25, DR).

Now, the sublimity of Eucharistic Communion was expressed by St. Thomas as follows:

Thus Angels' Bread is made
the Bread of man today:
the Living Bread from heaven
with figures dost away:
O wondrous gift indeed!
the poor and lowly may
upon their Lord and Master feed! (trans. Chambers)

{{236}} (5) *The mysteries of the future life*

A. THE BEATITUDE OF ETERNAL LIFE is described by Christ in various ways (see Matt 5:3–8; 16:27; 18:10, 43; 25:24) as being the kingdom of heaven that the righteous will possess, in which the pure of heart will see God, something like unto the angels who see the face of the Father. Each person will receive it in accord with his works. St. Paul (1 Cor 13:12) and St. John (1 John 3:2) say: "*We will see God face to face, as he is.*" This essential and inamissible beatitude, consisting of the immediate vision of God and

---

[24] [Trans. note: Though precisely as a sacrament it is more than this, for there it becomes a sign of the fidelity of Christ and the Church.]

[25] Even the naturalist Goethe admired the order of the sacraments that was preserved in the Catholic Church.

[26] Trent, *Decree on the Sacrifice of the Mass*, ch. 2 (Denzinger, no. 1743).

in beatific love, will not only satisfy our natural aspirations but, indeed, will surpass them: "Neither hath it entered into the heart of man, what things God hath prepared for them that love him" (1 Cor 2:9, DR).

B. ETERNAL PUNISHMENT will be inflicted on the wicked who die impenitent, and they will forever be deprived of eternal beatitude. "They will go into everlasting punishment . . . into the everlasting fire" (Matt 25:41, 46). Rationalists and liberal Protestants cry out with one voice that the idea of eternal punishment is opposed to God's wisdom, justice, and mercy: A sin committed in a passing moment should not lead to the fixing of an eternal punishment.

With St. Thomas,[27] we respond as follows in consideration of the impenitent person's sin as well as in relation to the various divine attributes. (1) After the impenitent person has died, *he remains irreparably fixed in his grave sin*, for it is fitting that the time of one's testing be brought to a close at the instant of death. He who in an instant makes himself blind will forever be blind, and he who kills himself cannot naturally rise again. Similarly, he who during his period of testing does not penitently convert, remaining turned away from God in spiritual death, will be deprived of beatitude forever, and because he irreparably rises up against God's justice,[28] he will forever suffer loss from it. This is all so because the punishment is not commensurate to the *duration of the sin committed*. "Indeed, the fact that murder is committed in a moment does not mean that only a momentary punishment is called for. In fact, such a fault is sometimes punished by imprisonment or lifelong exile, and sometimes even by death."[29]

(2) According to *justice*, a punishment is proportionate *to the weight of the fault*. Now, a mortal sin is a quasi-infinite offense against God, for it scorns God's infinite majesty and prefers some trifling good in place of him.

(3) Nor is the doctrine of eternal punishment opposed to the divine *mercy*, for "God, for His own part, has mercy on all. However, since His mercy is measured by the order of His wisdom, this means that it does not reach to those people who render themselves unworthy of that mercy, as do the demons and the damned who are obstinate in their wickedness."[30]

(4) Nor does *wisdom* require that punishments only be inflicted for the correction of the person who has done harm. (For example, the punishment of death is not for the correction of the person who has done harm but,

---

[27] See *ST* I-II, q. 87, a. 3; III *Suppl.*, q. 99, a. 1.
[28] [Trans. note: Reading *iustitiam* for *iniustitiam*.]
[29] *ST* I-II, q. 87, a. 3.
[30] *ST* III *Suppl.*, q. 99, a. 2, ad 1.

rather, is done in defense of the principles of social life and for the correction or tranquility of others, who remain in the city.) Thus, the eternal damnation of the wicked is for the correction of those who now live in the Church [on earth].[31] In fact, many are saved by fear of God, which is the beginning of wisdom.

{{237}} True, these arguments are not demonstrative. We must not believe dogmas on account of such arguments but, rather, on account of the authority of God who reveals. Nonetheless, they do offer a persuasive defense of their fittingness.

God's justice is infinite and does not leave a sin unpunished. *Nor is it surprising that God would punish, as God, just as he is merciful, as God.* There is nothing *sweeter* than the diffusion of the loftiest good and nothing *more terrible* than the inflexible proclamation of his right to be loved above all things. There is nothing *more sublime* than the harmony of these things that are separated by the greatest of distance.[32] Thus, already, we see that his mercy and justice are founded on the divine love of the Highest Good, though the *intimate* reconciliation of these attributes remains hidden. Hence, we desire to see the divine goodness in itself, that which is the root of his mercy and justice.[33]

This is expressed in the words read by Dante upon the gates of Hell:

Justice the founder of my fabric mov'd:
To rear me was the task of power divine,
Supremest wisdom, and primeval love.[34]

C. Finally, THE DOGMA OF PURGATORY and the universal practice of prayer for the dead manifest, at once, God's *justice* and his *mercy*. Indeed, nobody is granted eternal beatitude unless he is first freed from his venial

---

[31] See ibid., a. 1, ad 3.

[32] This utterly lofty harmony is expressed in the sequence, *Dies irae*:

O King of dreadful majesty!	Recall, dear Jesus, for my sake	O Judge of justice, hear, I pray,
grace and mercy You grant free;	you did our suffering nature take	for pity take my sins away
as Fount of Kindness, save me!	then do not now my soul forsake!	before the dreadful reckoning day.
		(trans. 1962 Missal)

[33] See *ST* I, q. 23, a. 5, ad 3: "God wills to manifest His goodness in men by predestining some by sparing them through His mercy, but also He manifests it in others whom He condemns by punishing them through His justice." Also see ibid., a. 3: "Condemnation includes the willingness to permit someone to fall into sin and to impose the punishment of damnation for sins."

[34] [Trans. note: See Dante, *The Divine Comedy*, trans. H. F. Cary, http://www.gutenberg.org/cache/epub/1008/pg1008.txt.]

sins and absolved of the temporal punishment owed to sins that have been remitted. However, God mercifully offers even after death a time of purification, and the souls detained in purgatory are aided by the prayers and offerings of the living, just as the latter are aided by the blessed, according to the *dogma of the communion of saints.*

This last dogma is the synthesis of all the others, for it signifies the communion that exists among the various members of the Church militant, suffering, and triumphant, whose moral [*sic*] head is Christ the Redeemer, the source of the whole of our supernatural life.

Thus, a marvelous harmony exists in the interconnection among the dogmas of Christianity. We will now turn to the precepts and the counsels, which themselves are no less intimately connected with these dogmas.

§3. The Excellence of the Law and the Christian Life

Precepts that are knowable by natural reason concerning God, ourselves, and other men are already contained in the Mosaic Law, especially in the Decalogue, though they are proposed more perfectly in the Christian law. In *ST* I-II, q. 101–108, St. Thomas shows at length how the New Law excels over the Old Law. His conclusions can be summed up as follows: No more eminent a law can be conceived of {{238}} (A) from the perspective of the principle of action (namely, divine grace); (B) from the perspective of its motive and end (love of God); (C) as regards the precepts; and (D) as regards the counsels.

A. *As regards the principle or source of action, the New Law is called "the law of grace."*

> That which is most powerful in it, that in which its full power consists, is the grace of the Holy Spirit, which is given through faith in Christ. Therefore, *the new law is principally the very grace of the Holy Spirit*, which Christ gives to believers. . . . Nonetheless, the New Law does contain certain things that, as it were, help to dispose us to receive the grace of the Holy Spirit and also pertain to the use of this grace. . . . Therefore, the New Law is primarily a law that is placed within us, *though secondarily it is a written law.*[35]

---

[35] See *ST* I-II, q. 106, a. 1.

Likewise, St. Augustine said: "In the Old Testament, the law is set forth in an external manner, so that the unrighteous might feel fear."[36] Therefore, as regards the principle of its activity, it is a "law of grace."[37]

B. *As regards the motive / end of its activity, it is called "the law of love,"* inasmuch as all things must be done for the sake of the love of God. No loftier motive could be thought up:

> Hence the Old Law, which was given to imperfect men, was called the "law of fear," inasmuch as it influenced men to observe its commandments by threatening them with penalties and is spoken of as containing certain temporal promises. However, those who are virtuous are inclined to do virtuous deeds through love of virtue, not on account of some extrinsic punishment or reward. Therefore, the New Law, whose preeminence comes from the spiritual grace which instilled into our hearts, is called the "Law of love," and it is said to contain spiritual and eternal promises, which are objects of the virtues, above all, charity.[38]

Thus, we have a response for those who say that Christians slave away for a future reward and not on account of virtue itself. We must say to such people that the principal reward is the supreme good, the object of the loftiest virtue, to be possessed inamissibly, without any danger of falling into sin.

C. *As regards the precepts.* The Evangelical Law is *especially concerned with interior acts,* for all of its precepts are included in the precepts of charity *concerning love of God and neighbor* and are ordered to these two: "Love the Lord your God with all your heart, with all your soul, with all your mind, and with all your strength" and "Love your neighbor as yourself." Christ does not command external acts, except those of the sacraments or those that are necessary for grace. Nor does he prohibit anything unless it is opposed to grace.[39] *Thus, as regards external and ceremonial things, the New Law is lighter than was the Old Law and hence is called a* "law of freedom"; *however, it prohibits disordered interior movements of the soul,* which were not expressly prohibited in the Old Law for all.[40]

---

[36] *De spiritu et littera,* c. 17.
[37] See *ST* I-II, q. 106, a. 3.
[38] *ST* I-II, q. 107, a. 1, ad 2.
[39] See *ST* I-II, q. 108, a. 2 and 4.
[40] See *ST* I-II, q. 107, a. 4.

You have heard that it was said to them of old: Thou shalt not kill. . . . But I say to you, that whosoever is angry with his brother, shall be in danger of the judgment. . . . You have heard that it was said to them of old: Thou shalt not commit adultery. . . . But I say to you, that whosoever shall look on a woman to lust after her, hath already committed adultery with her in his heart. . . . {{239}} If one strike thee on thy right cheek, turn to him also the other. . . . Do not judge. . . . *Love your enemies: . . . pray for them that persecute you* and calumniate you. . . . Take heed that you do not your justice before men, to be seen by them. . . . *Be you therefore perfect, as also your heavenly Father is perfect.* (Matt 5 and 6, DR)

Nothing more sublime than this could be proposed, and not only is it difficult for our powers of nature but, rather, it is impossible. Hence, Christ says, "Without me, you can do nothing" (John 15:5). The aid of grace is needed: "You must always pray" (Luke 18:1). However, when we are given divine aid, the words of Christ find themselves verified: *"For my yoke is sweet and my burden light"* (Matt 11:30, DR). For as St. Augustine says: "His commands are not heavy for the person who loves, but for him who does not, indeed they are."[41]

D. **The counsels.** Finally, in the Law of the Gospel, the counsels are fittingly added over and above the precepts. The latter are concerned with those things that are necessary for attaining the end of eternal beatitude, whereas the counsels are concerned with those things that enable man to *better and more readily* reach the aforementioned end. Indeed, making use of the things of this world, provided that he does not place his end in them, man can arrive at eternal beatitude. However, he arrives at it more readily by wholly setting aside this world's goods, and concerning this, there are the Gospel counsels regarding voluntary poverty, chastity, and obedience.[42] *"The counsels are ordered to the precepts of charity*, not so that these precepts could not be preserved without the counsels but, rather, *so that they may be observed more perfectly through the counsels."*[43]

Conclusion: Therefore, it is impossible to conceive of a more perfect law from the perspective of its principle, its end / motive, and that of its precepts and counsels. It is particularly marvelous inasmuch as through grace *we herein find to be reconciled a supra-human loftiness alongside something that*

---

[41] *De natura et gratia,* ch. 69.

[42] See *ST* I-II, q. 108, a. 4.

[43] *ST* I-II, q. 189, a. 1, ad 5.

is perfectly conformed to our nature: "My yoke is easy and my burden light." There is no defect found in it, but rather, *the virtues that are apparently opposed to each other here are admirably brought into agreement*: Love of God, by its great intensity, fosters—not harms—love of neighbor and indeed is its foundation; universal charity for all who are children of God perfects—not destroys—love for our homeland; we must acknowledge our own dignity as children of God but must do so with humility, for "we hold this treasure in earthen vessels." The Christian must be humble, though without pusillanimity, obedient without servility; all legitimate natural affections are permitted to him, whatever is honest, good, true (like science, the arts, commerce, etc.), whatever is delightful and useful, so long as all of this is subordinated to love of God and neighbor; but in order to increase this love, "if he wishes to be perfect," he is encouraged to give up his riches and take up absolute chastity along with religious obedience. Thus, he may arrive more easily at continuous contemplation of divine things and at the perfection of charity.

CONFIRMATION: No comparison can be made between the ethics of the best of paganism's philosophers and Christ's moral doctrine. The wise men among the Greeks said, "Know yourself; be a man; perfection is found in living in accord with reason." Jesus says: "Be perfect, as your heavenly Father is perfect." {{240}} The philosophers commended magnanimity, but they did not avoid pride. Christ speaks of a loftier dignity but commands humility. Epictetus teaches, "Put up with things and abstain," but Jesus says, "Blessed are those who suffer persecution for the sake of righteousness, for theirs is the kingdom of heaven." The wise wrote, "The greatest respect is owed to children [*pueris*]." However, Jesus preaches: "See that you despise not one of these little ones, . . . for their angels in heaven always see the face of my Father who is in heaven" (Matt 18:10, DR). He does not just say, "Help the poor," but rather says, "Blessed are the poor, for theirs is the kingdom of heaven." Nothing similar is found among the pagans.

Similarly, Christian ethics is far superior to the moral doctrine of modern philosophers, whether they be empiricists and utilitarians or idealists like Kant. Whatever is true and lofty in Kantian ethics is already found in Christ's doctrine, indeed, in a far more perfect manner.

§4. The Harmony of the Whole of Christian Doctrine

This harmony is made clear (a) in the conformity of supernatural mysteries with natural truth concerning God and man, (b) in the interconnection of the mysteries themselves, and (c) with man's ultimate end, to which the precepts and counsels lead.

(a) As has been said, *the supernatural mysteries manifest, in particular, the lofty goodness of God.* We showed their befittingness by making use of this principle: The Highest Good is maximally and intimately self-diffusive. There is the diffusion (or communication) of the intimate life of God *ad intra* (the Trinity) and *ad extra* (our elevation to the life of grace, the Incarnation, the Redemption, and our glorification).

(b) *However, the interconnection of the mysteries with each other* is clear inasmuch as one flows from another, and the supreme mystery cannot be denied without the others being undermined. Indeed, once we have admitted the loftiest mystery of the Holy Trinity, we can easily conceive (though, of course, not in a necessary manner) the way that those other things that depend upon God's freedom follow thereupon. However, by contrast, if we were to deny the mystery of the Trinity, we would bring to ruin the Incarnation of the Word of God who is distinct from the Father, as well as the sending of the Holy Spirit. Likewise, we would not understand our adoptive filiation, which is a participated likeness of the natural filiation in eternity.[44]

Now, the elevation of mankind to the life of grace is presupposed by original sin and, hence, by the Incarnation and the Redemption, from which come the Eucharist and all the sacraments.

Therefore, the loftiest mystery is that of the Trinity, the life of God *ad intra*: All things proceed from the Trinity and are ordered to it. However, below the Trinity, all the mysteries are referred to the Incarnate and redeeming Word of God. The Old Testament speaks of the fall of mankind and announces the Savior from whom proceeds the entire life of the Church militant, suffering, and triumphant. The Eucharist is the Incarnation's extension and radiation—that is, the sacrament of the body of Christ, forever present and life-giving. Finally, the communion of saints is nothing other than the mutual relations that exist among all the members of the Mystical Body of Christ. The universal synthesis of all of this can be expressed in the words of St. Paul: "For all things are yours, and you are Christ's, and Christ is God's" (1 Cor 3:22–23).

{{241}} This interconnection of the mysteries is confirmed by the fact that never have heretics attacked a Catholic truth of some importance without toppling over the entire edifice of doctrine, as can be clearly gathered from the history of Arianism, Pelagianism, Nestorianism, and Protestantism.

(c) *Finally, the precepts and counsels of Christianity logically flow from the dogmas.* For all things are reduced to love of God and neighbor. However,

---

[44] See *ST* III, q. 3, a. 8.

this love is born of contemplation of the infinite perfection or goodness, which is manifested in the Trinity, the Incarnation, the Redemption, and in our vocation to eternal life. In vain do rationalists labor, wishing to separate Christian ethics from the dogmas of faith. For nothing of Christian ethics remains once you set aside hope in eternal beatitude and supernatural charity; however, hope and charity necessarily presuppose faith and the mysteries of faith, and the whole of the Christian life is founded on the grace of Christ the Redeemer.

Mutual relations also exist between contemplation of the mysteries of faith and the active life of Christians, as St. Thomas sets forth in *ST* II-II, q. 182, a. 4: "According to its nature, the contemplative life is prior to the active life, insofar as it is concerned with things that are better and prior. Whence, it moves and directs the active life. However, from our perspective and by way of genesis, the active life is prior to the contemplative, for it disposes to the contemplative life," by measuring the passions that disturb the stillness of contemplation. Hence, although Christian ethics depends on the dogmas in an essential manner, we can, in discussing them apologetically with nonbelievers, first set forth Christ's moral teaching, as he himself did in the Sermon on the Mount. Then, if such nonbelievers are sincere, they will acknowledge this moral doctrine's purity and transcendence over the ethics of the philosophers, not only those who were sensualists but even spiritualists. And having been drawn in this way, they will look into the foundation of the Christian life and will find it in the mysteries of the Incarnation and the Redemption, which presuppose the Trinity. Thus, on account of its sublimity, Christian ethics will provide them with a motive of credibility for believing in the mysteries themselves.

Therefore, Christ's doctrine enjoys the greatest unity and harmony, marvelously joining together natural truth concerning God with the supernatural mysteries and precepts.

The synthesis of the whole of this doctrine, as we already said much earlier on, can be written out as follows so as to manifest how all the mysteries and our own life proceed from the Trinity and return to it:[45]

---

[45] [Trans. note: Here I am reproducing the full diagram from above (and referred to as such here), which is slightly more detailed.]

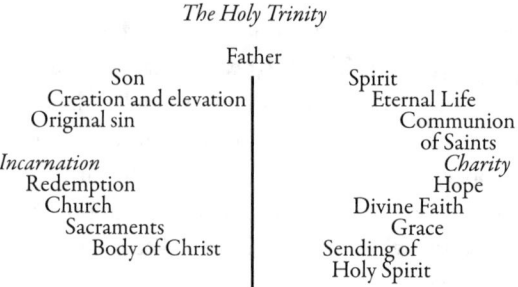

The Holy Trinity

Father

Son		Spirit
Creation and elevation		Eternal Life
Original sin		Communion
		of Saints
Incarnation		*Charity*
Redemption		Hope
Church		Divine Faith
Sacraments		Grace
Body of Christ		Sending of
		Holy Spirit

{{242}} The Father, the Creator of heaven and earth, was progressively manifested, as well as the Incarnate Son, the Savior, and the Holy Spirit, the sanctifier who leads souls to eternal life.

Conclusion. Considered in itself, this doctrine is, properly speaking, *sublime*—namely, something utterly lofty and extraordinary in the order of intellectual and moral beauty. Sublimity appears in it above all, inasmuch as it marvelously joins together *that which is highest* and *that which is lowest*, the riches of divine mercy and the misery of mankind, preserving the rights of justice: "God has restored peace in all things, reconciling in Himself, the lowest with the highest" (cf. Col 1:20). Similarly, this doctrine joins together *supernatural things* and *natural ones*, as well as *mystical contemplation* and *practical activity*. Likewise, Christ had the greatest of originality, and nonetheless, he did not come, as do innovators, to destroy but, rather, to fulfill, thus joining together in the best of ways, *the oldest* and *the newest* of things, the principle of all things and the end, α and ω, the alpha and the omega.

Hence, notwithstanding the obscurity of the mysteries, in them we have a verification for the words of St. Paul praying for believers: "That he (God) would grant you, according to the riches of his glory, to be strengthened by his Spirit with might unto the inward man, that . . . you may be able to comprehend, with all the saints, what is the *breadth* and *length* and *height* and *depth*, to know also the charity of Christ, which surpasseth all knowledge: that you may be filled unto all the fullness of God" (Eph 3:16–19, DR).

Such a doctrine, having marvelous qualities like this, contains a sign of its divine origin. It quite manifestly exceeds the powers of reason, which cannot morally know the sum of the natural truths of religion firmly, readily, and without error, and which *a fortiori* could not so fittingly order the loftiest mysteries and precepts in a way that is conformed to our nature but instead on its own, would fall into the deluded ravings of false mysticism, confusing exaltation of imagination with elevation of mind.

Moreover, on the basis of the goodness of the Christian doctrine, it is manifest that it is not from a wicked spirit, for it is radically opposed to forms of superstition, which themselves commend the most worthless estimation of God.

This conclusion is easily reached by men of good will, and hence we read in Matthew, at the end of the Sermon on the Mount, "when Jesus had fully ended these words, the people were in admiration at his doctrine" (Matt 7:28, DR; Mark 1:22; Luke 4:32).

This argument is confirmed through a consideration of the manner in which it was proposed and the way that this most eminent doctrine was constituted.

ART. 2: ON THE WAY THAT CHRIST PREACHED

As St. Thomas says,[46] the preacher of the faith should speak in such a way that (1) the Word of God may illuminate the intellect, (2) it might delight one's affect in a righteous manner, and (3) it may efficaciously move one's will to fulfill the divine commands. Now, these three manners of proposing doctrine are found in Christ's preaching in a most perfect and extraordinary manner.

§1. As Regards Illumination of the Intellect

{{243}} Jesus taught the loftiest mysteries *with the greatest authority*, together with *simplicity and humility*, marvelously joining together in his manner of teaching these two extremes.

Indeed, Christ's authority is unique and incomparable: "For he was teaching them as one having power, and not as the scribes and Pharisees" (Matt 7:29, DR). He did not argue from texts of Sacred Scripture and from glosses. He did not propose abstract demonstrations, as do philosophers. He did not deploy the instruments of rhetoric in order to stir up admiration. Rather, he brought forth brief, clear, and profound sentences, which gave offence to wicked inclinations and stirred up reason, immediately penetrating the mind, indeed, piercing like an arrow even the most stubborn of minds. These sentences were so new and beautiful that they could never fall into oblivion. They remain in the mind as the light of life or as a reproach.

He always spoke as *the supreme teacher*: "But do not be called teachers, for you have one teacher, Christ" (Matt 23:8). "You call me Master and Lord. And you say well, for so I am" (John 13:13, DR). Jesus understood

---

[46] See *ST* II-II, q. 177, a. 1.

well that he was above the judgment of all men, above every form of examination, above every censure, above every rejection: "For this came I into the world, that I should give testimony to the truth. Every one that is of the truth heareth my voice" (John 18:37, DR). He alone made use of these formulas: "Amen, Amen, I say to you." "I speak that which I have seen with my Father" (John 8:38, DR). "You believe in God: believe also in me" (John 14:1, DR). "I am the light of the world. He that followeth me walketh not in darkness, but shall have the light of life. . . . Although I give testimony of myself, my testimony is true: for I know whence I came and whither I go" (John 8:12–14, DR). "I am the way, and the truth, and the life" (John 14:6, DR). No greater doctrinal authority can be conceived.

Moreover, the *authority of Christ's life* confirmed his doctrine. Often, the moral character of philosophers does not agree with their own ethics. Likewise, among the prophets, even one as great as Moses sometimes sinned against God and hence did not enter the promised land (Deut 32:51). By contrast, Jesus perfectly fulfilled the precepts and the counsels that he taught. No imperfection was found in him. He was able to say to his foes: "Which of you shall convince me of sin?" (John 8:46, DR). And to his disciples: "For I have given you an example, that as I have done to you, so you do also" (John 13:15, DR).

The utter simplicity and humility are joined to this supreme authority. Now, this is indeed something sublime. Jesus is too great and powerful to be proud; in his majesty, we have an example of humility: "My doctrine is not mine, but his that sent me" (John 7:16, DR) and "learn from me, because I am meek, and humble of heart" (Matt 11:29, DR). He did not desire the title of teacher or honors. Whereas the Pharisees sat on the chair of Moses, Jesus chose to evangelize the poor who were despised by the pagan philosophers. He preached to all upon the mountain, on the seashore of the Sea of Tiberias, and in the temple portico. {{244}} Without rhetorical instruments or contention of soul, he spoke spontaneously in parables concerning the loftiest mysteries, *in a manner accommodated to all*, though never in a vulgar way. Nay, the loftier the object of consideration, the simpler did he preach with a calm soul. Sublime things are connatural to him, and he contemplated them ceaselessly, loving them with the greatest of love. However, those things that he possessed "without measure" (John 3:34) he handed on to us in a measured way so that our weakness might not be overwhelmed: "I have yet many things to say to you, but you cannot bear them now. But when he, the Spirit of truth, is come, he will teach you all truth" (John 16:12–13, DR). Finally, with a sweet simplicity, he commends humility to his disciples, saying, "Amen I say to you, unless you be converted, and become as little children, you shall not enter into the kingdom of heaven" (Matt 18:3, DR). Thus, in his manner of teaching, the greatest authority, simplicity, and humility are all reconciled with each other.[47]

§2. Jesus Not Only Illuminates but Also Delights the Affect in a Righteous Manner with a Marvelous Anointing

---

[47] This is expressed excellently by Bossuet in the same text cited above from the *Discours sur l'histoire universelle*, pt. 2, ch. 19: "Who wouldn't admire the condescension with which he tempers the loftiness of His doctrine? It is milk for infants and likewise bread for the strong. We look upon Him and see that He is full of God's secrets, but we see that He is not startled by this fact, as are other mortals to whom God communicates Himself. He speaks about these secrets naturally, as though He existed within this secret and within this glory; indeed, *'what he has without measure'* (John 3:35), He pours out with measure so that our weakness might be able to bear it."

Similarly, Fr. [Jean-Nicolas] Grou, S.J., writes most excellently, in his *L'intérieur de Jésus*, ch. 24 (Jesus Christ's manner of teaching): "The mouth speaks from the abundance of the heart, not only in the things that it says but also in the way that it says them. A humble master can teach great things, but he will teach them with humility. He will put on no airs, nor use any word, which would bear witness to the feeling of prideful self-sufficiency. He will know how to lower himself to the level of those to whom he is speaking and how to proportion himself to their intelligence. If he places weight and authority in what he says, he does not do this in order to draw some sort of worth to himself but, rather, in order to raise up the person in whose name he speaks and in order to make a greater impression upon the minds before him. Such was the way taken up by Jesus Christ in His teaching. He spoke as the God-Man, as mankind's teacher and law-giver, with a sovereign wisdom, an infallible authority, and nonetheless, He never lost His characteristic humility. . . . There is no way to express in a simpler way things which are so lofty and divine. The prophets seem astonished and struck by the great truths that they announce. Jesus remains self-possessed when He speaks, for he draws everything from His depths. . . . The treasury of his knowledge is found in Himself, and He does not exhaust it when He communicates it. . . . All proportions maintained, this is likewise the manner of teaching taken up by those who have an interior spirit. Their air, their tone, their style, their manner has something which belongs to them alone, something that those who are not interior cannot imitate. They speak with assurance, and at the same time, with humility, for they do not speak of themselves. Artifice, reasoning, and methodology have no part in their discourses, and nonetheless, they are convincing, bearing their proofs within their statements. They illuminate the mind, but they also go deeper, to the heart: they are simple, easy, familiar. However, in their simplicity, they have a sweet majesty, one that is gripping and charming. When you look upon them, you do not see striking figures, nor the great traits of eloquence; but for hearts that are well-prepared, they have a persuasive power and efficacy that can only come from the grace which spoke them. This is the distinctive character of those who preach in God's Spirit, and interior persons—or those who are called to become such—can never be deceived regarding this character. . . . (Other hearers do not taste of this preaching.) If they were of good faith, they would admit, as St. Augustine confessed about himself prior to his conversion, that they find Scripture too simple, that the narratives in the Gospel are too bare and too dry, and that they understand nearly nothing about its morality."

Indeed, "He speaks from the abundance of his heart" (Matt 12:34), always preaching through the greatest love of God for men. He himself came "that they have life and may have it more abundantly" (John 10:10, DR), saying, "Come to me all you that labor and are burdened, and I will refresh you" (Matt 11:28, DR). {{245}} This marvelous anointing appears above all when he came to speak to the Samaritan woman: "If thou didst know the gift of God and who he is that saith to thee, Give me to drink, thou perhaps wouldst have asked of him, and he would have given thee living water" (John 4:10, DR). Likewise, it is found in the beatitudes, in his final conversation with his disciples before the Passion, and so forth.

This anointing is manifestly opposed to vain "sentimentalism," for Jesus at once troubles our inordinate inclinations and profoundly draws our heart. *His anointing is united with austerity, self-denial,* and due severity: "And if thy eye scandalize thee, pluck it out, and cast it from thee" (Matt 18:9, DR). "If any man will come after me, let him deny himself, and take up his cross" (Matt 16:24, DR). Sometimes, toward the proud and unbelieving, he insists upon the loftiness of the mysteries: "Murmur not among yourselves. No man can come to me, except the Father, who hath sent me, draw him. And I will raise him up in the last day" (John 6:43–68, DR). Nay, the same Jesus, who with such an anointment mercifully speaks to men of good will, justly discloses the intention of the Pharisees and vehemently rebukes them: "Woe to you, hypocrites, because you shut the kingdom of heaven against men. . . . Woe to you blind guides. . . . Fill ye up then the measure of your fathers. You serpents, generation of vipers, how will you flee from the judgment of hell?" (Matt 23:13–33, DR). Christ spoke in this way because, in their perversity, the Pharisees impeded the salvation of the multitude.[48]

This terrible justice does not diminish Christ's anointing and mercy but, rather, on the contrary, shows its great worth. Sometimes the words of Jesus flow like dew, lightly laying in small drops upon the grass (Deut 32:2), though at other times his words are like devouring flames (Ps 118[9]:140). Now he says, "Peace I leave with you: my peace I give unto you: not as the world giveth, do I give unto you" (John 14:27, DR), but then he likewise says, "I came not to send peace, but the sword" (Matt 10:34, DR)—that is, "the sword of the Spirit, which is the word of God" (Eph 6:17). His word is living, "reaching unto the division of the soul and the spirit, . . . and is a discerner of the thoughts and intents of the heart" (Heb 4:12, DR). It is impossible to unite a greater anointing with a holier justice. Here, in this

---

[48] See *ST* III, q. 42, a. 2.

union, we see a likeness of the loftiest harmony that is found in the unity of the divine attributes.

§3. By His Preaching, Jesus Efficaciously Moves Wills to Act in a Right and Holy Manner

"The words that I have spoken to you are spirit and life" (John 6:64, DR). Many, notwithstanding the great difficulties and persecutions involved, believed in him. The servants of the Pharisees, not daring to lay hold of him, themselves said: "Never did man speak like this man" (John 7:46, DR). Up to the point of martyrdom, his apostles defended the faith. Through it, the moral life has been renewed in countless generations, arousing ardent love of God and neighbor, all the way to the point of sacrificing one's life, and leading to unmistakable holiness. After twenty centuries, Christ's words retain the same extraordinary efficacy. *By contrast, the most sound of the philosophers of antiquity* were not able to set aright the interior dispositions of men, and their books are no longer read, except by the learned. However, most men know the Gospel and its principal passages. {{246}} And yet this book was not even written by Christ himself: "Christ, as a most excellent teacher, adopted a manner of teaching (not through the writing of books, but rather,) by impressing His teaching on the hearts of His hearers."[49] He wrote in the minds of his apostles, and by means of these poor fishermen he renewed the face of the earth. *He alone was able to perpetually preserve his living teaching through the ages*, and forever arouse an unending series of apostles, just as he said: "However, my words will not pass away" (Matt 24:35). (On the fecundity of this doctrine, see the next chapter devoted to the marvelous life of the Church.)

Having considered all of these things in Christ's preaching regarding his way of illuminating, drawing, and efficaciously moving souls, how could we not conclude with the Apostle Peter: "Lord, to whom shall we go? Thou hast the words of eternal life" (John 6:69, DR).

However, we must consider another confirmation.

ART. 3: How Is Christ's Doctrine Constituted? It Is Not a Form of Syncretism

It is historically clear that this doctrine was constituted *without any human preparation*. That is, it was not elaborated by the human genius of some

---

[49] *ST* III, q. 42, a. 4.

teacher, nor through an eclecticism composed out of other materials. This is known on the basis of Christ's own testimony, as well as that of his fellow men, and it is confirmed by the impossibility of reducing Christianity to a kind of *syncretism* of Judaism, Eastern religions, and ancient philosophy.[50]

§1. On the Basis of Christ's Testimony and That of His Fellow Men

Those who deny Jesus's divinity say that he was a disciple of John the Baptist and of learned Jews, especially the Essenes. However, this is opposed to Christ's own express declarations, as well as to historically certain facts.

These declarations are found in the Synoptic Gospels, though they find particularly clear expression in John, which relates at greater length Christ's words to the priests of the synagogue asking him from whom he received his teaching.[51]

In Matthew 11:27 (DR) and Luke 10:22, we read: "All things are delivered to me by my Father. And no one knoweth the Son but the Father: neither doth anyone know the Father, but the Son, and he to whom it shall please the Son to reveal him."

In John 3:31–34 (DR), we see John the Baptist's testimony concerning Jesus: "He that cometh from heaven is above all. And what he hath seen and heard, that he testifieth. . . . For he whom God hath sent speaketh the words of God: for God doth not give the Spirit by measure." And in John 7:16–18 (DR), on the Feast of Tabernacles, Jesus says to the Jews: "My doctrine is not mine, but his that sent me. If any man will do the will of him, he shall know of the doctrine, whether it be of God, or whether I speak of myself. He that speaketh of himself seeketh his own glory: but he that seeketh the glory of him that sent him, he is true and there is no injustice in him." On the same day, Jesus says: "But he that sent me, is true: and the things I have heard of him, these same I speak in the world. . . . {{247}} But as the Father hath taught me, these things I speak. . . . But now you seek to kill me, a man who have spoken the truth to you, which I have heard from God" (John 8:26, 28, 40, DR). Just before his Passion, he again said in the temple: "For I have not spoken of myself: but the Father who sent me, he gave me commandment what I should say and what I should speak" (John 12:49–50, DR). Similarly, and indeed more intimately, he says to disciples: "The words that I speak to you, I speak not of myself. . . . And the word which you have heard is not mine; but the Father's who sent me" (John 14:10–24, DR). "But I have

---

[50]   See Pierre Battifol, *L'enseignement de Jésus* ([Paris: Bloud et Cie,] 1905).

[51]   See bk. 2, ch. 3 above (Christ's testimony concerning his divine mission).

called you friends because all things, whatsoever I have heard of my Father, I have made known to you" (John 15:15, DR). "Father . . . the words which thou gavest me, I have given to them" (John 17:8, DR).

All of the apostles preached this divine origin of Christ's doctrine. And the first hearers of these words said, "*How came this man by this wisdom* and miracles?" (Matt 13:54, DR; Mark 6:2). And the Jews marveled at him and said, "How doth this man know letters, having never learned?" (John 7:15, DR).

§2. Christian Doctrine Is Not a Syncretistic Mixture of Judaism, Eastern Religions, and Ancient Philosophy

Some *rationalists*[52] held that Christ's teaching was borrowed partly from Jewish teachers and partly from Greek or Latin philosophers. Others have said that Christianity arose from the doctrine of Zoroaster thriving in Persia, a claim that openly contradicts the facts, for at the time of Christ's apostles, this doctrine was unknown in Judea and, moreover, in its dualism, significantly differs from Christianity. Some have contended that Christianity is an imitation of Buddhism, which is clearly false historically, as well as merely through a comparison of the two religions. Today, a number of rationalists say that the Gospel's teaching already existed before the apostles came to know Greek philosophy but, rather, Christianity arose from Judaism and pagan notions that had already been known by all before Christ's own time. [Hermann] Gunkel taught that the principal aspect of this syncretism is pagan mysticism, which appeared in the Greeks under the influence of Eastern religions.[53]

Now, the fact that Christ's doctrine is not a syncretistic teaching can be proven from the fact that it was not borrowed (A) from Jewish teachers, (B) Greek or Latin philosophers, or (C) Eastern religions.

A. *Christ's teaching was not borrowed from Jewish teachers.* Although Christianity is related to the Mosaic covenant as the perfect is related to the imperfect, nonetheless, they are too distinct from each other for the transition from one to the other to be able to be made without a special, new intervention by God.

Indeed, (1) the Mosaic religion properly belonged to but one people, whereas Christianity is universal: "Preach the Gospel to every creature."

---

[52] For example, see [Ernest] Havet, *Le christianisme et ses origines*, bk. 1, pt. 1, ch. 1.

[53] [Hermann] Gunkel, *Zum religiongeschischtlichen Verständnis des Neuen Testaments* (1903), 95.

(2) The Jews expected a temporal Messiah, who would restore the kingdom of Israel, whereas Jesus came as a spiritual Messiah. (3) The fundamental dogmas of Christianity (the Trinity, the Incarnation of the Word, the Redemption through the Cross,[54] and justification through faith and good works) had been unknown to the Jewish people. {{248}} (4) In its ethics, Jesus's teaching, especially as regards the internal demands of justice, differed greatly from the traditions of the elders and the Pharisees.

Nor did the Gospel arise from the preaching of John the Baptist, which was only a preparation, leading men to do penance for the coming of the Messiah.

Nor did Christ borrow his teaching from the Essenes, for they recommended external purity in particular, adhering to Mosaic legal observances that were stricter than those followed by the Pharisees, likewise keeping away from the Gentiles and despising marriage.

Jesus's words cannot be compared with Jewish conceptions, as liberal Protestants themselves confess.[55]

Unless we wish to admit that an effect can be superior to its cause, we cannot say that the Gospel arose from the aforementioned conceptions.

B. *Nor was Christ's teaching borrowed from Greek or Latin philosophers.* (a) *As regards dogmas*, the pagans were unaware of the Trinity,[56] the Redemption, and sanctification through grace. Nay, many of the most excellent ones were in doubt concerning the immortality of the soul and concerning providence. These doubts are expressed in the books of Cicero,

---

[54] The mystery of the Trinity was adumbrated in a number of texts of the Old Testament, especially Wisdom 7–9. However, the Jews had only obscure and vague concepts concerning this matter. See [Jules] Lebreton, *Les origines du dogme de la Trinité*, 125.

Likewise, at first, the apostles did not wish to listen to Christ when he announced the mystery of the Redemption through the Cross, and up to the day of the Ascension, they asked Christ, "Lord, wilt thou at this time restore again the kingdom of Israel?" (Acts 1:6, DR).

[55] See Edmond Louis Stapfer, *La Palestine au temps de Jésus Christ* (Paris: Fischbacher, 1885), 472: "Nobody was less a man of his own era than was Jesus; nobody was less subject to the influence of his environment than he; nobody, was freer from prejudices and more independent than was he." Likewise, on 24: "An abyss separates the most admirable treatise of the Mishna, the *Pirké Aboth*, from evangelical morality." Likewise, see Harnack, *Das Wesen des Christentums* (Lepzig, 1900), 21–24; and Franz Julius Delitzsch, *Jesus und Hillel* (Erlanger: Deichert, 1867).

[56] For Plato, God is the Self-Subsistent Good. For Aristotle, he is Pure Act, Understanding of Understanding. For the Stoics, he is the soul of the world. In a way, the Neo-Platonists joined the three aforementioned conceptions together and thus admitted a kind of trinity; however, this sort of trinity is comparable to the Christian Trinity in name only. For the Neo-Platonists, three hypostases are unequal (One Good, the Intellect, and the World Soul), and their doctrine is pantheistic in nature.

who preceded Christ, and in those of Seneca, who came after him.[57]

(b) *The ethics of the philosophers* is no less different from Christ's moral teaching. The whole of Christian ethics is founded on the love of God and neighbor for God's own sake. Many philosophers proposed nothing for themselves, even were they to do good for others, unless it was done for one's own felicity. They knew not humility, and indeed, in the Stoics, pride was a virtue. Seneca wrote, "There is something that gives the wise man an advantage over God, for the latter has no fear through nature's own bounty, whereas the wise man has it from his own." "Hence, have faith in yourself, not in God, nor weary God with your prayers, but, rather, through your own powers, attain virtue and felicity. Indeed, alms must be given, but do so with a peaceful mind and a serene countenance, for you are not permitted to feel the pangs of sorrow."[58]

(c) *Nor did philosophers care about truth to be preached to the people.* A number said, like Horatius: "I hate the common man and keep my distance from him." They had no hope that they would change the morals of the people. Philosophy was sterile in this regard. {{249}} By contrast, Christ evangelized the poor, teaching them in parables. Sinners did not cause him to despair. Rather, he efficaciously led them to a better life and reformed the whole world.[59]

Hence, Christ's doctrine was in no way borrowed from Greek or Latin philosophers. Nay, it was new, seeming to be *foolishness to the Gentiles.* Hence, in the midst of the Areopagus, when the philosophers heard St. Paul preach the resurrection of the dead, "some indeed mocked. But others said: We will hear thee again concerning this matter" (Acts 17:32, DR). And Paul wrote to the Corinthians:

For the word of the cross, to them indeed that perish, is foolishness: but to them that are saved, that is, to us, it is the power of God. For

---

[57] See Cicero, *Contra academicos*, bk. 2, no. 48; *De natura deorum*, bk. 1, no. 6 and bk. 3, no. 39; *Tusculan disputations*, bk. 1, no. 49. Seneca, *De consolatione ad Marciam*, d. 19; *Ep.* 31 and 65. The latter letter denies the usefulness of prayer. Also see G. Boissier, *La religion romaine*, vol. 2, bk. 2, chs. 3–4.

[58] Seneca, *Ep.* 31 and 52.

[59] Havet himself, in *Le christianisme et ses origines*, confesses: "In Christianity, there are ideas and sentiments that indicate that it comes from another origin. All of Greek morality, including that of Plato himself, is a morality for the strong. By contrast, the Gospel is also and, indeed above all, a morality for the weak, through the twofold power of charity, which is connected to weakness and to human misery, and of grace, this foreign and supernatural power which replaces the internal spring which all the schools of Greek morality strive to attain and maintain."

it is written: I will destroy the wisdom of the wise: and the prudence of the prudent I will reject. Where is the wise? Where is the
scribe? Where is the disputer of this world? Hath not God made
foolish the wisdom of this world? For, seeing that in the wisdom of
God, the world, by wisdom, knew not God, it pleased God, by the
foolishness of our preaching, to save them that believe. For both *the
Jews require signs, and the Greeks seek after wisdom. But we preach
Christ crucified: unto the Jews indeed a stumbling block, and unto the
Gentiles foolishness.* But unto them that are called, both Jews and
Greeks, Christ, the power of God and the wisdom of God. (1 Cor
1:18–24, DR)

C. *Christ's doctrine was not borrowed from Eastern religions.* As was
said above, *Gunkel* holds that Christianity is a syncretistic mixture, drawing
its principal part from the pagan mysticism that, under the influence of
Eastern religions, appeared among the Greeks after Aristotle, Epicurus, and
Zeno the Stoic, with philosophical skepticism. In fact, in the first century,
there was a pagan syncretism combining together the ancient cults of the
Greeks and the Eastern religions, simultaneously worshiping Zeus and
Jupiter, Bacchus, Serapis, and Mithras. However, Gunkel is only able to note
very few, quite external and material, likenesses between this pagan syncretism and Christianity. And he says that there is a kind of likeness regarding
the death and resurrection of a given god; likewise, he claims a likeness in
regard to certain initiation rites that have a kind of agreement with the sym-
bolism involved in Baptism; and also, he points to the sacred banquets in
which the pagans draw close to Mithra or Dionysius.

However, we must respond to such claims as follows.[60] Some of these likenesses are false, whereas others are far too exaggerated, and they can easily
be explained by the fact that all religions intend to establish, in some way,
communication with the invisible world. And the likeness of the symbols
employed by pagan syncretism and Christianity is far less profound than is the
likeness between Mosaic religion and Christian religion, for the ceremonies of
the Mosaic Law were figures of our sacraments, as the pascal lamb was a figure
of the Eucharist and, similarly, the various ablutions and purifications [were
figures of Baptism].

{{250}} However, we find that Gunkel's theory is completely ruled out
if we consider (1) the effects of such pagan rituals, (2) the opposition of
the doctrines in question, (3) the irreducible opposition that exists between

---

[60] See Bernard Allo, *L'évangile en face du syncrétisme paien* (Paris: Bloud, 1910).

356

Christian and pagan mystics, and finally, (4) the effects of this syncretism and those of Christianity in the world.

(1) *The pagan rituals* aroused only one's imagination and nerves and thus provoked many people to shameful acts. By contrast, in Christianity, external worship is subordinated to the internal worship by which "God is adored in spirit and in truth."

(2) *The teaching of pagan* mystics is polytheistic—or, rather, if we consider it more deeply, pantheistic or dualistic, while also representing a form of fatalism, reflected in the worship of the stars. By contrast, from its beginnings, Christianity appears as being entirely unified, and all of its mysteries are subordinated to the dogma of the one God who is supreme and infinitely perfect.

(3) *There has forever been an irreducible opposition* between Christian and pagan mystics. Indeed, already at the time of St. Paul, we see this in his letters: "Bear not the yoke with unbelievers. For what participation hath justice with injustice? Or what fellowship hath light with darkness? And what concord hath Christ with Belial? . . . And what agreement hath the temple of God with idols? For you are the temple of the living God" (2 Cor 6:14–16, DR). "But the things which the heathens sacrifice, *they sacrifice to devils and not to God.* And I would not that you should be made partakers with devils. You cannot drink the chalice of the Lord and the chalice of devils: you cannot be partakers of the table of the Lord and of the table of devils" (1 Cor 10:20–21, DR; also 1 Cor 8:10). "But then indeed, not knowing God, you served them who, by nature, are not gods. But now, after that you have known God, or rather are known by God: how turn you again to the weak and needy elements which you desire to serve again?" (Gal 4:8–9, DR).

And as regards the charismatic gifts, which do have an appearance deceptively like certain things that can be found in pagan mysticism, we must say with St. Paul that these charismatic gifts come to no profit without charity: "If I speak with the tongues of men and of angels, and have not charity, I am become as sounding brass, or a tinkling cymbal . . . and if I should deliver my body to be burned, and have not charity, it profiteth me nothing" (1 Cor 13:1–4, DR).

However, pagan asceticism, which frequently led to shameful acts, was completely condemned by Christianity, as we see in a particularly strong way in the letter of St. Jude, vv. 4–13. Nor were Christians able to unconsciously undergo the influence of those who held to such mysticism, for they were always absolutely opposed to each other.

The Church continuously opposed those who, like the Gnostics, tried to mix Christian dogmas with foreign religions, and when they were pertinacious, excommunicated them.

(4) *Pagan mysticism produced no moral effect*. Nay, it perverted souls and toppled them over into misery, whereas by contrast, Christianity converted the world.

It is quite surprising that scientific persons wish to explain the origin of religion in this way. Indeed, the obvious disproportion between the causes proposed by it and the effect is a new confirmation of Christ's testimony.

Hence, Christ's teaching was not borrowed from others. It is something truly new and handed on for the first time by Jesus himself. {{251}} Nor is this *newness* diminished on account of the fact that Christianity was prepared through the Mosaic covenant, for by being reconciled with tradition, true and profound originality differs from the inventions wrought by innovators. And it is especially true in matters of religion, for the greatest and, indeed, true novelty must be reconciled with the greatest *antiquity* of religion, for there must be but one true religion for all men, be it imperfectly or perfectly established. Hence, Christ said, "I did not come to do away with the old but, rather, to fulfill it."

General conclusion: Christ's teaching, considered (1) in itself in relation to its perfection, harmony, and sublimity, (2) in Christ's manner of preaching, with his loftiest authority, simplicity, humility, anointing, and efficacy, (3) and in the manner in which it was established—namely, without human preparation—leads us to say that this doctrine appears to be, and indeed is rightly said to be, supernatural.

This conclusion is already *morally certain*, inasmuch as on the basis of what has been said, men cannot morally, by their own powers, without the divine aid of grace, arrive at the full array of truths of natural religion.[61] *A fortiori*, the one man Jesus of Nazareth, who never was able to spend time studying in schools of science, was not able, without extraordinary help coming from God, to discover such a religious doctrine that so fully satisfies all the aspirations of [our] rational nature, that so perfectly and harmoniously joins together that which is loftiest and that which is lowliest (the supernatural and the natural, justice and mercy, contemplation and action, the old and the new), that, finally, has so profound an influence upon mind and soul, indeed, renewing society.

The origin of such a doctrine *does not need to be explained through natural causes*. Nay, looking on it, we can see an *effect that properly belongs to God*—namely, the extraordinary harmony of things separated by the

---

[61] See vol. 1, ch. 13, a. 2, §2.

greatest of distance, which God alone can reconcile with each other, just as, in himself, the attributes of utter mercy and infinite justice are reconciled. Indeed, this doctrine is a resplendent expression and image of the Deity. Hence, according to St. Thomas, "it is more marvelous" than miracles of the physical order that "simple men, filled with the gift of the Holy Spirit, arrived, in an instant, at the greatest of wisdom and eloquence."[62] Such is the general position held by apologetes.[63]

---

[62] *SCG* I, ch. 6, §1.

[63] See Cardinal Zigliara, *Propaedeutica ad sacram theologiam*, bk. 2, ch. 9, 179: "Morally speaking, it is impossible that the man who speaks from himself, that is, solely from the light of his reason, would always and in all things reach the truth. . . . Add to this the preaching of the loftiest truths, which are above the thoughts of man."

Perrone teaches in *Praelectiones theologicae, De vera religione*, pt. 1, prop. 2: "The excellence and holiness of the evangelical doctrine confirms the divine and supernatural mission of Christ in an unassailable manner."

And Hurter, *Theologia generalis, Apologia religionis christianae*, thesis 15: "However, already a sufficient origin of so wise a religion cannot be assigned outside of a divine origin, one which does not come from some human teaching, since nothing so pure and sublime appeared before Christ. It came from no human institution or study, for Christ did not have such learning [*litteras non didicerit*]. Hence, unless we wish to admit a causeless effect, this doctrine can have no other cause than what our most holy master assigned to it when saying to the amazement of the Jewish people: 'My doctrine is not my own but, rather, is that of Him who sent me.'"

Likewise, see Hettinger, *Apologie du christianisme*, vol. 3.

Similarly, see Auguste Nicolas, *Études philosophiques sur le christianisme* (Paris, 1846); Monsabré, *Exposition du dogme catholique*, Lent 1879, 45th conference.

Christian Pesch, [S.J.,] also teaches in *Praelectiones dogmaticae*, vol. 1, prop. 23, 177: "A doctrine can be so excellent that its origin could not be explained by natural conditions, therefore meaning that recourse must be had to divine revelation. Now, such is true for Christ's doctrine. . . . Thus, since this doctrine not only infinitely surpasses pagan philosophy but also contains many things that are clearly opposed to the earlier opinions held by men, the only sufficient reason that can be assigned to it is divine revelation. However, although it is not easy in this way to demonstrate with certitude the divinity of the Christian religion, nonetheless, this argument is of great assistance in helping to dispose the minds of men so that they may then more easily admit its divine origin."

Ottiger holds, in *Theologia fundamentalis*, bk. 1, thesis 30: "Christ's dogma is so worthy of God that it openly bears witness to its divine origin, at least in a very probable manner. Indeed, it is most probable that Christ did not discover it solely through His own genius, nor did He accept it from the gentiles, nor did He draw the whole of it from the sacred books of His own people." However, in another place, Ottiger teaches in thesis 31: "The divine origin of Jesus Christ's mission and doctrine *is morally certain* on the authority (and holiness) of Christ Himself bearing witness to Himself." And in thesis 37, he shows that the divinity of Christ's revelation is confirmed by its astounding efficacy in emending the morals of people. Along these lines also see André Bovet, *De la science de Jésus Christ comme argument apologétique* (Fribourg: Fribourg imprimerie de l'oeuvre de Saint-Paul, 1895), 86–87.

With the authors cited above, we believe that the sublimity of Christ's doctrine is not insuf-

{{252}} All men do not perceive the power of this argument, but this is *on account of the exceedingly great sublimity* of Christ's teaching, not on account of its insufficiency.

Finally, *it is metaphysically impossible* that divine providence would permit this doctrine, which is so fruitful in all good things, to have been founded on an error as regards its divine origin. For God can permit evil to be done only in order to draw something better therefrom. Now, no greater good can be drawn from the aforementioned error. On the contrary, error would receive the greatest of commendations if the aforementioned fruits were attributed to it.

The value of this conclusion will be clear after we resolve the objections that can be raised against it. However, if it seems to be non-apodictic to some, being only quite probable, nonetheless, it will help many to dispose their minds so that they might more willingly consider the other motives of credibility.

§3. Objections

First objection: There is something unknown that is hidden in the origin of Christian doctrine, as the modernists profess. In order to explain this fact, Catholics have recourse to divine revelation, but this is only an explanatory hypothesis, not a certain conclusion.

Response: We do not have recourse to revelation as to a hypothesis that we have invented. Christ himself affirmed that his teaching was revealed by God, and his testimony is perfectly confirmed by his holiness and wisdom, which appear in a miraculous way in his sublime doctrine. He who preached to men such a doctrine so uprightly and holily *manifestly could not have been* insanely deceived or looking to proudly deceive us concerning the divine origin of his teaching. And how could an ignorant Jewish carpenter, by his natural powers, come up with a doctrine that so greatly surpasses all the ideas proposed by philosophers, even the greatest of them?

---

ficient for bringing forth a certain argument [on behalf of the credibility of revelation]. Even independent of Jesus's holiness, it gives moral certitude, and not only probability, concerning its divine origin, especially if one takes into consideration this teaching's efficacy in bringing about the reformation of morals. However, in general, it is considered together with the holiness / moral authority of Christ the teacher.

[Trans. note: Slight issues in the final sentence in Hurter required consultation with Hugo Hurter, *Theologia Dogmaticae compendium in usum studiosorum theologiae*, vol. 1 (Innsbruck: Libraria Academica Wagneriana, 1876), 57. Note, also, that on consultation with other uses of "citra" in the same volume, Hurter seems to use it in a somewhat extended sense of meaning "without" (as an extension of "short of having").]

It is urged, however: It would suffice to admit that Jesus was endowed with a splendid natural genius.

Response: As we already said, this explanation would be contrary to Jesus's own testimony. Moreover, experience bears witness to the fact that, unless one experiences favorable circumstances of place, time, and education, a splendid genius does not suffice for arriving at great knowledge of the truth. {{253}} Finally, eminent genius for manifesting natural truths of religion is still a natural gift of God, but a superior inspiration to preach the loftiest divine mysteries is a supernatural gift.

Second objection: The preceding conclusion only holds negatively, on the basis of the impossibility of preaching Christ's doctrine through natural causes.

Response: This would already be a sufficient argument, for this doctrine needs to have a cause. Now, if natural causes do not suffice, then a supernatural one is required. However, as we said, in this doctrine we also find a positive effect that is proper to God alone—namely, the marvelous reconciliation of things that are utterly distant from each other, things that God alone can bring together.

Third objection: If this doctrine were so perfect, it would not be perpetually fought by countless philosophers, learned men, and lawmakers. In fact, Christianity was fought not only by utterly evil emperors like Nero and Domitian but also by noble and generous ones like Trajan and Marcus Aurelius, and so too into our own days just as in the early ages of Christianity.

Response: (1) "A countless host of people, not only the simple but also *the wisest* of men, have flocked to the Christian faith,"[64] among whom we must indeed cite the great Doctors of the Church. However, let us also be sure to recall St. Paul's words:

> For see your vocation, brethren, *that there are not many wise according to the flesh*, not many mighty, not many noble. But the foolish things of the world hath God chosen, that he may confound the wise: and the weak things of the world hath God chosen, that he may confound the strong . . . that no flesh should glory in his sight. (1 Cor 1:26–29, DR)[65]

(2) *Among the persecutors* of the Christians, *many were so perverse that their man-*

---

[64] *SCG* I, ch. 6.

[65] See H.-D. Lacordaire, 16th conference, 318: "Indeed, where would the divinity of our mission be if the only knowledge that we had was an exceptional form of the kind of knowledge that the whole world has. If our books were imprinted on each page with the mark of genius, we would be nothing more than one more human power. We must be little men, fools for Christ, because thus, people who have good sense and men of genius who also have it when they wish, will say to themselves: 'Indeed, it is quite extraordinary that these little men, after eighteen centuries, would be the masters of all things, and that we would need to gather together the powers of the world to fight against them.'"

ifest and extraordinary wickedness provide a new sign of Christianity's divinity. And this was announced by the prophets and by Christ: "The kings of the earth stood up, and the princes met together, against the Lord, and against his Christ" (Ps 2:2, DR). "Behold this child (the infant Jesus) is set for the fall and for the resurrection of many in Israel and for a sign which shall be contradicted" (Luke 2:34, DR). "Do not think that I came to send peace upon earth: I came not to send peace, but the sword. For I came to set a man at variance against his father, and the daughter against her mother, and the daughter in law against her mother in law. . . . He that loveth father or mother more than me, is not worthy of me" (Matt 10:34–37, DR). Indeed, he did not come to give worldly peace but, rather, a superior form of peace, which requires self-denial: "The brother also shall deliver up the brother to death, and the father the son. . . . And you shall be hated by all men for my name's sake: but he that shall persevere unto the end, he shall be saved" (Matt 10:21–22, DR).[66]

{{254}} (3) *Among the adversaries* of the Christian faith, those who seem to be more noble and more generous, such as Marcus Aurelius, considered the propagation of Christianity and the destruction of paganism as representing the *overthrowing of the empire.* Moreover, *they were scandalized by Christ crucified* (Gal 5:11; 1 Cor 1:23), wishing only to admit that which is measured by reason, feeing oppressed by a loftier truth that to their eyes seemed to be foolishness. Hence, Jesus had said, "And blessed is he that shall not be scandalized in me" (Matt 11:6, DR; Luke 7:23), and "then shall many be scandalized and shall betray one another and shall hate one another" (Matt 24:10, DR). They fought Christianity because of its exceedingly great loftiness and austerity, because they do not wish to be humbly subjected to receive the sublime truth that is at once corrective and alluring. Thus, the truth and holiness of Catholicism is confirmed inasmuch as it is at once a principle of the greatest attractive force and one that is utter repellant. Given men's dispositions, if Christianity were not to produce these contradictory effects, it would not be a holy, true, and divine religion. Therefore,

---

[66] See Fr. Lacordaire, 15th conference (On the feeling of repulsion produced in the spirit by Catholic doctrine), 289–291: "Everyone knows that today the greatest majority of men of state in Europe are hostile to the Catholic religion and combat it by all the means that they have at their disposal. . . . This is also true for men of genius. . . . You know well the attacks made by the philosophers of Alexandria, then the succession of heresiarchs, Arius, Photius, and Luther. Still, this was only a prelude. I am passing rapidly over these facts in order to arrive at this capital fact, at this conspiracy of men of genius gathering together to declare war on Christianity, calling, in current language, the Son of God, before whom every knee must bend upon the earth, in heaven, and in hell, calling Him by the name '*L'infame*', gathering together all of humanity to cast down his altars, and Europe, responding to this conspiracy of unbelief, has established it into a true power. This fact is something unseen elsewhere, neither among the pagans, nor among the Muslims, nor in any other religion, no matter how paltry it may have been. It is particular to Christianity and, assuredly, I have the right to be astonished by it and to ask you as well to be so astonished."

it finds confirmation in the very fact that it is "A SIGN WHICH SHALL BE CONTRA-DICTED." *The mystery of the hatred expressed against the Christian religion confirms the mysteries of grace.* "If you had been of the world, the world would love its own: but because you are not of the world, ... therefore the world hateth you" (John 15:19, DR). On this, see Bossuet[67] and Lacordaire.[68]

{{255}} *Fourth objection*: The sublimity of Catholic doctrine can only be known under the infused light of faith and, hence, is not a motive of credibility leading one to believe.

Response: This sublimity is indeed more firmly and profoundly known by believers,

---

[67] See Bossuet, *Elevations sur les mystères*, 18th elevation: "Everything altogether lofty and simple is contradicted. Its loftiness cannot be attained. Its simplicity is disdained. One finds oneself to be vexed and lost in pride. However, the humble of heart enter into the depths of God without being bothered." And see 13th *elevation*: "What gives birth to these contradictions? 'You are from below, but I am from on high' (John 8:23). I come to bring men lofty things which surpass them, and prideful men do not wish to humble themselves in order to receive them. 'You belong to the world, but I am not of the world' (ibid.). You are of the flesh and sensual, and what I announce to you, this spiritual word, cannot enter into your spirit. You must be reborn; I must renew you; I must give you a new foundation: 'For that which is born of the flesh is flesh' (John 3:6) and one is spiritual only by being reborn and by renouncing his former life. 'The light came into the world, and men loved the darkness more than the light because their works were wicked. For he who does evil hates the light, and he does not live in the light, for fear lest his works be manifested' (John 3:19). . . . 'You cannot only hear my word' (John 8:43) because it is living, convincing, and beyond reproach. This is the great contradiction that Jesus suffered."

Also see 20th elevation (The contradictions of Christ uncover the secrets of the heart): "The secret thoughts which must be uncovered by Jesus Christ are principally those with which we deceive ourselves by believing that we are doing for God things which, in fact, we are doing only for our own interests, jealously holding on to our own authority, defending our own particular opinions. For these are the thoughts that we exert the greatest energy in hiding, since we strive to hide them from ourselves."

[68] H.-D. Lacordaire, 15th conference, 295–300: "*It is a question of knowing why Catholic doctrine is at once hated and loved*, why it is the *center of attraction and that of repulsion*. . . . This is the question. Shall we resolve it by saying that Catholic doctrine contains both good and evil, good which attracts and evil which repulses? However, when something contains both good and evil, this thing is mediocre, it is neither sovereignly loved nor sovereignly hated. It is tolerated; it is left alone, just as we allow a common man to pass by unseen. Now, humanity does not pass by Catholic doctrine. It grasps hold of it so that it may either attack it or adore it. Mankind becomes its adorer or its enemy, indeed constantly, for eighteen centuries. Once again, this is the question. . . .

"If man has an intelligent soul, he also has a corrupted heart. He loves his freedom and his vices. He impatiently suffers when he is condemned, and *given that there is nothing more perfect in all the world than Catholic doctrine, given its utterly eminent holiness, it naturally must excite against itself just as strong of a reaction as the love that it inspires and obtains.* See, good sirs, in two words, the resolution to the problem. . . . If Catholic doctrine did not produce these two contradictory phenomena, given what man is, this doctrine would not be holy, true, and divine."

but it already appears to men of good will, who diligently inquire into the saving truth, just as Christ's holiness is manifested to them in its effects.[69]

---

[69] Actual grace soliciting and arousing a good will thus precedes the grace of faith. See Clement XI, *Unigenitus Dei Filius*, nos. 26ff (Denzinger, no. 2425ff); Pius VI, *Auctorem fidei*, no. 22 (Denzinger, no. 2622).

CHAPTER NINE

Confirmation of Christ's Testimony through the Church's Miraculous Life

{{256}} The Church herself proposes her own miraculous life as being a moral miracle and fulfillment of the prophecy of Christ who established her with her visible notes (see vol. 2, ch. 5, a. 1 above). Earlier, we cited this declaration by the [First] Vatican Council: "The Church by herself, with her marvelous propagation, eminent holiness, and inexhaustible fruitfulness in everything that is good, with her catholic unity and invincible stability, is a great and perpetual motive of credibility and an irrefutable testimony of her divine mission."[1]

We draw the division of this chapter from what is said in this declaration. In short, we must consider the marvelous life of the Church according to its four causes and its effects. Indeed, (1) *her astonishing propagation*, like its apostolicity, is taken as being her efficient cause. (2) *Her extraordinary holiness* is taken as being her end, and this shines forth in her effects, especially in the perseverance of the martyrs and in her inexhaustible spiritual fecundity. (3) *Catholic unity* indicates the form and matter of the Church—namely, the social bond of her members. Finally, her *unconquered stability* corroborates all of the preceding marks (*notas*) and coincides with her apostolicity. Hence, the Catholic Church is distinguished from false churches and appears as being a moral miracle.[2]

---

[1]   [First] Vatican Council, *Dei filius*, ch. 3 (Denzinger, no. 3012).

[2]   See *SCG* I, ch. 6. Lacordaire, 29th conference. Albert de Broglie, *L'église et l'Empire romain au 4th siècle*, preliminary discourse. Paul Allard, *Le christianisme et l'Empire romain de Néron à Theodose* (Paris: Lecoffre, 1898); *Histoire des persecutions*; *La persecution de Diocletien et le triomphe de l'église*; *Dix leçons sur le martyre*. Jean Rivière, *La propagation du christianisme dans les trois premiers siècles* (Paris: Bloud, 1907). Léonce de Grandmaison, "L'expansion du christianisme d'après M. Harnack," *Etudes* (1903). Charles Journet, *L'église du verbe incarné*, vol. 1 (Paris: Desclée de Brouwer, 1941), 647–678 (Apostolicity as a sign of the true Church).

ART. 1: THE ASTONISHING PROPAGATION OF THE CHURCH

As we said in book 1, ch. 18, this argument draws its strength from the disproportion that exists between this propagation and natural causes. Now, this disproportion is made manifest through a consideration of four things: {{257}} (1) the utterly rapid way that Christianity spread, (2) the loftiness of the end obtained, (3) the great impediments it faced, and (4) the debility of natural means.

§1. The Utterly Rapid Way That Christianity Spread

We can consider this from two perspectives: (A) numerically and geographically and (B) as regards the different classes of societies that it spread to.

A. *Its numerical and geographical diffusion.* From the Acts of the Apostles, it is clear that after Pentecost, through Peter's preaching, first "approximately three thousand souls" (Acts 2:41) and then "five million men" (Acts 4:4) converted to the faith, and each day "the multitude of men and women who believed in the Lord was more increased" (Acts 5:14, DR). However, on the day when Stephen was stoned, a persecution began in the city of Jerusalem, and the believers "were dispersed through the regions of *Judah* and *Samaria* . . . and they preached the word of God" (Acts 8:1–4). Some "went about as far as Phoenicia and Cyprus and Antioch . . . and a great number believing, were converted to the Lord" (Acts 11:18–21, DR). Barnabas and Saul were sent to Antioch for a year, and "they taught a great multitude, so that at Antioch the disciples were first named Christians" (Acts 11:26, DR).

However, after this, the apostles founded churches *throughout the whole of the Roman Empire*, even *beyond the borders of the empire*. Hence, approximately twenty [*sic*] years after the Ascension (63–64), Peter writes in his letter "to the elect dispersed through *Pontus, Cappadocia, Asia, and Bithynia*" (1 Pet 1:1). At around the same time, Paul wrote to the Romans, "Your faith is spoken of in the whole world" (Rom 1:8, DR). Under Domitian, John writes in Revelation, at around the end of the first century, "to the seven churches which are in *Asia*: to *Ephesus* and to *Smyrna* and to *Pergamus* and to *Thyatira* and to *Sardis* and to *Philadelphia* and to *Laodicea*" (Rev 1:11, DR). Therefore, already before the death of the apostles, there were many Christians.

After the death of the apostles, the number of believers grew to be so great that *St. Justin, in the middle of the second century*, declared that all peoples, whether barbarian or Greek, counted among them people who raised up prayers in the name of Jesus Christ crucified.[3] And at the same time, *St. Irenaeus* testified that there were churches built in *Germany, Spain, France, in the East, Egypt, Libya, Jerusalem, and Judea.*[4] At the beginning of the third century, Tertullian wrote: "We are but of yesterday, and we have filled every place among you—cities, islands, fortresses, towns, market-places, the very camp, tribes, companies, palace, senate, forum—we have left nothing to you but the temples of your gods"[5] Others declare that nearly the greater part of Carthage is Christian.[6]

Similarly, pagan witnesses like *Tacitus*[7] speak of the "enormous multitude of Christians." *Pliny the Younger*, who was the proprietor in Bithynia, already found countless Christians.[8]

Hence, as the rationalist Harnack himself admitted,[9] at around the beginning of the fourth century, Christianity prevailed in the territories of Asia Minor, Thrace, Cyprus, and Edessa. {{258}} It diffused throughout Coele-Syria, Egypt, southern and central Italy, proconsulary Africa and Numidia, Spain, Greece, and central Gaul.

B. *Social diffusion.* The Christian religion soon diffused throughout all classes of society.

Indeed, many Christians were from among the common people, thus confirming the prophecy: "The poor will be preached to."

Hence, St. Paul writes: "For see your vocation, brethren, that there are not many wise according to the flesh, not many mighty, not many noble. But the foolish things of the world hath God chosen, that he may confound the wise: and the weak things of the world hath God chosen, that he may confound the strong" (1 Cor 1:26–27, DR). In this, Christianity differed from Greek philosophy and did not draw the proud. Hence, it is more marvelous that even the wealthy and the wise were converted to it.

There were *wealthy* numbered among the early Christians.

For example, there were the proconsul Sergius Paulus, Dionysius the Areopagite (Acts 13:12; 17:34), Titus Flavius Clemens and his family, along with many *from Caesar's house* (Phil 4:3, 22). Hence, at the time of Valerian, St. Cyprian states that there were

---

3   Justin, *Dialogue with Trypo*, no. 117 (PG 6, 749–750).
4   Irenaeus, *Adversus haereses*, 1.10.2 (PG 553ff); 3.3.2 (PG 848ff).
5   *Apology*, ch. 37, trans. S. Thelwall (PL 1, 462ff).
6   *Libellus ad scapulam*, ch. 5 (PL 704).
7   See Tacitus, *Annales*, 15.44.
8   See letter 97. On the authenticity of this letter by Pliny, see Gaston Boissier, *La fin du paganisme* [Paris: Hachette, 1903,] 383.
9   See Adolf Harnack, *Die Mission und Ausbreitung des Christentums in den ersten drei Jahrhunderten*, 2nd ed. (1906), vol. 2, bk. 4.

no few Christians numbered among the "Caesarianos."[10] In St. Paul's letters and in the Acts of the Apostles, we find a number of noble women, including Priscilla, the wife of Aquila (Acts 18:2–26; 17:4–12; 1 Cor 7:12; 11:5; Rom 16:1, 3, 7, 13, 15). Similarly, there was Pomponia Graecina,[11] and Eusebius[12] cites the wives of illustrious men, like Domitilla, Marcia, Julia Mammaea, and Severa the wife of Philip. Indeed, there is the wife and daughter of Diocletian, the wife of the prefect of Rome during the reign of Maxentius. Many suffered martyrdom for their faith.

Finally, no few *learned people* came to faith and defended it with all of their powers.

Thus, there was Dionysius the Areopagite, Apollo Alexandrinus (who in Paul's own days preached to the Corinthians), Justinus, Athenagoras, Aristides, and other apologetes. Similarly, there was Irenaeus, Tertullian, Cyprian, Clement of Alexandria, Origen, and the entire school of Alexandria. Concerning this matter, Arnobius is commonly cited: "Men endowed with so great abilities, orators, critics, rhetoricians, lawyers, and physicians, those, too, who pry into the mysteries of philosophy, seek to learn these things, despising those in which but now they trusted."[13]

On the basis of all this, we can infer that, during the first three centuries, Christianity spread very quickly throughout the whole Roman Empire and indeed even beyond the empire's borders, throughout all the orders of society. In this, it differs from Mithraism, which was defended nearly exclusively among soldiers and only in a few regions in the empire.

§2. Having Thus Spread throughout the World, Christianity Marvelously Restored Its Mores

A great number of men were converted from the defilement of vices, from crimes against nature, and from the pride of secular wisdom to chastity, humility, and poverty. And contemplating what they saw, they adhered with their whole soul to mysteries that surpass all the human intellect could understand. It is utterly marvelous how so many people in such a condition could come to so firmly *believe in such towering things, to perform such difficult tasks, and to hope in such lofty things.*[14] {{259}} Renewal came to family life, the dignity of wives, the condition of servants—nay, the whole of society was renewed in the spirit of charity and justice. (See what we say

---

10 See Cyprian, *Epistola*, 80.1.
11 Tacitus, *Annales*, 13.32.
12 Eusebius, *Historia ecclesiastica*, 6.21 and 36.
13 Arnobius, *Against the Heathens*, 2.5, trans. Hamilton Bryce and Hugh Campbell (PL 5, 816).
14 See *SCG* I, ch. 6.

below concerning the marvelous life of the Church and her inexhaustible fecundity in all good things.)

Hence, *St. Justin wrote*: "We who formerly delighted in fornication, but now embrace chastity alone. We who formerly used magical arts, dedicate ourselves to the good and unbegotten God. . . . We who hated and destroyed one another . . . now, since the coming of Christ, live familiarly with them, and pray for our enemies."[15] Likewise, *Latantius* writes:

> What the philosophers could not effect is accomplished only by divine instruction; for that only is wisdom. Were they able to persuade anyone who do not even persuade themselves of anything? . . . But what influence is exerted on the souls of men by the precepts of God, because of their simplicity and truth, is shown by daily proofs. Give me a man who is passionate, scurrilous, and unrestrained; with a very few words of God, "I will render him as gentle as a sheep." Give me one who is grasping, covetous, and tenacious; I will presently restore him to you liberal, and freely bestowing his money with full hands. Give me a man who is afraid of pain and death; he shall presently despise crosses, and fires, and the bull of Phalaris. Give me one who is lustful, an adulterer, a glutton; you shall presently see him sober, chaste, and temperate. . . . Give me a man who is unjust, foolish, an evil-doer; immediately he shall be just, and wise, and innocent: for by one laver all his wickedness shall be taken away.[16]

Eusebius also writes:

> Persians who have become His (Jesus Christ's) disciples no longer marry their mothers, nor Scythians feed on human flesh, because of Christ's word which has come even unto them, nor other races of Barbarians have incestuous union with daughters and sisters, nor do men madly lust after men and pursue unnatural pleasures, nor do those, whose practice it formerly was, now expose their dead kindred to dogs and birds. . . . The Bactrians also used to cast those who had grown old alive to the dogs. These however were customs of a former age, and are now no longer practised in the same manner, the salutary law of the power of the Gospel having alone abolished the savage and inhuman pest of all these evils.[17]

As regards all the absurd superstitions and depraved actions of the pagans before the

---

[15] Justin, *First Apology*, ch. 14, trans. Marcus Dodds and George Reith (PG 4, 348).
[16] Lactantius, *The Divine Institutes*, trans. William Fletcher, 3.26 (PL 6, 431ff).
[17] Eusebius, *Preparation for the Gospel*, trans. E. H. Gifford, 1.4 (PG 21, 39).

preaching of the Gospel, also see what St. Paul says in Romans 1:21–32.

Moreover, we have an utterly irrefutable testimony of the virtue of Christians in the enormous number who suffered martyrdom during this time, as we will discuss below in relation to the holiness of the Church.

Pagan writers themselves spoke of the eminent virtue of Christians. Pliny the Younger did in his famous letter to Trajan concerning the Christians.[18] Similarly, see Lucian's remarks in what he wrote about the death of Peregrinus.[19] The emperor himself, Julianus, praised the kindness of Christians toward foreigners, the way they took care to bury the dead, and the sanctity of their life.

This emendation of morals, not only in this or that man but in so great a host and *in the midst of all peoples, is utterly marvelous*, especially if it is compared with the virtues of the Gentiles. Thus, Vincenzo Maria Gatti, O.P., writes:

> Among the pagan philosophers, moderation, perseverance, mercy, justice, fortitude, prudence, and temperance are all praised very highly. But they found themselves in the midst of great excesses and defects that should be fled, things which at that time were common both for the common pagan man and even for citizens. {{260}} No virtue was ordered to the glory of God, none to please Him, none to the ultimate end which is beyond time and this world. What pagan fortitude can compare with the fortitude of the martyrs? What benevolence can be compared with Christian love? What temperance can be compared with Christian parsimony and sobriety, along with its incredible contempt for pleasures? What Fabrician frugality can be compared with the contempt for riches expressed by countless Christians, who distributed their wealth to the poor so that they may speed on more quickly to Christ? Humility, which is found in man's full subjection to God the Creator and is the foundation of all the virtues, was utterly unknown. The same must be said of charity, without which no saving virtue can be established, that virtue from which all others receive their form. Christianity filled the world with this virtue.[20]

§3. The Impediments to Christianity Were Utterly Great

Christianity faced the greatest of impediments (A) as regards the acceptance of its doctrine and worship, (B) as regards the reformation of morals, and (C) especially in the mist of the tyranny of persecutors.

---

18 Trajan, *Libr.*, 10, ep. 97.

19 See Lucian, *Opera* (ed. Dindorf), 691, no. 12.

20 Vincenzo Maria Gatti, *Institutiones apologetico-polemicae de veritate ac divinitate religionis et ecclesiae catholicae* (Rome: Typographia Forensi, 1867), vol. 3, 217.

A. *Regarding the acceptance of Christian doctrine and worship,* the words of St. Paul are of importance: "But we preach Christ crucified: unto the Jews indeed a stumbling block, and unto the Gentiles foolishness" (1 Cor 1:23, DR).

(a) Indeed, the *Jews* were expecting a temporal Messiah and did not wish to adore as true God this Jesus whom they had crucified. They were scandalized by Christ's weakness. Moreover, they did not wish to do away with the rites and ceremonies of the Law of Moses to which they were extremely devoted.

(b) However, *to the Gentiles,* Christianity was foolishness, for it seemed contrary to human wisdom that God would die and that a just and wise man would expose himself voluntarily to the most disgraceful kind of death. Hence, in the middle of the Areopagus, some of the Greek philosophers, hearing St. Paul speaking about Christ's Resurrection, "indeed mocked; But others said: We will hear thee again concerning this matter" (Acts 17:32, DR). Moreover, in the case of the Gentiles, the empty likenesses that they had heretofore used in honor of the gods had to be burned up, their temples overturned, and the sacrifices and superstitions to which they had become accustomed over the course of many centuries had to be fought with the greatest hostility.

B. *Regarding the reformation of morals,* although Christian ethics is admirable in itself, it was offensive to corrupt pagan society, for it proclaimed open war on all forms of passionate excess and pride. Indeed, it repressed wicked movements of the soul, commanded bodily mortification, gave preference to poverty over wealth, preached self-contempt, commanded love of enemies, and ordered that one must forgive the injuries done to them. It taught all people: "Love not the world, nor the things which are in the world. ... For all that is in the world is the concupiscence of the flesh and the concupiscence of the eyes and the pride of life" (1 John 2:15–16, DR). All of this was absolutely contrary to the opinions held by the philosophers and to the morals of the people more broadly. Among the Epicureans the most foul of vices thrived, and the Stoics, who despised worldly pleasures, held pride to be virtue and humility a vice.

C. *Persecutions. The pagans,* so greatly devoted as they were to the worship of the gods, *were accustomed to tolerating foreign superstitions,* which they were able to associate with their own ancestral worship;[21] *however, the Christian religion, exclusive of all others, displeased them greatly.* {{261}} The

---

[21] See Acts 17:22–23 (DR): "But Paul, standing in the midst of the Areopagus, said: Ye men of Athens, I perceive that in all things you are too superstitious. For passing by and seeing your idols, I found an altar also, on which was written: *To the Unknown God.*"

emperors, who were worshiped as gods, were not able to tolerate a religion that openly condemned such a cult. *Hence, throughout the whole world, for three centuries, they strove to destroy Christianity through utterly savage persecutions.* According to the law, among those Christians who did not wish to offer incense to the emperor, "the humbler are to be thrown to the beasts or burned alive; the more upright [*honestiores*] are to be beheaded."[22] Christianity was prohibited as being a new illicit religion, or as Pliny said, "a pertinacious, inflexible obstinacy, a wicked and immoderate superstition."[23] Sacred Scripture was held as being a book of magic and, according to the law,[24] "those who are devoted to the magical arts are to receive the worst of punishments, namely, by being thrown to the beasts or undergoing crucifixion. However, magicians themselves are to be burned alive."[25] Now, Jesus had foretold these persecutions: "And you shall be hated by all men for my name's sake. . . . And fear ye not them that kill the body, and are not able to kill the soul" (Matt 10:22, 28, DR). "If you had been of the world, the world would love its own: but because you are not of the world, but I have chosen you out of the world, therefore the world hateth you" (John 15:19, DR). Christians bore in mind the words of St. Paul: "*We suffer persecution: but are not forsaken. We are cast down but we perish not*" (2 Cor 4:9, DR). "Who then shall separate us from the love of Christ? Shall tribulation? Or distress? Or famine? Or nakedness? Or danger? Or persecution? Or the sword? . . . But in all these things we overcome, because of him that hath loved us" (Rom 8:35, 37, DR). These persecutions did not snuff out Christianity but instead made manifest its utterly great vigor. Nay, as we will discuss below, the number of Christians grew all the more as they suffered persecutions.

Therefore, the impediments faced by Christianity in relation to its teaching and the reformation of morals that it required were utterly great and extraordinary, all while it was being persecuted for its first three centuries of existence.

§4. The Natural Means That Christianity Employed Were Weak

A. Christianity did not spread *by violence of arms, nor by the promise of delights*—as St. Paul writes, "For the weapons of our warfare are not carnal

---

22 Paulus, *Sententia*, 5.39.1.
23 Pliny, *Epistulae*, 10.97.
24 Paulus, *Sententia*, 5.28.17.
25 Also see Paul Allard, *Histoire des persecutions*, 2nd [ed.,] vol. 1–5 (Paris: Lecoffre, 1892ff); *Le christianisme et l'Empire romain*, 4th ed. (Paris: Lecoffre, 1898).

but mighty to God" (2 Cor 10:4, DR)—but, rather, in opposition to allurements of the flesh and fear of torments.

B. *Nor did it spread by natural eloquence or wisdom.* What erudition,
philosophy, or eloquence did the apostles have? As St. Augustine said:

> And the very manner in which the world's faith was won is found
> to be even more incredible if we consider it. Men uninstructed in
> any branch of a liberal education, without any of the refinement
> of heathen learning, unskilled in grammar, not armed with dialec-
> tic, not adorned with rhetoric, but plain fishermen, and very few
> in number—these were the men whom Christ sent with the nets
> of faith to the sea of this world, and thus took out of every race so
> many fishes, and even the philosophers themselves, wonderful as
> they are rare. . . . And if the world has put faith in a small number
> of men, of mean birth and the lowest rank, and no education, it is
> because the divinity of the thing itself appeared all the more mani-
> festly in such contemptible witnesses.[26]

St. Paul himself wrote to the Corinthians: "And I, brethren, when I came
to you, came not in loftiness of speech or of wisdom, declaring unto you
the testimony of Christ. {{262}} For I judged not myself to know anything
among you, but Jesus Christ: and him crucified. *And I was with you in weakness and in fear and in much trembling.* And my speech and my preaching
was not in the persuasive words of human wisdom, but in shewing of the
Spirit and power, that your faith might not stand on the wisdom of men, but
on the power of God" (1 Cor 2:1–5, DR).

Conclusion. The disproportion between the use of such natural means
and the marvelous propagation of Christianity is manifestly clear. Thus, we
must conclude, with St. Thomas:

> And, what is most miraculous of all, in the midst of the tyranny of
> persecutors, an innumerable host, not only of the simple but also
> of the wisest of men, flocked to the Christian faith. In this faith,
> things exceeding every human intellect are preached, the pleasures
> of the flesh are restrained, and it is taught that all things that are
> in the world are to be held in contempt. In order for the minds of
> mortals to assent to such things this involves both *the greatest of
> miracles* and a manifest work of divine inspiration so that, spurning

---

[26] Augustine, *City of God*, 22.5, trans. Marcus Dods (PL 41,756).

visible things, men should only desire invisible ones. . . . Indeed, it would be more marvelous than all signs if the world were led by simple and humble men without miraculous signs to believe such difficult things, to perform such difficult actions, and to have so lofty a hope.[27]

Therefore, such an effect could only come from an extraordinary intervention by God, who alone can interiorly move man's intellect and will to such lofty things. However, God cannot spread error by way of a special action, above all in a matter of religion. Therefore, like a kind of divine seal, the marvelous propagation of Christianity confirms its divine origin with utter certainty. In this way, we have a confirmation for the words of St. Paul: "But the foolish things of the world hath God chosen, that he may confound the wise: and the weak things of the world hath God chosen, that he may confound the strong . . . that no flesh should glory in his sight" (1 Cor 1:27–29, DR). The marvelous conversion of the world is a greater miracle than the resurrection of someone from the dead, for it is the resurrection of the world itself.

§5 Resolution of Objections

Rationalists contend that Christianity's propagation came from natural causes (both intrinsic and extrinsic ones), taking up anew the argument that was made once upon a time by the English historian *Edward Gibbon*.[28]

A. According to them, the *intrinsic* natural causes of Christianity's propagation are (1) the obvious truth of Christian ethics and its purity of life; (2) the promise of a future life; and (3) the zeal with which Christians propagated their religion as the only true one that is necessary for salvation, along with their strict discipline.

Response to the first objection:[29] *Christian doctrine* is not evident in all ways. It contains mysteries that are obscure and incomprehensible. Its precepts are difficult for the intellect and, indeed, even more so for the will, while its counsels are utterly difficult. Likewise, the purity of the Christian life did not naturally convert men of degenerate morals, especially during the persecution of believers.

---

[27] *SCG* I, ch. 6. And, as St. Augustine had said, in *City of God*, 22.5: "If you do not believe that miracles were performed . . . this one great miracle suffices for us, that the entire world believed without any miracles."

[28] See Edward Gibbon, *The Decline and Fall of the Roman Empire*, ch. 15. Also see Harnack, *Die Mission und Ausbreitung des Christentums in den ersten drei Jahrunderten*, 73.

[29] As regards the resolution to these objections, see Gatti, *Institutiones apologetico-polemicae*, vol. 3, 192ff.

Response to the second objection: *The promise of a future life* does not suffice without the special aid of God, for many men are more moved to visible things in the present than they are to invisible things in the future. {{263}} Therefore, other contemporaneous religions and philosophical systems that taught the immortality of the soul did not manage to spread very far. Moreover, the Christian religion not only preached the eternity of the blessed life for the good but also preached that eternal punishment awaits the wicked, something that is a great mystery that remains unbelievable for many.

Response to the third objection: How were the Jews and pagans led to believe *that Christianity is the only true religion* if they did not see evident signs of its truth? How would the Jews desert their religion in order to embrace Christianity, toward which they were so hostile? How would the Gentiles admit "the foolish preaching" of Christians?

B. However, rationalists *insist* that many *extrinsic* natural causes were also at hand at the same time. (1) There was the gathering of peoples under the single authority of the Roman Empire, thus enabling the Christian religion to easily propagate itself through paths open in every direction. (2) Then there was the insufficiency of philosophy at that time. (3) Finally, there were sometimes wars, as well as the long-lasting ravaging that allowed countless barbarians into the empire, and thereafter, they took on the name of being Christians.

Response to the first objection: The size of the Roman Empire did indeed make the propagation of Christianity easier. Nay, we hold that it was ordered to precisely this end by divine providence. However, it also made the destruction of Christianity easier, as well as the propagation of Stoicism, which was embraced by a number of emperors.

Response to the second objection: Nor should we exaggerate the decline of philosophy during this time, for the Pythagorean, Platonic, and Stoic doctrines remained among some learned men. Nay, especially in the century of Anthony, Marcus Aurelius, and other leaders who were honored with the name "pious," Stoicism was held in the highest esteem, being honored and protected by the emperors themselves. Nonetheless, never did Stoicism, nor any other philosophical school, penetrate into the whole of society. However, Christianity overshadowed these schools and led the whole of paganism into contempt.

Response to the third objection: When the barbarians, who brought the Roman Empire to ruin, embraced Christianity, the latter was already spread out quite broadly within the bounds of the Roman Empire, as well as outside of it. Indeed, they came to the Church of Christ as did the Romans and Greeks, on account of the motives of credibility—namely, miracles, the sublimity of its doctrine, and the holiness and heroic fortitude of its martyrs.

And yet *rationalists continue to insist*: The words of ecclesiastical writers, especially St. Irenaeus and Tertullian, must be read as using rhetorical amplifications that were quite common at that time. Therefore, they prove very little, or even nothing, for the quickness and divinity of the propagation of Christianity.

Response: Even if it were admitted that Christian writers sometimes wrote *in a rhetorical manner*, nonetheless, the fact is their testimony has the greatest of strength, as is

CHRIST'S TESTIMONY THROUGH THE CHURCH'S MIRACULOUS LIFE

clear on two heads. First of all, there is the unanimous character of testimony from the Patristic era, which itself agrees with pagan accounts, as we discussed above. Moreover, there is the aim proposed by these Fathers themselves, for on this matter, we are not adducing the works of the Fathers aimed at preaching to the people but rather are concerned with the Fathers who narrated facts to the emperors (as did Tertullian, St. Justin, and others) or those who took this up as a proof offered against heretics, as St. Irenaeus did against Valentinus.[30]

Final objection: The fact of quick propagation is something common to Islam and other false religions. Therefore, an argument drawn from the quick propagation of a religion has no weight.

Response: Islam (as St. Thomas shows in *SCG* I, ch. 6) and other pseudo-religions[31] were propagated by the authority of rulers, using all sorts of human assistance, like violence, shrewdness, honors, wealth, and the coaxing of illicit pleasures. {{264}} By contrast, Christian religion restrained fleshly desires, fought against the spirit of worldliness, and notwithstanding the violence of persecutors, penetrated into the whole of society. Thus were fulfilled the ancient prophecies, which we will discuss at greater length later: "Arise, be enlightened, O Jerusalem: for thy light is come, and the glory of the Lord is risen upon thee. . . . And the Gentiles shall walk in thy light . . . : thy sons shall come from afar, and thy daughters shall rise up at thy side. Then shalt thou see, and abound, and thy heart shall wonder and be enlarged, when the multitude of the sea shall be converted to thee" (Isa 60:1–5, DR). Likewise, we here have a confirmation of Christ's own words: "And I say to you that many shall come from the east and the west, and shall sit down with Abraham, and Isaac, and Jacob in the kingdom of heaven" (Matt 8:11, DR), and "this gospel of the kingdom shall be preached in the whole world, for a testimony to all nations" (Matt 24:14, DR). In general, the fulfillment of prophecy confirms the other motives of credibility.[32]

---

[30] See Irenaeus, *Adversus haereses*, 1.3.

[31] See our discussion below concerning how Christianity compares to Buddhism and Islam. Also see Fr. Ambroise de Poulpiquet, *L'objet integral de l'apologétique* [Paris: Bloud, 1912/1913], 263–266.

[32] See Pascal, *Pensées*, fr. 783 [*sic*]: "Everything that is great on the earth is united together: the learned, the wise, and kings. The first write, the second condemn, and the last kill. And notwithstanding all of these oppositions, these simple men, without any force, resist all of these powers, subduing even these kings, these learned men, and these wise men, removing idolatry from the whole world. And they did all of this by the power that had foretold it." And fr. 599: "While Mohammed's path of success was human, Jesus took the way of humanly perishing. And instead of concluding that since Mohammed succeeded Jesus Christ may well have succeeded, we must instead say that since Mohammed succeeded, Jesus Christ should have perished" (ed. Havet, 301). See Gavino Spanedda, *Il mistero della chiesa nel pensiero di*

Art. 2: The Extraordinary Holiness of the Church Shining Forth in Her Inexhaustible Spiritual Fecundity and Especially in the Perseverance of the Martyrs

State of the Question—Already above (in bk. 1, ch. 17, vol. 2), when we speculatively discussed the value of the motives of credibility, we showed *that extraordinary and manifest holiness is a divine sign* because it can only come from God. Indeed, holiness is a virtue implying perfect purity from worldly things and utterly firm union with God, ordering all of the acts of the virtues to God. Now, the order of agents must correspond to the order of ends. Therefore, holiness can only come from God, and extraordinary holiness comes from God, extraordinarily intervening in the world.

In the same place, we enumerated *the signs of heroic holiness*: that it promptly, easily, and regularly performs difficult deeds that exceed the common powers of men; that the connection / harmony of all the virtues (even those that seem utterly dissimilar, like great prudence and remarkable meekness) would appear in charity and prudence.

However, after this (in vol. 2, bk. 2, ch. 5), when we discussed Christ's testimony, we saw *that Christ willed his Church to be manifest and outstanding in such holiness*. In other words, the Church must continually have in herself the principles and efficacious means for producing eminent holiness—that is, superior virtues in many of her members, and, in some, heroic virtues that manifestly surpass the natural moral powers of men.

{{265}} Now, however, we must show that this eminent holiness exists in *the Catholic Church* inasmuch as (1) *she always provides to all the principles and means of salvation*, (2) *she shines forth with the heroic perseverance of the martyrs*, (3) *she ceaselessly brings forth great saints*, (4) *and she is fruitful in all good things*.

§1. The Church Provides the Principles and Means of Holiness for All

This is manifest as regards the doctrine, worship, and laws of the Church.[33]

Sant'Agostino (Sassari: Cordella, 1944), 59–100 (The Church: Mother of Saints, One, Catholic, and the Ark of Salvation).

[33] In his *De symbolo apostolorum*, St. Thomas shows the causes of the Church's holiness, which comes forth from Christ's holiness and from the indwelling of the Trinity. Thus, from on high, we must treat of the holiness of the Church in the properly theological treatise on the Church that must be placed after the treatises on the Incarnation and the Redemption, following the order of the Creed.

Thus, Cardinal Juan de Torquemada, O.P., in his *Summa de ecclesia*, bk. 1, ch. 9, theolog-

A. *As regards doctrine.* The Roman Catholic Church,[34] today, as in the first centuries, teaches *the whole doctrine* of Christ as it is found in Scripture and tradition. This is not difficult to see merely by reviewing the writings of the apostolic Fathers, who openly hand on Catholic dogmas that are denied by Protestants. The Church forever has defended and set forth the integrity of this sublime doctrine, and it is like a *peak of truth* between errors that are opposed to each other. (For example, it is set between Monophysitism and Nestorianism as regards Christ, between Arianism and Sabellianism as regards the Trinity, between Pelagianism and Jansenism as regards grace, and between rigorism and laxism as regards matters of conscience.) Nay, the Church has had to fight against the most powerful of princes in order to preserve the *integrity of the evangelical law,* for example, as regards the union of marriage. By contrast, the pseudo-reformers taught that there is no free will, spoke of the horrid notion of a positive decree of reprobation not based upon foreseen demerits, and held that justification is through faith alone with works being utterly useless, while likewise confirming the divorce of princes. Moreover, the Church always has proposed evangelical *counsels,* self-denial, and the way of the cross to nobler souls, whereas Luther and his disciples, condemning virginity and drawing back from mortification and self-denial, rejected the counsels.

B. *As regards worship.* The Church preserves the *sacrifice of the Mass,* in which, according to Scripture and Tradition, "the same Christ who offered Himself once in a bloody manner on the altar of the Cross is contained and is offered in an unbloody manner"[35] so that the merits of the Passion may be applied to us and so that we may continually experience the fruit of the Redemption. Likewise, the Church preserves the seven *sacraments,* which according to the same testimony contain and confer the grace that they signify: Penance reconciles sinners with God and remits their sins; Eucharistic Communion is spiritual food for the soul and a

---

ically discusses the causes of the Church's holiness and, in chs. 10 and 11, resolves objections against it. In ch. 12, he expresses disapproval for the way that certain people speak of the Church's holiness, showing that integrity of faith does not suffice for calling a Church holy but, rather, requires that there be effects of holiness in many of the faithful, even if not all of them are good.

[34] [Trans. note: As noted in the translator's introduction in the first volume, this dated expression potentially can be read in line with a distorted ecclesiology that would implicitly reduce the whole of Catholicity to Roman Catholicity, making all the various *sui iuris* Churches mere branches of the Roman Church. For the sake of flow and consistency, I have left this phrase as he has written it, though it would be better articulated "the One Church, in union with the pope of Rome."]

[35] Trent, *Decree on the Sacrifice of the Mass,* ch. 2 (Denzinger, no. 1743).

pledge of future glory. Frequently, she commends *prayer* and other acts of worship, without either the excesses of superstition or disdain for external worship.

By contrast, Protestants reject the sacrifice of the Mass and nearly all of the sacraments. They preserve Baptism and a commemoration of the Last Supper, but only as mere signs, not as founts of grace. Worship, properly so-called, deprived of every kind of sacrifice, remains frigid so that believers gradually abandon their churches and establish new sects or fully fall into naturalism. {{266}} However, certain sects acknowledge the defects of Protestant worship and imitate Catholic worship.

C. *The precepts of the Church* manifestly foster the fulfilling of the divine law. Such is clear in the precept to hear Mass, to receive Communion annually, as well as in those concerned with fasting and abstinence. Therefore, the Church provides the principles and means of holiness to all.

§2. The Church's Extraordinary Holiness Shines Forth in the Heroic Perseverance of the Martyrs

As apologetes commonly note, when we consider this matter, we must take into consideration historical testimony concerning (1) the *number of martyrs*, not only in the first centuries but also in those that followed, (2) their *condition*, (3) *the motive* for the sake of which they died, (4) *the kind of torments* they underwent physically and morally, and (5) their *heroic patience*. In this way, we can gather together what is historically certain concerning the four causes of martyrdom so that we may thereby show the disproportion that exists between natural human powers and the heroic perseverance of the martyrs, which manifests an extraordinary intervention of God giving them aid.[36]

(1) *The number of martyrs.* From the year AD 64 under Nero until 313, when Constantine promulgated the Edict of Milan, great persecutions raged against the Christians. Normally, they are numbered as being ten, though Lactantius reduces them to six. There were also many local persecutions. According to tradition and history, there were countless martyrs. The first voice raised in contradiction appeared in 1684. H[enry] Dodwell contended that there were few martyrs. In his work, *De paucitate martyrum*, he intended to show that the persecutions were not general in nature and that Christians generally fled from them. Thierry Ruinart, in his work, *Acta primorum martyrum sincera*, refuted these assertions and confirmed the ancient

---

[36] See De Poulpiquet, *L'objet integral de l'apologétique*, 148–187 (The witness of the martyrs).

testimony of the Fathers and pagan authors by making use of recently found documents, especially from the catacombs. Hence, rationalists themselves today admit that the number of martyrs was utterly great.[37] *We can certainly say that there were many thousands for Rome alone.*[38]

According to Tacitus,[39] under Nero in AD 64 *a huge multitude* of Christians underwent martyrdom. Under Trajan (98–117), even after the edict ordering that only Christians who were accused were to be punished, there were many martyrs, as Eusebius relates.[40] According to the latter,[41] under Marcus Aurelius (161–180) *an almost countless number of martyrs* shone forth *throughout the world.* Likewise, he says that under the persecution at the time of Severus (193–211), martyrdoms occurred throughout all of the churches, especially that of Alexandria.[42] According to St. Dionysius of Alexandria, the same can be said for the Decian persecution.[43] Especially under Diocletian and Maximian (284–305) the persecution was more ferocious for a number of years, and *Christians were burned up together in groups,* as Lactantius,[44] Eusebius,[45] and Sulpicius Severus[46] all relate. In the catacombs we find inscriptions like "Marcella and the 550 Martyrs of Christ," "150 Martyrs of Christ,"[47] and similar. Cyprian affirmed that the number of Christian martyrs was beyond counting.[48]

{{267}} Moreover, as rationalists acknowledge, the Christians who did not perish needed the greatest fortitude in order to embrace and preserve their faith throughout these persecutions.

Finally, there were many martyrs in Persia (190,000 Christians perished under King Shapur II)[49] and so too among the Muslims, as well as more recently among the Japanese, the Chinese, the Vietnamese, and most recently in Asia and Africa.[50] Without cease, the Church has borne

---

[37] See Boissier, *La fin du paganisme*, vol. 1, 393: "Even supposing that at each time and in each particular place only a few gathered victims perished, they would form a considerable number."

[38] According to Roman martyrology, there were 13,825 martyrs for Rome alone.

[39] See Tacitus, *Annales*, 15.43–45.

[40] See Eusebius, *Historia ecclesiastica*, 3.33.

[41] See ibid., 5.1.

[42] See ibid., 6.1.

[43] See ibid., 7.2.

[44] Lactantius, *De morte persecute.*, ch. 16: "The whole world was shaken, and besides Gaul, from the East to the West three savage beasts raged."

[45] See Eusebius, *Historia ecclesiastica*, 8.3–13.

[46] Sulpicius Severus, *Historia sacra*, 2.32.

[47] P. Allard, *Rome souterraine*, 216.

[48] Cyprian, *De exortatione martyrii*, ch. 11

[49] See Sozomen, *Historia ecclesiastica*, 2.14 (PG 67, 970).

[50] See Edmond Le Blant, *Les persécuteurs et les martyrs aux premiers siècles de notre ère* (Paris: Ernest Leroux, 1893), 343.

witness through the shedding of blood.

(2) *Condition of the martyrs.* They were not only *uncultured* and ignorant people, like Theodotus and Serenus, but also included *nobles like* Flavius Clemens, Apollonius, and *learned men* like Justin, Irenaeus, and Cyprian. Not only did they include *vigorous males* like Victor, Sebastian, and Mauritius but also *women* like Perpetua, Cecilia, Agatha, the slave women Blandina and Potamiana, as well as *old men* like Polycarp and both Simeons—nay, also including *boys* and *girls*, like Tarcisius, Quiricus, Eulalia, and Agnes.

(3) *The motive* for which they were killed was *religion*, or piety, in order to preserve their devotion to God and *faith in Christ the Son of God*.[51] Indeed, they were not killed for love of the world, nor for some advantage, nor for wealth, nor honors, nor for any worldly allurement but, rather, properly speaking, for their Christian faith, indeed, as atheists[52] because they did not wish to worship the gods of paganism. Thus, they were accused as though their religion were a form of magic and the cause of various calamities.[53] As Tertullian attests, "If the Tiber rises as high as the city walls, if the Nile does not send its waters up over the fields, if the heavens give no rain, if there is an earthquake, if there is famine or pestilence, straightway the cry is, 'Away with the Christians to the lion!'"[54] Such was often the cry of the Roman people, who enjoyed the sight of such cruel spectacles.

Indeed, the emperors sometimes persecuted Christians *for political reasons*—namely, for the preservation of the empire. Nay, sometimes, they did so in order to cover up their crimes, as did Nero after the fire of Rome.

---

[51] As St. Thomas says in *ST* II-II, q. 124, a. 5: "Martyrs bear this name for they are, as it were, witnesses, for by enduring bodily suffering to the point of death they bear witness to the truth. Now, they do not bear witness to any truth whatsoever but, rather, to *the truth which is in accord with piety*, the truth that was made known to us by Christ. Thus, Christ's martyrs are said to be, as it were, His witnesses. Now this kind of truth is *the truth of faith*. However, the truth of faith includes not only inward belief in the heart but also outward profession, which is expressed not only by the words by means of which one confesses his faith but also by the deeds by which a person shows that he has faith. . . . Therefore, *inasmuch as they are referred to God, all virtuous deeds are kinds of professions of the faith*, by which we come to know that God requires these works of us and rewards us for them. And *in this way they can be the cause of martyrdom*. For this reason, the Church celebrates the martyrdom of Blessed John the Baptist, who suffered death, not for refusing to deny the faith, but for criticizing adultery.

[52] As is related by Pliny, Christianity was held to be "a pertinacious, inflexible obstinacy, a wicked and immoderate superstition" (*Ep.*, 10.97), as a form of sacrilege and magic. (See Ulpian, *Digesta*, bk. 48, t. 13.6.)

[53] See Minucius Felix, *Octavius*, ch. 9.

[54] Tertullian, *Apology*, ch. 40 (trans. S. Thelwall).

However, the Christians provided a cause for their persecution and never conspired against the empire. They spent time in the military like others, fighting in a manly manner. {{268}} They kept all just laws in good conscience. However, they were Christians, and behold their crimes: They despised polytheism, did not sacrifice to the gods, and did not eat that which was burnt in offering to them. This is what their religion commanded them. And hence the emperors persecuted them *on account of religion, not for the sake of political goods.* Indeed, if someone were to deny that he was Christian, he would be sent away, but he who confessed himself to be such was condemned. Hence, Tertullian, in his *Apology*, said to the Roman emperors: "We lay this before you as the first ground on which we urge that your hatred to the name of Christian is unjust."[55] In his first apology, St. Justin says the same to Antoninus Pius.

Now, THE OBJECT *of the testimony of the martyrs was the truth of the Christian faith and the divine signs confirming this faith.* Indeed, the martyrs were *witnesses* who, in the midst of torments, preferred to die rather than to deny the Christian faith.[56] This is clear from the responses that they made during their punishment.[57] Among them, those who had not seen Christ's miracles were not, properly speaking, witnesses to these miracles but, rather, made manifest how great their certitude was in the divine origin [*divinitatem*] of Christianity. And this certitude cannot be explained unless they had been presented with utterly firm motives of credibility.

Jesus had said: "For they will deliver you up in councils, and they will scourge you in their synagogues, and you shall be brought before governors, and before kings for my sake, for a testimony to them and to the Gentiles" (Matt 10:17–18, DR) and "the hour cometh, that whosoever killeth you will think that he doth a service to God" (John 16:2, DR).

(4) *Torments.* Tyrants think up all kinds of physical and moral torments so that they might assail the perseverance of Christians and terrorize them.

PHYSICAL TORMENTS are described by Tacitus as follows: "Mockery of every sort was added to their deaths. Covered with the skins of beasts, they were torn by dogs and perished, or were nailed to crosses, or were doomed to the flames and burnt, to serve as a nightly illumination, when daylight had

---

[55] Ibid., ch. 1.

[56] Martyrdom is an act of fortitude, as regards its elicitive principle, charity as its commanding principle, and faith as its end. See *ST* II-II, q. 124, a. 1, along with no. 11 of Cajetan's commentary on art. 2. [Trans. note: Fr. Garrigou-Lagrange refers to another number as well, though it is actually missing. The text reads "in art. 2, n. et 11".]

[57] See [Henri] Leclercq, *Les martyrs*, vol. 1, [Paris: Oudin, 1903,] 52ff and vol. 2, 280ff.

expired."[58] According to apologetes[59] and historians,[60] many martyrs were condemned *to be killed by beasts.* Others were *impaled on sharp spikes.* Many were *burned upon fiery torches* or rotated upon coals *to slowly burn* on every side. Some had such *broken bones* and ruptured viscera and were so torn up on all sides that there was no more room for them to suffer injury. Now, already *all of this was suffered, even by boys and girls, as well as by the weak, indeed for long stretches of time,* for the martyrs were so subjected to suffering in the hope that, conquered by such pains, they might deny the faith.

MORAL TORMENTS were not minor affairs either. Not only were they deprived of offices, dignities, and external goods so that their entire families were cast into distress, but often, *against the profound affections of nature, they had to fight against the tears of parents, wives, or children.*[61] In them was Christ's prophecy fulfilled: "Do not think that I came to send peace upon earth: I came not to send peace, but the sword. For I came to set a man at variance against his father, and the daughter against her mother, and the daughter in law against her mother in law. And a man's enemies shall be they of his own household. {{269}} He that loveth father or mother more than me, is not worthy of me; and he that loveth son or daughter more than me, is not worthy of me" (Matt 10:34–37, DR). Indeed, many parents stayed away from their children lest they suffer. Or, by contrast, many were handed over by their parents, like Hermenegild by his father, as Christ had foretold: "Brother also shall deliver up the brother to death, and the father the son; and the children shall rise up against their parents, and shall put them to death. And you shall be hated by all men for my name's sake, but he that shall persevere unto the end, he shall be saved" (Matt 10:21–22, DR). Christian virgins knew another moral torment and were not uncommonly sent to brothels, which they abhorred more than death.

(5) *Heroic fortitude.* Formally speaking, martyrdom is an act of the virtue of fortitude,[62] which confirms man in the good of virtue, especially when the danger of death is at hand. However, fortitude principally holds fear in check (namely, by patiently suffering it), which is something more difficult than moderating one's boldness.[63] Thus, it is *a middle and peak* above vices that are opposed to each other (namely, above inordinate fear

---

[58] Tacitus, *Annals*, 15.44 (trans. Alfred John Church and William Jackson Brodribb).

[59] Tertullian, *Apology*, ch. 12; Lactantius, *The Divine Institutes*, 5.12.

[60] Eusebius, *Historia ecclesiastica*, 7.10–11.

[61] See Leclercq, *Les martyrs*, vol. 1, 126ff (The passion of St. Perpetua).

[62] See *ST* II-II, q. 124, a. 2.

[63] See *ST* II-II, q. 123, a. 6; q. 125–127.

and irrational boldness or fearlessness).[64] Moreover, fortitude is a virtue only if it is *connected with the other virtues*. For example, it must be under the direction of prudence so that it may truly confirm man in the good of virtue and not, however, in prideful obstinacy.[65] Finally, in order for fortitude to be *heroic*, it must fulfill works that exceed the common powers of men, doing so promptly, eagerly, on the occasion when they are given, frequently if necessary, and with constancy.[66]

Thus, the martyrs suffered utterly savage torture. (1) Indeed, they were not unaware of fear prior to the time of their suffering—Jesus himself *began to become frightened* and weary)[67]—but indeed prayed and pressed back against this passion. (2) They are not motivated by impetuous boldness but, rather, go to their torment *with a peaceful soul*. By contrast, certain presumptuous Christians who had announced themselves rashly were filled with fear at the time of their suffering and ended up denying the faith.[68] (3) Moreover, the fortitude of the martyrs appears as being *connected* with charity, faith, hope, prudence, justice, chastity, humility, and even *meekness*, as is clear especially from their responses, nay, like that of Jesus and of St. Stephen who *prayed for their torturers* (Acts 7:60). {{270}} (4) Finally, they hurry off *readily* to their sufferings as though they were heading off to victory, enduring them just as though they were a host of delights, not cruel torture, doing so with a joyful soul, not merely for an hour but, rather, *with constancy*, often for many days.[69] The apostles, thrown into prison and

---

[64] See *ST* I-II, q. 65.

[65] See Benedict XIV, *De canonizatione sanctorum*, bk. 3, ch. 21.

[66] See Mark 14:33.

[67] See Dom Leclercq, *Les martyrs*, vol. 1, 68–69 (The martyrdom of St. Polycarp): "Only one faltered, a Phrygian named Quintus, who recently came from his province. Looking upon the beasts, he began to tremble. And he had been the one who had urged the others to come and denounce themselves along with him. The proconsul managed to overcome him, and make him swear an oath and offer sacrifice."

[68] Allard, *Dix leçons sur le martyre*, 330: "Nothing (in the nature of the testimony rendered by true martyrs) smacks of artificial enthusiasm and overheated emotions. Theirs is not the ardor of those who morbidly look for death, such as we find in sectarians. Rather, it is the firm determination of men who have thought things out, who do not voluntarily expose themselves to danger, who are wisely self-questioning, obedient to the rules which are supported by the solicitude of religious authority but who, when faced with peril, do not falter, all the more fearless as their testimony is not given in a trifling manner, being instead, the result of all their faith, all their virtue, and all their reason."

[69] See Lactantius, *The Divine Institutes*, bk. 5, ch. 11 (trans. Fletcher): "They contend, therefore, that they may conquer and inflict *exquisite pains* on their bodies, and *avoid nothing else but that the victims may not die under the torture*. . . . But they with obstinate folly give orders that diligent care shall be given to the tortured, that their limbs may be renovated for other

being scourged, were told that they were no longer to speak of Christ, "and they indeed went from the presence of the council, rejoicing that they were accounted worthy to suffer reproach for the name of Jesus" (Acts 5:41, DR). As Sulpicius Severus recounts, "In fact, they vied with each other in rushing upon these glorious struggles, and martyrdom by glorious deaths was then much more keenly sought after than bishoprics are now attempted to be got by wicked ambition."[70] Similar testimony can be found in St. Hilary[71] and Tertullian.[72]

Commonly, the most illustrious examples are cited. *St. Ignatius of Antioch*, fearing lest the Roman Christians might impede his martyrdom, beseeched them saying:

Allow me to become food for the wild beasts, through whose instrumentality it will be granted me to attain to God. I am the wheat of God, and let me be ground by the teeth of the wild beasts, that I may be found the pure bread of Christ. Rather entice the wild beasts, that they may become my tomb, and may leave nothing of my body; so that when I have fallen asleep [in death], I may be no trouble to anyone. . . . Now, I begin to be Christ's disciple. . . . Let fire and the cross; let the crowds of wild beasts; let tearings, breakings, and dislocations of bones; let cutting off of members; let shatterings of the whole body; and let all the dreadful torments of the devil come upon me: only let me attain to Jesus Christ.[73]

Likewise, *St. Polycarp*, at the moment of his suffering, gave thanks to God for having judged him worthy of being a martyr.[74] Equally, upon being led to the place of their martyrdom, *St. Cyprian and St. Felix* gave "thanks to God."[75] *St. Irenaeus said*, "I will rejoice if you give me the opportunity to be a partaker in my Lord's sufferings."[76] *Victor*,[77] *Vincent, Theodorus*, and many others faced with the most awful of torments praised God with a ready countenance. Vincent said, "This is what I have always desired; this is what I

---

tortures, and fresh blood be supplied for punishment."

[70] Sulpicius Severus, *Sacred History*, bk. 2, ch. 32 (trans. Alexander Roberts).

[71] Hilary, *Tract. in Ps.* 65 no. 21.

[72] Tertullian, *To Scapula*, ch. 5.

[73] Ignatius of Antioch, *Letter to the Romans*, nos. 4–5 (trans. Alexander Roberts and James Donaldson). See Leclercq, *Les martyrs*, vol. 1, 50.

[74] See Polycarp, *Letter to the Church at Smyrna*, nos. 12 and 14. See Dom Leclercq, *Les martyrs*, vol. 1, 67ff.

[75] See [Thierry] Ruinart, *Acta martyrum* (ed. Verona, 1731), 310.

[76] Ibid., 357.

[77] See ibid., 260.

have sought after with all of my vows."[78] And Theodorus sang out: "I will bless the Lord at all times, with His praise ever on my lips."[79] *Lucian and Marcian*, dying under Decius, surrounded on all sides with flames, began to chant aloud hymns of thanks to God.[80] Similarly, the Forty Martyrs of Sebaste with joy hurried onward toward their suffering, filled with prayer.[81]

This heroic fortitude was not any less in the cases of women martyrs either. *SS. Perpetua, Felicity*, and their companions "set forth from prison into the amphitheater as though they were in heaven, filled with joy, and with faces shining with beauty. . . . Perpetua followed with a peaceful countenance and even gait, like a beloved matron of Christ God, casting down the lively glance of her eyes so that it might not be seen by anyone there present. Likewise, Felicity rejoiced that she had been safely brought forth, that she may go forth to do battle with the beasts."[82] Nay, in the midst of her suffering, St. Perpetua, thrown high in the air by the furious onset of a bull, was rapt in ecstasy and felt nothing.[83] *St. Claudina*, having suffered every sort of torment throughout an entire day, losing the very sense of pain, said to her astonished and exhausted torturers: "I am a Christian, and we do nothing evil."[84]

{{271}} Indeed, there were Christians who, overcome by pain, denied the faith. However, this merely makes clearer the perseverance of those who unconquerably suffered all kinds of torments for Christ. Finally, we must note *that it would have been utterly easy for the martyrs to avoid these torments.* Indeed, all it would have taken was a simple oath, and that would have sufficed. Nay, not only were they able to avoid this torture very easily, but indeed they were encouraged to do so by means of promises, flattery, and all kinds of allurements. But they spurned all of these things, preferring disgrace to honors, sufferings to delights, and poverty, want, and the loss of all goods and life itself to wealth.

(6) *All things considered, this heroic fortitude is a miracle of the moral order.* Indeed, this fortitude, connected with the other virtues, implies *heroic acts* of the *principal virtues,* frequently repeated by a wide assortment of people (men, women, and youths), *performed with eager readiness* and *constancy*, carried through *in the midst of torments* both physical and moral in character, without any hope for temporal retribution—nay, notwith-

---

[78] Ibid., 325.
[79] Ibid., 327.
[80] Leclercq, *Les martyrs*, vol. 2, 101.
[81] Ibid., vol. 2, 379.
[82] See Ruinart, *Acta martyrum*, 87; Dom Leclercq, *Les martyrs*, vol. 1, 136.
[83] Leclercq, *Les martyrs*, vol. 1, 137–8.
[84] Eusebius, *Historia ecclesiastica*, bk. 5, ch. 1; Dom Leclercq, *Les martyrs*, vol. 1, 95.

standing all sorts of worldly promises and allurements.

Now, heroic acts of the principal virtues cannot be performed so often or so readily and constantly, in the midst of the fiercest sufferings, by men of every kind of condition, age, and sex, without any human motive, unless there is present here some extraordinary intervention by God giving aid to such people.

Therefore, all things considered, the fortitude of the martyrs is a miracle of the moral order.

The major premise of this argument is clear from the former historically certain points.

However, *the minor premise* is made manifest in two ways: indirectly, by excluding natural causes that seem, to some, to sufficiently explain these matters; and directly, by showing that the aforementioned perseverance of the martyrs is an effect properly belonging to God—namely, extraordinary holiness.

(a) *Indirectly*. According to many rationalists, the patience of the martyrs can be explained by natural causes—namely, by fanaticism and the hope of receiving praise.

Now, *fanaticism* cannot explain this perseverance, for fanaticism is a kind of blind obstinacy that flees from discussion and excludes wisdom, prudence, modesty, and meekness. Now, the martyrs did not flee from discussion but, rather, freely gave accounts of their faith. Nay, many of them were learned, such as St. Justin, St. Irenaeus, and St. Cyprian who all wrote apologies for their faith. Wisdom and prudence are clearly testified to in all of their responses, and they fulfilled what Christ himself had foretold: "But when they shall deliver you up, take no thought how or what to speak, for it shall be given you in that hour what to speak. For it is not you that speak, but the Spirit of your Father that speaketh in you" (Matt 10:19–20, DR). For example, when the judge commanded the Alexandrian virgin Potamiana to take off her clothes and cast herself into a cauldron filled with burning pitch, she said instead, lest she be laid bare: "Command that I be *gradually* lowered into the burning pitch so that you may see how lavishly I have received the patience of Christ, whom you do not know."[85] Nor do the martyrs bear witness to frenzied enthusiasm but, rather, to modesty, as is seen, for example, in the account of St. Perpetua's martyrdom. Finally, fanaticism implies indignation and anger, whereas by contrast, the martyrs were meek. In them, we find *a marvelous union of the greatest fortitude with the greatest meekness*. Only God can join together these extremes. {{272}} As St. Thomas says, "Properly speaking, meekness diminishes anger. . . . Anger, however, comes

---

[85] In Ruinart, *Acta martyrum*, 103; also, regarding the responses of the martyrs, refer to the accounts found all throughout Leclercq's work.

from some injury inflicted upon the soul or [*seu*] on account of injustice."[86] Therefore, the greater the injustice suffered, the more are we inclined to anger and vengeance and, indeed, it is all the more difficult to repress this passion. However, there is no greater injustice than the inflicting of the most awful torments upon an innocent person on account of religion. Now, the martyrs affirm the truth of the faith in the midst of the most bitter of torments without, however, expressing any indignation, anger, or hatred for their persecutors and executors. Nay, they bless them and pray to God for them. As he died from being stoned, St. Stephen said, "Lord, lay not this sin to their charge" (Acts 7:59, DR), just as Christ himself had said, "Father, forgive them, for they know not what they do" (Luke 23:34, DR). Likewise, many of the martyrs have shown meekness and charity toward their persecutors (e.g., the martyrs of Lyons, Cyprian, Maximilian, Marcellus the Centurion, et al.[87]) In them, the words of St. Paul find a confirmation: "We are reviled: and we bless. We are persecuted: and we suffer it. We are blasphemed: and we entreat. We are made as the refuse of this world, the offscouring of all, even until now" (1 Cor 4:12–13, DR). And Christ himself had said, "Pray for them that persecute and calumniate you" (Matt 5:44, DR). Finally, the impulse of fanaticism would not have lasted through three centuries. As Gatti notes, "Indeed, there are some who, imbued with some kind of error, scorn death and sufferings, but this rarely happens, nor do they last throughout such sufferings except for a brief time, and at the same time they blaze up with anger and spite. They come to hate their adversaries, alter their countenance, are obstinate, inconstant, and lack strength." The virtues obviously are not interconnected in cases of fanaticism.

Nor can the perseverance of the martyrs be explained through *hope of praise, for they were no less humble than they were magnanimous.* They were so humble that, even if they suffered many torments for the faith, they nonetheless would not allow themselves to be called martyrs for the faith.[88] Moreover, many were killed in secret. Finally, just as Christ died between two thieves, they were held to be notorious wrongdoers. This great humility was marvelously joined to magnanimity, which appeared in their responses, for they spoke with the greatest authority and certitude. This union of such dissimilar virtues at so lofty a degree indicates that they had received a special form of help from God, without which they would have instead fluctuated between pusillanimity and pride. In the martyrs, we find the loftiest verification for what St. Thomas says concerning the two aforementioned virtues: "Magnanimity makes man think himself deserving of great things in view of the gifts that he has received from God. . . . Humility, however, makes man give little weight to himself, in view of his own short-

---

[86] *ST* II-II, q. 157, a. 2 and *ST* I-II, q. 46, a. 6. Also see De Poulpiquet, *L'objet integral de l'apologétique*, 183.

[87] See Leclercq, *Les martyrs*, vol. 1, 105; vol. 2, 106, 155, 158.

[88] See Eusebius, *Historia ecclesiastica*, bk. 5, ch. 2.

comings."[89] For the martyrs did not count upon their own powers but, rather, upon God's aid, praying without ceasing.

(b) *Directly*. Martyrdom bears witness to a perseverance that is an *effect properly belonging to God*. Indeed, as we said, this fortitude presupposes the connection of the principal virtues, all had at the loftiest degree, and this harmony bears witness to extraordinary holiness.

Now, holiness cannot exist without God's aid, for it is a virtue implying perfect purity from earthly things and utterly firm union with God, ordering all the acts of the virtues to God.[90] However, the order of agents must correspond to the order of ends. Therefore, holiness cannot exist without divine aid, and extraordinary holiness cannot exist without extraordinary aid from God.

{{273}} Concerning this matter, St. Thomas says:

> To endure death is not praiseworthy in itself but, rather, is so only insofar as it is directed to some good consisting in an act of virtue, such as faith or the love of God. . . . And it is in this respect that an act comes to pertain to the perfection of life, for, as the Apostle says (Col 3:14, DR), "charity . . . is the bond of perfection." Now, of all virtuous acts martyrdom is the greatest proof of the perfection of charity, since a man's love for something is proved to be all the greater, to the degree that what he despises for its sake is something that he holds to be dear or to the degree that what he chooses to suffer for its sake is more odious to him. Now, it is clear that of all the goods of the present life man loves life itself most, and on the other hand, he hates death more than anything, especially when it is accompanied by the pains of bodily torment, "from fear of which even dumb animals refrain from the greatest pleasures," as Augustine says (in q. 36 of *83 Different Questions*). Indeed, from this perspective, it is clear that martyrdom is the most perfect of human acts as regards its genus, as being the sign of the greatest charity, according to John 15:13 (DR): "Greater love than this no man hath, that a man lay down his life for his friends."[91]

The extraordinary holiness of the martyrs is manifested in particular inasmuch as they rejoice in their sufferings, as we see in the aforementioned *acta* of St. Ignatius, St. Polycarp, St. Irenaeus, St. Vincent, St. Laurence, St. Perpetua, St. Felicity, St. Blandina, and others. In a marvelous way, we see a fulfillment of what Christ had foretold: "Blessed are ye when they shall revile you, and persecute you, and speak all that is evil against you,

---

[89] *ST* II-II, q. 129, a. 3, ad 4.
[90] See *ST* II-II, q. 81, a. 8.
[91] *ST* II-II, q. 124, a. 3.

untruly, for my sake. Be glad and rejoice for your reward is very great in heaven. For so they persecuted the prophets that were before you" (Matt 5:11–12, DR). This represents the pinnacle of holiness.

Therefore, all things considered, the perseverance of the martyrs is a miracle of the moral order.

Confirmations are added to this by a number of apologetes like, for example, Adolphe Tanquerey.[92]

(1) *The martyrs declared that they received divine aid, for otherwise they would not have been able to overcome their torments.* Polycarp said: "Leave me as I am; for He that gives me strength to endure the fire will also enable me, without your securing me by nails, to remain without moving in the pile"[93] And St. Felicity suffered many pains while giving birth in prison, and when one of her guards said to her, "You, who are now suffering in such a manner, what will you do when you are thrown to the beast?" she responded faithfully, "I will suffer what I suffer in this manner; however, there will be *another who will suffer in me, He who will suffer for* me, for I am also about to suffer for him."[94] Likewise, Andronicus said to his judge: "*Armed by my God*, I stand before you in faith and the power of the all-powerful Lord God."[95] The deacon Vincent, in the midst of the utterly harsh torments of the rack, said: "Rise up and rage with the full spirit of your wickedness. You will see that I can do more *through God's power* when I am tortured than you who torture me can yourself do." Many other examples could be cited.[96]

(2) *It was not uncommon for miracles to manifest this divine aid.* Sometimes, in the midst of the torments themselves, there was no (or, in any case, very little) pain sensed by the martyrs, as is said of St. Laurence and St. Perpetua, who was in a state of ecstasy throughout her suffering, like St. Polycarp.[97] {{274}} Sometimes their wounds were suddenly healed, and many beasts were tamed by the martyrs and spared them; some pagans, terrified by these wonders, embraced the Christian faith.

---

[92] See Tanquerey, *Synopsis theologiae dogmaticae*, 14th ed., vol. 1, 289.

[93] *Martyrdom of St. Polycarp* (trans. Roberts and Donaldson), ch. 13.

[94] Ruinart, *Acta martyrum*, 86.

[95] See Leclercq, *Les martyrs*, vol. 2, 281: "The martyr responded, 'Strengthened by my God, whom I serve, I scorn all the tortures that you would like to inflict upon me. Therefore, come up with new torments and you will see what power dwells within me, through the strength of Christ my Lord."

[96] Ruinart, *Acta martyrum*, 325; likewise see 103, 135, 136, 163, 260, 303, and 339. Similarly see Leclercq, *Les martyrs*, vol. 2, 105, 123, 221.

[97] See Leclercq, *Les martyrs*, vol. 1, 73 (On St. Polycarp's martyrdom): "As soon as the flames began to burn him, we witnessed a miracle. . . . The flames seemed to encircle him, taking the form of a ship's sail, filled with wind. The old man, placed at the center of this burning chapel, did not look, to our eyes, like someone whose flesh was burning but, rather, looked like baked bread or like a gold bar or silver in a furnace. During this time, we smelled a delightful odor that was like that of incense or of the most precious of perfumes." Likewise, see vol. 1, 138.

(3) *Nay, the blood of Christians is like a seed*, as Tertullian said: "Kill us, torture us, condemn us, grind us to dust. . . . Nor does your cruelty, however exquisite, avail you; it is rather a temptation to us. The oftener we are mown down by you, the more in number we grow; the blood of Christians is seed."[98] Indeed, immediately after the persecution, Christianity underwent a prodigious amount of growth, as the Fathers mention,[99] along with ecclesiastical historians. Christ had said, "Unless the grain of wheat falling into the ground die, itself remaineth alone. But if it die, it bringeth forth much fruit" (John 12:24–25, DR); and speaking of his own death, he said, "And I, if I be lifted up from the earth, will draw all things to myself" (John 12:32, DR). Likewise, St. Paul said, "For which cause I please myself . . . in persecutions, in distresses, for Christ. For when I am weak, then am I powerful" (2 Cor 12:10, DR). Thus, as Cyprian said, "The tortured stood forth with greater strength than did their torturers."

(4) *Christ had foretold this victory of the martyrs*: "Blessed are ye when they shall revile you . . . for my sake. Be glad and rejoice, for your reward is very great in heaven" (Matt 5:11–12, DR). And likewise: "And you shall be brought before governors, and before kings for my sake, for a testimony to them and to the Gentiles. But when they shall deliver you up . . . brother also shall deliver up the brother to death, and the father the son. . . . And fear ye not them that kill the body, and are not able to kill the soul. . . . Every one therefore that shall confess me before men, I will also confess him before my Father who is in heaven" (Matt 10:17–33, DR). Similarly, St. Paul had said, "If God be for us, who is against us? . . . Who then shall separate us from the love of Christ? Shall tribulation? Or distress? Or famine? Or nakedness? Or danger? Or persecution? Or the sword? . . . But in all these things we overcome, because of him that hath loved us. For I am sure that neither death, nor life, nor angels, nor principalities, nor powers, nor things present, nor things to come, nor might, nor height, nor depth, nor any other creature, shall be able to separate us from the love of God which is in Christ Jesus our Lord" (Rom 8:31–39, DR). Likewise, speaking of the ancient martyrs, it is said in Hebrews 11:33–38 (DR): "Who by faith conquered kingdoms, wrought justice, obtained promises, stopped the mouths of lions, quenched the violence of fire. . . . They were stoned, they were cut asunder, . . . being in want, distressed, afflicted: of whom the world was not worthy." And similarly St. John said: "For whatsoever is born of God overcometh the world. And *this is the victory which overcameth the world: Our faith*. Who is he that overcometh the world, but he that believeth that Jesus is the Son of God?" (1 John 5:4–5, DR).

---

[98] Tertullian, *Apology*, ch. 50 (trans. Thelwall).

[99] See Justin, *Dialogue with Trypho*, ch. 9; Eusebius, *Historia ecclesiastica*, 1.4, saying that Christians were "the most numerous of people among the nations."

Therefore, the heroic fortitude of the martyrs is a sign of the truth of the Christian faith, a sublime sign combining within itself a sensible and moral miracle, for sometimes the martyrs prayed in their ecstasy, like St. Stephen, who "saw the glory of God . . . and said: Behold, I see the heavens opened and the Son of man standing on the right hand of God" (Acts 7:55, DR).

Resolution of Objections

{{275}} Rationalists object: The perseverance of the martyrs can be explained by natural causes, for they can be compared with many examples of natural fortitude, which have often been shown by soldiers in battle, as well as by the *heroes* of paganism, such as Regulus and Scaevola, and indeed by certain wrongdoers in the midst of their own punishments. Moreover, many religions have their own martyrs. Thus, in *India*, almost to our own days, widows have the duty to kill themselves through fire upon the deaths of their husbands. Besides this, many burn themselves with naked feet upon fiery coals in order to please their gods, and they lay themselves out before carts filled with idols in order to be crushed by them. Similarly, the *Babystae* [*sic*] in Persia would prefer to undergo torments than to desert their religion. Finally, in particular among ancient heretics like the *Montanists* and among modern Protestants like the *Anabaptists*, there are not lacking those who would undergo death for their faith.[100] Even recently in 1856 in Uganda, Protestants handed over their lives for their religion.

Response: These examples of natural fortitude or fanaticism cannot be compared with our own martyrs on a number of heads. (1) They cannot be compared as regards

---

[100] Thus, Gaston Boissier (in *La fin du paganisme*, 5th ed., vol. 1 [Paris: Hachette, 1907], 344) denies the apologetic value of the martyrs' perseverance. He writes: "We can conclude with much more assurance that the question was not, properly speaking, a religious question. It would be such if we could affirm that the truth of a doctrine is measured by the steadfastness of those who defend it. There are Christian apologists who have claimed that this is so. They have wished to draw from the death of the martyrs incontrovertible evidence that the opinions for which they sacrificed themselves would need to be true. One does not allow oneself to be killed, they tell us, for a false religion. However, this reasoning is not correct, and moreover, the Church has undermined its strength by treating her enemies like how her own children have been treated. She has made herself out of martyrs, and it is not possible to claim for her own members that which she does not wish to accord to others. In the presence of the courageous death of the Waldensians, the Hussites, and the Protestants whom she burned or hung, without being able to extract from them any disavowal of their belief, she finds that she must renounce the claim that one only dies for a true doctrine." In reality, by contrast, we argue from the *perseverance of martyrdom* inasmuch as it appears to be *miraculous* and is clearly distinct from the *obstinacy* of fanatics.

the very number of such martyrs through the first three centuries of the Church's life, as well as into our own days. (2) Nor can they be compared as regards the conditions of such martyrs, for ours have included old men, feeble women, and little girls who have all suffered the fiercest torments. (3) Then also there are the various kinds of torments, whether physical or moral, which likewise were undergone for such long times. (4) Nor can a comparison be drawn with regard to the readiness and serenity in which these torments were suffered in patience, in connection with all the other virtues, so that heroic fortitude finds itself to be united to the greatest charity, humility, meekness, and prayer for persecutors. (5) Finally, no comparison can be drawn as regards the miracles that confirm this holiness.

Concerning this, St. Thomas states:

> Two things must be heeded in the deeds of the virtues, namely, *that which is done* and *the way that it is done*. Now, it happens that the same thing that is done according to a perfect virtue is also done not only by someone with little virtue but even by someone who does not have [that] virtue, as when someone not having the virtue of justice can do some work of justice. However, if we heed the way that it is done, the person who does not have the virtue of justice cannot perform this act in the same way as does the person who has it; nor does he who has little virtue perform the act in the same way as the person who has great virtue, acting with ease, promptly, and with delight, a way of acting that is not found in him who lacks virtue or who has little in the way of virtue. Therefore, we must say that this deed, namely, the offering of oneself as a martyr, or even suffering martyrdom, can be performed not only by someone having perfect charity but also by him who lacks charity, in accord with the words of St. Paul in 1 Corinthians 13:3 (DR): {{276}} "if I should deliver my body to be burned, and have not charity, it profiteth me nothing." However, perfect charity does this *promptly* and *with delight*, as is clear in the cases of SS. Laurence and Vincent, who joked while being tormented. However, the person with imperfect charity cannot do this, as well as the person who lacks charity.[101]

And likewise, "sometimes a person performs the external act of a virtue without having that virtue, doing so from some other cause than virtue. . . . For example, through the choice of an undue end."[102]

Benedict XIV says the same thing when he discusses *false martyrs*.[103]

In particular, the heroic fortitude of *soldiers* can be explained from natural causes,

---

[101] St. Thomas, *Quodlibet* IV, q. 10, a. 1 (Whether someone can offer himself as a martyr without perfect charity).

[102] *ST* II-II, q. 123, a. 1, ad 2.

[103] Benedict XIV, *Doctrina de servorum Dei beatificatione et beatorum canonizatione*, bk. 3, ch. 20.

inasmuch as they are moved by love of country, zeal for glory, wrongful desire for vengeance, ardently rushing into danger because of their anger, attacking with blindness of soul, reassured by the instruments of war, with many striving out of necessity or fear of dishonor, not exposing themselves to certain death but, rather, to probable death, and, finally, often dying in a sudden manner, thus doing so without severe suffering.[104] However, the perseverance of the martyrs cannot be explained by these natural causes.

Heroes like Regulus and Scaevola were very rare and were also hardened through the labors of war, inordinately desirous of glory, and the greatest peril of their homeland vehemently aroused their souls. As Benedict XIV says:

> If true moral virtues can be found among Gentiles, nothing seems to prohibit them from even being able to arrive at a heroic degree of virtue, considering the nature of the thing done. However, *since the establishment of a true hero requires the presence of all the moral virtues,* however many people among the pagans have obtained the name of being heroes on account of the excellence of some moral virtue, they were so greatly lacking in other virtues and attached to vices that none of them should be accounted heroes, as is proven at length by Cardinals de Lauraea and Aguirre, and at great length by Theophilus Raynaudus and, likewise, by St. Basil.[105]

Wrongdoers condemned to death cannot flee from it and sometimes, on account of desire for fame, even show fortitude—or, rather, unconquered obstinacy.

As regards the Indians mentioned earlier, who cast themselves under the tires of carts drawing their idols so that they may be crushed, their death is not martyrdom as a witness to the truth of their religion but, rather, is a form of suicide so that they may manage to reach *nirvana* more quickly. This clearly arises from superstition. Likewise, women who climb upon the funeral pyres containing the corpses of their dead husbands are moved by fanatic ardor in order to avoid the fate befalling widows, which is utterly gloomy in India. Nor do they suffer this torment without groaning and lamentation. And if they wished to flee from it, they would be prevented by bystanders.[106]

Babystae [*sic*] also were seized by fanatic madness, as is admitted by adversaries like Renan.[107] Moreover, they fought against civil authority with force and arms, whereas, by contrast, the martyrs defeated their persecutors through meekness and patience.

---

[104] See Ottiger, *Theologiae fundamentalis, De revelatione,* 888.

[105] Benedict XIV, *Doctrina de servorum Dei beatificatione et beatorum canonizatione,* bk. 3, ch. 21. Likewise, see the full text for references to the authors cited by Benedict XIV.

[106] See Ottiger, *Theologiae fundamentalis, De revelatione,* 891; Gatti, *Institutiones apologetico-polemicae,* vol. 3, 211.

[107] See Renan, *Les apôtres* (Paris, 1882), 378ff.

Among the heretics of old, few were killed through torments for the sake of religion. The Gnostics, the Basilidians, and the Valentinians did not know of martyrdom. By contrast, the Montanists were moved to suffering through their fanatic ardor, and in Africa during St. Augustine's days, *the Circumcellions* threw themselves off of cliffs. However, no comparison can be drawn between their frenzied enthusiasm and the virtues, prudence, modesty, and humility of the martyrs.[108] {{277}} Moreover, as Ottiger remarks,[109] since the existence of wicked spirits is not contradictory in nature, one cannot demonstrate the impossibility that these fanatics were compelled and enabled to voluntarily undergo such tortures by a preternatural power coming from wicked spirits so that superstition might imitate the effects of the true religion. This kind of diabolical power, together with unbridled love for the most disgraceful of sins, seems to have been the cause of the obstinacy of many of the Gnostic sects of the eleventh, twelfth, and thirteenth centuries.

As regards more recent heretics, Benedict XIV notes:

> Finally, we must admit that some have fearlessly faced their death. Poggio Bracciolini recounts [such things] concerning Jerome of Prague, as does Jacques Auguste de Thou [Thuanus] concerning Anne de Bourg, and [there also is the case] of the Anabaptists.[110] In the twelfth century, St. Bernard referred to the patience and readiness of those who were led to death, attributing it to a power that was exercised in their hearts by a demon. The New Adamites, the offspring of Wycliff and Huss, were also driven to a joyful death, as well as other more recent heretics, according to Alanum Copum [*apud Alanum Copum*]. None-

---

[108] See Allard, *Dix leçons sur le martyre*, 322–330: "The heretics of the first centuries varied a great deal concerning the matter of martyrdom. Some of them refused it. This is true on the whole for the Gnostics, as well as the sects of the Basilidians and the Valentinians.... The enthusiasm for martyrdom animated other heresies to the point of excess, however.... Fanatics holding to Montanism sought martyrdom ... in a feverish manner which will find its final form in the Circumcellions of the fourth century.... By contrast, on the question of martyrdom, the Church's entire position is holy and well-measured. In the East and in the West, everywhere that she makes her voice heard, she does so for the sake of the maintenance of the language of immutable faith and that of eternal good sense.... If she requires courage of her members, the Church does not call for rashness. For many motives, she counsels prudence during the time of persecutions.... One of the most formal rules is the prohibition that Christians denounce themselves to their enemies.... A second rule: do not irritate the pagans by insulting their worship.... Many of the weightiest men in the Church in the third century, Clement of Alexandria, Cyprian ... counselled believers to withdraw through flight from material danger and, above all, moral danger of persecution, themselves giving examples of this act of Christian modesty, though such flight does not prevent believers, if they are then arrested, ... from dying for their faith in the midst of the cruelest tortures."

[109] Ignatius Ottiger, *Theologia fundamentalis, De revelatione*, 893.

[110] [Trans. note: Here, for some reason, the text has a parenthetical notation that does not make chronological sense: "(Saec. XII)".]

theless, no matter how much this is so, by no means can the number of heretics' pseudo-martyrs be compared to the multitude of our martyrs from the beginning of the Church until our own days, all the more so since the number of the former is drawn from sects that are divided from each other, whereas ours shed their blood for truths that are one and the same.[111]

The Anabaptists showed utterly clear signs of fanatical furor, pride, and brutishness—nay, of cruelty.[112]

Finally, as Benedict XIV writes:[113] "Led by St. Thomas, theologians commonly teach that a heretic dying for a true article [of faith] cannot be a martyr, inasmuch as he lacks both unformed and formed faith. They add that such a person can be a martyr before God, though not for the Church, if he is invincibly a heretic and is disposed to believe everything that would be legitimately proposed to him [as being revealed]." Thus, according to Tanquerey:

> Those who were killed in *Uganda* from between 1885 and 1887 [literally 1885–186], believed *in good faith*, so that, as is clear from [their] truthful narrations, the religion that they embraced was the religion divinely revealed by Christ. And therefore, they were able to be aided *by divine grace* so that they were able to hand over their lives for the sake of religion which, although incompletely, they embraced in those truths which are necessary for salvation. In this case, through a divine intervention, they demonstrated *the truth of Christianity*, though not of Protestantism inasmuch as the latter is opposed to the Catholic Church.[114]

§3. The Church Ceaselessly Brings Forth Heroic Saints

This is clear (1) in the lives of the saints, (2) in the history of the various religious orders that have been established through the Church's history, and (3) in the whole of society, which is ceaselessly renewed by Christian virtues.

{{278}} (1) ***The Catholic Church is the fruitful mother of saints*** whose virtues surpass whatever human nature could ever produce. Indeed, among her host of members there are numbered all the holy confessors, fathers,

---

[111] Benedict XIV, *Doctrina de servorum Dei beatificatione et beatorum canonizatione*, bk. 3, ch. 20, no. 12.

[112] See the article by A. Baudrillart in *Dictionnaire de théologie catholique*, vol. 1, 1128–1134.

[113] Benedict XIV, *Doctrina de servorum Dei beatificatione et beatorum canonizatione*, bk. 3, ch. 20, no. 6.

[114] See Tanquerey, *Synopsis theologiae dogmaticae*, 14th ed., vol. 1, 291.

doctors, apostles, hermits, and virgins, all of whom, not only in the first age of the Church but also continuously down through all the subsequent ages, have shone with heroic zeal and have led countless souls to Christ more through their holiness than through their preaching.

As Gatti notes, since Protestants profess that the Roman Church was the true Church up to the time of Constantine (that is, up to the fourth century), to what church do they ascribe all the saints who have flourished up to the present day, other than to the Roman Church? There are St. Ambrose, St. Augustine, St Jerome, St. Cyril, St. Chrysologus, and others. To what church belong the Holy Roman Pontiffs like St. John I, St. Felix IV, St. Agapitus, St. Sylvester, St. Gregory the Great, St. Martin I, St. Eugenius I, St. Vitalianus, St. Agatho, St. Leo II, St. Benedict II, and St. Sergius I? And we could add so many other saints, the enumeration of whose names would go on for great length, though it is not necessary, saints like St. Apollinaris, St. Eulogius, St. Fulgentius, St. Gregory of Turin, and others. Likewise, among countless martyrs, there is the renowned host of apostles who spread the Christian faith throughout the various parts of the world and founded various churches, men like St. Patrick in Ireland, St. Augustine in England, St. Methodius in Russia, St. Boniface in Frisia, St. Willibald in Germany, and others who propagated the Christian faith far and wide. Then there are the holy founders of the religious orders, like St. Benedict, the patriarch of Western monks, St. Bernard, St. Norbert, St. Dominic, St. Francis, and so forth. Then too, great preachers of the faith like St. Vincent Ferrer, and illustrious virgins like St. Gertrude, St. Hildegard, St. Clare, St. Catherine of Siena, and others. Likewise, there are holy kings like St. Stephen, St. Louis, St. Henry, St. Leopold, and St. Stanislaus.

Nor is it the case that after the Protestants broke off, the Church ceased to bring forth heroic saints. Nay, following upon the calamity of this secession, and similarly at the start of the nineteenth century after the French Revolution, there was a great flourishing of saints, religious orders, and missionaries to nonbelievers. Thus, we have as witnesses to this St. Ignatius, St. Teresa, St. John of the Cross, St. Francis de Sales, St. Francis Xavier, St. Louis Bertrand, St. Philip Neri, St. Charles Borromeo, St. Vincent de Paul, St. Paul of the Cross, St. Alphonsus de Liguori, and St. Margaret-Mary Alacoque. Likewise, following upon the French Revolution, there is John Vianney, Don Bosco, and many founders of religious congregations, along with many martyrs in the missions, for example, Bl. [St.] Jean-Théophane Vénard and Bl. [St.] Jean-Gabriel Perboyre.

Frequently, many canonizations were performed only after an utterly accurate investigation into the heroic holiness of the person, as can be seen in the accounts gathered by the Bollandists (*Bollandianorum volumina*) and in Benedict XIV's work *Doctrina de servorum Dei beatificatione et beatorum canonizatione*.

From the earliest days of the Christian religion, the invocation of the saints has been a received fact, inasmuch as the Church believes that the saints, reigning together with Christ, offer their prayers for men to God.

By contrast, the principal authors of *Protestantism* were not saints but, rather, scorned the evangelical counsels, virginity, fasting, and, indeed, the cult of the saints—nay, giving the worst example of depravity.

Luther was an aggressive man who was insulting to those closest to him [*conviciosus in proximum*], prideful, transgressing his vows, a defiler of the divine books, a man who drank far too much, holding authority in contempt, stirring up the people, and speaking the most shameless of words.[115] {{279}} Calvin was a cold, caustic, and cruel man, an arrogant defender of his own infallibility, looking down upon the ancient Fathers of the Church, and called Luther an eminent apostle of Christ.[116] Zwingli was a slave to his desires. Henry VIII was cruel, addicted to luxury, an adulterer, and a murderer. Elizabeth was an unchanged copy of her father, Henry, in dissimulation. Therefore, it is not surprising that the heroic virtue of the saints is lacking in Protestantism.

Likewise, *Photianism* had perverse authors. It is historically clear that Photios was full of falsities and trickery, ambitious, a man at one time contemptuous of power and at another a flatterer, a man who devoured the things of the poor, the priests, and orphans. Likewise, Michael Cerularius, George of Cyprus, and Mark of Ephesus gave manifest signs of ambitious and trickery.[117]

---

[115] See Luther's works as a whole, not excluding the book *Tischreden*. Likewise, see [Heinrich] Denifle, *Luther und Luthertum*, 2 vols. (Mainz: Kirchheim, 1905–1906); Alfred Baudrillart, *L'église catholique, la Renaissance, le protestantisme* (Paris: Bloud, 1904); Nikolaus Paulus, *Die deutschen Dominikaner im Kampf gegen Luther* (Freiburg: Herder, 1903).

[116] Resp. contra Pugium [*sic*], *De libero arbitrio*. See Jean-Marie-Vincent Audin, *Histoire de la vie, des ouvrages, des doctrines de Calvin* [Paris: Maison, 1850]; Bossuet, *Histoire des variations*, bk. 9: "If we must compare these two men, there is nobody who would love better to wipe away the impetuous and insolent anger of the one (Luther) than the profound malignancy and bitterness of the other, who boasted of being cold-blooded when he disseminated such poison in his discourses."

[Trans. note: The language used by Fr. Garrigou-Lagrange here is not proposed for setting the tone for contemporary relations between the Church and our separated brethren.]

[117] See Hergenröther, *Photius, Patriarch von Constantinopel: Sein Leben, seine Schriften und das griechische Schisma* [Regensburg: Manz, 1867;] Karl Hefele, *Konziliengeschichte*, vol. 4 [Freiburg: Herder, 1855–1890]; Louis Duchesne, *Les églises séparées* (Paris : Albert Fontemoing, 1905), 223. In particular, read the work of a son of one of the schismatic churches who nonetheless admitted the primacy of the Roman Pontiff, Vladimir Soloviev, *La Russie et l'église universelle*, 2nd ed. (Paris: Stock, 1906), xlv and onward. Speaking of the origin of the schismatics, he writes (trans. Herbert Rees [London: Geoffrey Bles, 1948], 25): "The Emperors permanently embraced 'Orthodoxy' as an abstract dogma, while the orthodox prelates bestowed their benediction *in saecula saeculorum* on the paganism of Byzantine public life. And since '*sine sanguine nullum pactum*,' a magnificent hecatomb of one hundred thousand Paulicians sealed the alliance of the Second Rome with the 'Second Church.'... Religious society was separated from secular society, the former being relegated to the monasteries, while the *forum* was abandoned to pagan laws and passions."

[Trans. note: For an overview of the complex history of the Photian Schism, see Francis Dvornik, *The Photian Schism, History and Legend* (Cambridge: Cambridge University Press, 1948). Also, as regards Orthodox saints and miracle workers, one should bear in mind the

If men born into Protestantism or into schismatic churches and remaining therein in good faith do indeed cultivate virtues, even supernatural ones, this is an effect of God's mercy, which does not deny grace to him who does what is in his power; however, we cannot infer from this that the sect to which such a person adheres in good faith is a part of the true Church. Nor can these souls of good will be compared, as regards the heroic character of their virtues, to the saints canonized by the Catholic Church.[118]

(2) *Institutions and religious orders.* Among the institutions, an eminent place belongs to the *Catholic priesthood*, whose members [in the West] have been devoted to perpetual celibacy so that they may give themselves totally in service to God and souls. Now, this perpetual continence, which is faithfully kept by many priests, presupposes heroic acts [of virtue]. By contrast, Protestant ministers contract marriage and teach that it is not better or more blessed to remain in virginity than to be joined in matrimony.[119] In the Greek Church,[120] the majority of clerics are scorned by their faithful

---

dated nature of Fr. Garrigou-Lagrange's comments.]

[118] In 1882, Yahontov wrote a book entitled *Vita sanctorum Russiae septentrionalis*. Martinov judged that this book is of little importance for Westerners, writing in *Revue des questions historiques* (Oct. 1883), 639, "given that the work is overly-localized interest, treating of people who, for the most part, are unknown, if not problematic in their holiness."

[119] See Trent, *Canons on the Sacrament of Matrimony*, nos. 10 and 11 (Denzinger, nos. 1810 and 1811). On this matter, see Joseph de Maistre, *Du pape*, bk 3, ch. 3, §2: "In Christianity, there are things that are lofty and sublime. Between the priest and his flock, there are relations so holy and so delicate that they can only belong to men absolutely superior to other men. Confession by itself requires celibacy. . . . Who could believe, that, in a (Protestant) country where the excellence of married priests is seriously maintained, the epithet, *son of a priest*, is a formal insult? What is a minister in so-called 'reformed' worship? A man dressed in black who ascends a pulpit every Sunday in order to deliver an honest discourse. Every honest man can succeed in this profession, and it excludes no weakness proper to *honest men*. . . . The only thing required of them is probity. However, what therefore is this human virtue when placed before the formidable ministry which requires *divinized probity*— that is, *sanctity*?"

[120] [Trans. note: Although Fr. Garrigou-Lagrange is not wholly clear here concerning whether or not Eastern clerical marriage practices are in his crosshairs in making such claims, as a formator of men in the Ruthenian and Melkite Catholic Churches, among whom are numbered very holy married men, I cannot in good conscience allow comments like this to stand without noting their gravely problematic character, treating—as so often happens in polemics surrounding questions of clerical celibacy—this as an at-best-tolerated practice of the Eastern Churches. Great hurt has been caused by Roman Catholic clergy, bishops, and theologians (even to the point of prompting schism in the United States) because of such an unmeasured approach to the question of celibacy and marriage among the clergy of the Eastern Churches, even those in union with Rome. Indeed, even as regards our Orthodox brethren, I cannot justify remaining silent when Fr. Garrigou-Lagrange (for whose cause I have dedicated many hours in translation, and for whom I feel great affection) here casts insults that could apply, sadly, to priests in any jurisdiction. I should add, as well, that the anti-Protestant polemics

on account of their ignorance and drunkenness, as well as other vices, often lacking zeal, with religion thereby languishing.[121]

{{280}} Moreover, in the Catholic Church, *religious orders* are a school of perfection for the pursuit of holiness through the practice of the evangelical counsels and the imitation of Christ. Through the three vows of poverty, chastity, and obedience, one is led to do away with concupiscence of the eyes (or wrongful desire for external things), concupiscence of the flesh, and the pride of life. Thus, the religious state is an exercise in tending toward the perfection of charity, calming the soul from external cares, and is a kind of sacrifice through which someone offers himself and his belongings to God.[122]

Certain orders, like the *Brothers of St. John of God*, who serve the sick in hospitals, are concerned with works of the active life. Likewise, there are the *Sisters of Charity*, who renounce all things so that they may be devoted to the necessities of the poor and the needy. Many other sisters give themselves over totally to care for the elderly. Countless religious men and women are dedicated to the education of the young, like the *Brothers of Christian Instruction* and the *Brothers of St. Vincent de Paul*.

Other orders, like the *Carthusians, the Trappists, the Carmelites*, and others spend their time in the works of the contemplative life, dedicating themselves to the worship of God, prayer, and making satisfaction for sinners.

Finally, there are orders that have been instituted for the sake of teaching and preaching, which are derived from the fullness of contemplation, like the *Dominicans*, the *Franciscans*, and various *Clerics Regular*, who devote themselves totally to the service of God and the salvation of souls, to the propagation of Christianity, the evangelization of barbarian peoples, and fostering and preserving the civil order [*civilitatem*] together with religion.

There are also confraternities for fostering the piety of the faithful and purity of conscience, thus preserving the cultivation of the evangelical counsels and the ascetical life, whose principles and means are set forth in the saints' writings.[123]

---

of this section are, truth be told, words that also must be measured by their era. I write this without minimizing any of the traditional teaching that undergirds Fr. Garrigou-Lagrange's generally correct convictions, which, however, indulge in somewhat uncharitable Roman-centric rhetorical excesses here.]

[121] See Vladimir Soloviev, *La Russie et l'église universelle*, 2nd ed., 53–55.

[122] See *ST* II-II, q. 186, a. 7; q. 188, a. 6.

[123] See St. Cyprian, *On the Dress of Virgins*; St. John Chrysostom, *On Compunction*; St. Ambrose, *On Virgins*; St. Augustine, *Confessions*; John Cassian, *Conferences*; Bernard of Clairvaux, *On Loving God*; Richard of St. Victor, St. Bonaventure, Johannes Tauler, and Henry Suso;

These institutes even arouse the admiration of adversaries.

By contrast, Luther and his disciples rejected religious vows and taught that [canonical] regulars, who had solemnly professed chastity, can become married and that this marriage contract is valid, notwithstanding their vows. He even placed the married state before the state of virginity.[124] {{281}} *Nay, overturning all of the principles of sanctity, Luther taught: "Sin boldly, but believe more boldly still."*[125] In *Photianism*, religious institutes and pious societies either enjoyed nearly no vitality or have taken their guidance more from political prudence than from religion.[126]

The holiness of the Catholic Church is also made clear through the perseverance of the grace of miracles, as is spoken of in the lives of the saints, whereas, by contrast, Luther said, "Miracles must not be required by us, who deny free choice of the will."[127] And Calvin wrote to the king of France: "Those who demand miracles from us act wickedly."[128] Erasmus affirmed: "Nobody exists today who could heal a lame horse."[129] Likewise, no true miracles have been performed for schismatics, and whatever facts some refer to can be explained by natural causes, as Martinov shows.[130]

Fr. Lacordaire shows this,[131] drawing particular attention to the Christian virtues of chastity, humility, and charity, by which humanity is freed from "the concupiscence of the flesh and the concupiscence of the eyes, and the pride of life" (1 John 2:16, DR). For chastity represses the fleshly desires [*libinides*] that corrupt the very springs of life, thus preserving the holiness of matrimony. *Humility* casts out ambition, boasting, and arrogance, which

---

Thomas à Kempis, *The Imitation of Christ*; St. Catherine of Siena, *Dialogue*; Luis de Granada and St. Teresa; St. Ignatius, *Spiritual Exercises*; St. Francis de Sales, *Treatise on the Love of God*; St. Alphonsus Liguori; Bl. [St.] Louis-Marie Grignion de Montfort, and others.

[124] See Trent, *Canons on the Sacrament of Matrimony*, nos. 9 and 11 (Denzinger, nos. 1809 and 1811).

[125] On this Lutheran doctrine, see [Franz] Hettinger, *Apologie du christianisme* (French trans.), vol. 5, 50. He cites these words from the Pseudo-Reformer: "We necessarily sin for as long as we are alive. However, the Lamb of God takes away the sins of the world, and sin cannot separate us from him, even were we to commit, every day, a thousand adulteries and as many acts of homicide" (Luther, *Epist. ad Iac. Aurifabr* [Letter to Johannes Aurifaber]). See *De captivitate babylonica ecclesiae*, vol. 2, 284: "The more infamous you are, the more God will freely give you His grace" (Leipzig edition, vol. 12, 128).

[126] See Peter the Great, *Règlement ecclésiastique de Pierre-le-Grand*, trans. Cesare Tondini de Quarenghi (Paris: Société Bibliographique, 1874).

[127] Luther, *On the Bondage of the Will*.

[128] See Calvin, *Institutes of the Christian Religion*, preface.

[129] Erasmus, *Diatribe or Discourse on Free Will*.

[130] See Martinov in *Revue des questions historiques* (Jan. 1884): 272.

[131] Se Lacordaire, *Conférences de Notre Dame*, 1884.

all give rise to dissensions and discord. *Charity* conquers egoism, not only rendering to each person what justice already requires, but going beyond what is owed to one's neighbors, especially to the weak, the sick, and the poor, to the point of even remitting offenses and injuries. In this way, charity destroys social dissensions, which justice alone does not suffice for setting in order.

Now, there is no society that has inculcated these virtues so diligently in word and deed as has the Catholic Church. This appears not only through a comparison of Catholicism with dissolute paganism, Islam (which permits polygamy), and Buddhism (which allows the populace to practice polytheism with many repulsive idols), but even in comparison with Protestantism.

Indeed, the pseudo-reformers did not commend the three aforementioned Christian virtues. They held virginity in contempt, drew back from humility and obedience—teaching that private spiritual insight suffices as the supreme rule of faith, requiring no higher authority—and finally, regarding charity, held that faith without works (that is, without charity) suffices for salvation.[132]

{{282}} Hence, Luther himself confessed: "The world becomes worse every day. There are now men who are more eager for vengeance, greedier, more distant from every kind of mercy, more immodest and undisciplined, and much worse than they were under the papacy."[133] Melanchthon spoke similarly.[134] It is a sound claim to say that the doctrine of the Protestants led to such corruption.

Certainly, many good things remain in Protestantism, inasmuch as it preserves something of Christianity, but the special action of the Holy Spirit is not manifested in it.

However, if supernatural social morality remains in Photianism, it is nonetheless certainly very much debilitated and cannot be compared with the vitality of the Roman Church.

Indeed, we cannot deny that vices and scandals are found in Catholic nations; however, those who are evil are such because they depart from the

---

[132] See Trent, *Decree on Justification*, nos. 9–12 (Denzinger, nos. 1559–1562).

[133] Luther, *Postilla in Evang. Dom. I Advent.*

[134] On this, see [Johann Joseph Ignaz von] Döllinger, *Die Reformation* [Regensburg: Manz, 1851–1853]; Johannes Janssen, *Geschichte des deutschen Volkes seit dem Ausgang des Mittelalters*, vols. 2 and 3 (Freiburg: Herder, 1894); Albert Maria Weiss, *Apologie des Christentums vom Standpunkt der Sitte und Cultur* (Freiburg im Breisgau, 1889), bk. 5; [Auguste] Nicolas, *Du protestantisme* [*et de toutes les hérésies dans leur rapport avec le socialisme: Précédé de l'examen d'un écrit de M. Guizot* (Paris: Vaton, 1869),] vol. 2, bk. 3, ch. 4; Baudrillart, *L'église catholique, la Renaissance, le protestantisme*, 8th conference.

Catholic faith or do not keep the Church's precepts, not making use of the means of holiness offered by her. However, those who are holy are made to be such because they obey her commandments.

§4. The Church's Unexhausted Fecundity in All Good Things

As Fr. Lacordaire shows, along with many contemporary apologetes,[135] this fecundity is clear as regards: (1) men's private lives, (2) family life, and (3) social life.

(1) *The Church freed private men*, and continues to do so, from errors concerning God, the world, the soul, and morals—namely, from polytheism, dualism, materialism, determinism, utilitarianism, and so forth. She preaches the Gospel and proposes the means of salvation to all men, even uncultured men and the poor, whom philosophers often ignore. She has forever condemned luxurious extravagance, drunkenness, and other crimes against nature that were tolerated by pagan philosophers. Likewise, as we have already discussed, she has promoted, in a marvelous manner, both natural and Christian virtues.

(2) *She restored the family* by protecting wives, children, and servants. She defends the dignity *of wives* against the cruel domination or licentiousness of men, which thrived under the pagans, as well as against polygamy and divorce [*repudiationem*], which were tolerated by the Mosaic Law.[136] The Church has always imposed, even sometimes notwithstanding the great difficulties involved, the Christian law concerning the unity and indissolubility of marriage. By contrast, Protestants have taught: "The marriage bond can be dissolved because of heresy or difficulties in cohabitation, or because of the willful absence of one of the spouses."[137] {{283}} This is also clear in the decisions and "dispensations" by Luther, Bucer, and Melanchthon for Philip, the Landgrave of Hesse, in 1540, while his legitimate wife, Christina, was still alive, so that he might join himself to Margarethe von der Saale in marriage. Moreover, in the Catholic Church, the cult of the Blessed Virgin Mary, rejected by Protestants, forever is a source of renewal for virginity and perfect conjugal chastity.[138] Recently,

---

[135] See Antonin Sertillanges, *L'église* (Paris; Gabalda, 1917), bk. 5 (The Church's attitude toward this world, intellectual civilization, art, social life, political life, international life, and peace).

[136] See *ST* III, suppl., q. 65 and 67.

[137] Trent, *Canons on the Sacrament of Marriage*, canons 5 and 7 (Denzinger, no. 1805 and 1807).

[138] See Lacordaire, *Conférences de Notre-Dame*, 34th conference: "Jesus Christ wished to be born of a woman who was at once a virgin and a mother, an ineffable model of maternal and virginal devotion. . . . For eighteen centuries, woman has not ceased to look upon this sublime type,

many apologists have most excellently developed this argument.[139]

The Church defends the life of *children* by prohibiting and punishing—indeed with the gravest forms of penalty—abortion and the exposing, selling, and killing of children, which were not rare occurrences among the pagan Greeks and Romans, something that is clear when you read the laws of Lycurgus and the law of the Ten [*sic*] Tablets: "The Father has the power to immediately kill a child that is notably deformed."

The Church has heard the words of Christ: "Suffer the little children to come to me . . . for the kingdom of heaven belongs to such as these. . . . But he that shall scandalize one of these little ones that believe in me, it were better for him that a millstone should be hanged about his neck, and that he should be drowned in the depth of the sea." Hence, the Church provides, in many different ways, for the education of children and youths, especially for orphans. At great expense, she has established schools, colleges, and universities. She urges parents to educate their children in religion by word and example. And she has founded associations for the sake of perseverance and the apostolate.

No comparison can be drawn between all of these institutions and those

---

which is that of her regeneration. She has drawn from her the double courage of chastity and love. She has become worthy of the respect which the world needed to have for her. . . . The honoring of flesh and blood has given way to the honoring of affections. . . .

"In the world, there are three kinds of weakness: the weakness of destitution, befalling the poor; the weakness of sex, befalling women; and weakness of age, befalling children. These three kinds of weakness form the strength of the Church, who has allied herself with them, taking them under her protection by placing herself under theirs. This alliance has changed the face of society, for prior to its formation, the weak were sacrificed to the strong, the poor to the rich, woman to man, and the infant to all. . . .

"By a kind of special delegation, all the poor have been entrusted to Christian women. The pagan and Christian worlds differ from each other just as much as the Priestess of Venus differs from the sister of St. Vincent de Paul. . . . Two worlds stand before you: choose!"

Similarly, Joseph de Maistre says in *Du pape*, bk. 3, ch. 2: "In all countries where Christianity does not reign, we can see a kind of tendency toward the degradation of women. . . . It is possible, even, to assign the reason for this degradation, which can only be combated by a supernatural principle. Everywhere our sex is able to command vice, there can be no true morality, nor real dignity in mores. Woman, who is omnipotent in her power over man's heart, returns to him in full measure the perversity she receives at his hands, and nations languish in this *vicious circle*, from which they are utterly unable to escape solely by means of their own powers. . . . By means of a wholly contrary activity, though one that is also wholly natural, the most efficacious means for perfecting man is to ennoble and exalt women. And Christianity alone works to this end without cease."

[139] See Martin Stanislaus Gillet, O.P., *L'église et la famille* (Paris: Desclée de Brouwer, 1917): Sociologism and individualism; the Church, the family, and society; the moral, social, and familial causes of individualism (depopulation); religious education of tomorrow.

founded by Protestants, wherein modern naturalism frequently prevails.

The Church gradually tempered the condition of *slaves*, for Christ preached that all men are children of the same Heavenly Father and that all are equally heirs of the kingdom of God. St. Paul had taught: "For as many of you as have been baptized in Christ have put on Christ. . . . There is neither bond nor free. . . . For you are all one in Christ Jesus" (Gal 3:27–28, DR). {{284}} And likewise, "Masters, do to your servants that which is just and equal: knowing that you also have a master in heaven" (Col 4:1, DR).

Therefore, the Church embraced within one and the same charity both slaves and lords. All shared in the same baptism, the same sacrifice, and the same Eucharist, and some slaves were exalted to the rank of the priesthood, indeed, with someone like Callistus becoming pope. The manumission of slaves frequently took place on the Lord's Day and was commended as being an illustrious deed of charity. Moreover, the remembrance of the fact that Christ himself worked with his own hands helped to ennoble the labor of workers. Finally, slavery came to be abolished among Christians.[140] In this, we have a clear example of the way that Christian charity excels the natural ethics set forth by philosophers, like Aristotle, who explained the suitability of servitude, saying it is beneficial for the slave to thus be ruled by a wiser man and, likewise, for the latter to be aided by the former.[141] And, in fact, in all peoples prior to the diffusion of Christianity, slavery was considered to be something necessary, for, as legislators said, many men are not sufficiently wise and rightly disposed to enjoy civil liberty. Indeed, only the true religion can confer upon uncultured people sufficient rectitude of judgment and will so that they may not misuse their freedom.[142]

---

[140] See Augustin Cochin, *L'abolition de l'esclavage* (Paris: Lecoffre, 1862); Paul Allard, *Les esclaves chrétiens depuis les premiers temps de l'église jusqu'à la fin de la domination romaine en occident* (Paris: Lecoffre, 1900).

[141] See Aristotle, *Politics*, bk. 1, ch. 3.

[142] See Joseph de Maistre, *Du pape*, bk. 3, ch. 2: "At all times and in all places, until the establishment of Christianity and, indeed, even until this religion had sufficiently penetrated into men's hearts, slavery was ever held to be a necessary aspect of the government and political state of nations, in republics as it was in monarchies, without it falling into the head of any philosopher to say that slaves should not exist, nor into that of any legislator to attack this institution by means of fundamental laws or by circumstantial opportunities.

"Indeed, as is well known, one of the most profound philosophers of antiquity, Aristotle, went so far as to say that there were men *who are born slaves*, and there is nothing truer. I know that in our own days he has been blamed for this assertion; however, it would have been better to try to understand than to criticize him. His position is founded on the whole of history, which is the experimental basis of politics. . . . If left to himself, man in general is *too wicked to be free*. . . . Everywhere, a very small number of men have ruled the masses, for without a more

{{285}} (3) *Civil society* is also renewed by the Church.

A. *The due relation between social authority and civil liberties* is established by the Church, who teaches that all power comes from God and is ordered to the common good. In this way, *authority is strengthened*, not in accord with the leader's egoism but, rather, in accord with justice: "He that resisteth the power resisteth the ordinance of God" (Rom 13:2, DR). *She also ennobles obedience*, inasmuch as obedience offered to a legitimate and just authority's commands is a mediated form of obedience to God himself.

---

or less powerful aristocracy, sovereignty is no longer sufficiently strong. . . . There were far fewer free men in antiquity than there were slaves. . . . *Until the era of Christianity, the entire world was forever covered with slaves, and wise men never blamed this custom.* This is all an unshakeable assertion.

"However, the Divine Law finally appeared upon the earth and, at once, took possession of men's hearts, changing it in a way made to excite the eternal admiration of every honest observer. Religion began, from its very start, to apply its tireless energies above all to the abolition of slavery. . . . It acted divinely and, for this very reason, slowly. . . . The majority of mankind is *naturally* subject to serfdom and can only be drawn from this state *supernaturally*. . . . Wherever any other religion than our own reigns, slavery maintains its rights, and wherever this religion wanes, the nation becomes, in an exact proportion, less capable of liberty in general. We recently beheld the social state of Europe shaken to its foundations because Europe had too much liberty and not enough religion. . . . Government alone cannot govern. . . . There is need . . . either of slavery, which diminishes the number of wills acting within the state, or of Divine power, which, by a sort of spiritual *grafting*, destroys the natural bitterness of these wills and enables them to act together without harming each other."

St. Thomas explains that slavery is contrary to nature and, nonetheless, can be said to be natural in some manner. Indeed, he says in *In IV Sent.*, d. 36, a. 1, ad 2: "*Slavery is contrary to the first intention of nature, though not to the second*, for natural reason has an inclination leading one to be good, something nature desires too; however, on account of the fact of one's sins, nature also is inclined such that it brings with itself a penalty on account of this sin, and in this way *slavery was introduced as a penalty for sin*." And the Holy Doctor also explains, in *ST* II-II, q. 57, a. 3, ad 2, how slavery can be called *natural*, not indeed in an absolute way but, rather, on account of some consequent usefulness: "Absolutely considered, the fact that this man is a slave rather than another has no natural basis but, instead, is based on some consequent usefulness, inasmuch as it is useful for the slave to be ruled by a wiser man and the latter to be aided by the former, as Aristotle says in *Politics* bk. 1, ch. 3. Therefore, the slavery which belongs to the *ius gentium* is natural in the second manner, not the first." Also see *ST* I-II, q. 94, a. 5, ad 3; I-II, q. 2, a. 4, ad 3: "Slavery is an impediment to the good use of power, and therefore, men naturally flee from it." Also see *ST* II-II, q. 10, a. 10 (Whether unbelievers can have dominion over believers.) Finally, see the entries for "Esclavage" in the *Dictionnaire de théologie catholique* and *Dictionnaire apologétique de la foi catholique*.

In his 33rd conference, Lacordaire shows *that socialism leads to universal servitude*: "Take away from the individual his domain of land and labor, and what will remain but a slave? . . . Transfer that twofold domain to society—in other words, *to certain men who govern and represent society*—and what will remain of one's country but *universal servitude*? . . . The citizen will no longer be anything more than a valet of the republic."

However, if a law is unjust and godless, "we ought to obey God rather than men" (Acts 5:29, DR), as Peter, the apostles, and the martyrs have all responded throughout history. In this way, *just and due freedom is promoted*, thus enabling tyranny to be avoided without, however, the danger of falling into license, thereby leading to the establishment of *peace*—that is, the tranquility of order in society. They themselves must obey the commands of God and of the Church and confess their sins. In this way, Christian monarchy was established, giving rise to princes like Charlemagne and St. Louis.[143]

---

[143] See Pope Leo XIII's encyclical *Immortale Dei*.

Likewise, see Lacordaire's 35th conference: "No society can be conceived of without unity, without order, and without power. . . . But who will give it this unity? Who will create for it this order and this power? We must always come to a few men and even, in general, to a single man, in whom power is gathered up and resides, along with order and unity. (As he says in the 33rd conference: 'Whether a society be called a monarchy, an aristocracy, or a democracy, it is always represented and led by two or three men. . . . When we are twenty years old, we do not believe this, but when we reach forty, we no longer doubt this fact.') . . . However, how will one man, or several men, be able to firmly appropriate to themselves such grandeur and bear it from one century to the next, forever subsisting and forever equaling the needs of society . . . charged with forming form, with the fragility of a life, the immortality of a nation? . . . What is authority? *Authority is a superiority which produces obedience and veneration* . . . (and, consequently, order and unity). However, how can one man, or a group of men, inspire obedience and veneration in thirty million men? This is the mystery. On this point, prior to the coming of Jesus Christ, the world was divided into two systems: the Eastern system and the Western system.

"The Eastern system consists in this: . . . authority must be enveloped with the prestige of omnipotence; between the subject and the sovereign there must be so wide a gulf that our very eyes should not dare to look beyond it. . . . But a time comes when society yields under the burden of crowned madness, and then is fulfilled . . . what the Comte de Maistre felicitously expressed in these accurate words: 'Do what you will, and when we are tired, we will slaughter you.' Rarely have nations failed to come to this end. . . .

"The Western system calculates, weighs out, and limits, power. . . . We have a memorable model of this regime, indeed the most complete of all, in the Roman Republic. The Roman senate was the most marvelous assembly which ever governed a people. . . . Well, how long did this profane masterpiece of the Western world last? Five hundred years! Slightly more than a third of the time that the French monarchy endured? Therefore, there was insufficient obedience and veneration in this system, and, consequently, insufficient unity, order, and power.

"But what was the cause of these two different pitfalls, which were so different from each other, into which both the East and the West have fallen? It is because in both East and West, there was only man, nothing more than man. . . . Man is too little for so great a work. . . . And when power is uncertain and so poorly founded, society itself staggers about like a drunken man. . . .

"*Catholic society has laid open in the world two inexhaustible sources of obedience and veneration.* One is public: *the authority of its hierarchy*, which has endured for eighteen hundred years, . . . and without any other resource than persuasion, it draws obedience and veneration to itself as no other human majesty has been obeyed or venerated in any time or place. . . .

{{286}} B. *The poor and the sick* have their needs provided for by the Church. To this end, *institutes of charity* have been founded in all places in order to give aid to orphans, the weak, and the old, as even our adversaries willingly admit. Nay, Julian the Apostate and many nonbelievers after him have striven to imitate Christian charity, though in vain. Philanthropy cannot reach the perfection of charity. Thus, we have a confirmation for Christ's doctrine, which teaches that charity for our neighbors is nothing other than an extension of our charity toward God, inasmuch as our neighbors are to be loved as children of God and for God's own sake.[144] Christ had said, "Blessed are the merciful: for they shall obtain mercy" (Matt. 5:7, DR) and "When the Son of man shall come in his majesty . . . Then shall the king say to them that shall be on his right hand: Come, ye blessed of my Father, possess you the kingdom prepared for you from the foundation of the world. For I was hungry, and you gave me to eat: I was thirsty, and you gave me to drink; I was a stranger, and you took me in: naked, and you covered me: sick, and you visited me: I was in prison, and you came to me. . . . Amen I say to you, as long as you did it to one of these my least brethren, you did it to me" (Matt 25:31–46, DR).

Inspired by this motive coming from charity, the popes have striven to improve the conditions of workers, defending their rights and driving home to the wealthy the fact that charity must go beyond what is called for in justice in beneficence and almsgiving. {{287}} Moreover, the Church also

---

"The secret source of obedience and veneration opened up in the world by Catholic society is *confession* (which is required of princes just as much as of their subjects). . . .

The Catholic spirit has (thus) produced in the world, even as regards human authority, something altogether new and altogether unknown to antiquity, the middle term between the Western and the Eastern systems: it has produced Christian monarchy, . . . where obedience and veneration are changed into a fidelity that is tempered by honor. One finds oneself here to be far from the mores of Asia and no less far from the mores of Greece and Rome. . . .

"And how was this transformation brought about? How did power become at once divine and human? . . . *The Gospel had said that we must obey God in man*, 'Servientes sicut Domino et non hominibus' (Eph 6:7). The prince was no longer the proxy of the people but, instead, was the proxy of Jesus Christ. . . . The Gospel did not determine whether the government should be a monarchy, an aristocracy, or a democracy. . . . It said to the nations: . . . Remember that as soon as you have seated your supreme magistracy, God will come within it. . . .

"No Catholic prince, even the worst, even in the era of decadence, has left behind a name like the names of the East or of Rome in its decay. This sad glory was reserved for heresy. Catholic society had to be separated from in order for a Christian land to bear kings like Henry VIII of England and like all those monsters who inaugurated in Europe the reign of Muscovite power."

[144] See *ST* II-II, q. 25, a. 1: "The formal character for our love of our neighbor is God, for what we should love in our neighbor is that he might be in God."

defends, against socialism, the right to property and divided ownership of goods.[145]

C. *Among diverse peoples*, the Church has introduced just relations, prohibiting war that is motivated solely by the desire to plunder and determining what is licit and illicit in just wars, always affirming the necessity and excellence of the law of charity and of Christian fraternity above the particular laws of various nations. In this way, *Christendom* is formed as something that cannot be compared to internationalism, which contemporary unbelieving pacifists strive in vain to establish.

Indeed, the progress of justice and peace was great under the influence of Christianity. As St. Augustine said, "Among the true worshipers of God, wars are looked upon as being peaceful when they are waged not out of greed or cruelty but, rather, with the goal of securing peace, so that evil-doers may be punished and the good raised up." Indeed, as St. Ambrose says, there are "certain rights of war and compacts which must be observed even among enemies."[146] Hence, dread was gradually diminished, especially for

---

[145] A. *As regards the improvement of the condition of workers*, see the *Acta* from the papacy of Leo XIII, especially his encyclicals *Rerum novarum* (May 15, 1891) and *Graves de communi* (Jan. 18, 1901), which commend various means for this amelioration: equitable payment of a salary that provides for a suitable subsistence for oneself and one's children; workers' associations (syndicates) in order to claim their own rights efficaciously without, however, doing injury to the rights of their employers; moderation of labor, giving attention to the age and sex of the worker; giving permission for workers to devote sufficient time to their religious duties.

Also see *ST* II-II, in the treatise on *charity*, q. 31–[32] (On beneficence and almsgiving), q. 36–38 (On envy, discord, and contention, etc.). Likewise, in the treatise on *justice*, see q. 78 and 79 (On fraud and usury). Also see *ST* I-II, q. 60, a. 3 and II-II, q. 58, a. 6 and 7, *on legal / social justice*, which are ordered to the common good, whereas particular justice is ordered to the private good.

B. *On the other hand, against socialism*, see Leo XIII, *Quod apostolici muneris* (Dec. 28, 1878; Denzinger, no. 3130ff), no. 9: "For, while the socialists would destroy the 'right' of property, alleging it to be a human invention altogether opposed to the inborn equality of man, and, claiming a community of goods, argue that poverty should not be peaceably endured, and that the property and privileges of the rich may be rightly invaded, the Church, with much greater wisdom and good sense, recognizes the *inequality* among men, who are born with different powers of body and mind, inequality in actual possession, also, and holds that the right of property and of ownership, which springs from nature itself, must not be touched and stands inviolate. For she knows that stealing and robbery were forbidden in so special a manner by God, the Author and Defender of right, that He would not allow man even to desire what belonged to another, 'and that thieves and despoilers, no less than adulterers and idolaters, are shut out from the Kingdom of Heaven' (1 Cor 4:10). But not the less on this account does our holy Mother not neglect *the care of the poor* or omit to provide for their necessities. But rather, drawing them to her with a mother's embrace, and knowing *that they bear the person of Christ Himself*, . . . holds them in great honor. She does all she can to help them."

[146] These texts from St. Augustine and St. Ambrose are cited by St. Thomas in *ST* II-II, q. 40, a.

the unarmed, captives, and those who were injured. Often, even bishops and popes helped to settle disputes among various nations, and on a number of occasions, there has been confirmation at hand for what St. Thomas taught: "Peace is a proper effect of *charity* inasmuch as we love God with our whole heart and our neighbor as ourselves . . . ; peace is indirectly a work of justice, namely inasmuch as it removes the impediments that prevent its establishment."[147]

By contrast, the pseudo-reformers worked to destroy *Christendom*— that is, the union of Christian nations, which was established in the Middle Ages. {{288}} Now, from the time of the French Revolution onward, non-believers have wished to establish a new *society of nations*, founded on the principles of humanitarianism. However, we see the brutality of this contention, for never has there ever been so universal an upheaval of nations in Europe and throughout the whole world. In recent years, people have risen up against other peoples, and king against king. Moreover, even in given nations, various classes fight with each other, and there is permanent danger of domestic strife and war.[148]

Among those who draw back from the Christian faith, many, like Kant, intend to promote universal peace without the aid of God. However, looking on the outcome of such plans, we have a verification in the words of Scripture: "Saying: Peace, peace: and there was no peace" (Jer 6:14, DR). "For when they shall say, peace and security, then shall sudden destruction

---

1 and 3. In this question *on war*, St. Thomas determines (1) the conditions required for determining whether a war is just, (2) that clerics are absolutely not permitted to take part in war, which is ordered to the spilling of blood, (3) that certain kinds of ambushes are permitted, and (4) as soon as the need to fight on a feast day ceases, it is no longer permitted that one go to war on feast days.

[147] *ST* II-II, q. 29, a. 3, ad 3.

[148] See Soloviev, *Russia and the Universal Church*, trans. Herbert Rees (London: Geoffrey Bles, 1948), 29–30: "The nations and states of modern times, freed since the Reformation from ecclesiastical surveillance, have attempted to improve upon the work of the Church. The results of the experiment are plain to see. The idea of *Christendom* . . . has vanished; the philosophy of the revolutionaries has made praiseworthy attempts to substitute for this unity the unity of the human race—with what success is well known. A universal militarism transforming whole nations into hostile armies and itself inspired by *a national hatred such as the Middle Ages never knew*; a deep and irreconcilable social conflict; *a class struggle* which threatens to whelm everything in fire and blood; and *a continuous lessening of moral power* in individuals, witnessed to by the constant increase in mental collapse, suicide and crime—such is the sum total of the progress which *secularized Europe* has made in the last three or four centuries. . . . I am speaking here of the general result; that there has been progress in certain directions is unquestionable. . . . If class war were to break out one day with all the fury of a long-restrained hatred, we should witness remarkable happenings."

come upon them, . . . and they shall not escape" (1 Thess 5:3, DR). In reality, no firm peace will be found among nations without the aid of him who is called "the God of peace" (Rom 15:33; 16:20; 1 Cor 14:33, etc.). His Christ was announced as being the "Prince of peace" (Isa 9:6), the "King of kings, and the Lord of lords" (Deut 10:17; 1 Tim 6:15; Rev 19:16). Therefore, the nations that have received the Gospel have in themselves a principle of peace that is not only individual or familial but also social and international.[149]

---

[149] Thus, Lacordaire remarks in his 32nd conference: "In extending and constituting itself from one end of the world to the other, has not Catholic society carried with itself the *evangelic law*? Has it not imposed that law upon all its dispersed and united members? Has it not formed the foundation of general mores so that pagan actions, even if they perhaps have not been repressed by the laws of each and every country, have become something impossible, inspiring a feeling of horror? It is so. . . . He who does not adore God in Jesus Christ, reveres Him as a wise man; and none of His enemies contests giving Him the title of the greatest of legislators. . . . The Gospel law has not destroyed the rights properly belonging to each city, no more than has Catholic society destroyed human society. . . . Nations make laws as before, with this single difference, namely, that, nourished by the substance of the Gospel and emancipated from ancient egotism by a sentiment of general benevolence, which is now, as it were, innate to them, they do not soil their legal code with articles which are unworthy of a Christian heart. The Gospel has not passed over the world like a violent tempest, which uproots institutions; it has gently rained down upon it, like a healing stream, penetrating down to the sources of life, purifying and rejuvenating them. Everything that comes from God is forever marked with a double sign: in them unity joined to diversity, universality to individuality, and domination to liberty. This is why the Gospel, in freeing the human race from the bonds of a constricting form of justice, has not attacked the existence of nations. *A universal law for a universal empire would have been the fulfillment of man's dreams; however, God has done better. He has created a common law for a host of peoples who are separated* by their origins, their territories, and their institutions. He has left them to their own free self-disposition, saying to them: . . . Go. . . . Increase and multiply, declare war and peace, but remember that you are but one in truth and charity. . . .

"Every people which does not submit to the evangelical law is condemned, by the force of things, to barbarism. How unbelievable—and yet, also, how visible a claim! Before Jesus's coming, Athens and Rome arrived a state of civilization, but with the promulgation of the Gospel law, all peoples that have not recognized it have remained, in comparison with Christian peoples, in a state of inferiority which even now inspires scorn more than compassion. Consider the Muslims: he came along six hundred years after us. . . . What has even the cultivation of the fields become under them? . . . God has given them the most beautiful lands, after having given them the very posterity of His Gospel (which Mohammed had copied), in order to show us, through this nearby and illustrious example, the state into which nations fall when they reject the promulgated and known Gospel. . ."

"The Gospel was promulgated. . . it was then necessary that it be defended. . . that its immutability be assured. . . *God took up this task in a most profound manner. He has given us the Gospel law, not directly in the form of right but, rather, directly in the form of a duty.* He did not tell us: Here are your liberties. No, he said: Here are your obligations. This is a capital difference. . . . Right is the egoistic side of our relations, whereas duty is their generous and devoted side. And this is why between a society founded upon duty is as far from one founded on rights as there

{{289}} Thus, in various ways, the holiness of the Church and her fecundity in all good things can be seen, showing how greatly she transcends other religions.

Objection: Often, there have been many Protestants of upright character and eminent morality. Indeed, they have founded godly institutions, orphanages, and so forth. Therefore, Protestantism is holy.

Response: The holiness of Protestant men and institutions is either *natural* or *ordinary*, though not heroic, as something extraordinarily supernatural. They have set aside the evangelical counsels. They have no priests like St. Vincent de Paul, no monks like St. Bernard, no kings like St. Louis, and no doctor like St. Thomas.

Urging the point: There are Catholic nations that are inferior to Protestant nations in their *morals*. Prussia and England excel France, Spain, and Italy in their morals.

Response:

I will let pass the claim that Catholic nations are inferior in their morals to the degree that they depart from the Catholic faith. However, I deny this to the degree that they retain the Catholic faith. . . . (1) Adversaries in no way prove that in kingdoms that they call non-Catholic there is more done for God and out of love of Jesus Christ than in Catholic kingdoms by those *who keep the Catholic faith*. (2) In fact, among non-Catholics, religion itself becomes lethargic. We see far fewer heroic sacrifices made for God; religious and missionary vocations are lacking; and in no way is it clear that in such kingdoms wickedness fails to be widespread. (3) Moreover, statistics are silent when it comes to internal acts. . . . To the eye of the statistician, the Pharisee returns to his home justified, whereas in the Gospel, the publican does. And a number of statistics are gathered according to a norm that differs from that which is in accord with the words of the Gospel: "Harlots shall go into the kingdom of God before you" (Matt 21:31, DR). (4) Finally, *the worst sorts of principles* are spread among non-Catholics, whereas the Roman Church has sanctifying principles . . . forever serving as the means for the rebirth of morals in her.[150]

---

is between heaven and earth, as well as between devotion and selfishness. *Therefore, the Gospel . . . was not a declaration of the rights of man but, instead, a declaration of his duties.* From this flows the whole system of the evangelical defense against heathen persecution. . . . Therefore, whether the evangelical law is attacked in the person of a child, a virgin, of an old man, they are all armed. The reed will answer like Pius VII, of such sweet and benevolent memory: 'Sire, I can indeed yield my rights to you, but not my duties.'"

[150] Johannes Vincentius De Groot, O.P., *De ecclesia*, q. 7, a. 3. Also see Jacques Balmés, *Le protestantisme comparé au catholicisme dans ses rapports avec la civilisation Européene*; Lacordaire's conferences from 1844 to 1845; Albert Maria Weiss, *Apologie des Christentums*, passim.

{{290}} *Continued urging*: Nonetheless, there is greater *temporal prosperity* in Protestant nations than in Catholic ones.[151]

Response: (1) The truth of a religion is not especially manifested by the fact that it fosters temporal prosperity, for religion is directly concerned with fostering goods of the soul and only indirectly with the temporal good. Nay, on account of having too much temporal prosperity, men often turn more easily toward sensible goods and away from God. Hence, Christ said: *Blessed are the poor, the meek, those who mourn, those who hunger for justice, the merciful, and those who suffer persecution*. Likewise, before Christ's coming, the Jewish people certainly had a loftier religion [than others] and at least for many years did not reach the degree of material civilization that was enjoyed by some of the surrounding Gentile peoples.

(2) As many modern apologists point out:[152]

Three things are involved in the social good: the production of earthly goods and equitable distribution of them; the intellectual culture of the talented; and the right ordering of wills along with the interior satisfaction of souls. (a) Now, this *harmony and peace*, to which the others are ordered, finds itself best fostered by Catholicism, both in its precepts and in the sacraments, which enable the precepts to be more easily fulfilled, something which many Protestants acknowledge. (b) As regards the pursuit of *intellectual culture*, the theory of *private judgment* perhaps provides more vigorous stimulation for certain activities, but it simultaneously highly favors the budding of errors and, hence, the ruin of such work. (c) As regards *earthly works*, their *production* is perhaps more efficaciously fostered by Protestantism, for given that it raises souls less to heavenly things, it thereby *urges them on more ardently to earthly ones*. However, Catholicism is much better at procuring their *equitable distribution*, on account of the spirit of self-denial and fraternal charity, thus helping it to heal the plague of poverty and more fully follow the true common good.

Therefore, through the resolution to these objections, we have a confirmation for the fecundity of the Church in all good things. Now, however, we must consider her catholic unity.

---

[151] Thus, for example, see É[mile] de Laveleye, *L'avenir des peuples catholiques* (1875).

[152] See Tanquerey, *Theologia fundamentalis*, 14th ed., vol. 1, 431; Balmés, *Le protestantisme comparé au catholicisme* [Paris: Bray et Retaux, 1875,] ch. 9; Anatole Flamérion, *De la prospérité comparée des nations catholiques et des nations protestantes au point de vue économique, moral, social* (Paris: Bloud, 1908).

ART. 3: THE CHURCH'S CATHOLIC UNITY AND UNCONQUERED STABILITY

State of the Question—Already above, in bk. 1, ch. 18, when we speculatively discussed the value of the motives of credibility, we showed *that a sign of the divine origin* of a religion can be found in its catholicity / universality (from the perspective of its material cause / members) and in its unity (from the perspective of its formal cause). It is fitting to treat these two marks (*notas*) of the Church in a unified manner here in apologetics, for unity is all the more marvelous to the degree that the Church is more universal. Nay, catholicity is not formal unless it is joined to unity, which it presupposes. For if men of all times and from among all peoples, from barbarians to city-dwelling men—notwithstanding the profound *diversity* and opposition of languages, inclinations, conceptions, regimes, and so forth—are gathered together in *unity* of faith, worship, and ecclesiastical rule, and, moreover, if, notwithstanding countless impediments and causes of ruin, this catholic unity *remains unconquered and alive*, whereas by contrast other religions or sects alter and founder into the immobility of death, then this is a sign of God's special intervention, for he alone can produce and preserve this kind of intimate unity in the midst of so great a diversity.

{{291}} However, later on, in bk. 2, ch. 5, when we discussed Christ's testimony, we saw *that Christ willed that his Church be one, catholic*, and *indefectible*: *one* with a unity of faith, rule, and worship; *catholic* not only *de iure* but also *de facto* so that, in particular, known peoples, a noteworthy number of men would gradually become members of the Church; and *indefectible* so that the gates of hell would never prevail over her. Christ announced to his apostles: "Behold I am with you all days, even to the consummation of the world" (Matt 28:20, DR).

Now, however, we must set forth this catholic unity and unconquered stability of Christ's Church:[153]

§1. The Roman Church, and she alone, is one.

§2. The Roman Church, and she alone, is catholic.

§3. The Roman Church, and she alone, enjoys unconquered stability.

§4. The aforementioned marks cannot be explained through natural causes, and the prophecies are fulfilled in them.

---

[153] [Trans. note: See note 34 above concerning the phrase *Roman Catholic Church* and *Roman Church* used liberally throughout these sections.]

This represents an apologetic consideration of the marks of the Church—namely, inasmuch as they point out to us the true Church of Christ. However, in the properly theological treatise on the Church, they are considered more profoundly and loftily as properties that flow from the intimate constitution of the Church.[154]

§1. The Roman Church, and She Alone, Is One

(1) *The Roman Church enjoys perfect unity of faith, rule, and worship.* Unity is the non-division of a being, and the unity of a religious society comes from its social body, which according to Christ's will, is found in unity of faith, rule, and worship.

A. *Unity of faith* is manifested inasmuch as all believers profess their adherence to one and the same object of faith. Now, all the believers in the Roman Church believe, at least implicitly,[155] all the revealed truths, such as they were handed on from the apostles. They accept *one and the same symbol of faith, interpreted in one and the same manner.* If all the catechisms that circulate within all the churches that have Rome as their center were compared, one would find none that does not hand on the common doctrine of faith.

As regards matters that the Church has not yet defined, Catholics do sometimes disagree with each other, but this disagreement does not stand in the way of unity, for while Catholics dispute among themselves concerning things that have not yet been defined, they are prepared in soul and will to obey the Church. Nay, controversies of this kind enable dogmas to be understood more fully. Nor should it be objected that there were Jansenists numbered among Catholics and now that there are many Indifferentists. Indeed, Jansenists, Indifferentists, and so forth, are either hidden or out in the open. In the former case, they are only Catholics in appearance, though they are in fact outside of the Church as heretics, and in the latter case, they do not even belong in appearance to the Church.

{{292}} B. *Unity of rule* is manifested in the Roman Church inasmuch as all faithful are subject to the bishops and all bishops to the Roman Pontiff as to their supreme head. All obey the same general laws, and when settling

---

[154] See St. Thomas, *De symbolo apostolorum*; Torquemada, *Summa de ecclesia* (the words *unitas, holiness,* and so forth, in the table of this work); Cardinal Billot, *De ecclesia Christi.* This properly theological treatise on the Church must be logically set forth following upon the treatises on the Incarnation and the Redemption, as is done in the Creed.

[155] Even though each person, according to his particular condition, explicitly believes a given number of truths [of faith], nonetheless, every true believer believes all of them implicitly and is prepared to explicitly believe them all, if he comes to know them.

legal cases, they all accept with veneration the decrees of the sacred congregations or of the pope himself.

C. *Unity of worship* is had inasmuch as the reception of the same seven sacraments is admitted by all. There is also the same sacrifice of the Mass, and even though there is ritual diversity, one and the same victim is offered to God in an unbloody manner, producing the same effects in believers. Unity stands forth perfectly in the Eucharistic Communion of all believers.

There is also *a unity of charity / communion*, for all Catholic churches are in communion with each other either immediately or mediately and all of them are in communion with the Roman Church, whom they acknowledge and venerate as their mother and teacher. Indeed, the disagreements that arise, dividing some individual [churches] from each other, do not divide the Church.[156]

This unity already stands forth as being miraculous inasmuch as it is brought about strongly and sweetly, without tyranny, ruling and elevating countless intellects and freedoms. It is even more miraculously found if other churches that are separated from the Pope have not been able to preserve their unity.

(2) *Formal unity is lacking in other churches.*

A. AMONG THE PROTESTANTS, *unity is completely lacking*, for in Protestantism, there is no firm principle of unity. By contrast, its fundamental principle is *the spirit of private judgment*, which, excluding authority, gives birth to subjectivism and individualism. In fact, Protestantism is clearly divided in the profession of faith, in rule, and in worship. (a) *In the profession of faith*, there has been a succession from one variation to the next from the first pseudo-reformers up to this very day. Lutherans, Calvinists, and Anglicans brought forth divisions among themselves, dividing into many sects, not only concerned with accidental matters but, indeed, with essentials as well (e.g., regarding the Trinity of Persons in God, Christ's divinity, and the satisfaction he made for our sins).[157] (b) Similarly, *unity of rule* is rejected by

---

[156] In his *De symbolo apostolorum*, St. Thomas shows that the unity of the Church is caused by three things: (1) the unity of faith, (2) the unity of hope, (3) the unity of charity. Also see Torquemada, *Summa de ecclesia*, bk. 1, ch. 6 (the unity of the Church is gathered from the unity of the head by which she is ruled, from unity of faith, the sacrament of baptism, hope, charity, that of the life-giving Spirit, and unity of her ultimate end); chs. 7 and 8 (resolution of objections against the unity of the Church); chs. 60 and 65 (the union of the members of the Church with one another and with their head).

[157] See Jacques Bénigne Bossuet, *Histoire des variations des églises protestantes* [Paris: Garnier, 1921]; Johann Adam Möhler, *Symbolik oder Darstellung der dogmatischen Gegensätze der*

Protestants. Their sects are independent and, indeed, members of one and the same sect, if they belong to different kingdoms, obey different heads. Often among Protestants we find the admission of the principle "Cuius regio, eius religio"—the religion of a realm follows that of its ruler. Episcopalian Anglicans believe that authority resides in validly consecrated bishops, whereas others believe it resides in the presbyters. (c) *In worship*, there is no agreement on the sacraments. Some hold that baptism and the Lord's Supper are sacraments, whereas others hold that only baptism is, and others make use of no sacraments at all. The divisions forever grow, without any hope for union.[158] And since there are so many different Gospels preached, Protestants gradually come to give up every form of religion, as is clear in liberal Protestantism, whose number increases by the day. And for their part, they not only reject Christ's divinity but also his teaching authority. {{293}} Therefore, they [i.e., such very liberal Protestants] cannot be legitimately called Christians.

B. AMONG THE GREEKS, *formal unity is also lacking*, for none of their patriarchs is, by divine right, the head of the whole church. Their synod itself, even when gathered as a whole, lacks a divine principle of unity, given that it has rejected its visible supreme head. Nay, on account of the growing number of autonomous schismatic churches—there are fourteen—the difficulty of convoking a council grows by the day. Who will call it? Who will preside over it? In point of fact, what manifestly prevails in the Photian churches is a [merely] *natural* profession of what the Church is. [*De facto professio naturalis ecclesiae in Photianis ecclesiis manifeste praevalet.*] Thus, there are at least four Photian unions: Constantinople [*Cpolitanus*], Russian, Greek, and Bulgarian, with fourteen patriarchs separated from each other.[159]

Having considered the division of all these Protestant sects and the unions of Greek [Churches], the unity of the Roman Church appears as being an even greater marvel, for she has always preserved it, notwithstand-

---

Katholiken und Protestanten nach ihren öffentlichen Bekenntnisschriften [Regensburg: Manz, 1894]; Ernest Naville, *Le témoignage du Christ et l'unité du monde chrétien: Études philosophiques et religieuses* [Paris: Cherbuliez, 1893]. [Trans. note: Fr. Garrigou-Lagrange also cites "G. Goyau, *L'allemagne et la Réforme.*" This title, however, seems to be for Jean Janssen, *L'allemagne et la Réforme* (Paris: Plon, 1887). It is not clear if he meant to cite this text or to cite the multivolume Georges Goyau, *L'allemagne religieuse* (Paris: Perrin, 1909).]

[158] See the articles "Alliance evangelique" and "Alliance presbyterienne" in *Dictionnaire de théologie catholique.*

[159] See Paul Pierling, *Papes et tsars* [Paris: Retaux-Bray, 1890.]; Césaire Tondini de Quarenghi, *La Russie et l'union des églises* [Paris: Plon, 1876]; Vladimir Soloviev, *La Russie et l'église universelle*, 2nd ed. [Paris: Stock, 1906], 53–72.

ing countless causes of division, especially the obstinacy of human genius firmly adhering to its own opinions and the passions that stand in opposition to the Christian law.[160] However, the unity of the Roman Church will be even clearer if we consider it in conjunction with her catholicity.

§2. *The Roman Church, and She Alone, Is Catholic*

(1) *The Roman Church is catholic.*

A. VIRTUAL / DE IURE CATHOLICITY is the Church's aptitude to have a universal extension among all peoples. A universal (*unus versus alia*, one thing turned toward others) is one thing *that is apt* to exist in many, inasmuch as it transcends their individual conditions. There, our concern is not with distributive universality but, rather, collective universality, which is common to many things taken as a whole, not individually. Thus, a state [*civitas*] designates a collection of cities [*civium*]. This aptitude of the Roman Church to have a universal extension is made clear in a number of ways. Indeed, she overcomes every form of individualism and nationalism in regard to doctrine, rule, and worship.[161]

(a) *According to Christ's own will, her doctrine must be preached to all people.* It transcends the particularities of individuals, human conditions, peoples, places, and eras. No dogma, nor any precept, is limited to the conventions of this or that people, according to the particular conditions of this time or era.[162]

---

[160] See Jacques Bénigne Bossuet, *Sermon sur l'unité de l'église* [Paris: Delusseux, 1735]; also see the first part of "Lettre sur la mystère de l'unité de l'église et les mervelles qu'il renferme" [in *Oeuvres complètes de Bossuet*, vol. 17 (Besançon: Outhenin-Chalandre, 1841), 544–552].

[161] See Torquemada, *Summa de ecclesia*, bk. 1, chs. 13–17. The Church is called Catholic / universal: (1) *as regards place*, through the whole world; (2) *in relation to all time*; (3) in relation to *all people*; (4) in relation *to the conditions of men* because nobody is cast out of the Church, neither lords nor servants; (5) in relation to *the universality of the articles of faith* (for she rejects none of them); (6) as regards the universality *of the doctrine of faith*, which is concerned with all things, visible and invisible; (7) on account of the universality *of the precepts* that are proposed to all; (8) on account of the universality *of the means of salvation*—that is, the sacraments.

[162] See Cardinal [*sic*] Billot, S.J., *De ecclesia Christi*, q. 5, p. 226 (On the mark of catholicity). Here, see the note insisting on virtual catholicity: "Surely it can't be a question of speaking of number here *in a material sense.*" See De Poulpiquet, O.P., *La notion de catholicité* (Paris: Bloud, 1909): "The true norm of the Church's catholicity is not found so much in her progress spreading throughout the world but, rather, in the supernatural character of her conquests. As was said so well by Canon J. Didiot of blessed memory, 'the Church will not be more Catholic than she was before merely because she will have a thousand more adherents, because she will have sent missionaries into a country which heretofore had been unexplored'" (37); and "The Roman Church is Catholic, in other words, universal, in the profound and evangelical sense of this

{{294}} Catholic doctrine can illuminate all men, and it responds to all of man's legitimate aspirations, even those that are most lofty. In this, the Gospel differs from the Mosaic Law, which was given to one people only for a given time. Hence, as St. Paul said: "Wherefore the law was our pedagogue in Christ: that we might be justified by faith. But after the faith is come, we are no longer under a pedagogue.... For as many of you as have been baptized in Christ have put on Christ. There is neither Jew nor Greek: there is neither bond nor free: there is neither male nor female. For you are all one in Christ Jesus" (Gal 3:24–28, DR). The preaching of the Roman Church is the preaching of the "kingdom of God," whose loftiness and universality surpasses all the kingdoms of the world.

(b) *In her rule*, the Roman Church *is not national but, instead, international* or *supranational*. She is subordinated to no State, to no Caesar. With the apostles, she teaches: "We ought to obey God rather than men" (Acts 5:29, DR). And with Christ: "Render therefore to Caesar the things that are Caesar's; and to God, the things that are God's" (Matt 22:21, DR). The pope is not designated by the civil authority but instead is elected by cardinals who are chosen from among all nations, and the bishops receive their jurisdiction from the head of the Church himself.[163] Thus, the Roman Church, by her very constitution, transcends the various forms of civil rule and is opposed to none [that are legitimate]. She is properly supranational and therefore can extend to all nations.[164]

(c) *In her worship*, the Roman Church is *universal* inasmuch as she offers all the means of salvation—namely, the seven sacraments—caring for all souls. All souls are called to one and the same Eucharistic Communion, no matter what their nation, condition, or time, for they are all sons of God "who are born, not of blood, nor of the will of the flesh, nor of the will of man, but of God" (John 1:13, DR).

---

word, because she has forever known, throughout the already-lengthy course of the centuries, how to preserve herself from particularisms which, in the various dissident sects, have altered, humanized, and materialized the spiritual universalism of Jesus's religion and, by a necessary consequence, hindered the progress of its spread" (30).

[163] See Pius IX, *Syllabus of Errors*, nos. 19–55 (Denzinger, nos. 2919–2955).

[164] The nonbeliever, Auguste Comte, wrote in his work *Cours de philosophie positive*: "The Catholic system in the Middle Ages formed the political masterpiece of human wisdom which has not been surpassed up to the present day. The eminently social genius of Catholicism has consisted, above all, in establishing a purely moral power which is distinct and independent from political power, properly so-called, in order to gradually make morality penetrate as far as possible into politics, to which, on the contrary, morality heretofore had ever been essentially subordinated.... The spiritual power most often has struggled only to fittingly maintain the just independence which it required in order to fulfill its principal mission."

No positive religion can be conceived of that would be more apt to have a universal extension.

B. ACTUAL / DE FACTO CATHOLICITY

This can be considered in three ways: "(a) as regards place; (b) as regards men's conditions; (c) as regards time."[165] However, we will speak about the third aspect later on, when we come to treat of the Church's unconquered stability.

{{295}} (a) *As regards place*, the Roman Church exists throughout the whole world. Christ had said, "Go ye into the whole world and preach the gospel to every creature" (Mark 16:15, DR), and St. Paul wrote in Romans 1:8 (DR), "Your faith is spoken of in the whole world." In the harsh lands of the Gentiles and barbarians, the Roman Church prepared the way of the Lord. After the arising of heresies, she was always much more numerous than all other sects.

Prior to the Lutheran rebellion, the Roman Church led the whole of Europe to the Christian faith and life. And when the pseudo-reformers wrenched a number of nations from Catholicism in the sixteenth century, the Catholic faith was propagated through the great missionaries who traveled to America, India, the Chinese Empire, and Japan. According to recent statistical tables [at the turn of the twentieth century], which deserve to be believed, among those who are counted as Christians, already 270–300 million men belong to the Roman Church. One hundred ten million belong to the schismatic churches, including those that are dissidents. And to the various Protestant groups, nearly 150 taken together, there are 167 million adherents.[166]

Now, the Roman Church, diffused through each and every region, *completely prevailed in Europe* and indeed in Central and South America. In North America, there are nearly 25 million Catholics, in *Asia* 3.5 million, in *Africa* 3 million, in *Oceania* 2 million, and in the *Philippine Islands* 6 million. In Protestant regions, the Roman Church counts no few believers as well: in Great Britain 5.2 million, in Germany 20.321 million, in Holland 1.79 million, and in Switzerland 1.38 million. Certainly, today, these numbers are smaller than the true count.

This diffusion is not only material but also is *formal*—that is, a diffusion in the unity of faith, rule, and worship. Indeed, it is not physically universal but, instead, *morally* universal so that in particular known countries, a notable number of men become members of the Church. And as we said

---

[165] See St. Thomas, *De symbolo apostolorum*.

[166] See H. A. Krose['s article in] *Stimmen au M. Laach*, 1903.

above, we must consider the superhuman mode of this diffusion more so that than number of believers, materially considered.

However, this superhuman mode of diffusion is made manifest through the following points.

(b) *As regards the conditions of men.* Today, just as in her first centuries, the Roman Church embraces throughout the world persons coming from all walks of life. *The poor* and workers have the Gospel preached to them. In the missions, the slaves are freed and lepers cured. The wealthy make use of their power in order to promote various works of charity. Many Catholics are counted among the *wise* and the learned. It suffices to cite the following: Among mathematicians, there are Augustin-Louis Cauchy and Charles Hermite; among those who are most well versed in astronomy, there are Urbain Le Verrier, Hervé Faye, and Angelo Secchi; in matters of chemistry [and physics], there are Alessandro Volta, André-Marie Ampère, Jean-Baptiste Dumas, Michel Eugène Chevreul, Henri Étienne Sainte-Claire Deville; and among the masters of physiology, Claude Bernard, Louis Pasteur, and René Laënnec; and others could be named.

Therefore, the Roman Church gathers within herself men from among all peoples and of all conditions. But, nonetheless, in the midst of so great a diversity of nations, tongues, inclinations, and political institutions, she does not lose her unity of faith, rule, and worship. This unity is truly something marvelous, overcoming all the natural divisions that exist among peoples and orders of society. Thus, we can see the supra-human character of her unity, which can be made even more manifest by considering the short-comings of catholicity found in other churches.

{{296}} (2) *Catholicity is lacking in other churches.*

A. IN PROTESTANTISM. (1) Even virtual catholicity is lacking, on account of Protestantism's spirit of *individualism*. Indeed, very quickly, it came to be divided. Hence, *one* society of believers was not propagated, and *the diffusion of one* church was not brought about. Rather, there was the cohabitation of disharmonious sects gathered under the one broad tent of non-Catholicism. (2) In Europe, Protestantism was at first propagated *in a far too human manner*, through fire and sword. (3) The majority of Protestant sects in Germany, England, and Scandinavia depend upon the State and, therefore, are *national*. (4) The entire grouping of Protestants, making up 150 sects when taken together, *are far less in number than* Catholics, as was said above. (5) For three centuries, they did not think of *missionary* work, though they recently have sent forth many missionaries.[167] But even if

---

[167] Paul Pisani, *Les missions protestantes à la fin du XIXe siècle* (Paris: Bloud, 1908).

they expend immense sums of money each year and receive much aid from the civil authority, they convert few pagans to the faith. No comparison can be made between the action of Protestant missionaries and the zeal, self-denial, and sacrifice of Catholic missionaries, as Protestants themselves admit.[168]

B. AMONG THE GREEKS. (1) The Photian Church is not *one* and, therefore, is not Catholic. (2) The Photian churches are *national*, being distinguished into the Cpolitana [*sic*], Russian, Greek, and Bulgarian churches, which are not dependent upon each other and are more or less subject to the civil power in any given region. (3) The Photian churches are not eminent in *number*, *extension*, or *power of propagation*. Given that they are devoid of vitality,[169] they hardly shift beyond their original boundaries.

Conclusion. Because of the lack of catholicity in Protestantism and the Greek churches, we can see all the better how much difficulty is involved in preserving the unity of faith, rule, and worship in the mist of the diversity of all nations. Therefore, catholic unity appears as something extraordinary, something utterly unique in the whole world. If we moreover consider the Church's unconquered stability, we will clearly see that she manifestly and

---

[168] See De Hübner, "Six semaines en Océanie, pt. 2 (Samoa)," *Revues des deux mondes* (Jan. 1, 1886), 101 and 102: "The Protestant missionary brings his family with him, the comfort of life, and part of the native air which he has breathed from the time of his youth. Most often, he leaves a modest environment, which he leaves in exchange for a more conspicuous existence, in exchange for a more prominent place among Europeans, if any such place exists where he exercises his ministry; and those are the ones that they prefer to choose. In a very short time, he becomes an important figure with whom the representatives of the Crown must deal. This is a wondrous humanitarian and civilizing career.

"The Catholic priest who is dedicated to the apostolate follows a vocation. Leaving Europe, he knows that he will probably never see it again. He separates himself forever from his family and from his friends. He unites two elements together in his soul. He is an ascetic who repudiates worldly enjoyments and an explorer who thirsts for vast and unknown horizons. He arrives alone and poor, seeking out souls whom he hopes to win to the faith within the depths of the county which has been assigned to him as his sphere of activity. To the degree that it is possible, he adapts himself to the ideas, as well as to the customs, and food of the indigenous people. Sometimes (in China, for example), he dresses after the manner of the people who live in that land. He returns to civilized countries only briefly and only when he absolutely must do so."

Also see Philibert Ragey, *Les missions anglicanes* (Paris: Bloud, 1900), 2 and 4.

[Trans. note: The current translator, while wishing for the Catholic Church to spread throughout the world and among all people, and with a deep appreciation for the self-sacrificial activity of missionary priests and religious, cannot help but comment also on the dated and polemical nature of these quotes. I would be dishonest to the knowledge I have of very devout and self-sacrificing Protestant (indeed, evangelical Anglican) missionaries, whom I have known, were I to allow this text to pass into the twenty-first century without comment.]

[169] [Trans note: Reading *vitalitate destituta* for *vitalitate destitutae*.]

clearly bears witness to an effect that must come from a special intervention by God.[170]

§3. The Roman Church, and She Alone, Enjoys Unconquered Stability

{{297}} (1) *Notwithstanding the countless persecutions she has undergone, the Roman Church forever stands unconquered.* Established now for nineteen centuries, the Roman Church has forever overcome all causes of ruin, hostilities from nonbelievers, heresies, and quarrels that sometimes arise from the baseness of her own pastors.

During the first three centuries of her existence, she suffered cruel persecutions and, nonetheless, spread forth throughout the world very quickly, as we showed earlier. As Tertullian said, "The blood of Christians is seed," as was Christ's blood shed upon the Cross.

The Arians bitterly fought against Jesus's divinity, and many believers went off to that sect. However, Arianism gradually died off, while the Church's faith remained. *Julian the Apostate*, with the greatest cleverness, marshalled all the powers of pagan philosophy against the Christian faith, but paganism faded away, while the Church extended her reach.

Barbarians invaded the Roman Empire and were prepared to destroy all monuments of morality and religion, and the end of the world seemed

---

[170] See St. Augustine, *De vera religione*, ch. 7: "Whether or not they will it, those who are brought up as heretics and schismatics, when they speak not among themselves but with those outside their ranks, themselves use nothing other than the word 'Catholic' in speaking of the Catholic Church. Indeed, they cannot be understood, unless they separate it off by means of this name, by which it is named by the whole world."

See Joseph de Maistre, *Du pape*, bk. 4, ch. 5 (It is impossible to give the churches that are separated a common name that expresses unity): "A great and magnificent European city lends itself to an interesting experiment, which I propose to all thinking men. Within relatively close proximity, we find all the various Christian communions. There is a Catholic Church, a Russian Church, an Armenian Church, a Calvinist Church, and a Lutheran Church. A little further on, we find an Anglican Church. I believe the only community missing is a Greek Church. Say, then, to the first person you shall meet with on your way, 'Show me the ORTHODOX Church,' and each Christian will point to his own. And here is already a great proof of a common orthodoxy. But if you say, 'Show me a CATHOLIC Church,' all will reply, pointing all to the same building: 'There it is!' What a great and profound subject for meditation! It alone has a name concerning which all men agree, for given that this name is used to express unity—which is nowhere to be found except in the Catholic Church—this unity cannot be ignored where it exists, nor can we suppose it is found where it does not exist. Friends and enemies all agree on this point. There is no dispute about the name, which is as evident as the reality it expresses. From the beginning of Christianity, the *Church* has borne the name it bears today, and never has its name varied, given that it is impossible that any essence should disappear, or even be changed, without losing its name."

imminent. Yet the pope, the bishops, and religious converted the barbarians themselves to Christianity.

In the ninth century, *Photius* established the schism among the Greeks, but the schismatic churches remain lifeless, whereas the Roman Church extended into northern Europe, into Scandinavia, Bulgaria, Moravia, Bohemia, Poland, and Hungary.

In the Middle Ages, the Church was fought by *Muslims, Arab philosophies*, and *various sects of heretics* (e.g., the Albigensians, who revived a form of Manichaeism). However, in response, new orders arose, those of St. Dominic and St. Francis, along with great doctors like St. Thomas. Indeed, it was the golden age of sacred theology.

In the fifteenth and sixteenth centuries, *Luther* and *Calvin*, impatient with authority, wished to reform the Church in accord with the spirit of free examination, offering salvation to men through faith alone, despising God's precepts. They handed over the Church's goods to the unmeasured desires of princes, thus turning Europe into confusion, especially in Germany and England, so that some were able to believe that the end of the Roman Church was near. {{298}} However, in reality, the Church herself undertook the true reformation at the Council of Trent. There arose many holy founders of new orders—St. Ignatius, St. Vincent de Paul, St. Alphonsus Maria de Liguori, and St. Paul of the Cross. The whole of America, both North and South, accepted the Catholic faith. Among the missionaries of this era, there stand out in eminence names like Bartolomé de las Casas, St. Louis Bertrand, and St. Francis Xavier.

In the eighteenth century, *the philosophers* in France, England, and Germany fought against the Catholic faith with all of their strength, in particular hurling insults at the Roman Catholic Church. *The French Revolution* revived the most dreadful persecutions against Catholic priests and intended to institute a false likeness of religion in a natural religion [of Reason]. However, gradually, Catholic worship returned, along with works of charity and the religious orders. Indeed, even new congregations were instituted, and the vitality of the Church was manifested at the [First] Vatican Council, wherein the pope's infallibility was defined, and evangelization extended into Asia, Africa, America, and Oceania.

Thus, the Roman Church forever remains the same in her doctrine, her rule, and her worship, notwithstanding the objections raised by human science,[171] heresies, the vexations of secular power, and countless other causes

---

[171] See Joseph de Maistre, *Du pape*, bk. 4, ch. 2: "No religion, save one, can stand *the test of science.* Science, a kind of acid, that dissolves all metals, except gold. . . . Science and faith will never be

of ruin, which would have destroyed a merely human society. Nay, not only does she remain unconquered but, in accord with the words of St. Vincent of Lerins, "the understanding of the whole Church grows and progresses with vigor, though in the same dogma, in the same meaning, and in the same judgment." Thus, the mysteries of salvation are proposed more explicitly, along with the cult of the Sacred Heart of Jesus and the Immaculate Conception of the Virgin Mary, and likewise, the works of charity extend further abroad, as is seen above all in the fruits of the missions.

Thus, in her immutability, the Roman Church forever remains living, forever renewed in her youth.[172]

---

allied outside of unity. . . . I have already said why we ought not to attach any importance to the preservation of faith in the Photian churches, even although it be real, for they have not passed through the ordeal of science. The great acid has not yet touched them."

[172] See Joseph de Maistre, *Du pape*, bk. 4, conclusion: "Scarcely is Christianity established in the world when relentless tyrants declare against it a ferocious war. They bathe the new religion in the blood of its children. Heretics attack it in all its dogmas successively. Arius outshines them all, spreading dismay throughout the world, *making it doubt whether it is Christian.* Julian, with his power, cunning, science, and philosophical accomplices, deals against Christianity blows which would have proved mortal to anything that could be destroyed. Immediately thereafter, the North pours its barbarian hordes over the Roman empire. They come to avenge the martyrs, and it might be supposed that they come to extinguish the religion for which those martyrs died. However, quite an opposite result takes place. They themselves are tamed by this divine worship, which takes the leading place in their civilization, and mingling with all their institutions, begets the great European family and its monarchy, of which the world had not yet the remotest notion. However, the darkness of ignorance follows the invasion of the barbarians. And yet, the torch of faith shines more brightly on this dark ground, and science even, concentrated in the Church, does not cease to produce men eminent for their time. The noble simplicity of those ages, illustrated by lofty characters, was of infinitely more value than the half-learning of their immediate successors. In the latter's days there arose that fatal schism which reduced the Church to the necessity of seeking its visible head during forty years. This scourge of all who were contemporary with it is a treasure for us in history. It serves to prove that the Chair of St. Peter can never be moved. What human establishment could resist such an ordeal, which, nevertheless, was nothing compared to that which the Church was yet destined to undergo!

"Luther appears and Calvin immediately follows. In a fit of frenzy, without example in the annals of mankind, the direct consequence of which was an internecine war of thirty years, these two insignificant men, with sectarian pride, plebeian acrimony, and fanaticism which in truth belongs in taverns, proclaimed *the reformation of the Church*, and did in effect reform it without understanding either what they said or what they did. When men without mission presume to undertake the *reformation* of the Church, they *disfigure* their own party, while they really *reform* only the true Church, which is obliged to defend itself and to act with greater circumspection. This is exactly what took place, for there is no other real *reformation* than the immense chapter of *reformation* which we read in the Council of Trent. The supposed *reformation* having remained out of the Church, without regulation, without authority, and in a short time without faith also—such as we behold it today. But by what fearful convulsions

{{299}} (2) *Stability of life is lacking in other churches.*

A. PROTESTANTISM is a new church, established by innovators, set against the Roman Church, which through the uninterrupted succession of popes goes all the way back to Peter.[173] However, the innovators' church *in no way enjoys a principle of stability,* for, having rejected authority, it is founded upon the very principle of free examination, from which arises individualism and, hence, endless alterations in faith, rule, and worship. In fact, Protestantism continually alters its doctrines. Already in the seventeenth century, Bossuet, in his work *Histoire des variations des églises protestantes,* showed the countless variations that existed among the professions of faith offered by the pseudo-reformers, especially concerning the sacraments. {{300}} However, later on, many came to reject the mysteries of the Incarnation, the Redemption, and the Trinity. Every day, new sects appear, and liberal Prot-

---

has it not fallen to that state of nullity of which we are now the witnesses? Who can call to mind without shuddering the fanaticism of the sixteenth century, along with the terrible scenes it exhibited before the face of mankind? In particular, with what rage did it not wage war on the Holy See! We still blush for human nature as we read in the writings of the time the sacrilegious insults uttered against the Roman hierarchy by those coarse innovators. No enemy of the Christian faith was ever mistaken: all strike in vain, as they fight against God; but all know where their blows should fall. It is in the highest degree remarkable, that, in proportion to the passage of time, attacks on the Catholic edifice become *forever* more formidable, so that, in saying always, 'there can be nothing worse,' we always find ourselves *forever* mistaken. Following upon the dreadful tragedies of the sixteenth century, it must have been said, no doubt, that the tiara had undergone its greatest trial; this trial, nevertheless, was only the preparation for another. . . . Philosophism could only be erected on the vast basis of the Reformation. . . .

"Recall how many unbelieving books were written through the course of the eighteenth century. They are all aimed against Rome, as if there were no real Christians beyond the Roman pale, which, strictly speaking, is quite true. This can never be sufficiently repeated: there is nothing so infallible as the instinct of infidelity. If there be anything it hates, that excites its anger, and which it always attacks everywhere, and with fury, it is truth. . . . The Church arose victorious out of the three ordeals which no false institution can ever resist: the syllogism, the scaffold, and the epigram. . . .

"It is well known that the mania of predicting the downfall of the Pontifical power was a weakness of Protestantism as ancient as itself. Nothing could correct it, neither errors, nor the most enormous blunders, nor the highest degree of ridicule. It invariably returned to the charge. . . . In beholding the Sovereign Pontiff persecuted, exiled, imprisoned, outraged, deprived of his states by a preponderating and almost supernatural power, *before which the earth was silent,* it was not difficult for those *prophets* to foretell that the end had come to the Pope's spiritual supremacy and temporal sovereignty. . . . While the false prophets spoke with greater assurance, . . . an obvious interposition of Omnipotence, made manifest by the unaccountable agreement of the most discordant powers, bore back the Pontiff to the Vatican."

[173] [François] Guizot, a Protestant, says: "I bear profound respect for the Catholic Church. *She was, for centuries, the Christian Church of the whole of Europe.*" See *Meditations et études morales* (Paris: Didier, 1851).

estantism slides into a kind of vague deism, no longer being able to be called a form of Christianity. Without persecutions, Protestantism passes away in virtue of its own subversive principle: It cannot resist incredulity, laicism, and the spirit of insubordination and license, but, rather, traveling along the paths of liberalism, it increasingly accommodates to naturalism / irreligion.

B. THE GREEK CHURCHES, from the time of Photius, have been separate from the Roman Church. They do indeed subsist, though not as an organic body but, rather, like scattered members. Moreover, their permanence is not found in a stability of life, unconquered by persecutions but, rather, is a *quasi-immobility of death, for they lack vitality*. They express no progress in the understanding of dogmas, nor in their defense against rationalism. In their rule, they are national churches, unable to resist undue demands placed upon them by secular powers and finding themselves to be more or less subject to them. They lack the apostolate of the missions, and their institutes of charity proceed more from civil prudence than from religion.

Therefore, in churches outside of the Roman Church, true stability of life is lacking, something that coincides with the mark of apostolicity—that is, identity with the Church of the apostles.

§4. The Aforementioned Marks Cannot Be Explained through Natural Causes, and in Them, We Have a Confirmation of the Prophecies

(1) *These four marks*, since they are found only in the Roman Church, exceed all natural means, which are brought forth in other churches in order to preserve and propagate Christianity.

(2) *The holiness* of the Roman Church is manifest in her saints and martyrs, as we showed in the previous article, and her fecundity in all goods, if compared with the fruits of other religions and sects, appears to be *extraordinary and superhuman*. Therefore, it indicates a special intervention by God, for the order of agents must correspond to the order of ends, and only as God's minister can the Church lead souls to an utterly holy end—that is, to love of God himself above all things.

(3) *Catholic unity* also surpasses natural causes, which are incapable of establishing so profound a unity of faith, rule, and worship in the midst of so great a diversity of peoples.

Indeed, as Gatti writes:

People who are separated so far from each other, speaking such different languages, and having mores that are so different, cannot be joined together in one profession of faith and under the rule of one head unless there is some intelligent and efficacious power which orders and directs them thus. Otherwise, it would be impossible for there to be agreement among so diverse a group in relation to one and the same end, indeed to the point that they would arrive at accomplishing it. Now, that power cannot be human, for clearly human realities, which are united to one end by a human and material power, not only fall into dissolution immediately upon the cessation of material strength, but also do not persevere for a long while in one and the same existence, even while one and the same power is employed; rather, after a more or less lengthy period of time they wholly come to ruin, as is manifestly clear if we merely consider the kingdoms and empires which have existed in the world.[174]

{{301}} In other words, *in a given society, unity is all the more difficult to the degree that the society in question is more universal,* for man is inclined to his own judgment and his own will, and often obstinately adheres to them. Moreover, *this universality is all the more difficult to the degree that it must be more profound.* Now, in the Roman Church, there is not only unity as regards external obedience or external worship, but also obedience regarding the internal and utterly affirm assent to be made to the obscure mysteries and loftier precepts that are opposed to the inclinations of the flesh and pride.

(4) *The unconquered stability* of the Church for nearly two millennia cannot be explained through natural causes if we consider: (a) the utterly great mutability of minds, human institutions, religions, and systems of philosophy, especially in Europe;[175] (b) the utterly dreadful and countless persecutions that have been launched against the Church, as well as

---

[174] Gatti, *Institutiones apologetico-polemicae*, vol. 3, 696.

[175] See Joseph de Maistre, *Du pape*, Conclusion (§12): "No human institution has lasted eighteen hundred years. So wonderful a thing, calculated to arrest attention everywhere, is all the more marvelous in the midst of our changeful Europe. Rest is painful to the European, and this character forms a striking contrast with Oriental immobility. The European is essentially active and enterprising. He must innovate. He must change everything that comes within his reach. Politics in particular has never ceased to exercise the innovating genius of the daring sons of Japhet. In the restless mistrust which keeps them always on their guard against sovereignty, there is much pride no doubt, but there is also a just awareness of their dignity. God alone knows in what proportion these two elements respectively exist. Here, we merely need to call attention to the character, which is incontestable, and to ask ourselves what hidden power has been able to maintain the Pontifical throne in the midst of so many ruins and against all the laws of probability."

the undue demands of secular powers,[176] as well as the critique of religion that has been set up by human science; and (c) the debility of the natural aids on which the Church relies—nay, the sometimes-grave defects of her ministers.[177]

No proportion exists between these weak natural means and the unconquered stability of the Church against so many causes of ruin.[178]

{{302}} (5) *The prophecies are fulfilled in this marvelous life of the Church.* The holiness, unity, and unconquered stability of the Church not only

---

[176] Even the rationalist Harnack writes in *L'essence du christianisme*, 14th conference [(Paris: Fischbacher, 1907)], 261: "This (Roman) Church has maintained in the West the idea that religion and the Church are independent, doing so against the State's own tendencies toward dominion in the spiritual domain. . . . The religious and moral domain is connected to nothing worldly and does not allow itself to be invaded. This is one reason for the recognition that we grant to the Roman Church."

[177] See Joseph de Maistre, *Du pape*, Conclusion (§17): "Thousands upon thousands of times have its (the Holy See's) enemies reproached us with the weaknesses, indeed even the vices, of those by whom it has been occupied. They have not reflected on the fact that every sovereignty must be viewed as a single individual, possessing all the good and all the bad qualities that have belonged to the entire dynasty, and that the succession of Popes, thus considered in regard to its general merit, surpasses all others without difficulty, indeed beyond comparison. Moreover, they have overlooked the fact that while they insisted most complacently on certain blots, they argued powerfully in favor of the indefectibility of the Church. . . . God promised us that he would found, *on a succession of men like ourselves*, an eternal and indefectible Church. He did so, as he said he would, and this wonderful thing, which is becoming every day more dazzling, is already incontestable for us, who are placed more than eighteen centuries from the time of when this promise was made. Never did the moral character of the Popes influence the faith. Liberius and Honorius, both eminent in their piety, do however require an apology in regard to dogma; the bullarium of Alexander VI is irreproachable. Once again, why do we delay to acknowledge this miracle and to all attach ourselves to this center of unity, apart from which there is no Christianity?"

[178] Ibid.: "What, then, are our brethren, so unfortunately separated, waiting for? . . . And what do they mean by a miracle, if they will not acknowledge the greatest, most manifest, and the most incontestable of all, in the preservation, and in our days above all—if I may use the word—the resurrection, of the Pontifical throne. . . . Of the wreckage of the Roman empire have been formed a multitude of empires, all differing from one another in manners, language, and prejudices. The discovery of new lands has incalculably multiplied this variety of peoples—all independent in relation to each other. What other than a Divine Hand could retain them under the same spiritual sceptre? Meanwhile, this is a reality of which we are all witnesses. The Catholic edifice, composed of politically discordant (and even hostile) parts, and, moreover, attacked by the most wicked, the most ingenious, and most formidable inventions that human power, aided by time, was capable of having recourse to, at the very moment it appeared to have fallen into irretrievable ruin, is reestablished on its ancient bases more firmly than ever, and the Sovereign Pontiff of Christians delivered from the most relentless persecution and consoled by new friends, by illustrious conversions, by the most cheering hopes, raises his august head in the midst of astonished Europe."

cannot be explained through natural causes but, indeed, were announced as a divine work by the ancient prophecies as well as by Christ himself.

The prophets foretold the universal propagation of the kingdom of God through Israel—that is, that the God of Abraham, Isaac, and Jacob was to reign over the whole earth. Isaiah had said: "Arise, be enlightened, O Jerusalem: for thy light is come, and the glory of the Lord is risen upon thee. . . . And the Gentiles shall walk in thy light, and kings in the brightness of thy rising" (Isa 60:1–3, DR; see Isa 2:2–5; 18:7; 19:23–25; 23:15–18; 42:6–7; also see the argument below drawn from the prophecies fulfilled by Christianity). In the Psalms, we read, "Ask of me, and I will give thee the Gentiles for thy inheritance, and the utmost parts of the earth for thy possession" (Ps 2:8, DR).

Jesus had said even more explicitly: "Thou art Peter; and upon this rock I will build my church, and the gates of hell shall not prevail against it" (Matt 16:18, DR). "And other sheep I have that are not of this fold: them also I must bring. And they shall hear my voice, and there shall be one fold and one shepherd" (John 10:16, DR). "And for them do I sanctify myself, that they also may be sanctified in truth. And not for them only do I pray, but for them also who through their word shall believe in me, that they all may be one, as thou, Father, in me, and I in thee; that they also may be one in us: that the world may believe that thou hast sent me" (John 17:19–21, DR). "And you shall be witnesses . . . even to the uttermost part of the earth" (Acts 1:8, DR). "Going therefore, teach ye all nations: baptizing them in the name of the Father and of the Son and of the Holy Ghost, teaching them to observe all things whatsoever I have commanded you. And behold I am with you all days, even to the consummation of the world" (Matt 28:19–20, DR; see Mark 16:15).

Therefore, by considering how all of these prophecies were fulfilled, we have a confirmation that the marvelous life of the Church, made manifest through her marks (*notis*) is "a great and perpetual motive of credibility and an irrefutable testimony of her divine mission."[179]

However, in accord with the requirements of the critical spirit, *Protestants* hold that the unconquered stability of the Catholic Church cannot be admitted as being a miracle. Yet they themselves do not see *that they themselves absolutely lack a critical spirit*, while they admit, for example, that *Luther*—whose manifest pride, hot temper, petulance, and all of his mores were radically opposed to Christ's life and that of the saints—*was a true reformer of Christianity*.[180]

---

[179] [First] Vatican Council, *Dei filius*, ch. 3 (Denzinger, no. 3013). See Bossuet's *Instruction pastorale sur les promesses de Jésus-Christ à son église*.

[180] See Denifle, *Luther und Luthertum*, 2 vols.

{{303}} We already resolved above the objections raised by modernists against the value of this argument.[181]

---

[181] See bk. 1, ch. 18 in this second volume. Modernists say: *Something unknown* is concealed in the marvelous life of the Church, but this does not prove that this unknown thing is a supernatural intervention by God. In fact, they can say nothing else, given their agnostic prejudices. Indeed, they doubt the ontological and transcendent value of the first principles and, hence, doubt the value of the demonstration of the existence of a God who is essentially distinct from the world. Nay, for them, a miracle cannot be an abrogation of the laws of nature, but instead must only be an abrogation of what we subjectively are accustomed to experiencing in our knowledge of the phenomena of nature. Therefore, even when it comes to obvious physical miracles, they say that this fact is not yet explained, given our current knowledge of the laws of nature. It contains something unknown. Therefore, they must say the same thing concerning the marvelous life of the Church. By contrast, once the ontological and transcendent value of the first principles of reason are presupposed, the miracle of the Church's life can be discerned with certitude, just like the clearest cases of a physical miracle.

Confirmation of Christ's Testimony through Miracles and Prophecies

Ch. 10. On Christ's Miracles {{304}}
  Art. 1. On the Miracles Performed by Christ before His Death
  Art. 2. On Christ's Resurrection
  Art. 3. On the Continuation of Miracles in the Catholic Church
    and in Her Alone

Ch. 11. On Christ's Prophecies
  Single Article

Ch. 12. Confirmation of Christ's Divine Mission by the Messianic
    Prophecies
  Single Article

Having considered internal motives of credibility (i.e., taken from the marvelous fulfillment of humanity's aspirations), as well as the motives that are external to human awareness, though intrinsic to religion (i.e., taken from the sublimity of Christian doctrine and from the extraordinary life of the Church), we must now consider the motives that are external to human awareness and, likewise, extrinsic to religion—namely, miracles and prophecy: (1) the miracles of Christ and the apostles; (2) Jesus's prophecy; (3) and the messianic prophecies of the Old Testament. Thus, we will proceed by using a regressive method, going from what is more known to us to what is less known—that is, from what is more recent to what is more ancient. Therefore, there will be three chapters in this section.

CHAPTER TEN

On Christ's Miracles

ART. 1: ON THE MIRACLES PERFORMED BY CHRIST BEFORE HIS DEATH

§1. The state of the question. {{305}}
§2. The classification of the miracles narrated in the Gospels.
§3. These miracles are historically certain.
§4. They are truly supernatural.
§5. They confirm Christ's divine mission with utter certainty.

§1. State of the Question

Although many rationalists admit the majority of the facts recounted in the Gospels, they nonetheless reject the miracles spoken of therein because, according to them, miracles are *a priori* impossible. Therefore, they deny either the historicity or the supernaturality of these facts.

As we discussed earlier, the rationalist *Paulus* (†1851) said that Jesus cured the man who was blind from birth but did so by means of an eye salve that he mixed with mud. Likewise, the five loaves of bread filled the five thousand inasmuch as their example led other men who had bread to give some to those who did not have any. He walked upon the sea—that is, upon the shore, above the sea. *Strauss* (†1874) rejected these ridiculous inventions, which are opposed to the honesty of the Evangelists, contending instead that all the accounts of the miracles must be classified as *myths*, as facts that have been augmented and adorned by the imagination. Now, since myths could only be formed after the passage of some time, Strauss said that the Gospels were not contemporaneously written accounts but, rather, must have been written a hundred or a hundred and fifty years after Christ's death.

However, critics had to acknowledge that the Synoptic Gospels were

435

written after the first letters of St. Paul but before the end of the first century. As we discussed earlier, *Harnack* today holds that the Gospel according to Mark was composed between AD 65 and 70, the Gospel according to Matthew between AD 70 and 75, and the Gospel according to Luke between AD 78 and 93 or perhaps between AD 60 and 70. {{306}} Therefore, many contemporary rationalists and liberal Protestants admit the historicity of certain miracles recounted in the Gospels, which they contend can be explained by *mental suggestion* and hypnotism, holding that the accounts concerning the other miracles were gradually constituted *through a kind of process of idealization* inasmuch as a natural fact that was more or less extraordinary was elevated by faith by being transfigured beyond its historical conditions.[1] Such was the position held by the *modernists*.[2] However, conservative Protestants defend the traditional position concerning the miracles of Christ.[3]

The [First] Vatican Council defined, "If anyone says that no *miracles are possible and that, therefore, all accounts of them, even those contained in Sacred Scripture, are to be dismissed as fable and myths; let him be anathema.*"[4]

Already, at the beginning of this second book, we defended the historical authority of the Gospels in general. Now, we must consider the historicity of the miracles recounted therein, along with their supernaturality and probative force.

---

[1] See Ernest Renan, *Vie de Jésus*, ch. 16; Albert Reville, *Jésus de Nazareth*, vol. 2, 61–85; Edmond Louis Stapfer, *Jésus-Christ pendant son ministère*, 125–149; Oskar Holtzmann, *Leben Jesu*, 58–59; Adolf Jülicher, *Einleitung in das Neue Testament*, 3rd ed., 291 and 292; [Paul Wilhelm] Schmiedel, in *Encyclopaedia biblica* (Cheyne); Adolf Harnack, *L'essence du christianisme*, trans. André-Numa Bertrand (Paris: Fischbacher, 1907), 42; (English trans., Thomas B. Saunders, 1902), 31: "So far as I can judge, the stories may be grouped as follows: (1) Stories which had their origin in an exaggerated view of natural events of an impressive character; (2) stories which had their origin in sayings or parables, or in the projection of inner experiences onto the external world; (3) stories such as arose in the interests of the fulfilment of Old Testament sayings; (4) stories of surprising cures effected by Jesus' spiritual force; (5) stories of which we cannot fathom the secret." For a critique of Harnack's theory, see Hermann van Laak, S.J., *Harnack et le miracle*, trans. Charles Senoutzen (Paris: Bloud, 1911).

[2] See Pius X, *Pascendi dominici gregis*, no. 30 (Denzinger, no. 3494); also see Marius Lepin, *Les theories de M. Loisy*, 183–196.

[3] See Edmond de Pressensé, *Jésus Christ*, 4th ed., 373; Frédéric Godet, *Commentaire sur l'évangile de saint Luc* and *Commentaire sur l'évangile de saint Jean*; Jules Bovon, *Theologie du nouveau testament.*, vol. 1, 296–309; Sanday's article in Hasting's *Dictionary of Christ and the Gospels*, vol. 2, 624–628.

[4] [First] Vatican Council, *Dei filius*, can. 3.4 (Denzinger, no. 3034).

§2. The Classification of the Miracles Narrated in the Gospels

Beyond the extraordinary signs that were accomplished in Christ's birth, baptism, and death, the Gospel refers to many miracles performed by Christ in confirmation of his divine mission. More than forty are specifically recounted in the Gospels, and many more are mentioned in passing in a general manner, for example, as is said in Luke 6:19, "power went out from him and healed all."

In *ST* III, q. 44, St. Thomas divided Christ's miracles from the perspective of how they show his power over all kinds of creatures.

(1) *Over spiritual substances.* He freed many who were possessed by demons. In Acts 10:38 (DR), St. Peter said that he "went about doing good and healing all that were oppressed by the devil." Eight miracles of this kind are referred to in the Gospels: The demoniac was healed in the synagogue of Capernaum (Mark 1:23–28; Luke 4:33–37); in the region of the Gerasenes two were freed, and the demons were cast out into pigs nearby (Matt 8:28–34; Mark 5:1–20; Luke 8:26–39); the man who suffered seizures [*lunaticus*] was cured (Matt 17:14–20; Mark 13–28; Luke 9:37–44); likewise, he healed the man who was born deaf and mute (Matt 9:32–34; Luke 11:14–15), the man who was born blind and mute (Matt 12:22–23), the daughter of the Canaanite woman (Matt 15:21–28; Mark 8:24–30), and the woman who had a spirit of weakness (Luke 13:1–16). Of Mary Magdalene, it is said that "he cast seven demons out of her" (Mark 16:9; Luke 8:2). Finally, we read in the Gospel that "they brought to him many that were possessed with devils, and he cast out the spirits with his word" (Matt 8:16, DR; Luke 6:17–18). {{307}} By contrast, the angels in the desert ministered to Christ, and one of them appeared to him in the Garden of Gethsemane in order to give him comfort (Matt 4:11; Luke 22:43).

(2) *Over heavenly bodies.* He performed two miracles of this kind: The star appeared at Christ's birth (Matt 2:2), and at his death, darkness covered the whole of the land from the sixth to the ninth hour (Luke 23:44).

(3) *Over men. Three resurrections* are recounted: the widow of Nain's son, the daughter of Jairus, and Lazarus, who had been in the tomb for four days (Matt 9:18–26; Luke 7:11–17; John 11:1–45). There are many accounts of him *curing* people, for example: the ten lepers (Matt 8:1–4; Mark 1:40–45; Luke 5:12–14; 17:12–19); the three paralytics (Matt 9:1–7; Mark 2:1–12; Luke 5:18–26; Matt 8:5–13; Luke 7:2–19; John 5:1–9); at least seven blind people, one of whom was blind from birth (Matt 9:27–31; 20:29–34; Mark 8:22–26; 10:46–52; Luke 18:35–43); the woman who suffered from a flow of blood (Matt 9:20–22; Mark 5:25–34; Luke 8:43–48); St. Peter's mother-

in-law (Matt 8:14–15; Mark 1:29–31; Luke 4:38–39); the son of a certain princeling (John 4:46); the man with the withered hand (Matt 12:9, 13); the man with dropsy (Luke 14:1–6). And in a general manner, it is said more than once, "a very great multitude of people from all Judea and Jerusalem and the sea coast, both of Tyre and Sidon, who were come to hear him and to be healed of their diseases" (Luke 6:17–18, DR).

(4) *Over irrational creatures.* The Gospels refer to the sudden conversion of water into wine at Cana in Galilee (John 2:1–11), the miraculous catches of fish (Luke 5:1–11; John 21:1–13), the discovery of the silver coin in the mouth of the fish (Matt 17:23–26), the two multiplications of the loaves (Matt 14:15–21; Mark 6:39–44; Luke 9:12–17; John 6:5–15; Matt 15:32–38; Mark 8:1–9), the calming of the storm (Matt 8:18–27; Mark 4:35–40), the walking on the water (Matt 16:23–33; Mark 6:47–52; John 6:16–21), and the sudden drying up of the fig tree (Matt 21:18–21; Mark 11:12–14, 20–22).

(5) *Christ gave his apostles the power to perform miracles* (Luke 10:9; Matt 10:8; Mark 16:17; John 14:12), and after the first sending, the seventy-two disciples returned, joyfully saying: "Lord, even the demons are subject to us in your name" (Luke 10:17). Similarly, after the day of Pentecost, many of the apostles performed miracles, which are recounted in *Acts* (Acts 2:43; 5:12; 9:34–40; 19:11–12; 20:9–12).

§3. Christ's Miracles Are Historically Certain

A defense of the historicity of each of these miracles in particular falls to a course in Sacred Scripture;[5] however, for this apologetic thesis, it is briefer and more efficacious that we consider them all together, especially by making clear the way that these miracles are connected with other facts whose historicity (something admitted by most rationalists) we proved earlier. Thus, concerning this matter, we must argue, as do many authors, as follows.[6]

(1) *The witnesses who refer to these miracles are the same as those who recount the other facts* and, hence, are equally deserving of belief. {{308}} Nay, these witnesses *suffered death* for asserting the truth of the extraordinary facts that they recounted concerning Christ.

---

[5]   See Joseph Knabenbauer, *Comm. in S. Matth. et S. Luc*; Marie-Joseph Lagrange, *S. Marc*; Marius Lepin, *L'origine du quatrième évangile*; Leopold Fonck, S.J., *Die Wunder des Herrn im Evangelium exegetisch und praktisck erklärt* (Innsbruck: Rausch, 1907); Louis-Claude Fillion, *Les miracles de Notre Seigneur Jésus-Christ* (Paris: Lethielleux, 1909), vol. 1 (General, overall study), vol. 2 (The miracles of Jesus studied individually).

[6]   See Adolphe Tanquerey, *Synopsis theologiae dogmaticae*, 14th ed., vol. 1, 228.

(2) *Like other facts, these miracles can be discerned as easily as other events, given that they are sensible.* Nor are they unbelievable, like extraordinary things, unless one gratuitously already denies the possibility of miracles, though they do call for greater attention.

(3) *However, due attention to the events in question is not lacking,* for Christ's most well-known miracles were done *in public,* in cities and in broad daylight, often being performed in Jerusalem itself in the sight of the people. Among their witnesses, many were of influence in matters of science and authority, like Nicodemus, Jairus, the centurion, Zacchaeus, Lazarus, the scribes and Pharisees, the priests, and the Sanhedrin. Not all of them were inclined to admit these miracles, for the scribes and Pharisees made use of all possible means in order to deny their existence.

(4) *Nay, Christ's own enemies undertook a juridical inquiry into certain miracles* (John 5:10–16; 9:1–34). The clearest example of this is found in the account of the curing of the man born blind recounted in John 9. (a) After the miracle was performed, immediately the neighbors who knew that he had been blind diligently asked, "How were your eyes opened?" (b) They led him to the Pharisees, who first asked him how it was that he came to see, but they did not wish to believe that he had been blind. (c) The Pharisees themselves called in his parents, who asserted, "We know this because he is our son, and he was born blind." (d) Once again, the Pharisees called in the man who was born blind and, again, like judges, interrogated him:

> They said to him: Give glory to God. We know that this man (who is called Jesus) is a sinner. He said therefore to them: If he be a sinner, I know not. One thing I know, that whereas I was blind now I see. They said then to him: What did he to thee? How did he open thy eyes? He answered them: I have told you already, and you have heard. Why would you hear it again? Will you also become his disciples? They reviled him therefore and said: Be thou his disciple; but we are the disciples of Moses. We know that God spoke to Moses; but as to this man, we know not from whence he is. The man answered and said to them: Why, herein is a wonderful thing, that you know not from whence he is, and he hath opened my eyes. Now we know that God doth not hear sinners, but if a man be a server of God and doth his will, him he heareth. From the beginning of the world it hath not been heard, that any man hath opened the eyes of one born blind. Unless this man were of God, he could not do anything. They answered and said to him: Thou wast wholly born in sins; and dost thou teach us? And they cast him out. (John 9:24–34, DR)

In this juridical inquiry, the miraculous fact is so clear that the Pharisees could not deny it without utterly obvious malice. Therefore, Jesus, by way of conclusion, said, "For judgment I am come into this world: that they who see not may see; and they who see may become blind. And some of the Pharisees, who were with him, heard, and they said unto him: Are we also blind? Jesus said to them: If you were blind, you should not have sin; but now you say: We see. Your sin remaineth" (John 9:39–41, DR).

Similarly, we read in John 12:9–11 (DR), following upon the resurrection of Lazarus, many Jews "came, not for Jesus' sake only, but that they might see Lazarus, whom he had raised from the dead. But the chief priests thought to kill Lazarus also because many of the Jews, by reason of him, went away and believed in Jesus." {{309}} Similarly, as we see in Acts 4:14–17 (DR), following upon the miracle performed by St. Peter, the leaders and the priests "*could say nothing against it* . . . and they conferred among themselves, saying: What shall we do to these men? For indeed a miracle hath been done by them, known to all the inhabitants of Jerusalem. *It is manifest, and we cannot deny it*. But that it may be no farther spread among the people, let us threaten them that they speak no more in this name to any man."

(5) *We must take note of the simplicity of these narrations in the Gospels,* which are completely different from what we read in the apocryphal gospels.[7] Hence, all these things considered, these accounts cannot be rejected, unless we were to reject the very honesty of the Gospels as a whole.

(6) *Moreover, these miraculous facts were intimately connected with other facts recounted in the Gospels* so that they cannot be denied without leading us to reject the entire historicity of Christ. Indeed, (a) we often read, "Many believed in his name, seeing signs which he performed" (see John 2:23; 11:45; 12:42; 20:29; Acts 5:12). This is how the *conversion of many people* is explained, like that of Nicodemus (John 3:2), as well as the apostles' vigorous faith. After the miracle of Cana, "his disciples believed in him" (John 2:11, DR), and after the calming of the storm, they said among themselves, "Who is this, thinkest thou, that both wind and sea obey him?" (Mark 4:40, DR). (b) Likewise, many of *Christ's words* were spoken at the time of a given

---

[7] See Marius Lepin, "Évangiles canonique et évangiles apocryphes," *Revue pratique d'apologétique* (Dec. 15, 1905): 241–256. As many apologetes note: "The marvels recounted in the apocryphal gospels have a completely different character. In them, Jesus performs such miracles in order to astonish, frighten, or exact revenge. He is a kind of insubstantial supernatural specter. His wonderworking is material, mechanical, and immoral, like the tricks of a magician. Everywhere he goes, he is like a magnetic force. Nature is put into panic, falling into nonsense, merely by his presence. Each of his words is followed by miraculous effects for both good and evil." See "The Gospel of Thomas" 4–5 and "The Gospel of Pseudo-Matthew" 26 in Constantin von Tischendorf, *Évangelia apocrypha*, 2nd [ed.,] 9ff, 164ff, 181.

miracle. For example, when he had healed the paralytic, Jesus set forth his divine mission and filiation to the Jews (John 5); likewise, the entire bread of life discourse is connected with the multiplication of the loaves (John 6). (c) Finally, on the occasion of these miracles, especially the raising of Lazarus, *the priests and the Pharisees took counsel together*, saying, "What do we, for this man doth many miracles? . . . But one of them, named Caiaphas, being the high priest that year, said to them: You know nothing. Neither do you consider that it is expedient for you that one man should die for the people and that the whole nation perish not. . . . From that day therefore they devised to put him to death" (John 11:47–53, DR). Thus, since Christ's miracles are intimately connected with the details of his life, preaching, Passion, and death, you could not undermine their veracity without simultaneously undermining that of the whole of the Gospel.[8] {{310}} Indeed, certain rationalists admit this fact, and because miracles are forever found in Christianity, the only thing that they can do is reject the possibility of miracles *a priori*.

(7) *The letters of St. Paul* can also be argued from. Their authenticity is admitted by nearly all rationalist scriptural critics, especially the letters to the Galatians, to the Romans, and the two letters to the Corinthians, which according to Harnack and Jülicher were written in either AD 53 or 54. Now, these letters formally assert that miracles were performed by the apostles in Christ's name. However, if the apostles performed miracles in Christ's name, *a fortiori*, Christ himself performed miracles. It suffices to cite the words of Romans 15:18–19 (DR): "For I dare not to speak of any of those things which Christ worketh not by me, for the obedience of the Gentiles, by word and deed, by the virtue of signs and wonders, in the power of the Holy

---

[8] *As regards Lazarus's resurrection*, Théophane Calmes notes in *Évangile selon saint Jean* [Paris: Lecoffre, 1906], 341: "Up to this point, the conflict between Jesus and the Jews followed an ascending path. The miracle of Bethany is the ultimate terminus of this upward gradation, and the Savior's death will be its immediate consequence. . . . Now, critics agree that the passion narrative found in the fourth Gospel is of equal historical value to the accounts which are found in the Synoptic Gospels. Therefore, we must recognize the reality of the fact that was its proximate cause. . . . The precision and abundance of the historical details (mentioned earlier) rule out the idea that this is an allegory. It is true that, in the mind of the author, the resurrection of Lazarus symbolizes the mystical resurrection of the soul that clings to Jesus (John 11:25). However, it is striking to see the sobriety with which the miracle is recounted in 41–44. This kind of expositional richness is found only in historical passages preceding this one. The contrary is the case for allegorical teachings. Moreover, many of the features of the narrative are quite gripping. Can we think that the author, using allegory to express the doctrine of the mystical resurrection through faith, would insist thus upon the human details, mentioning as he does in verses 33–35 the emotion, disturbance, and tears of Jesus?"

Ghost." Likewise, see 2 Corinthians 12:12. In 1 Corinthians 12:28, among all the charismata, he speaks of the grace of healing and of powers (that is, the grace of miracles). In Galatians 3:5 (DR), he takes up the argument from miracles: "He therefore who giveth to you the Spirit and worketh miracles among you."

(8) *The apostles and Fathers would not have been able to call upon Christ's miracles with such confidence* unless they were entirely certain concerning them. How could St. Peter have said to the Jews in Acts 2:22 (DR), "Ye men of Israel, hear these words: Jesus of Nazareth, a man approved of God among you, by *miracles* and *wonders* and *signs*, which God did by him, in the midst of you, as *you also know*"?

(9) If Christ's miracles were only pious inventions made up by his disciples, their contemporaries, especially their *adversaries*, would have openly declared this fact. However, the contemporary Jews, who wrote the Talmud, or pagan authors like Celsus[9] did not deny the miraculous works of Christ but, rather, attempted to explain them as being magical artifices.

From all of these points, we must conclude that miracles of this kind cannot be *historically* denied. They are certain, as are the other facts recounted in the Gospels, whose historicity is admitted by rationalists.

§4. Christ's Miracles Are Truly Supernatural

Rationalists do not deny that certain miracles recounted in the Gospels properly speaking exceed natural powers (e.g., the resurrections recounted therein). Hence, as we already have said, they hold that we must reject the historicity of these miracles *a priori*. As regards other signs, they concede that facts of these kinds truly stirred up amazement in those who saw them at that time, but they contend that they were recognized as being supernatural only because people were unaware of the laws of nature, along with the fact that men in these days had the propensity to admit miracles quite easily. Now, in response to this, we must say the following.

(1) *The Pharisees were not inclined to acknowledge Christ's miracles, and nonetheless, they were not able to deny them.* For example, there was their threefold investigation into the healing of the man who was born blind. {{311}} Likewise, there was their inquiry following Lazarus's resurrection, which took place before the eyes of many Jews, with many of them believing, though others went away to the Pharisees, and gathering together evidence, they held counsel and said: "What do we, for this man doth many miracles?

---

[9] See Origen, *Contra Celsum*, 1.38.

If we let him alone so, all will believe in him; and the Romans will come, and take away our place and nation" (John 11:47–48, DR). The same thing took place in Acts 4:16, after the miracle performed by St. Peter.

(2) Earlier, after Christ's first miracle, which clearly exceeded the powers of sensible nature, *the scribes had said*, "He hath Beelzebub, and by the prince of devils he casteth out devils." And Jesus responded to them, "How can Satan cast out Satan? And if a kingdom be divided against itself, that kingdom cannot stand. . . . And if Satan be risen up against himself, he is divided, and cannot stand, but hath an end. . . . Amen I say to you that all sins shall be forgiven unto the sons of men, and the blasphemies wherewith they shall blaspheme; but he that shall *blaspheme against the Holy Ghost*, shall never have forgiveness, but shall be guilty of an everlasting sin" (Mark 3:22–29, DR; see Matt 12:27ff; Luke 11:15). St. Mark explains the nature of the sin against the Holy Spirit by adding, "Because they said: He hath an unclean spirit," and they said this having seen the miracles that clearly manifested the Holy Spirit's intervention.

(3) *The extraordinary facts themselves* that are presented in the Gospels as miracles, *when their nature and physical circumstances are considered attentively,* are clearly supernatural. There are many such cases: the instantaneous healing of a person who was born blind solely by means of spit and mud, the full curing of leprosy solely by touch, healings brought about at a distance by a mere word, the sudden conversion of water into wine, the multiplication of loaves, and *a fortiori* the raising of a dead man who was already beginning to rot. All of these facts, without falling into absurdity, cannot be called natural, as was said in bk. 1, ch. 19, where we showed at length, in our thesis concerning the discernibility of miracles (especially resurrection, the multiplication of loaves, and the healing of the man born blind), that they certainly exceed not only the powers of sensible nature but also those of created spirits. Moreover, among the physical circumstances of miracles, we must consider the fact that Christ performed these miracles instantaneously by his mere word. The winds responded immediately to his utterly certain command, and as Quadratus tells us, these healings were so stable that the sick who were thus cured or called back to life from death led a long life thereafter.[10]

(4) *The moral circumstances and fruits* of these signs confirm their divine

---

[10] Citing Quadratus, see Eusebius, *Historia ecclesiastica*, bk. 4, ch. 3: "But the works of our Savior were always present, for they were genuine: those that were healed, and those that were raised from the dead . . . were also always present; and not merely while the Savior was on earth, but also after his death, they were alive for quite a while, so that some of them lived even to our day."

origin. In general, seven moral circumstances are enumerated for human acts: who, what, where, by what aids, why, how, and when. As we said earlier in this volume,[11] the principal circumstance is the end, which appears first in the intention and declaration made by the wonderworker, though it comes later in execution—namely, in the moral fruits of the miracles performed. {{312}} (a) *Why?* Christ always said that he acted for the glory of God and the salvation of souls. And this is utterly clear on the basis of the fruits of the miracles—namely, the emendation of the lives of the disciples, along with the conversion of many Jews and Gentiles, the correction of vices, and the regeneration of humanity. Christ himself said, concerning false prophets: "By their fruits, you shall know them. . . . Every good tree brings forth good fruits, whereas every bad tree brings forth bad fruit" (Matt. 7:16–17). The fruits of Christianity are clearly conformed to right reason and to the nobler aspirations of our nature. (b) *What?* In the very nature of these miracles, we find nothing that appears ridiculous, indecent, violent, and irrational. On the contrary, all of them are good, morally befitting, beneficent, and worthy of God. (c) *Who?* Jesus, who performs these miracles, teaches a doctrine that honors God, is conformed to right reason, and leads to good morals. He himself appears to be utterly holy and endowed with a full host of heroic virtues. (d) *How?* Nothing unbefitting is grasped in his manner of acting, nor any ostentation, but rather, he acts with humility and modesty, indeed, often saying to those whom he healed, "Tell no one" (Matt 8:4; 16:9; Mark 5:43; 7:36; 8:26; etc.). Indeed, not wishing to vainly enkindle souls, he chose not to "show a sign from heaven" to the Pharisees and Sadducees (Matt 16:1–3). (e) *By what aids?* Christ performed miracles by commanding, after prayer, with majesty joined to humility. (f) *Where?* He did not perform these miracles among vain and unworthy men. Thus, he did not wish to perform a miracle before Herod in order to fulfill his curiosity. (g) *When?* He performed miracles at suitable times but not at others, thus showing that miracles must not be multiplied for the sake of the temporal necessities of this life. For example, in John 6:26 (DR), after the multiplication of the loaves, when the crowd from Capernaum gathered and sought after Jesus, he said to them: "Amen, amen, I say to you, you seek me, not because you have seen miracles, but because you did eat of the loaves and were filled." On the basis of all of these circumstances, we have a clear confirmation that Christ was a minister of God, not of the devil.

(5) *We have an additional confirmation by considering the foolishness or impossibility of the hypotheses to which rationalists make recourse* in order to

---

[11] See vol. 2, bk. 1, ch. 19, a. 2.

deny these miracles. As we said in our discussion of the state of the question, the explanation proposed by Paulus is held to be ridiculous by rationalists themselves. Likewise, the mythicism invented by Strauss has been rejected by all critics, who are forced by historical evidence to admit that the Gospels were written much earlier than Strauss wished. However, rationalists today contend that Christ's miracles can be explained by suggestion or hypnosis.

Earlier, when we discussed hypnosis,[12] we showed *the limits of the powers of suggestion*. Now, however, it suffices to say the following. (1) Only those who are disturbed with a nervous condition can be healed by means of suggestion.[13] However, Christ also healed lepers, those who could not hear or speak, and people born blind, and indeed he raised up dead people, calmed storms, multiplied loaves, and so forth. All such phenomena lay beyond the bounds of what can be brought about by means of hypnosis. (2) When it is efficacious, suggestion works only gradually, not immediately, so that the sick may have a kind of persuasion concerning the healing to be obtained.[14] {{313}} By contrast, Christ healed suddenly with a mere word or touch and, in many cases, did not gain the trust of these sick people whom he cured (Matt 12:22; Luke 17:12–14; 7:2–10; John 11:6). (3) Moreover, suggestion does not act at a distance.[15] However, Jesus sometimes performed miracles at a distance, without any preparation, as he did, for example, when he healed the centurion's son and the Canaanite woman's daughter (Matt 8:5–13; 15:22–28).

Therefore, the rationalists' hypotheses cannot explain the historical miracles of Christ, and their supernaturality remains certain.[16]

§5. Christ's Miracles Confirm His Divine Mission with Utter Certainty

A. *In general*, this was declared by Jesus in many places. For example, when John the Baptist sent two of his disciples to him to ask whether he was the Messiah, Jesus responded: "Go and relate to John what you have heard and seen. The blind see, the lame walk, the lepers are cleansed, the deaf hear, the

---

[12] See vol. 2, bk. 1, ch. 19, a. 3, §4.

[13] See Joseph Grasset, *L'hypnotisme et la suggestion* (Paris: Doin, 1904), 398–400: "There is no proof that hypnotherapy would be able to modify bodily lesions."

[14] See ibid., 124, 127, 128, 377.

[15] See Grasset, *L'hypnotisme*, 130: "A subject who neither sees nor hears his magnetizer, who is not in communication with him in any natural sensorial manner, nor by any artificial manner, ... cannot be put to sleep, nor undergo suggestion."

[16] See Fonck, [*Die Wunder des Herrn im Evangelium exegetisch und praktisch erläutert,*] and Fillion, *Les miracles de Notre Seigneur Jésus-Christ*, vol. 2.

dead rise again, the poor have the gospel preached to them. And blessed is he that shall not be scandalized in me" (Matt 11:4–6, DR; Luke 7:18–23). These signs had been announced by Isaiah as being messianic (Isa 35:5; 61:1). Similarly, when Jesus walked in the temple, in Solomon's Portico, the Jews surrounded him and said, "How long dost thou hold our souls in suspense? If thou be the Christ, tell us plainly," and Jesus responded to them, "I speak to you, and you believe not: *the works that I do in the name of my Father, they give testimony of me.* . . . If I do not the works of my Father, believe me not. But if I do, though you will not believe me, believe the works: that you may know and believe that the Father is in me and I in the Father" (John 10:24–38, DR). And because this argument was irresistible, the Jews, as the Evangelist adds, "sought therefore to take him, and he escaped out of their hands."

B. *In particular,* on many occasions, Jesus explicitly declared the connection of his miracles with the mission to be confirmed thereby, prior to the performance of that miracle. For example, before the raising of Lazarus, "Jesus lifting up his eyes, said: Father, I give thee thanks that thou hast heard me. And I knew that thou hearest me always: but because of the people who stand about have I said it, *that they may believe that thou hast sent me*" (John 11:41–42, DR). And indeed, as is often said in the Gospel, many believed upon seeing the miracles (John 2:11; 3:2; 9:35–38).

C. Nay, Jesus declared that this proof of his divine mission is *utterly firm* and *clearly manifest* when he said concerning his enemies, in John 15:22–25 (DR): "If I had not come and spoken to them, they would not have sin: but now they have no excuse for their sin. He that hateth me hateth my Father also. If I had not done among them the works that no other man hath done, they would not have sin; but now they have both *seen* and *hated* both me and my Father. But that the word may be fulfilled which is written in their law (Ps 24:19): They hated me without cause." {{314}} Thus, as the [First] Vatican Council says, the divine origin of the Christian religion is *legitimately proven* on the basis of utterly certain signs that are accommodated to the intelligence of all. Nothing could be clearer, except for the very Resurrection of Christ, which we will discuss in the next article.[17]

---

[17] See Jacques-Bénigne Bossuet, *Discours sur l'histoire universelle,* pt. 2, ch. 29: "[There were] countless healings, the resurrection of the dead, and that of Christ Himself attested to by those who saw it and held it to be true up to the point of death, in other words, everything that one could wish for in order to assure the truth of a fact, since God Himself—I will not fear to say it—could perform no clearer action in order to establish the certitude of a fact than to reduce it to sensual testimony, nor could he provide it with a stronger proof for the sincerity of its witnesses than that of a cruel death."

Objection: Christ himself seemed to have given little weight to the probative force of his miracles. He rebukes the scribes and Pharisees when they ask for a sign from heaven (Matt 12:38), whereas he says to the Apostle Thomas that they are blessed "who have not seen but have believed" (John 20:24). Sometimes he himself forbade that his miracles be announced publicly (Matt 9:30; 12:16; Mark 1:44; etc.).

Response: Christ rebukes the Pharisees who seek sign after sign, hiding their malice by feigning ignorance, whereas from then on he promises the great sign of his Resurrection. And he rebukes Thomas, who does not wish to believe the apostles' testimony, even after so many great signs, but moreover demanded to see with his eyes and feel with his hands. Sometimes Christ prudently prevented his miracles from being spoken of publicly, in order to flee from the wrath of the Pharisees, to avoid arousing the commotion of political messianism among his followers, or to offer an example of the virtue of humility.

ART. 2: ON CHRIST'S RESURRECTION

§1. State of the question.

§2. The importance of this motive of credibility.

§3. Christ truly died.

§4. It is historically certain that Christ was raised from the dead and that his Resurrection was perfectly manifested.

§1. State of the Question

Not only is Christ's Resurrection narrated in the Gospels but also, in the Acts of the Apostles as well as in St. Paul's letters, it is said that it was preached by the apostles as being the greatest motive of credibility.

Rationalists, in order to weaken the strength of this fact, have thought up many different systems, which they themselves have been forced to successively cast aside. There are at least *four distinct theories*—namely, *that holding it was fraudulent, saying that it was a kind of amplification, that asserting it was a hallucination,* and *that which asserts it was a spiritual vision.*

(1) With the deists in the eighteenth century, *Reimarus* revived the explanation that was invented by the Jewish priests and then by argued on behalf of by Celsus, holding that *the apostles were deceivers* in saying that Christ had risen from the dead. However, other rationalists reject this *fraud theory* because it does not explain how a religion founded upon lies could have renewed the world, nor how the apostles, who had been timid and fickle, fought on behalf of this fraud to the point of martyrdom.

{{315}} (2) However, certain rationalists, like *Weizsäcker* and *Martineau*,[18] preserved part of this first theory, saying that the apostles declared that they *saw* the Lord only in a general manner, inasmuch as they firmly believed in his immortality. However, afterwards, their disciples amplified these words and gradually believed that Christ truly rose from the dead. However, like the first theory, this *amplification theory* (or evolution theory) was rejected by many, indeed for nearly the same reasons: For if the apostles declared that they saw Jesus when they did not in fact see him but only believed in his immortality, then they were deceivers. Therefore, their zeal, along with the renewal of the world, remain unexplained, and likewise, this would destroy St. Paul's argument concerning the future resurrection of bodies, which has the bodily Resurrection of Christ as its pledge (1 Cor 15).

(3) Admitting the perfect honesty of the apostles, many have said that they were deceived by a kind of *hallucination*. Such was the position of people like *Strauss, Renan, Harnack, Réville,* and *Meyer*.[19] According to them, the apostles could not believe that Jesus had been defeated by his enemies. Therefore, they pored over the Scriptures, finding therein predictions concerning the resurrection of the Messiah, and therefore, ardently desiring his resurrection, they were deceived by hallucinations.

(4) No few rationalists, like *Keim, Ewald, Schenkel,* and *Stapfer*,[20] reject the last explanation as being insufficient, for it is clear that the apostles did not expect the Resurrection and, considering the number and character of its witnesses, as well as the various circumstances of the apparitions, the hallucination hypothesis is unfounded. Therefore, these rationalists thought up a fourth theory, holding that *Jesus truly appeared to the apostles*, not indeed in a bodily manner but, rather, *in a spiritual manner*, for although he did not rise from the dead, his soul, which was united to God, was able to comfort the disciples by making them more certain concerning his immortality.[21] Among the modernists, *Édouard Le Roy* proposed a similar theory, for he denied the "reanimation of a corpse" as being something impossible, teaching that Christ was resurrected in some sense, inas-

---

[18] See Karl Heinrich Weizsäcker, *Das Apostolische Zeitalter der christlichen Kirche* [Freiburg: Mohr, 1886], 5; James Martineau, *The Seat of Authority in Religion* [London: Longmans, 1890], 363ff.

[19] See Albert Réville, *Jésus de Nazareth*, vol. 2, 453–478; Arnold Meyer, *Die Auferstehung Christi* (Tubingen: Mohr, 1905).

[20] See [Daniel] Schenckel, *Das Charakterbild Jesu* [Wiesbaden: Kreidel, 1864], 231ff; Stapfer, *La mort et la résurrection de Jésus-Christ*, 2nd ed., 231–322.

[21] See Stapfer, *La mort et la résurrection de Jésus-Christ*, 255 and 261: "Paul saw no difference (indeed, much to the contrary, he likened them completely) between the apparitions to the twelve and that which he had been granted.... Now, he was convinced that Jesus Christ really appeared to him. However, Jesus of Nazareth's material body is not what was shown to him. Rather, God had revealed Jesus Christ "in him." He says this in the most explicit manner, without us being able to give another meaning to the term that he makes use of in Galatians 1:15."

much as he did not cease to act after his death and inasmuch as his soul retained a kind of virtual matter in the next life. He intended to reconcile this with Catholic dogma, for according to the pragmatism of the modernists, dogmas must be held *only* in their practical sense—that is, as preceptive norms of acting: One must comport oneself in relation to Jesus as though he rose in a bodily manner.[22]

(5) The partisans of the comparative history of religion say that the idea of the Resurrection, along with the temporal description of this taking place "on the third day" in the Evangelists and St. Paul must have depended upon other religions wherein we find the idea of a god who dies and rises again, namely, divinity of growth [*numinis vegetativi*]. Thus, Heinrich Zimmern, Peter Jensen, and Charles Virolleaud related this to Marduk in Assyrian myths; Otto Pfleiderer, Thomas K. Cheyne, Hermann Gunkel, Richard Reitzenstein, Wilhelm Bousset, and James G. Frazer had recourse to Eastern, Egyptian, Iranian, and Hellenistic myths (Osiris, Dionysus-Zagreus, Adonis, Attis, and others). Contemporary authors, at least those who hold the doctrine of the Resurrection, deny that the apostles themselves borrowed from pagan ideas, though the early communities, especially those made up of pagan Christians, underwent significant influence from pagan religions.

{{316}} *The Church* condemned this last proposition,[23] along with the two following modernist theses: "*The Resurrection of the Savior is not properly a fact of the historical order.* It is a fact of merely the supernatural order, neither demonstrated nor demonstrable, which Christian conscience gradually derived from other facts" and "In the beginning, faith in the Resurrection of Christ was not so much in the fact itself of the Resurrection as in the immortal life of Christ with God."[24] These theses are found in the works of Alfred Loisy.[25] Among the Catholic exegetes who wrote against the aforementioned theories, we should cite Ladeuze, Chauvin, and Mangenot.[26] The traditional thesis is also defended by conservative Protestants.[27]

Thus, we see the state of the question. Rationalists forever think up new theories to set up against the traditional teaching, doing so in particular (as

[22] See Le Roy, *Dogme et critique* [Paris: Bloud et Cie, 1907], 155–257.
[23] Pius X, *Lamentabili*, no. 26 (Denzinger, no. 3426).
[24] Ibid., nos. 36 and 37 (Denzinger, nos. 3436 and 3437).
[25] See Alfred Loisy, *Les évangiles synoptiques*; *Le quatrième évangile*.
[26] Paulin Ladeuze, *La résurrection du Christ* (Paris and Brussels: Maison de l'Action catholique, 1909); Constantin Chauvin, *Jésus Christ est-il ressuscité?* (Paris: Bloud, 1905); Eugène Mangenot, "La résurrection de Jésus-Christ" in *Revue pratique d'apologétique* (1908); Vincent Rose, *Études sur les évangiles* (Paris: Welter, 1902), ch. 8.
[27] See Frédéric Godet, *Commentaire sur l'évangile de saint Luc* [Paris: Fischbacher, 1872]; *Commentaire sur l'évangile de saint Jean* [Paris: Fischbacher, 1876]; Edmond De Pressensé, *Jésus-Christ* [Paris: Fischbacher, 1881]; François Bovon, *Théologie du N.T.*, vol. 1 [Lausanne: G. Bridel, 1902]; Sanday in *Hasting's Dictionary of Jesus Christ*, vol. 2, 638ff.

they themselves admit) on account of their *a priori* denial of the possibility of miracles.[28] However, they object that many contradictions are found in the Gospel accounts of the Resurrection, inasmuch as the sacred authors disagree with each other concerning the appearance of the angels, following the time when the women came to the tomb, and so forth.[29]

In order to resolve this question, we will see what Christ's own declarations as well as those of the apostles tell us about the importance of the Resurrection as a motive of credibility. This is the starting point for debate admitted by many rationalists. Then we will ask about the foundation for this certitude that the apostles had. In other words, we will prove historically that Christ truly died and truly rose on the third day.

§2. The Importance of This Motive of Credibility

As we can see from the Gospels, *Christ himself had chosen this sign as the seal of his miracles* and as *an irrefutable argument of his divine mission.*

(a) After performing many miracles, *speaking to the Pharisees,* who heretofore asked him, "Master, we would like to see a sign from you," Jesus responded, "An evil and adulterous generation seeketh a sign: and a sign shall not be given it, but the sign of Jonas the prophet. For as Jonas was in the whale's belly three days and three nights: so shall the Son of man be in the heart of the earth three days and three nights" (Matt 12:39–40, DR; Luke 11:29). Jesus affirmed this again when the Pharisees asked for a sign from heaven (Matt 16:4). Likewise, he said to them: "Destroy this temple; and in three days I will raise it up," speaking (as St. John says) of the temple of his body (John 2:19, DR; Mark 14:58).

(b) Likewise, *at least four times Jesus predicted to his disciples his Resurrection.* {{317}} Immediately after Peter's confession, "Jesus began to shew to his disciples, that he must go to Jerusalem, and suffer many things from the ancients and scribes and chief priests, and be put to death, and the third day rise again" (Matt 16:21, DR; Mark 8:31; Luke 9:22). Likewise, he did so immediately after the transfiguration (Matt 17:22; Mark 9:30) and again before his triumphal entry into Jerusalem (Matt 20:19; Mark 10:34; Luke 18:33). In all of these three synoptic accounts of his prediction of his death and Resurrection we read: "He will rise on the third day." Finally, after the last supper, Jesus announced it again (Matt 26:32; Mark 14:28).

(c) Nay, while he was on the Cross, the people passing by blasphemed, saying: "Ha! Thou that destroyest the temple of God and in three days buildest it up again. Save thyself,

---

[28] For example, see Réville, *Jésus de Nazareth,* vol. 2, 435: "The idea of the real resurrection of a body that has really died would only have been adopted in such a time when men were lacking the physiological notions that we have since then acquired."

[29] See Fillion, *Les miracles de Notre Seigneur Jésus-Christ,* vol. 2.

coming down from the cross" (Mark 15:29–30, DR; Matt 26:61). And after his death, the chief priests and Pharisees gathered before Plate, saying, "Sir, we have remembered, that that seducer said, while he was yet alive: After three days I will rise again. Command therefore the sepulcher to be guarded until the third day: lest perhaps his disciples come and steal him away and say to the people: He is risen from the dead. And the last error shall be worse than the first" (Matt 27:63–64, DR).

The apostles invoked this miracle of Christ's Resurrection in particular[30] in order to confirm the truth of their preaching.

Matthias was chosen to be an apostle so that he might be a witness to the Resurrection (Acts 1:22). *Peter*, in his first sermon to the people, argued from the Resurrection of Christ predicted by David in order to prove the truth of the faith: "*This Jesus hath God raised again*, whereof all we are witnesses, being exalted therefore by the right hand of God and having received of the Father the promise of the Holy Ghost, he hath poured forth this which you see and hear. . . . Therefore let all the house of Israel know most certainly that God hath made both Lord and Christ, this same Jesus, whom you have crucified" (Acts 2:32–36, DR). Similarly, *St. Paul*, before the Athenians in the Areopagus, after speaking of God the Creator said, "Because he hath appointed a day wherein he will judge the world in equity, by the man whom he hath appointed, giving faith to all, *by raising him up from the dead*" (Acts 17:31, DR). Likewise, in 1 Corinthians 15:5–8 (DR), St. Paul refers to the Resurrection of Christ, who "was seen by Cephas, and after that by the eleven. Then was he seen by more than five hundred brethren at once: of whom many remain until this present. . . . After that, he was seen by James: then by all the apostles. And last of all, he was seen also by me." And twice he declares, "*If Christ be not raised, then your faith is in vain*" (1 Cor 15:13–17).

St. Paul does not mean that other miracles are insufficient motives of credibility but, rather, only means to say (and expressly affirms): "And if Christ be not risen again, then is our preaching vain. . . . *Yea, and we are found false witnesses of God*" (1 Cor 15:14–15, DR); that is, our preaching is false, for it is based upon this fact that was alleged by all the apostles. Moreover, "And if Christ be not risen again, your faith is vain: *for you are yet in your sins*" (1 Cor 15:17–19, DR). That is, if Christ did not rise, then your faith in the resurrected Christ, which is the root of faith (Rom 4:25), is false and does not cleanse you from sin. Nay, according to John Chrysostom,[31] Theophylact, and Ecumenius,[32] Christ's

---

[30] [Trans. note: Reading *praecipue* for *praecique*.]

[31] See John Chrysostom: "If the dead cannot rise then nor is sin abolished, nor is death destroyed, nor the reproach borne away" (PG 61, 335). Likewise, see Theophylact, PG 124, 759ff.

[32] Ecumenius: "For if He Himself remained detained by death in some way, then how will he be able to free others from death, which has come about on account of sin? Consequently, therefore, *nor could sin be destroyed by Christ's death, for if it were, then all the more certainly would death, which came about through sin, also have been destroyed*. But if this were the case, it would then be wholly necessary that he who freed others from death would have first been

death was inefficacious for bringing about the remission of sins, and if Christ remained in death, he would have been conquered by it. {{318}} If he was not able to conquer death through his Resurrection, then neither was he able to conquer sin. Indeed, it is weightier and more difficult to conquer sin than to conquer death. Therefore, *sin is fully destroyed only if its effect—namely, death—is destroyed.*[33]

In this last declaration by St. Paul, we have an excellent statement of *the importance of Christ's Resurrection and its intimate connection with the principal mysteries of Christianity.* This connection can be expressed thus: If Christ did not conquer death by rising again, then we cannot be certain that he conquered death upon the cross and that our redemption has been accepted by God. Why? Because, as is explained at length in the Old Testament, as well as in the letter to the Romans, "as by one man *sin entered into this world and by sin death*: and so death passed upon all men, in whom all have sinned" (Rom 5:12, DR), "for the wages of sin is death," (Rom 8:10) and "the body indeed is dead because of sin" (Rom 8:10, DR). Therefore, he who invisibly takes away the sins of the world must visibly destroy death—that is, the effect of sin—so that we may have an utterly certain sign of his victory over sin and of our redemption. Christ did not appear sensibly upon the Cross as victor but, rather, as one who has been conquered. By contrast, through the Resurrection, he is manifested as the conqueror of death, and thus, we know how he was able to tell his disciples, "In the world you shall have distress. *But have confidence. I have overcome the world*" (John 16:33, DR). Hence, Christ's Resurrection is the greatest motive of credibility inasmuch as it is, according to divine providence, the most resplendent sign of Christ's victory over sin and the devil.[34]

Nay, as St. Paul shows in the same text, in relation to the future, it is the sign and pledge of our future resurrection: "But now Christ is risen from the dead, the first fruits of them that sleep, for by a man came death: and by a man the resurrection of the dead. And as in Adam all die, so also in Christ all shall be made alive. . . . And the enemy, death, shall be destroyed last: For he hath put all things under his feet" (1 Cor 15:20–26, DR). "And when this mortal hath put on immortality, then shall come to pass the saying that is written: Death is swallowed up in victory. O death, where is thy victory? O death, where is thy sting? Now the sting of death is sin. . . . But thanks be to God, who hath given us the victory through our Lord Jesus Christ" (1 Cor 15:54–57, DR). Thus, Christ appeared as

---

raised, becoming the one who would lead others to the resurrection."

[33] This is how Cornelius a Lapide set forth this interpretation and cites the aforementioned authors. See PG 118, 867ff.

[34] See Paulin Ladeuze, *La résurrection du Christ devant la critique contemporaine*, 4th ed., [Bruxelles: Maison de l'Action catholique, 1910]1; Jacques-Marie Vosté, O.P., *Studia Paulina* (Rome: Collegio Angelico, 1928), 56ff (2nd ed., 62).

the savior of the whole of humanity, not only as regards the soul but also as regards the body, in which the soul's glory will be manifested.

From this utterly lofty aspect, Christ's Resurrection, thus connected to the redemption of humanity, is a mystery intrinsically pertaining to Christianity and is an object of faith, whereas, from an external perspective, as we will discuss, it is simultaneously a historical fact. {{319}} This gives rise to a number of apologetic points concerning the importance of the Resurrection.

(1) Rationalists hold that the Resurrection is impossible because it would lack a sufficient reason and would be opposed to the laws of nature. St. Paul, by contrast, assigns the supreme reasons for this miracle, its place in the counsel of providence, showing that this sign is not opposed to the laws of nature but instead is above them, likewise being maximally conformed to the supernatural laws of the salvation of souls.

(2) Liberal Protestants and modernists teach that miracles are signs that are far too extrinsic to religion that cannot be of use in leading men to interior faith. However, St. Paul makes clear that Christ's Resurrection is a sign that is not extrinsic to religion but instead is connected with the other mysteries in an utterly profound and marvelous way.

(3) All adversaries object: There can be no true certitude concerning any fact founded upon apparitions. Therefore, let them deign to explain how the apostles had such great certitude concerning the fact of Christ's Resurrection. Not only did they preach this to the point of martyrdom as being the greatest motive of credibility, but in confirmation of it, they performed *new miracles*.[35] Afterwards, for nineteen centuries, Christ's Resurrection has been preached as being the principal sign of his divine mission.

Therefore, we must look into the historical origin of this certitude that the apostles had.

§3. Christ Truly Died

For the Jews themselves, as well as for the other enemies of Christianity, Christ's death has been perpetually held to be an utterly incontrovertible fact. Nay, the Jews and the pagans were so certain about this fact that even though they fought against the reality of Christ's Resurrection, they never

---

[35] See Acts 3:15–16 (DR). Peter heals a lame man in the name of Jesus Christ, the Nazarene, and then adds: "But the author of life you killed, whom God hath raised from the dead: of which we are witnesses. And in the faith of his name, this man, whom you have seen and known, hath his name strengthened. And the faith which is by him hath given this perfect soundness in the sight of you all." Likewise, see Acts 4:10–33.

claimed that he did not die. Nevertheless, at the beginning of the nineteenth century, the rationalists Paulus, Schleiermacher, Hase, and Herder did not fear to affirm that Christ did not die on the Cross but only became unconscious, afterwards showing himself to the apostles after he came back to consciousness, then dying later on in some unknown place. Today, this explanation is rejected by rationalists themselves as being materially and morally impossible.[36]

(1) *All four Evangelists*, whom we have proven to be deserving of faith, unanimously state that Jesus Christ suffered and died, was anointed with spices, and was buried. Moreover, other New Testament authors testify to this fact as being utterly certain. All Christians from the beginnings of Christianity held it to be an indubitable fact. Nay, indeed, they held that it was the cause of mankind's redemption, and many of them rested upon this with the firmest faith, to the point of pouring out their blood.

{{320}} (2) *Many were eyewitnesses* of his death, with their witness being preserved in the Gospels: the centurion, along with a number of soldiers; John; the mother of Jesus, as well as godly women. Pilate did not permit Jesus's body to be buried until after he learned from the centurion that Christ was already dead (Mark 15:39, 44–45). Nay, soldiers were sent so that they might break the legs of those who were crucified: "But after they were come to Jesus, when they saw that he was already dead, they did not break his legs. But one of the soldiers with a spear opened his side: and immediately there came out blood and water" (John 19:33–34, DR). Then, Joseph of Arimathea and Nicodemus "took therefore the body of Jesus and bound it in linen cloths, with the spices, as the manner of the Jews is to bury" (John 19:40, DR). Moreover, as Renan himself admits,[37] the only explanation for Christ's death is the hatred of the Jews, for since they so ardently desired his death, they would not have let their victim remain alive.

Objection: Christ's death is rendered doubtful by Pilate's admiration: "Pilate wondered that he should be already dead" (Mark 15:44, DR).

Response: That admiration is a sign of its authenticity, for crucified people sometimes lived for a whole day (and sometimes longer). Pilate probably did not pay enough attention to everything that Christ suffered beforehand or, holding that he was a demigod, expected something extraordinary to be done on his behalf.

---

[36] See the work of the rationalist Réville, *Jésus de Nazareth*, vol. 2, 445: "This theory held by Paulus, which was in the vogue last century, . . . is nothing more than a patchwork of material and moral implausibilities."

[37] See Renan, *Vie de Jésus*, ch. 26.

(3) *It is materially impossible* that Jesus remained alive after his Crucifixion. Indeed, he had been hewn with the cruelest scourging, was pierced with the sharp spikes upon the crown of thorns, was put into agony for three hours, and was finished off by the most horrific suffering. However, if he did not die, the soldier's lance, which opened up his side, would have killed him. Nay, his body was placed in a tomb, was wrapped in linen, and was covered with so great an amount of spices that even by themselves they would have been enough to suffocate Jesus if he were not already dead. Then the tomb was visited by the Jews and had a large stone placed over its opening, lest someone would be able to enter it, and guards were placed at the mouth of the tomb, lest the apostles steal his body. All of this surely makes it quite clear that Jesus truly was dead when he was taken down from the cross.

(4) *Finally, it is morally impossible* that Jesus, whose sincerity, utterly great perfection, and zeal remain unquestioned, would have lived in some unknown place after his Crucifixion, deceiving his apostles concerning his Resurrection or allowing them to be deceived and preach this error as being an utterly certain argument for the truth of faith.[38] Many rationalists admit that this is impossible. Therefore, there can be no doubt concerning Christ's death on the Cross.

§4. It Is Historically Certain That Christ Was Raised from the Dead and That His Resurrection Was Perfectly Manifested

Let us consider St. Paul's testimony, which was read in his letters before the Gospels were written. Then we will consider the testimony of the Evangelists, drawing this section to a close with an examination of the objections raised by rationalists.

(1) **St. Paul's testimony.** In 1 Corinthians 15, written around AD 57–58, St. Paul refers to various appearances by the resurrected Christ, which he had already handed on himself to the Corinthians in around 52 or 53:

{{321}} For I delivered unto you first of all, which I also received: how that Christ died for our sins, according to the scriptures, and that he was buried, and that he rose again the third day, according to the scriptures, and that *he was seen by Cephas*, and after that *by the eleven*. Then was he seen *by more than five hundred brethren* at once, of whom many remain until this present, and some are fallen

---

[38] See, for example, Réville, *Jésus de Nazareth*, vol. 2, 455ff.

asleep. After that, he was seen by *James*, then *by all the apostles*. And last of all, *he was seen also by me*, as by one born out of due time. (1 Cor 15:3–8, DR)

St. Paul did not intend to refer to all of Christ's appearances but, rather, in particular to those that were made to the apostles, without, however, excluding others. The final appearance is that by which he himself was converted near Damascus, four or five years after Christ's death. This event is referred to in Acts 9:3ff, 17, and 21; 22:14; and 26:14. This vision was not merely spiritual. Indeed, St. Paul says that he saw Jesus *last of all*, which would have been false if it were a question of a merely spiritual vision, for afterwards, Christ appeared spiritually to Ananias. Nor can it be said that St. Paul is speaking only about the immortality of Christ's soul, which would not have ceased to act after his death, for in this chapter he expressly affirms, time and again, the Resurrection of Christ's body, which he proposes as an exemplar of our future bodily resurrection. Likewise, St. Paul frequently mentions the Resurrection in other letters.[39] As will be at once clear, there is no disagreement between St. Paul's texts and the testimony offered by the Evangelists.[40]

(2) *The testimony of the Evangelists.* Most of the appearances are enumerated by authors *independently from each other*: St. Matthew, St. Mark, St. Luke, and St. John, for St. Matthew and St. John himself were the witnesses of a number of appearances. St. Mark hands on the preaching of St. Peter, and St. Luke probably accepted from Joanna, the wife of Chusa, Herod's procurator, many points concerning Christ's Passion, for he names her

---

[39] For example, see 1 Thess 1:10 and 6:13.

[40] By contrast, when St. Paul speaks about mystical visions brought about in an inexplicable manner (2 Cor 12:2–4), he does not then consider anything of the vision of another kind near Damascus. This vision established him as an apostle, a witness to Christ's Resurrection, like the other apostles (see 1 Cor 9:1–5, etc.).

Adversaries object that when Paul speaks of the Resurrection of Christ, he does not make mention of the empty tomb, which the Evangelists later on will mention. Hence, they hold that he was unaware of this fact and that the message of the empty tomb must be attributed to a later tendency in the development of Christian apologetic preaching.

Response: This argument "from silence" proves nothing unless it is proven that St. Paul should have spoken about that fact. However, he takes up the cause on behalf of the Resurrection of Christ not directly with regard to the proof of an empty tomb but with respect to even stronger proofs, n.p. [*sic*] proofs of apparitions, after which he but once more gives an accounting of the aforesaid facts to the ecclesiastical authority [viz., the pillars in Jerusalem]. Finally, by means of the sequence, "*he died . . . was buried . . . and rose on the third day*," St. Paul implicitly teaches that the tomb was empty on the third day.

among the women going to the tomb, and he is particularly aware of things pertaining to Herod's court (Luke 8:3; 23:7–12; 24:10).

However, the four Evangelists agree concerning the very fact of the Resurrection, for they all hold that the tomb was found empty and that Christ appeared to the eleven apostles.

A. *They all affirm the tomb was found to be empty.* {{322}} According to all of them, Joseph of Arimathea asked Pilate if he might have Jesus's body, wrapped it in pure linen, and placed it in his new grave, which was dug out of the stone, then placing a large stone at the mouth of the grave (Matt 27:56–66; Mark 15:42; Luke 23:53; John 19:38). Nay, with Pilate's permission, the Pharisees protected the tomb, sealing the stone and setting guards there (Matt 27:66). Now, according to the four Evangelists, on the first day after the Sabbath, when the women and disciples came to the tomb, the stone had been removed from the mouth of the grave, and they could not find the Lord's body. An angel appeared to them and announced that Christ had risen (Matt 28:1ff; Mark 16:1ff; Luke 24:1ff; John 20:1ff). St. John relates that the linen and the napkin remained in the tomb, separately folded up. However, if Christ had really been buried in the grave as is narrated in the Gospels but was afterwards not found therein, then a strong confirmation can be had for the Evangelists' later account concerning his bodily Resurrection.[41]

The chief priests themselves, not knowing how to explain the way that the tomb was found to be empty, thought up a false story, which St. Matthew refers to: "They gave a great sum of money to the soldiers, saying, 'Say that his disciples came by night and stole him away when we were asleep, . . . and this story was spread abroad among the Jews even unto this day." However, this invention, as even some rationalists admit,[42] is obviously

---

[41] See Rose, *Études sur les évangiles*, ch. 8 (The empty tomb).

[42] See Réville, *Jésus de Nazareth*, vol. 2, 459. Réville thinks that the chief priests themselves carried away Jesus's body so that it would not be venerated by his disciples. However, other rationalists have a response to this claim. See Edmond Stapfer, *La mort et la résurrection de Jésus-Christ* [Paris: Fischbacher, 1898], 283: "Nothing can be cited in support of this hypothesis: no fact, no text, no allusion, however fleeting, is brought forth to give it some value. It is utterly improbable, for it would have been a unique blunder for the high priest to come himself to provide the apostles with a pretext for believing in the resurrection."

See Oskar Holtzmann, *Leben Jesu* (Tübingen: Mohr, 1901), 392ff. Holtzmann thinks that Joseph of Arimathea did indeed at first permit Christ's body to be placed in his grave but that then, afterwards, it was carried away in a way that was unknown to all to be buried elsewhere, as it were, in an undignified manner, in a grave among the members of his own family. However, beyond the difficulties involving the grave's guardians and Joseph's impunity in relation to the Jews and to Pilate, this gratuitous assertion runs into difficulties trying to explain how such a change would be brought about following on his pious burial. Moreover, when the

a false story. As St. Augustine asked, "If the soldiers were asleep, what could they see? If they saw nothing, how were they witnesses?" Moreover, had the disciples carried away the body, they would have been accused before the judge; however, to the contrary, the apostles, who publicly preached the Lord's Resurrection, never were condemned as being despoilers of his tomb. Moreover, we would not have an explanation for how the apostles believed in the Resurrection and preached it to the point of suffering martyrdom.

{{323}} Nor can it be said that Christ's body was engulfed by the rending of the earth, for in that case the linens and the napkin would have been absorbed as well.

No more should we give credence to the hypothesis invented by Loisy holding that Christ's body would have been thrown into a common grave. This hypothesis enjoys no foundation and stands in open contradiction to the testimony of all the Evangelists. St. Paul and St. Peter also speak about Christ's burial in a way that expresses honor.[43]

B. *All the Evangelists agree with St. Paul that Jesus appeared to the eleven apostles.* Twelve appearances are mentioned in total; namely, he appeared to Mary Magdalene when she sat next to the tomb crying (Mark 16:9; John 20:11); to the women returning to the tomb (Matt 28:9–10); to Simon Peter (Luke 24:34; 1 Cor 15:5); to the two disciples on the road to Emmaus (Luke 24:15–35); to all the apostles except Thomas, gathered in the upper room (Mark 16:14; Luke 24:36–43; John 20:19–23); to all of them, with Thomas present, whom he ordered to place his finger in the nail wounds and his hand into Christ's side (John 20:24ff; 1 Cor 15:5); to five apostles and two disciples at the Sea of Tiberius (John 21:1–24); to the eleven apostles who had gone to Galilee (Matt 28:16ff); to more than five hundred brothers gathered together (1 Cor 15:6); to James (1 Cor 15:6); to the eleven apostles in Jerusalem and in Bethany on the day of the Ascension (Mark 16:19; Luke 24:50–52; Acts 1:1–12); and finally, to St. Paul on the road to Damascus (Acts 9:3ff; 1 Cor 11:8). Nay, in Acts, we read: "To whom (namely, the apostles) also he shewed himself alive after his passion, by many

---

apostles preached Christ's Resurrection, deceived as they were by this removal, Joseph himself, whether as a friend or as a foe, would certainly have felt the need to speak up.

Adversaries call attention to the "Decree of Caesar" sent from Nazareth to the West in 1878 and made public in 1930, in which the punishment of beheading is stated as holding for the violation of tombs. Such a decree would have been for the particular case of the violation of Christ's tomb, pronounced by Tiberius and proscribed in Nazareth, Christ's homeland. However, experts in this matter are sure neither concerning the place where this decree was found, nor concerning whether it was authored by Tiberius, nor concerning the particular object treated in it. If it was already decreed before Christ's death, then this would mean that the removal of Christ's body would be even less likely than it already is. See Giuseppe Ricciotti, *Vita di Gesù Cristo* (Milan / Rome: Mondadori, 1942), §628; François-Marie Braun, O.P., *Où en est le problème de Jésus?* (Paris: 1932), 403n2.

[43] See 1 Cor 15:4; Rom 6:4; Col 2:12; Acts 2:24–32.

proofs, *for forty days appearing to them, and speaking of the kingdom of God*" (Acts 1:3, DR).

Thus, all of the Evangelists and St. Paul hold that Jesus appeared to the eleven apostles after his Resurrection.

Objection: Many rationalists push back, saying that *Matthew* and *Mark* seem to presuppose that Christ only appeared to his disciples in Galilee.[44] *Luke* and *John*, however, assert that he was seen by his disciples in and around Jerusalem. On the basis of this discrepancy, it is inferred that the apparitions in Jerusalem are not historical.[45]

Response: Matthew and Mark have the particular intent to refer to the Galilean appearances, which were both more frequent as well as the place where the institution of the apostles was complete. However, they do not deny the appearances in Jerusalem. Nay, St. Matthew recounts how Christ appeared to the godly women (Matt 28:9–10), and Mark refers to appearances to Mary Magdalene (Mark 16:9), to the two disciples going to the town of Emmaus (Mark 16:12), to the apostles gathered in the upper room (Mark 16:14), and to the apostles on the day of the Ascension (Mark 16:19).[46] On this matter, also refer to commentators on the Gospel.[47]

---

[44] According to Matt 28:7 (DR) and Mark 16:7, the angel said to the women standing by the tomb: "And going quickly, tell ye his disciples that he is risen. And behold he will go before you into Galilee. There you shall see him."

[45] See Édouard Le Roy, *Dogme et critique* (Paris: Bloud, 1907), 192–217.

[46] Many do indeed deny the authenticity of the end of this chapter in Mark, from verse 9 onward. However, they do not sufficiently disprove it. The majority of critics admit this authenticity.

[47] See Ladeuze, *La résurrection du Christ*, 43–47. On this matter, Brassac says, "Many rationalist critics (e.g., Stapfer and Réville) hold that at the beginning there were two mutually-independent traditions concerning Christ's appearances, one *Galilean* and the other centered on *Jerusalem*. It is difficult to reconcile these two traditions with each other, though St. John joined them together, and St. Paul would, on this score, write prior to the formation of any tradition. . . . The existence of a number of distinct and opposed traditions which formed progressively is not, however, an established fact. St. John, who reproduces a true line of apostolic tradition, places, like St. Luke, the first appearances in Judah and likewise reports the appearances in Galilee. St. Paul enumerates the appearances in their chronological order and gives them as a proof of Jesus's Resurrection in 1 *Cor* 15:3–8. Now, he says, 'Christ arose on the third day and was seen by Peter and then by the twelve [*sic*]. . . .' It seems that the first appearance dates from the very day of the Resurrection and that it consequently took place in Jerusalem. Two days did not suffice for the apostles to gather in Galilee." "St. Matthew gives preference to the Galilean appearances, just as he gives preference to the ministry of our Savior in Galilee. He himself reports the appearances that gave encouragement to the holy women in Jerusalem. Moreover, when he adds, 'The eleven went to the mountain which Jesus had appointed' (Matt 23:16), this must be seen as being an allusion to an order given by Jesus in Jerusalem after His appearances. We do not encounter Him fixing such a meeting place prior to His passion."

[Trans. note: In this note, Fr. Garrigou-Lagrange seems to be quoting, at least in part, from Auguste Brassac, *Manuel biblique ou cours d'écriture sainte à l'usage des séminaires* [Paris:

{{324}} *Rationalist will insist, however*: There are many contradictions in the Gospels—for example, as regards the appearances of the angels. Luke and John speak of two angels, whereas Matthew and Mark speak of one. According to Luke, the angels stood alongside the godly women, whereas according to Matthew, the angels sat upon the stone. Likewise, the authors do not always agree regarding the order of the appearances.

Response: The Evangelists agree concerning the substance of the account, the fact of the Resurrection, and the most important circumstances. However, they are not easily reconciled regarding certain accidental circumstances, for they do not recount all of the interconnections of the facts. We do not concede that there are true contradictions between them, but even if there were such regarding these tiny details, their historicity would not thereby be destroyed, for frequently, when many witnesses recount one and the same complex fact, they agree on what is substantial concerning it and disagree about its minor circumstances. Nonetheless, their testimony is commonly admitted. Nay, these apparent points of disagreement manifest the Evangelists' honesty, for if they wished to deceive their readers, they would have avoided such points of disagreement.

Others object: Christ announced, "So shall the Son of man be in the heart of the earth three days and three nights" (Matt 12:40, DR). Now, in fact, he remained only two nights and one day in the tomb.

Response: This prediction, made to the Pharisees, is only found once in this form in the Gospels—namely, in Matthew 12:40—whereas by contrast, as we read in the Synoptics, Jesus announces three times to his disciples: "He will rise on the third day" (Matt 16:21; 17:22; 20:19; 27:63; Mark 8:31; 9:30; 10:34; Luke 9:22; 18:33; 1 Cor 15:4). The expression "three days and three nights" is easily explained through the likeness to the sign of the prophet Jonah that is made by Jesus here. Indeed, as we read in Jonah 2:1 (DR): "And Jonas was in the belly of a fish for three days and three nights." Hence, Jesus said: "For as Jonas was in the whale's belly three days and three nights: so shall the Son of man be in the heart of the earth three days and three nights." As St. Thomas explains, following St. Augustine, "Sometimes in Scripture, the part is taken for the whole. Therefore, we must say that Christ, making use of a synecdoche, was in the tomb for three days and three nights, for Friday is counted as being a full day, and even the previous night, with no doubt existing regarding the second day, though the third is counted regarding the night as well as the following day."[48] This was his manner of speaking because of the likeness being drawn between the figure and reality.

{{325}} (3) **The apostles were not hallucinating.** Now, we must consider the nature of these appearances.

As we said earlier, Strauss and Renan, having rejected the theory that the apostles were deceivers, taught that they themselves were deceived by hallu-

---

Chernoviz, 1907].]

[48] St. Thomas, *In XII Matth.*, lect. 3.

cination. Renan says[49] that the apostles were not able to believe that Jesus was conquered by his foes. Therefore, they pored over the Scriptures and there found predictions of the Messiah's Resurrection. Thus, inflamed with a great desire for the Resurrection, they were deceived by a hallucination. Today, the rationalist Meyer speaks along nearly the same lines.[50]

This theory, which comes from an *a priori* denial of the possibility of miracles, completely contradicts the historical testimonies as well as what psychology teaches concerning hallucination.

A. *It is historically certain that the apostles and disciples did not expect the Resurrection.* Indeed, Nicodemus and Joseph of Arimathea placed Jesus's body in the tomb as though it were going to remain there in perpetuity, and they placed a stone at the mouth of the grave. And when the Sabbath had passed, Mary Magdalene and the godly women brought aromatic spices so that they might anoint Jesus's body. Therefore, they too did not expect the Resurrection. Nay, Mary Magdalene, seeing the empty tomb, said, "They have taken away my Lord: and I know not where they have laid him" (John 20:13, DR). Then, later on, she did not immediately recognize Jesus when he spoke to her, "for she thought he was the gardener." When the godly women announced the Resurrection to the apostles, "these words seemed to them as idle tales, and they did not believe them" (Luke 24:11, DR). The disciples on the road to Emmaus had lost all hope. St. Thomas said to the apostles, "Except I shall see in his hands the print of the nails and put my finger into the place of the nails and put my hand into his side, I will not believe" (John 20:25, DR). From all of these various testimonies, which are all deserving of belief, it is quite clear that the apostles did not expect the Resurrection. Nay, Christ said to them, "O foolish and slow of heart to believe" (Luke 24:25, DR), and "he upbraided them with their incredulity and hardness of heart" (Mark 16:14, DR).

B. *Taking into account all of the circumstances, it is psychologically clear that the apostles were not hallucinating.* (a) Indeed, nobody is deceived by hallucinations unless he is *disposed* to flights of fancy, by vehement desires or out of fear. However, we find nothing like this in the apostles, for as St. John says, "as yet they knew not the Scripture, that (Jesus) must rise again from the dead" (John 20:9, DR), and therefore they were filled with sorrow and despair. (b) *Many people who are awake cannot simultaneously have the same sort of hallucinations involving all of the same sensory experiences* so that they would all see, hear, and touch something that never took place.

See Renan, *Vie de Jésus*, ch. 26; *Les apôtres*, ch. 1.
[50] See Meyer, *Die Auferstehung Christi* (Tübingen: Mohr, 1905).

(c) *Long-lasting hallucination are a true form of madness*, and no traces of such insanity are seen in the apostles. Therefore, how would they be able to imagine that for forty days (but no longer thereafter) they saw someone who had risen from the dead, hearing his instructions, accepting commands from him, eating with him, touching him, and finally seeing him, with their own eyes, ascend into heaven? (d) Once the given excitation of one's nerves and imagination comes to an end, *an experience of hallucination is corrected by reflection.* {{326}} By contrast, the apostles remain convicted, even to the point of martyrdom, that they had seen the Lord in a bodily manner. (e) Moreover, how could such preaching, which renewed the face of the earth, be founded upon such a sickly kind of hallucination? (f) Finally, this does not explain how the tomb was found to be empty.

(4) **Christ appeared to the apostles in a bodily manner, not a merely spiritual one.** As we discussed earlier, certain rationalists, like Keim and Schenkel, rejected the hallucination theory as being insufficient, holding instead that Jesus appeared to the apostles in a merely spiritual manner. They denied the "reanimation" of a corpse, but according to them, Christ's soul, united to God after his death, comforted the apostles and manifested itself to them.

This new theory comes from a gratuitous denial of the possibility of bodily resurrection and cannot be admitted without denying the honesty of the Evangelists and the apostles. As St. Luke recounts, at first sight, the apostles, "being troubled and frightened, supposed that they saw a spirit. And he said to them: . . . See my hands and feet, that it is I myself. *Handle, and see, for a spirit hath not flesh and bones, as you see me to have.* And when he had said this, he shewed them his hands and feet. But while they yet believed not and wondered for joy, he said: Have you here any thing to eat? And they offered him a piece of a broiled fish and a honeycomb. And when he had eaten before them, taking the remains, he gave to them" (Luke 24:37–43, DR).

In fact, the apostles, especially St. Thomas, not only saw but also touched the Lord's body. Moreover, if the reanimation of a corpse had not taken place, the tomb would not have been empty. Finally, this would bring to ruin St. Paul's own argument concerning the future resurrection of bodies, which he holds is pledged to us in Christ's own bodily Resurrection. St. Paul himself, on the road to Damascus, saw Jesus *bodily*, for he says, "And last of all, he was seen also by me" (1 Cor 15:8, DR). As we already hinted above, this proposition would be false if this were merely a spiritual apparition, for Christ afterwards appeared spiritually to others, like, for example, to Ananias.[51] Finally, St. Paul speaks in a different way about his own spiritual visions, indicating that they were spiritual. (Acts 18:9; 22:17; 23:11; 2 Cor 12:1).

St Thomas says:[52]

Through given *evident signs*, Christ showed that He had resurrected. . . .

Christ manifested His Resurrection in two ways, namely, by means of testimony (by the angels and Sacred Scripture) and by way of argument or sign. And each kind of manifestation sufficient in its own kind. . . . *The arguments (or signs) were sufficient for showing that the Resurrection was true and glorious.*

He first showed that it was a *true resurrection on the part of the body*, doing so in three ways. (1) He showed that it was a *true and solid body*, not imaginary or rarefied, like the air, establishing this fact by offering His body to be handled. Whence, at the end of Luke, He states, "Handle and see; for a spirit hath not flesh and bones, as you see Me to have." (2) He showed that it was a *human body* by presenting His true features for them to behold. (3) He showed that this body was *numerically identical to* the body which He had before by showing them the scars of the wounds. Whence, as we read at the end of Luke, he said to them, "See My hands and feet, that it is I Myself."

{{327}} In another way, he showed them the truth of His Resurrection *on the part of His soul* reunited with his body, doing so by means of the activities of the three kinds of life exercised by the soul. (1) He did so in the activities of the nutritive life by eating and drinking with His disciples, as we read at the end of Luke. (2) He did so *in the activities of sense life* by replying to His disciples' questions and by greeting them when they were in His presence, thus showing that He both saw and heard. (3) He did so in the activities of intellectual life by conversing with them and discussing the Scriptures. Indeed, in order that nothing might be wanting to make the manifestation complete, he also showed that He had the Divine Nature, by performing the miracle by which they caught the huge load of fish and, moreover, by ascending into heaven while they looked upon Him. . . .

He also showed his disciples the glory of his Resurrection by entering into

---

[51] See what is said by conservative Protestants like Godet in *Commentaire sur l'évangile de saint Luc*, 3rd ed., vol. 2, 595.

[52] See *ST* III, q. 55, a. 5 and 6.

the upper room and joining them *while the doors were closed.* . . . Likewise, it belonged to his property of glory that "he vanished suddenly from their eyes," as we are told at the end of the Gospel of Luke, for in this way, we are shown that He had the power to be seen or not seen, a power belonging to a glorified body (see 1 Cor 15:42, 44).

(Likewise, St. Thomas concludes in ad 1): Although each of these arguments (or signs), taken separately, would not suffice on its own to perfectly make manifest Christ's Resurrection, nonetheless, *when they are all taken together, they fully manifest it,* above all on account of the Scriptural testimonies, the sayings of the angels, and also Christ's own assertion supported by miracles. However, regarding the angels who appeared, they did not assert that they were men, as Christ asserted that He was truly a man.

Objection: There are many accounts in the Gospel that seem to bear witness to merely spiritual apparitions, for Jesus's body does not have the same nature as his first body. He enters into the upper room through closed doors, suddenly vanishes from before the eyes of the apostles, and indeed, as we read at the end of Mark, "he appeared in another shape" (Mark 16:12, DR) to the disciples on the way to Emmaus.

Response: These were not merely spiritual apparitions, for the apostles touched the hands and feet of Jesus after the Resurrection (Matt 28:9; Luke 24:39–40; John 20:27). The facts that are alleged in this objection show that after the Resurrection his glorified body enjoyed special endowments, but they did not, however, diminish his body's reality or identity. As regards the appearance in another shape, St. Thomas notes: "After his Resurrection, Christ appeared in his own shape to some who were well-disposed to belief, while he appeared in another shape to those who seemed to be already growing tepid in their faith. Hence, the latter said, at the end of Luke's Gospel, 'We hoped that it was he that should have redeemed Israel.' Thus, Gregory the Great said that 'he showed himself to them bodily such as he was in their minds, for because he was still a stranger to faith in their hearts, he put on the pretense that he had to go on further,' that is, as though he were a foreigner."[53]

Likewise, "In order to manifest the glory of his Resurrection, Christ did not wish *to continually* converse familiarly with His disciples as He did before, lest it seem that he had risen to the same life as that which he had prior to this."[54] For the same reason, he did not manifest himself immediately to all, for that which pertains to the glorious life is not known in a general manner by the natural law (that is, by common knowledge) but, rather, through a special gift of grace.[55]

---

[53] *ST* III, q. 55, a. 4.
[54] *ST* III, q. 55, a. 3.
[55] See *ST* III, q. 55, a. 1.

(5) *The reality of his appearances is confirmed by the miraculous way the apostles were changed, as well as by the conversion of St. Paul.* Indeed, at first, the apostles were in many ways uncertain, fearful, and as it were, despairing. After the Resurrection and the pouring forth of the Holy Spirit, we see them being wise in divine matters, steady, fearless, and constant in all persecutions. {{328}} Peter, who during the Passion denied the Lord because of his fear, says before the Sanhedrin, "For we cannot but speak the things which we have seen and heard," (Acts 4:20, DR) and "We ought to obey God rather than men" (Acts 5:29, DR). The apostles "went from the presence of the council, rejoicing that they were accounted worthy to suffer reproach for the name of Jesus" (Acts 5:41, DR). Likewise, the sudden and persevering conversion of St. Paul is explained if the Lord truly appeared to him, as he himself recounts. Otherwise, this conversion and the vigorous faith of the apostles remains inexplicable. The tree shall be known from its fruits.

Objection: According to St. Thomas, the apostles *believed* in Christ's Resurrection, and he teaches in another place that one and the same thing cannot be simultaneously seen and believed, nor known and believed. Therefore, the apostles were not able to be visual witnesses of Christ's Resurrection.

Response with the Holy Doctor: The apostles did not see Christ resurrect in the same way that they saw Lazarus's resurrection, for "upon His rising, Christ did not return to the familiar manner of life, but instead, to a kind of immortal and God-conformed condition. . . . Therefore, it was fitting that Christ's Resurrection was not directly witnessed by men but, instead, was proclaimed to them by angels."[56] Nonetheless, "the apostles were able *to witness* the Resurrection even *by sight*, for *on the faithful testimony of their own eyes (fides occulata)* they saw that Christ, whom they had known to be dead, was now alive. However, just as man arrives from the hearing of faith to the beatific vision, so too did men arrive at sight of the risen Christ through the message already heard from angels."[57]

What is meant by these words, *fides occulata*?

This is explained by a distinction given by St. Thomas: "Christ manifested his Resurrection in two ways, namely, by means of testimony (by the angels and Sacred Scripture) and by way of argument or sign. And each kind of manifestation was sufficient in its own kind."[58] That is, sensible signs sufficed for producing certitude of the same order, which is called physical certitude: "Touch and see." The testimony of the angels, of Christ himself, and of the Scriptures sufficed with internal grace for having certitude of a loftier

---

[56] See *ST* III, q. 55, a. 2.
[57] Ibid., ad 1.
[58] *ST* III, q. 55, a. 6.

order—namely, for having the supernatural certitude of faith. "Thus, the apostles arrive at sight of the risen Christ through the message already heard from angels." And faith in the Resurrection remains here, for Christ's Resurrection is not only a *miracle*, which is naturally knowable on the basis of signs (e.g., his wounds), but at the same time is *a mystery of faith*. Indeed, not everything about the Resurrection could be sensed by the apostles and many things remained hidden (e.g., the fact that it was not only the mere reanimation of a corpse but the self-resurrection of the Son of God, connected with the mysteries of the Redemption and future glory). These transcend both the senses and reason and are believed on account of the authority of God who reveals. Hence, in speaking of the Apostle Thomas, St. Thomas says: "*He saw one thing and believed another*: he saw the wounds and believed in God."[59] Therefore, *faith* is said to be *ocular* when a given mystery is made visible regarding some external aspect. Thus, we can say that the apostles had the faithful testimony of their eyes (*fidem oculatam*) concerning the very fact of divine revelation through Christ, on account of Christ's miracles, while nonetheless, this very revelation, precisely as God's uncreated, essentially supernatural action, is a hidden mystery, believed together with the other mysteries, at once *that* which is believed and *that by which* we believe, just as light is what we see and that by which we see (see vol. 1, ch. 14, a. 3).

The idea of the Resurrection did not arise from a kind of syncretism of pagan religions.[60] {{329}} Adversaries call upon the idea of the death and revivification of a solar divinity or divinity of growth found in other religions, derived from the morning rising of the sun and from the death of plants in winter with their subsequent rebirth in the spring. They claim that this is confirmed by the description of time in the Gospel accounts: "in the morning, once the sun had risen" (Mark 16:2) and "on the third day" (1 Cor 15:4), which is a sacred number in various Eastern religions, determining the victory of the good principle of light and of the fruit-bearing power over the evil principle, which also would have entered into the Old Testament through the influence of various mythologies thereupon (Gunkel).

However, the historical fact of Christ's Resurrection stands in firm opposition to this theory. His Resurrection was recounted, by witnesses who are deserving of faith, in the New Testament, where we find nothing vague, nor any abstraction, nor any allusion to yearly cycle of rebirth or to the victory over chaos and the dragon. Rather, all of the details recounted here are concrete, being concerned with a historical man, described in accurate terms concerning time and place, and other circumstances as well. Moreover, before the influence of Christianity, the true sense of the resurrection is not indeed found in other religions, which instead only present a continuation of some hero's life in another

---

[59] *ST* III, q. 55, a. 5, ad 3.
[60] See Léonce de Grandmaison, S.J., [*Jésus Christ,*] vol. 2, [Paris: Beauchesne, 1931], 428–434, 506–522.

world or in another person. Indeed, it was so much the case that the pagans were not familiar with the idea of the true resurrection, that the Athenians, having knowledge of the mysteries, ridiculed St. Paul (or doubted his words) when he preached that Christ's Resurrection is the pledge of the bodily resurrection of all men (Acts 17:32). Moreover, the various elements in these "resurrections"—such as the intervention of a woman (Mother Earth), who occupies a central location in such narratives, as well as of a generative power and of sexual love along with the impure worship connected with them—make any comparison with the Gospel accounts ridiculous.[61]

As regards the confirmation drawn from the temporal descriptions deployed in mythological accounts (e.g., "on the third day," which adversaries number along with "on the fourth day" and "three and a half times"), it is certain that this description never is concerned with a true bodily resurrection. Finally, it is clear from the Gospels themselves that the apostles in no way expected Christ's Resurrection on the third day.[62]

{{330}} Therefore, the manifestation of Christ's Resurrection was utterly perfect in every order. It was the object of natural certitude on account of evidence as a sign and the object of supernatural certitude on

---

[61] See ibid., 531ff: "The career of these two 'dead and resurrected' demigods does not, in fact, involve either a passion or a resurrection in the received sense of these words. Shattered by a tragic and involuntary accident, it is followed by an enduring recovery—and that is where the analogy ends. As soon as one wishes to press upon one or another of its terms, everything fades away. Osiris retrieves life and a kingdom, though in another world. Dionysius-Zagreus is assassinated and devoured, and only a relic remains. Pallas saves the heart and carries it to Zeus, who takes it, marries Semele, the daughter of Cadmus, who gives him a second Dionysius. Each year, after his winter reclusion in Hades, Adonis takes up anew a regular period of life and of earthly love. The sorrowful Attis, forced to be faithful, will henceforth take his place on the chariot, and in the worship, of the Great Mother Goddess."

Elias Bickermann (in 1924), applying morphological methodologies, discerned in the Gospel accounts the motifs of heroic aphansism and theophany taken from popular literature and was thus led to hold that the first ministers had been persuaded not, properly speaking, concerning Christ's Resurrection but, rather, concerning his aphansis and assumption body and soul into glory by God, using the examples of Enoch, Romulus, and Ganymede. The faith in the resurrection from the dead expressed by St. Paul would have been a later infiltration coming from Hellenistic mysteries, wherein dead and risen gods are worshiped.

Against this kind of invention stands the true redemptive death of Christ, openly testified to in the Gospels, as something accepted, without any difficulty, as a fundamental dogma of Christianity in the earliest centuries, not only by St. Paul, but by all believers.

[62] See ibid., 509: "In sum, the mention of 'the third day' has no connection with these distant mythologies. It figured into Christ's predictions, themselves being conformed to the belief, which had surely been widespread in Israel at that time, holding that God hears and brings aid quickly, on 'the third day,' to the righteous who trust in him. However, neither were the Lord's prophecies understood by His disciples, nor did the belief in the divine aid coming on 'the third day' imply a fixed and determinate lapse of time. This is a completely clear fact which was set forth in the primitive catechesis which St. Paul, entering into the Church, himself received and transmitted to his followers."

account of the testimony of the angels, Christ, and the Scriptures, in which it had been foretold. Afterwards, it was confirmed by new miracles (Acts 3:15; 4:10–33). For us, *this is historically certain, with moral certitude*, as well as *supernaturally certain on account of the Church's own infallible testimony.* See *Lamentabili* (Against the modernists), no. 36.[63]

ART. 3: ON THE CONTINUATION OF MIRACLES IN THE CATHOLIC CHURCH AND IN HER ALONE

§1. Jesus Christ's promises.

§2. Miracles forever continued in the Roman Catholic Church and even today continue.

§3. This sign of God is lacking in other churches.

§4. Thus, we have a confirmation for the divine origin of the Roman Catholic Church.

§1. Jesus Christ Promised That Miracles Would Be Performed in His Church

This can be shown from many declarations by Christ. (a) He said to his disciples: "But the Father who abideth in me, he doth the works. Believe you not that I am in the Father and the Father in me? Otherwise believe for the very works' sake. Amen, amen, I say to you, *he that believeth in me, the works that I do, he also shall do: and greater than these shall he do.* Because I go to the Father" (John 14:10–13, DR). As St. Thomas remarks,[64] this is as though

---

[63] See Ladeuze, *La résurrection du Christ*, 58: "Conducted merely in accord with historical methodologies, criticism forever leads to a defense of our faith, indeed with an armament which is appropriate to our era and irrefutable in the face of our adversaries. The examination of the Gospel texts cannot make us perceive, beyond these texts, an era that would be closer to the facts, a belief different from our own, functioning as the evolutionary basis for the latter. On the contrary, through St. Paul, we reach the most ancient testimony possible, and this testimony is conformed to our faith. Given that it is concerned with an object that can be perceived by witnesses, the historian can only bow before it. In order to avoid doing so, recourse to considerations from outside the historical order will be necessary. Historical criticism is not what is destructive for faith but, rather, what is so destructive is criticism which is inspired by a false philosophy, a criticism which thereby denies its own principles.... The propositions held by this kind of philosophical criticism are what were clearly condemned by the Holy Office in its decree *Lamentabili sane exitu*, no. 36 (Denzinger, no. 3436): 'The Resurrection of the Savior *is not properly a fact of the historical order.* It is a fact of merely the supernatural order (neither demonstrated nor demonstrable) that Christian consciousness gradually derived from other facts.'"

[64] See St. Thomas, *In XIV Ioan.*, 14:12.

he said, "When I will be more greatly glorified, then it will be fitting that I do even greater things and even give you power to greater things." Thus, before Jesus was glorified, the Spirit was not given in fullness, as he was given later. (b) Jesus, after saying to the apostles, "Go ye into the whole world and preach the gospel to every creature," immediately continues, "*In my name they shall cast out devils. They shall speak with new tongues. They shall take up serpents: and if they shall drink any deadly thing, it shall not hurt them. They shall lay their hands upon the sick: and they shall recover*.... {{331}} But they going forth preached everywhere: the Lord working withal, and confirming the word *with signs that followed*" (Mark 16:15–20, DR).

§2. Miracles Forever Continued in the Roman Catholic Church and Even Today Continue

This is clearly proven from historical records, whose honesty cannot be denied lest the whole of historical certitude were to perish. Thus, in the first century, this was clear, especially in the Acts of the Apostles and likewise in St. Paul's letters. For example, we read in Acts: "And by the hands of the apostles were many signs and wonders wrought among the people.... Insomuch that they brought forth the sick into the streets and laid them on beds and couches, that, when Peter came, his shadow at the least might overshadow any of them and they might be delivered from their infirmities ..., bringing sick persons and such as were troubled with unclean spirits: who were all healed" (Acts 5:12–16, DR). Likewise, "Stephen ... did great wonders and signs among the people" (Acts 6:8, DR). St. Paul speaks about miracles that he himself performed (Rom 15:18; 2 Cor 12:12), and he numbered the grace of miracles among the charismatic gifts (1 Cor 12:28; Gal 3:5). In the second century, no few wonders were handed on by the apostolic Fathers, who had orally learned the teaching of the apostles. In the third century, miracles are recounted by writers who are deserving of belief, affirming that they speak about them as eyewitnesses, like St. Irenaeus, St. Justin, St. Cyprian, Origen, Tertullian, and others. In the fourth and fifth centuries, approved historians of the faith testify to them, as well as teachers who were famed for their holiness and teaching, among whom are numbered Eusebius and St. Jerome and then St. Ambrose, St. Augustine, and others. And there is no age in which the Catholic Church did not shine forth with men of holiness and the glory of miracles. It suffices that one look through the volumes of *Ruinart* and the *Bollandists*, as well as other historical accounts, which have gathered them together from authentic accounts. In our own

ON CHRIST'S MIRACLES

days,[65] the *Sacred Congregation for Rites*, in the process for the canonization of saints, inquires into the truth of miracles with great subtlety and severity so that when it approves them, they may be held to be utterly certain facts.[66]

Today, many miracles are performed in the sanctuary of *Our Lady of Lourdes*, where there is a commission of doctors, whose examination bears witness to the fact that many utterly certain miracles are performed there in any given year.[67]

---

[65] [Trans. note: Note that this is no longer the case, as the Sacred Congregation for Rites was split, in 1969, into the Congregation for Divine Worship and the Congregation for the Causes of Saints.]

[66] See Benedict XIV, *De canonizatione sanctorum* (especially bk. 4). Note, for example, what Daubenton refers to in *La vie du révérend père Jean François Régis* (Paris, 1716): "An English gentleman came to Rome. It happened—I know not how—that a Roman prelate with whom he was in contact, had him read a proceeding containing the proof offered for a number of miracles. The Protestant read it with much attention and pleasure. Then, he gave it back to the prelate, saying: 'This is certainly the surest manner of proving miracles. If all such miracles which are received in the Roman Church were established on proofs that are so evident and authentic as these ones, we would have no difficulty subscribing to them, and in that way, you would save yourselves from all the ridicules that we launch against all of your supposed miracles.' The prelate replied, '*Now, heed well that none of these miracles which seem so well proven and so strongly supported have been admitted by the Congregation of Rites because they have seemed to be insufficiently proven.*' Astonished at this response, which he had not expected, the Protestant admitted that only a blind, *a priori* bias could contest the canonization of the saints and that he would never have thought that the Roman Church's attention would go so far in its examination of miracles." (Cited in Perrone, 31.) [Trans. note: This was translated with an eye to the French translation published in Lyon in 1853. No further details are provided for the Perrone citation.]

[67] See Georges Bertrin, *Histoire critique des événements de Lourdes: Apparitions et guérisons* (Paris: Lecoffre, 1905), 120: "Even if we were to gather together all the various kinds of nervous conditions, including the worst of them, this would not furnish an explanation for even *one thirteenth* of these healings. (See the appendix on pages 376–477: there are around 180 out of a set of 2,600, in rounded numbers.) Tuberculosis, in all of its various forms, presents by itself a rather sizeable contingent of cases. Pulmonary tuberculosis, bone tuberculosis, intestinal tuberculosis, white tumors, lupus, Pott's disease, coxalgia, and so forth have given place to 571 healings, among those which have been able to be identified. . . . Moreover, we find 394 cases for digestive diseases and those connected to them, 68 for circulatory illnesses, among which are numbered 34 pertaining to the heart, 99 for respiratory diseases (bronchitis, pleurisy), . . . 383 for brain diseases, 95 for bone disease, . . . 15 for cancers, 27 for sores. . . . Let us also note in particular 34 blind people who have had the good fortune of seeing once more and 28 deafmute people who have recovered their ability to speak and hear. See no. 9 in the appendix."
In particular, note on 207–232 the healing of *Pierre de Rudder*, who had a broken bone instantaneously healed. Prior to the healing, "Peter was able to rotate his heel totally around to the front and his toes such that they pointed backwards. . . . He made two extremities of the broken bone come out through the wound" (212–213). See 278–291 on the healing of *Marie Lemarchand* whose tuberculosis-lupus was healed suddenly. Likewise, see 330–358 concerning the sudden healing of *Gabriel Gargam*, who was paralyzed from the waist down, only being

§3. This Sign of God Is Lacking in Other Churches

{{332}} No miracles are seen in Protestantism, nor any hope for miracles. Luther said: "Miracles must not be required by us, who deny free choice of the will."[68] And Calvin wrote to the king of France: "Those who demand miracles from us act wickedly."[69] He said that his doctrine does not stand in need of miracles, for he was preaching the Gospel of Jesus Christ, not a new gospel for which faith would need to be solidified through signs.

Likewise, no true miracles are found in Photianism, and those that are sometimes brought forward as having been performed on behalf of the separated church and against the union of the Ruthenians with the See of Peter are not facts of such a nature as to require a supernatural cause. [Ioannes] Martinov, an expert in Russian matters, affirms with certitude that these miracles are not at all supernatural.[70]

---

able to be fed through a tube, and already had gangrene in his feet.

See Dr. Edouard Le Bec, *Preuves médicales du miracle* (Bourges: Tardy-Pigelet, 1917), 31 (examination of the healing of Pierre de Rudder, whose broken bone was instantly healed): "We can estimate that the bone piece that repaired the substantial loss of the bone was five grams. This large quantity of phosphoric salts was deposited all of the sudden. It is utterly clear that this quantity was not found ready in the body at the moment of the miracle.—Need we say that an unknown natural force could have instantaneously extracted from the blood much more phosphorus than it contained?—Where would it have been able to draw this quantity which did not, in fact, exist? Need we say that it *formed* them? This is to admit the supernatural Power—could we not say 'creative Power'—that nonbelievers push back against, while Christians know it quite well!" And on 67: "Therefore, it is quite clear that *the temporal factor was lacking* and one cannot contemplate that this would have been a natural, physiological healing." And finally, on 110: "(Unknown) natural forces acting upon a tumor will no more destroy it than they would destroy matter. They will only be able to transform this living substance. . . . Now, in the supernatural healing of *cancer*, what we see is *not a transformation but, instead, an absolute disappearance*, something which is quite different indeed. This can only be brought about by the action of a power that differs from natural ones, for *there is only one supernatural power possessing the power to bring about the integral suppression of matter*."

[68] Luther, *On the Bondage of the Will*.

[69] See Calvin, *Institutes*, preface.

[70] *Revue des questions historiques* (Jan. 1884), 272.

[Trans. note: For an overview of the complex history of the Photian Schism, see Francis Dvornik, *The Photian Schism, History and Legend* (Cambridge: Cambridge University Press, 1948). Also, as regards Orthodox saints and miracle-workers, one should bear in mind the dated nature of Fr. Garrigou-Lagrange's comments.]

§4. Thus, We Have a Confirmation for the Divine Origin of the Roman Catholic Church

{{333}} Indeed, these same signs, like the raising of the dead and the curing of the sick, which were found in the primitive Church, also have remained into the present in the Roman Catholic Church and in it alone, as may be ascertained from records that are authentic and wholly worthy of belief. For this reason, since, as the Protestants conceded, the primitive Church, at least up to the third or the fourth century, was the true Church, then the present-day Roman Catholic Church must also be true.

God never has allowed miracles to be lacking in the true religion. This is clear from history, be it of the patriarchal period, the time of the Jews, or even much more so from Christian history. Already now, to the extent that the miracles that have been performed in the three states of the Church demonstrate her truth and divinity, so too, by contrast, does their absence from Protestantism, Photianism, and Judaism after Christ demonstrate the falsity of the latter.

Why were many miracles performed in the earlier centuries of the Church's existence, while fewer were performed in later times?

St. Thomas responds: "This marvelous conversion of the world to the Christian faith is the most certain evidence of the signs from the past, such that it is no longer necessary that they be further repeated, since they are evidently apparent in their effect. . . . Nevertheless, God does not cease, even in our days, to work miracles through his saints in confirmation of the faith."[71] Indeed, in the first centuries of the Church's existence, the Christian religion had to be founded and paganism destroyed. The apostles, men who were lacking in all human means, stood in need of aid, and Christians needed to be defended against the ferocity of their persecutors, as well as against being seduced by magical deeds of heretics. Therefore, it was necessary that miracles be produced by God in order to show that the Church is divine. Thus, even now, in the evangelization of unbelievers or in certain sanctuaries in Christian regions, they are performed in order to strengthen believers against contemporary naturalism and to manifest the truth of the faith, as well as the supernatural power of God, Jesus Christ, and the Blessed Virgin Mary. Indeed, having seen these miracles, many unbelievers and many Protestants have been converted to the Catholic Church.

---

[71] *SCG* I, ch. 6.

CHAPTER ELEVEN

On Christ's Prophecies

SINGLE ARTICLE

§1. State of the question. {{334}}

§2. Christ distinctly and particularly predicted many future contingents, which were fulfilled to the letter.

§3. Christ's prophecies are utterly certain motives of credibility.

§4. Resolution of objections against the supernaturality of Christ's predictions.

§1. State of the Question

Earlier, in vol. 2, bk. 1, ch. 20, we discussed prophecy (or the making of predictions) in a speculative and general manner, there saying that it is *the certain prediction of a future contingent that cannot be naturally foreseen.* Having proven the possibility of prophecy, we showed that it can be distinguished with certainty from human conjecture and from the divinization of spirits, especially if *the future contingent in question is remote and determinately predicted with all of its minute circumstances,* if it is *complex and free* (nay, depending on *the freedom* of many people, who do not intend to fulfill a prediction), and *a fortiori* if it is a *miracle* depending solely upon the divine freedom and exceeding all possible natural foresight. Prophecies of this kind, if they are fulfilled, quite clearly can only come from God and, thus, *provide a radiant indication of his infinite foresight.* Therefore, if they are proposed as signs of revelation, they are utterly certain motives of credibility.

Now we must consider Christ's prophecies and then, next, the messianic predictions made in the Old Testament.

As regards Christ's prophecies, rationalists and modernists hold that Jesus erred in his preaching of the destruction of Jerusalem, for according to them, he also then announced the end of the world as being imminent. Hence, this prophecy concerning the end of the world would be false, thus greatly diminishing the importance of the other. Thus, based on some difficulty or obscurity, adversaries strive to deny even those things that are utterly clear. By contrast, according to a right method, we must proceed from what is more known to what is less known—that is, from manifest things to obscure ones. Otherwise, the whole of knowledge would be brought to ruin.

When we bring forth Christ's testimony, we set forth in passing his prophecies concerning the Church as well as the end of the world, and in treating of his Resurrection, we saw how he announced it. Now we must gather together Christ's principal predictions.

§2. Christ Distinctly and Particularly Predicted Many Future Contingents, Which Were Fulfilled to the Letter

{{335}} As is recounted in the Gospels, Christ knew the secrets of hearts and predicted many future events concerning himself, his disciples, and the Church, as well as concerning unbelieving Jews and the city of Jerusalem.

(1) *Christ had certain knowledge of the secrets of the heart.* "And Jesus seeing their thoughts, said: Why do you think evil in your hearts?" (Matt 9:4, DR; also 12:24–25; 16:7–8; Mark 2:8; Luke 6:8; 7:39–40; 11:17). "But Jesus knowing their wickedness, said: 'Why do you tempt me, ye hypocrites?'" (Matt 22:18, DR; also 26:10; Luke 5:21–22; 9:46–47). "For he knew what was in man" (John 2:25, DR). "But there are some of you that believe not. For Jesus knew from the beginning who they were that did not believe and who he was that would betray him" (John 6:65, DR; also 7:29; 13:11; 16:19). Similarly, he knew *remote facts*, as well as nearby ones. For example, he said to Nathanael, "Before that Philip called thee, when thou wast under the fig tree, I saw thee" (John 1:48, DR). And he told the Samaritan woman everything that she had done (John 4:29). Likewise, he said to Peter, "Go to the sea, and cast in a hook: and that fish which shall first come up, take: and when thou hast opened its mouth, thou shalt find a stater. Take that, and give it to them for me and thee" (Matt 17:26, DR).

(2) *Christ predicted his Passion and Resurrection many times.* John notes, "He himself knew what he would do" (John 6:6, DR). "[He knew] all things that should come upon him" (John 18:4, DR). In fact, Jesus announced his Passion and Resurrection *at least three times*, not in an ambiguous and doubtful way but, rather, *clearly, in minute details*, and *with certitude, at a time when all of these things could not have been foreseen*—namely, after Peter's confession (Matt 16:20–23; Mark 8:30–33; Luke

9:21–22), after the curing of the crazed man (Matt 17:21–22; Mark 9:29), and after the parable of the workers sent into the vineyard (Matt 20:17–19; Mark 10:32–34; Luke 18:31–34). The first time, this prediction seemed so extraordinary to Peter that he himself said, "Lord, be it far from thee, this shall not be unto thee."

In Mark, this prediction is recounted thus: "The Son of man shall be betrayed to the chief priests and to the scribes and ancients. And they shall condemn him to death and shall deliver him to the Gentiles. And they shall mock him and spit on him and scourge him and kill him: and the third day he shall rise again" (Mark 10:33–34, DR).

In Matthew, we read the same thing, and moreover, his *Crucifixion* is predicted (Matt 20:17–19). The Pharisees themselves said to Pilate, "Sir, we have remembered, that that seducer said, while he was yet alive: After three days I will rise again" (Matt 27:63, DR). Now, all of these were fulfilled down to the smallest of details (Matt 27:57; Mark 14:64; Matt 27:2, 26, 30).

(3) *He announced many things to his disciples.* (a) *In general,* he foretold to his disciples *the graces of the Holy Spirit,* "which they should receive who believed in him" (John 7:39), as well as *persecutions*: "If the world hate you, know ye that it hath hated me before you. . . . If they have persecuted me, they will also persecute you" (John 15:18–20, DR). "For they will deliver you up in councils, and they will scourge you in their synagogues. And you shall be brought before governors, and before kings for my sake, for a testimony to them and to the Gentiles. {{336}} But when they shall deliver you up, take no thought how or what to speak: for it shall be given you in that hour what to speak. For it is not you that speak, but the spirit of your Father that speaketh in you. The brother also shall deliver up the brother to death, and the father the son" (Matt 10:17–22, DR; also 24:9–13; Mark 4:17; 10:39; Luke 11:49; 12:1–11; 21:13). All these were fulfilled to the letter, as is related in the Acts of the Apostles (Acts 4:1–8; 5:17–41; etc.) and in the history of Christianity's first centuries.

(b) Jesus foretold *to the apostles* that they would *flee and scatter during his Passion,* as well as the fact that *they would gather together in Galilee* following upon his Resurrection: "All you shall be scandalized in me this night. For it is written: I will strike the shepherd: and the sheep of the flock shall be dispersed. But after I shall be risen again, I will go before you into Galilee" (Matt 26:31–32, DR; John 16:32). In fact, after Jesus was apprehended by the soldiers, "then the disciples, all leaving him, fled. . . . (And after his Resurrection) the eleven disciples went into Galilee, unto the mountain where Jesus had appointed them" (Matt 26:56; 28:16, DR). He also promised to them the gift of converting sinners, the grace of miracles, the gift of tongues, the gifts of the Holy Spirit (Matt 4:18–20; 10:1–19; Mark 1:17; 16:17; Luke 10:19; 21:14, 15), oppression and struggle against the spirit of the world, and finally a great victory: "Fear not, little flock, for it hath pleased your Father to give you a kingdom" (Luke 12:32, DR; Matt 19:18; John 7:31; 15:16).

(c) *To St. Peter*, Christ announced his *apostolate*: "Fear not: from henceforth thou shalt catch men" (Luke 5:10, DR). His *primacy*: "Thou art Peter; and upon this rock I will build my church . . . and I will give to thee the keys of the kingdom of heaven" (Matt 16:18–19, DR; John 1:42–44). *His threefold denial*: "Amen I say to thee that in this night before the cock crow, thou wilt deny me thrice" (Matt 26:34, DR; Mark 14:30, 71). *His martyrdom*: "Whither I go, thou canst not follow me now: but thou shalt follow hereafter. . . . When thou wast younger, thou didst gird thyself and didst walk where thou wouldst. But when thou shalt be old, thou shalt stretch forth thy hands, and another shall gird thee and lead thee whither thou wouldst not" (John 13:36; 21:18, DR). And St. John adds, "This he said, signifying by what death he should glorify God."

(d) Likewise, Jesus predicted in Bethphage to his disciples, whom he sent to a certain village: "You shall find an ass tied and a colt with her" (Matt 21:2, DR). And, likewise, he announced to them who were to prepare the dinner, and they ate all the food that they discovered had been [miraculously] made [in the multiplication of the loaves and fishes] (Matt 14:13). And *concerning Mary Magdalene*, he said, "Amen I say to you, wheresoever this Gospel shall be preached in the whole world, that also which she hath done shall be told for a memory of her" (Matt 26:13, DR; Mark 14:9).

(4) *Jesus predicted many marvelous things about the Church.* At the time when he made such predictions about the church, they were hardly likely, but nonetheless, he announced them with utter certitude, and Christians firmly believed in them. Among them, we must note, in particular, (a) *the sending of the Holy Spirit*: "But you shall receive the power of the Holy Ghost coming upon you, and you shall be witnesses unto me in Jerusalem, and in all Judea, and Samaria, and even to the uttermost part of the earth" (Acts 1:8, DR). In fact, "they were all filled with the Holy Ghost, and they began to speak with divers tongues, according as the Holy Ghost gave them to speak" (Acts 2:4, DR). {{337}} (b) *The marvelous propagation of the Church throughout the whole of the world, along with her indefectibility*: "Thou art Peter; and upon this rock I will build my church. . . . Going therefore, teach ye all nations; . . . and behold I am with you all days, even to the consummation of the world" (Matt 16:18; 28:19–20, DR). However, who at Christ's own time could have foreseen this marvelous propagation

and unconquered stability of the Church? (c) *The conversion of nonbelieving peoples* was announced in a variety of ways—for example, in the parable of the murdering vintners, the lord "will give the vineyard to others" (Luke 20:16, DR); in the parable of the mustard seed (Matt 13:31–32); in the parable about the people invited to supper (Luke 14:24); and elsewhere clearly and expressly, for example: "I have not found so great faith in Israel. And I say to you that many shall come from the east and the west, and shall sit down with Abraham, and Isaac, and Jacob in the kingdom of heaven" (in Matt 8:10ff, DR; also 24:14; Luke 13:29).

(5) *Jesus also announced many things to the Jews.* As we already said, he foresaw the crime of the Pharisees and the chief priests. *Concerning Judas,* he said: "Amen I say to you that one of you is about to betray me. . . . [W]oe to that man by whom the Son of man shall be betrayed. It were better for him, if that man had not been born" (Matt 26:21–24, DR; likewise in Mark, Luke, and John). In various ways, he announced terrible chastisements *to the Jews*: "What therefore will the lord of the vineyard do? He will come and destroy those husbandmen and will give the vineyard to others. . . . And they sought to lay hands on him. . . . For they knew that he spoke this parable to them" (Mark 12:9–12, DR). "*Therefore I say to you that the kingdom of God shall be taken from you* and shall be given to a nation yielding the fruits thereof. . . . The stone which the builders rejected, the same is become the head of the corner . . . *and on whomsoever it shall fall, it shall grind him to powder*" (Matt 21:42–44, DR, order altered). "*Behold I send to you prophets* and wise men and scribes, and *some of them you will put to death* and crucify, and some you will scourge in your synagogues and persecute from city to city, that upon you may come all the just blood that hath been shed upon the earth. . . . Amen I say to you, all these things shall come upon this generation" (Matt 23:34–39, DR). "Behold, your house shall be left to you, desolate" (Matt 23:38, DR). "*And thou Capharnaum . . . shalt go down even unto hell.* For if in Sodom had been wrought the miracles that have been wrought in thee, perhaps it had remained unto this day" (Matt 11:23, DR). And this was completely fulfilled, for only ruins remain of this city.

(6) **The destruction of Jerusalem.** Finally, Jesus expressly announced the destruction of Jerusalem, along with its various antecedent signs. First, he somewhat obscurely said: "The hour cometh, when you shall neither on this mountain, nor in Jerusalem, adore the Father" (John 4:21, DR), and "Woe to you, Scribes and Pharisees, hypocrites. . . . You are the sons of those who killed the prophets, and now fill up the measure of your fathers" (Matt 23:32). However, a few days before his death, Jesus clearly predicted the overthrow of Jerusalem (see Matt 24; Mark 13; Luke 21).

In order to understand this prophecy, as many commentators note, we must distinguish it into a number of parts: (1) the prediction itself, (2) the twofold questioning of the apostles concerning the time of the downfall of Jerusalem and the signs of the end of the world, {{338}} (3) Jesus's response to the first question, and (4) his response to the second question. This final part is not easily determined in Matthew's text. It probably begins in verse 23 therein. It is briefer in Luke 21:25–28 because elsewhere, in 17:20, St. Luke refers to the apostles' second question and the Lord's response.

(1) Jesus says, concerning the building of the temple: "Do you see all these things? *Amen I say to you, there shall not be left here a stone upon a stone that shall not be destroyed*" (Matt 24:2, DR; likewise in Mark and Luke).

(2) "The disciples came to him privately, saying: *Tell us when shall these things be? And what shall be the sign of thy coming and of the consummation of the world?*" (Matt 24:3, DR). St. Thomas notes, "In Luke alone is this question touched upon, namely, the destruction of Jerusalem, which they did not believe would be destroyed until after the second coming. Whence, they said, in Acts 1:6 (DR), 'wilt thou at this time restore again the kingdom of Israel?'"[1]

(3) In response, Jesus announces *three signs of the destruction of Jerusalem*—namely: (a) "For many will come in my name saying: I am Christ. And they will seduce many" (Matt 24:5, DR; Mark 13:3–6; Luke 21:7–8), and *many false prophets shall rise,*[2] like Elymas and Simon the Magician (Acts 13:6–11; 8:9–10), as well as his disciples, the pseudo-liberators like Theodas (Acts 5:36). (b) "And you shall hear of *wars* and rumors of wars.... For nation shall rise against nation, and kingdom against kingdom: And there shall be *pestilences* and *famines* and *earthquakes* in places. Now all these are the beginnings of sorrows" (Matt 24:6; Mark 13:7–8; Luke 21:9–11). In fact, as Josephus recounts, before the overthrow of Jerusalem there were civil wars in nearly every city in Palestine.[3] And Gentiles rose up against one another in the Roman Empire, in Gaul, in Germany, in the regions of the Danube, in Britain, and in the confines of the region of Parthia.[4] Between the years AD 60 and 70, there were many earthquakes, leading to the destruction of Laodicea in AD 61 and Pompeii in AD 63.[5] There also

---

[1] St. Thomas, *In* XXIV *Matth.*

[2] See 2 Pet 2:1–20 (DR): "But there were also false prophets among the people . . ."; 1 John 2:18 (DR): "Even now there are become many Antichrists, whereby we know that it is the last hour."

[3] See Josephus, *The Jewish War*, 2.17.10 and 2.18.1–8.

[4] See Tacitus, *Histories*, 1.2.

[5] See Tacitus, *Annals*, 14.27; 15.12.3; 6.1.1.

were plagues and famines not only in Judea but throughout the empire.[6] In the year 65, terrible signs appeared above Jerusalem.[7] (c) "Then shall they deliver you up to be afflicted and shall put you to death: and you shall be hated by all nations for my name's sake. And then shall many be scandalized and shall betray one another and shall hate one another" (Matt 24:9–14, DR; Mark 13:9–13; Luke 21:12–19). In fact, as is recounted in Acts and St. Paul's letters, between AD 30 and 67, St. Paul, St. John, and all the apostles were thrown into prison or interrogated by the Jewish Sanhedrin, Christians were dispersed, and Stephen and James the brother of John were killed. St. Paul was thrown into prison, his staff was cut down, and he was judged by Gallio, Felix, Festus, Agrippa, and Nero. At the same time heresies sprouted, but as the Lord predicted (Matt 24:14; Mark 13:10), "the apostles preached everywhere" (Mark 16:20)—that is, throughout the whole world known at that time.

{{339}} (4) The ruin of Jerusalem was foretold: "*When therefore you shall see the abomination of desolation*, which was spoken of by Daniel the prophet,[8] *standing in the holy place*—he that readeth let him understand— then they that are in Judea, let them flee to the mountains" (Matt 24:15–22, DR; Mark 13:14–20). "For these are the days of vengeance, that all things may be fulfilled, that are written. But woe to them that are with child and give suck in those days: for there shall be great distress in the land and wrath upon this people. *And they shall fall by the edge of the sword and shall be led away captives into all nations: and Jerusalem shall be trodden down by the Gentiles till the times of the nations be fulfilled* (Luke 21:22–24, DR). Earlier, when he wept over Jerusalem, Jesus stated the cause of this terrible chastisement: "If thou also hadst known . . . the things that are to thy peace. . . . For the days shall come upon thee: and *thy enemies shall cast a trench about thee and compass thee round* and straiten thee on every side, and *beat thee flat to the ground, and thy children who are in thee*. And they shall not leave in thee a stone upon a stone, *because thou hast not known the time of thy visitation*" (Luke 19:42–44 (DR).

All of these things were fulfilled. In the years AD 66 and 67, the Jewish people rose up against the Romans. Vespasian, with a massive army, invaded Galilee and Judea, killing many Jews. Then, having been made emperor in

---

[6] Acts 11:28; Tacitus, *Annals*, 16.13; Josephus, *The Jewish War*, 5.13.

[7] Josephus, *The Jewish War*, 6.5.3; Tacitus, *Histories*, 5.13.

[8] Dan 9:26–27 (DR) predicted: "Christ shall be slain . . . and there shall be in the temple the abomination of desolation: and the desolation shall continue even to the consummation, and to the end." Likewise, see Dan 12:11.

69, he demanded that his son Titus take over this war. *Christians fled and arrived at the town of Pella.* Titus encircled Jerusalem with a palisade and during the time of the siege (as is reported by Flavius Josephus, who was an eyewitness and is wholly worthy of belief),[9] *one million, one hundred thousand Jews died by sword or famine, and ninety-seven thousand were carried off to hard slavery*; they who nevertheless survived such a huge massacre were sold at military auctions during the reign of Emperor Hadrian like low-priced sheep. As Flavius Josephus recounts,[10] after Titus had conquered the city of Jerusalem, *the temple was consumed by fire and demolished, and the whole city was leveled to the ground.* Truly, the "abomination of desolation" was in the temple, for at the time of the siege, the temple was converted into a citadel,[11] and after the siege *the Romans offered sacrifices to their gods in the holy place.*[12] This took place in AD 70, thus fulfilling what Jesus had said: "Amen I say to you that this generation shall not pass till all these things be done" (Matt 24:34, DR).

These facts are utterly certain historically. In memory of them, there remains the triumphal arch elevated in honor of Titus, and the testimony of Flavius Josephus is conformed to what is said by Tacitus[13] and Suetonius.[14]

§3. Christ's Prophecies Are Utterly Certain Motives of Credibility

Indeed, they are true prophecies that exceed the powers of natural foresight: *They announce clearly and certainly complex future contingents along with all of their smallest circumstances*—nay, *future things that are dependent upon the free wills of many individuals* who do not intend to fulfill the prediction. For example, "the Son of man shall be betrayed to the chief priests and the scribes: and they shall condemn him to death. And shall deliver him to the Gentiles to be mocked and scourged and crucified: and the third day he shall rise again" (Matt 20:18–19, DR). {{340}} *In particular, Christ's Resurrection and the unconquered stability of the Church could not have been naturally foreseen since they are miracles*, depending immediately upon God's freedom. Nor was this fulfillment fortuitous, for many minute details correspond perfectly to the prediction, and in particular, the miracles announced

---

[9] See Josephus, *The Jewish War*, 4.9.3.

[10] Ibid., 7.

[11] Ibid., 6.3.6.

[12] Ibid., 6.6.1.

[13] See Tacitus, *Histories*, 5.1–13.

[14] See Suetonius, *Vespasian*, 4; *Titus*, 4.

could not have been something fortuitous. On the contrary, in all of these things, God's providence is made manifest. Therefore, in the words of the [First] Vatican Council, these prophecies "manifestly display the . . . infinite knowledge of God."

Moreover, Christ clearly connected these predictions with the Christian religion, for they are concerned with Christ himself, the Church, and the divine chastisements to be inflicted in punishment upon nonbelievers. Nay, sometimes, Christ said explicitly to his disciples: "At present I tell you, before it come to pass: that when it shall come to pass, you may believe that I am he" (John 13:19, DR; 14:29). Therefore, if Christ's mission were not divine, God, the principal author of prophecy, would be a false witness, which is impossible. Thus, as the [First] Vatican Council states, these prophecies, like miracles, are "the most certain signs of the divine revelation, adapted to the intelligence of all men."

Nor is the gift of prophecy lacking in the Church. St. Paul wrote, "And the manifestation of the Spirit is given to every man unto profit. To one indeed, by the Spirit, is given the word of wisdom. . . . To another, the working of miracles, to another, prophecy" (1 Cor 12:7–10, DR). *The Book of Revelation* is one great prophecy that announces the principal events of the life of the Church in a symbolic manner, like what was prophesied by Ezekiel, Daniel, and Zechariah. Some of these symbols are explained in the book itself, whereas others can be explained through analogy with what is found in the prophecies of the Old Testament. However, many remain obscure for us. Nonetheless, all commentators admit that the Book of Revelation is a prophecy concerning the definitive victory of the Church, first against paganism and then against the world at the end of time. Moreover, as can be seen in the volumes written by the *Bollandists* and other historians, *many saints were illuminated with the gift of prophecy*. For example, the founders of religious orders often announced the future to be fulfilled by their sons. Just as miracles have never ceased to exist in the Roman Catholic Church, so too has this gift of prophecy remained.

§4. Resolution of Objections Against the Supernaturality of Christ's Predictions

Objections are raised especially by rationalists against the value of the prophecy concerning the destruction of Jerusalem.

(1) Many contend that it could only have been written after the event. Why? Because it seems too complete and too perfectly fulfilled. Nonetheless, many adversar-

ies admit that Jesus foresaw the ruin of Jerusalem,[15] though not distinctly with all of its minute circumstances. And most hold that the Synoptic Gospels were written after AD 70 because the destruction of Jerusalem is described in them in exact detail.

Response: (1) This rationalist opinion arises from their gratuitous denial of the possibility of any truly supernatural prophecy. (2) It would already be quite extraordinary if Christ foresaw the destruction of Jerusalem, for during his life, the Jews lived in peace under the Roman Empire, as Pliny recounts.[16] {{341}} Jerusalem was by far the most illustrious of the cities of the East. The temple of the Mosaic religion seemed as though it would remain intact forever. (3) This prophecy was known prior to the destruction of the city, for three years prior to its destruction, the Christians in Jerusalem fled the city, as Christ warned, and arrived at Pella.[17] (4) If this prediction by Christ was only written after the event, then its writers would not have mixed with it those things that pertain to the end of the world. They would not have written, "And immediately after the tribulation of those days, the sun shall be darkened" (Matt 24:29, DR), but would have noted the fulfillment of the events, as they were accustomed to do (John 21:19; Acts 11:28). In particular, they would have said that the temple was burnt up prior to its destruction. Hence, certain rationalists, like Bernhard Weiss,[18] admit that St. Mark wrote this prediction prior to the event.

(2) Rationalists, taking up the opposite objection, argue not from the fact that the prediction is too perfect but, rather, from the fact that Jesus supposedly would have erred in it by announcing the end of the world at the same time as something immanent. Indeed, in the Synoptic Gospels, after the preaching of the signs of the end of the world, we read: "Amen I say to you, that this generation shall not pass till all these things be done" (Matt 24:34, DR; Mark 13:30; Luke 21:32).

Response: Already, we have said much concerning this when we set forth (in ch. 4, vol. 2) Christ's testimony concerning the end of the world. The following points are to be recalled and developed.

A. These texts are indeed difficult, for in this discourse Christ spoke about both the

---

[15] See the writings of Stapfer, Oskar Holtzmann, Renan, and Réville. Cf. Marius Lepin, *Jésus, messie et fils de Dieu d'après les évangiles synoptiques*, 3rd ed. (Paris: Letouzey et Ané, 1907), 381.

[16] See Pliny [the Elder], *N[atural] H[istory]*, vol. 15.

[17] Eusebius, *Historia ecclesiastica*, 3.5; St. Epiphanius, *Adv. haereses*, 11:28.

[18] See Bernhard Weiss, *Das Leben Jesu* (Stuttgart: Cotta, 1902), vol. 2, 439: "Every doubt concerning the authenticity of this prophetic declaration should be ruled out. . . . If Mark wrote after the ruin of Jerusalem, how is it that the prophecy that he recounts contains absolutely nothing that reflects the event which would have happened, for in reality, the temple was destroyed by fire and not at men's hands."

And Edmond Stapfer, *La mort et la résurrection de Jésus-Christ* (Paris: Fischbacher, 1898), 53–60: "The authenticity of the whole of the great eschatological discourse seems incontestable to us. Who, therefore, would have invented Mark's account?"

ruin of Jerusalem and the end of the world. However, since the first event is the figure of the second, it is not easy to discern what pertains to the first and what to the second. Nevertheless, the words of a given author, especially a wise one, must be understood, if possible, as though they are not contradictory. However, if, as rationalists contend, Jesus would have announced the end of the world as something immanent, he would have contradicted himself, for in many other places, he said things that stand in opposition to this:

(a) He said about the day of judgment: "*But of that day or hour no man knoweth, neither the angels in heaven, nor the Son, but the Father.* Take ye heed, watch and pray. For ye know not when the time is" (Mark 13:32–33, DR; Matt 24:36). Up to the Ascension, he said to his disciples, "It is not for you to know the time or moments, which the Father hath put in his own power" (Acts 1:7, DR).

(b) He had announced the future diffusion of the Gospel among all the Gentiles: "And this gospel of the kingdom shall be preached in the whole world, for a testimony to all nations: and then shall the consummation come" (Matt 24:14, DR; Mark 13:10; 16:15). However, the kingdom of heaven must gradually grow, for it is compared to a grain of wheat or a seed that gradually grows.[19]

(c) Let it not be said that the full evangelization of all the Gentiles is to be fulfilled, according to the prophecy, prior to the destruction of Jerusalem, for we read in the same sermon in Luke: "They . . . shall be led away captives into all nations, *and Jerusalem shall be trodden down by the Gentiles till the times of the nations be fulfilled*" (Luke 21:24, DR). {{342}} Hence, Jesus would have contradicted himself if he had announced the end of the world as something imminent. He only spoke by exhorting his hearers to vigilance: "*Watch ye therefore*, because you know not what hour your Lord will come. But this know ye, that if the goodman of the house knew at what hour the thief would come, he would certainly watch and would not suffer his house to be broken open. *Wherefore be you also ready, because at what hour you know not the Son of man will come*" (Matt 24:42–44, DR; Mark 13:33; Luke 12:39). As St. Jerome said, the Lord therefore wished for the end to remain uncertain so that man would forever expect. In other words, Christ intended for Christians to live as though the end were close at hand. In fact, the first generation lived thus, ever vigilant. This has been true in every era for all souls, for the end of this life is close at hand. Indeed, we must consider this world as being something utterly unstable and fleeting, for this world is passing away.[20]

B. With all of these points in place, we can more easily explain the words, "this generation shall not pass till all these things be done." Many interpreters, with Chrysostom, Theophylact, and Euthymius understand this "generation" as applying to all the faithful.

---

[19] See Lepin, *Jésus messie et fils de Dieu d'après les évangiles synoptiques*, 385–388.
[20] See Marie-Joseph Lagrange, "L'avènement du fils de l'homme," *Revue biblique* (1906): 400–401.

Jerome says, "Either it signifies all of mankind or the Jews in particular."[21] Many[22] today hold that these words do not clearly refer to the end of the world but, perhaps, only to the destruction of the city. Jesus would have been responding to the question posited above by the apostles: "Tell us when shall *these things* (namely, the destruction of the temple) be? And what shall be the sign of thy coming and of the consummation of the world?" (Matt 24:3, DR). Maldonat[23] notes, in line with St. Augustine's thought,[24] "That Christ responded to both in a vague manner, just as the apostles asked their question in a vague manner. Since I judge that he did it by a certain and divine counsel, lest someone be able to know the end of the world . . . It is up to a diligent and prudent reader to distinguish what are said about Jerusalem's destruction and about the end of the world." However, in many ways these two events agree as figure and the reality thereby figured. Finally, if it is only a question concerning the present generation, it can be said that "it shall not pass till all *these things be done*"—namely, until the first take place *in reality* and the latter *in figure*. Others hold that the words *this generation* have two senses. In relation to the ruin of Jerusalem, they designate the present generation, whereas in relation to the end of the world, they designate the *Jewish people*.[25] On this, St. Augustine says, "There are certain things that are manifest but others that are so obscure that it is either a laborious affair to judge them, or indeed, rash to define something about them for as long as they are not understood."[26]

St. Peter, explaining this prediction by the Lord, says: "But of this one thing be not ignorant, my beloved, that *one day with the Lord is as a thousand years, and a thousand years as one day*. The Lord delayeth not his promise, as some imagine" (2 Pet 3:8–9, DR). In other words, God sees present and future things simultaneously in eternity. {{343}} Likewise, in a way, prophetic knowledge foresees things from on high and, involving a

---

[21] Jerome, *Commentary on Matthew*, 24:34.

[22] See Marie-Joseph Lagrange, *S. Marc*, 325.

[23] See Maldonat, *In Matth.*, 24:5. [Trans. note: This likely is referring to the Spanish Jesuit, Juan Maldonado (1533–1583).]

[24] See St. Augustine, *Letter* 80.

[25] See Fillion, *Évangile selon saint Matthieu*, 24:34: "We believe, with other exegetes (in particular, with Reischl and Bisping) that it is better to make a distinction. . . . It seems to us that the words *generatio haec* have a double sense, depending on whether they fall upon one or the other of these events. Inasmuch as Jesus is making illusion to the troubles befalling Jerusalem, they represent the Jews who then lived; inasmuch as He wished to describe the end of the world, they designate the whole Jewish people who will persevere until the end of days in order to render homage to the truth of Jesus. Thus, there would be, in v. 34, a prophecy having a dual perspective, something we encounter so often in the sacred texts." In fact, often in Sacred Scripture is the word *generatio* used for *gente* (see Num 10:30; 11:28; Lev 20:18; Ps 44:19; etc.). Also, concerning this expression *generatio haec*, see what is said by Cardinal Billot in *La Parousie* (Paris: Beauchesne, 1920).

[26] St. Augustine, *Letter* 80.

kind of obscurity, at least in its expression, does not always determinately consider all things that are in a given interval of time.[27]

C. According to ancient interpreters, the other words, "there are some of them that stand here, that shall not taste death, till they see the Son of man coming in his kingdom" (Matt 16:28, DR), must be understood as being concerned with Christ's transfiguration, for they were said prior to it.[28] However, it is better to refer them to the destruction of the Jerusalem temple and the expansion of the Church, just like the words said about the death of John the Apostle (John 21:21ff). The end of the world is not in question here, for Jesus said, "Nobody knows that day . . . except the Father."

D. Some, reading 1 Thessalonians 4:15,[29] have thought that Paul announced the end of the world as being immanent. He himself wrote in 2 Thessalonians 2:2–4 (DR): *"Nor be terrified . . . as if the day of the Lord were at hand.* Let no man deceive you by any means: for *unless there come a revolt first,* and the man of sin be revealed, the son of perdition . . . so that he sitteth in the temple of God, shewing himself as if he were God." Therefore, according to the testimony of Christ and the apostles, the time of the final coming would remain completely uncertain.[30]

What, then, should we conclude? There are indeed certain obscure words in Christ's

---

[27] See Lepin, *Jésus messie et fils de Dieu d'après les évangiles synoptiques,* 401–403: "It is likely we experience such difficulties in perspective precisely because of the very literary genre of the selection here occupying us. Indeed, it usually happens that sacred prophecy proceeds by way of *descriptive depictions of the future, passing from one to another without a transition,* whatever may be the various times to which they refer, above all when the events have a cause-effect relationship between them or a relation of symbol to that which is prefigured. . . . Now, an anticipation and, as it were, *a first act of the ultimate judgment* will be realized before the end of the present generation: the faithless generation will receive punishment for its crimes. The Son of Man will come to begin his reign as the great law keeper. . . . The destruction of Jerusalem and of the temple, by *placing an end forever to the ancient order of things,* marks . . . in some way, the true point of departure for the Church . . . the beginning of the kingdom of God on earth, in the form of a universal society having a public and definitive organization."

[28] See Maldonat, *In Matth.,* ibid.

[29] "For the Lord himself shall come down from heaven with commandment and with the voice of an archangel and with the trumpet of God, and the dead who are in Christ shall rise first" (1 Thess 4:15, DR). On June 18, 1915, the *Pontifical Biblical Commission* responded negatively to the question, "Whether . . . it is lawful to reject as farfetched and destitute of solid foundation the interpretation traditional in Catholic schools (also retained by the sixteenth-century Reformers themselves), which explains the words of St. Paul in the fourth chapter of the First Letter to the Thessalonians without in any way implying the affirmation of a Parousia so imminent that the apostle counted himself and his readers among those of the faithful who would survive to meet Christ?" Also see the other responses given on the same day by the Biblical Commission to questions concerning the Parousia. See Denzinger, nos. 3628–3630).

[30] As regards the other difficulties involving this matter in this Pauline letter, see Jacques Marie Vosté, O.P., *Commentarius in epistolas ad Thessalonicenses* (Rome: Ferrari, 1917).

prophecies, but this obscurity cannot be the reason for denying what is most clearly predicted and has been fulfilled. Nay, this obscurity, joined as it is with so great clarity, is a sign of Sacred Scripture's loftiness, as St. Augustine and St. Thomas often note.[31] Therefore, we must apologetically conclude, as Tanquerey says: "Thus, the aforementioned words (from which our objection is drawn) can be rightly understood, without imputing any error or open contradiction to the Lord. If this is how things stand, the laws of exegesis require that this interpretation be preferred. Thus, nothing proves that Jesus would have been in error; moreover, it is clear that all of the essentials of His prediction of the temple's destruction were fulfilled. Therefore, Christ was truly a prophet, sent by God."[32]

---

[31] See *De potentia*, q. 4, a. 1.
[32] Tanquerey, *De vera religione*, 14th ed., 245.

CHAPTER TWELVE

Confirmation of Christ's Divine Mission by the Messianic Prophecies

Single Article

§1. State of the question and methodology {{344}}
§2. Exposition of messianic prophecies in general and in particular
§3. The fulfillment of the messianic prophecies
§4. The probative force of the messianic prophecies
§5. Resolution of objections

§1. State of the Question and Methodology

Let us consider (A) the value of this confirmation, according to Christ and the Church, (B) the objections raised by rationalists, and (C) how one should argue concerning such things in apologetics.

A. *According to Christ and the Church.* Jesus, when speaking against the unbelieving Jews, invoked in confirmation of his divine mission the prophetic testimony given in the Old Testament, as well as the testimony of John the Baptist: "Search the Scriptures, . . . and the same are they that give testimony of me. . . . For if you did believe Moses, you would perhaps believe me also: for he wrote of me" (John 5:39–47, DR). Also, "Abraham your father rejoiced that he might see my day" (John 8:56, DR; Gen 12:3). Nay, Jesus explained the prophecies to his disciples on the road to Emmaus: "And beginning at Moses and all the prophets, he expounded to them in all the scriptures the things that were concerning him" (Luke 24:27, DR). Likewise, he said to the apostles after his Resurrection: "All things must needs be fulfilled which are written in the law of Moses and in the prophets and in the psalms, concerning me. Then he opened their understanding, that they might understand the scriptures, and he said to them: Thus it is written: and thus it behooved Christ to suffer and to rise again from the dead, the third day'" (Luke 24:44–46, DR).

All the apostles argued from the messianic prophecies (2 Pet 1:19; Acts 8:30). The Evangelists, narrating Jesus's life, often say: "So that the Scriptures might be fulfilled" (e.g., John 19:24–27). This is a traditional argument that has been perpetually set forth by the Fathers of the Church and by theologians.

At the [First] Vatican Council, the Church numbers the Old Testament prophecies among the most certain signs of revelation inasmuch as they "manifestly display the . . . infinite knowledge of God."[1] {{345}} And at the time of Advent, as well as in Passiontide, the [Roman] liturgy commemorates, especially in the lectionary of the Mass, the principal Old Testament prophecies.

B. *Rationalist objections.* Rationalists *a priori* deny the possibility of supernatural prophecy and intend to explain the Old Testament predictions through natural causes and the particular genius of the Hebrew people. According to them, the Old Testament, taken as a whole, supports the claims of supernaturalism. However, any given part taken separately, considered under the light of modern criticism, is clearly natural. Hence, prophecy is nothing more than the natural phenomenon of ecstasy, which can be explained by specific circumstances.[2] For example, according to James Darmesteter,[3] the Jewish people gradually arrived at monotheism and acknowledge the obvious superiority of this religious faith. However, notwithstanding this religious superiority, they underwent oppression, thus giving rise to the persuasion among them that there was reserved for them a future era of glory and universal domination. Thus, *their messianic hope would have appeared as something merely natural.* And, as Renan wishes,[4] *their messianic hope inflated their idea of the Messiah.* In other words, the Jews' ardent imagination and expectation of a universal Messiah so stirred up their minds that, at the time of Christ's coming, his contemporaries imposed upon him the title of Messiah as well as the characteristics that were supposed to accompany such a person. For his own part, Jesus was at first somewhat unaware of this, though he gradually persuaded himself that he was the Messiah, and his disciples strove to show that the prophecies were fulfilled in Jesus's life.

---

[1] See [First] Vatican Council, *Dei filius*, chs. 3 and 4 (Denzinger, nos. 3009 and 3017).

[2] Such is the position of Ewald, Reuss, and Kuenen.

[3] See James Darmesteter, *Les prophètes d'Israël* [Paris: C. Lévy, 1895].

[4] See Ernest Renan, *Vie de Jésus*, ch. 1.

Before his own apostasy, Alfred Loisy refuted these theories.[5]

CRITIQUE. Already, in our earlier discussions, we examined at length the rationalistic principles in relation to prophecy in general.[6] Now, however, in relation to his specific question, we must say, with many apologetes,[7] that the firm expectation of the Messiah, which was especially strong among the Jews at the time of Christ,[8] was not created by Christians, since this expectation certainly existed before them. Nor did it naturally develop from the aspirations of the Jewish people, for this expectation refers to the propagation of monotheism throughout the whole world by the Messiah. However, how could such an idea be conceived of naturally and without revelation by a people who so often fell back into idolatry, who abhorred the Gentiles and did not wish to share its privileges with them? In fact, the messianic expectation arose from the messianic prophecies, as is clear looking at the New Testament (Matt 2:5; Luke 1:7; John 1:45), as well as from the books and traditions of the Jews.[9] The rationalists' hypothesis struggles from its own deficiency in critical awareness, as will be clear in light of what we will discuss below.

{{346}} C. *How are we to argue from the prophets in apologetics?* We will indicate (1) what is not necessary, (2) what is not expedient, and (3) what is suitable for this proof.

(1) *It is not necessary that we defend the authenticity of the prophetic books.* We will leave these questions to an introductory course in Sacred Scripture.[10] *It suffices to know that all the messianic prophecies were written at least three hundred years before Christ.* Indeed, they were in the collection of the books of the Old Testament, which, according to all, even our adversaries, had been completed at least three centuries prior to Christ. Also, it is clear upon reading the Prologue of *Sirach* (ca. 130 BC) that *the law, the prophets,* and the other books were already translated into Greek by that time. Therefore,

---

[5] See Alfred Loisy, "L'espérance messianique d'après Ernest Renan," *Revue d'histoire et de littérature religieuses* (Sept.[-Oct.] 1898): [385–406].

[6] See vol. 2, ch. 20 above (On the notion, possibility, and discernibility of prophecy, as well as concerning its probative force).

[7] For example, see Adolphe Tanquerey, *De vera religione*, 12th ed. (Rome: Desclée, 1908), 232–235.

[8] The existence of this expectation is proven by a number of testimonies drawn from the Gospels. See Herod's consultation of the teachers (Matt 2:2–6), the canticle of Simeon (Luke 2:26–32), the deputation of Jews sent to John the Baptist (John 1:19–20), as well as many other facts of Jesus's life (e.g., John 6:14 and 7:31).

[9] This is clear in the *Talmud*, as well as in the *liturgical books* of the Jews.

[10] See Jean-Baptiste Pelt, *Histoire de l'Ancien Testament* [Paris: Lecoffre, 1930].

they existed before this, for this is the only way they could have then been successively translated.

(2) *It is not expedient to argue from prophecies that are applied to the Messiah only according to their spiritual or typological sense but not according to their literal sense.* The literal sense is that which is immediately expressed by the words according to the author's own intention. The typological sense is that which is not immediately expressed by the words but instead is only mediately expressed by the persons or things that they signify.[11] The Evangelists and apostles, who wrote under the light of inspiration, apply to Christ many things that were only *typologically* predicted concerning him.[12] However, when we argue against rationalists, it is not expedient to make use of the typological sense, unless it is historically clear that this sense was known prior to the event. *A fortiori,* it is not fitting to argue by way of their accommodation sense,[13] which is not a sense of scripture but instead is ascribed to passages on account of a kind of analogy.[14] Therefore, we will only make use of prophecies that are applied to Christ in their literal sense. Nay, we will even omit certain obscure ones.

---

[11] St. Thomas says in *ST* I, q. 1, a. 10: "The author of Sacred Scripture is God, who has the power to signify His meaning not only by words, as man also can do, but also by means of things themselves. Thus, whereas in every other science things are signified by words, this science has the property that the things signified by words also themselves have a signification. Therefore, that first signification whereby words signify things belongs to the first sense, namely the historical or *literal sense.* That signification whereby the things signified by words themselves also have a signification is called the *spiritual sense,* which is founded on the literal sense and presupposes it.

"Now this *spiritual sense* has a threefold division. . . . Therefore, insofar as the things of the Old Law signify the things of the New Law, there is the *allegorical sense.* Insofar as the things done in Christ, or the things which signify Christ, are types of what we ourselves ought to do, there is the *moral sense.* However, insofar as they signify what relates to eternal glory, there is the *anagogical sense.*"

And in ibid., ad 1: "Thus, no confusion results in Sacred Scripture, for all the senses are founded on one, namely, *the literal, from which alone can any argument be drawn.* . . . Nevertheless, nothing is lost in Sacred Scripture on account of this, since nothing necessary to faith is contained under the spiritual sense which is not put forward clearly elsewhere by the Scripture in its literal sense."

[12] Thus, Matthew 2:15 (DR) cites Hosea, "Out of Egypt have I called my son," and in v. 18 (DR) Jeremiah, "A voice in Rama was heard, lamentation and great mourning; Rachel bewailing her children, and would not be comforted, because they are not." Likewise, from revelation, we know that David and Solomon are figures of Christ.

[13] [Trans. note: J. Corbette, "Biblical Accommodation," *Catholic Encyclopedia,* vol. 1 (New York: Robert Appleton Company, 1907), https://www.newadvent.org/cathen/01099b.htm.]

[14] See the section "Les Propheties" in Lesêtre's article "Jésus-Christ" in *Dictionnaire biblique,* 1435.

(3) *In order to suitably argue* against rationalists, *we must first set forth the prophecies in general*—namely, what the prophets all agree on, at least the most important ones (namely, on the prediction of the messianic reign). {{347}} In this way, we will construct an argument that cannot be denied by rationalists of good faith. This is how many authors approach these issues today, and we will here follow their expository methods.[15]

However, we must not overlook the classical exposition of the prophecies *in their particularities*,[16] considering their temporal progress, although they can only receive a complete critical defense in a course on the exegesis of the Old Testament.

Finally, we must consider *the fulfillment* of the prophecies *in general* and also *in their particular details*, as well as the probative force of the argument thus proposed.

---

[15] See [Jules] Touzard's article in *Revue pratique d'apologétique*, vol. 6, 906–933 and vol. 7, 81–116, 731–750; *Les prophêtes d'Israël et l'argument prophétique*; "Juif (peuple) dans l'Ancien Testament" in *Dictionnarie d'apologétique*; Tanquerey, *De vera religione*, 14th ed., 295–318; Marie-Joseph Lagrange, "Pascal et les prophéties messianique," *Revue biblique* (1909): 433.

[16] See Marie-Joseph Lagrange's review of Touzard's "Le peuple juif dans A. T." in *Dictionnaire apologétique*, published in the 1917 volume of *Revue biblique*. In his comments, Fr. Lagrange remarks: "Instead of a methodology devoted to detailed precisions, Touzard has preferred one which provides the broad outlines [of the prophetic message]. . . . If we have understood these broad outlines aright, they hold first of all the hope that the religion of Yahweh would one day become the religion of humanity. Now, all civilized peoples profess monotheism, and this monotheism came to them from Israel, not from Greece.

"The prophets' hope was also a program of interior religion, that which is practiced by Christianity. And Touzard does not stick merely to that. Indeed, in these terms, the conformity of the realization to the hope would certainly be astonishing, but one could be tempted to see, in the monotheistic hope, less a prophecy than a presentiment, felt by religious souls who were certain that they possessed a conception [of God and religion] superior to the others held in their times, likewise being rather confident in the truth's ability to overtake humanity, leading them to foresee its triumph. . . . Therefore, the master scholar took care not to exclude the Messiah from the messianic predictions: 'The prophets had predicted that, for the formation and government of the future kingdom, Yahweh would have a representative, a true king, a descendent of David, fully penetrated by divine influence, totally filled with the spirit, in order to accomplish the marvelous work to which he had been destined. Now, it was a descendent of David, who, at a moment when hopes were most lively, announced that the fullness of time had arrived' (col. 1646). This time, we have not only a solid proof but a topical [*topique*] proof, since the prophets' presentiment could not elevate itself so high in the [merely] human order.

"It would not be suitable to judge this exposition in a summary which reduces even further what the author rightly calls a broad outline. Nonetheless, I do wonder whether these terms are not at once too much and too little. For a convergence of the broad outlines proving a divine plan, the reader can consult (our work) *Le messianisme chez les Juifs*, 258ff."

§2. Exposition of Messianic Prophecies in General and in Particular

A. *In general.* Since the early prophets are more obscure, inasmuch as God gradually revealed to them the things that pertain to the Messiah, it is better not to argue from this or that prophet but, rather, from all of them taken together, just as, in order to recognize the likeness between a man and his image, it is better to consider the whole image than only a few features of it. Likewise, in order to understand the sense of a given book, it is necessary that we read all of its parts.

Now, if one were to ask what do all the Old Testament prophets agree on, we can find three things.

(1) *All the prophets*, for eleven centuries, *taught monotheism* and *the moral law* promulgated in the name of God. They preached faith in the one God, who is infinitely perfect, holy, just, merciful, provident, and just in giving out recompense. They drove home to the Hebrew people the need for religious worship that is both external and internal, purity of morals, justice, and charity.

{{348}} (2) *All the prophets announced the universal and spiritual kingdom of God.* Indeed, they foretold the propagation of monotheism throughout all peoples, as well as that of the kingdom of the God of Abraham, Isaac, and Jacob over the face of the earth inasmuch as God chose Israel to be a light of the nations (Isa 2:2–4; 18:7; 19:23–25; 23:15–18; 41:18–25; 42:6–7; Mic 4:1–5). This kingdom will not only be eternal but internal as well. Israel must do penance and return to God with their whole heart. Then the God of mercy will send them his spirit and fill them with his blessings (Hos 2:7–19; 11:1–5; 14:2–5; Isa 4:4–6; 30:18–22; Ezek 11:19–20; 36:25–27).

(3) *All the prophets announced the Messiah—that is, the ruler of the kingdom of God*, the mediator between God and men. In a more or less explicit manner, they described his origin, endowments, gifts, passion, and triumph. (a) He is to arise *from the offspring of David* (Amos 9:11–12; Isa 11:1; Jer 23:5; 33:14–18; Hos 3:5; Ezek 34:23–24) in the city of Bethlehem (Mic 5:2–3). (b) He will be called *the Son of God* (Ps 2:7), *Mighty God, Father of the future age, and the Prince of Peace* (Isa 9:5–7; 2:3–4). He will judge his people in justice and equity (Isa 11:3–5) and will write his law on the hearts of the faithful (Jer 31:33). (c) He will save his people through his utterly humble obedience, *his painful passion*, and *death*—"the chastisement of our peace was upon him, and by his bruises we are healed" (Isa 53:5, DR; also 42:1–4; 49:1–6; 50:1–9; 52:13–15; Ps 21; 68). (d) Finally, after "he shall lay down his life for sin, he shall see a long-lived seed, and the will of

the Lord shall be prosperous in his hand" (Isa 53:10, DR), and all will judge all the peoples (Ps 2:1–4; Isa 24–28).

B. *In particular, following a temporal progression.* So that the progress of the messianic idea in the Old Testament might be made clearer, we must exposit it according to the three successive periods of the Patriarchs, Kings, and Prophets.[17]

1. THE PERIOD OF THE PATRIARCHS. *During this era, the* SAVIOR OF THE WORLD *is announced; he will come from the seed of Abraham, Isaac, Jacob, and Judah.*

(1) Following Adam's sin, God, speaking to the devil, who tempted Eve in the form of a snake, says: "*I will put enmities between thee and the woman, and thy seed and her seed: she* (in Hebrew: he, namely 'your seed') *shall crush thy head, and thou shalt lie in wait for her heel*" (Gen 3:15, DR). (2) NOAH announces: "Blessed be the Lord God. . . . May He dwell in the tents of Shem" (Gen 9:26–27, DR). (3) Among the sons of Shem, ABRAHAM is chosen, and the Lord says to him: "Come into the land which I shall shew thee . . . and in thee shall all the kindreds of the earth be blessed" (Gen 12:1ff).[18] ISAAC, his son, receives the same blessing: "And in thy seed shall all the nations of the earth be blessed because Abraham obeyed my voice" (Gen 26:4–5, DR). {{349}} Likewise, JACOB, taking Esau's place, hears these words: "*And in Thee and thy seed, all the tribes of the earth shall be blessed*" (Gen 28:14, DR). (4) Jacob himself, near death, announces to his sons what will take place in the last days, promising Judah a kind of primacy over his brothers: "*The scepter shall not be taken away from Juda, nor a ruler from his thigh* (or, the staff of command from between his knees), *till he come that is to be sent* (*schiloh*), *and he shall be the expectation of nations*" (Gen 49:8–10, DR).[19] (5) Balaam predicts: "A star shall rise out of Jacob and a scepter shall spring up from Israel" (Num 24:17, DR).—(6) Finally, MOSES, the lawgiver and liberator of Israel, announces a great prophet who will be similar to himself: "*The Lord thy God will raise up to thee a prophet from thy nation* (Israel) and from thy brethren *like unto me; him thou shalt hear*" (Deut 18:15, DR).

*

* *

---

[17] See *ST* II-II, q. 174, a. 6 (Whether prophecies grew with the passage of time). Also see Bossuet, *Élevations sur les mystères*, 10th week (Elevation on the prophets).

[18] See Joseph Corluy, S.J., *Spicilegium dogmatico-biblicum*, vol. 1, 373; Michael Hetzenauer, O.P., *Theologia biblica*, vol. 1, 575.

[19] Eastern versions have the reading *schelok*—that is, "he whose scepter."

2. THE PERIOD OF THE KINGS. *During this era, the Messiah is now described as* a KING, THE SON OF GOD, A PRIEST, *and indeed his* PASSION AND SACRIFICE *are foretold.*

(1) *Anna,* the mother of Samuel, says in her canticle, "The Lord shall judge the ends of the earth, and he shall give empire to his king, and shall exalt the horn of his Christ" (1 Sam 2:10, DR). (2) God, through the mouth of *Nathan,* promises great things to David in the reward of the building the temple [by his offspring]: "He shall build a house to my name, *and I will establish the throne of his kingdom fore ever. I will be to him a father, and he shall be to me a son....* But my mercy I will not take away from him, as I took it from Saul, whom I removed from before my face" (2 Sam 7:13–15, DR; 1 Kgs 11:36).

(3) DAVID announces in the Psalms the universal kingdom of God and, in particular, describes the glories and sufferings of the Messiah.[20] The Messiah will be the KING *over all the peoples.* In Psalm 71 (DR): "In his days shall justice spring up, and abundance of peace, till the moon be taken away. And he shall rule from sea to sea, and from the river unto the ends of the earth. Before him the Ethiopians shall fall down.... The kings of the Arabians and of Saba shall bring gifts. *And all kings of the earth shall adore him: all nations shall serve him.* For he shall deliver the poor from the mighty, and the needy that had no helper.... He shall save the souls of the poor ... and they will forever adore him.... And in him shall all the tribes of the earth be blessed: all nations shall magnify him."

In Psalm 2 (DR), this King is called the MESSIAH / THE CHRIST—that is, he who is *anointed* by God. Nay, he is called the SON OF GOD: "The kings of the earth stood up, and the princes met together, against the Lord, and against his *Christ....* He that dwelleth in heaven shall laugh at them ... and trouble them in his rage. But I am appointed *king by him over Sion,* his holy mountain, preaching his commandment. {{350}} The Lord hath said to me: *Thou art my son, this day have I begotten thee.* Ask of me, and I will give thee the Gentiles for thy inheritance."

---

[20] See Augustin Calmet, *Commentarius litteralis in omnes libros Veteris et Novi Testamenti*; Louis-Claude Fillion, *Les psaumes commentés d'après la Vulgate et l'hébreu* (1893); Marie-Joseph Lagrange, "Notes sur le messianisme dans les psaumes," *Revue biblique* 2 (new series), nos. 1 and 2 (1905), 39–57 and 188–202. Fr. Lagrange numbers as directly belonging among the messianic psalms Psalm 2. See ibid., 41: "This psalm is the messianic psalm *par excellence,* and the first Hebrew document which contains the technical term, 'Messiah.'" He also numbers Ps 72 (71), 110 (109): 1–4. He numbers among the less directly messianic psalms Ps 22 (21), 40 (39):1–12, 45 (44), and 89 (88). Finally, he notes twenty psalms that announce the universal kingdom of God.

In Psalm 109 (DR), the Messiah is called a PRIEST and the LORD *of all*: "The Lord said *to my Lord: Sit thou at my right hand*. . . . With thee is the principality in the day of thy strength: in the brightness of the saints: *from the womb before the day star I begot thee*. The Lord hath sworn, and he will not repent: *Thou art a priest forever* according to the order of Melchizedek. The Lord at thy right hand hath broken kings in the day of his wrath."

However, the Messiah will also be *a voluntary* VICTIM *for sins*. We read in Psalm 39:7–9 (DR): "Sacrifice and oblation thou didst not desire, but thou hast pierced ears for me. Burnt offering and sin offering thou didst not require. Then said I, Behold I come. In the head of the book it is written of me that I should do thy will." Psalm 21 (DR) describes his torments: "O God my God, look upon me: why hast thou forsaken me? . . . *But I am a worm, and no man: the reproach of men, and the outcast of the people.* All they that saw me have laughed me to scorn: they have spoken with the lips, and wagged the head. . . . For many dogs have encompassed me: the council of the malignant hath besieged me. *They have dug my hands and feet.* They have numbered all my bones. . . . *They parted my garments amongst them; and upon my vesture they cast lots.*"[21] And in Psalm 68:22 (DR): "*And they gave me gall for my food, and in my thirst they gave me vinegar to drink.*"[22]

Also, the *fruits of this sacrifice* and *the glory of the Messiah* are announced during this period too. See Psalm 15:10 (DR): "Because thou wilt not leave my soul in hell; nor wilt thou give thy holy one to see corruption."[23] Likewise, Psalm 21:23–29 (DR): "I will declare thy name to my brethren: in the midst of the church will I praise thee. . . . With thee is my praise in a great church. . . . The poor shall eat and shall be filled: and they shall praise the

---

[21] See Joseph Knabenbauer, *Commentarius in Psalmos* (Paris: Lethielleux, 1912), 97.

[22] On the Davidic origin of this psalm, as well as Psalms 2, 15, 17, 31, and 109, see the response of the *Pontifical Biblical Commission* from May 1, 1910. This commission also responded affirmatively to this twofold question: "On the basis of the many testimonies of the holy books of the New Testament, the unanimous agreement of the Fathers, [and] also the statements of the writers of the Jewish people, must many prophetic and messianic psalms be recognized that foretell the coming, kingdom, priesthood, Passion, death, and Resurrection of a future Redeemer? And is it necessary for this reason to reject completely the opinion of those who, perverting the prophetic and messianic character of the psalms, limit these prophecies concerning Christ to mere predictions of the future lot of the chosen people?" (Denzinger, no. 3528).

[23] See Marie-Joseph Lagrange, "Le messianisme dans les Psaumes," *Revue biblique* (1905), 192: "The only literal explanation for Ps 16 (15):10, above all in the Greek, is that given in Acts (2:25–32 and 13:35–37): he who speaks in this psalm hopes for resurrection, even before having descended into Scheol. The Apostles, who witnessed Jesus Christ's resurrection, quite naturally applied this to Him."

CHRIST'S DIVINE MISSION BY THE MESSIANIC PROPHECIES

Lord that seek him. . . . All the ends of the earth shall remember, and shall be converted to the Lord: And all the kindreds of the Gentiles shall adore in his sight."

*

* *

3. THE PERIOD OF THE PROPHETS. *During this period, a much more explicit description is provided for* the ORIGIN, ENDOWMENTS, GIFTS, AND SACRIFICE OF THE SAVIOR.[24]

{{351}} (1) OBADIAH 21 (DR) announces: "And saviors shall come up into mount Sion." Joel 2:28–32 (DR) says, in the name of the Lord: "I will pour out my spirit upon all flesh: and your sons and your daughters shall prophesy. . . . And I will shew wonders in heaven. . . . The sun shall be turned into darkness, and the moon into blood: before the great and dreadful day of the Lord doth come. And it shall come to pass, that every one that shall call upon the name of the Lord shall be saved: for in mount Sion, and in Jerusalem shall be salvation, as the Lord hath said, and in the residue whom the Lord shall call." Amos 9:11 (DR) predicts: "In that day I will raise up the tabernacle of David, that is fallen: . . . and I will rebuild it as in the days of old." Hosea 3:5 and 11:10 announce the conversion of Israel and the calling of the Gentiles. Micah 4 shows many nations coming to Jerusalem and to the worship of God (cf. Isa 2:2ff and Zech 8:20ff), also designating the very place where the Messiah will be born: "*And thou, Bethlehem* Ephrata, art a little one among the thousands of Juda: out of thee shall he come forth unto me that is to be the ruler in Israel: and his going forth is from the beginning, from the days of eternity" (Mic 5:2, DR).[25]

(2) ISAIAH, in his great prophecy, describes the birth of the Messiah, his divine attributes, his universal dominion, his salvific sacrifice on behalf of all the peoples, and his triumph. (We will cite from the text by following the order of the chapters.)

(a) *His nativity.* Isaiah 7:14 (DR): "*Behold a virgin* (alma) *shall*

---

[24] The following texts are cited according to the probable chronology of the prophets, as is held by a number of scholars. For example, see Fulcran Vigouroux, *Manuel biblique*, 8th ed., vol. 2, no. 907. However, according to others, Joel must be numbered among the later prophets. See Marie-Joseph Lagrange, "Notes sur les prophéties messianiques des derniers prophètes," *Revue biblique* 3 (new series), no. 1 (1906): 67.

[25] See Albin Van Hoonacker, *Les douze petits prophètes* (Paris: Gabalda, 1908), 346 and 388–392; "La prophètie relative à la naissance d'Emmanuel," *Revue biblique* (April 1905): 213ff. Also see Marie-Joseph Lagrange, "La vierge et Emmanuel," *Revue biblique* 1, no. 4 (1892): 481.

conceive,[26] and bear a son and his name shall be called *Emmanuel*."[27] According to Matthew 1:23, as well as the whole of Catholic tradition, this text is applied to Christ's nativity.

(b) *His divine gifts.* Isaiah 9:6–7 (DR): "For a child is born to us and a son is given to us, and the government is upon his shoulder: and his name shall be called Wonderful, Counsellor, *God the Mighty*,[28] the Father of the world to come, *the Prince of Peace.* His empire shall be multiplied, and there shall be no end of peace." {{352}} Isaiah 11:1–4 (DR): "And there shall come forth a rod out of the root of Jesse, and a flower shall rise up out of his root. *And the spirit of the Lord shall rest upon him*: the spirit of wisdom, and of understanding, the spirit of counsel, and of fortitude, the spirit of knowledge, and of godliness. . . . He shall judge the poor with justice, and shall reprove with equity for the meek of the earth." Chapters 24–26 announce his universal dominion. Isaiah 28:16 (DR): "Therefore thus saith the Lord God: Behold I will lay a stone in the foundations of Sion, *a tried stone, a corner stone, a precious stone*, founded in the foundation. He that believeth, let him not hasten." Chapter 35 describes the joy of the time of the Messiah's coming. In verses 4–10 (DR), it is said: "*God himself will come and will save you. Then shall the eyes of the blind be opened, and the ears of*

---

[26] See Albert Condamin, S.J., *Le livre d'Isaïe* (Paris: Lecoffre, 1905), 59–72: "The messianic sense [of this] is admitted by all Catholic exegetes, and with a few exceptions, it is admitted by them as being the literal sense of the passage. This is also accepted by a good number of Protestants, though it is interpreted in a variety of ways."

See Joseph Knabenbauer, *Commentarius in Isaiam prophetam*, vol. 1, 172, regarding the meaning of the Hebrew term *almah*: "Whatever may be the etymology of this term (which is uncertain), the meaning can be sought by seeing how it is *used.* . . . The word *almah* is used for expressing *an unmarried woman.* . . . Besides, this use must be determined primarily and essentially from the dialect being looked into, hence, for the Hebrew language, from the use which is discerned in writings of the ancient Hebrews, that is, in the sacred texts. Now, nothing refers to how this *use* which would have been made of this ancient term after many centuries either in the writings of the rabbis or in those of the Arabs, or to what notion this term ultimately would have passed over into. However, the use made of it in the sacred texts is beyond the pale of doubt." Likewise, in the Greek version, we read ἰδοὺ ἡ παρθένος, "Behold the virgin."

[27] The meaning of this term *Emmanuel* is more explicitly determined from the subsequent chapters. Already in 9:8, concerning the land of Judah (which subsequently is called the land of the Lord and the inheritance of God) is called, "Your land, O Emmanuel." Hence *Emmanuel* designates the Lord himself or the Messiah. Likewise, in 8:10, it is announced that all the power and pride of the peoples are to be cast away, "Because Emanuel" (Hebr.) or "because God is with us" (Vulg.). Therefore, this name is not used for a certain son of the king, nor for a human king who would be the savior, but only him to whom the theocracy belongs, the Lord himself or the Messiah.

[28] See Condamin, *Le livre d'Isaïe*, 58. Also see Franciscus Ceuppens, O.P., *Isaiae prophetiarum, collection prima* (Rome, 1931), 133–136.

the deaf shall be unstopped. . . . And the redeemed of the Lord shall return, and shall come into Sion with praise, and everlasting joy shall be upon their heads." In Isaiah 40:1–11, the preaching of John the Baptist is announced (at least typologically), according to SS. Matthew, Mark, and Luke, in these words: "The voice of one crying in the desert: Prepare ye the way of the Lord, make straight in the wilderness the paths of our God. . . . And the glory of the Lord shall be revealed, and all flesh together shall see, that the mouth of the Lord hath spoken."

(c) *The virtues and deeds of the servant of Yahweh.* Isaiah 42:1–9 (DR):

Behold my servant, I will uphold him: my elect, my soul delighteth in him: I have given my spirit upon him, he shall bring forth judgment to the Gentiles. He shall not cry, nor have respect to person, neither shall his voice be heard abroad. *The bruised reed he shall not break, and smoking flax he shall not quench.* He shall bring forth judgment unto truth. . . . I the Lord have called thee in justice. . . . And *I have given thee for a covenant of the people, for a light of the Gentiles*, so that thou mightest open the eyes of the blind, and bring forth the prisoner out of prison, and them that sit in darkness out of the prison house.

Isaiah 49:3–6 (DR): "And he [the Lord] said to me: Thou art my servant Israel,[29] for in thee will I glory. . . . Behold, I have given thee to be the light

---

[29] See Knabenbauer, S.J., *Commentarius in Isaiam prophetam*, vol. 2, 231–232: "The name 'Israel' is lacking in one Hebrew manuscript (cf. De Rossi), and some critics have judged that this term needs to be done away with. Indeed, it is not difficult to explain why the servant of the Lord is called by this name. Indeed, the reason for this is declared in the words that follow upon this, wherein the servant himself comes to personify the people, washing the sins of people through his vicarious satisfaction. . . . However, the fact that the people were not able to understand is immediately clear from verse 6, in which the same servant is said to be taken up by God in order to rouse the tribes of Jacob and to convert the dregs of Israel, where, therefore, *the servant as a redeemer of the people of Israel is distinguished from Israel*, and indeed so that it would be clearly inconsistent and as foreign as possible to the whole prophecy to say that the people is its own redeemer. . . . Then, in verse 8, it is said that there is a 'covenant of the people . . .' However, the people cannot be conceived as being *a mediator in a covenant with itself*."

Also see Condamin, *Le livre d'Isaïe*, 297: "'Israel,' gloss: see the discussion concerning *the servant of Yahweh* on p. 325–344." "According to some, the servant of Yahweh is a moral personality, the personification of the people of Israel. According to most contemporary critics, this refers to a *real* person. Catholic exegetes are unanimous in seeing in this passage a prediction of the passion of Jesus Christ. Among Protestant exegetes, not only are there some who interpret chapter 53 as being a literal prophecy of the Messiah's suffering (Franz Delitzsch, etc.), but many of them interpret the Servant as representing, in a direct manner,

of the Gentiles, that thou mayst be my salvation even to the farthest part of the earth."

{{353}} (d) *The Savior's sacrifice.* Isaiah 50:5–7 (DR): "The Lord God hath opened my ear, and I do not resist; I have not gone back. I have given my body to the strikers, and my cheeks to them that plucked them: I have not turned away my face from them that rebuked me, and spit upon me. The Lord God is my helper, therefore am I not confounded." Isaiah 53:1–7 (DR):

> Who hath believed our report?... And we have seen him, and there was no sightliness, that we should be desirous of him. Despised, and the most abject of men, a man of sorrows, and acquainted with infirmity, and his look was as it were hidden and despised, where-upon we esteemed him not. *Surely, he hath borne our infirmities and carried our sorrows,* and we have thought him as it were a leper, and as one struck by God and afflicted. *But he was wounded for our iniquities,* he was bruised for our sins: the chastisement of our peace was upon him, and *by his bruises we are healed.* . . . The Lord hath laid on him the iniquity of us all. He was offered because it was his own will, and he opened not his mouth: he shall be led as a sheep to the slaughter, and shall be dumb as a lamb before his shearer, and he shall not open his mouth.

(e) *Finally, the triumph of the Messiah and the conversion of many.* Isaiah 53:10–11 (DR): "If he shall lay down his life for sin, he shall see a long-lived seed, and the will of the Lord shall be prosperous in his hand. Because his soul hath labored, he shall see and be filled; by his knowledge *shall this my just servant justify many,* and he shall bear their iniquities." Then, in chapters 54–55, as well as in 60–62, the prophecy announces a new Jerusalem, calling all men to faith. God will forever protect and secure it, giving an abundance of spiritual gifts, as the holy spouse of the Lord: "*Behold . . . the nations* that knew not thee *shall run to thee,* because of the Lord thy God, and for the Holy One of Israel, for he hath glorified thee" (Isa 55:5, DR) "*Arise, be enlightened, O Jerusalem: for thy light is come,* and the glory of the

---

Israel, thus recognizing that these oracles are fulfilled in Jesus incomparably better than in Israel" (ibid., 341). Genenius remarks, "The Jews abandoned this (messianic) interpretation only in later times, doubtlessly following on their controversies with Christians" (326). Later on in this chapter, see the resolution to objections presented in §5. [Trans. note: The "Genenius" referred to might be Wilhelm Gesenius.]

Lord is risen upon thee. . . . *And the Gentiles shall walk in thy light,* and kings in the brightness of thy rising" (Isa 60:1–3, DR). "Thy sun shall go down no more, and thy moon shall not decrease: for the Lord shall be unto thee for an everlasting light" (Isa 60:20, DR). Likewise, see Isaiah 64:10–14.[30]

    (3) JEREMIAH predicts the coming of a Savior from the seed of David. See Jeremiah 23:3–8 (DR): "Behold the days come, saith the Lord, and I will raise up to David a just branch: and a king shall reign, and shall be wise: and shall execute judgment and justice in the earth. In those days shall Juda be saved, and Israel shall dwell confidently: and this is the name that they shall call him: The Lord our just one." Likewise, see Jeremiah 33:14–15. Ezekiel 34:23–31 (DR) hands on the words of the Lord: "I will set up one shepherd over them (my sheep), and he shall feed them, . . . and he shall be their shepherd." {{354}} Likewise, in Ezekiel 37:24 (DR): "And my servant David shall be king over them, and they shall have one shepherd." Daniel[31] sees a stone come down from the mountains, broken off from there without any hands, striking a great and frightening statue upon the latter's clay feet, breaking them, then afterwards becoming a great mountain, filling the whole earth. This is interpreted as meaning that the statue represents the reign of idolatry, and *the God of heaven will set up a kingdom that shall never be destroyed, and his kingdom shall not be delivered up to another people: and it shall break in pieces, and shall consume all these kingdoms: and itself shall stand for ever*" (Dan 2:34–44, DR). Afterwards, he says:

> I beheld, therefore, in the vision of the night, and *lo, one like the Son of man came with the clouds of heaven,* and he came even to the ancient of days; and they presented him before him. And he gave him power, and glory, and a kingdom: and *all peoples, tribes, and tongues shall serve him.* His power is an everlasting power that shall not be taken away: and his kingdom that shall not be destroyed. . . . *But the saints of the most high God shall take the kingdom:* and they

---

[30] See Condamin, *Le livre d'Isaïe,* 361: "In this magnificent poem, Jerusalem is represented as the center of a *universal kingdom* extending to all nations (54:3; 55:4–5; 60:4, 11, 16; 61:6), *a religious kingdom* where all will come together to worship Yahweh (60:7, 13; 61:6), composed of the righteous and the saints (60:21; 62:12), and *everlasting* (55:3; 60:15, 19, 10; 61:8). Theologians are correct in seeing the realization of these promises in the Church founded by Jesus Christ, since the *Servant of Yahweh* is Jesus Christ and since the vast posterity of the Servant, the multitudes of men who are given to Him in return for His suffering and death, must populate the new Jerusalem (52:10–12; 54:1–3)."

[31] See Marie-Joseph Lagrange, "Les prophéties messianiques de Daniel," *Revue biblique* (1904): 494.

shall possess the kingdom for ever and ever. (Dan 7:13–18, DR)

Likewise, in Daniel 7:27 (DR): "And that the kingdom, and power, and the greatness of the kingdom, under the whole heaven, may be given to the people of the saints of the most high: whose kingdom is an everlasting kingdom, and all kings shall serve him, and shall obey him." Daniel also predicts the times of the Messiah, the end of transgression and sin, the abolition of iniquity, and an anointing with the most excellent form of holiness. See Daniel 9:24 (DR): "Seventy weeks are shortened (that is, determined) upon thy people, and upon thy holy city, *that transgression may be finished, and sin may have an end, and iniquity may be abolished; and everlasting justice may be brought; and vision and prophecy may be fulfilled; and the saint of saints may be anointed.*" [32]

(4) THE LATER PROPHETS add certain details regarding the messianic kingdom and the Messiah himself.[33] To the Jews who have returned from captivity and were rebuilding the temple, Haggai predicts in 2:1–10 (DR) the future glory of this temple: "Thus saith the Lord of hosts: Yet one little while, and I will move the heaven and the earth, and the sea, and the dry land. And I will move all nations, and *the desired of all nations shall come, and I will fill this house with glory.* . . . Great shall be the glory of this last house more than of the first, saith the Lord of hosts: and in this place I will give peace." Zechariah prophesies in 2:10–13 (DR): "Sing praise, and rejoice, O daughter of Sion, for behold I come, and I will dwell in the midst of thee: saith the Lord. And many nations shall be joined to the Lord in that day, and they shall be my people, and I will dwell in the midst of thee." {{355}} "*I will bring my servant, the Orient*[34] (the sprout [*germen*]) . . . and I will take away the iniquity of that land in one day" (Zech 3:8–10, DR). "Thus saith the Lord of hosts, saying: Behold a man, the orient is his name. . . . Yea, he

---

[32] See Corluy, *Spicilegium dogmatico-biblicum*, vol. 1, 474–514. In this text, Corluy sets forth the ways the Fathers and contemporary critics resolve the difficult problem concerning how we are to understand the seventy weeks spoken of by Daniel in this text.

It is more probable that each week is seven years (Lev 25:8) and that they begin with the decree of Artaxerxes I, in the twentieth year of his reign (456), giving Nehemiah license to restore the city of Jerusalem (see Neh 2:2). From this year of 456 to the fifteenth year of Tiberius's rule—that is, to the year when Jesus was baptized—around 486 years would have passed, thus meaning that the seventieth week would have arrived, in the middle of which Christ was crucified.

[33] See Marie-Joseph Lagrange, "Notes sur les prophéties messianiques des derniers prophètes," *Revue biblique* (1906), 67.

[34] In Luke 1:78 (DR), Zechariah, the father of John the Baptist, says, "Through the bowels of the mercy of our God, *in which the Orient from on high hath visited us.*"

shall build a temple to the Lord: and he shall bear the glory, and shall sit, and rule upon his throne: and he shall be a priest upon his throne" (Zech 6:12–15, DR). "Rejoice greatly, O daughter of Sion, shout for joy, O daughter of Jerusalem, *behold thy king will come to thee, the just and savior; he is poor, and riding upon an ass,* and upon a colt, the foal of an ass. . . . *And he shall speak peace to the Gentiles,* and his power shall be from sea to sea, and from the rivers even to the end of the earth" (Zech 9:9–10, DR). "In that day *there shall be a fountain open to the house of David,* and to the inhabitants of Jerusalem, *for the washing of the sinner* and of the unclean woman. . . . I will destroy the names of idols out of the earth" (Zech 13:1–2, DR). "And all they that shall be left *of all nations* that came against Jerusalem, shall go up from year to year, to adore the King, the Lord of hosts, and to keep the feast of tabernacles" (Zech 14:16, DR).

The final prophet, MALACHI, announces the forerunner of the Lord: "Behold I send my angel, and he shall prepare the way before my face. And presently the Lord, whom you seek, and the angel of the testament, whom you desire, shall come to his temple. Behold, he cometh" (Mal 3:1, DR).[35] The entire Catholic tradition applies these words from Malachi 1:11 (DR) to the sacrifice of the New Law: "From the rising of the sun even to the going down, my name is great among the Gentiles, and in every place there is sacrifice. And there is offered to my name a clean oblation, for my name is great among the Gentiles, saith the Lord of hosts."

The divine origin of these prophecies was already clear before their fulfillment.

A. The Jews accepted these predictions as being divinely revealed. And they were not wrong in doing so, for the prophets' preaching was proposed as being divine and was confirmed by miracles or predictions that already had been fulfilled.[36]

---

[35] See Mal 4:5–6 and Luke 1:17.

[36] *The miracles of Moses* are recounted in Exod 7–12. Before Pharaoh the king of Egypt, the staff of Aaron was turned into a snake at Moses's command, and likewise the ten plagues caused great affliction throughout Egypt solely at Moses's command, without them affecting the land of Goshen where the Hebrews lived. Likewise, in Num 16, we are told about how, in accord with Moses's prediction, the earth suddenly swallowed Korah, Dathan, and Abiram, who roused sedition against Moses. Similarly, fire killed 250 men who illegitimately offered incense and another 14,700 who murmured against Moses. (See ch. 13 below.)

Later on, many miracles were performed on behalf of the Hebrew people. For example, *the miraculous passing of the Israelites through the Jordan* (Josh 3:15ff) and *the destruction of the walls of Jericho* (Josh 4). *Many prophets* ratified *their divine mission through miracles*, alongside their prophecies, to which subsequent events clearly corresponded, either while they were alive or soon thereafter. See 1 Kgs 17–18 (the miracles of Elijah), 2 Kgs 4 and 5; Jer 28:16ff;

B. Likewise, for us as well, giving careful consideration to the prophets' preaching, we must say that this preaching cannot be explained by natural causes.

(a) The prophets expressly affirm that they are proposing a divinely revealed doctrine. {{356}} However, their testimony is worthy of belief, for they were certainly morally upright and in sound mind [*compotes*]. Nor can someone disprove the existence and value of the signs by which their mission was confirmed.

(b) Nor can it be said that the prophets' preaching is an expression of what contemporary men thought, for often they preached a doctrine that was contrary to the prejudices of their fellow men, and for this reason they suffered persecutions. Nor did they announce, as the false prophets did, things that were pleasing to the rulers and the people.

(c) Nor were the prophets able to derive their teaching from the seers found among the neighboring peoples, for the latter were not familiar with pure monotheism, and they taught a natural ethics that was corrupted with many errors.

However, the divine origin of the prophecies is clearly manifested from their fulfillment, as we will now show.

§3. The Fulfillment of the Messianic Prophecies

A. *In general.* (1) In Christianity, the prediction *concerning the universal propagation of monotheism* among all the peoples finds its fulfillment. In fact, God chose Israel to be a light to the Gentiles and has diffused over the whole earth *the spiritual kingdom of the true God*—that is, the God of Abraham, Isaac, and Jacob. Indeed, the Gentiles have acknowledged the one God, the Creator and Lord of all things, he who repays deeds in justice and is full of mercy. And the worship in spirit and truth has prevailed over idolatry. This knowledge and worship truly, coming through Christ and the apostles who were of Jewish stock, has spread over the whole world, just as the prophets announced.

(2) Likewise, in Jesus, the predictions *concerning the Messiah himself* were fulfilled. For Jesus was born *from the stock of David*, in Bethlehem, was recognized as the *Son of God*, the Mighty God, and the Prince of Peace. He

---

Ezek 4–12; Mic 1–4; Dan 2, 4, and 14 (the preservation of Daniel from harm after being cast into the lion's den). On the historicity and value of the miracles performed by Moses and the prophets, see Ottiger, *Theologia fundamentalis*, vol. 1, 478–514 and the first question responded to by the Pontifical Biblical Commission on June 27, 1906 (Denzinger, no. 3394).

saved his people not by an earthly triumph but, rather, through his utterly humble obedience, *painful Passion*, and death. Finally, he has seen his seed last for ages, and all the peoples have adored him.

Already considered in a general manner, this fulfilment of the prophecies manifests their divine origin. *Indeed, only God could have foreseen and affirmed with certitude, many centuries beforehand, the passion of the Messiah and the conversion of the peoples,* just as he alone was able, according to his own good pleasure, to confer such great holiness upon his Christ and marvelously renew the morals of the peoples.[37]

Nor can it be said that these two principal predictions naturally came forth from the Jewish peoples' natural desires and expectations, for they were contrary to their desires. Indeed, the Jewish people did not wish to share their privileged religion with the Gentiles, and the apostles themselves only with difficulty understood the need for the painful Passion in order to establish the spiritual and universal kingdom of God.[38]

{{357}} B. *In its specific details.* We can set out an exposition, part by part, concerning the fulfillment of the most important prophecies by enumerating the principal facts of Christ's life as recounted in the Gospel.[39]

(1) *The homeland of the Savior*: Bethlehem (Mic 5:2; Matt 2:6; John 7:42).

(2) *The lineage of the Messiah*: the family of Abraham, Isaac, Jacob, Judah, and David (Gen 12:3; 22:18; 26:4; 28:14; 49:8–12; Matt 1:2–6; Luke 3:31–34).

(3) *The Virgin Mother* (Isa 7:14; Matt 1:18–25; Luke 1:27–34).

(4) *The subjection of external kings*: "The kings of Tharsis and the islands shall offer presents: the kings of the Arabians and of Saba shall bring gifts." (Ps 71:10, DR; Isa 60:3–6; Matt 2:1–11).

(5) *His forerunner* (Mal 3:1; 4:5; Luke 1:5–27, 57–80).

---

[37] See what was said earlier in this volume concerning the extraordinary holiness of Christ and concerning the marvelous conversion of the world (vol. 2, bk. 2, chs. 6 and 9).

[38] See Matt 16:22–23 (DR). After the first prediction of the Passion, "Peter taking him, began to rebuke him (Jesus), saying: Lord, be it far from thee, this shall not be unto thee. Who turning, said to Peter: Go behind me, Satan, thou art a scandal unto me because thou savorest not the things that are of God, but the things that are of men." And in Luke 24:25–26 (DR), Jesus says to his disciples on the road to Emmaus: "*O foolish and slow of heart to believe in all things, which the prophets have spoken.* Ought not Christ to have suffered these things and so to enter into his glory?" St. Paul says in 1 Cor 1:23 (DR): "But we preach *Christ crucified: unto the Jews indeed a stumbling block,* and unto the Gentiles foolishness."

[39] See Vigouroux's concordance of the prophets and the Gospels in *Manuel biblique*, vol. 2, no. 903, which also refers to the predictions that can be applied to the Messiah in their spiritual or typological sense.

(6) *The beginning of the preaching of the Gospel*: "The land of Zebulon, and the land of Naphtali . . . the way of the sea beyond the Jordan of the Galilee of the Gentiles. . . . The people that walked in darkness, have seen a great light: to them that dwelt in the region of the shadow of death, light is risen" (Isa 9:1–2, DR; Matt 4:13–15).

(7) *The miraculous healings*: "Then shall the eyes of the blind be opened, and the ears of the deaf shall be unstopped" (Isa 35:5–6, DR; Matt 11:5).

(8) *The preaching of the Gospel*: "The spirit of the Lord is upon me, because the Lord hath anointed me. He hath sent me to preach to the meek, to heal the contrite of heart, . . . to proclaim the acceptable year of the Lord, . . . to comfort all that mourn" (Isa 61:1–2, DR; Luke 4:18).

(9) *The Savior's mercy and humility*: "The bruised reed he shall not break, and smoking flax he shall not quench" (Isa 42:1–3, DR; Matt 3:17; 12:18; 17:5).

(10) *The triumphal entry into Jerusalem*: "Tell ye the daughter of Sion: Behold thy king cometh to thee, meek and sitting upon an ass and a colt" (Zech 9:9; Matt 21:4–5, DR).

(11) *The institution of the new sacrifice and the new priesthood*: "For from the rising of the sun even to the going down, my name is great among the Gentiles, and in every place there is sacrifice, and there is offered to my name a clean oblation: for my name is great among the Gentiles, saith the Lord of hosts" (Mal 1:11, DR). " The Lord hath sworn, and he will not repent: Thou art a priest forever according to the order of Melchizedek" (Ps 109:4, DR). "The poor shall eat and shall be filled: and they shall praise the Lord that seek him: their hearts shall live for ever and ever. All the ends of the earth shall remember, and shall be converted to the Lord: And all the kindreds of the Gentiles shall adore in his sight" (Ps 21:27–30, DR). Also see Matthew 26:26–29 and Luke 22:15–20.

(12) *The infidelity and accusation of the Jews.* Jesus says: "Therefore do I speak to them in parables: because seeing they see not, and hearing they hear not, neither do they understand. And the prophecy of Isaias is fulfilled in them, who saith: By hearing you shall hear, and shall not understand: and seeing you shall see, and shall not perceive" (Matt 13:13–14, DR; likewise see Mark, Luke, and John; Isa 11:9). {{358}} Jesus also says to the Pharisees: "Have you never read in the Scriptures: The stone which the builders rejected, the same is become the head of the corner? By the Lord this has been done; and it is wonderful in our eyes" (Matt 21:42; Ps 117:22; Acts 4:11; Rom 9:33; 1 Pet 2:7).

(13) *The disgrace and anguish of the Passion*: "Unjust witnesses rising up have . . . repaid me evil for good" (Ps 34:11–12, DR). "I have given my body

to the strikers, and my cheeks to them that plucked them: I have not turned away my face from them that rebuked me, and spit upon me" (Isa 50:6, DR; Matt 26:67–68; likewise see Mark and Luke). "And they gave me gall for my food, and in my thirst they gave me vinegar to drink" (Ps 68:22, DR; Matt 27:48; likewise Mark and Luke).

In the Passion, two of the most important prophecies of David and Isaiah are fulfilled. Psalm 21 (DR): "All they that saw me have laughed me to scorn. . . . Many calves have surrounded me: fat bulls have besieged me . . . . *They have dug my hands and feet.* They have numbered all my bones. . . . They parted my garments amongst them; and *upon my vesture they cast lots.*" (See Matt 27:35–44; likewise, Mark, Luke, and John).

Another great prophecy fulfilled in the Passion is Isaiah 53 (DR, slightly altered):

> We have seen him, and there was no sightliness, that we should be desirous of him. *Despised, and the most abject of men, a man of sorrows.* . . . *Surely he hath borne our infirmities and carried our sorrows*: and we have thought him as it were a leper, and *as one struck by God and afflicted.* But he *was wounded for our iniquities,* . . . and by his bruises we are healed. . . . And the Lord hath laid on him the iniquity of us all. He was offered because it was his own will, and he opened not his mouth: he shall be led as a sheep to the slaughter, and shall be dumb as a lamb before his shearer. . . . The Lord was pleased to bruise him in infirmity: if he shall lay down his life for sin, *he shall see a long-lived seed.* . . . *My servant shall justify many*, and he shall bear their iniquities . . . , and hath prayed for the transgressors.

The prophecies concerning the Messiah's passion are among those that are the most eminent and clear, not only as regards the end, cause, and fruits of the Passion but also as regards its particular circumstances. Why? Because in the Passion, the work of the Savior "is brought to consummation" (John 19:30) and hence, the mystery of the Cross, "a scandal to the Jews" (1 Cor 1:23), should be made manifest in a singular manner. Therefore, at the beginning of the Passion, Jesus said to Peter, who wished to defend him with a sword, "How then shall the Scriptures be fulfilled, that so it must be done?" (Matt 26:54, DR; John 19:28).

(14) *The Resurrection of the Messiah*: "Thou wilt not leave my soul in hell; nor wilt thou give thy holy one to see corruption" (Ps 15:10, DR). In Acts 2:29–31 (DR), St. Peter, referring to this prophecy, says: "Ye men,

brethren, let me freely speak to you of the patriarch David: that he died and was buried. . . . Whereas therefore he was a prophet and knew that God hath sworn to him with an oath, that of the fruit of his loins one should sit upon his throne. Foreseeing this, he spoke of the resurrection of Christ. For neither was he left in hell: neither did his flesh see corruption." Likewise, in Acts 13:36, St. Paul explains this prophecy as well.

{{359}} (15) *The remission of sins*: "On that day there shall be a fountain open to the house of David, and to the inhabitants of Jerusalem: for the washing of the sinner, and of the unclean woman" (Zech 13:1, DR; Matt 9:2; Acts 2:38; etc.).

(16) *The Ascension*. In Acts 2:34–36 (DR), St. Peter says: "For David ascended not into heaven; but he himself said: The Lord said to my Lord, sit thou on my right hand, until I make thy enemies thy footstool (Ps 109:1). Therefore, let all the house of Israel know most certainly that God hath made both Lord and Christ, this same Jesus, whom you have crucified."

(17) *The sending of the Holy Spirit*. As is recounted in Acts 2:17ff (DR), when the Holy Spirit was sent over the disciples on the day of Pentecost, the Jews marveled at the fact that they spoke in all tongues. However, Peter refuted those who said that they must be drunk on wine, citing, among the others in his sermon, Joel's prophecy: "For these are not drunk, as you suppose, seeing it is but the third hour of the day. But this is that which was spoken of by the prophet Joel (Joel 2:28–29): And it shall come to pass, in the last days, saith the Lord, I will pour out of my Spirit upon all flesh: and your sons and your daughters shall prophesy: and your young men shall see visions."

(18) *The conversion of the Gentiles*: "Arise, be enlightened, O Jerusalem: for thy light is come, and the glory of the Lord is risen upon thee. For behold darkness shall cover the earth, and a mist the people: but the Lord shall arise upon thee, and his glory shall be seen upon thee. . . . Thy sons shall come from afar, and thy daughters shall rise up at thy side. . . . The strength of the Gentiles shall come to thee" (Isa 60:1–5, DR). However, when Jesus's parents took him to the temple as a baby, Simeon took him into his arms, blessed the Lord, and said: "Now thou dost dismiss thy servant, O Lord. . . . Because my eyes have seen thy salvation. . . . A light to the revelation of the Gentiles and the glory of thy people Israel" (Luke 2:29–32, DR; see Acts 11:18 and 1 Tim 2:4–7).

(19) *The victory of Christ*: "Because his soul hath labored, he shall see and be filled. . . . Therefore will I distribute to him very many, and he shall divide the spoils of the strong" (Isa 53:11–12). "The Lord will send forth the scepter of thy power out of Sion: rule thou in the midst of thy enemies"

(Ps 109:2, DR). However, Christ said to his disciples: "In the world you shall have distress. But have confidence. I have overcome the world" (John 16:33, DR).

(20) *The eternal kingdom of Christ*: "His name shall be . . . the Father of the world to come, the Prince of Peace. His empire shall be multiplied, and there shall be no end of peace: he shall sit upon the throne of David, and upon his kingdom; to establish it" (Isa 9:6–7, DR; Ps 2:44). "With thee is the principality in the day of thy strength: in the brightness of the saints: from the womb before the day star I begot thee" (Ps 109:3, DR). Jesus said to Pilate: "My kingdom is not of this world" (John 18:36, DR). He had said to Peter: "Thou art Peter. And upon this rock I will build my church, and the gates of hell shall not prevail against it. And I will give to thee the keys of the kingdom of heaven" (Matt 16:18–19, DR).

§4. The Probative Force of the Messianic Prophecies

Already above (pt. 1, ch. 20, vol. 2), we determined how prophecy in general is distinguished from human conjectures and the divinization of spirits. {{360}} As we showed, it is impossible for one to naturally or fortuitously foretell an event long before it is going to happen, indicating all of its minute circumstances, involving many future contingents, with many of them depending up the freedom of men, along with other circumstances that are completely extraordinary that can only be produced by God's freedom, beyond men's natural expectations.

Now, in the messianic prophecies, which were fulfilled in Christ, many things of this sort were predicted, with firm certitude, at least three centuries before the event.

Therefore, these predictions are so many in number, so certain, and so extraordinary that they cannot be something merely fortuitous or something natural but instead obviously surpass human wisdom. Moreover, as is clear from their object, end, circumstances, and fruits, they are not diabolical but instead must be said to be divine.

In order to explain this argument, according to the principles that we laid out in pt. 1, ch. 20 in this volume, we here exclude: (a) chance and (b) natural necessity.

(a) *Chance* is *a per accidens cause* of those things that *rarely* take place, either happily or unhappily, outside of any intention, as though they were intended. Hence, the order of the world cannot be from chance (i.e., a privation of order), for otherwise those things that are natural and *per se* would be produced from that which is *per accidens* (that is, the more would be produced from the less). Likewise, *many things* cannot concur by chance *in some one contingent thing that is determinately predicted* (e.g., the virtues of the Messiah, the principal facts of his life, as well as the persecutions and all of the circumstances that concurred in Christ's Passion in fulfillment of Isaiah's prediction). *A fortiori, the series of messianic prophecies* cannot be from chance, for otherwise, the whole of Judeo-Christian religion would be something fortuitous, for this series begins with the primitive promise of the Redeemer, recounted in Genesis, and comes to its end in the marvelous life of Christ's Church. Moreover, all the prophets agree in the predictions concerning the universal kingdom of God and the Messiah, the ruler of this kingdom.

(b) *Nor can natural necessity* be the source of the messianic hope and its fulfillment. For just as the order of the world cannot arise from blind necessity (because then the more perfect would be produced from the less perfect and the intelligible from the unintelligible), so too the order of the prophecies and their fulfillment cannot come from natural necessity without the superior ordering of divine providence. Moreover, as was said earlier, it is not some necessary future fact, existing determinately in natural causes, but instead is a *future contingent*—nay, one that frequently depends on *the freedom of many men* who do not intend to fulfill the prophecy, as is clear in Christ's Crucifixion. Moreover, *extraordinary facts* were announced— namely, Christ's heroic virtues, miracles, the miraculous conversion of the Gentiles, and so forth—all of which can only be foreseen by God, for without his completely free and extraordinary intervention, they could not be brought about.

Nor, as we noted earlier, can it be said that the messianic faith naturally appeared among the Jewish people, for they frequently did not wish to believe the prophets and killed them. Moreover, among those things that were foretold, the sufferings of the Messiah and the entry of the Gentiles into the kingdom of God were in a way contrary to the Jewish people's natural desires and expectations.

Therefore, the messianic predictions cannot be explained without the extraordinary intervention of God. {{361}} Nay, as the [First] Vatican Council states, "They manifestly display the . . . infinite knowledge of God." This is what has been held by all the Fathers of the Church, her doctors, and apologetes.[40]

---

[40] See Pascal, *Pensées* (ed. Havet, 273): "The greatest of the proofs on behalf of Jesus Christ are found in the prophecies. Moreover, God made the greatest provision for them, for the event which fulfilled them is a miracle enduring from the birth of the Church up to the end

However, *the probative force* of the prophecies arises from the fact that they clearly come from a special intervention by God, as a properly divine sign. Indeed, this seal of God confirms, with the greatest of certainty, the revelation for the sake of which it was brought about, for otherwise God would be a false witness. (See our discussion of this in ch. 20, a. 4 of this volume). However, the *connection* between all the messianic prophecies and the Christian religion is clear of itself, for these prophecies are concerned with Christ himself and are fulfilled in him.

Therefore, the divine mission of Christ is confirmed, with the greatest of certitude, by the messianic predictions. This is already true of the prophesies when they are considered solely by the light of reason. However, under the light of supernatural faith, their strength, loftiness, and extension are more firmly, easily, and profoundly acknowledged, and therefore, *a fortiori*, under the illumination of the gifts of understanding and wisdom, they are penetrated even more profoundly.[41]

§5. Resolution of Objections

Already in §§1 and 4, we resolved a number of the objections raised by rationalists against the supernatural origin of the messianic hope. (Also see vol. 2, ch. 20, a. 3 and 4.)

(1) Rationalists will *insist*, however: The prophets did not announce a *personal Messiah* but instead a kind of gathering—namely, the better and holier part of Israel as a redeemed people.

Response: Certain *secondary* predictions are indeed suited to the holier part of the Jewish people, inasmuch as they function as a typological figure for the Messiah. However, the *most illustrious* of them, *as well as all of them taken together*, cannot be attributed to any group of people, nor to any

---

of time. Therefore, God raised up prophets for sixteen hundred years, and for four hundred years afterwards, He dispersed all these prophecies, which all the Jews who carried them, all through the world. . . . *Were a single man to have made a book of predictions concerning Jesus Christ*, as regards their time and manner, and were Jesus to have come in conformity with these prophecies, *this would be something of infinite strength*. But there is something much more here: *a succession of men for four thousand years, men who constantly and without variation come one after another to predict this same event.*"

Pascal objects to himself (289): "'If this was so clearly foretold to the Jews, why did they not believe? Or how were they not exterminated for resisting something so clear?' I respond as follows. First, it was indeed foretold that they both would not believe something so clear and also that they would not be exterminated. And (secondly), nothing redounds more gloriously to the Messiah, for it does not suffice that there should be prophets; but moreover, their prophets must be kept above suspicion. Now, etc."

[41] See *ST* II-II, q. 8, a. 2 and 6.

particular person other than Christ. Indeed, a group of people is not what is being spoken of in Isaiah: "Behold a virgin shall conceive, and bear a *son* and his name shall be called *Emmanuel*" (Isa 7:14, DR). "For *a child* is born to us, and a son is given to us, and the government is upon his shoulder: and his name shall be called Wonderful, Counsellor, *God the Mighty*, the Father of the world to come, the Prince of Peace" (Isa 9:6, DR). "And the spirit of the Lord shall rest upon him: . . . he shall judge the poor with justice" (Isa 11:1–4, DR). Likewise, we cannot merely attribute to a group of people the sufferings undergone by the *servant of the Lord* who, as is announced in Isaiah, chapter 53, suffers and dies for the salvation of all. Moreover, all the Israelites sinned to a greater or lesser degree and could not offer expiation for their own sins nor for those of others, nor did any of them die for the whole people. {{362}} Nay, Isaiah 49:6 (DR) clearly distinguishes the "servant of the Lord" from the people of Israel when the prophet says, in the name of the Lord: "It is a small thing that thou shouldst be my servant to raise up the tribes of Jacob, and to convert the dregs of Israel. Behold, I have given thee to be the light of the Gentiles, that thou mayst be my salvation even to the farthest part of the earth." In this text, *the servant of the Lord, understood as the redeemer of the people of Israel, is distinguished from Israel itself.* It is utterly foreign from every prophecy to say that the people is its own redeemer. Likewise, in the same chapter of Isaiah (49:8), the "servant of the Lord" is said to be given "as a covenant of the people." However, the people cannot be conceived of as being a mediator of the covenant with itself. The same can also be said concerning those things that are announced in Psalm 21 concerning the sufferings of the Messiah.

Finally, the true sense of the prophecies is made manifest from the fact that they are clearly and perfectly fulfilled in Christ's life but not in some partial group of the people of Israel nor in any other individual.

(2) Still, rationalists will *insist* against the fulfillment of the prophecies, for as they say, they foretell *temporal felicity and the restoration of the kingdom of Israel* (Amos 9:8–15; Hos 2:15, 23; Isa 11:10–16). By contrast, shortly after Christ's death, Jerusalem was overthrown and the Jews dispersed.

Response: As St. Thomas notes,[42] in Sacred Scripture, it is often the case that divine and spiritual things are handed on through likenesses to bodily realities, for God provides for all things in a way that is fitting to their natures. Now, it is natural to man that he arrive at intelligible things by way of sensible ones because all of our knowledge takes its beginning in our senses. Hence, two things must be distinguished in the messianic prophecies: (1) *future spiritual realities* (namely, the restoration of the universal kingdom

---

[42] See *ST* I, q. 1, a. 9.

of God through the Messiah-Savior, foretold by all the prophets one after another); and (2) *the material image used as a figure* of the predicted things (namely, the temporal prosperity of Israel).[43]

However, the fact that this latter element was only a figure is clear on at least three heads. (1) It is wholly lacking in certain predictions—for example, in the case of the servant of the Lord who is filled to the brim with reproaches, along with his sorrowful passion and death. In these prophecies, the Messiah in no way appears as being a king and temporal ruler. (2) In all the prophecies, the kingdom of God is announced as being *universal*, over all the peoples. Hence, it is presented as being possibly separated from the temple and city of Jerusalem. (3) Most especially, we see the prophets describe at length the hardness of Israel, along with the rejection of the greater part of the people and their destruction. See the end of St. Stephen's preaching in Acts 7:47–54.[44]

{{363}} (3) Finally, rationalists *object*: If the Messiah was so clearly announced, how is it that so many Jews did not acknowledge Christ?

Response: (a) Many Jews knew of the signs of the coming of the Messiah. When the Magi came to Jerusalem and asked Herod about the birthplace of Christ, the chief priests said: "In Bethlehem of Judea" (Matt 2:5). When Simeon took the child Jesus into his arms, looking upon him, he saw "a light for revelation to the Gentiles" (Luke 2:32). The same is true for Nicodemus and the disciples. In Jerusalem, "of the people many believed in him and said: When the Christ cometh, shall he do more miracles than these which this man doth?" (John 7:31, DR). Nay, the Samaritan woman and the Samaritans said:

---

[43] Hence, St. Paul, calling to mind the temporal blessings received by Israel in its exodus from Egypt, says in 1 Cor 10:1–11 (DR): "*Now these things were done in a figure of us.* . . . All passed through the sea. And all in Moses were baptized, in the cloud and in the sea. And did all eat the same spiritual food. And all drank the same spiritual drink: (And they drank of the spiritual rock that followed them: and the rock was Christ.) . . . Now all these things happened to them in figure."

Likewise, concerning how this state of the Old Law had been established as a figure of the mysteries of Christ, see Heb 8:4. Similarly, refer to *ST* I-II, q. 102, a. 4 (explanation of the most important ceremonial precepts of the ancient worship, inasmuch as they were figures of the worship performed under the New Law). Regarding the promises, see *ST* I-II, q. 114, a. 10, ad 1. St. Thomas cites Augustine (*Contra Faustum*, bk. 4, ch. 2): "*The spiritual things which were to come, which have been fulfilled in us, had been prefigured in these temporal promises*, for the carnal people were adhering to the promises of the present life. And not merely was their speech prophetic but even their life was so."

Regarding the prophecies concerning this matter, see Touzard, *Revue du clergé français* (1908): 538; *Dictionnaire apologétique de la foi catholique*, col. 1643.

[44] See Acts 7:47ff (DR): "You stiff-necked and uncircumcised in heart and ears, you always resist the Holy Ghost. As your fathers did, so do you also. Which of the prophets have not your fathers persecuted? And they have slain them who foretold of the coming of the Just One: of whom you have been now the betrayers and murderers. Who have received the law by the disposition of angels and have not kept it."

"This is indeed the Savior of the world" (John 4:42, DR).

(b) However, most of the Jewish people, forgetful of the prophecies concerning the sorrowful passion of the Messiah, expected a temporal liberator. Hence, it is not surprising that they did not acknowledge Christ.[45] Nay, this blindness on the part of the Jews was itself announced by the prophets, as Jesus said: "Therefore do I speak to them in parables: because seeing they see not, and hearing they hear not, neither do they understand. And the prophecy of Isaias is fulfilled in them, who saith: By hearing you shall hear, and shall not understand: and seeing you shall see, and shall not perceive" (Matt 13:13–14, DR; see Mark and Luke; Isa 6:9). John writes in John 12:37–40 (DR): "And whereas he had done so many miracles before them, they believed not in him, that the saying of Isaias the prophet might be fulfilled, which he said: Lord, who hath believed our hearing? And to whom hath the arm of the Lord been revealed? (Isa 53:1). Therefore, they could not believe, because Isaias said again: *He hath blinded their eyes* and hardened their heart, *that they should not see with their eyes*, nor understand with their heart and be converted: and I should heal them (Isa 6:9)."[46] Likewise, St. Paul says in Romans 11:7–9 (DR): "And the rest have been blinded. As it is written (in Isa 6:9): God hath given them . . . eyes that they should not see. . . . And David saith (in Ps 68:23): Let their table be made a snare and a trap and a stumbling block and a recompense unto them." Similarly, before this, St. Paul had said in Romans 9:32 (DR): "For they stumbled at the stumbling stone. As it is written (in Isa 8:14): Behold I lay in Sion a stumbling stone and a rock of scandal. And whosoever believeth in him shall not be confounded." Jesus himself had said to the Pharisees: "Have you never read in the Scriptures (in Ps 117:22): The stone which the builders rejected, the same is become the head of the corner? By the Lord this has been done; and it is wonderful in our eyes" (Matt 21:42, DR). Nay, Jesus, taking up the prophecy of Daniel anew (see Dan 9:26), wept over Jerusalem and said: "[Thy enemies will . . .] beat thee flat to the ground . . . and they shall not leave in thee a stone upon a stone, *because thou hast not known the time of thy visitation.*" Hence, the prophecies are also confirmed in this unbelief, just as it is in the faith of the disciples and the Gentiles, who, illuminated by the Holy Spirit, accepted Jesus as the Savior of the world.

As regards the strength of this argument, it is of little importance that many of the Jews understood the prophecies in a material manner. In general, predictions are not fully explained until after the event. And Christ came, lived, died, and has been glorified, just as the prophets foretold.

---

[45] Concerning how the rabbis understood the messianic prophecies prior to Christ and after him, see Marie-Joseph Lagrange, *Le messianisme chez les Juifs* (Paris: Gabalda, 1909), 137–256.

[46] See St. Thomas, *In Ioannem*, ch. 12: "The blinding and hardening of heart brought about by God must not be understood as though God caused wickedness or impelled them to sin. Rather, it must be understood as meaning that he did not infuse grace. Now, he does indeed infuse grace out of His mercy, but the reason why he did not infuse it is found on our side, namely, inasmuch as there is something in us which is opposed to divine grace."

Comparison of Christianity with the Mosaic Religion and with Other Religions

Having proven the divinity of Christianity, by way of confirmation, we will now take up (1) a comparison of Christianity with the Mosaic religion, which preceded Christ's coming and prepared for it, and (2) a comparison of true Christianity with other religions and sects. Therefore, there are two chapters in this comparative section.

CHAPTER THIRTEEN

Comparison of Christianity with the Mosaic Religion, with a Defense of Its Divine Origin

SINGLE ARTICLE

{{365}} Here, our concern will be simultaneously turned to the Mosaic religion itself as well as to primitive religion as it is testified to by Moses. The question of their divine origin is resolved in three ways:

§1. By means of extrinsic arguments (from the testimony of Christ and the apostles, and also from Moses's miracles and prophecies)
§2. By means of intrinsic arguments (from the substantial agreement of the primitive and Mosaic religions with Christianity)
§3. By weighing out matters concerning certain difficulties[1]

§1. Extrinsic Arguments

(1) *The testimony of Christ and the apostles.* Christ and the apostles in many places cite, *as divinely inspired,* the books of the Old Testament, in which the primitive and Mosaic religion are contained. Jesus calls these books *Scripture* or *the Scriptures,* as though they were books *par excellence,* asserting that they contain the doctrine of salvation and foretell himself: "Search the scriptures, for you think in them to have life everlasting. And the same are they that give testimony of me" (John 5:39, DR). Likewise, using the solemn formula *"It has been written,"* or "It was said by God," Christ

---

[1] See Joseph Huby, S.J., *Christus: Manuel d'histoire des religions* (Paris: Beauchesne, [1912/1934]), 586–681.

refers to the words of Exodus (Matt 22:31–32, DR: "Have you not read that which was spoken *by God, saying* to you: I am the God of Abraham . . . ?") and of Deuteronomy (Matt 4:4, 7, 10). He speaks in the same manner concerning the Law and the prophets (Luke 16:16; Matt 11:13; 22:40). Now, these are the principal parts of the Old Testament.

Similarly, Peter likewise asserts that the prophets were inspired: "For prophecy came not by the will of man at any time; but the holy men of God spoke, inspired by the Holy Ghost" (2 Pet 1:21, DR). And St. Paul says, concerning all the books that were then held by the Jews as being sacred: "All scripture, inspired of God, is profitable to teach, to reprove, to correct, to instruct in justice" (2 Tim 3:16, DR).

Nor is it only the case that the Old Testament in general was approved by Christ as being inspired, but, moreover, *it was held to be inspired in its particulars, as regards its principal historical facts, the Mosaic Law, and the prophecies.*

(a) Christ recalls many facts from the Old Testament as being certain— for example, the killing of Abel, the flood, the promises made to Abraham, the destruction of Sodom, the appearance of God to Moses, the giving of the manna in the desert, the bronze serpent, the miracles of Elijah and Elisha, and so forth (Matt 23:35; 24:37ff; 22:31ff; Luke 11:51; 17:26ff; 20:27; 4:27; Mark 12:26; John 6:49–57; 3:14).

(b) He says concerning the law of Moses: "Do not think that I am come to destroy the law, or the prophets. I am not come to destroy, but to fulfill. For amen I say unto you, till heaven and earth pass, one jot, or one tittle shall not pass of the law, till all be fulfilled" (Matt 5:17–18, DR; John 7:19). Indeed, he did not abolish the Mosaic Law, except as regards its ceremonial precepts, which were figures of the worship performed in the New Law.

(c) Finally, by invoking the principal prophecies of the Old Testament, Christ confirms and fulfills their own authority. Thus, he says of Moses's prophecies: "For if you did believe Moses, you would perhaps believe me also: for he wrote of me" (John 5:46, DR). Likewise, he commemorated the promise made to Abraham concerning the Messiah (John 8:56) and cites the various prophecies, especially Isaiah.

(2) *The miracles and predictions of Moses and the prophets.* The proof drawn from these signs, which were sensible and striking for their eyewitnesses, preserves its power on account of Christ's aforementioned testimony. Nay, the historicity of these miracles and predictions, when directly considered, cannot be disproven, and they are defended by Catholic

exegetes.[2] For our aims here, it suffices that we merely refer to the principal facts that are recounted in the Old Testament.

{{366}} A. MOSES was called by God, who appeared to him in the symbolic form of the *burning bush* that remained unscathed, to liberate the Israelite people from Egypt (Exod 3:1; 4:23). He performed many wonders in Egypt: he sent *ten plagues* to this land, each of which, as he predicted, began and ended at his command, leaving the Israelites intact, even though they lived among the Egyptians (Exod 7:1; 12:32). However, going forth from among the Egyptian people, Moses dried up the sea by striking it with his staff, thus leading the great host of the Israelites *through the midst of the sea* (Exod 14:16–31). Then, *through his very voice upon Mount Sinai,*

---

[2]   See Ignatius Ottiger, *Theologia fundamentalis*, vol. 1 [Freiburg: Herder, 1911], 472–514; also see Catholic commentaries on Deuteronomy, Exodus, and Numbers. According to the *Pontifical Biblical Commission* (June 23, 1905; Denzinger, no. 3373), "it must be held that the books of Sacred Scripture which are held to be historical, narrate *history properly so-called, which is objectively true,* . . . except in the case, however, not readily or rashly to be admitted, where without opposing the sense of the Church and preserving her judgment, it is proved with strong arguments that the sacred writer did not wish to put down true history, and history properly so-called, but to set forth, under the appearance and form of history, a parable, an allegory, or some meaning removed from the properly literal or historical sense of the words."

Likewise, according to the same commission answered negatively to the question (June 27, 1906; Denzinger, no. 3394): "Are the arguments accumulated by critics to impugn the Mosaic authenticity of the Sacred Books that are designated by the Pentateuch of such weight that, in spite of the very many indications *of both Testaments taken together,* the continuous *conviction of the Jewish people, and also the unbroken tradition of the Church* in addition to the *internal evidences* drawn from the text itself, they justify affirming that these books were not written by Moses but were composed for the most part from sources later than the time of Moses?"

Nonetheless, according to the same commission, "it can be granted . . . that Moses, for the composition of the work *made use of sources,* namely, written documents or oral tradition, from which, according to the particular goal set before him and under the influence of divine inspiration, he made some borrowings" (Denzinger, no. 3396). Likewise, it can be conceded that Moses, in order to compose his work, conceived by him under the divine inspiration, "*was committed to another or several to be put into writing* . . . and that finally when the work was composed in this way, it was *approved* by Moses" (Denzinger, no. 3395) Finally, "safeguarding substantially the Mosaic authenticity and the integrity of the Pentateuch, it can be admitted that over such a long course of ages, *it underwent some modifications*" (Denzinger, no. 3397).

Moreover, it is certain that Moses was neither deceived nor a deceiver. Indeed, he was not *deceived*, for so wise a lawgiver and worshiper of the True God who condemned every form of idolatry could not have been continually hallucinating through the course of forty years, nor have been deceived by a demon. Nor was he a *deceiver*; much to the contrary, his whole life manifests his sincerity. Nay, he persistently upbraided the people and its rulers for their vices and errors, confessed his own ignorance, referred to his own sins with humility, and is found to be utterly meek in suffering insults. Looking upon his life, we discover nothing comparable to a false reputation.

which all the people heard, *God* promulgated the ten precepts (Exod 19:16). Thereafter, new signs followed—for example, *the column that led them along the way* (Exod 13:21–22), *the manna in the desert* (Num 11:4–9; Deut 8:3; Exod 16:13–19), *the water that came forth from the rock that had been struck* (Num 20:7–13; Deut 1:37), and the destruction of Korah, Dathan, and Abiram, whom the earth swallowed up (Num 16:1–23).

Moreover, Moses *foretold these miracles, at least the principal ones*— namely, the plagues in Egypt (Exod 8–10), the passing through the Red Sea (Exod 14:13), the dreadful ruin of Korah, Dathan, and Abiram (Num 16:28), the abundance of manna appearing each day for all the people (Exod 16:4–5; 16:12), and many others that exceeded the powers of merely human foresight (Num 14:29–30; 26:64). However, these predictions of the miracles were concerned with the work of liberation undertaken by Moses or were given in order to encourage adherence to the Mosaic Law and therefore confirm its divine origin.

B. The prophets also performed many miracles in confirmation of their divine missions. *They healed the ill* without making use of natural means (2 Kgs 5:1–14), sent diseases to punish wrongdoers (2 Kgs 5:27), *prayed for abundant rain* after the skies had been closed for three years (1 Kgs 18:42–45), and *made fire descend from heaven* to devour their offerings (1 Kgs 18:37–39). *Daniel was preserved unharmed in the lion's den* (Dan 6). Many other examples could be cited as well.

{{367}} Likewise, the prophets[3] confirmed their mission *through predictions* that were borne out by the events that followed soon upon them. Thus, Elijah predicted the drought that lasted for three years and six months (1 Kgs 17:1). Isaiah foretold the overthrow of Sennacherib, which happened soon thereafter (2 Kgs 19:19–37). Likewise, Jeremiah predicted the death of Hananiah (Jer 28:16–17), the destruction of Babylon (Jer 50:1–52, 64), and the captivity of the Jews that was to last for seventy years (Jer 25:11). Likewise, Micah and Daniel announced the fates of various peoples (Mic 1:1–16; 3:12; 4:10; Dan. 7:1–12).

These various signs confirmed for the Jews the divine mission of Moses and the prophets, and for us as well, their value, confirmed by Christ's testimony, cannot be disproven. Moreover, we can also draw a significant confirmation of this from intrinsic arguments on its behalf.

---

[3] [Trans. note: Reading *prophetiae* as *prophetae*.]

§2. Intrinsic Arguments

The divine origin of primitive and Mosaic religion is manifested from their excellence, inasmuch as they are substantially in harmony with Christianity and predict it. In this section, we must (1) set forth the fact itself, and then (2) inquire into the reason for it.[4]

(1) *Mosaic religion and even primitive religion are substantially in harmony with Christianity and announce it.*

A. PRIMITIVE RELIGION, which was revealed to our first parents the patriarchs, is summarized as follows by the Book of Genesis:

(a) *God is one, the Creator of heaven and earth* and the Lord of all things (Gen 1:1ff), thus ruling out polytheism. All things that he has made were good from the beginning (Gen 1:10, 12, 21), thus ruling out dualism (i.e., the existence of an evil principle). He is the Provident Ruler of all things, the Supreme Lawgiver, a Judge who pays back the just and punishes the wicked (Gen 2:16, 17; 3:14ff).

(b) Man was made in the image of God (Gen 1:26–27) and therefore was endowed with a spiritual and immortal soul,[5] established at the beginning in a state higher than the present [fallen state] and endowed with dominion over all created things,[6] and he was made capable of good and

---

[4]   [Trans. note: Reading *ratio facit* as *ratio facti*.]

[5]   Frequently flesh (*basar*) and spirit / soul (ruah or *nephesh*) are opposed to each other.

   The spirituality of the human soul can be found in the text of Gen 1:27 (DR), "And God created man to his own image," and 2:7, "And the Lord God formed man of the slime of the earth: and breathed into his face the breath of life, and man became a living soul." Brute animals are said to be formed in their body and vital spirit *from the ground*, therefore, from matter (Gen 2:19). However, in the creation of man, a distinction is drawn between the body *made from the earth's soil* (and therefore formed from matter) and the spirit of life, which is immediately breathed into him by God (that is, created and joined with the body). See Gen 2:7; Michael Hetzenauer, *Theologia biblica*, vol. 1 [Freiburg: Herder, 1908], 531.

   The immortality of the soul follows on its spirituality, and the patriarchs considered themselves to be sojourners on this earth, speeding onward to the homeland in another world. Thus, they spoke of the time *of their sojourning* (Gen 47). Hence, St. Paul says in Heb 11:13–15 (DR): "All these (Abraham, Isaac, and Jacob) died according to faith, . . . confessing that they are pilgrims and strangers on the earth. For they that say these things do signify that they seek a country." Likewise, we must understand the words of Jacob, "I will go down to my son into hell, mourning," as being concerned with the immortality of the spirit, for Jacob believed that his son Joseph had been devoured bodily by beasts. The expression "to go to his fathers" (Gen 15:15) must be understood along the same lines. See Hetzenauer, *Theologia biblica*, 535.

[6]   Man was just—"and God saw all the things that he had made, and they were very good" (Gen 1:31, DR)—right, innocent, and without any disordered passions: "And they were both naked: to wit, Adam and his wife: and were not ashamed" (Gen 2:25, DR). He lived in a beautiful place (Gen 2:8–15). He was not subject to the necessity of death (Gen 2:17). He

521

evil so that he may find his end in being united to God through charity and freely willed obedience (Gen 2:15–16). {{368}} Marriage was instituted by God himself as a sacred contract of two people in an indissoluble bond (Gen 2:24). However, man unhappily transgressed the divine command and through sin fell from his first dignity into the worst misery, along with all of his offspring (Gen 3:1–24). Nevertheless, God gave him room for penance and *promised his liberation* (Gen 3:14–15).

(c) *The precepts* were either natural or positive. The first is that God is to be adored, loved, feared, and shown gratitude, and his commands must be followed (Gen. 2:16; 3:13; etc.). Already at the time of Abel, sacrifices were offered to God (Gen 4:3–4), and Abraham was commanded to perform circumcision as a sign of the covenant between God and the Chosen People (Gen 17).

The Christian religion can be observed in this primitive religion as though in a kind of nucleus. "All the articles of faith are contained in certain primary *credibilia*, namely, that it be believed that God exists and exercises providence concerning the salvation of mankind, according to the words of Heb 11:6 (DR), 'He that cometh to God must believe that he is: and is a rewarder to them that seek him.'"[7]

*
*　*

B. THE MOSAIC RELIGION. Since the primitive religion was gradually corrupted, leading to the appearance of various superstitions and forms of idolatry, in order to ensure that true religion might remain at least somewhere, God specially elected Abraham's family and the people of Israel as the guardian of revelation. Thence was the Mosaic religion born, as a kind of renewal of the primitive religion and a preparation for Christian revelation. Its principal headings can be expressed as follows:

(a) *God's nature and unity* is declared in such a way that nothing more sublime could be thought: *I am who am* (Exod 3:4). All idolatry and superstition are ruled out: "You will have no foreign gods before me" (Exod 20:3). God is preached everywhere to be the Creator and Governor of the universe, the Lord of all things (Deut 4:35–39), eternal, omnipotent, omniscient,

---

was endowed with eminent knowledge of all things, "for whatsoever Adam called any living creature the same is its name" (Gen 2:19, DR). He lived in perfect peace and familiarity with God (Gen 3:8–10).

7 *ST* II-II, q. 1, a. 7.

present to all men (Deut 15:1–19; 29:45; 32:1–43), most holy, zealous for his law (Exod 20:5; 34:14) but "merciful and gracious, patient and of much compassion, and true" (Exod 34:6–7, DR), and "He doth judgment to the fatherless and the widow" (Deut 10:18, DR).

(b) *Man* was created in God's image so that through love and fear of God and observation of the divine commands he might enter into a close relationship with God. Moses insists upon the temporal sanctions established for the whole of the Israelite people, but he is not unaware of the immortality of the soul but instead presupposes it, for example, when he expressly prohibits "seek[ing] the truth from the dead" (Deut 18:11, DR). {{369}} And Christ himself authoritatively declares the sense of Exodus 3:6 when, in opposition to the Sadducees who denied the immortality of the soul, he said: "Have you not read that which was spoken by God, saying to you: I am, ἐγώ εἰμι, the God of Abraham and the God of Isaac and the God of Jacob? He is not the God of the dead but of the living'" (Matt 22:31–32, DR; Mark 12:26ff; Luke 20:37ff).

(c) *The commandments.* The greatest and first commandment in the law is "Thou shalt love the Lord thy God with thy whole heart, and with thy whole soul, and with thy whole strength" (Deut 6:5, DR; 11:13). However, the second is "Thou shalt love thy friend (that is, thy neighbor) as thyself. . . . If a stranger dwell in your land and abide among you, . . . you shall love him as yourselves" (Lev 19:18, 33–34, DR). "On these two commandments dependeth the whole law and the prophets" (Matt 22:40, DR). From these two first precepts flow all the various obligations of the *Decalogue* (Exod 20), which is a compendium of the whole law.[8] These obligations toward God are: "Thou shalt not have strange gods before me. Thou shalt not make to thyself a graven thing. . . . Thou shalt not take the name of the Lord thy God in vain. . . . Remember that thou keep holy the sabbath day." Those toward our neighbors are: "Honor thy father and thy mother. . . . Thou shalt not kill. Thou shalt not commit adultery. Thou shalt not steal. Thou shalt not bear false witness against thy neighbor. Thou shalt not covet thy neighbor's house; neither shalt thou desire his wife." Likewise, the Mosaic Law commends kindness toward the poor, orphans, and widows (Exod 23:10–11; Deut 15:7; etc.), toward laborers, old men, the deaf and the blind, foreign peoples (Lev 19:13–33), enemies (Exod 23:4), and even toward animals too (Deut 25:4).

(d) *Worship* is ordered to the acknowledgment and adoration of God's supreme excellence, to the confirmation of faith, to penance, and to the

---

8   See *ST* I-II, q. 100, a. 5–7 (Whether the precepts of the Decalogue are suitably enumerated).

fostering of justice and love of God. In this way, various sacrifices are determined, in which we see none of the cruelty, obscenity, or superstition that is found in the Gentiles' worship of their gods (Lev 23 and 25). The priests, with the high priest who is in charge of them, along with the Levites, are consecrated to God through a special rite (Lev 8:1ff; Num 16:5ff).

However, since revelation had not yet come to a close but, rather, developed up to the coming of the Messiah, God promised that he was going to send prophets to the Israelite people (Deut 18:9ff).

(e) *The Mosaic religion announces Christianity.* Indeed, not only is it substantially in harmony with Christianity as regards its dogmas concerning God, the salvation of man, and the commandments, but as becomes increasingly clearer through the messianic prophecies, the whole of the Mosaic religion exists as a preparation and figure of Christianity. Indeed, even before the prophets, *Moses foretold Christ's coming*: "The Lord thy God will raise up to thee a prophet of thy nation and of thy brethren like unto me. Him thou shalt hear" (Deut 18:14–20; see John 1:45; 4:25; 5:46; 6:14; and 7:40; Acts 3:22ff; 7:37).

Nay, as St. Thomas shows:

> Although in some respects one or other of the prophets was greater than Moses, nonetheless, *simply speaking, Moses was greater than all (the prophets)....* {{370}} (1) First, as regards the intellectual vision, for ... as is said in Numbers 12:8, he saw God "plainly and not by riddles" (Num 12:8, DR). (2) As regards the imaginary vision that he, as it were, had at his beck and call, for not only did he hear words, but he also saw one speaking to him in the form of God. Indeed, this was so not only while he was asleep but took place even when he was awake. Whence, it is written in Exodus 33:11(DR) that "the Lord spoke to Moses face to face, as a man is wont to speak to his friend." (3) As regards his declaration, for he spoke to the whole people of believers in the person of God, as one proposing the law anew. However, the other Prophets spoke to the people in the person of God as people leading them to observe Moses's law, in accord with the words of Malachi 4:4 (DR), "Remember the law of Moses my servant." (4) As regards the working of miracles, which he performed for a whole nation of unbelievers. Whence it is written in Deuteronomy 34:10–11 (DR), "There arose no more a prophet in Israel like unto Moses, whom the Lord knew face to face: in all the signs and wonders, which he sent by him, to do in the land of Egypt to Pharaoh, and to all his servants, and to his whole land."[9]

---

[9] *ST* II-II, q. 174, a. 4.

Comparing Moses with David, St. Thomas adds: "Moses's vision was more excellent as regards his knowledge of the divinity, but David knew and expressed the mysteries of Christ's incarnation more fully." However, Moses did announce Christ.

Hence, Jesus said: "If you did believe Moses, you would perhaps believe me also, for he wrote of me" (John 5:46, DR). "Do not think that I am come to destroy the law, or the prophets. I am not come to destroy, but to fulfill" (Matt 5:17, DR). Hence, St. Thomas says, in sum: "The divine law is divided into the old and new law, not as into different species of law but, rather, as into that which is imperfect and that which is perfect in one and the same species."[10] Hence, St. Paul says in Galatians 3:24 (DR): "The law was our pedagogue in Christ."

(2) *The divine origin of Mosaic religion, as well as of primitive religion, is clearly manifest based on its excellence and its foretelling of Christianity.*

A. *The excellence of Jewish monotheism.*

(a) Negatively. Based on what was said above, it is clear that the Mosaic religion can in no respect be alleged to be unworthy of God as regards its dogmas, commands, and worship.

(b) Positively. Although, absolutely speaking, monotheism could be known and demonstrated by reason alone, nonetheless, as we showed earlier,[11] revelation is morally necessary so that men may know the sum of the natural truths about God readily, with firm certitude, and with no admixture of error. Now, through Moses's teaching, *only the Israelites*, despite the fact that they often were aroused to polytheism, nonetheless knew—readily, with firm certitude, and with no admixture of error—monotheism and the sum of the natural truths of religion. Therefore, divine revelation was morally necessary in order for them to arrive at this knowledge, which was perfect, not simply speaking but, rather, for their time.[12]

This argument, which is set forth by all apologetes,[13] heeding all circumstances, is utterly valid. Indeed, (1) no other people has adhered to the worship of the one God for a long time, but, rather, the whole world has dwelt in the errors of polytheism, idolatry, and superstition. {{371}} (2) Nay, the most illustrious Greek and Roman philosophers, even after the passing of many centuries, never arrived at such perfect knowledge concerning God. Their early philosophers were materialists, gradually entering into knowl-

---

[10] See *ST* I-II, q. 107 (Comparison of the Old and New Law, a. 1–3).
[11] See vol. 1, bk. 1, ch. 13, a. 2 (On the necessity of revelation).
[12] See *ST* I-II, q. 98, a. 2.
[13] See, in particular, Auguste-Théodore-Paul de Broglie, *Questions bibliques* (Paris: Lecoffre, 1897), 243–320.

edge of the truth. Plato and Aristotle did indeed affirm the existence of the one, utterly perfect God, but they did not manage to elevate themselves to the doctrine of creation,[14] above all free creation. Nor did they manage to arrive at a perfect notion of providence, ordering and permitting all things, even the most particular. (3) By contrast, Moses, a Jewish man educated among the Egyptians who were devoted to their fetishism and lacking Greek science, wrote at the beginning of Genesis: "In the beginning, God created heaven and earth. . . . And God said: let there be light. . . . " Likewise, he laid out the various divine attributes of wisdom, holiness, justice, mercy, and so forth, as well as the supreme duties of men and their secondary duties. (4) The necessity of divine revelation will appear with greater clarity if we consider the fact that *the Israelites were often roused to polytheism*, both by the example of the neighboring Gentiles, as well as on account of their own propensities, but nonetheless, on account of Moses's doctrine and zeal, they managed to preserve monotheism invincibly. At this time, when all true religion was at its lowest point, as well as all moral discipline, the Israelites could not have, without divine revelation and supernatural assistance, conceived of this perfect knowledge of God and, notwithstanding the innumerable difficulties involved, preserve it.[15]

Evolutionists, as will be discussed below, hold *a priori*[16] that Israel, like all peoples, was at first devoted to a form of animism, then polydaemonism, then totemism, then fetishism, and then finally polytheism, all before arriving at superior forms of religion and monotheism. However, this evolutionistic conception of things is nothing other than the gratuitous denial of the supernatural order, neglecting the testimony of the prophets who openly declare that they wish to do nothing more than restore the ancient form of worship. Moreover, even if Israel had at first been devoted to a form of idolatry, how then, later on, at the time of the prophets, eight centuries before Christ, when all peoples held a form of polytheism or dualism, did the Israelites alone, without any special intervention from God, manage to admit monotheism and preserve it unconquerably?[17] (See the final objection

---

[14] See *ST* I, q. 44, a. 2.

[15] See J. Touzard, "Juif (peuple) dans l'Ancien Testament" in *Dictionnaire apologétique de la foi catholique* (1915), col. 1606–1614: The origin of Jewish monotheism: (1) Jewish monotheism, a unique fact in the history of religion; (2) Jewish monotheism does not find its explanation in the natural conditions of the Israelite people.

[16] See Antoine Schmidt-Lemonnyer, *La revelation primitive et les données actuelles de la science* (Paris: Lecoffre, 1914).

[17] See Marie-Joseph Lagrange, *Études sur les religions sémitiques* (1905), 25: "Monotheism does not come from polytheism. Therefore, how did it enter into the world? . . . (Solely from the

discussed below in the resolution to the objections.)

{{372}} B. *The divine origin of the religion of Israel is clearly manifest from the way it foretells Christianity.* Indeed, not only does Moses's teaching contain the sum of the truths that pertain to natural religion but also includes truths that absolutely exceed created understanding, for Moses in fact speaks not only about the providence of God the author of nature but also about properly supernatural providence, which disposes and confers supernatural aids for the sake of salvation, likewise promising that prophets are to be sent to the Israelite people (Deut 18:9–22). Now, the prophets did in fact come as Moses announced, and as we set forth earlier, they themselves predicted with increasing clarity the universal propagation of monotheism and the kingdom of God through Christ, describing his characteristics, gifts,

---

historical perspective), one will hold that it is very probable that the seed of this idea was placed by God Himself into man's heart." Likewise, see Albert Condamin, S.J., "Babylone et la Bible," in *Dictionnaire apologétique de la foi catholique* (1909), vol. 1, col. 337ff. Likewise, Wilhelm Schmidt and Antoine Lemonnyer, *La revelation primitive et les données actuelles de la science* (Paris: Lecoffre, 1914), 265: "It is hard not to imagine anything more unlikely than the hypothesis holding that the living narrative of Sacred Scripture, which is so charged with meaning, even in its smallest details, while nonetheless remaining so easy to understand and so clear, would have come from these disparate (Babylonian) fragments which themselves are so obscure in their meaning." Also, see Huby, *Christus: Manuel d'histoire des religions*, 5th ed., 661.

Concerning this, see Berthau's article "Extrinsécisme" in *Revue pratique d'apologétique* (Dec. 1, 1908), 342–350: "Therefore, naturalistic history ends up running into inextricable difficulties here. Either Israel always was monotheistic—and this cannot be explained without the hypothesis of revelation, since all other peoples, including those who came from her own race, were, in fact, polytheists in the era when their own history begins. Or Israel, starting with the polytheism that was common to all other peoples, as well as to her own Semitic brethren, then arrived *by herself* at monotheism—and this is no more explained here, since not only is there no example of a similar evolution in any of the other peoples (as Renan himself notes) but even more so, all of them evolved in the opposite direction (something demonstrated by the facts themselves).

"In other peoples—in the Egyptians and Hindus in particular—we must turn to the most distant ages of their history to find the purest and loftiest religious sentiment, and by contrast, to the degree that these people grew great, polytheism indisputably is confessed (with the particular demands of each city, of each temple, and of each royal dynasty). And the facts show, moreover, that never did philosophical reflection manage to produce the contrary evolution, replacing polytheism by monotheism. . . .

"On this vast and utterly important question concerning Jewish monotheism, Gunkel seems, therefore, to have spoken the true word of history and of criticism in his famous debate with Delitzch: 'The popular monotheism of Israel was, in fact, *a veritable miracle* in the midst of the religions of the ancient East.'"

Likewise, see Pierre Daniël Chantepie de la Saussaye, *Manuel d'histoire des religions* (Paris: Armand Colin, 1904 / 1921), 11: "The only truly monotheistic religion that one finds is the Jewish religion, along with its two daughters, Christianity and Islam."

works, and Passion. However, this preaching, which was fulfilled in Christianity, exceeded all the powers of reason. Moreover, it cannot be said to be diabolical in origin but instead is clearly divine, in view of its object, as well as its end, circumstances, and fruits. As St. Thomas states, "It is clear that one and the same thing disposes something to its end and ultimately leads it thereto, and by 'the same,' I mean either by itself or through its subjects .... Therefore, the Old Law was given by the same God, by whom salvation is given to man through the grace of Christ."[18]

§3. Objections

A. *A priori objections* from evolutionism, as well as against the suitability of the divine election of the Jewish people.

1. *Objection*: Evolutionists hold that men gradually proceeded from animality to rational life and likewise hold that all peoples first were devoted to animism, then polydaemonism, then to totemism, and then to fetishism, afterwards passing through polytheism so as to arrive at the superior forms of religion. Now, they add: Israel is a people just like all others. Therefore, it first adhered to fetishism and idolatry thereafter, honoring their national deity, and finally, at the time of the prophets, came to hold that there is only one God.

{{373}} *Response*: As regards the major premise, (a) above, we refuted the principles of evolution, for the more cannot be produced from the less, nor the more perfect from the less perfect, nor rational life from animal life. Human intelligence and morality presuppose an intelligent and moral cause, the just and holy God. (b) The history of religions in no way proves that primitive religion was first inferior, taking on the form of animism, totemism, or fetishism. Indeed, these forms of idolatry could just as well arise from the corruption of primitive religion, as is asserted in Genesis 6:1.[19] (c) Nay, the history of many religions, especially those of the Egyptian and Babylonian peoples, bears witness not to ascending progress in their conception

---

[18] *ST* I-II, q. 98, a. 2 (Whether the Old Law was from God).

[19] See Schmidt-Lemonnyer, *La révélation primitive et les données actuelles de la science*, xiv: "Ch. 1 Detailed analysis of the intimate nature, content, and extent of primitive religion, according to inspired sources.—Ch. 2. Dedicated to establishing, in accord with results drawn from scientific investigations, the indisputable bodily and spiritual *aptitude* of the beings presented to us by prehistory, anthropology, and ethnology as *the most ancient types of humanity* that we know of *for receiving primitive revelation*, however elevated that one may wish to suppose it.—Ch. 3. Moreover, we find in the data furnished for us by the various sciences numerous confirmations of the historical reality of this revelation. (Refutations of the theories of Wellhausen, Delitzch, Gunkel, etc.)—Ch. 4. A final study concerning the destinies of primitive revelation following upon the fall, as men spread out and covered the surface of the earth."

of God but, on the contrary, regression from imperfect monotheism to polytheism.[20]

However, we deny the minor premise of the objection. As regards its religion, Israel was not like other peoples. It alone in antiquity gave expression to monotheism as its truly national and popular religion. However, as we have already said, this cannot be explained without there having been some special intervention by God, something that, in fact, is affirmed by Moses and the prophets.

Insistence: (a) However, if God were to have revealed monotheism from the beginning, then he would have preserved this religion, at least among a number of peoples. Nothing like this is found in the narrative of Genesis 4–9, which is concerned with the progressive corruption of humanity. Now, this seems to be contrary to the right order of divine providence. (b) Moreover, God would have been playing favorites if, among all the peoples, he had chosen to heap his benefits solely upon the Israelite peoples, rejecting all other nations.

Response: (a) It does not fall to man to determine the ways of God's providence. As St. Paul said, "How incomprehensible are his judgments, and how unsearchable his ways! For who hath known the mind of the Lord? Or who hath been his counsellor?" (Rom 11:33). It suffices that we know the general reason why God permits or does not impede evils to be done. As St. Augustine said, "Since God is the highest good, he would not permit any evil to exist in his works unless his omnipotence and goodness were such that he would also be able to draw good from evil."[21] For, as St. Thomas adds,[22] God permits evil to be done so that he might draw something better therefrom. Thus, it is said in Romans 5:20 (DR), "*Where sin abounded, grace did more abound*,"[23] and likewise, in the blessing of the paschal candle [in the Roman rite], we say, "O happy fault, which merited us so great a Redeemer!" {{374}} (b) *As regards the election of the people of Israel*, God does not play favorites, for, as St. Thomas says, "In things which are given gratuitously, someone can give more or less, as he pleases, provided he deprives nobody of what is owed to him, without thereby infringing justice in any way. Indeed, this is what the master of the house said: 'Take what is thine and go thy way. Is it not lawful for me to do what I will?' (Matt 20:14–15, DR)." However, God manifests himself to all men through his works: "For the invisible things of him from the creation of the world are clearly seen, being understood by the things that are made. His eternal power also and divinity: so

---

[20] See Huby, *Christus: Manuel d'histoire des religions*, ch. 14, §2, 600.

[21] Augustine, *Enchiridion*, ch. 11; *ST* I, q. 2, a. 3, ad 1; q. 23, a. 3, ad 3.

[22] See *ST* III, q. 1, a. 3, ad 3.

[23] On this matter, St. Paul shows in chs. 1–4 of Romans that the pagans were justly deserted by God. Both the Jews and the Gentiles were guilty for their sin, from which they can be freed only by faith in Christ: "For as by the disobedience of one man, many were made sinners: so also by the obedience of one, many shall be made just" (Rom 5:19, DR); God "endured with much patience vessels of wrath, fitted for destruction, so that he might shew the riches of his glory on the vessels of mercy which he hath prepared unto glory" (Rom 9:22–23, DR).

that they are inexcusable. Because that, when they knew God, they have not glorified him as God or given thanks: but became vain in their thoughts. And their foolish heart was darkened" (Rom 1:20–21, DR). Moreover, God manifested himself in a supernatural way to our first parents, and the vestiges of this primitive religion more or less remained in various peoples. Furthermore, the Gentiles were able, with the aid of grace, to have "implicit faith in the mediator concerning divine providence, believing that God is the liberator of men in ways that are pleasing to Himself, in accord with what the Spirit would reveal to those who knew the truth."[24]

However, why was the Law given to the Jewish people rather than to others? St. Thomas responds:

> *It was fitting that the people from whom Christ would be born should be marked out by a special sanctification*, in accord with the words of Leviticus 19:2 (DR): "Be ye holy, because I . . . am holy." Moreover, nor was it on account of Abraham's own merits that this promise was made to him, namely, that Christ should be born from his seed. Rather, it was on account of God's own gratuitous election and calling. . . . Therefore, it is evident that it was merely from a gratuitous election that the patriarchs received the promise and that the people who sprung from them received the law (see Deut 4:36–37). . . . However, if it is again asked why He chose this people and not another so that Christ might be born from them, a fitting answer is given by Augustine (in *Tract. super Joan.*, 26): "If you wish to avoid error, do not look to judge why he draws one man and not another."[25]

Insistence: However, the divine law must exclude nobody from the worship of God. Now, the Mosaic Law says: "The Ammonite and the Moabite, even after the tenth generation shall not enter into the church of the Lord forever" (Deut 23:3, DR).

Response: In sum, St. Thomas says[26] the Old Law excludes nobody from the worship of God but only from the temporal things that were proper to the Jewish people. Thus, it is said in Exodus 12:48 (DR): "If any stranger be willing to dwell among you, and to keep the Phase of the Lord, all his males shall first be circumcised, and then shall he celebrate it according to the manner: and he shall be as he that is born in the land."

B. *A posteriori objections.* These can be drawn from the imperfection of the Mosaic conception of God, the soul, and the moral law.

1. *Objection*: Moses presents God as being: (a) a kind of rival, greedy for sacrifices; (b) unjust, approving of the plundering of the Egyptians by the Israelites, rewarding the

---

[24] *ST* II-II, q. 2, a. 7, ad 3.

[25] *ST* I-II, q. 98, a. 4 (Whether the Old Law should have been given solely to the Jewish people).

[26] See *ST* I-II, q. 105, a. 3, ad 1 (On the judicial precepts, as regards extraneous matters).

lies of the Egyptian midwives, and punishing sins to the third and fourth generation; (c) the author of sins, blinding and hardening people's hearts at his good pleasure; (d) nay, a cruel God who ordered that the Canaanite peoples be extinguished by a bloody death.

Response: (a) Moses says that God is a zealous rival not on account of God's greed but, rather, inasmuch as he alone wishes to be loved, honored, and adored above all things from the whole of man's heart, something that God could never fail to wish, since he himself is the Highest Good, to be loved above all. As regards sacrifices, they are prescribed inasmuch as external cult is a due manifestation of interior religion. However, the Jews were thoroughly taught, from their infancy, that God does not have need of them.

{{375}} (b) As regards the Egyptian vessels spoken of in Exodus 12:36, it is not clear from the text itself whether they were given to the Israelites or were taken [*accomodata*] by them. However, even in the latter case, God, as the true and independent Lord of things and men, was able to take these vessels from the Egyptians on account of their sins and give them to the Israelites in reward for their labor.[27] God did not reward the midwives on account of their lies but, rather, as we read in Exodus 1:21: "Because they feared God and did not wish to follow Pharaoh's unjust command." However, the words by which God is said to "*visit the iniquity of the fathers upon the children, unto the third and fourth generation of them that hate me*" (Exod 20:5, DR) do not mean that God inflicts spiritual punishments upon innocent children. Rather, as St. Thomas says, the sins of fathers are said to be inflicted upon their sons, "because sons who are reared on the sins of their parents are themselves more prone to sin . . . and likewise are deserving of greater punishment if, seeing their parents' punishment they do not amend their way of life."[28] (c) If God is said to *blind* and *harden*, this must not be understood as meaning that God moves men to sin but, rather, that in punishment for their sin and perversity, he withdraws illumination of the soul and good inspirations.[29] The words *God tempts men* mean that he proves them. (d) As regards the objection drawn from *the annihilation of the Canaanites*, a response can be drawn from Wisdom 12:3–11 (DR): "For those ancient inhabitants of thy holy land, whom thou didst abhor, *because they did works hateful to thee . . . those merciless murderers of their own children* . . . it was thy will to destroy by the hands of our parents. . . . For it was a cursed seed from the beginning: neither didst thou for fear of any one give pardon to their sins."

Insistence: However, *Yahweh*, whom Moses proposed to the Jews as a God to be adored, was not the supreme Lord of heaven and earth but, rather, a God who was particular to the Jewish people, a national God,[30] indeed powerful and terrible, but cruel. In fact, he called for the sacrifice of the son of Abraham and accepted the son of Jephthah as a victim.

---

[27] See *ST* I-II, q. 100, a. 8, ad 3.

[28] *ST* I-II, q. 87, a. 8.

[29] See *ST* I-II, q. 79, a. 3.

[30] Concerning this objection, see Huby, *Christus: Manuel d'histoire des religions*, 618–623.

Response: (a) Although Moses referred Yahweh to the Jewish people in a special manner, nonetheless, he simultaneously and everywhere represented him as being the Most Perfect Being, the Creator, Ruler, and Governor of all things and men: "God said to Moses: *I am who am*" (Exod 3:14ff). "The Lord your God did great things for you in Egypt, before thy eyes. . . . That thou mightest know that the Lord he is God, and there is no other besides him" (Deut 4:35, DR, altered). "Behold heaven is the Lord's thy God, and the heaven of heaven, the earth and all things that are therein. And yet the Lord hath been closely joined to thy fathers, and loved them and chose their seed after them, that is to say, you, out of all nations, as this day it is proved. Circumcise therefore the foreskin of your heart, and stiffen your neck no more. Because the Lord your God he is the *God of gods, and the Lord of lords*, a great God and mighty and terrible, who accepteth no person nor taketh bribes" (Deut 10:14–17, DR). Then justice and mercy are immediately added among God's moral attributes: "He doth judgment to the fatherless and the widow, loveth the stranger, and giveth him food and raiment." Likewise, "*See ye that I alone am, and there is no other God besides me*" (Deut 32:39, DR). (b) As regards *human sacrifices*, they are neither prescribed nor permitted anywhere in the Mosaic Law. Nay, they are prohibited with threat of the gravest punishments: "Thou shalt not do in like manner to the Lord thy God. For they have done to their gods all the abominations which the Lord abhorreth, offering their sons and daughters, and burning them with fire" (Deut 12:31, DR). (c) However, "when Abraham consented to kill his son, he did not consent to commit murder, for it was just that his son be killed at the command of God who is the Lord of life and death."[31] {{376}} Moreover, since God supplied another victim once Abraham's obedience was proven, this shows well enough that human victims are in no way pleasing to him.[32] (d) Finally, regarding Jephthah, who offered his son as a victim on account of a rash vow (Judg 11:30–39), this fact is opposed to the command of the Law and nowhere was it declared that God accepted a victim of this kind.

2. *Objection*: The laws of Moses are too accurate in defining things, even minute and indifferent ones, especially for *many ceremonies*, as though these were a matter of the greatest importance. Now, *it is unworthy of God to be so scrupulously concerned with such insignificant things.*

Response: With St. Thomas, we can say:

It was expedient that the Old Law should contain many ceremonial precepts, for many of the people were prone to idolatry. Whence, they needed to be called back from the worship of idols to the worship of God by means of the

---

[31] *ST* I-II, q. 100, a. 8, ad 3.
[32] However, the killing of Christ, which was figured by the Old Testament sacrifices, was a voluntary sacrifice—not, however, for those who killed him, for whom it was an utterly grave sin. (See *ST* III, q. 48, a. 3, ad 3.)

ceremonial precepts. Likewise, since men served idols in many ways, it was moreover necessary that many means of repressing every single one be devised. . . . However, as to those who were inclined to good, it was again necessary there be many ceremonial precepts, both because their minds were thus turned toward God in many ways and more continually, and also, because the mystery of Christ, which was foreshadowed by these ceremonial precepts, brought many good and useful things to the world, giving men many things to consider, things which needed to be signified by various ceremonies.[33]

By contrast, "the New Law is called the law of faith insofar as its preeminence is derived from that very grace which is given inwardly to believers and for this reason is called the grace of faith. Nevertheless, it does consist secondarily in certain deeds which are both moral and sacramental. However, the New Law does not consist chiefly in these latter things, as did the Old Law."[34]

Hence, Christ said to the Samaritan woman: "The hour cometh and now is, when the true adorers shall adore the Father in spirit and in truth" (John 4:23, DR). True adorers will adore not in ceremonies and sensible figures but in spirit and truth. Thus, gradually, true worship rises from sensible things to spiritual ones, from the multiplicity of figures to the unity of the divine reality.

3. *Objection*: However, Mosaic religion seemed to teach nothing concerning *the immortality of the soul* and the future life, which nonetheless must be counted as belonging among the fundamental truths of religion. Rather, what is principally promised in the Old Testament are temporal goods.

Response: (a) St. Thomas says, "The Old Law disposed men to Christ, as the imperfect disposes to the perfect. . . . Therefore, the Jewish people is compared to a child that is still under a pedagogue (Gal 3:24). [Now, man's perfection consists in despising temporal things and cleaving to spiritual ones. . . .] However, those who are still imperfect desire temporal goods, though in subordination to God."[35] "Therefore, immediately at the start of the law, the people were invited to the earthly kingdom of the Canaanites (Exod 3:8–17) . . . , while at the very beginning of Christ's preaching, He invited men to the kingdom of heaven, saying 'Do penance, for the kingdom of heaven is at hand' (Matt 4:17, DR)."[36] However, the Old Testament's temporal promises were figures of the spiritual goods of the New Law, as St. Paul says in 1 Corinthians 10:6–11. (b) Moreover, even if the books of Moses do not say much about the immortality of the soul and the future life, they nonetheless suppose them, as we said above in §2. For they teach that man

---

[33] *ST* I-II, q. 101, a. 3.

[34] *ST* I-II, q. 107, a. 1, ad 3; q. 108, a. 1.

[35] *ST* I-II, q. 99, a. 6.

[36] *ST* I-II, q. 91, a. 5.

is made *in the image of God and that God "breathed into his face the breath of life"* (Gen 2:7, DR). {{377}} The patriarchs speak of the time "of their sojourning" (Gen 47:9), as it were, "sojourners and strangers on the earth," as St. Paul says (Heb 11:13–16). Mourning over his son Joseph, Jacob said, "I will go down to my son into hell (sheol)" (Gen 37:35, DR), which designates nothing other than the place prepared for the dead; nor is it a question merely of the grave, for Jacob thought that a wild beast had devoured Joseph. Likewise, as his death approached, he declared, "I will look for thy salvation, O Lord" (Gen 49:18, DR). In various places, the dead are said to *proceed and go to their fathers, to their people* (Num 20:26; 31:2; 30:24; etc.) Finally, Moses prohibited "seek[ing] the truth from the dead" (Deut 18:11, DR). The promulgation of the doctrine concerning the immortality of the soul was not made through Moses, for this truth was already had from primitive revelation and had been preserved not only in the families of the patriarchs but even in many Gentiles, as we see in the writings of the Egyptians, the Babylonians, and the Greeks.[37] However, at the time of Moses, much less had been revealed concerning the state of the soul after death and the future life of the just. Later on, Job said: "For I know that my Redeemer liveth, and in the last day I shall rise out of the earth. And I shall be clothed again with my skin, and in my flesh I shall see my God" (Job 19:25–26, DR). Then Daniel more clearly announced: "Many of those that sleep in the dust of the earth, shall awake: some unto life everlasting, and others unto reproach, to see it always. But they that are learned, shall shine as the brightness of the firmament: and they that instruct many to justice, as stars for all eternity" (Dan 12:2–3; likewise, 2 Macc 7:9; 12:44). Likewise, see Isaiah 26:19 and 25:8, as well as Daniel 12:1.

4. *Objection*: Finally, as regards morals, the Mosaic Law does not seem to be worthy of God, for it favors slavery and permits polygamy and divorce. Moreover, it is said to be "a law of fear." However, God should be loved more than feared.

Response: (a) Moses did indeed tolerate *slavery*, but he highly mitigated it. Hence, the state of slavery was much milder among the Jews than it was in all other nations: "If thou buy a Hebrew servant, six years shall he serve thee; in the seventh he shall go out free for nothing" (Exod 21:2, 11, DR). (b) Likewise, the Mosaic Law restricted *polygamy*, to the degree it was possible at that time and among that people; however, it did not at all foster it. As regards *divorce*, by God's own decree, under the law of Moses it was not permitted to repudiate one's wife; however, on account of the Jews' "hardness of heart," it was permitted to them so that a greater evil might be avoided.[38] Moreover, many restrictions were placed on divorce, and wives were protected against the caprices of men (see Deut 24:1–4). (c) Additionally, we do not contend *that the Mosaic Law was* perfect simply

---

[37] See Huby, *Christus: Manuel d'histoire des religions*, 666 (The future life in Israel and in the people close to them), 487 (in the Egyptians), 533 (in the Babylonians), 307, 316, and 331 (in the Greeks).

[38] This is based on Christ's declaration in Mark 10:4–12. See *ST* III, Suppl., q. 67, a. 3.

speaking but instead was *perfect for that time and for the Jewish people.* Thus, as a *law of fear*, it was the path to the Gospel Law, which is called the law of love: "The fear of God is the beginning of wisdom" (Ps 110:10). As St. Thomas says:

> Nevertheless, there were some in the state of the Old Covenant who, having charity and the grace of the Holy Ghost, looked chiefly to spiritual and eternal promises. In this respect they belonged to the New Law. Likewise, in the New Covenant there are some carnal men who have not yet attained to the perfection of the New Law, men who even in the New Covenant needed to be led to virtuous action by the fear of punishment and by temporal promises. However, although the Old Law contained precepts of charity, nevertheless it did not confer the Holy Ghost by Whom "charity . . . is spread abroad in our hearts" (Rom 5:5, DR).

{{378}} *Hence, notwithstanding these imperfections, the Mosaic religion was,* for a time of idolatry, so excellent as regards its dogmas, commands, and worship *that it cannot not be explained without divine revelation.*

5. *Objection:* Many rationalists, like Delitzsch (*Babel und Bibel*, 1902) hold that the biblical account of creation, the life of the first man in paradise, his sin, and so forth, were taken from *Babylonian and Assyrian myths.* They say that it is probable that these myths were accepted by the Israelites and were gradually cleansed of their polytheism.

Response: On this matter, many things have been written by Catholic critics. See, for example, the works of Fr. Marie-Joseph Lagrange, as well as those of Condamin, Schmidt-Lemonnyer, Hetzenauer, and Nikel.[39]

As is clear from all these works, although the Israelites were aware of the myths held by the Gentiles, the biblical narrative could not have been drawn from them for the following reasons. (a) In all of the various cosmogonies of the Gentiles, even in the laws of Hammurabi, *polytheism* was taught, whereas, by contrast, the biblical cosmogony teaches *pure monotheism.* (b) In all the myths, eternal material elements are presupposed, not created ones, whereas in Genesis, it is said that God created *ex nihilo,* at the beginning of time. Nor were any of the Gentile philosophers able to arrive at this conception of creation. (c) As regards man's original state and sin, there are certain likenesses here, though also evident differences, and nowhere do we find the moral and religious elevation and simplicity that appear in the first chapters of Genesis.

Now, *these likenesses* can be explained not only through the aspirations that are shared by all men but also through the primitive tradition that, according to Genesis, comes from Adam. As Hetzenauer says, "After the confusion of tongues and dispersion of the peoples, men conformed the accounts from primitive tradition to their times and

---

[39] We cited all of these works above in the main thesis of this chapter before the objections.

places, as well as their own thoughts and circumstances, so that various traditions came to be found among various peoples (cf. Dillman, Genesis 49). From these various traditions, the inspired author, illuminated by God, selected the pure and original account and opposed it to the depraved accounts."[40]

However, *the dissimilarities* and utterly lofty elevation of the biblical narrative are so obvious that it cannot be rationally explained how the Jewish people, less developed than other peoples, were able to arrive, through some natural development, at so perfect a conception concerning God, the production of the world, and man.[41]

In other words, from one perfect principle, many imperfect fragments arose, though not vice versa. To put it another way, the lofty, simple, and comprehensive biblical narrative was not naturally constituted from such imperfect fragments.

Therefore, this objection does not diminish the arguments by which the divine origin of Mosaic religion and primitive religion is proven. On the contrary, these new studies continually and more fully show the excellence and transcendence of the biblical account in comparison with all other ancient religions of the East. Now, however, we must compare Christianity with other religions existing today.

---

[40] Michael Hetzenauer, *Theologia biblica*, vol. 1 (Freiburg: Herder, 1908), 559.
[41] See ibid., 506.

CHAPTER FOURTEEN

The Divinity of Christianity Is Confirmed through a Comparison with Other Religions

{{379}} Having compared Christianity with Mosaic and primitive religion, we can compare it with other religions that exist today and ask whether it so *transcends* them that we may thereby find a new confirmation of its divine origin in the fact of this excellence.

There are two religions in particular that a few rationalists place on equal footing with Christianity—namely, *Buddhism* and *Islam*—which we must discuss briefly here, recalling points that are certain or at least probable, based on the history of religions.

ART. 1: ON BUDDHISM

§1. History
§2. The Doctrine of Buddhism
§3. Critique of Buddhism

§1. History

Buddhism[1] arose from Vedism and Brahmanism. The ancient Indians pro-

---

[1] See Barthélemy Saint-Hilaire, *Le Bouddha et sa religion* [Paris: Didier, 1866]; Abbé de Broglie, *Problèmes et conclusions de l'histoire des religions* [Paris: Putois-Cretté, 1886], ch. 6.—Hermann Oldenberg, *Le Bouddha* [Paris: Alcan, 1903] (a German work translated into French and English); Louis de La Vallée-Poussin, *Bouddhisme* (opinions concerning its dogmatic history) (Paris: Beauchesne: 1909); "Inde (Religions del')" in the *Dictionnaire apologétique de la foi catholique*, col. 653ff; Huby, *Christus*, 5th ed., 138[–]258; Joseph Bricout, *Où en est l'histoire des religions*, vol. 1 [Paris: Letouzé et Ané, 1912], 267; M. Ribaud, "Le bouddhisme et l'évangile" in *La Civiltà cattolica* (1934): 253–271 and 495–508; Pierre Johanns, *Vers le Christ par le*

537

fessed *Brahmanism*, which is contained in the very ancient texts known as the *Vedas*. They conceive of the divinity in a very obscure manner as being the supreme being to whom sacrifices are offered in order to obtain benefits. Philosophers reduced this popular religion into a more systematic form that, truth be told, is pantheistic in nature. According to them, *Brahma* (in the neuter gender) is the universal whole and indeterminate seed from whence God, the world, and all things evolve. God (in the masculine gender) comes forth, and from him emanate the various kinds of men: From his mouth are born the *Brahmans* (or priests), from his chest, soldiers, from his side, merchants, and so forth. {{380}} The gods demand sacrifices, and after death, men transmigrate into the bodies of animals until, at last, they acquire a kind of immutability and are absorbed by Brahma, the sole universal being. Since sins are a cause of sorrow and alteration, they must be carefully avoided. Hence, it teaches an ethic of rigid asceticism. However, for the common run of men, the number of gods increased, and worship fell into impure bacchanalia.

Nevertheless, in the sixth century before Christ's coming, Brahmanism was greatly changed by *Siddhartha*, who is called *Shakyamuni* (wise man from the house of Shakya) or *Buddha* (wise man). It is difficult to know the details of his life. It seems that Shakyamuni was born around 557 BC, of royal linage. He deserted his house, homeland, wife, and children in order to cultivate wisdom with the Brahmans. After this, he withdrew into retirement and through the practice of severe mortifications and assiduous meditation believed that he found true wisdom. He preached this doctrine and established an order of monks who joined him in teaching those who followed in the footsteps of the master. Thus, this religion gradually came to propagate itself, first in *India*, and today thrives on the island of *Ceylon* [Sri Lanka], in *Siam* [Thailand], among the *Chinese*, in the *Tibetan* region, and in the *Japanese* empire. Indeed, it has many adherents, nearly 120 million, though it is difficult to count them, for many Chinese people belong to multiple religions.

§2. The Doctrine of Buddhism

This doctrine is, in particular, practical in nature.

A. *Few dogmatic principles* are handed on. (1) Shakyamuni professed that we must not seek out the supreme being, for we can know nothing about it with certainty. In reality, Buddhism *teaches nothing concerning God*

---

vedanta, French translation (Louvain: Lessianum, 1933).

because either he does not exist or nothing is certain concerning his existence. (2) According to the Buddha, *all beings are essentially equal*, and all things *perpetually change*. The Buddha himself was at one time a common animal—hence, man does not essentially differ from other beings, thus meaning that the spirituality and immortality of the soul are ruled out, at least logically. (3) *Metempsychosis* (or the transmigration of souls) is one of its fundamental doctrines. (4) Nonetheless, there is something that is immutable, namely, *Law,* by whose force good actions necessarily are their own reward and evil actions bring punishment with themselves. (5) All existence is evil. Therefore, *all evil* arises from the desire to live. Hence, this desire must be completely uprooted, along with all the passions. Then man, after living many lives and having overcome his wicked inclinations, enters into *nirvana*, a kind of state of immobility and, perhaps, annihilation. (Contemporary phenomenalist Buddhists believe that, according to Buddha, nirvana is nothing other than the perfect annihilation of every form of personal existence. Personalist Buddhists hold that *nirvana* is a state of perfect quiet, wherein beings are free from every form of desire, labor, and relation with other beings.)[2]

B. *Its ethics* are deduced from the aforementioned principles. Since all evil arises from the desire to live and guilt from desire, *in order to avoid sorrow man must renounce desire completely*. This extinguishing of every form of desire represents the peak of perfection. In order to reach this end, harsh mortifications, like those practiced by the Brahmans, are not needed but instead only moderate ones, with meditations and confession of faults. {{381}} Believers are prohibited from committing theft, lying, becoming drunk, committing murder, and adultery. Celibacy and poverty are prescribed for their religious. However, Shakyamuni in his own law for these religious does not speak of prayer, nor of grace,[3] and this is not surprising since, according to him, God's existence is utterly uncertain. Good works possess only a dispositive value in relation to a better state in process of transmigration and, in the end, must be overcome.

Therefore, the ultimate end of this ethics is something negative and egoistical—namely, avoid pain. Nonetheless, in practice, Shakyamuni commended *universal sympathy*. Thus, the religious of Buddhism show other men the way by which they may be freed from the miseries of this life, and believers should give alms to the religious.

---

[2] See Vallée-Poussin, *Bouddhisme*, 156–157 (Personalists and phenomenalists).

[3] See ibid., 212: "In his law written for monks, the vehicle for *nirvana*, the master makes no room either for grace or for prayer."

Today, there are three sects of Buddhism in particular, designated by the name of "Lesser Vehicle" [Hīnayāna], "Greater Vehicle" [Mahāyāna], and the "Tantric Vehicle." The atheistic or agnostic teaching is not preserved among the masses, but rather, they hold a form of polytheism following many obscene idols.[4]

§3. Critique of Buddhism

In order to compare Buddhism with Christianity, we must consider their similarities and differences.

A. *Similarities* do indeed exist between the two religions *in certain rites or practices, though not in doctrine*. At first sight, certain ethical principles seem to be the same: a profound awareness of the hardships of this life, the mortification of the flesh and the desires [*concupiscentiae*], which are considered as being tinder for sin and a form of misery, monasticism, voluntary poverty and continence, benevolence toward men, meditation, confession of sins, and desire for attaining the ultimate end. However, in all of these likenesses of the practical order, there are also great differences encountered as well, for the way that Buddhism conceives of the final end is night and day different from the Christian conception of it. Indeed, Christianity leads to perfect life and the vision of God, through the grace of the sacraments, prayer, and supernatural merit. By contrast, Buddhism tends toward self-annihilation and likewise does not speak of grace, prayer properly so-called, and the supernatural moral life.

Hence, the aforementioned similarities are only external, more apparent than true, and are easily explained, without there being any mutual influence, on the basis of mankind's general aspirations, for which all religions intend to offer satisfaction.

B. *However, the differences* between Buddhism and Christianity are many in number and profound in nature, to the point that the two religions cannot be set on the same level.

(a) *The dogmas* of Buddhism manifestly do not surpass natural reason.

---

[4] See ibid., 206 and 275–413. Followers of *lesser vehicle* Buddhism are, in particular, the monks, holding that the way to salvation (which they call a vehicle) is found in the extinction of all desires. They profess agnosticism regarding the existence of God and man's nature. Followers of *greater vehicle* Buddhism are laypeople in particular, holding that the way of salvation is found especially in universal sympathy. In general, they hold a kind of ideal[istic] pantheism. *Tantrism*, which grew in strength from the seventh century AD onward, renewed ancient polytheism, with its obscene idols, and teaches a kind of magic to be used for obtaining transformation into the Buddha.

Nay, they are very inferior to the conclusions of sound philosophy. *For it teaches nothing concerning God.* {{382}} Likewise, it seems to be unaware of the spirituality of the human soul since it seems to place no *essential* difference between man and brute animals, as is clear from its doctrine of metempsychosis. Not only does it not know that providence orders all things to the good but it even professes a form of *pessimism*, teaching that all of life is evil and that the ultimate end that is desirable above all else is self-annihilation or something similar. This is obviously false. Meditation consists in thinking about nothing, lest something evil may be thought. Practices of this kind produce nervous overexcitement with quasi-pathological effects. By means of self-suggestion many monks arrive at a kind of ecstasy.

It does not know of creation and the conservation of all things, nor is God the judge of men's actions. Nay, the very existence of the soul is denied. The person or "self" is only a word expressing a collection of phenomena, sensations, perceptions, and so forth, which therefore lack a subject, for they have no ultimate identity.

(b) *Ethics* properly so-called does not exist in Buddhism, for just as religion cannot exist without truths concerning God, so too no ethics can exist without God, who is the foundation of obligation and the judge of human actions. Moreover, morality cannot be conceived of in a system that denies personality or the "self." Although the ethics of Buddhism is much more perfect than its dogma inasmuch as it contains given commands from the natural law (though only negative ones in the original forms of Buddhism), it nonetheless lacks not only a supernatural motive but even a natural motive, which was known of by the great philosophers [of Greece]. Indeed, the self-denial and benevolence that it fosters *do not proceed*, like Christian charity, *from love for God* and men inasmuch as they are children of God, *but rather from self-love* and from a kind of *natural sympathy*. However, even adversaries admit that this sympathy differs most greatly from Christian charity. For example, Oldenberg, an admirer of Buddhism, writes:

> Buddhism is unaware of this charity which, according to St. Paul, surpasses faith and hope and, without which, all that could be said by all the tongues of men and angels would be like empty sounds in the air or the clashing of symbols. Buddhism commands less so love of enemies than non-hatred for them. It arouses and nourishes a kind of inclination to goodness and compassion toward all creatures. However, this sentiment is not a spontaneous, mystical and unreflective effect of love but, rather, is a kind of reflex sentiment, a kind of rational persuasion, namely, that all things will proceed

better because of this benevolence, with the hope that the reward of the natural law will be procured by acting in this way.[5]

Moreover, Buddhism commends *pride*, not humility, *for* anyone, all by himself, without divine grace, can obtain salvation (or, rather, liberation from evils). Buddhism is not aware of the threefold foundation of Christian humility: that God created us in an utterly free manner *ex nihilo*, that we need grace for any saving act, and that we are sinners.

Finally, this ethics may be judged by its *fruits*, for among Buddhists we find a thriving culture of polygamy, divorce, and even polyandry. Monks often indulge in laziness, for they are prohibited from performing labor and they do not know of prayer, properly so-called. Hence, although some of them sometimes exhibit great zeal, they have established nothing similar to the countless works of Christian charity. The Buddha did not intend the amelioration of man's social condition.

{{383}} Hence, just as in its doctrine, there is nothing in Buddhism's moral practices that would indicate that it surpasses the powers of human nature.

(c) *True miracles are lacking* in Buddhism. The wonders that are cited are referred to only in books that were written long after the event, and are completely ridiculous and entirely unworthy of God. (For example, the Buddha ran through the entire circuit of the heavens, sending fire out of one of his eyes and water from the other. At another time, when he was to fight with the serpent king, his entire body turned into fire.) Moreover, these marvels are not referred to as being extraordinary works of God in confirmation of Buddhism's divine character, for this religion does not teach anything about God. Instead, they are cited in order to manifest the power that any man, by his own powers, can arrive at through self-denial.

(d) *Finally, the propagation* of Buddhism cannot be compared in any way with the miraculous propagation of Christianity but instead is sufficiently explained by the natural qualities of this religion (and even by its defects). Indeed, it is much less opposed to the passions than is Christianity, since Buddhism is in doubt concerning the existence of God the Supreme Lawgiver and judge. Hence, this agnostic, quasi-atheistic religion, lacking a supreme authority, was easily accepted by kings and propagated by them. Nor do we find in it unity, or unconquered stability, for some of its adherents are agnostics, others atheists, others pantheists, and others are even polytheists and profess a kind of belief in magic.

---

[5] Oldenberg, *Le Buddha*, 298.

From all of these manifest errors and defects, it is clear that Buddhism is not from God who reveals but, rather, came forth from human ingenuity and is highly inferior to Christianity.

ART. 2: ON ISLAM

§1. History
§2. The Doctrine of Islam
§3. Critique of Islam

§1. History

Islam[6] (or Mohammedanism [*sic*]) is the religion that was founded in Arabia by Mohammed in the *seventh century AD*.

The ancient Arabs received the patriarchal religion from Abraham and Heber (Gen 10:25; 16:15; 21:18) and preserved it for some time. However, gradually, with the passing of time, they fell into polytheism. Following the destruction of Jerusalem, many Jews and certain illiterate Christians came to Arabia. Mohammed, however, was born around the year 570 and for a long while was a shepherd, then, becoming a trader, married a wealthy widow, and, admiring Israelite and Christian institutions (though with little in the way of knowledge concerning Christian dogmas), began to preach a new doctrine. {{384}} He said the angel Gabriel appeared to him and affirmed that he was a prophet sent by God in order to renew the ancient patriarchal religion. In the year 622, he migrated from Mecca to Medina, reconciled himself with the people of Medina [*medinenses*], and with their aid imposed his religion through strength of arms upon many throughout the whole of Arabia. He died on June 8, 632. Afterwards, Islam also propagated, by strength of arms, into Asia, Africa, and parts of Europe.

Many today admit that Mohammed was sincere at the start of this but afterwards made use of made-up revelations that stood in line with his pas-

---

[6] See Bernard Carra de Vaux, *La doctrine de l'Islam* (Paris: Beauchesne 1909); "Islamisme et ses sectes," *Dictionnaire apologétique de la foi catholique*, col. 1135–1154; Ignace Louis Gondal, *Islamisme et christianisme* (Paris: Roger et Chernoviz, 1906); A. Palmieri's article "Coran" in *Dictionnaire de théologie catholique*; Huby, *Christus*, 541; Bricout, *Où en est l'histoire des religions*, vol. 1, 424; Henri Lammens, "Qoran et tradition: Mahomet fut-il sincère?" in *Recherches de science religieuse* (1901): 27[ff]; (1911): 25[ff] and 140[ff]; Michelangelo Guidi, "Storia della religione dell'Islam" in *Storia delle religioni*, ed. Tacchi Venturi (Turin, 1930), 227–359. [Trans. note: The final volume might be, in fact, the second volume of an edition published in 1939 by Unione tipografico - editrice torinese.]

sions. He took many wives and gave utterly certain signs of his ambition, cruelty, and lustfulness.

Various judgments have been made concerning his state of mind, leading various people to hold that he suffered from epilepsy or hysteria, or even that he was a great genius. Mohammed did not claim full moral perfection for himself; however, later dogmas (under the influence of the figure of Christ in the Gospels) elevated him to the status of being the ideal man. He was a man who was at once both religious and political.

The source for the doctrine of Islam is found in the Qur'an, which is the preaching of Mohammed, gathered in fragments by his followers, containing the divine revelation mediated by the angel Gabriel. Then, in order to fill the holes in this text, the *Sunna* (Customs) of the prophet, his associates, and his closest followers were added, and from this tradition, other sources for the religion were then composed.

§2. The Doctrine of Islam

Mohammed called his religion *Islam*, which means "submission" (resignation).[7]

A. *The dogmas* that are most important are as follows. (1) It professes the existence *of one God*, who is the Creator, *Allah*, who alone is to be adored, to the exclusion of a Trinity of persons. Just as every emanation and generation is excluded from belonging to God, so too is the possibility of God becoming incarnate. Christ was not the Son of God but, rather, a great prophet. He did not die upon the Cross but instead was elevated to heaven. (This is a form of Docetism.) Christians are held to be polytheists. (2) It professes the existence of angels, who are sent from God and are caretakers for men. (3) It professes the divine mission of the prophets, of whom Mohammed is the greatest and last, as well as the Paraclete promised by Christ to his disciples. God does not immediately enter into the mind of the prophet but, rather, only speaks through the mediation of an angel. (4) It professes the revelation of its sacred book, the Qur'an (the recitation). According to Islamic theologians, it far surpasses the ancient texts handed on by the patriarchs. (5) It professes the immortality of the soul and the resurrection of bodies. Paradise and hell are described in a very materialistic manner. It seems that the opinion prevails in Islam that the punishments of hell are not eternal. Mohammed promised believers that paradise would bring them sensible and carnal delights more so than the vision of God. (6) Finally, it teaches fatalism

---

[7] [Trans. note: Fr. Garrigou-Lagrange adds the qualifier in parenthesis in French.]

in many texts in its sacred book (though, perhaps, they may be explained in a different way), even if it sometimes affirms human freedom. Original sin is unknown of in Mohammed's doctrine, though a memory of it can be found in certain legends. Likewise, grace and redemption are unknown of as well.

B. *The commands* of the religion are little concerned with the interior acts of the soul but instead are mostly external prescriptions. Prohibitions are made concerning wine, the eating of pork, images, gambling, and so forth. {{385}} It commands the recitation of a kind of creed (wherein one says, "There is no God but God, and Mohammed is his prophet"), prayers five times a day, ablutions, fasting on one meal in Ramadan, pious pilgrimages, the giving of alms, and circumcision. It has no rights of sacrificial propitiation. Above all, it commends holy war against unbelievers, whom God, through the ministry of his warriors, wishes to convert or unite. Mohammed, who died in this warfare, immediately entered heaven. Thus, fanaticism was given a significant impetus for growth. Finally, it permits polygamy and divorce at the whims of men, and it allows that unbelievers may be reduced to slavery.

There are three particular sects among Muslims, divided in particular along the lines of those traditions and hierarchy that some admit and others reject.

§3. Critique of Islam

There are many true things contained in Islam, especially the monotheism that it propagated among a number of more or less barbarian peoples.[8] However, this can be easily explained from the fact that they drew such monotheism from Judaism and Christianity. Nonetheless, Mohammed did draw back from Christ's doctrine, denying the mysteries of the Trinity and the Incarnation. He was unaware of original sin and grace. No comparison can be made between the final retribution spoken of in Mohammed's doctrine and that which is found in Christianity. The rewards of heaven and the punishments of hell are highly physical and carnal in nature in Islam. There is no word about remorse of conscience and the punishment of being separated from God in hell, and while the beatific vision in heaven did come to be admitted by some orthodox Muslims later on, it is difficult to harmonize it with Mohammed's doctrine concerning the unknowability of God [*de Deo velato*]. The "revelations" in the Qur'an present themselves as being given for the advantage or needs of the prophet and the community. Moreover,

---

8 Islam also promoted some progress in philosophy, especially in the Arabic version and interpretation of the works of Aristotle.

many of them are political in character. Nothing proves that Mohammed was sent by God. He admitted that he cannot do miracles, adding that they are not necessary: The Qur'an itself was the greatest miracle. Later on, miracles will come to be attributed to certain mystics, many in the form of telepathic communication and knowledge of other persons' thoughts. Its worship is very poor in its prayers, and it has neither a priesthood nor sacraments. The ceremonies of Mecca at the end of the pilgrimage, prescribed to be taken at least once in one's own life or through a substitute, smack of an uncivilized character.[9]

Islam's fatalistic tendency encourages the physical disposition to fatalism found in eastern peoples. Endurance (resignation) overlooks the idea of humility, that of expiation, and the relation of man's sorrows to the Passion of the Incarnate God. The idea of holy war, especially in its offensive form, is contrary to the peaceful spirit of Christianity. {{386}} Soldiers who have fallen in war are undeservedly honored with the title of being martyrs, who, according to the loftier concept of martyrdom, found in Christianity pour out their own blood without any harm [*offensione*] to others. Likewise, in Islam, the fruits of great holiness are lacking. Nay, it gives signs of the contrary—namely, violence and unchecked lustfulness, the violation of the unity and sanctity of marriage, an inferior condition thrust upon women, negligence in the education of youths, who are thought to be good from birth, given Islam's ignorance of original sin.

The propagation of Islam is explainable in natural terms, as St. Thomas notes in *SCG* I, ch. 6:

> Mohammed enticed the peoples by means of promises of carnal pleasures. . . . He also handed on commands that were conformed to these promises, loosing the reins of carnal pleasure. . . . Also, in proof of truth of his doctrine, he brought forward only things that could be grasped by the natural abilities of anyone with a common and modest amount of wisdom. In fact, in his teaching, he mixed together truths with many fables and doctrines which were utterly

---

[9] See de Vaux, *La doctrine de l'Islam*, 130ff: "What impression has been left on pilgrims concerning this visit to holy places? Is it that of a God who is more immaterial, a religion that is purer, a morality that is holy? One is justified in doubting that. It is even astonishing that this impression is not more often than not negative. Indeed, it sometimes is. So many bizarre rituals, implausible traditions, poured out blood, torn flesh, deaths in the animal and human kingdoms, so many strange, incoherent, and barbaric spectacles—all of this are not made for raising our religious sentiments nor for refining our moral sensibilities. There were indeed spirits that were shocked by all of this, like the founder of the religion of Babism."

false. Moreover, he did not perform supernatural deeds . . . but, instead, said that he was sent in strength of arms.

As regards Islamic mysticism, which some people wish to say is equal to Christian mysticism, the following points must be noted. Some wrongly judge that this mysticism is proper to the Qur'an and comes from it alone.[10] Mohammed and his companions were not contemplatives but, rather, warlike men with a lively faith in a few religious ideas. Where a contemplative spirit is found in Islam, the idea of the absorption of the soul into God, especially in certain Persian poets, seems to call to mind the "Nirvana" spoken of in Buddhism, on account of Gnostic and Neoplatonic influences. In the writings of Islamic philosophers, the development of mysticism in Islam is owed in particular to the influence of Christianity. The first Islamic religious were called *râhib* and then *sufi*, names that were used for Christian monks. Islamic mysticism first manifested itself in Syria and Egypt, places where the Christian contemplative life had flourished. In the mystical doctrines of Islam, we can find many things that are similar to what is found in Christianity, arising from the hands of certain authors or through clear allusions to the Gospels, such as the parable of the sower and the calling of the apostles. Beginners are required to undergo various degrees of contrition and practice various spiritual exercises. Great insistence is placed upon the value of a spiritual

---

[10] See de Vaux, *La doctrine de l'Islam*, 227: "The doctrine of Islamic mysticism is not Quranic in inspiration. *Mysticism was added to Islam.* We do not find it incorporated into it from its start. It was not part of its first institution, and we do not see it in its holy book." Likewise, see Guidi, "Storia della religione dell'Islam," 300: "But the undeniable poverty of the mystical life of Mohammed is certainly in stark contrast with the rich flourishing of Muslim mysticism, which, it should be noted, becomes more complex as the set of forces that stimulate the life of the community become more complex. The more one studies these forces, the more insufficient appears the hypothesis of one spontaneous development arising from the influences of the Qur'an. One should also consider that the religious and cultural phenomena that arose within the unity established by Islam are the deepest reasons for this development; we can constantly observe how the original attitudes—or at least those which are to be considered such after they have become proper to the environment, even though they are the result of a synthesis with foreign values—then receive the fertilizing influence of other cultures and other religions. The result is a unique figure with only relative originality, not unlike what is encountered, for example, in the history of grammar; and these analogies are absolutely not to be overlooked. We must therefore conclude by affirming a rich stream that flows from the outside into the purely Quranic stream, also bearing in mind that the connection of mystical experiences with the Qur'an is partly the result of a harmonizing activity, which attempted, as in all fields of religious life, to coordinate every activity with the doctrine of the Qur'an."

[Trans. note: Thanks are owed to Dr. Thomas Howes for assistance translating this note from Italian.]

director, to whom, as a "father" and doctor of the soul, one is said to owe full and open subjection. {{387}} Poverty of spirit is commended, along with self-denial and denial of the things of the world, ascetical exercises, and spiritual warfare, all to the end of fully giving oneself over to God. In their analysis of the spiritual life, they enumerate various moments that are very similar to the descriptions found in Christian mystics.[11] Nonetheless, a great abyss separates Islamic mysticism from Christian mysticism, inasmuch as the former, unaware of the Incarnation, the redemptive Passion, and the infinite divine love, knows God only at a distance, like a Lord governing his servants, a God to whom one cannot be joined in union, a claim that is mollified by some through a kind of union that has a pantheistic character. This mysticism often has the effect of leading to pessimism and flight from work, while the legitimate authority needed for avoiding deliberation is lacking, as well as violent and abnormal practices. It is difficult to say whether Islam bears witness to mysticism in the true sense of the word, both on account of the difficulty involved in distinguishing true supernatural mysticism from a kind of natural analogue, as well as on account of the difficulty involved in discerning the true sense of the descriptions given by these "mystics," which can differ greatly from that which is expressed by Christians using the same terms. *Per se*, it is possible for supernatural mysticism to exist in those who live in a state of grace in good faith outside the visible Church. However, that it in fact exists outside should be greatly doubted because even in the Church, where the mystery of the Redemption is honored, the sacraments are obtained, and the guidance of infallible authority received, only a few who aspire to the mystical life fully reach it on account of the subjective indisposition of many.[12]

Finally, as St. Thomas says concerning Mohammed, in the same text as above:

> Moreover, no wise men trained in things divine and human believed in him from the beginning. Those who did were *brutal*

---

[11] De Vaux, *La doctrine de l'Islam*, 247ff: "Mystical theory seems to have developed simultaneously in the two religions, and it is possible that during this work, they were acquainted with one another. It also seems that the Islamic doctrine, which certainly in the middle ages, to the eighth or ninth century, imitated the doctrine of the Christian East, later on, in its own turn, exercised some influence, in the fourteenth and fifteenth centuries, on Christian mysticism in Spain. The latter influence, bearing more so upon form, imagery, and manner of expression of Spanish mysticism than on its foundations, cannot be ruled out."

[12] We have discussed this topic in "The Grace of Christ and Mystics Outside the Church" in Réginald Garrigou-Lagrange, *Our Savior and His Love for Us*, trans. A. Bouchard (St. Louis, MO: B. Herder, 1951), 355–384.

men and desert wanderers, utterly ignorant of all divine teaching, through whom, by violence of arms, Mohammed forced others to follow his law. *Nor is it true to say that the divine oracles from earlier prophets* bear witness to him in any way. Much to the contrary, he distorts almost all the testimonies of the Old and New Testaments by making them into his own fabrications, as is clear to anyone who examines his law. Therefore, he was shrewd indeed to forbid his followers from reading the Old and New Testaments, lest these texts might convict him of falsity. Thus, it is clear that those who place faith in his words do so foolishly.[13]

And let us add that fatalism also immediately fosters laziness, and the union of the spiritual and temporal power in one and the same leader begets absolute tyranny. Finally, Islam increasingly shows the signs of its age and corruption. In all things, it is very inferior to Christianity.

{{388}} ***Conclusion.*** From the certain conclusions of the history of religions, it is manifestly clear that Christianity transcends all other religions. Nay, based on this comparison with other religions, its absolute transcendence (that is, its divinity) is confirmed, since no other religion can equal its doctrine, institutions, miracles, prophecies, marvelous propagation, unconquered stability, unity, and fruitfulness in all good things. Thus, through the history of religions and the comparisons that can be drawn from it, all the motives of credibility on behalf of the mysteries of Christianity find themselves to be increasingly corroborated.[14]

---

[13] *SCG* I, ch. 6.

[14] See de Broglie, *Problèmes et conclusions de l'histoire des religions*, chs. 8–10.

On the Duty of Receiving Divine Revelation After It Has Been Proposed by the Church

{{389}} Having considered the value of the motives of credibility, we now must take up the question concerning the obligation to believe divine revelation after it has been proposed by the Church in a sufficient manner. Likewise, we must take up, in a general manner, the question concerning the foundation for our religious duties, to the degree that they can be known by reason alone. Thus, we have four topics to consider here:

Art. 1. On indifferentism and liberalism, along with how they are opposed to the Church's teaching

Art. 2. Proof, by reason, concerning individual men's duty to profess natural religion (or religion in general)

Art. 3. Proof, by reason, concerning any given person's duty to receive divine revelation that has been sufficiently proposed, or their duty to investigate into this matter

Art. 4. On the duty of civil authority and society to receive divine revelation, once it has been sufficiently proposed

ART. 1: ON INDIFFERENTISM AND LIBERALISM, ALONG WITH HOW THEY ARE OPPOSED TO THE CHURCH'S TEACHING

§1. On absolute indifferentism, as well as laicism, which denies the necessity of [holding] a particular religion, even natural religion

§2. On mitigated indifferentism or latitudinarianism, which holds that all religions (or at least all forms of Christianity) are good and provide a way for salvation

§3. On liberalism, which defends the [utter religious neutrality of the] civil order and its freedom of worship as something befitting to reason as well as to the spirit of Christianity

§1. On Absolute Indifferentism

Absolute indifferentism *denies the necessity of any given form of religion, even be it natural.* It is expressed in the third proposition condemned in Pius IX's *Syllabus of Errors*: "Human reason, without any consideration at all of God, is the sole judge of truth and falsehood, of good and evil; it is a law unto itself, and by its natural powers, it suffices to care for the good of men and nations."[1]

{{390}} This absolute indifferentism finds its source in atheism, pantheism, or agnosticism. Indeed, if God does not exist and is not distinct from the world, or if nothing can be known with certainty concerning him, then there can be no duties that exist in relation to him. However, those who, like a number of deists, admit that God exists, while however denying that divine providence extends to singular existing things, contend that God cares little concerning our acts of deference. Hence, they disregard religion as an indifferent and useless affair.

Therefore, according to such thinkers, what is religion? It is, like art, *something that proceeds from men's imaginations rather than from their reason.* Hence, even if it happened to be necessary once upon a time, and forever remains useful for certain people as a stimulus for them to act, religion nonetheless is opposed to the progress of the sciences, unless it is subordinated to science itself, as providing a symbolic conception of the Absolute, which has no need of proving its truth. For a number of people, religion (which they ultimately identify with mysticism) is something to be sought out as a kind of ornament for souls, or a kind of luxury, like the art of poetry.

Such is the general sentiment held by *absolute evolutionists*, though they set forth this general claim in a variety of ways, depending on whether they are materialists (like Haeckel) or idealists (like Hegel).[2]

---

[1] Pius IX, *Syllabus of Errors*, no. 3 (Denzinger, no. 2903).

[2] See our earlier discussion in vol. 1, bk. 1, ch. 8 (Examination of Pantheistic Evolutionism). As regards religious philosophy, Spinoza held that religion is something fabricated by the imagination, whereby God is conceived of as being a person distinct from the world, as someone who exercises providence and the remuneration of justice. Fichte, equally rejecting the existence of a personal God, said that religion should be nothing more than rational faith in the existence of the moral world, which we must conscientiously [*pie*] and freely prefer to the sensible order. For Hegel, religion is a symbolic (or imaginative) conception of the Absolute,

Agnostics bring forward nearly the same explanation of religion, doing so either in an empiricist form (as do positivists)[3] or in an idealistic form (as did Kant). Indeed, *Kant* said that, through a kind of moral faith, we must believe in God's existence, as well as in that of a future life. However, *he denied that we had any particular duties toward God and likewise denied the necessity of worship.* According to him, man only needs to fulfill all the moral duties he has in relation to himself and those that he has toward other men, doing so in a religious manner.[4] For, as he said, if God created us for his own glory, he would have been guilty of a kind of divine egoism. This last proposition, condemned by the [First] Vatican Council, was held by Georg Hermes and Anton Günther.[5]

{{391}} *Laicism.* Contemporary laicism puts these principles into practice. Nay, it constitutes *a religion of irreligion* as something that is obligatory for society and for the state. The fundamental principle of laicism is the absolute autonomy of reason and of the human will: "Human reason is so independent that faith cannot be enjoined upon it by God,"[6] as Kant said[7]

---

one that prepares the way for the philosophical conception thereof. Schopenhauer and [Karl Robert Eduard von] Hartman[n] treat of religion in their chapters on illusions.

3   See our earlier discussion in bk. 1, ch. 9, where we consider the implications of empiricist and idealist agnosticism as regards religious philosophy. However, *positivists* are themselves subdivided. *Sociologist-positivists* hold that religion arises from a kind of sense of dependence upon the collective, which unsophisticated people conceive of as some sort of Higher Being to be honored through religion. Such was the position held by neo-Comteans. However, because society does not suffice for providing a foundation for our moral obligations, other agnostics—namely *psychologist-agnostics*—believed that the religious sentiment arises from our subconscious in certain circumstances and at first is a kind of religious emotion from which we gradually develop symbolic representations and religious concepts (cf., for example, William James [*W. Iameò*]). Thus, those who hold that religion is useful can embrace it. However, this is not something positing an obligation, strictly speaking. See ch. 9 above.

4   See the remarks by Victor Delbos in Kant, *Fondements de la métaphysique des moeurs* [No edition], 62: "Religion consists in looking upon moral laws as though they were divine commands. Through its essential affirmations, it must claim to increase not our knowledge (either of God or of things) but, rather, only the efficacy of our duties as *mobile*: it is enclosed within the postulates of practical reason." Likewise, see Kant's *Religion Within the Bounds of Mere Reason*.

5   See [First] Vatican Council, *Dei filius*, can. 1.5 (Denzinger, no. 3025) and ch. 2 (Denzinger, no. 3002). Similarly, see Jean-Michel-Alfred Vacant, *Études théologiques sur les constitutions du Concile du Vatican d'après les actes du concile*, vol. 1 (Paris: Delhomme et Briguet, 1895), 270, 580, 608.

6   In this form, this principle was condemned by the [First] Vatican Council in *Dei filius*, can. 3.1 (Denzinger, no. 3031).

7   See Kant, *Religion Within the Bounds of Mere Reason*, bk. 4, chs. 5 and 6. Likewise, see Kant, *The Groundwork for the Metaphysics of Morals*, ed. Delbos, section 2, 170–178 (On the auton-

and as laicists profess today (for example, Ferdinand Buisson in his book, *La foi laïque*[8]).

See what we said above, in vol. 1, in ch. 7 (on the foundation, spirit, and consequences of naturalism), ch. 8 (on evolutionism), and ch. 9ff (on agnosticism).

§2. On Mitigated Indifferentism (or Latitudinarianism)

This form of indifferentism admits that there are certain duties owed to God, as well as the necessity of some form of worship, at least internal. However,

---

omy of the will as the supreme principle of morality).

[8] See Ferdinand Buisson, *La foi laïque*, [(Paris: Hachette, 1912),] 193: "The human person must be free: this commandment is addressed first to the human person. For his own part, he can no more annihilate his own freedom than he can allow it to be annihilated by another. *Every form of servitude is a crime against humanity, without exception, including servitude that one believes to be voluntary.*" The laicist spirit or [the unfettered claim on behalf of the rights of] free thought "*demands that its adherents expressly reject*, not only every form of imposed belief, but *every form of authority claiming to impose its beliefs*" (ibid., 198). "Faith in God is not one of the obligations that society can include among its laws. *Our laws and institutions are no longer founded on the Rights of God but, rather, on the Rights of Man.* . . . They no longer act or speak in God's name or through the grace of God but rather, in the name of the nation and with a purely human authority" (206). "Laicity is the corollary of popular sovereignty." "Can one be a free thinker without being a republican; and can one be a republican without being a socialist?" (196).

And Buisson adds: "In no way do we look to wage war against the religious idea; even less do we look to suppress religious liberty" (ibid., 159). Elsewhere, he praises liberal Protestants "for the effort they have undertaken in attempting to extract from traditional and ecclesiastical religion what could be called a form of eternal Christianity, a kind of gospel fashioned from the marrow of the old gospel, *a laic religion of the ideal, without morality, without dogmas, without miracles, and without priests.*" Kant already had said this in the text cited above.

Likewise, [Jean] Jaurès, in his "Discours à la Chambre des députés" on Feb. 11, 1895, said: "The greatest thing in the world is the sovereign freedom of the mind. . . . It is the fact that any truth that does not come forth from ourselves is a lie. . . . It is the fact that if the very ideal [*sic*] of God made itself visible, *if God Himself stood before the multitudes in a tangible form, man's first duty would be to refuse obedience to him* and to consider him as an equal with whom to dispute, not as a master to whom one would submit oneself."

On this point, see the article "Laicisme" in the *Dictionnaire apologétique de la foi catholique*, 4th ed., col. 1772: "The Apostle said, 'reprove, entreat, rebuke in all patience' (2 Tim 4:2, DR). There are some who would like the Church to be less restlessly active, less impassioned, *serene and even somewhat indifferent,* after the manner of a philosophical school. By adopting this attitude, the Church would be false to herself, to her mission, and to the interests that she watches over. Her priests are not professors of wisdom. They are ministers whose charge is the things of God. Their duty is to make His name respected. . . . to promulgate his commandments. They must defend and vindicate the blood of the God-Man, poured forth for the salvation of the world. They must lead their brothers' souls to eternal life."

it holds that *one can profess whatever positive religion one wishes*. This general category contains a great variety of particular positions.

(1) Certain[9] people holding such a mitigated indifferentism diminish the essential duties of natural religion, even if they do in fact admit its necessity. {{392}} Some *deny the usefulness and efficacy of prayer*, since it clearly is not fitting either to God or to man.[10] Others reject the necessity *of external and public worship* because God wishes to be adored "in spirit and truth." Likewise, they reject positive forms of religion.

(2) According to others, positive religions can be admitted, though among them (e.g., among *Christianity, Islam, and Buddhism*) one is free to choose whatever form of worship one so wishes. (One finds an example of this in "Profession de foi du vicaire savoyard" in Rousseau's *Émile*.)

This doctrine is formulated as follows in Pius IX's *Syllabus of Errors*: "Everyone is free to embrace and profess the religion that by the light of reason he judges to be true"; "Men can find the way of eternal salvation and attain eternal salvation by the practice of any religion whatever."[11]

Hugues-Felicité Robert de Lamennais ultimately arrived at this kind of indifferentism:[12] "Man can attain the eternal salvation of his soul by any profession of faith, provided his moral conduct conforms to the norms of right and good."[13] (See Fr. Lacordaire's examination of Lamennais's system.[14])

---

[9] [Trans. note: Reading *Quiadam* as *quidam*.]

[10] See Jules Simon, *La religion naturelle*, pt. 4, ch. 1.

[11] Pius IX, *Syllabus of Errors*, nos. 15 and 16 (Denzinger, nos. 2915 and 2916).

[12] See Hugues-Felicité Robert de Lamennais, *Essais sur l'indifférence en matière de religion*, vol. 2, ch. 20 (The Words of a Believer).

[13] See Gregory XVI, *Mirari vos*, no. 13 (Denzinger, no. 2730; also see 1670 [old numbering]).

[14] See Henri-Dominique Lacordaire, *Oeuvres complètes*, vol. 7 (in 12 vols), *Considérations sur le système philosophique de M. de Lamennais*. See ch. 10 (This system is useless in defense of Christianity); ch. 11 (It contains the broadest form of Protestantism that has ever been expressed). See the conclusion of ch. 12: "Monsieur de Lamennais's error consists in not wishing to allow us to evidentially discern authority, reducing all the elements of certitude to authority, and all authorities to one alone, namely mankind, of which Catholicism would be nothing more than a developed form" (154). "Thus, we can see the abyss which Lamennais involuntarily dug out below the edifice of Christianity. As he declared mankind to be infallible in philosophic and religious matters, one will have the right to say to him: let us go no further; we have certitude, truth, and faith; that is enough. . . . Through a kind of Protestant outlook, each man will remain free to turn mankind against the Church, to invoke against the Church's authority the infallible authority of mankind. . . . Where do the followers of [Henri de] Saint-Simon believe they can read the prophecy of their dreams? In humanity, which they claim to be infallible, in man's past and in the present hopes of mankind. . . . I am quite sure . . . that these are crazy assessments of how matters truly stand, just as I believe that Protestants incorrectly explain Holy Scripture. However, it is nonetheless true that the [so-called] infalli-

More recently, the modernists, who held that religion is ultimately found in man's religious sentiment, by that very fact more or less asserted that all religions are true, for man's religious sentiment is one and the same everywhere, at least substantially so.[15]

(3) Finally, others say: *It suffices that one embrace Christianity, without professing Catholicism.* Here, see what is said in nos. 17 and 18 of Pius IX's *Syllabus of Errors*: "At the very least, there must be good hope for the eternal salvation of all those who do not dwell in any way in the true Church of Christ. Protestantism is nothing else than a different form of the same true Christian religion, in which it is possible to serve God as well as in the Catholic Church."[16]

§3. On Liberalism

Inasmuch as it is distinct from the indifferentism that we discussed above, liberalism, which was admitted by Catholic liberals who were disciples of Felicité de Lamennais, *defends the civil freedom of any form of worship, not as an intrinsically [in se] disordered condition of society but, rather, as something conformed to the spirit of the Gospel and indeed of great use* [to society]. {{393}} Although liberal Catholics admitted that the Catholic Church was divinely instituted, they did indeed teach that full freedom must be conceded it, though nothing more is owed to it beyond that. "For the true religion," they said, "will spread and flourish solely by way of persuasion. It will be embraced by many, and indeed, with all the more freedom (and, therefore, with greater trust and love) to the degree that the coercion of believing is less, since the truth always prevails over errors."

The Church says: "What worse death is there for the soul than the liberty of error. . . . Thus, human nature, already inclined to evil as it is, is now rushing headlong [to its ruin]."[17] For not all men (indeed, not many) take interest [*sunt cultores*] in truth and virtue. And having granted freedom to teach errors that flatter passions or pride, the greater part of men will not be able, without great difficulty, to discover the truth that saves.

Such *liberalism* can be defined as follows: *the doctrine holding that the*

---

bility of mankind is, today, the logical foundation for one of the most formidable errors which has ever appeared in the world" (145–148).

[15] See Pius X, *Pascendi dominici gregis*, no. 14 (Denzinger, no. 2082 [old numbering]).

[16] Pius IX, *Syllabus of Errors*, nos. 17 and 18 (Denzinger, nos. 2917 and 2918). Likewise, see Denzinger, nos. 2805–2865 [nos. 1642–1677, old numbering]. [Trans. note: This seems off, as it contains a number of texts, some related, some not.]

[17] Gregory XVI, *Mirari vos*, no. 14 (cf. Denzinger, no. 2731).

civil and social authority is not bound to receive divine revelation that has been sufficiently proposed to it, but instead can remain *neutral* between true and false religions without submission to supernaturally revealed divine positive laws. It is a kind of social naturalism: Temporal society is not bound to subordinate its own proximate end to the supernatural end.[18]

The history of liberalism and its condemnation can be divided into three periods.[19]

First period. Felicité de Lamennais, along with his disciples, founded in 1830[20] the journal *L'avenir* for the sake of vindicating the rights of the Church. He proposed the separation of Church and the state as something of the greatest use for providing freedom for the Church and defended the civil freedom for any form of worship as a suitable means for reconciling science with faith.

{{394}} On August 15, 1832, Pope Gregory XVI, in his encyclical

---

[18] See Leo XIII, *Libertas*, no. 23–24 (Vatican trans.): "And this all the more surely, because by far the greater part of the community is either absolutely unable, or able only with great difficulty, to escape from illusions and deceitful subtleties, especially such as flatter the passions. If unbridled license of speech and of writing be granted to all, nothing will remain sacred and inviolate. . . . And the more so because the authority of teachers has great weight with their hearers, who can rarely decide for themselves as to the truth or falsehood of the instruction given to them."

Liberal apologetes do not give sufficient attention to man's inclination to evil, as though man were born good, as Rousseau said, without original sin. By contrast, in his own apologetics, Pascal exaggerated the consequences of original sin. Following the correct path laid down by tradition, St. Thomas avoided these two opposed extremes, as is clear in *SCG* IV, ch. 52 and *ST* I-II, q. 81–85. According to him, original sin does not completely destroy the good of nature, though it does diminish it (see *ST* I-II, q. 85). And the Holy Doctor notes in a number of places: "*In men alone does evil seem to be found in a great number*, for man's good as regards the bodily senses is not man's good inasmuch as he is man (that is, the good of reason). However, many follow their senses rather than their reason" (*ST* I, q. 48, a. 3, ad 5). Likewise, see *De malo*, q. 1, a. 3, ad 17; a. 5, ad 16.

Likewise, the Church Fathers in general provide a similar explanation for Rom 3:12 (DR): "All have turned out of the way: they are become unprofitable together: there is none that doth good, there is not so much as one." And in the words of St. John in 1 John 2:16 (DR): "For all that is in the world is the concupiscence of the flesh and the concupiscence of the eyes and the pride of life. And 1 John 5:19 (DR): "The whole world is seated in wickedness." Likewise, see Ps 110:10 (DR): "The fear of the Lord is the beginning of wisdom."

[19] See Leo XIII, *Libertas* (*AAS*, vol. 8), 228 and 231. Leo XIII notes that this doctrine leads to *social atheism*. Likewise, G. de Pascal's article "Liberalisme" in the *Dictionnaire apologétique de la foi catholique*: "It seems that we could define this liberalism as a system of political and social life holding that the civil and social element only belongs to the human order and can—indeed, certain bolder people go so far as to say *must*—consider itself and act without any obligatory relation of dependence on the supernatural order."

[20] [Trans. note: Reading this instead of *ann. 170.*]

Mirari vos,[21] condemned this teaching inasmuch as it paved the way for indifferentism:

> Indeed, this absolutely pestilential error paves the way of that complete and unrestrained liberty of opinion which rages far and wide to the ruin of sacred and civil communities, whereas some still claim with the greatest impudence that some advantage to religion is gained from it. But "what worse death is there for the soul than the liberty of error," [as] Augustine said. When all constraints are removed, by which man is kept upon the path of truth . . . then truly is "the bottomless pit" opened up. . . . Proud—or, rather, foolish—men are those who, relying [solely] upon our human reason, which given what human nature is, is weak and infirm, thus examine the mysteries of faith, which surpass all that the human mind can understand.

Lamennais's disciples subjected themselves [to the Church] with perfect faith. Indeed, Lamennais at first subjected himself to the condemnation, but he later on fiercely fought the Church and, in his *Les paroles d'un croyant*, argued on behalf of complete freedom of conscience.[22] He was likewise

---

[21] See Denzinger, nos. 2730–2732.

[22] [Trans. note: The first paragraph in this note is in a footnote in the original Latin without any actual mark in the body of the text. Everything after this is in the note associated with the text above attached to this note number.]

On this occasion, Lacordaire wrote to Montalembert in October 1833: "Conscience, which is everything in the course of living one's life, is nothing when it is opposed to authority. The greatest crimes are committed with false conscience. Even were yours without stain in this affair, you should not listen to it but, rather, the voice of the Church, which has already raised itself, and which will raise itself hereafter with a dominion that will cast down all pride."

In 1834, after the edition of Lamennais's book *Les paroles d'un croyant*, Lacordaire wrote in the conclusion to his work, *Considérations sur le système philosophique de M. de Lamennais*: "This suffices for me. . . . If I have helped one of my brothers emerge from a state of perplexity, from which I too have suffered, if I have warned the Church that *a war is being prepared—and indeed is already being fought—against her in the name of humanity*, then I will have done enough. . . . It does not fall to me to give counsels; however, one can always say, without pride, that one is not deceived and give glory to God who 'calls us from the darkness into His own wondrous light.'

"After striving for ten years to conceive of the true role to be played by philosophy in the Church, where have I arrived? At the same thought that was possessed without concern by those who had counted more so on the Church's mind [*esprit*] than on their own. . . . How much have I come to admire the superiority of the Church, the ineffable instinct that pushed her onward, the divine discernment which drew her from the shadow of an illusion. . . . In contrast with human things which, at first, have the appearance of grandeur while immediately

condemned in 1834.[23] He died in Paris on February 27, 1854, without having signed any retraction.

{{395}} *Second period.* This begins after the revolution of 1848. Many Catholic liberals, attempting to protect the Church's freedom, deviated from the directions set forth in the encyclical *Mirari vos.* The professor of theology, [Léon Nicolas] Godard, in his book *Les principes de 89 et la doctrine catholique* in 1861 wished to reconcile these principles with Catholicism, but he was condemned by the Sacred Congregation of the Index. And after the discourse of Count de Montalembert at the Malines Congress in 1863, Pius IX once more condemned liberalism on December 8, 1864, in the encyclical *Quanta cura.*[24] He condemned, as an application of naturalism, the doctrine of those who hold that "the best notion of public society and, likewise, civil progress wholly require that human society be constituted and governed without any consideration for religion, as though it did not exist, or at least *without making distinction between true and false religions.*" Now, Pius IX added that—in opposition to the teaching of Sacred Scripture, the Church, and the Holy Fathers—such people do not hesitate to assert

"that the best condition of society is that in which one does not

---

thereafter becoming small, the Church grows through the centuries, and she never stands in need of justification.

"I likewise reflected on another point. I asked myself how a philosophy, whose vice I perceive so clearly today, had for so long held my reason in suspense. I have come to realize that fighting against an intellect superior to mine, and wishing to fight alone against it, victory was impossible. For the truth is not a self-sufficient auxiliary for reestablishing the equilibrium of forces. Otherwise, error would never triumph over the truth. *Therefore, the world needs a power that sustains weak intellects against strong ones, delivering them from the most terrible oppression: oppression of the mind* [esprit]. This power did, in fact, come to my aid. I did not deliver myself. This power did. Arriving at Rome, at the tomb of the Apostles Peter and Paul, I knelt and said to God: 'Lord, I now begin to feel my weakness: my sight is covered. Error and truth both evade my sight. . . . Hear the prayer of the poor man.' I know not the day nor the hour, but I saw what I did not see before. I left Rome free and victorious. *I learned from my own experience that the Church is the liberator of the human mind* [esprit]. And as all other freedoms necessarily flow from freedom of the intellect, *I perceived, in their true light, the questions which divide the contemporary world.*

"Yes, the world looks for peace and freedom. But it seeks after them on a route that is troublesome and one of servitude. The Church alone has been the source of peace and freedom for mankind. . . . This is why a priest will not get involved in the violent and fruitless disputes of his era. He will pray for the present and the future. He will anoint the sorrows and pains of the world with charity, as much as he can. He will tirelessly preach to contemporary generations: *Neither peace nor freedom is possible outside the truth.*"

23 See Gregory XVI, *Singulari nos* (Denzinger, no. 1617 [old numbering]).

24 See Pius IX, *Quanta cura*, no. 3 (Denzinger, no. 1689 [old numbering]).

acknowledge that the society has the power of coercing, through penalties, those who violate the Catholic religion, except inasmuch as public peace requires this." And from this wholly false idea of social government, they do not fear to promote that false opinion, . . . namely, "that each man has a right to freedom of conscience and of worship, something which should be proclaimed in law and asserted. . . ." However, while they rashly assert this, they in no way note or consider the fact that they are thus preaching *a freedom of perdition*.[25]

Along with this encyclical, Pius IX's *Syllabus of Errors* was edited as a collection of modern errors, in which a number of propositions drawn from liberalism are found:[26] "In our age, it is no longer advisable that the Catholic religion be the only State religion, excluding all the other forms of worship. It is in fact false that civil freedom of worship and the full right granted to all to express openly and publicly any opinions and views lead to an easier corruption of morality and of the minds of people and help to propagate the plague of indifferentism."[27]

Third period. For a number of years following the encyclical *Quanta cura*, liberalism no longer seemed to exist in the form of a doctrine but instead continued to exist in the form of a kind of tendency. Therefore, on November 1, 1885, in his encyclical *Immortale Dei*, Leo XIII confirmed and cited the encyclicals *Mirari vos* and *Quanta cura*, as well as the *Syllabus of Errors*,[28] and likewise explained the nature of legitimate freedom and how false religions can be tolerated in order that a greater evil might be avoided:

{{396}} The Church, indeed, deems it unlawful to place the various forms of divine worship on the same footing as the true religion, but does not, on that account, condemn those rulers who, for the sake of securing some great good or of hindering some great evil, allow patiently custom or usage to be a kind of sanction for each kind of religion having its place in the State. And, in fact, the Church is wont to take earnest heed that no one shall be forced to embrace

---

25 Ibid. (Denzinger, no. 1690 [old numbering]).

26 See Pius IX, *Syllabus of Errors*, nos. 24, 55, and 77–80 (Denzinger, 2924, 2955, and 2977–2980).

27 Following a logical order, Pius IX's *Syllabus of Errors* condemns (1) *the absolute autonomy of reason* (prop. 1, whence follow 2–4), (2) the absolute autonomy of civil society (prop. 39); and (3) the absolute autonomy *of ethics* (props. 56–61).

28 See Leo XIII, *Immortale Dei*, nos. 33ff (Denzinger, nos. 3169ff).

the Catholic faith against his will, for, as St. Augustine wisely reminds us, "Man cannot believe otherwise than of his own will." ... Especially with reference to the so-called "liberties" which are so greatly coveted in these days, all must stand by the judgment of the Apostolic See, and have the same mind. *Let no man be deceived by the honest outward appearance of these liberties....* Experience has made Us well acquainted with their results to the State.[29]

Indeed, in liberalism, we find a kind of false charity toward nonbelievers. However, the corruption of the greatest virtue is always something intrinsically grave and in its countless consequences, for it constitutes a false spirit.

Likewise, on June 20, 1888, in his encyclical *Libertas*, Leo XIII wrote, anew:

From what has been said it follows that it is quite unlawful to demand, to defend, or to grant *unconditional freedom* of thought, of speech, or writing, or of *worship*, as if these were so many rights given by nature to man. For, if nature had really granted them, *it would be lawful to refuse obedience to God*, and there would be no restraint on human liberty.[30]

In relation to this question, this encyclical must be read with great care, for here we find said:

What *naturalists* or *rationalists* aim at in philosophy, that the supporters of *liberalism*, carrying out the principles laid down by naturalism, are attempting in the domain of morality and politics ...: in public affairs the commands of God may be passed over, and may be entirely disregarded in the framing of laws.[31]

And against this, Leo XIII wrote:

Wherefore, civil society must acknowledge God as its founder and parent, and must obey and reverence His power and authority. Justice therefore forbids, and reason itself forbids, the state to be godless;

---

[29] Ibid., nos. 36 and 42 (Denzinger, nos. 3169ff [old nos. 1874–1880]; taken from Vatican translation).

[30] Leo XIII, *Libertas*, no. 42 (Denzinger, no. 3252; Vatican translation).

[31] Ibid., nos. 15 and 18.

or to adopt a line of action which would end in godlessness—namely, to treat the various religions (as they call them) *alike, and to bestow upon them promiscuously equal rights and privileges. . . .*[32]

But, in spite of all this show of tolerance, it very often happens that, while they profess themselves ready to lavish liberty on all in the greatest profusion, (the partisans of liberty) are utterly intolerant toward the Catholic Church, by refusing to allow her the liberty of being herself free.[33]

In opposition to his teaching, Leo XIII presents the words of Jesus Christ: "You shall know the truth: and the truth shall make you free" (John 8:32, DR).[34]

Finally, liberalism reappeared among Catholics in the form of a doctrine in the writings of the modernists, and here once more, it was condemned by Pius X, in his encyclical *Pascendi dominici gregis*,[35] in his letter concerning the social errors held by the association "Le Sillon" (see his letter from August 25, 1910), and before this in his encyclical *Vehementer nos*.[36]

Therefore, liberalism's teaching here can be reduced to the following: The civil and social authority, in the laws and decrees it must make, is not bound to preserve conformity to supernaturally revealed divine laws; nor is it disordered to have civil freedom granted to any worship whatsoever, whether true or false. This principle of liberalism is found in the famed French *Declaration of the Rights of Men [and of the Citizen]*.[37]

---

[32] Ibid., no. 21.

[33] Ibid., no. 35. [Trans. note: Slightly expanded from the abbreviated form in which it is found in Fr. Garrigou-Lagrange's text.]

[34] See ibid., no. 27.

[35] See Pius X, *Pascendi dominici gregis*, no. 25 (Denzinger, no. 2093 [old numbering]).

[36] See Pius X, *Vehementer nos*, no. 13 (Denzinger, no. 1995 [old numbering]).

[37] *The Declaration of the Rights of Man*: "The representatives of the French People, gathered as the National Assembly, considering the fact that ignorance, neglect, or contempt for the rights of man are the only causes of public evils and of the corruption of governments, have resolved to set forth, in a solemn Declaration, the natural, inalienable, and sacred rights of man, etc. . . ." According to Catholic teaching, one would have needed to say: "ignorance, neglect, or contempt for the Rights of God and of man's duties are the causes of public evils." However, once God's rights have been set aside, it is not surprising that the rights of man would thus become sacred: "The sacred rights of man."

A society founded on man thus is substituted for that society which is founded on the Gospel.

Art. 3: "The principle of all sovereignty resides essentially in the nation; no [lower] body, nor any individual can exercise authority if it does not expressly emanate from the former."

{{397}} According to the Church, the condemnation of liberalism is nothing other than an application of the first principles—whether of reason or faith—inasmuch as freedom of error cannot be something right and ordered but, rather, is a freedom of perdition, as St. Augustine said.[38] This has been forever taught by the popes. For example, see Boniface VIII's bull *Unam sanctam*[39] and Martin V's condemnation of Jan Hus and John Wycliffe.[40] Likewise, see Leo X's ex cathedra condemnation of the errors of Martin Luther, among which the following is found: "That heretics be burned is against the will of the Spirit."[41]

What then will be the Church's authority?

Art. 4: "Freedom consists in being able to do whatever does not harm another person." Thus, the freedom of teaching atheism is not excluded as something unacceptable.

Art. 6: "Law is the expression of the general will," not, however, an expression of human reason in conformity with the divine law.

Art. 10: "Nobody should be harassed for his opinions, even religious ones, provided that their expression does not trouble the public order established by law." In other words, civil freedom of any form of worship, be it true or false, is not disordered and is one of man's sacred rights.

Against these principles *of the new rights of man*, see Leo XIII's encyclical *Immortale Dei*.

In his letter, *De hac declaratione* [(to the Master General of the Marists, on the one hundredth anniversary of their founding)], Benedict XV wrote, on March 7, 1917 (*AAS*, 172): "After those first three centuries near her beginnings, in which the blood of Christians flowed over the whole world's globe, never could one say the Church was in a state of crisis as much as she began to be at the end of the eighteenth century. Indeed, through the work of madly unsound philosophy, fabricated through heretical innovation and treason, spread abroad by foolish minds, there burst forth *that greatest upheaval of things*, touching not only on the aforementioned France but gradually throughout all peoples, so great that *it would have shattered the Christian foundations of society*. For *having publically rejected the authority of the Church*, although it would be the destruction of right and obligation (iuris), of duty and of order in society, whose security and legal claim belongs to religion, it is now pleasing [to the eyes of men] to hold that *power arises from the people and not from God*: all men are equal to each other by nature and therefore are such by right; what anyone would like to do is permitted, so long as it is not prohibited by law; law has no power if it has not been ordered by the multitude; most especially, so long as nobody is harmed, no limits are to be set on freedoms in regard to religious sentiments or in spreading abroad whatever [thoughts] one wishes. Thus, from then on, these come to be held, in general, as the principles on which society rests; however, the fact that this could be harmful to human society, when by them the blind lusts and partisanship come to arm the great multitude of people, never appears more clearly than when they were first declared."

[38] See Augustine, *Ep.* 105 (166), ch. 2, no. 9 (PL, 33, 399). Likewise, see Augustine, *Ep.* 155 (PL, 33, 669); *Contra Cresconium*, 3.51, 57 (PL, 43, 527); *Ep.* 134 (PL, 33, 801); *De civitate Dei*, 5.24 (PL, 41, 171).

[39] Denzinger, no. 874.

[40] See Denzinger, nos. 1214–1272.

[41] See Denzinger, no. 1483. From the condemnation of this proposition, it at least follows that a Catholic state, taking heed of the mores and circumstances of a given era, can legitimately inflict this punishment of death on account of the crime of heresy, following on the Church's

From these various condemnations, the following judgment of the Church is clear: Indifferentism (which is also often called liberalism) is a heresy against the dogma "outside the Catholic Church no salvation is possible for anyone."[42] {{398}} However, liberalism in the form in which it is admitted by Catholic liberals as something distinct from indifferentism, if not a heresy, is a theological error,[43] and it is numbered by Pius IX among those doctrines that, as he himself says, "must be thoroughly held by all the children of the Catholic Church as rejected, proscribed, and condemned."[44] For it is opposed to the necessary and certain application of the principles of faith, nay, of reason.

Art. 2: Proof, by Reason, concerning Individual Men's Duty to Profess Natural Religion (or Religion in General)

§1. Proof of thesis: Individual men have, in the form of a natural duty, a
  moral obligation to profess religion
§2. Corollaries
§3. The specific acts of natural religion[45]

§1. Proof of Thesis: Individual Men Have, in the Form of a Natural Duty, a Moral Obligation to Profess Religion

Earlier (in vol. 1, bk. 1, opening article), we set forth the traditional notion of religion in general, along with the heterodox notions thereof held by sensualists, pantheists, idealists, and agnostics.

As we said there, objectively considered, *religion is the complex of truths and precepts by which our life is ordered to God.* Subjectively considered, it is *the virtue by which man,* knowing that there is some supreme Divinity, *is*

---

judgment of the person's culpability and pertinacity.

  [Trans. note: This volume's translator wishes to note that he distances himself from the most extreme application of the principles being laid out here. However, note also that Fr. Garrigou-Lagrange himself also contextualizes this matter as well.]

[42] See Boniface VIII, *Unam sanctam* (Denzinger, no. 870); Council of Florence, *Cantate Domino* (Denzinger, no. 1351); Pius IX, *Singulari quadam* (Denzinger, 1646 [old numbering]).

[43] See "Libéralisme" in *Dictionnaire apologétique de la foi catholique*, col. 1840.

[44] Pius IX, *Quanta cura*, no. 6 (Denzinger, no. 2896).

[45] Natural religion is not, in fact, a genus, containing supernatural religion as a species, but instead can be treated in a unified manner at once concerning what belongs to it as a genus and as an inferior species [*sed per modum unius tractari potest de genere et de specie inferiori*].

inclined toward worship of him on account of his excellence and rule.

Now, there are two ways for proving our thesis. The first is drawn from the perspective of man's end, directly proving that man stands in need of religion, and indirectly that man is obligated to render worship to God. This opens the way for the second argument, which is drawn from the perspective of God's rights and directly proves this obligation.

Argument One: *Man stands in need of religion in order to achieve his natural end.* The ultimate end to which man is ordered is knowledge of the supreme truth and love of the supreme goodness—namely, God the Author of our nature. Now, in order to arrive at this knowledge and love, man must do what he can so as to truly know God and obey him, and likewise must bear witness to God internally and externally concerning his subjection and love, and religion is precisely this sort of bearing of witness. Therefore, in order to achieve his natural end, man stands in need of religion.

The major premise is easily proven by (a) the nature of intellect and (b) the nature of our will.

(a) *Indeed, the intellect is ordered to knowledge of the truth.* Now, knowledge of the truth that is utterly necessary concerning ourselves and the direction of life is not had unless we know the *first cause* of our nature, *the supreme law* of our moral activity, and *the source of assistance needed* (on account of our weakness) so that we may ceaselessly maintain rectitude of life. And this is knowledge of the supreme truth, namely, God the Author of all beings and the Supreme Lawgiver. {{399}} Therefore, our intellect is naturally ordered to knowledge of God, the Author of our nature, inasmuch as God is knowable from created things.

(b) *Likewise, the will is ordered to love of the true good* known by the intellect. Now, the intellect knows not only particular goods but moreover the universal good, not finding such fullness of the good except in the source of all goods—namely, *in the supreme goodness of God himself.* Therefore, the will is naturally ordered to love God the Author of nature, indeed doing so above all other things. We stretch forth toward stable and perfect beatitude, which cannot be found in created goods, and we already imperfectly enjoy this in the present life when we love God above all things.[46]

Minor premise: Now, in order to arrive at this knowledge and love, man *must* do what he can so as *to truly know God* and *obey* him, and likewise must *bear witness* to God internally and externally concerning his subjection and love.[47] Otherwise, our knowledge of God would remain merely speculative

---

[46] See *ST* I-II, q. 2, a. 8.

[47] The act of the virtue of religion (which is distinct from the acts of the theological virtues,

in nature, having no influence upon our life, and our love of God would be inefficacious, a kind of poetic pleasure concerning the divine goodness, though not bringing forth the means needed for preserving the precepts of the eternal law, nor removing impediments coming from sins.

In addition, secondarily, *we must offer external worship*, for "the human mind stands in need of the educative help of sensible things . . . so that it may be roused to the spiritual acts by which it is joined to God,"[48] for in this life, there is no intellection without us turning toward the phantasms. However, if external worship sometimes degenerates into superstition, this is *per accidens*, on account of men's own wicked dispositions.

Argument Two: *By a natural duty, God is owed internal, external, and social worship.* To the most excellent God, the greatest of all benefactors and the Highest Good, is due testimony of subjection, honor, gratitude, and love. Now, by his very nature, man depends on God (and naturally knows this fact) as Creator and most excellent Lord, by whom he is preserved and aided. Therefore, by a natural duty, man owes to God testimony in the form of subjection, honor, gratitude, and love—and this is divine worship.

Regarding the major premise: *Subjection or service is owed to a lord*; thus, "it is necessary that wherever we find a proper and specific notion of lordship, there is a proper and specific notion of servitude. . . . And such service (in relation to God) is designated by the term 'worship' [*latria*] by the Greeks."[49] "*However, honor is owed to someone on account of his excellence.* Now, a singular form of excellence belongs to God, inasmuch as He transcends all things through an excess holding true in all possible ways. Whence, a special form of honor is owed to Him,"[50] as well as reverence, to which *adoration* [*adoratio*] is ordered.[51] *Gratitude* is owed on account of one's beneficence, and thus is thanksgiving owed to God. Finally, *a devout[52] declaration of love* is owed to the Highest Good, and man is naturally inclined to love God above all things, "for otherwise, if he naturally loved himself more than God, it would follow that his natural love would be perverse and destroyed, not perfected, by charity."[53]

---

which are immediately concerned with God himself) properly consists in this sort of bearing witness. See *ST* II-II, q. 81.

[48] *ST* II-II, q. 81, a. 7.
[49] *ST* II-II, q. 81, a. 1, ad 3.
[50] *ST* II-II, q. 81, a. 4.
[51] See *ST* II-II, q. 84, a. 2.
[52] See *ST* II-II, q. 82.
[53] See *ST* I, q. 60, a. 5; *ST* II-II, q. 26, a. 3.

{{400}} And not only is internal worship owed to God but also *external worship*, for God is the Author not only of our soul but also of our body, and as such is to be glorified through external worship. Moreover, if internal worship is sincere, it necessarily must be expressed through deeds, words, and other external actions, by which internal devotion is increased.

Finally, *social worship* is owed to God because he is the Creator and Benefactor of human society, just as he is of any individual in particular. Therefore, society, as such, must acknowledge God as the Supreme Lord and must present him with worship. Otherwise, the people would not fear God and would despise social authority, soon leading to the overthrow of all things.

Because worship is properly *owed* to God, the virtue of religion is said to be a part of justice, or a virtue connected to justice.[54]

Objection: Indifferentists say *God does not need services rendered by creatures*. Therefore, the duties of religion are empty vanities. This objection is proposed by St. Thomas in the following way: "In those things which done by men, something seems to be all the more praiseworthy to the degree that there is a greater need that it be done. However, God has no need of anything which would be done for Him by us. Therefore, the virtue of religion seems to be less praiseworthy than the other virtues by which one comes to the aid of men."

Response: St. Thomas himself answers this objection: "In those things that are done for others for their own use, greater praise is owed to that action which is done for one in greater need, for it is of greater use. However, something is not done for God for the sake of giving Him something of use but, rather, *on account of His glory and for our use.*"[55]

Therefore, the objection presupposes the false premise posited by utilitarianism, which holds that something is good and to be done not because it is befitting but, rather, because it is useful. However, the reduction of the fitting good to the useful good represents the destruction of the whole of moral obligation, which is not founded in usefulness but, rather, in right. Therefore, the vacuity of this objection is quite clear before the bar of common sense, for if it were true, it would be true to say that a wealthy man does not need to be repaid by me, so therefore I will not repay him, for repayment is vain. Likewise, one could say that a benefactor does not need my gratitude, and therefore gratitude is vain; likewise, my father does not need my reverence, so therefore, it is not owed to him.

The point will be urged: However, God was not able to make all things for the sake of his own glory, for *this would be a form of divine egoism*. Instead, he created us solely for our own happiness. Such was the position held by Kant, Hermes, and Günther.

Response: This would be a form of egoism if God were not identical with the Highest

---

[54] See *ST* II-II, q. 80.

[55] *ST* II-II, q. 81, a. 6, ad 2.

Good, but, in reality, he is goodness itself, and if he did not do all things *for the manifestation of his goodness* (that is, for his glory), then he would not have ordered all things to the highest good but, rather, to some particular good, which would involve some form of sin on God's part (in other words, the greatest of absurdity) and the destruction of our own felicity.

Further urging: The characteristic property of egoism is that one subordinates all persons to oneself, as though all things were slaves and things to be used. However, God would act in this way if he were to have made all things for the sake of his own glory.

Response: This would be the case if men were not perfected and themselves glorified through this subordination to God.[56] Nevertheless, it is much more glorious for us to exist for the sake of God's glory than merely for the sake of our own felicity. {{401}} "However, on account of the fact that we revere and honor God, our mind is subjected to him, and its perfection consists in this. *For anything is perfected through the fact that it is subjected to its superior*, just as the body is perfected by the fact that it is vivified by soul, and the air through the fact that it is illuminated by the sun."[57] Hence, it is said in Psalm 113:9 (DR): "Not to us, O Lord, not to us; but to thy name give glory."

§2. Corollaries

(1) **Duties toward God are of central importance and primary.** This is proven in three ways: (a) on account of God's rights, (b) on account of man's dependence [upon God], and (c) on account of man's own final end.

(a) Primary and centrally important duties are those that *are immediately founded upon a supreme right*. Now, the rights of God, the First Cause, Supreme Lord, and Lawgiver, are the supreme rights, in which religious duties find their immediate foundation. Therefore, [they are primary and centrally important.]

(b) That which is *first in man is the fact that he is a creature* that is dependent upon God, the Supreme Lord. Now, our first and supreme duty is taken from that which is first in man. Therefore, [our first and supreme duty exists in relation to God.]

(c) First and centrally important duties are those that *are concerned with the ultimate end* or with means that are closely related to this end, for the end is prior in the order of intention. Now, religious duties are concerned with either the ultimate end itself (such as to know and love God) or with means that are closely related to this end (such as to serve God through the worship

---

[56] See *ST* I, q. 96, a. 4. What does it mean to be dominated by someone not as a slave but as a free man? It is to love him not for his own use but, rather, for his own good and for the common good.

[57] *ST* II-II, q. 81, a. 7.

that is owed to him). Hence, the theological virtues (which are specified by God himself) and, immediately below them, the virtue of religion (which is specified by divine worship) are superior virtues, for religion is loftier than the other moral virtues like justice, courage, and temperance, which are not immediately ordered to the divine honor.[58]

(2) *Duties toward God are the foundation for all other duties.*[59] This is proven in two ways: (a) from the perspective of the divine rights; and (b) from the perspective of our end.

(a) In the subordination of duties, once one does away with the primary duty, which *is founded upon the supreme right*, all other duties are done away with. Now, religious duties are primary duties. Therefore, [if they are done away with, all others are as well.]

(b) In the subordination of duties, once one does away with the first, which *is concerned with the ultimate end* to be sought out, all others are done away with too. Now, the duties of religion are concerned with the ultimate end, or with those means that are more closely tied to this end. Therefore, [once they are done away with, all the others are too.] Nay, man's true *rights* find their source in their duties owed to God.[60]

Objection: However, someone who doubts the existence of God still preserves the notion of obligation toward other men.

{{402}} *Response*: If we were to, *per impossibile*, do away with God's rights, all correlative rights and duties would be destroyed. However, once we do away with the knowledge of God's rights, we do away with *the ultimate foundation* of all duties, though someone can consider solely the *proximate foundation* for our obligation to others (namely, our neighbors' own rights). In that case, one will not form for oneself a full notion of moral obligation, which is founded on the eternal law.[61] Indeed, we are properly obligated to do

---

[58] See *ST* II-II, q. 81, a. 5 and 6.

[59] See Zigliara, *Summa philosophica*, vol. 3, 130 and 138.

[60] On Feb. 16, 1892, in his encyclical *Au milieu des sollicitudes*, Leo XIII wrote: "As soon as the State refuses to give to God what belongs to God, by a necessary consequence it refuses to give to citizens that to which, as men, they have a right; as, whether agreeable or not to accept, it cannot be denied that *man's true rights spring from his duty toward God*. Whence it follows that the State, by missing in this connection the principal object of its institution, finally becomes false to itself by denying that which is the reason of its own existence. These superior truths are so clearly proclaimed by the voice of even natural reason, that they force themselves upon all who are not blinded by the violence of passion."

[61] See Leonard Lehu, *Philosophia moralis et socialis* (Paris: LeCoffre, 1914), 250: "The *proximate* foundation of obligation is the essential order of things; however, this only is so as a second cause that is dependent upon the first cause. . . . The *ultimate* foundation of obligation is not something differing from God Himself but, rather, is the eternal law."

good and flee from evil, not on account of the *passive* ordering of our nature and will to the fitting good but, rather, on account of the *active* ordering by which God makes our nature and will for the sake of performing the moral good, and he has a completely strict right to be obeyed. For moral obligation is founded on a loftier right, and hence, God himself is not bound by obligation, though he himself must act wisely and cannot sin, for he is wisdom and holiness itself. Idealistic pantheists speak about man himself in terms that in fact only hold true for God: Man is not subject to obligation but, rather, owes it to himself that he act in accord with right reason. They do not heed the fact that our right reason is only a second cause, which does not obligate "except in virtue of the first cause. Now, the fact that human reason is a rule of the human will, by which its goodness is measured, is something that it holds from the eternal law, which is the divine reason."[62] Hence, the following proposition is condemned in the *Syllabus of Errors*: "Moral law needs no divine sanction, and there is not the least need that human laws conform to the natural law or *receive their obligatory force from God.*"[63]

§3. The Specific Acts of Natural Religion

These acts are most especially prayer and sacrifice. In *ST* II-II, q. 85, a. 1, St. Thomas teaches *that the offering of sacrifice pertains to the natural law* [*ius naturale*]. He says:

> Looking on the defects which man perceives in himself, seeing that he needs help and direction from someone above himself, natural reason declares to man that he is subject to some superior being, and whatever this superior being may be, all know it by using the name "God." However, just as in the case of natural beings, the lower are naturally subject to the higher, natural reason, in accordance with man's natural inclination, declares that he should render

---

[Trans. note: However, out of deference to Fr. Lehu, the present translator must note that he is very clear also about the rule of *reason* as the proximate measure (through prudence) of the moral act, though obviously grounded on the essential order of things. This topic engaged him in a profound and important debate against Fr. Edmund Elter, S.J., and Dom Odo Lottin, OSB. See Lehu, *Philosophia moralis et socialis*, 72–166; *La raison: Règle de la moralité d'après Saint Thomas* (Paris: Lecoffre, 1930). For a clear summary of the whole controversy, see Ludovicus N. Hamel, "Controversia Lehu-Elter, Lottin circa regulam moralitatis secundum S. Thomam," *Antonianum* 7 (1932): 377-384.]

62 *ST* I-II, q. 19, a. 4.

63 Pius IX, *Syllabus of Errors*, no. 56 (Denzinger, no. 2956).

submission and honor, in his own particular manner as a man, to that which is above himself. Now, in a way that is befitting to his nature, man should make use of sensible signs in order to signify anything, for his knowledge is drawn from things known through the senses. Therefore, natural reason declares that man should use some kinds of sensible things, offering them to God as signs of the subjection and honor owed to him, like those who make certain offerings to their lord in recognition of his authority. Now, this pertains to the formal character of what a sacrifice is, and hence, the offering of sacrifice belongs to the natural law [*ius naturale*].

The same must be said concerning the sacrifice of expiation required following upon sin, for by a strict right, reparation is owed to every case of injustice, indeed all the more strictly so to the degree that the right violated is more sacred in nature. Now, an offence inflicted against God by men is most wrong in character. Therefore, following upon sin, which is a kind of turning away from God, reparation is owed to God in the form of an expiatory sacrifice.

Confirmation: What is common among all seems natural. {{403}} Now, in all the world's ages, and in all given nations of men, there forever has been some kind of offering of sacrifice. Therefore, [it is something owed to God].

However, the offering of sacrifice is not among the first principles of the natural law [*ius naturale*] but, rather, among the secondary, because it proceeds from a number of premises. Hence, nothing forbids that this right could be unknown by certain people. Moreover, no matter how natural reason may declare, in general, that sacrifice is to be offered, nonetheless, it does not say that it should be done in this or that way. This depends either on a choice made by men or on some positive determination made by God. Finally, all men are bound to perform an internal sacrifice, for all are bound to offer their minds devoutly to God and to be joined to him through love. However, all are also bound to external sacrifice, which is a sacrifice properly so-called, though not *per se* (for not all are priests) but *per se* or *per alios*, through others, so that sacrifice is offered for all in every community.[64]

Is prayer something belonging to the natural law [de iure naturae]? The response here is the same as what we said for the case of sacrifice, which implies prayer. Indeed, the same principle holds here: Looking on the defects which man perceives in himself, seeing that he needs help and direction from someone above him, natural reason declares to man that he is subject to some superior being, and whatever this superior being may be, all know it

---

[64] See *ST* II-II, q. 85, a. 4.

by using the name "God." Moreover, prayer is found among all men.

Some *object*: God gives us the aid that we need, even if we do not ask for it. Now, the divine aid belonging to the natural order is not something free after the manner of grace but, rather, is something that is owed to us. Therefore, prayer is not necessary in the natural order.

Response: (1) Although God's aid is necessary for us, these various aids are gifts from God and are known by us as being such. Hence, it is fitting that we seek even necessary things from God. (2) In the natural order, the divine aid for doing the moral good and conquering inordinate passions is owed to human nature in general, but not to this man rather than to that man, for, according to the common laws of providence, God sometimes permits the human will, which, of itself, is able to fail, actually to fail. Hence, in relation to this or that particular man, the divine aid for doing the natural moral good can and must in some sense be said to be freely given.

The solution to the other objections against the use and efficacy of prayer do not *per se* exceed the powers of reason, but this solution becomes much clearer and more certain following on revelation. See *ST* II-II, q. 83, a. 2: From all eternity, divine providence has looked upon all things, and by it "not only are all effects that will take place disposed but even the causes by which they will be done, as well as the order in which they will be done." However, among other causes there is numbered prayer, which is foreseen and willed by God from eternity. Therefore, it is useful and befitting that men pray, not indeed so that through our prayers "we would change the divine disposition of things (for it is unchanging) but, rather, so that we may ask that which God has disposed might be fulfilled through our prayers, namely 'that by asking, men may deserve to receive what the Almighty, from all eternity, disposed to give, as Gregory the Great said in *Dialogue*, 1.8,'" as St. Thomas says in the same text.

What we have said suffices with regard to religion in general, as well as the acts of religion that belong to the natural law [*ex iure naturae*].

ART. 3: PROOF, BY REASON, CONCERNING ANY GIVEN PERSON'S DUTY TO RECEIVE DIVINE REVELATION THAT HAS BEEN SUFFICIENTLY PROPOSED, OR THEIR DUTY TO INVESTIGATE INTO THIS MATTER

§1. Proof from God's rights {{404}}

§2. Proof from man's end

§3. First corollary: Concerning the grave obligation to investigate into divine revelation when there already is at hand a serious probability that it exists

§4. Second corollary: No salvation outside the Church

§5. Resolution of objections

§1. Proof from God's Rights

This proof is set forth by the [First] Vatican Council, against the principle of the absolute autonomy of reason and the human will, holding that "human reason is so independent that faith cannot be enjoined upon it."[65] As the Council says: "Since man is totally dependent upon God, as upon his Creator and Lord, and since created reason is absolutely subject to uncreated truth, we are bound to yield by faith the full homage of intellect and will to the God who reveals."[66]

This provides us with the following argument. By the natural law [*iure naturae*], *created reason* is subject to God as to the *Creator, Lord, and Uncreated Truth* and is *bound to offer service* to him. Now, revelation that has been sufficiently proposed seems to proceed from God the Creator, Lord, and Uncreated Truth. Therefore, created reason, by the natural law [*iure naturae*], is bound to offer him service, once man has received revelation that has been sufficiently proposed. Indeed, this is not only owed to God as Lord in the form of a service of the will (or obedience) but, moreover, is owed to him as to the Uncreated Truth, for we owe him the service of our intellect through the intellectual adherence of faith.

Hence, he who refuses to receive divine revelation that has been sufficiently proposed to him acts against the natural law [*ius naturae*] and does injustice to God, as though such a person were to say, "In revealing, God can deceive or be deceived," or "I am not bound to be subject to God." This is a form of positive and freely willed infidelity, which is an act elicited by the intellect and commanded by the will out of pride. However, an injustice is all the graver to the degree that the right of the lord in question is holy and absolute.

And let it not be said that, because the obligation to receive the divine revelation is supernatural and not natural, infidelity is not *contrary to the natural law* [*ius naturae*]. Indeed, as St. Thomas responds: "To have faith is not something falling to human nature. However, it is befitting to human nature that man's mind not oppose the interior instinct [of grace] and external preaching of the truth. Whence, infidelity is opposed to nature in this respect."[67] Thus, he who *directly* transgresses the supernatural law *indirectly* transgresses the natural law.[68]

{{405}} Hence, Christ the Lord said: "Go ye into the whole world and

---

[65] [First] Vatican Council, *Dei filius*, can. 3.1 (Denzinger, no. 3031).

[66] Ibid., ch. 3 (Denzinger, no. 3008).

[67] *ST* II-II, q. 10, a. 1, ad 1.

[68] See Leo XIII, *Libertas*, 227 [cf. nos. 8–9, 17, 20].

preach the Gospel to every creature. He that believeth and is baptized shall be saved: *but he that believeth not shall be condemned.*"[69] Now, some say, "These words are hard," and think that the idea of eternal punishment is something unjust and utterly unworthy of God. However, these are frequently the same people who, seeing the most manifest of miracles (e.g., in the sanctuary of Our Lady of Lourdes[70]), do not wish to admit the divine origin of these signs and say that they are produced by unknown natural powers, just as the Pharisees said of Christ: "By the prince of devils he casteth out devils."[71] However, those who judge matters this way quite clearly do injustice to God and render judgment on themselves, as the Lord said: "He that believeth in him is not judged. *But he that doth not believe is already judged.*"[72] Nay, we must keep in mind Christ's words to the Pharisees, who attributed to the prince of demons the manifest works of the Holy Spirit: "But he that shall blaspheme against the Holy Ghost, shall never have forgiveness, but shall be guilty of an everlasting sin."[73] That is, he who speaks against the Holy Spirit when he performs a manifest miracle has no excuse, nor reason for pardon, and hence does not have, in his own power, the ability to be healed. And if he does happen to be healed thereafter, this will only be because of an entirely gratuitous offering of divine assistance.[74]

§2. Proof from Man's End

By the natural law, man is bound to efficaciously stretch out toward his ultimate end, in which he finds his beatitude. Now, without accepting divine revelation that has been sufficiently proposed, man cannot efficaciously tend toward his ultimate end but, on the contrary, *most greatly distances himself from it through infidelity.* Therefore, man is bound by the natural law [iure naturae] to receive divine revelation when it is sufficiently proposed, for it is the way toward his beatitude.

Major premise. The natural law *directly* commands that we stretch forth toward our natural end, which in particular consists in perfect knowledge of God on the basis of our knowledge of creatures and in natural love of God

---

[69] Mark 16:15–16 (DR).
[70] See vol. 2, ch. 10, a. 3 above. Some of these unbelieving people say, "These signs are not *sufficiently extraordinary*"; others, however, who know of them on the basis of others' testimony, assert, "They are *too extraordinary* for their existence to be admitted."
[71] Mark 3:22 (DR). Also see Matt 2:24–32; Luke 1:15ff.
[72] John 3:18 (DR).
[73] Mark 3:29 (DR). See Matt 12:31; Luke 12:10.
[74] See St. Thomas's commentary on Matt 12:31.

above all. However, the natural law also *indirectly* commands us to tend to the supernatural end, inasmuch as it orders us to be obedient to any legitimately commanding superior, especially God, who can give positive precepts for arriving at the supernatural end.

Minor premise. This is proven in our thesis concerning the necessity of revelation, for revelation is morally necessary in order for us to have firm, unencumbered, error-free knowledge of all the natural truths of religion, and is necessary without qualification for knowledge of the supernatural end, in the attainment of which is found our salvation. Hence, he who refuses to receive divine revelation that has been sufficiently proposed most greatly draws back from his ultimate end, for he cannot indeed have saving knowledge of God, nor, *a fortiori*, love for him.[75]

Now, speaking *per se*, as we did earlier,[76] the speculative judgment of credibility, as well as the speculatively-practical judgment of credentity (or that of the obligation to believe), can be had without grace, although ordinarily grace concurs with it. {{406}} Nay, sometimes it is had with absolute resistance to the grace of faith, as in the formal sin of positive infidelity committed in full awareness. Hence, Christ said of the Pharisees: "If I had not done among them the works that no other man hath done, they would not have sin: but now they have both seen and hated both me and my Father."[77]

However, the ultimate practically-practical judgment of credentity (namely, "here and now, I must believe this; it is good to believe") is essentially supernatural, for it represents the fittingness of the act of faith and of the good promised to those who believe, not only in the abstract but also in the concrete, *for me here and now*, and this presupposes that, under the influence of actual grace, my will is already inchoately moved to supernatural things to be believed.[78]

§3. First Corollary: Concerning the Grave Obligation to Investigate into Divine Revelation When There Already Is at Hand a Serious Probability That It Exists

(1) *From the perspective of God's rights.* Created reason is bound, by the natural law [*iure naturae*], to hold in the greatest reverence that which is taught by God, if something is taught by him. However, he who refuses to

---

[75] See *ST* II-II, q. 10, a. 3.

[76] See bk. 1, ch. 15, art. 3, §2.

[77] John 15:24 (DR); likewise, see Acts 4:16.

[78] See vol. 1, ch. 15, a. 3.

investigate into divine revelation, when he already sees that there is a serious probability that it may exist, does not revere the divine words. Therefore, this represents an action that is contrary to the natural law, at least indirectly, one doing injustice to God, as though one were to say the divine words are a trifling affair. This is positive infidelity that is at least indirectly willed, given one's voluntary negligence in inquiring into the true faith, for then the ignorance in question is not invincible but, rather, is culpable.

(2) *From the perspective of man's end.* When one is in doubt concerning the means that are necessary for salvation, *the safer path must be taken*; there cannot be too much security when eternity is at risk. Now, the Christian faith is proposed as being the means necessary for salvation, for it is said that "he who does not believe will be condemned,"[79] and "without faith it is impossible to please God."[80] Therefore, so long as doubt or probability remains concerning the divine origin of this faith, the safer path must be taken. In other words, it is necessary that, under pain of mortal sin [*sub gravi*], one must inquire further and also pray, to the degree that one knows of the fittingness of prayer. To deliberately and obstinately neglect such a means is utterly rash, since one would thus incur peril of eternal damnation. As Billuart wrote, "In such doubt, the nonbeliever is bound, under pain of mortal sin, to diligently inquire into the truth, for otherwise his ignorance of the true faith will be voluntary and culpable for him. No doubt, many heretics find themselves in this condition, especially those who live among Catholics."[81] Hence, the following proposition has been condemned: "An infidel who does not believe will be excused of infidelity, since he is guided by a less probable opinion."[82]

§4. Second Corollary: No Salvation Outside the Church

Now,[83] because all are bound to receive divine revelation when it has been sufficiently proposed to them, all have a grave [*gravis*] obligation [i.e., under pain of mortal sin] to enter the Catholic Church, for as is historically clear, Jesus Christ, sent by God, established the Catholic Church, which is

---

[79] Mark 16:16.
[80] Heb 11:6.
[81] Billuart, *Summa sancti Thomae, De fide*, diss. 3, a. 3, §2.
[82] Innocent XI, Decree of the Holy Office (March 2, 1679) against the "Laxists," no. 4 (Denzinger, no. 2104).
[83] See St. Thomas *In I Decretalem*, ch. 3; Tommaso Maria Zigliara, *Propaedeutica*, bk. 4, ch. 12; Edmund Dublanchy, *De axiomate: Extra ecclesiam nulla salus* (1895); Édouard Hugon, *Hors de l'Église point de salut* (1907).

discernable by her own proper notes, as the rule of faith.

{{407}} Indeed, on pain of damnation, Christ commands that all men, as a matter of doctrine, must accept the laws and sacraments from the body of apostles: "Preach the gospel to every creature. He that believeth and is baptized shall be saved: *but he that believeth not shall be condemned. . . .* Going therefore, teach ye all nations. . . . Teaching them to observe *all things whatsoever I have commanded you.*"[84] Likewise, the whole of the tradition affirms that salvation does not exist outside of the Church.[85]

Those who belong to the body of the Church are the baptized who externally profess the Catholic teaching, under the magisterium of the Roman Pontiff, in communion with the faithful. However, *those who belong to the soul of the Church* are all men who have internal faith and charity.[86]

Hence, he who culpably remains outside of the body of the Church to the end of his life will not be saved. Now, he is culpable who, faced with serious doubt concerning the matter, does not seek after the truth; and this holds, *a fortiori,* for him who knowingly and willingly does not enter the Church, which he acknowledges to be true.

However, he who *inculpably* remains outside of the body of the Church can be saved as long as he has faith and charity, or perfect contrition, and belongs to the soul of the Church.[87]

---

[84] Mark 16:15–16 (DR) and Matt 28:19–20 (DR). See Matt 10:14–15, 40; 18:17; Luke 10:16.

[85] One can cite, above all, the following. St. Ignatius of Antioch, to the Philadelphians, ch. 3: "Indeed, whoever belongs to God and to Jesus Christ are themselves *with the bishop*; and whoever returns, through repentance, to the unity of the Church shall themselves belong to God and live in accord with Jesus Christ." St. Irenaeus, likewise affirms this and adds, in *Adv. haeres.*, bk. 4, ch. 33 (PG 7, col. 1077): "The truly spiritual disciple, receiving the spirit of God, judges all things . . . and likewise will judge all those who are *outside of the truth*, that is, who are *outside of the Church.*" In his own terms, Origen expresses the axiom thus: "Therefore, let nobody persuade himself, nor deceive himself: outside of this house, that is, *outside of the Church, none are saved*" (Hom. III on Joshua, no. 5, PG, 12, 841–842). St. Cyprian says in *De unitate ecclesiae*, no. 6 (PL 4, 503): "He who does not have the Church as his mother cannot have God as his father." And finally, St. Augustine says in *De baptismo*, bk. 4, ch. 17 (PL 43, 170): "There is no salvation outside of the Church. Who denies this? And therefore, whoever is outside of the Church does not have salvation."

[86] [Trans. note: The language of soul and body are being used a bit loosely here, and while they are somewhat classical in post-Reformation theology, they must be understood in line with what is said from the time of Pius XII's encyclical *Mystici corporis*.]

[87] Hence, in the case of those who have heard nothing concerning the true faith and are invincibly ignorant of it, there is only merely negative infidelity, and as St. Thomas says, "This does not have the formal character of sin but, rather, of punishment, for such ignorance of divine things followed upon the sin of our first parents. However, those who are unfaithful in this way (and die in such infidelity) are indeed condemned on account of other sins which cannot be remitted without faith. However, they are not condemned on account of the sin of infidel-

Therefore, it is necessary, with a necessity of means for salvation, (1) to *really* belong to the soul of the Church, and (2) to belong to the body of the Church—for adults *in reality* or *in voto* (that is, through an implicit desire) and for children *in reality*.[88] For adults, to belong to the body of the Church is also something necessary with a necessity of precept.[89] However, this obligation does not diminish true freedom. On the contrary, by traveling upon this path, as St. Paul says, "the creature also itself shall be delivered from the servitude of corruption, into the liberty of the glory of the children of God."[90]

{{408}} And Pius IX taught: "By all means, however, it must be held, *de fide*, that outside of the Apostolic Roman Church, nobody can be saved, that it is the true arc of salvation, and that anyone who does not enter into her will perish in the flood waters. Nonetheless, one must hold that it is equally certain that he who labors in ignorance of the true religion, if such ignorance be invincible, is not bound by fault before the eyes of God."[91] And the same pope wrote in another encyclical:

> We know as well as you that those who suffer from invincible ignorance with regard to our most holy religion, by carefully keeping the natural law and its precepts, which have been written by God in the hearts of all, by being disposed to obey God and to lead a virtuous and correct life, can, *by the power of divine light and grace*, attain eternal life. For God, who sees, examines, and knows completely the minds and souls, the thoughts and qualities of all, will not permit, in His infinite goodness and mercy, anyone who is not guilty of a voluntary fault to suffer eternal punishment. However, also well-known is the Catholic dogma that no one can be saved outside the Catholic Church and that those who obstinately oppose the authority of the Church . . . and stubbornly remain separated . . . cannot obtain salvation. . . . But, God forbid that the children of the Catholic Church should in any way at all be unfriendly to those who are not at all joined to us by the same bonds of faith and charity. Nay, . . . let them ever be ready to aid them and, above all, . . . let them strive to bring them back to Catholic truth and to their most loving mother, the Church.[92]

---

ity" (*ST* II-II, q. 10, a. 1). Thus, the following proposition of Baius was condemned: "Purely negative infidelity in those among whom Christ has been preached is a sin" (St. Pius V, *Ex omnibus afflictionibus*, no. 68; Denzinger, no. 1968).

[88] Namely, through a valid baptism, which is conferred *per se* by the true Church, though *per accidens* by a sect inasmuch as the person baptizing wishes to do what the Church intends.

[89] See *ST* III, q. 68, a. 1 and 2.

[90] Rom 8:21 (DR).

[91] Pius IX, *Singulari quadam* (Denzinger, no. 1647 [old numbering]).

[92] Pius IX, *Quanto conficiamur moerore*, nos. 7 and 8 (Denzinger, nos. 1677ff [old numbering]).

§5. *Resolution of Objections*

Three series of objections can be distinguished: (A) those based on the principles of indifferentism; (B) those based upon the autonomy of reason; and (C) those based on the supernaturality of the act of faith.

A. *Objections based on the principles of indifferentism*

1. *Objection*: Anything that is true and befitting must be admitted. Now, in all religions something true and befitting can be found. Therefore, in order to preserve equity, all religions must be more or less admitted, even though Christianity is better and livelier than they.

Response: I make a distinction regarding the major premise. I concede that whatever is *true and good, without qualification*, must be admitted. However, I deny that we must admit that which is *true and good only in a qualified sense* (that is, from some given, accidental perspective) while being false and evil in an unqualified sense. I contradistinguish the minor premise in the same way. Indeed, as St. Thomas says:

> As the good is related to things, so is truth related to knowledge. Now, it is impossible to find something in things which would be completely deprived of goodness.[93] Hence, it likewise is impossible, for any form of knowledge to be completely false, without some mingling with the truth. . . . Whence, the teaching of the demons themselves, by which they instruct their prophets, contains some form of truth, by which it is rendered acceptable. Indeed, thus is the intellect led astray through an apparent truth, just as the will is led astray to evil through the appearance of goodness.[94]

Even in the Hegelian denial of the principle of contradiction there is a kind of apparent truth, inasmuch as that which undergoes becoming in a certain sense is and in a certain sense is not. Hence, those things that are false, without qualification, can be true in a qualified sense, at least in appearance. And *in a doctrine that is, without qualification, false, the truth is not found as the soul of that doctrine but, rather, as a servant of error.* Hence, in order to preserve equity, we do not need to consider Catholicism and Protestantism with equanimity. Nay, in order to profoundly know what is good, it is fitting that we love it, just as in order to perfectly know something evil that is opposed to holiness, it is necessary that we hate it, as do God and the saints. But this is not in any way opposed to scientific [*sic*] serenity. No, on the contrary, utter hatred of evil frees one from inordinate passions and prejudices.

---

[93] See *ST* I, q. 48, a. 4; q. 5, a. 1, ad 1. At least the subject in which this evil is found remains, as in the case of blindness in animals.

[94] *ST* II-II, q. 172, a. 6.

2. *Yet it will be insisted*: However, those things that are not essentially contradictory or contrary can be true at one and the same time. {{409}} Now, various religions are not essentially contradictory or [*seu*] contrary. Therefore, they can be simultaneously true, as are the various states of religious life in the Catholic Church.

Response: *There are many forms of contradiction and contrariety between the various religions.* (a) First of all, this is so *in relation to truths to be believed*, as between polytheism, pantheism, and monotheism. Moreover, it is found inasmuch as Christianity admits the divinity of Jesus Christ, something rejected by Judaism and Islam. Indeed, we find this where the infallibility of the Catholic Church is acknowledged and, on the contrary, denied by Protestants. (b) *As regards the precepts*, polygamy and divorce, which are permitted in many religions and prohibited in others, cannot be simultaneously licit and illicit in one and the same circumstances. (c) *In relation to worship*, some are pure and befitting, whereas others are intrinsically inhuman and wanton. It is unjust to say to God that all religions respect God in equal manners when one of them teaches what is true and another what is false, when one promotes what is good and another what is evil. This is the same as saying that God is indifferent concerning truth and falsity, as well as concerning what is morally befitting and what is not befitting.

3. *Still, one further point*: But the true religion cannot be discerned unless some religion is already admitted as a norm. Now, this involves a begging of the question (*petitio principii*).

Response: I deny the major premise. It is discerned on the basis of naturally known principles, inasmuch as the true religion cannot be contrary to reason and contrary to morality but, rather, must be in line with the loftier aspirations of our nature—nay, it must be an efficacious principle of the moral life and confirmed by divine signs.

B. *Objections based on the autonomy of reason*

First objection: Servitude is opposed to the autonomy of reason. Now, in believing, the intellect is reduced to servitude, as is said by St. Paul, "bringing into captivity every understanding unto the obedience of Christ" (2 Cor 10:5, DR). Therefore, the obedience of faith is contrary to the autonomy of reason.

Response: I make a distinction regarding the major premise. I concede that blind servitude, under the prejudice of errors, is opposed to the autonomy of reason in this way. However, I make a sub-distinction regarding the claim that the servitude (or obedience [*obsequium*]) that is obviously owed to the Uncreated Truth is opposed to the autonomy of reason. I concede that this is opposed to *an autonomy of insubordination*; however, I deny that it is opposed to *a legitimate and subordinate autonomy*. Hence, as St. Thomas says, "Inasmuch as infidelity is a sin, it is born of pride, whence man does not wish to subject his intellect to the rules of faith."[95] Nay, this blessed captivity, spoken of by St. Paul in the text cited above, is the beginning of a loftier freedom of spirit, which is found

---

[95] *ST* II-II, q. 10, a. 1, ad 3.

above inordinate passions and erroneous prejudices, in supernatural contemplation of the infinite truth. Hence, Christ said, "The truth will set you free."

2. *It will be insisted, however*: To serve God is nothing other than to obey God. Now, obedience pertains to the will and not to the intellect. Therefore, man is bound to bring forward obedience [*obsequium*] of will, not of intellect.

Response: "*Obedience* is said in two different ways. Sometimes, it includes an inclination of will for fulfilling the divine commands. And in this way, it is not a specific virtue but, rather, is included in a general manner in every virtue, for all the virtues fall under the precepts of the divine law. And in this way, obedience is required for faith. Obedience can be understood in another way . . . as a specific virtue which is part of the virtue of justice, which renders to a superior that which is due. . . . And in this way, obedience comes after faith."[96]

3. *Yet the point will be urged*: Nonetheless, the intellect cannot serve God except by judging him in accord with the evidence of truth. Now, faith requires that one have a firm judgment without evidence of the truth thus affirmed. Therefore, the intellect is not bound to the obedience [*obsequium*] of faith.

{{410}} *Response*: There is the evidence of credibility, which is extrinsic, and intrinsic evidence concerning the thing believed in is not required, for this is what distinguishes faith from science.

4. *It is, however, insisted*: Nonetheless, the *speculative* intellect can only affirm something on account of the intrinsic evidence of the thing thus affirmed. Now, the evidence of credibility is extrinsic. Therefore, so long as the evidence of credibility remains, there is no obligation to speculatively admit the revealed mysteries but instead only a *practical* requirement to do so. Thus, the modernists said: "The dogmas of the faith are to be held only according to their practical sense; that is to say, as preceptive norms of conduct and not as norms of believing."[97]

Response: I make a distinction regarding the major premise. I will let the point pass regarding *a scientific assent*. However, I deny it *for the assent of faith*. Thus, on the authority of a qualified teacher, the speculative intellect of a student affirms the truth of doctrines that are not directly ordered to action [*praxim*] and do not pertain to the practical intellect. However, the Uncreated Truth, which is the primary object of faith, is not an object that directly pertains to activity [*operabile*] but, rather, is an object of contemplation.[98] [Thus, the assent involved here also is not something merely limited to praxis.]

5. *Yet, pushing on*: Nonetheless, the speculative intellect cannot affirm something *with utter firmness* solely on account of the authority of a teacher.

Response: I concede this for the case of a human teacher. I deny it for the case of a

---

96 *ST* II-II, q. 4, a. 7, ad 4.
97 Pius X, Decree of the Holy Office, *Lamentabili*, no. 26 (Denzinger, no. 3426).
98 See St. Thomas, *De veritate*, q. 14, a. 5.

divine teacher, along with the assistance of grace within the soul.

6. *Objection*: Finally, immanentists object that revelation is *a free gift from God*, which is not necessary for the natural development of our faculties. Therefore, it can be spurned like a useless title of nobility.

Response: Revelation is indeed a grace, in the sense that God is not bound to reveal something to us. However, faith is *obligatory* if God wills it, and he obviously has the right to impose positive commands upon man. Moreover, revelation is morally necessary in order for us to know all the natural truths of religion and in order to rightly set up our life. Nay, once we presuppose man's elevation to his supernatural end, it is strictly necessary. This elevation is the highest of nobilities that could be given, and it must be received with the greatest gratitude.

C. *Objections based on the supernaturality of the act of faith*

1. *Objection*: The duty to fulfill a supernatural act does not belong to the natural law [*iure naturae*]. Now, the act of faith (or of receiving divine revelation, as is necessary for salvation) is a supernatural act. Therefore, the duty to receive divine revelation is not something belonging to the natural law [*iure naturae*] and is not commanded by the natural law.

Response: It is not *directly and immediately* commanded by the natural law but, rather, is *indirectly and mediately* (or hypothetically) commanded, for the natural law obligates one to obey a superior who legitimately commands something, especially God.

2. *It will be insisted, however*: Neither is this obligation founded upon the natural law. For this duty is known after revelation only through the judgment of credentity. Now, this judgment is substantially supernatural, (*quoad substantiam*), as is the pious affect of belief [*pius credulitatis affectus*—that is, the movement of will that accompanies the supernatural act of faith, in distinction from the motions of the will pertaining to supernatural hope and charity]. Therefore, this obligation, even when revelation has been proposed in a sufficient manner, is not naturally known.

Response: The speculatively-practical judgment of credentity is *per se* natural and can be had without grace. Nay, it can be had with resistance to grace in the case of the sin of infidelity committed with full awareness. However, the practically-practical judgment of credentity immediately ruling the pious affect of belief is essentially supernatural because it presupposes that my will is here and now, concretely and in an already inchoate way, moved toward supernatural things to be believed in.[99]

3. *The point will be pressed, though*: The speculatively-practical judgment of credentity has the same object as does the practically-practical judgment of credentity. Now, a judgment is specified by its object. {{411}} Therefore, the speculatively-practical judgment of credentity should likewise be supernatural *quoad substantiam*.

Response: I make a distinction regarding the major premise. I deny that they have

---

[99] See John of St. Thomas, *Cursus theologicus, De fide*, disp. 3, a. 2.

the same object formally considered in the same way. However, I concede that they have the same object considered in different ways. I contradistinguish the minor premise. I concede that a judgment is specified by its object and by the formal way in which its object is considered. Otherwise, I deny it.

Allow me to explain. In the speculatively-practical judgment of credentity, the duty to believe is considered in a general manner and in its naturally knowable principles. However, in the practically-practical judgment of credentity, this duty considered in a particular manner, *here and now*, inasmuch as it is unqualifiedly good for me to believe, notwithstanding the difficulties and passions involved. Hence, the formal object of this judgment is the goodness of the act of faith and the good promised to those who believe, attracting the person who forms such a judgment, overcoming, here and now, all the obstacles that lead those who believe not to come to belief. However, this goodness of the act of believing, as necessary for salvation, is supernatural. Hence, the practically-practical judgment of credentity is essentially supernatural and, in this way, it differs from the speculatively-practical judgment of credentity.

4. *One final point to be considered*: However, no essentially supernatural judgment can exist prior to faith itself. Now, this would be the case for the practically-practical judgment of credentity. Therefore, what you have said doesn't hold.

Response: I concede that, prior to the act of faith, there cannot be an essentially supernatural speculative judgment. However, I deny that there cannot be an essentially supernatural practically-practical judgment. For this ultimate judgment is not concerned with the mysteries on account of the authority of God who reveals things to be believed but, rather, with the very act of faith to be performed and with its goodness, notwithstanding the difficulties involved, a goodness that is supernatural. And, at the same time, this beginning of faith is the beginning of the true freedom of spirit spoken of by Christ when he said in John 8:32–34 (DR): "The truth shall make you free. . . . Whosoever committeth sin is the servant of sin." However, the absolute autonomy of reason and of the will is nothing other than the false freedom of the prodigal son and a form of true captivity. The spirit expands in the security of divine faith and in obscure contemplation of the infinite truth.

ART. 4: ON THE DUTY OF CIVIL AUTHORITY AND SOCIETY TO RECEIVE DIVINE REVELATION, ONCE IT HAS BEEN SUFFICIENTLY PROPOSED

§1. Proof from the rights of God, the author of civil society.
§2. Proof from the end of society and of civil authority.
§3. How must civil authority receive divine revelation?
§4. Resolution of objections.

Also, see the first article of this chapter, where we discuss liberalism and its opposition to the Church's teaching.[100]

§1. Proof from the Rights of God, the Author of Civil Society

The natural law requires [*iure naturae*] that we owe to God as Creator, Lord, Benefactor, and Uncreated Truth worship by way of natural religion and the obedience [*obsequium*] of faith, if he comes to manifestly reveal something supernaturally. Now, *God is no less the Creator, Lord, and Benefactor of society and of civil authority than he is of any man.* Therefore, civil authority and society, on the basis of the natural law [*ius naturae*], owe God worship in a social manner as well as the obedience [*obsequium*] of faith if he manifestly reveals something supernaturally.

The *major premise* was proven above in articles 2 and 3.

The *minor premise* is proven as follows. God is the Creator of man who, by his nature, is social—that is, a being that lives in society. {{412}} Hence, God is the creator of civil society itself as well as of authority, without which society would have no unity in existence nor in acting (that is, in promoting the common good). Therefore, civil authority depends upon God in an essential way, for otherwise it could not be obligatory for men, since nobody is, properly speaking, obligated by himself or by his equals. "For there is no power but from God: and those that are, are ordained of God."[101] Every authority comes from the first authority, just as all causality comes from the first causality. Such is the subordination of agents in the moral order just as much as in the physical.

Conclusion: Therefore, the civil authority cannot reject God's authority, lest it thereby deny itself. And, if there were no revelation, it would still need to acknowledge, defend, and foster natural religion. Among the ancient philosophers there was nearly unanimous consent concerning this matter, as can be seen in Plato (*Laws*, bks. 4, 7, and 10), Cicero (*Orat. pro Flacco*), and in Marcus Aurelius [*Valerium Max.*] (bk. 1).

And, therefore, the civil authority cannot reject the authority of God who reveals but, rather, is bound to receive divine revelation that has been sufficiently proposed to mankind. For if God were to determine a specific form of religion and manifest positive precepts, societies and rulers are [morally] bound to offer it obedience [*obsequium*], just as are individual men. It would be absurd to contend that when rulers enact laws they can act

---

[100] See Pius IX, *Syllabus of Errors*, nos. 77–80 (Denzinger, nos. 2977–2980).
[101] Rom 13:1 (DR).

as though no revelation existed when it, in reality, does exist, being able to command what is perhaps prohibited by it. This would be akin to saying the human legislator is greater than the divine legislator.[102]

Hence, Leo XIII said in his encyclical *Immortale Dei*: "For, men living together in society are under the power of God no less than individuals are, and society, no less than individuals, owes gratitude to God who gave it being and maintains it and whose ever-bounteous goodness enriches it with countless blessings."[103] Hence, a little before this he had said: "As a consequence, the State, constituted as it is, is clearly bound to act up to the manifold and weighty duties linking it to God, by the public profession of religion."[104]

Likewise, elsewhere, Leo XIII said: "Wherefore, civil society must acknowledge God as its Founder and Parent, and must obey and reverence His power and authority. *Justice therefore forbids, and reason itself forbids, the State to be godless; or to adopt a line of action which would end in godlessness—namely, to treat the various religions* (as they call them) *alike*, and to bestow upon them promiscuously equal rights and privileges."[105] {{413}} Hence, the state has the duty, before God, to receive divine revelation.

§2. Proof from the End of Society and of Civil Authority

He who must obtain a proximate end that is *per se* ordered to a higher end must attain it so that this essential subordination is preserved in his activ-

---

[102] On this thesis, see Cardinal Pie, *Instruction synodale sur les principales erreurs de notre temps*. Also see Msgr. Henry Sauvé, papal theologian at the time of the [First] Vatican Council, *Questions religieuses et sociales de notre temps: Vérités, erreurs, opinions libres*, 2nd ed. (Paris, 1888), ch. 3 (On Catholic liberalism). Also see Donoso Cortes, "On the Generative Principle of the Most Grievous Errors of Our Day," [in *Donoso Cortes: Readings in Political Theory*, trans. Vincent McNamara and Michael Schwartz (Ave Maria, FL: Sapientia Press, 2008), 141ff]. This letter was a report presented to Pius IX in 1850, showing that radicalism will follow upon liberalism, next giving rise to socialism, and ultimately materialistic and atheistic communism. These pages deserve careful reading.

Also see Dom Paul Benoît, *La cité antichrétienne au XIXe siècle: Les erreurs modernes*, vol. 2 (Paris: Palmé, 1887): 6–31 (*semi-liberalism* and its characteristics: the false spirit of reconciliation and of moderation, diminution of the truths and weakening of the Catholic sense, independence and presumption of spirit); 148–161 (*mitigated latitudinarianism*); 174–226 (*semi-liberal errors concerning the Church's magisterium and concerning coercive power*); 230–296 (*semi-liberal errors concerning the relations between Church and state*); 502–557 [*sic*] (*semi-liberal errors concerning the state*: the revolutionary dogma concerning the sovereignty of the people; the egalitarian spirit of semi-liberals; their enthusiasm for universal suffrage).

Finally, see Joseph-Louis Demeuran, *L'église* (Paris: Beauchesne, 1914), pt. 3 (Liberalism).

[103] Leo XIII, *Immortale Dei*, no. 6 (Vatican trans.).

[104] Ibid.

[105] Leo XIII, *Libertas*, no. 21 (Vatican trans.).

ity. Now, the civil authority must immediately tend to *the temporal good of the civic order, which is per se subordinated to our spiritual and eternal good*—namely, life lived in accord with virtue and true religion. Therefore, in seeking the temporal good of the civic order, civil authority is bound to preserve its essential subordination to life in accord with virtue and the true religion, and hence must not set out of consideration revealed religion that has been sufficiently proposed but instead must profit from it.

The major premise is obvious. For if a subordination is essential and one does not preserve it, one thus destroys the very essence of the immediate end. Hence, in his work *De regimine principum*,[106] St. Thomas says in bk. 1, ch. 15: "Now, anyone who must do something which is ordered to something else as to its end must see that his work is fitted to that end. Thus, a black-smith fashions a sword fit for use in battle, and a builder arranges the house so that it may be of use as a dwelling place." Likewise, the doctor immediately intends the healing of a man, something that is *per se* subordinated to the moral life. Hence, in what he counsels and prescribes, the doctor must be attentive to moral laws, like, for example, those related to abortion and to the use of hypnotism.

The minor premise can be made manifest both directly and indirectly.

(a) *Directly*, it is made manifest by considering man's nature, for *just as the body is per se subordinated to the soul*, so too the temporal good is subordinate to the spiritual and eternal good (that is, to life lived according to virtue and the true religion).[107]

(b) *Indirectly*: However, once this subordination is rejected, *order, and peace itself, comes to be destroyed in civil society*, just as disease often follows upon vice. Indeed, there can be no society without morality, and there is not true morality without religion—that is, without due subordination to God the Author of our nature. Therefore, he who fights against religion overturns the very foundations of society itself. Likewise, without God's assistance, society cannot attain its own end, for a second cause cannot do anything without the concurrence of the first cause, and the order of agents corresponds to the order of ends.

Conclusion: Hence, the state, by its own subjects, as well as itself, must

---

[106] This work was written by St. Thomas up to bk. 2, ch. 4. Ptolemy of Lucca wrote from chapter 5 of this book to the end of book 4.

[107] See *ST* II-II, q. 83, a. 6: "It is permitted that we desire temporal things, not indeed principally, such that we would place our end in them, but rather, as a kind of support, by which we are aided in tending to beatitude (namely, inasmuch as our bodily life is sustained by them and inasmuch as they serve us as instruments in the acts of the virtues, as the Philosopher says in *EN* 1.8)."

acknowledge not only God but also the true religion.

This reason, taken from the end of civil society, is developed by St. Thomas as follows in the text cited above from {{414}} *De regimine principum*:

> Therefore, because the end of the life that we live aright here-below is heavenly beatitude, the king has the duty for this reason to promote the good life of the multitude, such as is befitting in relation to the achievement of heavenly beatitude, namely, so that he may command those things that lead to heavenly beatitude and, to the degree that it is possible, forbid those things that are contrary to it. However, those things that provide the way to true beatitude, as well as those things that are impediments thereunto, are known from divine law, the teaching of which belongs to the duties of the priesthood.

Similarly, St. Augustine had said in *Epist.* 185, *ad Bonifac.* no. 19: "For a man serves God in one way because he is a man, and in another way because he is a king. . . . In this way, kings serve God inasmuch as they are kings when they do those things that they can only do because they are kings."

The same reason is presented by Leo XIII in his encyclical *Libertas*: "For public authority exists for the welfare of those whom it governs; and, although its proximate end is to lead men to the prosperity found in this life, yet, in so doing, it ought not to diminish, but rather to increase, man's capability of attaining to the supreme good in which his everlasting happiness consists: which never can be attained if religion be disregarded."[108]

And let it not be said that the end of society is not subordinated to the supernatural end but only the end of natural religion, for the natural law commands that society itself obey God, thus manifestly imposing a positive law. Hence, the obligation that society has to receive divine revelation is founded on "that necessary cohesion which exists by the will of God between both orders, both natural and supernatural."[109]

Confirmation from the true notion of freedom. Freedom is indeed a power that is indifferent to opposed [choices], but if we wish to express its perfection and exclude its defect, we must say with St. Thomas that *freedom is a power able to choose between means, preserving the order of the end*. Indeed:

---

[108] Leo XIII, *Libertas*, no. 21 (Vatican trans.).

[109] Pius IX, *Allocution* from June 9, 1862. However, one must not say, with a few theologians and canonists (e.g., Augustino Triumpho and Nicolò de' Tudeschi), that the state is directly subordinated to the Church and the civil magistrates are only vicars of the Roman Pontiff. No, indeed, each society is highest in its own order.

Free choice is related to the things to be chosen, which are ordered to the end, as the intellect is related to conclusions. However, it is manifest that the intellective power can draw a variety of conclusions in accord with given principles; however, when it happens to proceed to a conclusion outside of the order established by its principles, this is from its own defect. Whence, it pertains to the perfection of free choice's own freedom that it is able to choose various things, *so long as the order of the end is preserved*; however, by choosing something turning aside from the order of the end, it sins, and this pertains to *a defect in freedom.*[110]

Hence, freedom of choice is greater and more perfect in God, who cannot sin, than it is in us, for we can sin.

Therefore, man's true freedom is reconciled in a marvelous way with the authority of God who reveals. Nay, it cannot remain without this subordination. For insubordination (or license) leads to the servitude of corruption and to the tyranny of the passions, as Christ shows in the parable of the prodigal son, which holds true not only in our own individual lives but also in societies that choose not to obey God. And once this obedience has been rejected, all things are thrown into confusion, good men are oppressed by evil ones, and true freedom and dignity pass away, {{415}} whereas, by contrast, those who obey God find true freedom, with hearts that are enlarged in holiness, as is said in the Psalms: "I have run the way of thy commandments, when thou didst enlarge my heart."[111]

§3. How Must Civil Authority Receive Divine Revelation?

To this question, Pope Leo XIII responds in his encyclical *Immortale Dei*, saying:

> Hence, civil society, established for the common welfare, should not only safeguard the well-being of the community, but have also at heart the interests of its individual members, in such mode as not in any way to hinder, but in every manner to render as easy as may be, the possession of that highest and unchangeable good for which all should seek. Wherefore, for this purpose, care must especially be taken to preserve unharmed and unimpeded the religion whereof

---

[110] *ST* I, q. 62, a. 8, ad 3. Also see *ST* I, q. 83, a. 4.
[111] Ps 118:32 (DR).

the practice is the link connecting man with God. Now, it cannot be difficult to find out which is the true religion, if only it be sought with an earnest and unbiased mind.[112]

And directly before this, Leo XIII had said: *"All who rule, therefore, would hold in honor the holy name of God, and one of their chief duties must be to favor religion, to protect it, to shield it under the credit and sanction of the laws,* and neither to organize nor enact any measure that may compromise its safety."

Hence, the civil authority (or the state) cannot set divine revelation out of consideration but, rather, must receive it in three ways: (1) negatively (by doing nothing contrary to revealed religion); (2) positively and indirectly (by defending it); (3) positively and directly (by fostering it).

(1) *Negatively—the state must not establish or do anything contrary to the revealed religion.* It cannot promote irreligion nor pass laws by which the preaching of the true faith would be impeded, as well as the administration of the sacraments, the celebration of divine worship, its judgment concerning the morality of human acts, the education and instruction of ministers of worship, and the preservation of religious orders [*religiosarum familiarum*]; likewise, it cannot deny the indissolubility of matrimony or sanction divorce (properly so-called) in various cases, and so forth.[113]

(2) *Positively and indirectly—the state must defend, in the temporal order, not only natural religion but also revealed religion.* It is bound to prohibit that which is contrary to the natural law and unjust to God. Already Plato himself had said, once upon a time: Atheists are to be punished by death because they overturn the ultimate foundation of every order and of society itself. St. Louis, king of France, punished blasphemers by searing their tongues, and Clement IV asked him to soften these punishments.

St. Thomas says: "*Nonbelievers* who never have received the faith, such as Pagans and Jews, in no way are to be compelled to make an act of faith so that they would believe, for belief is something that must be freely willed. However, they are *to be compelled* by believers, if possible, *to not impede the faith, whether through blasphemies, or wicked persuasions, or even through open persecutions.*"[114] However, as regards coercion of heretics, see the doctrine of the Church set forth in Boniface VIII's bull *Unam sanctam,*[115] in the

---

[112] Leo XIII, *Immortale Dei,* nos. 6 and 7 (Vatican trans.).

[113] Pius IX, *Syllabus of Errors,* nos. 39–53 and 67 (Denzinger, nos. 2939–2953 and 2967).

[114] *ST* II-II, q. 10, a. 8.

[115] See Denzinger, no. 873.

condemnation of the errors of Jan Hus and of Martin Luther,[116] and what St. Thomas teaches on this matter.[117]

{{416}} (3) *Positively and directly—the state must foster revealed religion* not only by showing favor to the preaching and propagation of the true faith, the building of churches, and by acknowledging clerical immunity from secular services (e.g., military service), but also by publicly professing the true faith (e.g., through participation in true worship, *through public veneration of the holy name of God and of Jesus Christ*). Nay, the state can even compel citizens to perform certain religious acts, especially in circumstances wherein such omissions would represent a form of contempt for religion in some way (e.g., the denial of oaths before a tribunal).

Nonetheless, since the state is not infallible, it cannot set itself up as the judge in religious matters but, rather, in such things must acknowledge direction from religious authority, whose divine institution is presupposed as being proven. Thus, Constantine the Great wished to be called a "bishop *ad extra*," and Charlemagne, "devoted defender of the Church, and her

---

[116] See Denzinger, nos. 1214 and 773 [old numbering].

[117] See *ST* II, q. 10, a. 8. In speaking about the Catholic state, as it existed in the Middle Ages, St. Thomas said, not of nonbelievers who never had received faith, but rather, about apostates: "Such people are also to be compelled, in a bodily way, so that they may fulfill what they promised, and hold what they already received" (*ST* II-II, q. 10, a. 8). For religion must not be impeded, nor externally despised, to the detriment of society: "*For it is much graver that faith, which gives life to the soul, be corrupted, than for money, by which temporal life is sustained, to be counterfeited.* Hence if monetary counterfeiters or other wrongdoers are immediately handed over to death by secular leaders, much more can heretics be immediately handed over by those who convict them of heresy so that they may not only be excommunicated but even justly killed. However, on the part of the Church, mercy is to be given to those who err. And therefore, she does not immediately condemn but does so only after a first and second correction, as the Apostle teaches. However, afterwards, if this person is still found to be obstinate, the Church, no longer hoping in his conversion, providing for the salvation of others, separates him from the Church through a sentence of excommunication. And, furthermore, she hands him over to the judgment of the secular order to be expelled from the world through death." (*ST* II-II, q. 11, a. 3).

Moreover, the will of this offending party can be corrected through fear of sensible evils. However, in this, prudence must be consulted, as well as religious authority, so that one may see what is more expedient to the temporal and spiritual good, for often evil must be tolerated in order to avoid a greater evil.

Jean-Jacques Rousseau himself, in his *Social Contract*, trans, G. D. H. Cole (London: Everyman's Library, 1920), bk. 4, ch. 8, even though he proposes freedom and license of conscience against the Catholic Church said: "Therefore, there is a purely civil profession of faith whose articles should be fixed by the Sovereign, not exactly as religious dogmas, but as social sentiments without which a man cannot be a good citizen or a faithful subject. . . . If anyone, after publicly recognizing these dogmas, behaves as if he does not believe them, let him be punished by death, for he has committed the worst of all crimes, namely, that of lying before the law." Thus, Rousseau, in rejecting the authority of the Church, admitted the omnipotence of the state and statolatry.

humble supporter."

A doubt: But what can the Church demand of a heretical, indifferent, or unbelieving state?

She can demand that Catholics spread throughout *a heretical state* be free in the profession of their religion and that the juridical personality of the ecclesiastical society be acknowledged. Indeed, since such a state cannot claim infallibility for itself, it thus cannot reasonably contend that the religion that it professes is the only true one and that Catholics cannot live their lives in good faith.

However, an indifferent state does not care more for one religion than for another. Hence, according to its own principles, it must hold that the Church is a legitimate society, doing nothing against her but, rather, protecting her.

An unbelieving state cannot rationally deny that the Christian religion at least probably teaches the truth. Hence, it would act against reason and the natural law [*ius naturae*] if it were to impede the preaching and propagation of this religion. {{417}} Indeed, Christian nations often intervene with unbelievers in order to obtain freedom for Catholic missionaries and for their believers.

Conclusion: In this question (and something similar is found in all of the great questions), *Christian truth and perfection* are at once *the golden mean* and *peak* between and above the excesses opposed to it, here the *liberalism* of indifferentists and the *fanaticism* of sectarians. It likewise transcends the fluctuations of opportunistic *modérantisme*,[118] which strives to establish a kind of middle position between truth and falsity and between good and evil. We can diagrammatically represent this peak of truth, placed above the errors that are opposed to each other and likewise above a kind of empty reconciliation of these excesses:

> Love of God
> and of souls
>
> Opportunistic
> *modérantisme*
>
> Liberalism   Sectarianism

Human passions frequently fluctuate between two errors; sometimes they wish to ascend higher and find stability and peace. However, true tranquility

---

[118] [Trans. note: This particular political phenomenon (*modérantisme*) from the French Revolution is perhaps what Fr. Garrigou-Lagrange is referring to by the term *moderantismus*, though it is possible that he may merely be using this Latin term to refer to a general kind of "moderationism," an opportunistic "splitting the balance" between sectarianism and liberalism.]

of order is only found in the peak where truth is found. This peak is attained, not only speculatively but also practically, in particular by *the saints*, who simultaneously avoid liberalism and fanaticism, with a zeal, however, that is utterly distinct from the mild warmth of mere *modérantisme*.[119]

In this complex practical question, a role is to be played not only by the moral virtues (such as prudence, justice, courage, and temperance) but also and especially by the theological virtues of faith, hope, and charity. Hence, in order to find the correct direction, one must always have before one's eyes what St. Thomas teaches (in *ST* I-II, q. 64) *concerning the virtuous mean*: *The moral virtues*, which rule the passions and activities, *consist in a mean* between excess and deficiency, and this mean, as something rational, overcomes these irrational extremes, just as courage overcomes not only inordinate fear but also rashness. {{418}} *However, the theological virtues*, which are concerned with the ultimate end of our life, *per se do not consist in a mean*:

> Never can a man love God as much as he ought to be loved, nor believe nor hope in him as much as he ought to be. Whence, much less can there be some form of excess here, and thus the good of such a virtue does not consist in a mean but, rather, the better that it is, all the more does it draw close *to the heights*. However, from our perspective, there is another rule or measure for the theological virtues, for even if we cannot be borne to God as much as we ought to be, nonetheless, we can be borne to him by believing, hoping, and loving in accord with the measure of our condition. Thus, *per accidens*, a mean and extremes can be considered in the case of the theological

---

[119] St. Thomas reconciles this firmness with charity by saying in *ST* II-II, q. 11, a. 3: "*As regards heretics*, two things must be taken into consideration. (1) *On the side of those who have sinned*, thereby deserving to be separated from the Church through excommunication but also to be removed from the world through death. . . . (2) *On the side of the Church, there is mercy* for the conversion of those who err. And therefore, she does not immediately condemn them." And in a. 4: "Heretics who return, no matter how many times they have fallen, are received by the Church for penance, through which the way of salvation is opened up for them." Also in q. 10, a. 5–12: "However, *unbelievers*, who never have received the faith, *are in no way to be compelled to faith: their rites can be tolerated in order to avoid some evil*. The children of Jews are not to be baptized against their parents' wills."

A noble Christian soul, who in our own days led many unbelievers to faith, wrote: "I am struck by the fact that unbelievers experience more sympathy for persons having profound faith [*les êtres de foi profonde*] than for those whose convictions are flexible and utilitarian. . . . However, the indomitable affirmation must be enveloped in the most intelligent sympathy, the most lively and delicate charity" (Elisabeth Leseur, *Journal et pensées de chaque jour* [Paris: J. de Gigord, 1920], 162).

virtues when we consider them from our perspective (thus, hope is found between and above desperation and presumption).[120]

Above all, in all things, our intellect must affirm that which *is*—no more, no less. In Christ's words, "But let your speech be yea, yea: no, no."[121]

These matters must receive attentive practical attention so that we might avoid mediocrity, which is opposed to zeal for God and souls, and which wishes to reduce both the theological and the moral virtues to an inferior sort of mean. Hence, we said in this question, as in other similar ones, Christian truth and perfection are at once a golden *mean* and *a peak*, between and above extreme errors. Therefore, true peace must not be sought after in a kind of mediocrity, which would diminish Christian holiness but, on the contrary, must be sought, with full sincerity, in the peak of truth and virtue, to which all the legitimate aspirations of our heart tend.

This is how, under the Church's own direction, true Christian theologians and philosophers have spoken concerning these matters.[122]

---

[120] *ST* I-II, q. 64, a. 4.

[121] Matt 5:37 (DR).

[122] What, however, practically speaking, is *the peak of truth* above the opposed excesses of liberalism and sectarianism, as well as above *modérantisme* or tepid opportunism, which oscillates back and forth at a middle altitude? This is set forth, with great indulgence for those erring, by Léon Ollé-Laprune in *Le prix de la vie*, 456: "Bearing human nature within himself, as well as what he adds to it, though, while adding to it, adapting it, *the Christian* rejects nothing, despises nothing, hates nothing that is human as such, and consequently, he is *at once the most accommodating and the most intractable of men. Never putting a principle at stake, he is uncompromising*; and thus, it is not only his Christian faith but, moreover is his reason, his conscience, his very honor which find him to be unshakably resolved to maintain them before and against all. In this respect for, and fidelity to, all that is true, good, fitting, just, and sacred, he is full of kindness, of jealousy, and if I may so dare to say, all forms of daring. His energy is indomitable. However, where principles are not at stake, he is easy, and moreover, *for men he has all possible outlooks*, even all forms of indulgence: does he not have the most profound awareness of his own weakness? This intimate humility makes him clairvoyant, just, and good; and, out of respect for the truth, through the spirit of justice, and through charity, he strives to understand others, to understand them even in their errors and their faults, and knowing that he must condemn that which is false and evil, he never has contempt or scorn for persons.

"Thus, we can see what we must, more than ever, indeed better than ever, see and do. Contemporary youth seem to strive to acquire understanding and practice of this course of action. They aspire to *clear, precise, and strong ideas*, which they wish to be *vast and great*. They speak of *sympathy, harmony, and union*, and they desire all souls to be open in some way to all things and nonetheless to be vigorous too. They wish that one be firm without being enclosed. What a beautiful program of action: to renounce unmoored and changing outlooks as much as ones that are cramped and narrow; to be on guard against bitterness and anger, as much as against flaccid opinions and banal indulgence. . . .

"Peace will be brought about by light and frankness. . . . *Peace through the effacement* of ideas

{{419}} Therefore, according to Catholic doctrine, not only individual men but also society itself is bound to receive revelation when it has been proposed in a sufficient manner. It does not suffice to say that this is the *thesis* that indeed must be preserved in schools of sacred theology as a speculative truth; however, in practice, we must act in accord with the *hypothesis* of the freedom of all forms of worship in order to attain all the advantages of this hypothesis. In reality, the *thesis* cannot be considered as being only a merely speculative ideal that can be set aside in practice, for *this thesis enunciates the very* END TO BE ATTAINED—namely, the true religion must be embraced by all, not only individually but also socially. In order to attain this end, circumstances must be considered. Hence, in a particular case, that is, *per accidens*, prudence may declare that *some evil is to be tolerated* in order to avoid a greater evil. However, to relinquish the thesis as something that is merely ideal, only to be preserved in the schools, *would be to turn aside from the very end to be attained*. This would be to fall into opportunism and to draw evermore back from love for God and for souls. Finally, the thesis, in enunciating the weightiest obligation, would come to be considered an empty word and, hence, nothing at all.

Thus, on account of the abuse of this distinction between *thesis* and *hypothesis* (as though the thesis were merely speculative and the hypothesis the sole practical rule), Catholic social action gradually has been destroyed. Today, many Catholics are seen ignoring society's obligations toward God and holding that it is a normal state of affairs that one accept the neutrality of the state, the neutrality of school[s], and utter freedom of conscience. However, by traveling along this path, society becomes, at its very root, irreligious and atheistic.

Hence, on account of this abuse of the distinction between thesis and hypothesis, a number of theologians substitute for it the distinction between the *end* and *the means that are suitable* here and now in relation to the end, in accord with the judgment of prudence. In this way alone can we preserve that which must indeed be preserved as a matter of greatest importance— namely, *the efficacious intention of the end*, whence proceeds rectitude and efficacy in choice, as well as that of the execution of the means ordered to the end. Nay, one also thus preserves, in due harmony, God's authority and

---

or through the annihilation of persons, even if this were possible, or at least by forgetting what separates people, is not a true form of peace. *Rather, it is by pushing onward to the very peak of all your thoughts*, and in your relations with other persons, to the depths and heights of the other and of yourselves, *by means of sincerity and frankness, that, wishing for peace, you will have it*, and that, thus truly established in peace, you will possess the world."

man's freedom, inasmuch as the latter differs from mere license, which leads to the servitude of corruption.

Thus, in accord with this subordination of ends, the Church forever proceeds *fortiter et suaviter*, strongly and sweetly. Notwithstanding the utterly great difficulties involved, so too do the saints press onward to restore all things in Christ—namely, so that God's reign may come about not only in the hearts of certain most excellent believers but in human society itself.

Kind charity and absolute firmness of faith are not opposed to each other but, rather, on the contrary, mutually support each other, and thus, they must be united in us so that they may not be separated, lest the former come to an end and fall into liberalism, and the other be diminished or decline into sectarianism. They must be joined on high and intimately, in the ardor of the same love, which is zeal for the glory of God and the salvation of souls. So united, they in reality are in the Church, as in Christ, an image of the reconciliation of the divine perfections: "Mercy and truth have met each other: justice and peace have kissed."[123]

§4. Resolution of Objections

{{420}} 1. *Objection*: He who cannot judge concerning revelation is not bound to acknowledge it. Now, the civil authority cannot judge concerning the fact of revelation, nor concerning things pertaining to religion, but only about those things that are ordered to the temporal good. Therefore, [it cannot be bound to receive revelation.]

Response: In order for civil authority to be bound to receive divine revelation, it is not necessary that it be able to *authoritatively judge* concerning the fact of revelation and about those things that pertain to religion. Rather, it suffices that it be able to judge concerning the motives of credibility *in accord with common sense*, as well as concerning the truths of faith, in the way that the faithful judge. For already, in accord with common sense, the state admits truths of natural ethics, such as the notion of moral obligation, free choice, responsibility, and property rights, even if philosophers deny these truths theoretically.

2. *Objection*: The state cannot command something against the conscience of its subjects. Now, the performance of any religious act is contrary to the conscience of citizens who reject God's existence. Therefore, the state never can compel citizens to certain religious acts (e.g., to the taking of oaths before tribunals).

Response: I concede that the state cannot command anything contrary to true and

---

[123] Ps 84:11 (DR). We have written about a number of these things in another work, Réginald Garrigou-Lagrange, *God: His Existence and His Nature*, vol. 2, trans. Bede Rose (St. Louis: B. Herder, 1949), 397–445.

certain conscience. However, I deny that this is so for erroneous and hardened conscience. For there are those who hold that it is permissible that one perform the gravest of crimes. Hence, just as men who do not admit property rights can be compelled to act as though they acknowledge those rights, so too the state can and must prohibit that which is contrary to the natural law and unjust to God and, indeed, compel citizens to perform certain acts of religion, the omission of which would involve contempt of religion (e.g., the taking of oaths before a tribunal).

3. *Objection*: Nonetheless, an authority whose proximate end is the temporal and external good must set out of its consideration internal acts. Now, acts of religion are internal. Therefore, [it must set them out of its consideration.]

Response: I make a distinction regarding the major premise, conceding if the temporal good were not essentially subordinated to the spiritual good in an essential manner. Otherwise, I deny it. Thus, the doctor in his prescriptions cannot set morality out of consideration (e.g., with regard to abortion, craniometry, etc.). Moreover, acts of religion are not merely internal, for worship must be external. Finally, social worship is owed to God, as Author of society, and religion supports temporal society in a number of ways, by directing souls not only in spiritual things but also in the use of spiritual things.

Indeed, only God can judge purely internal acts. However, when opinions and religion are manifested through external acts, the ecclesiastical authority, as well as the civil authority, have the right and duty to prohibit those things that are harmful to the social good.

4. *Objection*: However, society, which intends a good that is in no way proportioned to the supernatural end, is not bound to attend to the supernatural end. Now, the state intends a temporal good, which is in no way proportioned to the supernatural end. Therefore, [it is not bound to attend to the supernatural end.]

Response: The temporal good is indeed not a means *proportioned* to the attainment of the supernatural end but, rather, is *subordinated* to it, for "we are aided *by temporal things* in tending to beatitude (namely, inasmuch as our bodily life is sustained by them and inasmuch as they serve us as instruments in the acts of the virtues)."[124] Nay, once this subordination is set aside, temporal things come to be desired as the principal things desired so that we would then place our end in them, as happens in irreligious or atheistic societies.

5. *Objection*: Nonetheless, it seems to suffice that the state be related negatively to the Church, doing nothing against her, though remaining neutral. For indeed, the civil authority is bound to attend to the *very end of activity* of society itself, though *not to the ultimate end of the agents in society* (namely, that of individuals). Now, life in accord with the true religion is not the very end of the activity of society but, rather, only that of the individual agents in society. {{421}} Therefore, the civil authority is not bound to posi-

---

[124] *ST* II-II, q. 83, a. 6.

tively attend to the Catholic religion in a positive manner, nor to the supernatural end.[125]

Response: If the civil authority did not come from God and if *the very end of the activity of society itself* were not subordinated to the spiritual life, I would concede this point. Otherwise, however, I deny it. As Leo XIII said, "Therefore, the name of God must be held to be holy by those who rule." Likewise, liberals and semi-rationalists err in saying, in words that were condemned in the *Syllabus of Errors*: "As there is a distinction between the philosopher and his philosophy, he has the right and the duty to submit himself to the authority he acknowledges as legitimate; but philosophy neither can nor must submit to any authority."[126] Moreover, in practice, natural and supernatural things are not to be *separated* from each other, as they are distinguished in speculative consideration, for the *speculative* intellect abstracts from singulars in order to consider universals, whereas, by contrast, *the practical* intellect tends toward a work to be done in particular. And we cannot concretely and efficaciously intend the ultimate natural end in abstraction from the supernatural end, for man is bound by the natural law [*iure naturale*] to obey God when he commands. Therefore, one cannot turn away from the ultimate supernatural end without simultaneously turning away from the ultimate natural end.

6. *Objection*: However, then the state would not need to tolerate the worship of nonbelievers and of heretics. Now, this intolerance would lead to great public discord.

Response: The state must not *per se* tolerate (that is, without any just cause) that which in itself is evil and unjust to God. However, the worship offered by nonbelievers and heretics must *per accidens* be tolerated (that is, in order to avoid a greater evil). *For to tolerate is not to prohibit an evil, though an evil per se must be prohibited.*[127] Hence, although the civil authority can sometimes tolerate freedom of worship, nonetheless, it cannot in any way [positively] sanction this through its laws, for to sanction freedom of worship is to sanction impiety, since false forms of worship are superstition and impiety.

7. *Objection*: Nonetheless, the good is that from which a good effect follows. Now, a good effect follows from freedom of worship—namely, juridical freedom for the true religion. Therefore, freedom of worship is good. This is the argument brought forth by that form of liberalism that wishes to be called Catholic.

Response: I make a distinction regarding the major premise. I concede that this is good either *per se* or *per accidens*. However, I deny that it is always *per se* good. I likewise

---

[125] Some have proposed a similar objection in relation to the professional unions, as though a union should remain neutral and is not positively bound to attend to the supernatural laws of the Christian life. However, in reality, in order to avoid the errors of socialism, corporations of workers of this kind must promote, by legitimate means, the professional, physical, intellectual, moral, and religious good of workers. See Adolphe Tanquerey, *Brevior synopsis theologiae moralis et pastoralis*, no. 616.

[126] Pius IX, *Syllabus of Errors*, no. 10 (Denzinger, no. 2910).

[127] See *ST* II-II, q. 10, a. 11 (on tolerance for nonbelievers); q. 11, a. 3, ad 2 (on tolerance for heretics).

distinguish the conclusion. I deny that *freedom of worship is per se good*, for it is intrinsically impious. However, I concede that it is a *per accidens good*—namely, on account of the freedom offered to the true religion. However, this true freedom of religion is not necessarily founded on freedom of all forms of worship. Nay, rather, it *per se* excludes it.

8. *Objection*: However, the principle by which the freedom of the true religion is defended must be admitted. Now, the freedom of the true religion is defended on the basis of the principle of the freedom of worship. Therefore, [the freedom of worship must be admitted.]

Response: I make a distinction regarding the major premise. It must be admitted either *absolutely* as a thesis or *ad hominem*, as a hypothesis. I will let the minor pass. I make a distinction regarding the conclusion, denying it as a thesis, conceding it as a hypothesis.

For we can argue *ad hominem*[128] from the freedom of worship against those who proclaim the freedom of worship and nonetheless harass the true Church and directly or indirectly prohibit its worship. This kind of *ad hominem* argumentation is right, and the Catholic Church does not disdain it but, rather, urges that it be used in defense of her own right to freedom. However, this does not mean that freedom of worship, considered in itself, can be defended in an absolute manner by Catholics, for in itself it is absurd and impious. Indeed, truth and error cannot have the same rights. {{422}} Nor must falsity be spoken in defense of truth, just as evil must not be done in order to bring about good. Hence, St. Paul says in Romans 3:7–8 (DR): "For if the truth of God hath more abounded through my lie, unto his glory, why am I also yet judged as a sinner? And not rather (as we are slandered and as some affirm that we say) let us do evil that there may come good? Whose damnation is just."

9. *Objection*: In the order of acting, only that which is practical is true, without qualification. Now, the thesis spoken of above is not practical but, rather, a speculative ideal, which may well be taught in the schools, whereas the hypothesis of the freedom of worship is a practical fact. Therefore, this hypothesis is true, speaking without qualification [*simpliciter*].

Response: I make a distinction regarding the major premise. I concede that only that which is a due end or as a means that is of itself fitted to it is practical. I deny, however, this is so for a *per accidens* suitable means. I contradistinguish the minor premise in like manner. Indeed, as we said above, *the thesis sets forth the end to be attained* (namely, the true religion is to be embraced by all, not only individually but also socially). However, in order to attain this end, the circumstances must be considered. Hence, in a given case, that is, *per accidens*, prudence may declare that some evil is to be tolerated in order to avoid a greater evil. However, *we cannot consider the aforementioned thesis as being a merely spec-*

---

[128] [Trans. note: That is, taking the terms of argument accepted by a given person.]

ulative ideal that can be set aside in practice, for this would be to turn away from the end to be attained. Hence, the aforementioned objection arises from nominalism or empiricism, which reduces universal principles to some particular fact and morality to success. In that case, it would be true to say, "Right consists in a material fact; all the duties of men are an empty name, and all human deeds have the force of right,"[129] which is one practical consequence of nominalism. In these sometimes-difficult matters, the immutable firmness of faith must be reconciled on high with the sweetness of Christian charity and diligent prudence considering the suitable means.[130]

{{423}} 10. *Objection*: Then there would be no freedom of thought, speech, con-

---

[129] Pius IX, *Syllabus of Errors*, no. 59 (Denzinger, no. 2959).

[130] Léon Ollé-Laprune, *La vitalité chrétienne* (Paris: Perrin, 1901), 41, writing about Catholic liberals says: "There are men who are convinced that recourse to human means, provided that there be nothing culpable in them, is not only permitted but, indeed, is good; and there are other men for whom everything that resembles clever and political conduct in the slightest way is unworthy of God. For the former, it is a duty that one seek out alliances, engage all honest men from all parties in Catholic interests, and make use of public freedoms in service of the Church; others call these cowardly accommodations, disgraceful transactions, and even treason. Finally, the first know how to remain below their ideal and to confine themselves to what is possible in the given state of affairs; the others' motto is, 'All or nothing.'"

However, the same author says, afterwards, on 45: "Nonetheless, so-called 'liberalism' contains a poison which corrupts it. . . . It is very difficult to make a doctrine out of the liberal attitude. Why? Because one risks transforming contingent maxims into eternal truths, the necessities of the moment into absolute rules. When one remains in the heights, there is nothing to fear. Everything that one says about the right to freedom for the very honor and advantage of the truth is indeed incontestable. When one then begins to descend down to applications and enter into the details, danger begins to show itself, one that is all the more redoubtable to the degree that it is more hidden. It begins with a kind of noble disdain for every narrow way of serving the truth. One thus has such great confidence in the divine power of truth that in order to enable it to be accepted one no longer comes to count on anything other than it alone. All well and good, but *the temptation here is delicate for good souls.* There is no need to fear that they themselves would ever become indifferent to truth and falsity; however, they risk *no longer being well enough aware of and armed against the precautions that one must take against error.* If they do not take care, they will practice the fatal maxim of liberalism: 'Do whatever; let it pass.' Thus, through their imprudence, minds will come to hold the idea that in a society, error as such has rights, that freedom as such is always inviolable, and that it is a most criminal assault to limit freedom so as to protect it against its own excesses. Thus, only one step remains for one to make a troubled and transitory social state into the very ideal of every society and to hold that intellectual division is a positive form of progress, treating every union of spiritual power with temporal power, in whatsoever condition, as being something chimerical, a danger, and even erroneous. And soon thereafter, in less lofty minds, there comes to be, under the pretext of intellectual largess, *a growing unawareness of the worth of the truth.* In less certain minds, *there comes to be a so-called charitable tendency to not contradict anyone and to leave everyone play with fire* and, in the end, in minds that are weak and soft, a *disposition to judge that all positions can be held* and that, moreover, he who says, 'I do not believe. I cannot believe,' is more than half excused."

science, and worship. However, this is false, for man is free to embrace what seems to be true to him and to choose among opinions that are free and open.

Response: *A true freedom of thought* does indeed exist—namely, the right to embrace everything that is true, especially the true religion, and to admit only that which is obviously true or credible, as well as to choose among free and open opinions. Likewise, there is a legitimate form of freedom of speech, so long as one speaks the truth and not what is harmful to others.

However, there cannot be an absolute moral freedom of thinking or speaking, for a right to admit or teach error does not exist. Indeed, we can err and be excused on account of our good faith; however, objectively speaking, the right to accept error as one pleases is contrary to action itself. Likewise, no right exists for one to reject the truth that has been either intrinsically or extrinsically made manifest (that is, a right to reject the true religion that has been sufficiently proposed and embrace some other that is more pleasing to oneself). Hence, it would be better to speak about the duty to profess the true religion, rather than about the freedom to profess it.

11. *Objection*: The Catholic Church contradicts herself, for she demands freedom—nay, even a kind of protection—from heterodox states, and she herself teaches that the Catholic state cannot concede such freedom and protection to the heterodox. If the Church can exclude heterodox believers, so too can a heterodox state exclude the Church.

How can one admit these words of Louis Veuillot to the Church's adversaries: "I demand of you, in the name of your principles, freedom, which I refuse you in the name of my own"?

Response: There is no contradiction here. Indeed, the Church has the right to claim her exclusive right—that is, the protection *on behalf of the truth*, and hence on behalf of herself, for it is certain that she exclusively possesses the complete truth. In fact, if she lives in a region where freedom is granted to all sects, the Church herself certainly can demand that she be accorded the privileges that are conceded to error. However, in a heterodox state, the Church would present testimony to her divine mission so that she may show such a state that it should at least show her tolerance. And in a Catholic state, she herself often makes use of tolerance for heterodox believers so as to avoid a greater evil. Hence, the Church demands freedom for herself, on the basis of the very rights of the truth, and *per accidens ad hominem*, on the basis of the freedom of conscience that her adversaries proclaim. And she denies, *per se*, freedom of error, which is not a right to error.[131]

12. *Objection*: It would be better to concede complete freedom to any given reli-

---

[131] Hence, certain people have not said without some justification: "The Church is intolerant in principle because she believes. She is tolerant in practice because she loves. The enemies of the Church are tolerant in principle because they do not believe, and intolerant in practice because they do not love." However, in the writings of the enemies of the Church, theory and practice contradict each other. But in the Church, principles themselves direct her action *fortiter et suaviter*.

gion and to refute error solely through the exposition of the truth. Then the true religion would be propagated and would flourish solely through intimate persuasion, since truth always prevails over error. Such was Lamennais's position.

Response: It is not better to give freedom to error, for such freedom leads to perdition, for "the greater part of the community is either absolutely unable, or able only with great difficulty, to escape from illusions and deceitful subtleties, especially such as flatter the passions."[132] {{424}} Nor is it true that the majority of men are interested in truth and virtue. Rather, as is said in 1 John 2:16 (DR): "For all that is in the world is the concupiscence of the flesh and the concupiscence of the eyes and the pride of life." Hence, "the fear of the Lord is the beginning of wisdom" (Ps 110:10, DR).

Man needs *to be freed* from his corrupted passions, his egoism, his pride, his errors, and his doubts. And persecution, which does away with true freedom, does not come from the truth but, rather, from error and wickedness. Hence, St. Paul says in 2 Timothy 3:12 (DR): "And all that will live godly in Christ Jesus shall suffer persecution."[133] Hence, there is no true

---

[132] Leo XIII, *Libertas*, no. 23 (Vatican trans.).

[133] See H.-D. Lacordaire, 7th Conference (1835), "On the Coercive Power of the Church": "The accusation is raised, saying that the truth is intolerant, and one readily speaks of tolerance as though it were the prerogative of error. There is no prejudice which is more widespread, none that is more readily contradicted by history and by the very spectacle of contemporary facts. If history has a dogma to proclaim, it is that error is a ruthless and atrocious persecutor, indeed always, as soon as it can and to the degree when it can.... As St. Paul said, 'All those who wish to live piously in Jesus Christ will suffer persecution,' (2 Tim 3:12), and Jesus Christ, He who was the great sacrifice offered for the truth, the victim *par excellence* of error, himself said to the Jews: 'See, I send you prophets, wise men, and teachers; some you will kill and crucify, and others you will have whipped in your synagogues....' This prophecy did not delay in being fulfilled, not only in Judah, but throughout all the world. Who persecuted during the first three centuries of the Christian era?... Who persecuted under the emperors of the East? Were they not the Arians, the Donatists, and the Iconoclasts? Up to the time of Charlemagne the Church never ceased to defend herself against murder, torture, and fiery conflagration.... With the resurrection of error, the sixteenth century was witness to a renewal of all these bloody dramatics; it witnessed the Protestants breaking our images, demolishing our church[es], toppling over our tombs ... and slaying our priests and our religious.... And now that the ideas of tolerance seem so widespread, who persecutes in Europe, who imprisons, who banishes people ...? Is it the Church ...? The battle between error and truth is forever that between Cain and Abel. Cain does not cease to say to his brother: come, let us go down together to the field of freedom.... But he does so in order to betray and murder him....

"The truth tends to prevail through understanding and error through bodily force. If civil society wishes to defend the truth—that is, to prevent violence from disturbing it in its efforts at persuasion—this is its duty. If it wishes to go further still, once again make truth the fundamental law of the state, this is its right.... And certainly, if there is a great and powerful idea, one that is worthy of man, it is to make the truth the fundamental law of his life. (Nay, this is even obligatory.) ... However, human passions, which had respected this state of affairs in antiquity because then religion was erroneous, went on the attack with vigor in modern

freedom, the image of the God of freedom, except in charity. Therefore, we must conclude this treatise on revelation with the words of Jesus Christ found in John 8:31–32 (DR): "If you continue in my word, you shall be my disciples indeed. And you shall know the truth: and the truth shall make you free." {{425}} Thus, as St. Paul said in Romans 8:21 (DR), "the creature also itself shall be delivered from the servitude of corruption, into the liberty of the glory of the children of God."

*

* *

May the Blessed Virgin Mary deem what we have written concerning revelation, with St. Thomas as our guide, worthy of her blessing and protection. Moreover, may she pray for us and for each of our readers so that, arriving at the revelation of God in glory, we may praise and exalt Jesus Christ above all others forever.

---

times because religion was wholly pure, holy, and true. And the passions were victorious. Civil society, profoundly divided, today rests on an absolutely contrary principle, complete and utter freedom of worship. At the very least, may this freedom no longer be an empty promise, and may the Church once more obtain from error full and peaceful exercise of her spiritual rights, that is, the right to persuade mankind. This is our sweetest hope and dearest desire."

And we must add what Cardinal Pie said elsewhere in his *Instruction synodale sur les principales erreurs de notre temps*: "What of the principles from which one can indefinitely fail to draw the consequences? *Does this not represent the practical elimination of the thesis, relegating it indifferently to memories of the past or the mists of the future?* What of the fundamental laws of society, without which society nonetheless can [not] subsist and prosper.... No, never will I accept for France the absolute and definitive necessity of what has been called 'the hypothesis.' ... I think too highly of my country, I have too lofty an idea of her divine predestination, I know too well how easily she can return to the good after having served evil to declare that she is irremediably fixed in falsehood. No, France is not an apostate forevermore!"

Definitions and Declarations of the Church on the Sources of Revelation (Namely, on Sacred Scripture and Tradition)

TEXTS FROM THE COUNCIL OF TRENT

SESSION IV (APRIL 8, 1546)

{{426}} "The holy, ecumenical, and general Council of Trent, lawfully assembled in the Holy Spirit, . . . has always this purpose in mind that in the Church errors be removed and the purity of the gospel be preserved. This gospel was promised of old through the prophets in the Sacred Scriptures;[1] our Lord Jesus Christ, Son of God, first promulgated it from his own lips; he in turn ordered that it be *preached through the apostles to all creatures*[2] as the source of all saving truth and norms of conduct. The council clearly perceives that this truth and rule are contained in *written books* and *unwritten traditions* that have come down to us, having been received by the apostles from the mouth of Christ himself or from the apostles[3] by the dictation of the Holy Spirit, and have been transmitted, as it were, from hand to hand.

"Following, then, the example of the orthodox Fathers, it receives and

---

[1] See Jer 31:22ff.
[2] Matt 28:19ff; Mark 16:15.
[3] 2 Thess 2:15: "Now our Lord Jesus Christ himself, and God and our Father, who hath loved us and hath given us everlasting consolation and good hope in grace." Also see 2 Tim 2:1–2.

venerates with the same sense of loyalty and reverence *all the books of the Old and New Testament—for the one God is the author of both*—together with all the *traditions* concerning *faith and practice* [*mores*], as coming from the *mouth of Christ or being inspired by the Holy Spirit and preserved in continuous succession in the Catholic Church.*

"The council has thought it proper to insert in this decree a list of the sacred books, so that no doubt may remain as to which books are recognized by the council. They are the following:

"*Old Testament*: The five [books] of Moses, that is, Genesis, Exodus, Leviticus, Numbers, Deuteronomy; Joshua, Judges, Ruth, four [books] of Kings [i.e., two books of Samuel, two books of Kings], two of Chronicles, the first [book] of Ezra, the second [book] of Ezra called Nehemiah, Tobit, Judith, Esther, Job, the Psalter of David containing 150 psalms, Proverbs, Ecclesiastes, the Song of Songs, Wisdom, Ecclesiasticus [i.e., Sirach], Isaiah, Jeremiah with Baruch, Ezekiel, {{427}} Daniel, the twelve minor prophets, that is, Hosea, Joel, Amos, Obadiah, Jonah, Micah, Nahum, Habakkuk, Zephaniah, Haggai, Zachariah, and Malachi; two [books] of Maccabees, that is, the first and the second.

"*New Testament*: The four Gospels according to Matthew, Mark, Luke, and John; the Acts of the Apostles, written by Luke the evangelist; fourteen Epistles of the apostle Paul, that is, to the Romans, two to the Corinthians, to the Galatians, Ephesians, Philippians, Colossians, two to the Thessalonians, two to Timothy, to Titus, Philemon, and the Hebrews; two [Epistles] of the apostle Peter, three of the apostle John, one of the apostle James, one of the apostle Jude, and the Revelation of the apostle John.

"If anyone does not accept all these books *in their entirety, with all their parts*, as they are being read in the Catholic Church and are contained in *the ancient Latin Vulgate* editions,[4] as *sacred* and *canonical* and knowingly and deliberately rejects the aforesaid traditions, let him be anathema.

"Hence, let all understand the order and manner by which the council will proceed after laying down the foundation of the profession of faith and what witnesses and supports it will especially use in strengthening its teachings and renewing morals in the Church" (Denzinger, nos. 1501–1505).

---

4 [Trans. note: As an Eastern Catholic, the translator feels the need to point out that the primarily intra-Western focus of the Council of Trent should not be taken as wholly normative for how to interpret the reception of scriptural text within the Church. The concerns here, stressing the Vulgate, are tied to concerns in Europe surrounding the claims of Protestants and Renaissance textual scholars. No doubt, the Vulgate has a special place in the Western Church, even today, given the long history of interweaving between its various editions and the liturgical life of the Western liturgical-ritual traditions.]

"Moreover, because the same holy council thought it very useful to the Church if it were known which of all the Latin editions of the sacred books now in circulation is to be regarded as the authentic version, it declares and decrees: *this same ancient vulgate version* which has been preserved by the Church for so many centuries is to be regarded as *authentic* in public readings, disputations, sermons, and examinations, and let no one dare or presume to reject it on any grounds.

"Furthermore, to restrain irresponsible minds, it decrees that no one, relying on his own prudence, may twist Holy Scripture *in matters of faith and practice* [*mores*] that pertain to the building up of Christian doctrine, according to his own mind, contrary to the meaning that the Holy mother the Church has held and holds—since it belongs to her to judge the true meaning and interpretation of the Holy Scripture—and that no one may dare to interpret the Scripture in a way contrary to the *unanimous consensus of the Fathers*, even if such interpretations are not intended for publication. Those who oppose this shall be declared such by the Ordinaries and punished by the penalties established by law" (Denzinger, nos. 1506–1507).

TEXTS FROM THE [FIRST] VATICAN COUNCIL

SESSION III

Dei filius, Constitution on the Catholic Faith, ch. 2

"Further, this supernatural revelation, according to the universal belief of the Church, declared by the sacred Council of Trent, 'is contained *in the written books and unwritten traditions* that have come down to us, having been received by the apostles from the mouth of Christ himself or from the apostles themselves by the dictation of the Holy Spirit, and have been transmitted as it were from hand to hand.' {{428}} These books of the Old and New Testaments are to be received as sacred and canonical *in their integrity, with all their parts*, as they are enumerated in the decree of the said council and are contained in the ancient Latin edition of the *Vulgate*. These the Church holds to be sacred and canonical, not because, having been carefully composed by mere human industry, they were afterward approved by her authority or merely because they contain revelation with no admixture of error, but because, *having been written by the inspiration of the Holy Spirit, they have God for their author* and have been delivered as such to the Church herself (see can. 4).

"Since, however, what the holy Council of Trent has laid down concerning the interpretation of the divine Scripture for the good purpose of restraining undisciplined minds has been explained by certain men in a distorted manner, we renew the same decree and declare this to be its sense: In matters of faith and morals, affecting the building up of Christian doctrine, that is to be held as the true sense of Holy Scripture which Holy Mother the Church has been and holds, to whom it belongs to judge of the true sense and interpretation of Holy Scriptures. Therefore, no one is allowed to interpret the same Sacred Scripture contrary to this sense or contrary to the unanimous consent of the Fathers" (Denzinger, nos. 3006–3007).

Can. 2.4: "If anyone does not receive as sacred and canonical the books of Holy Scripture, entire and with all their parts, as the sacred Council of Trent has enumerated them or denies that they have been divinely inspired, let him be anathema" (Denzinger, no. 3029).

Based on these points, we see that *in matters of faith and morals the authority of the Fathers is of the highest degree.* On this, also see Denzinger, nos. 517ff, 600–602, 625, 650, 2330, 2830, 3007, 3289, 2083 [old numbering]; *likewise, the commonly held teachings of the theologians is to be held* (Denzinger, nos. 1179, 2676, 2679, 2814, 2876ff); modern authors are not to be rashly preferred (Denzinger, no. 2047); the customs of the Church are norms of belief (Denzinger, nos. 247 and 1863): "Let the law of prayer establish the law of belief" (Denzinger, no. 246).

COLLECTION OF DECLARATIONS AND DEFINITIONS
BY THE CHURCH ON THE INSPIRATION AND INERRANCY
OF SACRED SCRIPTURE

In the following chronologically ordered texts, we always find the same, firmly held doctrine, which has come to be expressed more and more explicitly.

- We already have the canon of the books of Sacred Scripture in the fourth century, devised and edited by [Pope] St. Damasus I (366–384), but repeated by [Pope] St. Gelasius I (492–496) in the famous document "*De libris recipiendis vel non recipiendis*," which is called the Gelasian Decree. See Denzinger, nos. 180, 353ff [literally 162, old numbering].

- In his *Symbol of the Faith*, Pope St. Leo IX (1049–1054) professed: "I believe also *there is one author* of the New and Old Testament, of the law both of the prophets and of the apostles, namely the omnipotent God and Lord" (Denzinger, no. 685).

- Likewise, under Innocent III, in the profession of faith prescribed to Durand of Huesca and his fellow Waldensians (Dec. 18, 1208): "We believe that one and the same God is the author of the Old and New Testaments" (Denzinger, no. 790).

- Similarly, in the profession of faith given to Michael Palaiologos at the Second Council of Lyons in 1274.

- {{429}} Likewise, the Council of Florence (1438–1445), in the decree for the Jacobites: "[The Holy Roman Church] . . . professes that one and the same God is the author of the Old and New Testament, that is, of the law and the prophets and of the Gospel: since the saints of both Testaments spoke under the inspiration of the same Holy Spirit, she accepts and venerates their books, whose titles are as follows: [the canonical books follow here]" (Denzinger, no. 1334).

- The Council of Trent (1545–1563): "The holy, ecumenical, and general Council of Trent . . . receives and venerates with the same sense of loyalty and reverence all the books of the Old and New Testament—for the one God is the author of both" (Denzinger, no. 1501).

- [First] Vatican Council (1869–1870), *Dei filius*, ch. 2 (On Revelation): "These the Church holds to be sacred and canonical, not because, having been carefully composed by mere human industry, they were afterward approved by her authority or merely because they contain revelation with no admixture of error, but because, *having been written by the inspiration of the Holy Spirit, they have God for their author* and *have been delivered as such to the Church herself*" (Denzinger, no. 3006; also see can. 2.4, Denzinger, no. 3029).

This definition is of the greatest importance. It excludes two opinions concerning the nature of Sacred Scripture: (1) if a given book had been put together through human industry, *the subsequent approval of the Church* would not suffice for it to be holy and canonical; (2) nor does the fact that *it happens to contain revelation without error* suffice. Thus (3), in order for a book to be holy, it must be written through the inspiration of the Holy Spirit, thus having God as its author, and in order for a book to be canonical, it needs to be handed on by the Church herself as such (that is, as inspired).

In his encyclical *Providentissimus Deus*, Leo XIII developed this dogmatic formula further still.

The sovereign pontiff showed how the inerrancy of Sacred Scripture is to be preserved and defended against historical objections, noting:

> But *it is absolutely wrong and forbidden, either to narrow inspira-*
> *tion to certain parts only of Holy Scripture, or to admit that the sacred*
> *writer has erred.*

For the system of those who, in order to rid themselves of these
difficulties, *do not hesitate to concede that divine inspiration regards*
the things of faith and morals, and nothing beyond, because (as they
wrongly think) in a question of the truth or falsehood of a passage,
we should consider not so much what God has said as the reason
and purpose which He had in mind in saying it—*this system cannot*
be tolerated. For all the books which the Church receives as sacred
and canonical, are written wholly and entirely, with all their parts,
at the dictation of the Holy Ghost; *and so far is it from being possi-*
ble that any error can co-exist with inspiration, that inspiration not
only is essentially incompatible with error, but excludes and rejects
it as absolutely and necessarily as it is impossible that God Himself,
the supreme Truth, can utter that which is not true. This is the
ancient and unchanging faith of the Church, solemnly defined in
the Councils of Florence and of Trent, and finally confirmed and
more expressly formulated by the [First] Council of the Vatican. . . .

Hence, because *the Holy Ghost employed men as His instruments,*
we cannot therefore say that it was these inspired instruments
who, perchance, have fallen into error, and not the primary author.
{{430}} *For, by supernatural power, He so moved and impelled them to*
write—He was so present to them—that the things which He ordered,
and those only, they, first, rightly understood, then willed faithfully
to write down, and finally expressed in apt words and with infallible
truth. Otherwise, it could not be said that He was the Author of the
entire Scripture. (Leo XIII, *Providentissimus Deus,* no. 20, Vatican
trans; see Denzinger, nos. 3291–3293)

On *sound exegetical principles,* in accord with which Sacred Scripture is
to be interpreted, see the same encyclical and later decrees and encyclicals
(Denzinger, nos. 3372ff, 3394ff, 3412ff, 3461, 2100 [old numbering]).

The aforementioned definitions and declarations by the Church are
opposed by the following *Modernist Theses* condemned in the Holy Office's

Decree *Lamentabili* (July 3, 1907) in numbers 9–12 (Denzinger, nos. 3409–3412):

> 9. They display excessive simplicity or ignorance who believe that *God is really the author of the Sacred Scriptures.*

> 10. The *inspiration* of the books of the Old Testament consists in this: The Israelite writers handed down religious doctrines under a certain particular aspect that was either little or not at all known to the Gentiles.

> 11. Divine inspiration does not extend to the whole of Sacred Scriptures in such a way that each and every one of its parts is protected from all error.

> 12. If he wishes to apply himself usefully to biblical studies, the exegete must first put aside all preconceived opinions about the supernatural origin of Sacred Scripture and interpret it the same as any other merely human doctrine.

Therefore, the ninth and tenth theses deny the divine origin of Sacred Scripture; the eleventh denies its inerrancy; the twelfth subverts the way that it is to be interpreted.

The tenth thesis must be compared with the naturalistic teaching concerning inspiration condemned in Pius X's encyclical *Pascendi* (Sept. 7, 1907):

> God does indeed speak in these books—through the medium of the believer, but only, according to Modernistic theology, by *vital immanence and permanence.* Do we inquire concerning *inspiration?* Inspiration, they reply, is distinguished only by its vehemence from that *impulse which stimulates the believer to reveal the faith that is in him by words or writing.* It is something like what happens in poetical inspiration, of which it has been said: There is God in us, and when he stirreth he sets us afire. And it is precisely in this sense that God is said to be the origin of the inspiration of the Sacred Books (no. 22; cf. Denzinger, no. 3490).

The eleventh thesis denying the universal inerrancy of Sacred Scripture must be compared with the responses expressed by the Biblical Commission concerning "implicit citations" and on the historical character of Sacred Scripture (Denzinger, nos. 3372 and 3373).

Alphabetic Index of Subjects and More Notable Persons

Citations are in the original Latin pagination, as noted inline throughout
these two volumes in translation.
(For example: {{1.42}} means: Volume 1, Latin page {{42}})
On occasion, entries expanded slightly for clarity.

Agnosticism. What it is {{1.259}}; empiricist agnosticism {{1.261–264}}; idealistic agnosticism {{1.265ff}}; critique of agnosticism {{1.274–298}}

Analogy. What it is and how many kinds of analogy there are {{1.283ff}}
Defense of the analogical and transcendent value of the first notions
and principles of reason {{1.282–298}}
Explanation of how to defend the analogical value of the notions by
which the supernatural mysteries are expressed {{1.174, 289, 349}}

Apologetics. What it is: state of the question {{1.1–6}}; definition from its
object and its *end* {{1.40ff}}; how apologetics *argues from reason*, though
under the direction of faith {{1.41–43}}; division of apologetics {{1.44,
2.125ff}}; how it is related to sacred theology and to the sciences
belonging to the natural order {{1.49ff}}; apologetics is a particular
office of sacred theology and thus has a specific object while, nonetheless, remaining part of sacred theology and not distinct therefrom {{1.9,
41ff, 50, 58ff}}; the nature of integral and potential parts of a given
science or virtue, according to St. Thomas {{1.33n82}}
Its methodology, which is analytic-synthetic, especially external though
also internal {{1.66–76}}; on the method of immanence {{1.117–
124, 359ff, 376, 407, 435, 481, 2.3ff, 26, 77–124}}; historical
overview as regards methodology {{1.8–132}}
When it comes to a historical exposition of the motives of credibility,
preference should be given to a regressive method, which considers
Christ's teaching and deeds prior to consideration of primitive revelation {{2.125–129}}
How one should propose a unified demonstration that at once defends

Christianity and Catholicism {{1.45ff, 2.127ff}}

The unity of the whole of apologetics {{2.29ff, 1.45}}

On the spirit of apologetics {{1.1–4, 41ff, 50ff, 57, 95, 430, 480}}

Apostolicity. As a mark of the True Church {{2.202}}; only belongs to the Roman Church [that is, the One Church, in union with the pope of Rome] {{2.297–300}}

Apostles. Christ gave the apostolic college the threefold power of teaching, ruling, and sanctifying believers {{2.191–195}}; in what way the apostles knew everything that is in the deposit of revelation {{1.177n77}}

Aristotle. Conception of metaphysics as the supreme science that defends its principles, and sacred theology must be considered along these lines in the supernatural order {{1.15}}; in accord with Aristotle's teaching, a defense of the ontological and transcendent value of the first notions of reason, registered against agnostics {{1.274–298}}

Aspirations of man. How one can argue from them in apologetics {{2.2–10}}

Assent of faith. {{1.443–457}}. Specifically, as regards the grace needed for the act of faith {{1.414ff}}; how freedom of the act of faith is reconciled with its utter certitude {{1.422ff}}; how the believer adheres to the First Truth (i.e., the formal motive of faith) {{1.427–478}}; relationship between the assent of faith and the judgment of credibility {{1.503ff}}

Attributes of God. How they are identified in the eminence of the Deity and, nonetheless, are formally found there {{1.296–298, 322}}

Authenticity. Of the Gospels {{2.140ff}}

Authority of God Revealing. As the formal motive of faith {{1.408–414}}; in what way is it known supernaturally and infallibly {{1.427–478}}

Authority of the Church. When she proposes revelation, she nonetheless is not the formal motive of faith but only the necessary condition for it {{1.413}}; Christ established the Church's infallibility in order to preserve and propose revelation in perpetuity {{2.195}}

Authority in the civil order. Must receive revelation that has been sufficiently proposed {{2.411}}; how it must do so {{2.413–425}}

St. Augustine. An outstanding apologete {{1.90}}; cited throughout this work, especially as regards the mode of knowing the formal motive of faith {{1.434ff}}

Authenticity. Of the books of the New Testament {{2.133–152}}

Autonomy. The principle of rationalism based on the absolute autonomy of reason {{1.206ff, 215ff, 303, 307, 402ff}}

Baius, Michael. His pseudo-supernaturalism {{1.184, 361ff}}

On the value of miracles {{2.32–95}}

On the value of prophecy {{2.98–124}}

Existence of these various motives of credibility {{from 2.205 to the end of volume 2}}

Criteria of revelation. See *Credibility, motives of*

Criticism [*biblical*]. {{2.135}}

Demons. What is said about them in the Gospel {{2.173}}; what can they do in imitation of miracles {{2.86ff}}; on divination by demons {{2.120ff}}; the nature of the natural faith had by demons and whether it has the same formal motive as does infused faith {{1.447}}; comparison between the sin of the demons and the naturalistic principle asserting the absolute autonomy of reason {{1.215}}

Deschamps, Cardinal Victor Auguste Isidore. As an apologete {{1.116, 2.126}}

Deism. Admits the existence of God, but it does away with his providence or otherwise diminishes it, denying the possibility of miracles {{1.97, 118}}

Deity. The formal notion of the Deity is utterly eminent, above being, one, and so forth, identifying in itself all simply simple perfections, which are formally-eminently found there {{1.295ff, 324}}; God, considered from the formal perspective of the Deity, is the subject of supernatural theology, whereas God, considered from the formal perspective of being, is the subject of natural theology {{1.9}}

Demonstration. The fact of revelation is demonstrated apodictically from signs, by means of a *reductio ad absurdum* {{1.514–515, 2.92–97, 122ff, 300, 313, 333, 339, 359}}

Desire. Natural desire to see God through his essence is elicited (not innate), conditional, and inefficacious {{1.359–376}}

Discernability. Of miracles {{2.58–92}} and of prophecy {{2.115–122}}

Dogma. Notion thereof, as well as concerning its immutability and our progressive understanding of it {{1.160–179}}

Eclecticism. As favored by rationalism {{1.104}}

Emanantism. Refutation thereof, as it overthrows the supernatural order {{1.225, 257}}

Empiricism. See *Agnosticism* (empiricist) and *Evolutionism*

End. End of apologetics {{1.39–45, 2.30}}; principle of finality {{1.240}}; in what the ultimate natural end and the ultimate supernatural end differ {{1.361ff}}. See also *Desire*

Essence. What it is {{1.185, 278}}. See also *Nature*

Fortune and chance. Discussed in general {{2.117–118}}. See also *Prophecy* (fulfillment thereof)

Franzelin, Cardinal Johann Baptist. Regarding the question concerning whether God would have revealed the sum of all the natural truths of religion if man had been created in a state of mere nature {{1.390}}

Freedom of conscience and worship. See *Liberalism*

Frohschammer, Jakob. See *Semi-rationalism*

Future contingents. Proper object of prophecy or prediction {{2.101}}

Gardeil, Ambroise. On the nature of apologetics and its relationship with sacred theology {{1.62}}; on the mode of knowing the formal motive of faith {{1.464}}; regarding credibility {{1.497}}; concerning the genesis of the act of faith {{1.503}}

Gnostics. Brief exposition of their doctrine {{1.225}}

God. How God as the author of nature is distinguished from God as the author of the supernatural order (that is, of the order of grace and glory) {{1.135, 198ff, 324–331, 345, 448, 463ff, 467, 515}}

How to defend the existence of an order of strictly supernatural mysteries in God {{1.318–330}}

Whether God, as the author and Lord of nature, can perform miracles {{1.200}}; on the possibility of miracles {{2.45ff}}

How we know the authority of God revealing, inasmuch as it is the formal motive of essentially supernatural faith {{1.427–478}}

Gonet, Jean-Baptiste. Frequently cited throughout the work. As regards the notion of supernaturality {{1.205, 464}} and that of credibility {{1.492}}

Gospel. By many means of confirmation that are historically certain, it is clear that the Gospels are authentic and historical {{2.133ff}}; the doctrine taught in the Gospels is not a form of syncretism {{2.246ff}}; the Gospel accounts of miracles are historically certain {{2.305ff}}

Grace. Necessary for faith {{1.417ff}} and for the practically-practical judgment of credentity {{1.503ff}}

Frequently aids in the judgment of credibility {{1.499ff}}

See also *Supernatural* and *Supernatural Life*

Günther, Anton. See *Semi-rationalism*

Haeckel, Ernst. Exposition and refutation of his evolutionistic doctrine concerning religion {{1.221ff, 252}}

Heretical formulas. The faith (or, rather, opinion) that they preserve concerning certain revealed truths does not rest on the formal motive of infused faith, even if they say that they believe on the authority of God

{{1.417–422}}

Luther, Martin. His notion of faith and the influence of this notion on Protestant apologetics {{1.99}}; his pseudo-supernaturalism {{1.184}}; his testimony concerning Protestant morals {{1.281ff}}

Magisterium. Revelation is divine speech after the manner of a teaching authority [magisterii] {{1.143}}; what is a human teaching authority {{1.145}}; what is a divine teaching authority {{1.148}}; the infallible teaching authority of the Church {{2.195}}

Magnetism. Phenomena of this kind are not the same as miracles {{2.79}}

Maistre, Joseph de. On the marks of the Church {{2.279, 283ff, 297, 299, 301}}

Malebranche, Nicolas. His ontologism {{1.342}}; his theory of miracles {{2.34}}

Man. The nature of the human powers of knowledge do not extend to knowledge of God's intimate life {{1.325ff}}

    Our nature contains an obediential (i.e., elevable) capacity for the supernatural order {{1.351–377}}

    How man can accept revelation {{1.346ff}}

    How revelation is befitting to him {{1.377ff}}

    Man's legitimate aspirations are miraculously fulfilled in Christianity {{2.215ff}}; man is bound, by the natural law, to receive revelation has been sufficiently proposed to him {{2.404ff}}

Marks of the Church. Discussed variously {{2.197, 264, 290ff}}

Mary, Blessed Virgin. Her veneration always renews perfect chastity {{2.283}}

Martyrs. Their constancy is a motive of credibility {{2.266–275}}

Materialism. See Evolutionism (empiricist / materialistic)

Messiah. Christ's testimony concerning his messiahship {{2.154ff}}

Metaphysics. Supreme science of the natural order, therefore defending the value of its principles, an office shared by sacred theology in the supernatural order {{1.14ff}}

Methodology. Of theology {{1.33}}; of apologetics {{1.65}}; how the method of apologetics must be determined {{1.65}}; it is analytical and synthetic, in particular external, though also internal {{1.66}; the Church upholds a determinate apologetic methodology {{1.70}}; the methodology of apologetics according to the Fathers {{1.87–90}}, according to the scholastics {{1.91–96}}, according to contemporary Catholics {{1.114ff}}, according to the first Protestants {{97ff}}; according to liberal Protestants {{1.109}}, according to semi-rationalists {{1.111}}, according to the modernists {{1.72}}; on the methodology of immanence {{1.117ff, 259ff, 376, 407, 487, 2.2, 30, 215ff}}; the union of various methodologies and the unity of apologetics {{2.26–31}}

Miracles. The notion of a miracle {{2.32}}; the division thereof {{2.42}}; the possibility thereof {{2.43ff}}; discernibility as regards the supernaturality of a fact and as regards is existence {{2.62ff}}; its probative force {{2.92}}

 Christ's miracles are historically certain {{2.307}}, truly supernatural {{2.310}}, and they irrefutably confirm his testimony {{2.313}}

Modernism. It hardly differs from liberal Protestantism {{1.72}}; what it says concerning the methodology of apologetics {{1.72ff}}, revelation {{1.141}}, faith {{1.406}}, credibility {{1.486}}, miracles {{2.38}}, and the Gospels {{2.139, 155, 184, 330}}

Molina, Luis de. Position that infused faith is not essentially supernatural through its formal object {{1.449, 456}}

Monotheism. As held by the Hebrew people {{2.368, 370, 378}}

Mosaic religion. Proof of its divine origins {{2.364}}

Motives of credibility. Their notion {{1.517}} and division {{1.518ff}}

 Value of the motives that are internal to us {{2.2, 215}}, and of the motives intrinsic to religion (the miraculous life of the Church and the sublimity of her teaching) {{2.11, 226, 257}}

 Value of miracles {{2.92ff, 305ff}}

 Value of prophecies {{2.122, 334, 397}}

Mysteries, the true notion of supernatural mysteries {{1.160}}; how this differs from natural mysteries {{1.165}}; on the intelligibility of the mysteries {{1.169}}; defense of the existence of an order of mysteries in God that are not merely natural but indeed supernatural {{1.315ff}}

Mythism. Exposition and refutation {{2.134, 305}}

Myths. Babylonian myths compared with the Book of Genesis {{2.378}}

Naturalism (or *rationalism*). Its definition, foundation, spirit, and consequences {{1.206ff}}; division of the systems of naturalist thinkers {{1.216}}

Nature. How the natural differs from the supernatural {{1.185}}; the hypothetical necessity of the laws of nature {{2.47}}; the natural order {{1.197}}. See also *God*

Necessity of revelation. Discussed in detail {{1.377–396}}

Nominalists. Their denial that sanctifying grace and infused faith are essentially supernatural {{1.202, 420, 451}}

Nonbelievers. Discussed in general {{1.394, 396ff}}

{{2.344ff}}; their value {{2.359}}; Christ's prophecies {{2.334}}

Protestantism. Its notion of faith {{1.99, 405}}, of credibility {{1.485ff}}; errors of liberal Protestantism {{1.109ff, 268, 406}}; Protestantism lacks the true marks of the Church {{2.278, 292, 295, 299}}

Reason, human. The limits of its natural power of knowledge {{1.320ff}}; what is morally possible for it to know concerning natural religion {{1.380–386}}; on the value of reason {{1.274–298}}; the mutual relationship between revelation and reason: between natural truths and supernatural ones there can be neither disagreement between natural and supernatural truths, nor confusion, but rather, there is harmony between them {{1.332–345, 2.225–242}}; on the rational obedience of faith {{1.482–519}}; revelation frees reason from errors, illuminates it, and strengthens it {{1.377–386, 224–247}}

Rationalism. Its origin {{1.96ff}}; definition {{1.206}}; its foundational principle upon the supposed autonomy of reason {{1.207–209}}; its spirit {{1.212–217}}; philosophical rationalism {{1.97, 104, 206}}; biblical rationalism {{1.98, 107, 2.130ff}}

Religion. Notion {{1.126, 2.398}}; comparison of principal religions existing today to Christianity

Resurrection of Christ. Historically proven and defended {{2.314–330}}

Revelation. Notion {{1.130–152}}; species {{1.153–159}}; possibility {{1.301–376}}; necessity {{1.377–390}}; signs of revelation {{1.517–519, 2.1–128}}; existence of revelation {{2.129–388}}; obligation to receive divine revelation when it has been sufficiently proposed {{2.389}}; fact of revelation known from one perspective from signs, and from another by faith {{1.441, 463–476, 493}}; the fonts of revelation in Sacred Scripture and Tradition {{2.426ff}}

Revolution (French). Benedict the XV's {{2.397}} and Leo XIII's {{2.401}} words concerning the "Declaration of the Rights of Man"

Ritschl, Albrecht. His teaching concerning revelation and miracles {{1.268}}

Ripalda, Juan de. Did not rightly determine the difference between the natural and supernatural orders, thinking that a created supernatural substance is not evidently impossible {{1.317, 340, 456}}

Rule of the Church. A visible rule, in relation to spiritual ends, not solely eschatological in question {{2.191ff}}

Sabatier, Auguste. What he said, as a liberal Protestant, concerning revelation itself {{1.296}}, prophecy {{2.100}}, and miracles {{2.37}}

Sacred Scripture. How it is considered in apologetics {{2.133}}; as a fount

451, 456, 472ff, 476}}

Tanquerey, Adolphe. Cited variously {{2.273, 290, 343}}

Tertullian. As an apologete {{1.88}}

Theological conclusion. Properly so-called and improperly so-called {{1.18–20 and 175–179}}

Theology. Definition {{1.5–17}}; its formal subject (or object) *quod* {{1.9}} and formal object *quo* {{1.11}}, extension {{1.14}}, unity {{1.31}}, division {{1.28}}, methodology {{1.33–38}}, and relationship with other sciences {{1.22}} and with faith {{1.18}}

Theology (fundamental). Is sacred theology itself inasmuch as it is concerned with the foundations of faith and the theological sources {{1.49–62}}; contains apologetics and the treatise on theological sources (*De locis theologicis*) {{1.9, 38–50}}; thus, apologetics is a *part / office* of sacred theology and not something separate. See also *Apologetics*

St. Thomas Aquinas. Cited in nearly all articles of the text, especially his texts concerning the question of the mode of knowing revelation, as the formal motive of infused faith {{1.438–449}}; his apologetics {{1.91ff}}

Thomism. Compared with other systems {{1.283, 317, 341, 404, 449, et passim.}}

Toleration (religious). In what sense it can be admitted {{2.395, 419, 421}}

Tradition. As a font of revelation {{2.426ff}}

Traditionalism. Exposition and refutation {{1.378ff}}

Trinity. Brief exposition of this mystery's harmony with reason {{2.228}}

Torquemada, Juan de. Exceptional theologian and apologete who wrote the first and distinguished *Summa de ecclesia* {{2.265, 292ff}}; reference to his works, regarding his teaching concerning the Church's power in temporal matters, precisely as consequence of their relation to the Church's supernatural end (see *Summa de ecclesia*, chs. 90–92, 113, 116)

Unity. Of the Church of Christ {{2.198}}; only belongs to the Roman Church [that is, the One Church, in union with the pope of Rome] {{2.290}}

Unity of sacred theology {{1.31}} and of apologetics {{2.29ff}}

Vacant, Alfred. Frequently cited throughout. His comparison of the Thomists and the Scotists concerning the distinction between the natural and supernatural orders {{1.341, 428, 450}}

Wilmers, Wilhelm. His position concerning how revelation is known, as the formal motive of faith {{1.465}}

Virtue. How the Christian virtues differ from the natural, acquired virtues {{2.175, 183, 220, 281}}; on the golden mean in the virtues {{2.417}}; on heroic virtues {{2.19, 22}}; in the martyrs {{2.266–277}}; in Christ {{2.207–213}}

Worship. Variously discussed in relation to oneself and the civic order {{2.216, 220, 234, 398ff, 411–425}}

Zahn, Theodor. A Protestant. The chronology he admitted concerning the Gospels, in comparison with that admitted by many rationalists {{2.145}}

Zigliara, Cardinal Tommaso Maria. Teaching, along with all Thomists, that revelation, as the formal motive of infused faith, is at once that by which we believe and that which we believe (*id quo et quod creditur*), even if, from an inferior perspective (i.e., considered solely as modally supernatural), the fact of revelation is rationally and certainly knowable on the basis of sensible signs {{1.467}}; cited elsewhere {{1.46, 319, 391}}